▪▪▪ HALLMARK FEATURES: A COMPLETE LEARNING PACKAGE

Through this unique and highly praised set of learning tools, your students come away ready to understand the material. Learning objectives set clear expectations, frequent review sections keep students on track, and boxed features engage students in critical thinking.

PREP, CHECK, AND REVIEW

- **Learning Objectives** based on Bloom's Taxonomy (with Bloom's cognitive domain and difficulty level noted for each question) are created specifically for the text, with references to chapter learning objectives.

- **What Have I Learned?** section breaks offer a brief quiz with an answer key so students can gauge their comprehension, ensure they understand concepts, and know they are making connections between key terms and broader questions.

- **Chapter Review** sections offer additional opportunities to review core concepts, connect ideas to stories, think critically about the issues, and master key terms—all conveniently organized around learning objectives.

- **Telling Stories with Data** shows students how data can explain—or distort—political phenomena, and improves their ability to interpret facts and figures. What Do YOU Think? questions encourage students to challenge the narratives constructed around the data. *Explore this feature in Chapter 5 on page 168.*

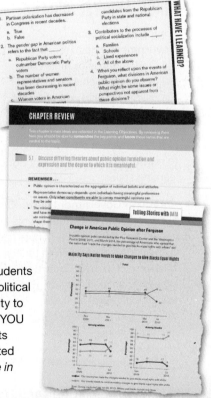

"This feature will help students process the material better, and help them think critically about a topic."

–Timothy Nokken, *Texas Tech University*

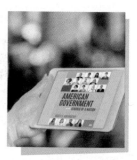

▪▪▪ SAGE COURSEPACKS FOR INSTRUCTORS

OUR CONTENT TAILORED TO YOUR LMS

SAGE coursepacks makes it easy to import our quality instructor materials and student resources into your school's learning management system (LMS). Intuitive and simple to use, **SAGE coursepacks** allows you to integrate only the content you need and requires no access code.

A RICH SET OF TEST QUESTIONS

- **The test bank** built on Bloom's Taxonomy (with Bloom's cognitive domain and difficulty level noted for each question) is created specifically for the text, with references to chapter learning objectives (and the page number). It includes **more than 1,500 multiple choice, short answer, essay, fill-in-the blank, and true-false questions**.

- **Assessment questions for SAGE Premium Video** in the Interactive eBook offer high-quality video assignments and test students on comprehension as well as analysis and application.

- See **more SAGE coursepacks features** at **sagepub.com/storiesofanation**.

ANALYTIC SKILL-BUILDING

- **Assignable data exercises** in each chapter help students build essential data literacy skills using interactive data visualization tools from **SAGE Stats** and **U.S. Political Stats**. Drawing on a series of key data ranging from demographic patterns to state budgets to voting behavior, these exercises offer students a dynamic way to analyze real-world data and think critically about the stories behind the numbers.

CUSTOMIZED AND CURATED FOR USE IN:

⑤SAGE coursepacks

BRIEF EDITION

AMERICAN GOVERNMENT

For Sadie and Dylan

BRIEF EDITION

AMERICAN GOVERNMENT

STORIES OF A NATION

SCOTT F. ABERNATHY
University of Minnesota

Los Angeles | London | New Delhi
Singapore | Washington DC | Melbourne

FOR INFORMATION:

CQ Press

An imprint of SAGE Publications, Inc.

2455 Teller Road

Thousand Oaks, California 91320

E-mail: order@sagepub.com

SAGE Publications Ltd.

1 Oliver's Yard

55 City Road

London, EC1Y 1SP

United Kingdom

SAGE Publications India Pvt. Ltd.

B 1/I 1 Mohan Cooperative Industrial Area

Mathura Road, New Delhi 110 044

India

SAGE Publications Asia-Pacific Pte. Ltd.

3 Church Street

#10-04 Samsung Hub

Singapore 049483

Executive Publisher: Monica Eckman

Development Editor: Elise Frasier

Editorial Assistant: Zachary Hoskins

Content Development Editor: John Scappini

Production Editor: Kelly DeRosa

Copy Editor: Megan Markanich

Typesetter: C&M Digitals (P) Ltd.

Proofreader: Laura Webb

Indexer: Will Ragsdale

Cover Designer: Gail Buschman

Marketing Manager: Erica DeLuca

Printed in Canada

Library of Congress Cataloging-in-Publication Data

Names: Abernathy, Scott Franklin, 1966- author.

Title: American government : stories of a nation / Scott Abernathy.
Other titles: American government (Brief edition)

Description: Brief edition, First edition. | Los Angeles : Sage/CQ Press, 2019. | Includes bibliographical references and index.

Identifiers: LCCN 2017040100 | ISBN 978-1-5443-0736-7 (pbk. : alk. paper)

Subjects: LCSH: United States—Politics and government—Textbooks.

Classification: LCC JK31 .A23 2019 | DDC 320.473—dc23
LC record available at https://lccn.loc.gov/2017040100

This book is printed on acid-free paper.

MIX
Paper from
responsible sources
FSC
www.fsc.org   FSC® C011825

18 19 20 21 22 10 9 8 7 6 5 4 3 2 1

BRIEF CONTENTS

PART III: INSTITUTIONS

PART IV: POLICY

DETAILED CONTENTS

left: Andrew Burton/Getty Images; *center*: First Liberty Institute; *right*: MPI/Getty Images

STORIES OF...

left: The Granger Collection, New York; *center*: The Granger Collection, New York; *right*: The Granger Collection, New York

STORIES OF...

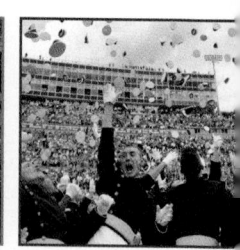

left: The Granger Collection, New York; *center*: AP Photo/Max Whittaker; *right*: RJ Sangosti/The Denver Post via Getty Images

STORIES OF...

left: The Granger Collection, New York; *center*: Afro American Newspapers/Gado/Getty Images;
right: Franklin D. Roosevelt Presidential Library & Museum

4. Civil Liberties and Civil Rights: Building and Defending Fences

STORIES OF...

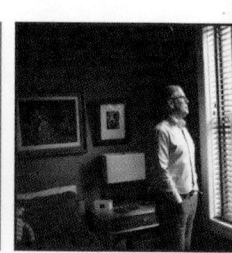

left: Andrew Harrer/Bloomberg via Getty Images; *center*: Neville Elder/Corbis via Getty Images; *right*: Maddie McGarvey/For The Washington Post via Getty Images

STORIES OF…

PART II: POLITICAL BEHAVIOR AND MASS POLITICS

STORIES OF...

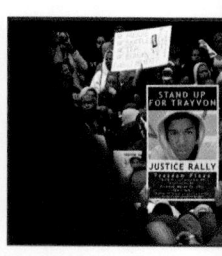

left: The Granger Collection, New York; *center*: Bilgin Sasmaz/Anadolu Agency/Getty Images;
right: NICHOLAS KAMM/AFP/Getty Images

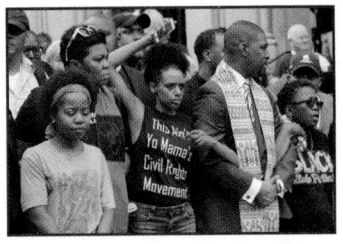

STORIES OF...

6. The Media: Truth, Power, and American Democracy 175

STORIES OF...

left: Jaap Arriens/NurPhoto via Getty Images; *center*: World History Archive / Alamy Stock Photo;
right: Courtesy of the Library of Congress, Prints and Photographs Division

7. Parties, Elections, and Participation: The Insurgents versus the Establishment   207

STORIES OF...

left: BRENDAN SMIALOWSKI/AFP/Getty Images; *center*: Victor J. Blue/Bloomberg via Getty Images;
right: JIM WATSON/AFP/Getty Images

STORIES OF...

left: Ricky Carioti/The Washington Post via Getty Images; *center*: Scott Olson/Getty Images;
right: Vanessa Carvalho/Brazil Photo Press/LatinContent/Getty Images

STORIES OF...

PART III: INSTITUTIONS

STORIES OF...

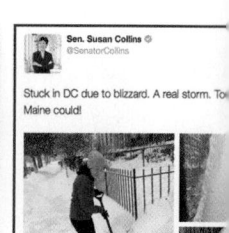

left: REUTERS/Eduardo Munoz; *center*: Bill Clark/CQ Roll Call; *right*: Senator Susan Collins/Twitter *left*: AP Photo/Greg Gibson, File; *center*: AP Photo/Andrew Harnik; *right*: REUTERS/Jonathan Ernst

STORIES OF...

10. The American Presidency: Individuals, Institutions, and Executive Power 317

**The Killing of an American Citizen
Tests the Limits of Presidential Powers** **318**

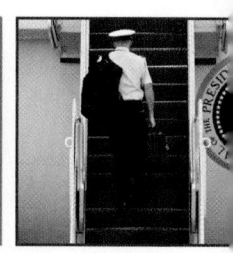

left: Mark Wilson/Getty Images; *center*: Tracy Woodward/The Washington Post via Getty Images; *right*: AP Photo/Cliff Owen *left*: ullstein bild via Getty Images; *center*: AFP/Getty Images; *right*: AP Photo/Doug Mills

STORIES OF...

STORIES OF...

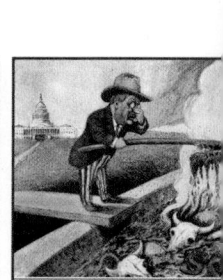

left: AP Photo/Andy Newman; *center*: AP Photo/LM Otero; *right*: North Wind Picture Archives via AP Images

12. The Federal Judiciary: Politics, Power, and the "Least Dangerous" Branch — 378

STORIES OF...

left: ©Copyright 2011 Eric Allie – All Rights Reserved; *center*: Alex Wong/Getty Images; *right*: The White House via Getty Images

STORIES OF...

left: Olivier Douliery/picture-alliance/dpa/AP Images; *center*: Bettmann / Contributor; *right*: The Granger
Collection, New York

PART IV: POLICY

  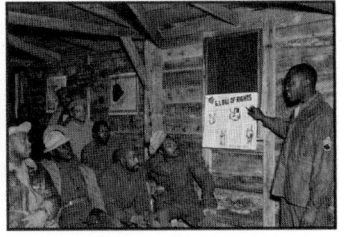

STORIES OF...

left: Kevork Djansezian/Getty Images; *center*: Jessica Rinaldi/The Boston Globe via Getty Images; *right*: Library of Congress/Corbis/VCG via Getty Images

STORIES OF...

left: GraphicaArtis/Getty Images; *center*: Kremlin Press Center /Anadolu Agency/Getty Images;
right: AHMAD AL-RUBAYE/AFP/Getty Images

PREFACE

REAL PEOPLE, REAL STORIES, REAL POLITICS

Stories are powerful things. They help shape the political world in which we all live. They help define who we are as individuals and as a people. And stories are also excellent teaching tools, making the material relatable, memorable, and real. This book harnesses the full power of narrative to draw students into the study of American politics, highlighting the unpredictable outcomes of people's actions and strategies.

The Benefit of Real Stories

This textbook tells stories about real people: their strategies, the actions they took, the contingencies surrounding those actions and their outcomes, and the struggles they faced. The topics and scope of coverage in this brief edition are consistent with other brief, introductory American government texts and equally comprehensive. What is different about our storytelling approach is that stories help drive the themes of the book in a way that engages students to interact more directly with the material, one of the biggest challenges in any introductory class.

A Richer Understanding of Political Dynamics

With this approach, students will better understand that political outcomes are not predetermined but are instead the results of strategic choices made by political actors, usually undertaken in an uncertain environment, often amid unequal relationships of power. The approach in this book is designed to show students how others have wrestled with similar questions of power, action, and change, whether in very different times and circumstances or in situations ripped from today's headlines. How some have succeeded, others failed, but, more importantly, how many have operated in the space between success and failure, adjusting their strategies along the way.

Stronger Connections through Engagement

A second benefit is that your students will actually read the book. In doing so they will be doing much more than skimming for key terms or IDs. By combining the deep dives into one or a few key stories in each chapter with solid research-backed core content, *Stories of a Nation* will guide your students to a genuine engagement with the material, the theories that try to explain political outcomes, and the enduring questions of American representative democracy. And, they will connect the dots between those elements. The first chapter of the book, for example, clearly identifies and explains the founding ideals of American democracy—liberty, equality, natural rights, the American Dream, American exceptionalism. But those ideas are each situated within a set of vivid stories about people and groups coming from different times, places, and experiences who claimed their rights as citizens. Together, these stories help students understand so-called "key terms" in ways no ordinary descriptive text can.

Greater Instructional Flexibility

Third, *American Government: Stories of a Nation* is adaptable to the approach that *you* want to use. This is not a book that pushes a specific perspective or one that envisions a teacher as a repository of fact. These narratives allow for an emphasis on institutions, behavior, or a combination of both. The stories can also be used to focus on American political development, ideas, or an approach that focuses on people, or their efforts to secure their own rights and liberties.

In addition, the variety of sources used to present the material in the book—textual, visual, and data-based—as well as the self-assessment tools, make the content accessible to students with a variety of learning strengths. As a teacher, that kind of book is what I always wanted, but I never found one that completely fulfilled that promise. That is another reason that I wrote it.

Stories help students connect to people who come from different places and times, and who have had different experiences. Chapter 1 begins with a story about how two different groups claimed their First Amendment rights through the Equal Access Act: Nebraska high school student Bridget Mergens, who wanted to start a Bible study club, and students in Boyd County, Kentucky, who wanted to start a Gay-Straight Alliance club. Their actions made it possible for students today to do the same. Above left is Liz Loverde, sophomore at Wantagh High School in Long Island, New York, who several years ago successfully pressured her school to allow a Christian Bible study club. Right is Jennifer Villasana, president of the Gay-Straight Alliance at Richland High School, holding a badge she wore at the White House LGBT Conference on Safe Schools and Communities at the University of Texas at Arlington in 2012. *left:* First Liberty Institute; *right:* Rodger Mallison/Fort Worth Star-Telegram/MCT via Getty Images

Greater Inclusiveness

The fourth reason is just as important and closely connected to the narrative approach in this book. In spite of efforts by the authors, editors, and publishers of American government textbooks to address the diversity of Americans' lived experiences, the majority of books on the market do not fully embrace that diversity. A mounting body of scholarship analyzing the text, image, content, and context of those works arrives at strikingly similar conclusions: depictions and considerations of members of traditionally marginalized groups are sparse and, when presented, placed in a specific set of chapters and topics.

Covering the efforts of women to achieve rights in a chapter on civil rights, for example, makes perfect sense. But it doesn't make sense that that would be the only place we'd hear stories of political actions taken by women or members of other groups who have acted to secure their rights. Therefore, the chapter on Congress focuses on stories about women representatives and senators in their efforts to achieve a more complete realization of political representation in American democracy.

In this book, diversity is not a list of boxes to check off. Americans' diverse identities have powerfully shaped political processes and outcomes even when not successful in any given struggle. It includes a broad vision of the diversity of Americans' lived experiences, including the reality that any one American may have multiple conceptions of their own identities, and that those self-understandings shape their participation in the political process. Through the power of narrative and of stories, my goal is that *all* students—reading and using this book—will find that they are also a part of the American experience, whether or not their voices have been heard.

THE ORGANIZATION OF THE BOOK

In this brief edition, we begin our study of American government by looking at the foundations, covering basic ideas in American democracy (Chapter 1), the Constitution (Chapter 2), American federalism (Chapter 3), and efforts to protect civil liberties and secure civil rights (Chapter 4). Then we move on to American political behavior and mass politics, with an exploration of public opinion (Chapter 5), the media (Chapter 6), parties, elections, and political participation (Chapter 7) and interest groups and social movements (Chapter 8). Moving on to American political institutions, we examine Congress (Chapter 9), the presidency (Chapter 10), the federal bureaucracy (Chapter 11) and the federal judiciary (Chapter 12). Finally, we conclude with American public policy (Chapter 13). Though time constraints often mean that policy is not covered in the course of a term, I encourage instructors to include it. The focus on American dreamers and immigration policy is one that I think will resonate with your students.

Each chapter in *Stories of a Nation* begins with a focused narrative that sets up and integrates the subject matter that follows, subject matter that is tied to four to six learning objectives. The nuts and bolts sections that follow the initial narrative refer back to that story, with figures, tables, and images chosen to connect the narrative with the subject matter. Each major section concludes with a set of quiz questions (with answers) to reinforce the learning.

How does this approach work in practice? In Chapter 5, for example, on Public Opinion, I focus the narrative on the aftermath of the fatal police shooting of Michael Brown in Ferguson, Missouri in 2014. The basic question is this: has public opinion about the way that African-Americans are treated by police changed since that event and others related to it?

The chapter begins by setting up the story, focusing on the one-year anniversary of the tragic event. Learning objectives guide students to a full set of issues that political scientists consider when presenting the topic of American public opinion—assessing the components and formation of opinions, ways of measuring it, patterns of change in people's attitudes, and the larger meaning and impact of public opinion in American democracy. The nuts and bolts material covered in the chapter explores debates over the stability, coherence, and meaning of American public opinion. A section on political socialization fuses the narrative and the research-based content into one section, with an in-depth consideration of the partisan divides in opinion on the core issues of race and policing.

The chapter concludes with a section that challenges students to continue to explore the meanings of public opinion. Finally, like every chapter, this one also has a comprehensive guide for review that connects the learning objectives, take-home points of the stories, major political science themes, and key terms, to help students confirm that they have fully comprehended the material.

As you can see, no political science content gets "lost" at the expense of the narrative—and with plenty of built-in guidance, no student gets lost in the coverage.

PEDAGOGY: DIFFERENT WAYS OF TELLING STORIES

This book acknowledges the challenges of dealing with the political world that students will inevitably have to confront in their own lives. To that end, it also provides students with specific skills with which to bring the deeper understandings that they will develop to bear on their own political realities. Each of the pedagogical features of the book is designed to harness the power of narrative in the service of teaching students to be critical readers of image, data, and text.

Telling Stories with Data

In an increasingly data-driven world, the ability to act as a critical interpreter of data—and perhaps most importantly—of the stories told based on the sometimes-competing interpretations of those data is a fundamental skill. Data, and their interpretation, constitute an exercise of power. By engaging with the recurring feature *Telling Stories with Data* students will understand that data-stories can be just as important in the political process as any other narrative. Students will critically reflect on how the data were obtained, how they were interpreted, and how political narratives were constructed around them. In doing so, students will engage with the use of data to advance a particular political objective and become more thoughtful and critical readers of the stories constructed around numbers and statistics.

A Variety of Voices

When writing a textbook, any author exercises power by the necessary act of writing some stories in and leaving others out. Even as we try to remain neutral or objective, we inevitably impose a particular point of view on events, or even a false coherence to actions and consequences that may in fact be incoherent and messy. Another key feature of the textbook is the inclusion of oral and written statements by people, historical and contemporary, in which they reflect on key issues or the impact of their words on their own story and on American political history. These writings, speeches, and communications, have been chosen to challenge any one dominant narrative in the text, rather than to reinforce it.

Intentional Use of Images

Image literacy is as crucial to the pedagogical objectives of this book as textual literacy. Instead of solely offering images as illustrative enhancements to the text, the book also examines the ways in which images themselves have played and continue to play a role in the development of American government and politics. Through a critical presentation of the use of images, students will gain skills in interpreting images as they gain a deeper understanding of the political world of which they are part, and which they will help to shape.

Reinforcing the Fundamentals

Several smaller features of the book also serve to reinforce the nuts and bolts materials and also help students understand why the chosen narratives will help them gain a deeper and more memorable understanding of this material.

- *Learning Objectives* at the start of each chapter guide students' reading of and engagement with the material, signposting the goals and setting clear expectations for what they will master.
- *What Have I Learned?* section breaks offer a brief quiz with an answer key so students can gauge their comprehension, ensure they understand concepts, and know they are making connections between key terms and broader questions.
- *Chapter Review* sections conclude each chapter by offering students additional opportunities to review core concepts, connect them to the stories, think critically about the issues, and master key terms—all helpfully framed around the chapter's learning objectives.

BRINGING IT ALL TOGETHER: TEACHING AND A NARRATIVE APPROACH

I have taught incarcerated youths, homeless adolescents, fourth graders, seventh graders, undergraduates, and graduate students. Across all these experiences I have learned that narrative is a powerful educational tool. People are born to be storytellers and story-hearers; it seems to be in our make-up. We are wired to respond to narrative and its ability to convey the contingency, complexity, and uncertainty of collective human action, and the hopes of what might be accomplished if it succeeds. Our students care about these stories. They are also already talking about them—all the time. My goal, in this book, is to give students both a framework and set of tools with which to discuss the complexities and contradictions of American government and politics. The stories told within this book will resonate with and engage your students.

With so much to cover in an introductory course like this, we instructors want to make sure to convey all the important material central to our course goals. You might wonder if students will get "lost" in the narratives and fail to sufficiently attend to the "nuts and bolts," or that conversations in your classes might become sidetracked into debates on the narratives themselves rather than discussions about the underlying political processes and institutions. Though these are reasonable questions, rest assured that we have taken a very thoughtful and proactive approach to this issue, efforts that, based on results from class-testing, work.

The book consciously strives to avoid weighing in on one side or another of heated debates but instead guides students to use their own engagement with them to more deeply understand American politics. A set of instructors' resources offer concrete tips on guiding successful and focused class discussions. The pedagogical features within each chapter have been designed to reinforce the nuts and bolts in a way that preserves the immediacy of the narratives without sacrificing all of the coverage that you expect.

Stories that are devoid of people, their actions, aspirations, and mistakes are not very interesting. Fortunately, as teachers of American government, we rarely encounter stories like that. The political world that we teach our students about is vibrant, fascinating, and charged. The description of the chapter content above and a glance at the table of contents of the book shows that this book takes up stories that emerge directly from that political world, stories that will draw your students in to a *real* understanding of their political worlds, and their places in it.

That is why stories are such powerful things.

SUPPORTING YOUR TEACHING

SAGE edge is a robust online environment featuring an impressive array of tools and resources for review, study, and further exploration, keeping both instructors and students on the cutting edge of teaching and learning. SAGE edge content is open access and available on demand. Learning and teaching has never been easier! We gratefully acknowledge Jeneen Hobby, Cleveland State University; Andrew Levin, Harper College; Nick Pyeatt, Penn State Altoona; John Seymour, El Paso Community College; and Theresa Marchant-Shapiro, Southern Connecticut State University for developing the ancillaries on this site.

SAGE edge for Students at **http://edge.sagepub.com/abernathybrief1e** provides a personalized approach to help students accomplish their coursework goals in an easy-to-use learning environment.

- **Chapter summaries** with **learning objectives** reinforce the most important material.
- Mobile-friendly **eFlashcards** strengthen understanding of key terms and concepts, and make it easy to maximize your study time, anywhere, anytime.
- Mobile-friendly practice **quizzes** allow you to assess how much you've learned and where you need to focus your attention.
- Carefully selected **video resources** bring concepts to life, are tied to learning objectives, and make learning easier.
- **Exclusive access to influential SAGE journal and reference content,** ties important research and scholarship to chapter concepts to strengthen learning.

SAGE edge for Instructors at **http://edge.sagepub.com/abernathybrief1e** supports teaching by making it easy to integrate quality content and create a rich learning environment for students.

- The **Test bank** built on Bloom's taxonomy (with Bloom's cognitive domain and difficulty level noted for each question) is created specifically for this text, with references to chapter learning objectives (and page number) and ExamView test generation. It includes more than 1,500 multiple choice, short answer, essay, fill-in-the-blank, and true-false questions, as well as the opportunity to edit any question and/or insert personalized questions to effectively assess the students' progress and understanding.
- Editable, chapter-specific **PowerPoint® slides** offer complete flexibility for creating a multimedia presentation for the course, so you don't have to start from scratch but you can customize to your exact needs.
- An **instructor's manual** features chapter overviews and learning objectives, lecture starters, ideas for class activities, and discussion questions.
- A set of all the **graphics from the text,** including all the maps, tables, and figures in PowerPoint, PDF, and JPG formats for class presentations.
- Carefully selected chapter-by-chapter **video and multimedia content** that enhances classroom-based exploration of key topics.

Enriched Learning through Technology

Students today are connected, wired, and networked in ways previous generations could not have imagined, and they process information in ways that go way beyond reading the printed word on a paper page. To keep up with them and their quickly evolving world, *American Government: Stories of a Nation* is also a full-fledged, integrated media experience. When students purchase a new print copy of the book they receive access to an enhanced ebook. This interactive ebook uses the VitalSource Bookshelf®, where students can read the eBook online, on any device, and download it to read offline. They can also share notes and highlights with instructors and classmates, and "follow" friends and instructors as they make their own notes and highlights. Through a series of annotated icons on select pages, students can quickly link to multimedia on the page where a topic is discussed, pointed to articles and background pieces, to audio clips of interviews, to video clips of news stories or satirical commentary, to reference and biography material, to CQ Researcher policy backgrounder reports, to important current data on such topics as approval ratings and public opinion polls.

In addition to the curated multimedia content discussed above, two excited types of **SAGE Premium Video** truly set this ebook apart:

- **Topics in American Government** videos recap the fundamentals of American politics in every chapter—from the Bill of Rights to voter turnout to the powers of the presidency. Each animated video is paired with chapter learning objectives and tied to assessment in our **SAGE coursepacks**, offering a more complete way to **reinforce mastery of key concepts** while meeting your students' diverse learning styles.
- **American Government News Clips** bring extra coverage of current events into the book, connecting
- multiple, brief 2- to 4-minute news clips to core chapter content. With multiple-choice assessment in **SAGE coursepacks**, these clips offer an ideal way for students to practice using higher level analysis and application skills to apply chapter concepts to recent political events.

Altogether, these resources allow students to explore an important topic or idea while reading—a reinforcing exercise as well as vetted content that provides depth and added context. It's an enhanced, enriching, and interactive learning experience.

SAGE Coursepacks for Instructors

The **SAGE coursepack** for *American Government: Stories of a Nation* makes it easy to import our quality instructor materials and student resources into your school's learning management system (LMS), such as Blackboard, Canvas, Brightspace by D2L, or Moodle. Intuitive and simple to use, **SAGE coursepack** allows you to integrate only the content you need, with minimal effort, and requires no access code. Don't use an LMS platform? You can still access many of the online resources for *Stories of a Nation* via the SAGE edge site.

Available SAGE content through the coursepack includes:

- Pedagogically robust **assessment tools** that foster review, practice, and critical thinking, and offer a more complete way to measure student engagement, including:

- o Diagnostic chapter pre tests and post tests that identify opportunities for improvement, track student progress, and ensure mastery of key learning objectives
- o **Test banks** built on Bloom's Taxonomy that provide a diverse range of test items with ExamView test generation
- o **Activity and quiz options** that allow you to choose only the assignments and tests you want
- o **Instructions** on how to use and integrate the comprehensive assessments and resources provided

- **Chapter-specific discussion questions** to help launch engaging classroom interaction while reinforcing important content
- **Assessment questions for SAGE Premium Video** from the Interactive eBook offer high-quality video assignments and test students on comprehension as well as analysis and application.
- **Assignable data exercises** in each chapter help students build essential data literacy skills using interactive data visualization tools from **SAGE Stats** and **U.S. Political Stats**. Drawing on key data series ranging from demographic patterns to state budgets to voting behavior, these exercises offer students a dynamic way to analyze real-world data and think critically about the stories behind the numbers.
- Additional **video resources** that bring concepts to life, are tied to learning objectives and make learning easier
- EXCLUSIVE, influential **SAGE journal and reference content**, built into course materials and assessment tools, that ties important research and scholarship to chapter concepts to strengthen learning
- Editable, chapter-specific **PowerPoint® slides** that offer flexibility when creating multimedia lectures so you don't have to start from scratch but you can customize to your exact needs
- **Integrated links to the interactive eBook** that make it easy for your students to maximize their study time with this anywhere, anytime mobile-friendly version of the text. It also offers access to more digital tools and resources, including SAGE Premium Video
- **All tables and figures** from the textbook

A number of instructors helped to guide the development of the above resources. We appreciate the time and thoughts our reviewers put into their feedback, which helped us to refine the material and ensure that we provide content useful to both instructors and students. We offer special thanks to Justin S. Vaughn, Boise State University, and to:

Richard A. Almeida, Francis Marion University

John A. Aughenbaugh, Virginia Commonwealth University

Madelyn P. Bowman, Tarrant County College, South Campus

Marla Brettschneider, University of New Hampshire

Mark A. Cichock, University of Texas at Arlington

Amy Colon, SUNY Sullivan

Victoria Cordova, Sam Houston State University

Kevin Davis, North Central Texas College

Michael J. Faber, Texas State University

Terry Filicko, Clark State Community College

Patrick Gilbert, Lone Star College

Andrew Green, Central College

Sally Hansen, Daytona State College

Alyx D. Mark, North Central College

David F. McClendon, Tyler Junior College

Michael P. McConachie, Collin College

Patrick Moore, Richland College

Tracy Osborn, University of Iowa

Carl Palmer, Illinois State University

Melodie Pickett, Tarleton State University

Daniel E. Ponder, Drury University

Nicholas L. Pyeatt, Penn State Altoona

Paul Rozycki, Mott Community College

Deron T. Schreck, Moraine Valley Community College

Tony Wohlers, Cameron University

ACKNOWLEDGMENTS

There are many, many people who have helped to make this book a reality, some of whom probably have, or have had, no idea that they did so. I am grateful to all of them. Just as the Ninth Amendment makes it clear that Americans' fundamental rights and freedoms can never be fully enumerated, this will be a necessarily incomplete statement of my gratitude.

First, I would like to thank my teachers over the years. I owe each of these individuals much more than I can repay. Colleagues at the University of Minnesota, past and present, have offered their knowledge, feedback, and support over the years. I owe special thanks to W. Phillips Shively for not trying to talk me out of writing an American government textbook and supporting me throughout the process. Thanks to the many students over the years who inspired and motivated me to write the book. Members of the staff in the Department of Political Science have been invaluable over the years.

To the many talented, warm, and professional people at SAGE/CQ Press I owe much. The book began with an idea floated to Earl Pingel who then passed it along to Charisse Kiino. Though Charisse has moved on from the role of acquisitions editor to other responsibilities, her stamp is very much on this book, and I am grateful for it.

In addition, many thanks to Carrie Brandon, Gail Buschman, Matthew Byrnie, Sarah Calabi, Erica DeLuca, Monica Eckman, Eric Garner, Jade Henderson, Zachary Hoskins, Jennifer Jones, Nancy Matuszak, Dianne Nabrzeski, Michele Rhoades, John Scappini, Michele Sordi, Rose Storey, and Amy Whitaker. All made me feel like part of the SAGE/CQ family in addition to doing their jobs superbly. Though not technically part of the SAGE/CQ group, I am indebted to Chuck McCutcheon for collaborating on the Parties chapter.

I would like to thank the many colleagues who very helpfully offered their time, praise, criticisms, and support throughout the process of writing this book. They offered feedback in reviews, surveys, focus groups, and class testing. In addition to several who wish to remain anonymous, they include:

Milan Andrejevich, Ivy Tech Community College

Stephen Anthony, Georgia State University

Juan Arzola, College of the Sequoias

Yan Bai, Grand Rapids Community College

Thomas J. Baldino, Wilkes University

Patricia Bodelson, St. Cloud State University

Seth Bordner, Kent State University

Christopher Borick, Muhlenberg College

Madelyn Bowman, Tarrant County College South

Todd Bradley, Indiana University Kokomo

Mark Brewer, University of Maine

Jeffrey Brown, Wayne County Community College

Susan Burgess, Ohio University

James D. Buthman, Hartwick College

Timothy Campbell, Labette Community College

Mary Carver, Longwood College

Kimberly Casey, Northwest Missouri State University

LaTasha Chaffin, College of Charleston

Ben Christ, Harrisburg Area Community College

Dewey Clayton, University of Louisville

Diana Cohen, Central Connecticut State University

Kathleen Cole, Metropolitan State University

Todd Collins, Western Carolina University

Michael Coulter, Grove City College

Kevin Davis, North Central Texas College

Chris Deis, Depaul University, Lincoln Campus

Joseph S. Devaney, East Georgia State College

Richardson Dilworth, Drexel University

Agber Dimah, Chicago State University

Cristina Dragomir, SUNY Oswego

Lauren Elliott-Dorans, Ohio State University

Bond Faulwell, Johnson County Community College

Daniel Franklin, Georgia State University

John Frendreis, Loyola University of Chicago

Frank Fuller, Chestnut Hill College

Maria Garcia-Acevedo, California State University Northridge

Sarah Gershon, Georgia State University

Tobias Gibson, Westminster College

Patrick Gilbert, Lone Star College

Andra Gillespie, Emory University

Frederick Gordon, Columbus State University

George Gordon, Illinois Wesleyan University

Andrea Graff, Lincoln Land Community College

Greg Granger, Northwestern State University of Louisiana

Matthew Green, The Catholic University of America

Matthew Gritter, Angelo State University

Gloria Guevara, California State University Northridge

Homer Guevara, Northwest Vista College

Paul Henri Gurian, University of Georgia

Mel Hailey, Abilene Christian University

Therese M. Hammond, Pennsylvania State University Lehigh Valley

Jeneen Hobby, Cleveland State University

Tom Hoffman, Spring Hill College

Michael Hoover, Seminole Community College

Jennifer Hopper, Washington College

JoyAnna Hopper, University of Missouri

Tony Horton, Arkansas State University

William Housel, Louisiana Scholars' College

Robert Housner, Everett Community College

Mark Jendrysik, University of North Dakota

Caitlin Jewitt, Virginia Tech

April Johnson, University of Illinois at Chicago

Gabe Jolivet, Ashford University

Jeff Justice, Tarleton State University

Mily Kao, Mesa Community College

Kimberly Keenan, City College of San Francisco

Christopher Kelley, Miami University

Athena King, Eastern Michigan University

John Klemanski, Oakland University

Lisa Krasner, Truckee Meadows Community College

Andrew Levin, Harper College

La Della Levy, College of Southern Nevada Henderson Campus

Eric Lomazoff, Villanova University

Benjamin Lundgren, Santa Clara University

James Malone, Hillsborough Community College

Alyx Mark, North Central College

Mack Mariani, Xavier University

Shane Martin, Fitchburg State University

Wendy Martinek, Binghamton University

Valerie Martinez-Ebers, University of North Texas

Michael McConachie, Collin College

Karen McCurdy, Georgia Southern University

Mary McHugh, Merrimack College

Stephen Meinhold, University of North Carolina, Wilmington

Melissa Merry, University of Louisville

Keesha Middlemass, Trinity University

Mark Miller, Clark University

Patrick Moore, Richland College

Samantha Mosier, Missouri State University

Brian Naples, Panola College

Sharon A. Navarro, University of Texas at San Antonio

Brian Newman, Pepperdine University

Timothy Nokken, Texas Tech University

Hyung Park, El Paso Community College

Sara Parker, Chabot College

Scott Parker, Sierra College

Lisa Perez-Nichols, Austin Community College

Robert Peters, Western Michigan University

Clarissa Peterson, DePauw University

William Pierros, Concordia University Chicago

Blayne Primozich, El Paso Community College

Nicholas Pyeatt, Pennsylvania State University, Altoona

Judd Quarles, Tyler Junior College

Andree Reeves, University of Alabama, Huntsville

Ted Ritter, John Tyler Community College

Joseph Robbins, Shepherd University

Jason Robles, Colorado State University

Michelle Rodriguez, San Diego Mesa College

James Ronan, Rowan University

Jon Ross, City Colleges of Chicago

Paul Rozycki, Mott Community College

Mikhail Rybalko, Texas Tech University

Ray Sandoval, Richland College

Erich Saphir, Pima Community College

Deron Schreck, Moraine Valley Community College

Eric Schwartz, Hagerstown Community College

Allen Settle, California Polytechnic State University

John Seymour, El Paso Community College

Brent Sharp, University of Central Oklahoma

Amy Shriver Dreussi, University of Akron

Abha Singh, University of Texas, El Paso

Sue Ann Skipworth, University of Mississippi

Gwyn Sutherland, Elizabethtown Community and Technical College

Nate Steffen, Bismarck State College

Bob Switky, Sonoma State

Barry Tadlock, Ohio University

Chris Thuot, SUNY Onondaga Community College

Anip Uppal, Central New Mexico Community College

Troy Vidal, Columbus State University

Danny Vyain, Ivy Tech Community College

Kimball Waites, Big Bend Community College

Adam Warber, Clemson University

Jessica Webb, Kalamazoo Valley Community College

Zach Wilhide, Tidewater Community College

Mark Williams, St. Charles Community College

Claire Wofford, College of Charleston

Tony Wohlers, Cameron University

Patrick Wohlfarth, University of Maryland

Laura Wood, Tarrant County College

Tyler Young, Collin College

Kimberly Zagorski, University of Wisconsin-Stout

Penultimately, I am deeply grateful to the other members of our little band: Elise Frasier on editing, development, and general excellence, Megan Markanich on copyediting, Kelly DeRosa on production editing, and Monica Eckman on executive publishing, vision, and project oversight. This book is theirs as much as it is mine.

Finally, I would like to thank my family: Mom, Dad, Julie, and Jeannette, to whom I am deeply thankful. And to Dylan and Sadie, who have grown—too quickly—into wonderful and wonderfully different people. And lastly my wife, Sara: In spite of the hours, days, and weeks away from you and the kids, I am still here, and I am still yours.

Scott
Minneapolis, Minnesota
September 2017

ABOUT THE AUTHOR

Scott F. Abernathy was born and raised in Fort Worth, Texas. While an undergraduate at Dartmouth College he volunteered for three months with Mother Theresa's Missionaries of Charity in Calcutta, India. After graduation, hoping to do service work closer to home, Scott worked as an on-street counselor with homeless adolescents in Boston, Massachusetts.

Scott then received a Master of Curriculum and Instruction and taught fourth and seventh grades in Wisconsin public schools. Hoping to learn more about the underlying systems that drove the educational outcomes he was trying to change, Scott completed an M.P.A. in Domestic Policy and then a Ph.D. in Politics from Princeton University. Scott is now an associate professor of political science and a University Distinguished Teaching Professor at the University of Minnesota. He is also the author of *School Choice and the Future of American Democracy* and *No Child Left Behind and the Public Schools*, both from University of Michigan Press.

While Scott says that being a street outreach worker was the most transforming job he ever had, he admits that the chance to teach students, not in a subway stop or a squat, but through the writing of this textbook, is pretty cool as well.

Sara Miller McCune founded SAGE Publishing in 1965 to support the dissemination of usable knowledge and educate a global community. SAGE publishes more than 1000 journals and over 800 new books each year, spanning a wide range of subject areas. Our growing selection of library products includes archives, data, case studies and video. SAGE remains majority owned by our founder and after her lifetime will become owned by a charitable trust that secures the company's continued independence.

Los Angeles | London | New Delhi | Singapore | Washington DC | Melbourne

1 AMERICAN POLITICAL STORIES
Claiming Rights, Demanding to Be Heard

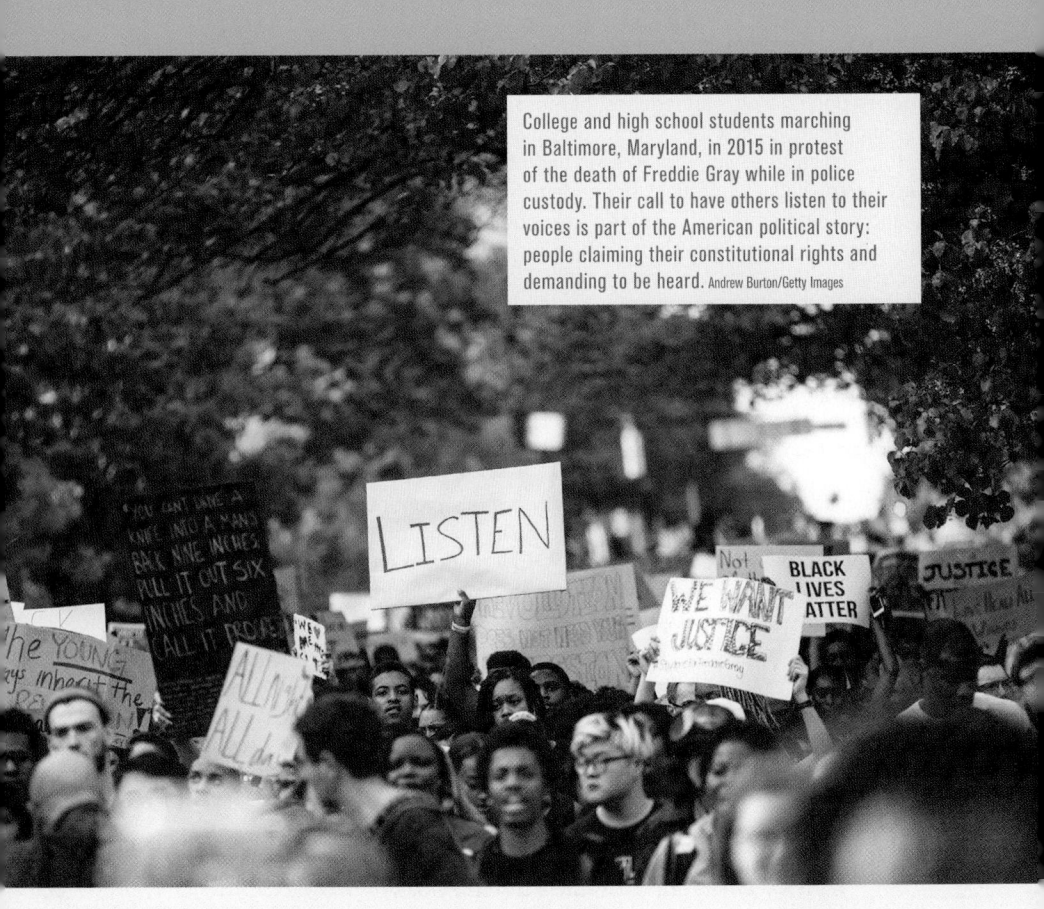

College and high school students marching in Baltimore, Maryland, in 2015 in protest of the death of Freddie Gray while in police custody. Their call to have others listen to their voices is part of the American political story: people claiming their constitutional rights and demanding to be heard. Andrew Burton/Getty Images

In my undergraduate Introduction to American Government course here at the University of Minnesota, on the first day of class, I tell my students, "I don't care *what* you think," which does tend to generate some uncomfortable silence. But I mean it. Before things get too out of hand, though, I quickly follow up with, "However, I care very much about *how* you think. That is what this course is about."

This book is no different. My hope is that you will use this book to question what everyone tells you that you *should* know or think, to become more confident in making your own ideas known, and to sharpen your ability to interpret for yourself the political world around you. This book uses stories to help accomplish those goals. These stories are very much a central part of the book's structure and objectives. In each chapter, you will be presented with stories that illustrate important concepts in the study of American politics. They are meant to make those ideas come to life—to help you understand that American government is not something that exists apart from you. And because they are *real* stories, in all their messy, complicated glory, they will also force you and your classmates to think in ways that are not either-or and to walk in the shoes of people who may be very different from you.

This book, therefore, is going to be difficult at times, although not in the sense of being difficult to read and follow—far from that, I hope. I mean that many of the stories don't have clear heroines, heroes, or villains. Hardly any of them have tidy endings. In this book, I will quote individuals whose words or ideas some will strongly disagree with, maybe even find objectionable. This book will not offer any one political, theoretical, or academic perspective. There will be no magic wand waved in the final chapter of this book that announces, "Here! We've got it!" Welcome to the world of American politics and government.

Read the stories; absorb the nuts-and-bolts facts and concepts that emerge along the way in these chapters. Most importantly, however, connect the two. Use the stories to more deeply understand the complexity of American politics, then and now. Use them to understand the diversity of the voices that are a part of the national conversation. Use the stories to make your own voices stronger, better informed, more politically savvy, and more effective.

In this chapter and in the book generally, we raise fundamental questions when we try to define what we mean by a "good government" or a bad one. Whose rights get protected? Whose get restricted? How do these questions get resolved? Who gets to decide? The stories told in this book illustrate how big questions like these are resolved, revisited, and re-resolved through **politics**, the process of influencing the actions and policies of a **government**. Politics and government are closely connected, but they are not the same thing. Politics describes processes; government describes the rules and institutions that arise from political action and conflict and that structure future political action. Throughout the book, we'll hear from people who have engaged with those institutions and who have taken part in those processes.

We will begin with two stories: one about a young woman in Nebraska who fought for the right to establish a Christian Bible study group at her school and the other about a group of Kentucky students who claimed their rights to establish a Gay-Straight Alliance (GSA). We will then go back in time to the American Revolution and Thomas Jefferson's drafting of the Declaration of Independence.

What could these stories possibly have in common? In them we will witness the efforts of vastly different people who have wrestled with what fundamental rights mean in American democracy and see how they as individuals and groups have tried to answer that question, staking their own claims upon their rights.

By connecting to those stories about the foundations of American government, you will be able to do the following:

1.1 Define the key elements of American political culture.

1.3 Describe the core features of American political institutions.

1.2 Identify the political, social, and economic events and institutions that gave rise to the American Revolution.

AMERICAN STUDENTS CLAIM THEIR RIGHTS

Bridget Mergens walked into the office of her school principal in Omaha, Nebraska, with a request. She wanted to start a student group—a Christian Bible study club.

"I thought he liked me and I was sure he'd say yes," Mergens later recounted.[1] As one reporter noted, "Principal James Findley did like her . . . but he didn't say yes. 'An informal get-together over lunch at the cafeteria would be fine,' Findley [recalled] saying, 'but a school-sponsored club? Don't ask me that, Bridget, because I have a problem with that.'"[2]

Mergens's high school sponsored many other extracurricular clubs, including a photography club and a scuba diving club. Was her proposal fundamentally different from these sanctioned student groups? This became a question with which her principal and her local school board had to wrestle, and they ultimately denied her request. To Mergens, the school board's arguments were fundamentally flawed.

The legal basis of Mergens's claim was a national law, the Equal Access Act (EAA), which was passed in 1984. The law's primary intent is to restrict the ability of public high schools to exclude faith-based religious extracurricular clubs. The act states, "It shall be unlawful for any public secondary school which receives Federal financial assistance . . . to deny equal access or a fair opportunity to, or discriminate against, any students who wish to conduct a meeting . . . on the basis of the religious, political, philosophical, or other content of the speech at such meetings."[3]

In 1981, prior to the act's passage, the U.S. Supreme Court had already affirmed these rights for students at public colleges and universities, but it had not yet done so for those in public high schools. As Mergens's case proceeded, it was far from certain that the Court would now affirm those same rights for high school students. The reason was the potential "impressionability of high school" students, compared to those in college and beyond.[4] Would high school students be mature enough to distinguish between their school's efforts to provide an open forum for voices and the possibility that the school itself endorsed the club members' beliefs?

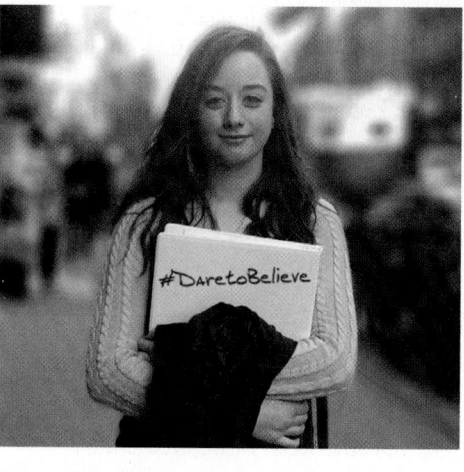

Liz Loverde, a sophomore at Wantagh High School in Long Island, New York, in 2014. Loverde successfully pressured her school to allow a Christian Bible study club, thus following in the footsteps of others, such as Bridget Mergens, in claiming rights under the Equal Access Act (EAA). First Liberty Institute

In June 1990, five years after Bridget Mergens tried to start the Bible club, the Supreme Court ruled in her favor. The Court upheld high school students' rights to have the same access for their faith-based extracurricular clubs as that granted to other student groups. It also upheld the constitutionality of the EAA. In her majority opinion in *Board of Education of Westside Community Schools v. Mergens*, Supreme Court justice Sandra Day O'Connor wrote, "There is a crucial difference between government and private speech endorsing religion, and, as Congress recognized in passing the Act, high school students are mature enough and are likely to understand that a school does not endorse or support student speech that it merely permits on a nondiscriminatory basis."[5]

To some, Mergens's efforts harkened back to the civil rights movement, in which African Americans claimed their own rights. The director of the Christian-based National Legal Foundation said so explicitly: "Just as officials in the 1950s shut the doors of the schoolhouse to black children, some school officials of the 1980s have attempted to keep out Christians who want to form a Bible club. Such arbitrary censorship is anti-religious discrimination, pure and simple."[6]

To others, including some of the members of the Supreme Court, the worry was more about the limits of Mergens's claims on her rights. Who else might make a claim based upon her efforts? Justice Anthony Kennedy raised a concern about the constitutionality of the EAA: that other students with other voices might also use the act to gain access for their student clubs, even if some of their issues of interest might make school administrators uncomfortable.[7] The free speech provisions of the EAA might also guarantee access for student groups with much more controversial agendas. It was this possibility that especially worried school administrators. Reflecting back upon his decision to deny Mergens's request and the Supreme Court's ruling, Omaha principal James Findley recounted, "I didn't have a concern about the five or six kids having a Bible study club. I was concerned about what and who it opens the doors to. I've had students say they'll start a Satanist club or a skinheads group."[8]

As it turned out, other groups of high school students *did* test the system but perhaps not in the ways that Congress intended when it passed the EAA in the first place or in the ways that Principal Findley or members of the Supreme Court worried about. These groups were not Satanists or skinheads. One was a collection of young people in Boyd County, Kentucky, who wanted to start a gay-straight alliance club. In 2002 they circulated a petition declaring their intent. Driving the formation of GSAs was the desire not only to create solidarity between high school students with diverse sexual identities but also to provide a safe space for students who had not yet chosen to make public their own sexual identities, perhaps because of the potential of harassment by their fellow students.

School officials turned down the student's request to form the GSA. Of twenty-one student group applications, theirs was the only one denied. Requests from groups such as the Future Business Leaders of America and the Fellowship of Christian Athletes were approved.[9] The students then contacted the American Civil Liberties Union (ACLU) for help. One month after the ACLU sent a letter to the school board in which it referred to the EAA, the board reversed itself and approved the formation of the GSA.[10]

But that didn't fully settle the case. Back at Boyd County High, GSA club founders' fears of harassment turned out to be valid. According to testimony from the school's principal, at the first official meeting of the GSA, a crowd "directly confronted the GSA supporters 'with facial expressions, hand gestures . . . some very uncivil body language . . . people were using loud voices and angry voices.'"[11] Two days later, a group of students protesting outside the school "shouted at [GSA] students as they arrived, 'We don't want something like that in our school.'"[12]

In an emergency meeting held in December, the school board, following the recommendation of the district superintendent, decided to "ban all noncurricular clubs for the remainder of the 2002–03 school year."[13] After the decision, members of the GSA stopped using school facilities to meet, but other groups, including the school's drama and Bible clubs, continued to use the high school's facilities. The members of the GSA went to court.

Their case did not make it to the Supreme Court; it did not have to. In 2004 the ACLU announced a settlement with the Boyd County public schools and claimed victory: "The settlement requires that the district treat all student clubs equally and conduct an anti-harassment training for all district staff as well as all students in high school and middle school."[14]

The GSA was not the first or the only case brought by student groups focused on challenging discrimination based on a student's sexual identity, but the efforts of these students highlight the ways in which individuals have used the political tools available to them to secure their own rights. In filing her lawsuit and pursuing her claims all the way to the Supreme Court, Bridget Mergens had help from the National Legal Foundation, a Christian public interest law firm.[15] The Boyd County High GSA had the help of the ACLU. While Mergens and the members of the Boyd County High GSA differed in the particular rights they asserted, they both staked their claims on the same federal law, the EAA. With help, they harnessed the power of the American judicial system to realize their goals.

Both groups' efforts were undertaken with knowledge of the complicated ways in which laws and policies are enacted in the United States and a strategic understanding of the political process. In this book we will consider those dynamics in detail. We will also dive into the stories of many other individuals and groups who have sought to claim their rights and reshape the laws of the land. In a very deep sense, however, whether or not any of the others whose stories you will read "won" or "lost" is not the most important consideration. By adding their voices to the American conversation, they mattered.

The EAA is just one of many political instruments that individuals have used to claim their rights. Underpinning all of these instruments are the political ideals drawn from thinkers throughout history, expressed in the Declaration of Independence and affirmed as rights by the Framers of the Constitution of the United States. These rights form the basis for the story of this evolving thing we call American democracy, whether or not the Framers fully envisioned how others would use their ideas and the institutions that they created. These efforts are central to the subjects and approach of this chapter and of this book.

WHAT HAVE I LEARNED?

1. Why have high schools, colleges, and universities struggled with the expression of student voices in cases as diverse as those involving Christian Bible study clubs and Gay-Straight Alliances (GSAs)?

2. How did Bridget Mergens and the members of the Boyd County High GSA make use of the same law, the Equal Access Act (EAA), to claim their rights?

3. What other rights might students in high schools, colleges, and universities claim?

....

Answer Key: 1. Students might reflect upon the rights of all students to have their voices made present in their educational institutions as well as on concerns of school officials that groups might form promoting unpopular, or even hateful, ideas; 2. Answers should focus on fundamental ideas such as freedom of expression; 3. Answers will vary and might focus on speech, safety, or many other areas.

AMERICAN POLITICAL CULTURE IS BUILT ON A SET OF SHARED IDEAS

• Understand the key elements of American political culture.

When they asserted their rights, Bridget Mergens and members of the Boyd County High GSA did so on the basis of a handful of ideas that form the foundation of the American Republic itself. Indeed, these ideas were affirmed in the Declaration of Independence in 1776, making them part of the country's basic DNA: "We hold these truths to be self-evident, that all men are created equal, that they are endowed by their Creator with certain unalienable Rights, that among these are Life, Liberty, and the pursuit of Happiness." These were revolutionary ideas, but they were not original ones. They weren't supposed to be.

In drafting the Declaration of Independence, Thomas Jefferson and his coauthors drew upon a set of ideas about liberty and government that were widely known in the colonies and Great Britain—ideas Jefferson knew needed to be persuasive and compelling enough to successfully launch a revolution. From the histories and philosophical works of ancient Greece and Rome, they borrowed the idea of **democracy** (from the Greek *demos*, meaning "people," and *kratos*, or "power"), whereby power is held by the people.

They borrowed from English Enlightenment philosopher John Locke, who had argued against the divine, or God-given, right of kings to rule with absolute power. Locke claimed that people are born with **natural rights** that kings cannot give or take away. A legitimate government, to Locke, is one that involves a **social contract**, in which people give to their governments the ability to rule over them to ensure an orderly and functioning society. If a government breaks that social contract by violating people's natural rights then the people have the right to replace that unjust government with a just one.

From the French Enlightenment, Jefferson and his colleagues drew on the works of Baron de Montesquieu, who gave an institutional form to the ideas of natural rights and the social contract in proposing that power in government should be divided between different branches so that no one branch could become too powerful.

Jefferson also drew upon Scottish Enlightenment thinkers such as David Hume. Given the historical tendency of leaders to abuse political power, Hume believed a just government should be carefully designed and the lessons of science and history carefully applied to its structure to keep the greedy and ambitious from using political power to their own advantage.

Later in the chapter we will see how those ideas gave rise to a revolution and helped form the basis for the institutions of modern government. Those ideas of liberty, equality, rights, happiness, and others also endure in other ways. Today they shape the shared set of beliefs, customs, traditions, and values that define the relationship of Americans to their government and to other American citizens. We call those shared beliefs **American political culture**.

Equality Is about Having the Same Rights or Status

Central to all of this—and the first key idea expressed in the Declaration of Independence—is a commitment to equality, to having the same rights and status. This might involve **social equality**, in which no individuals have an inherently higher social status than others. Unlike Europe, with its nobility and royalty, America was founded on the idea that all individuals could reach the social status that they sought based on their own efforts. **Political equality** exists when members of a society possess the same rights under the laws of the nation. Finally, **economic equality** refers to a situation in which wealth is relatively evenly distributed across society. America does not have economic equality. In fact, differences in wealth and incomes are as stark today as they have ever been in the nation's history. Rather than emphasizing equality of economic *outcomes*, American political ideas tend to focus on ensuring equality of economic *opportunity*.

These are two very different concepts. For example, think about American public education in high schools. Equality of opportunity would mean that every student had a right to attend equally good public high schools. Equality of outcomes, however, might point to their right to achieve the same graduation rates or test scores. Americans weigh the differences between opportunity and outcomes all the time when they seek to resolve many important civil rights issues and make choices about domestic public policy options.

Inalienable Rights Exist above Any Government Powers

The thinking behind the Declaration of Independence and the government that was eventually based upon it is that some truths and some rights are *self-evident*. These are called **inalienable rights** in the sense that they exist before and above any government or its powers. Thomas Jefferson names "life, liberty, and the pursuit of happiness" as among those inherent, self-evident rights. Since they—unlike *privileges* that a government might grant—may not rightly be taken away by a government, a just system of political rule must be constructed in such a way as to protect rights and their expression. The desire to safeguard individuals' rights led to the complex structure of American political institutions in the Constitution, which we will explore in the next chapter.

Liberty Involves Both Freedom from Interference and to Pursue One's Dreams

Another foundational American ideal expressed in the Declaration is a commitment to **liberty**, to social, political, and economic freedoms. That liberty might involve freedom *from* interference by a government or a freedom *to* pursue one's dreams. The degree to which the government should focus on freedom *from* or freedom *to* remains a hotly debated topic in American politics. There is often also a tension between these two visions of liberty. In the case of Bridget Mergens's Bible study club, the tension between these two freedoms came into sharp relief. Mergens and her fellow students claimed the freedom *to* explore their faith in an extracurricular club. By allowing the group, however, Omaha public school officials risked violating other students' freedoms *from* having a government endorse a particular religious faith, or endorse religious over nonreligious beliefs.

The Pursuit of Happiness Is at the Core of the American Dream

When Thomas Jefferson wrote about "the pursuit of Happiness," he was tapping into another core American political value: the belief that individuals should be able to achieve prosperity through hard work, sacrifice, and their own talents. The idea of the **American dream** has drawn immigrants to the nation's shores and borders since its founding, and it continues to do so today. Some observers, however, question whether the American dream remains alive and well in an era of such profound economic inequality.

American Political Culture Has Many Roots

America's religious traditions have also helped shape American political culture in ways more significant than in many modern democratic governments.

Millennials and the American Dream

The state of the American dream in the twenty-first century is actually something that we can study. Words are not the only ways to tell stories, nor are images and videos. Data can tell political stories as well. In this book, we will investigate data—numbers, statistics, and survey results—as well as the stories that political actors and reporters construct around the numbers. Make no mistake, data stories can be and are used for political purposes. In investigating data stories in this book, the goal is twofold: to help you become more capable and confident interpreters of data and to help you gain the skills to critically examine the narratives constructed around data.

Is the American Dream Alive or Dead for You?

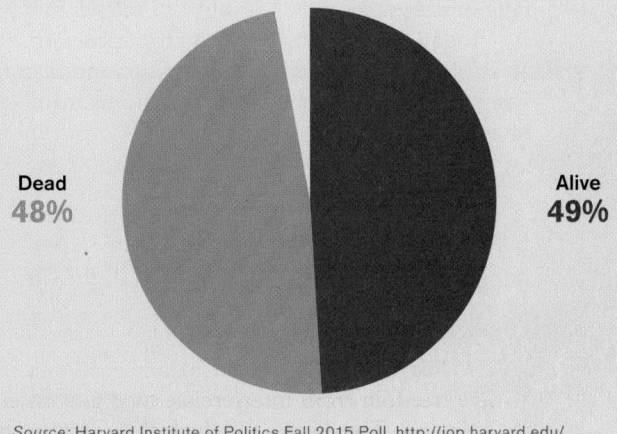

Dead
48%

Alive
49%

Source: Harvard Institute of Politics Fall 2015 Poll, http://iop.harvard.edu/survey/details/harvard-iop-fall-2015-poll.

We start with what at first glance seems like a very simple data story—one taken from the results of a Harvard University survey of eighteen- to twenty-nine-year-olds conducted in December of 2015.[16]

In the 2015 Harvard survey, Americans between the ages of eighteen and twenty-nine were just about equally split between those who believed that the American dream was still alive (49 percent) and those who did not (48 percent).

WHAT DO YOU THINK?

The authors of the survey report placed these results in context and went into much more detail about other factors. But let's assume that they did not. What conclusions might you draw from this figure alone? Does it reflect your experience? What other data from this survey would you want to know? If you could break out groups of young adult Americans based upon identities and characteristics, what would you examine?

As it turns out, in the Harvard survey, college graduates (58 percent) were more likely than those who had not graduated or ever enrolled (42 percent) to say the American dream was still alive. Young adult Americans in the survey who said that they were supporters of Democratic presidential candidate Bernie Sanders (56 percent) or Republican Party candidate Donald Trump (61 percent) reported that they felt the American dream was dead. What might these results mean for your understanding of the political attitudes of young adult Americans in 2016?

Some of the very first British colonies were founded by groups of individuals fleeing persecution for their religious beliefs and hoping to practice their faiths without interference. While the diversity of religious faiths represented in American society continues to expand, America was, and is, a nation partly defined by religious faith and expression. In this book, we will continue to explore the theme of how a nation founded upon liberty, especially religious liberty, wrestles with decisions about if, or how, to place boundaries on religious expression.

Today, questions about the proper role of religion in the nation endure. What kinds of holiday displays are acceptable for a community to officially sponsor? Would a ban on immigration by members of specific religious faiths be constitutional?

American Exceptionalism Flows from the Nation's Historical Development

Finally, when Americans tell stories about themselves, their politics, and their histories, they often refer to the ways in which the nation is different because of the historical patterns of the nation's development. **American exceptionalism** refers to these historical and cultural differences, shaped in many ways by the voices of those who have contributed to the national chorus but also by the fact that America was an experiment, starting anew, without the legacy of the European monarchies to constrain its promise.[17] The idea of an exceptional America is not a new one. In 1630 Puritan leader John Winthrop delivered a sermon to a group of immigrants from Britain onboard their ship as they waited to land in New England. In it he exhorted, "We must Consider that we shall be as a City upon a Hill, the eyes of all people are upon us."[18]

Americans Hold Diverse Political Ideologies

Americans may not always agree on a set of foundational concepts that constitute a shared political culture, and they also may disagree sharply about what the desired outcomes of the political processes should be. A person or group's **political ideology** is a set of beliefs about *what* should happen as the result of the process of governance. Individuals' political ideologies may differ on, for example, the degree to which government should regulate economic activity, how deeply government should be involved in individuals' decisions in their private lives, how much government should act to ensure equality of opportunity, or an almost endless list of other policies and issues. As with questions about religious faith, contemporary debates based upon competing American political ideologies endure, with some observers and scholars arguing that the nation had become deeply divided. In this book, we will explore these debates and discussions in detail.

1. The Declaration of Independence _____ the residents of the rebellious British colonies.

   a. Granted fundamental political privileges to
   b. Recognized the fundamental rights of
   c. Granted colonial women the right to vote along with
   d. Placed strict limits on the expression of rights of

2. The term *American exceptionalism* refers to _____.

   a. The fact that America is unique in its democratic form of government
   b. America's inability to protect individual rights
   c. The belief that America's unique history contributed to its special political culture and institutions
   d. All of the above

3. American society is characterized by _____.

   a. Relative social equality and economic inequality
   b. Relative economic equality and social inequality
   c. Relative social equality and economic equality
   d. Relative social inequality and economic inequality

4. What are some of the key components of American political culture?

5. What is the difference between political culture and political ideology?

Answers: 1. b; 2. c; 3. a; 4. Answers should include a discussion of inalienable rights, liberty, religious beliefs, and American exceptionalism; 5. Answers should cover how political culture refers to a shared set of beliefs about how political processes should work, while political ideology refers to preferred outcomes from those processes.

POLITICS AND POLITICAL ACTION SET THE STAGE FOR REVOLUTION

In April of 1607, three British ships made their way up what would later become known as the James River in Virginia. After deciding on a spot far enough up the river to avoid Spanish warships, these individuals created the settlement of James-

- Explain the political, social, and economic events and institutions that gave rise to the American Revolution.

town, the first permanent British settlement in the modern-day United States of America.[19] Over the course of the next 170 years, the turbulent political, economic, and social experiences they faced would shape the conditions that led to their eventual separation from Great Britain and establish the foundations of a set of formal and institutions that continue to shape America today.

Colonial Settlements Establish a Precedent for Independence

The colonists who established Jamestown did not set out on their own. They were backed, funded, and supported by the Virginia Company, chartered in 1606 to exploit the resources of North America for the benefit of Great Britain and the company's investors. They hoped to find gold, harvest forest products, and maybe find a valuable trade route.[20] In terms of the subsequent development of the thirteen British colonies and the free American states that later grew out of them, the initial political and economic structure of the colonies proved to be as important as any other factor. From the beginning, the British colonies in North America were used to doing things for themselves without much oversight or interference from the British government.

In 1619 the Virginia colony developed its own legislative assembly, the House of Burgesses, which was the first elected assembly in colonial America.[21] Each of the other thirteen colonies eventually did the same. These assemblies instilled in their colonies a tradition of self-governance and a resistance to being told what to do by Great Britain, especially by Parliament.

In addition, unlike France and Spain, Great Britain initially lacked a coherent colonial policy. Later, in the face of significant national debts incurred in part to protect its colonies from its European rivals, Great Britain tried to exert more centralized control over what it saw as ungrateful and entitled colonies and get them to pay their fair share of the costs of their own protection.[22] This move likely came too late, however; colonial governments were not about to give up the independence that they had enjoyed for so long.

A Global War Forces Change in Colonial Policy

The Treaty of Paris in 1763 ended the fourth major military conflict between two global powers, France and Great Britain, in less than seventy-five years. In Europe, this conflict was known as the **Seven Years' War**.[23] In the American colonies, it was known as the French and Indian War. It was a global war; fighting took place in North America, the Mediterranean Sea, the Indian Ocean, the West Indies, and the Philippines and involved most of the European powers of the time, including Great Britain, France, Austria, Prussia, Spain, and Sweden.

The North American part of the war began when members of the Ohio Company, a land speculation company established by a group of wealthy Virginians, pushed Virginia's claims on Native American lands in the Ohio River Valley into lands claimed by France. In 1754 a young officer named George Washington was sent to the territory to challenge French control and assert colonial claims. After an initial attack, Washington retreated to a hastily constructed fort, called Fort Necessity, in western Pennsylvania. Washington was later forced to surrender to the French but was allowed to withdraw with his surviving men.

Hoping to coordinate alliances with Native American peoples—and to keep them from allying with the French—Great Britain requested that its colonies meet at a conference in Albany, New York, in the summer of 1754. Seven colonies sent representatives there.[24] The so-called Albany Congress accomplished very little. However, one of its delegates, Benjamin Franklin, who later became America's first international celebrity, presented to the Congress a plan for closer coordination between the colonies. The **Albany Plan** called for a "Plan of Union," in which colonial legislatures would choose delegates to form an assembly under the leadership of a chief executive appointed by Great Britain.[25] This governing body would have power over dealings with Native American peoples and collective self-defense. And, in a premonition of an issue that would return again in debates over governance of the victorious United States, it would have the power to tax the colonies to pay for their collective defense.

Benjamin Franklin's proposal for a unified legislative body was not adopted by the colonial governments. It was not an idea whose time had come. Great Britain was better off dealing with its North American colonies individually rather than as a potentially powerful unified colonial legislature. For their part, many colonies did not want to give up their own sovereignty, especially when it involved land claims that might make a lucky few colonies (especially Virginia) grow even larger and more powerful than they already were at the expense of the small coastal colonies, such as Rhode Island and Delaware, whose boundaries were constricted by the ocean and those of neighboring colonies.

Benjamin Franklin may not have expected his plan to be adopted. He was a very savvy politician. But his plan did plant the seeds for an American union. Writing four years later, Franklin discussed the "impossibility" of an American union at that time, stating, "When I say such a union is impossible, I mean without the most grievous tyranny and oppression."[26] In the minds of many American revolutionaries, they would get just that.

Economic Conflicts Grow between Great Britain and Its Colonies

After the Seven Years' War, Great Britain was the unquestioned European power in North America, in Canada, and in the modern United States east of the Mississippi River. With victory, however, came problems: Great Britain had to now confront increasingly assertive colonies. It had acquired a vast new territory that now had to be administered, defended, and paid for. But money was scarce. War had left Great Britain with a significant amount of debt. With bankruptcy a possibility, the British government fully expected its thirteen colonies to pay for their own costs to the British Crown so as not to make the debt problem even worse.[27] See Figure 1.1.

Beginning in 1763, a series of acts and proclamations began to enlarge the scope of Great Britain's involvement in colonial affairs, producing a backlash from colonists who felt that Great Britain was going too far. To make matters worse, these acts were instituted during an economic depression in the colonies. Colonial legislatures became increasingly resistant to having Parliament interfere in areas of economic life that the colonies, not Great Britain, had been in charge of for decades.

It was an environment full of misunderstanding and anxiety, vulnerable to the efforts of those who would capitalize on these fears to promote their own ideas about relations with Great Britain. This instability was made worse by the inability or refusal of Great Britain to fully understand what was happening in its thirteen North American colonies.

The Idea of Independence Is Given Voice in Political Propaganda

In this uncertain political environment, there were a few who advocated for resistance to Great Britain, some who remained loyal to Great Britain, and many more who were undecided and afraid of actions that might lead to a hopeless

FIGURE 1.1

European Territorial Claims before and after the Seven Years' War

Following the Seven Years' War, Britain laid claim to much of the territory once held by the French, thus consolidating its power in the eastern portion of North America. Administering those colonies and finding ways to fund expansion was enormously difficult.

war against the greatest military power in the world. It was this last group of colonists, the undecided, who found themselves in the crosshairs of a radical few. Those few had a powerful, cheap, and flexible technology on their side. It was called the printing press, and the American radicals used it very well.

From the printing presses came inexpensive and easy-to-produce papers called pamphlets; the printers came to be called pamphleteers. Enough people had access and the ability to read their products to make the pamphlet a revolutionary technological innovation.[28] The pamphleteers were engaged in **political propaganda**, "which is simply the attempt to control the actions of people indirectly by controlling their attitudes."[29] Their goal was to change public opinion— the distribution of people's attitudes and preferences on the issues of the day. American pamphleteers were not trying to show their intelligence or literary skill. They were trying to mobilize people in support of their cause. Words and ideas, as the pamphleteers knew well, could also constitute strategic political action.

Of all of the American pamphleteers, the most widely read was Thomas Paine's 1776 pamphlet *Common Sense*, which sold perhaps more than one hundred thousand copies in its first year alone. *Common Sense* ultimately "had more influence in focusing the spirit of revolt than the writings of all the intellectuals taken together."[30]

Calling King George III the "royal brute of England," Paine challenged the legitimacy of the British monarchy, refuted arguments in favor of reconciling differences with Great Britain, and announced that "the period of debate is closed."[31] He used the dreaded *I* word, *independence*, writing that independence from Great Britain was not only possible but that it was sure to come to pass.[32] Drawing on the idea that the American colonists had a unique destiny in the world and in history, Paine called the colonists into action at just the time when many were ready to receive his message.

Revolutionaries Take Action, Their Eyes on Increasing the Powers of Colonial Legislatures

Words alone, however powerful, were not enough to mobilize the colonists to make a final break from Great Britain. Colonial radicals began a planned strategy of resistance—one that involved propaganda; organization; and, occasionally, violence. A common phrase associated with resistance to British tax policy was, "No taxation without representation!" While it was used at the time, the phrase did not fully capture the struggle between colonial governments and Great Britain.

American radicals generally did not want to be represented in Parliament in Great Britain. Representatives would have been out of communication with the colonies during debates and consistently outvoted in Parliament even if some arrangement for their representation could be worked out. Instead, the colonists argued that the power of taxation should be held by colonial legislatures, not British Parliament. In many ways, colonial opposition to British policies was conservative. Its adherents wanted to go back to the way things had been prior to the Seven Years' War, when British colonial policy was more hands-off. Economic and political realities, however, made this an unrealistic goal.

The Sons of Liberty Attempt to Mobilize Colonists around British Tax Policies

In 1765, in response to Great Britain's tax policies, a group of merchants and workingmen, including Sam Adams, formed the **Sons of Liberty**. It was a working-class organization, with a potentially much larger appeal to the general public than the revolutionary elites. That potential made the Sons of Liberty both attractive and scary to the wealthy elites in the revolutionary movement. Their fear was that they might not be able to control the actions of the Sons of Liberty. Through rallies, sermons, protests, and heavy use of the newspapers, the Sons of Liberty tried to mobilize public opinion in support of resistance to Great Britain and its tax policies. They also resorted to violent protest. Acts of mob violence, including rioting and looting, in response to British policy only reinforced elite fear, causing "some conservative American political leaders . . . to worry more about the danger of mobs than they did about British policies."[33]

The group's violent actions backfired as a political strategy. Uncommitted colonists looked on the mob violence fearfully, wondering how bad things might get if the crisis were to deepen. In response, radicals changed their strategy. They planned and organized boycotts of British goods, pressuring fellow colonists to comply.

In October 1765, at the invitation of Massachusetts's colonial legislatures, nine of thirteen colonies sent representatives who met in New York to debate and prepare a colonial response to Britain's policies.[34] This so-called Stamp Act Congress (named after the Stamp Act, another British tax, that required the purchase of a stamp for nearly everything involved in trade) issued a Declaration of Rights and Grievances, which was, in many ways, quite mild. It affirmed colonial loyalty to the Crown. It did, however, protest against the imposition of taxes

Crispus Attucks and four others were shot and killed at the Boston Massacre. MPI/Getty Images without colonial consent. Most importantly, the Stamp Act Congress was an early assembly of representatives across, not just within, the British colonies. In 1766 Great Britain repealed the Stamp Act, mostly due to the pressure of British merchants concerned about its effects on their profits. In fact, the Stamp Act had never been effectively enforced.

The Crisis Accelerates as Protests Intensify

In spite of continuing tensions, the years following the repeal of the Stamp Act were relatively quiet politically with radicals losing power and influence and moderates able to keep them in check. Beginning in 1770, however, radical responses to British policies—and British responses to these radical responses—began to shift power and support away from the moderates and into the radical camp.

The exact sequence of events leading up to the Boston Massacre in 1770 is not entirely clear, nor is the exact role of radicals in escalating the situation. It involved a confrontation between a mob of Bostonians and a small group of British soldiers, beginning with taunts and snowballs and ending in the deaths of five American colonials. One of those killed was Crispus Attucks, a young man of African and Native American descent. Sam Adams and other radicals quickly mobilized to use the press to rally support for their cause, describing "the blood of our fellow citizens running like water through King Street."[35]

The Boston Tea Party Adds Fuel to the Revolutionary Fire

In 1773 the Boston Sons of Liberty seized upon an even greater crisis to push away the possibility of reconciliation with Great Britain: the Boston Tea Party. It began over a corporate bailout of the East India Tea Company by the government of Great Britain. The British company was nearly bankrupt, and it had large stocks of unsold tea. Though corrupt and poorly managed, the East India Tea Company was no ordinary company. It ruled much of India with its own private army. It could count among its investors some of the wealthiest and most powerful men in Great Britain. It was—in modern terms—too big to fail.

It needed a bailout, and it got one with the Tea Act, passed by Great Britain in 1773. The act gave the East India Tea Company a tax-free monopoly on the tea trade to the colonies. New England merchants, some of whom were profiting handsomely by smuggling tea from Netherlands merchants into the colonies, were not pleased. The Tea Act cut out the middlemen in the colonial tea trade— the New England merchants—who saw "ruin staring them in the face."[36]

It was the fear of what Great Britain might do next as much as what it actually *had* done that drove many merchants into the radical camp. In November 1773, the *Dartmouth* entered Boston Harbor loaded with tea. Two other ships soon followed. With the merchants increasingly on their side, the Sons of Liberty provoked a crisis, dumping the tea from the ships into the harbor.

Not everyone in the American colonies cheered the actions of the radicals. That it was an act of lawlessness worried many. The violence that accompanied the protest seemed to some completely unjustifiable. The strategic actions of the Boston radicals placed the British government in a very difficult situation.

It could not ignore the attack on British property and commerce. Asserting control, however, risked driving moderate colonials into the radical camp.

Parliament, with the support of King George III, clamped down. Hard. In a series of actions in 1774, known in the colonies as the **Intolerable Acts**, Britain sought to make an example of Massachusetts and its radicals. If Parliament and the Crown thought that this show of resolve, backed if necessary by force, would quiet the colonies, they were wrong. Writing many years after the Revolution, John Adams observed this:

> The colonies had grown up under constitutions of government so different, there was so great a variety of their religions, they were composed of so many different nations . . . that to unite them in the same principles in theory and the same system of action, was certainly a very difficult enterprise. . . . Thirteen clocks were made to strike together—a perfection of mechanism which no artist had ever before effected.[37]

The actions of the British government and the Boston radicals had both helped to synchronize these thirteen clocks.

The Institution of Slavery Denied the Natural Rights of African Americans

The first group of twenty Africans arrived in Jamestown, Virginia, in 1619 aboard a Dutch ship. Like the native peoples whose lands had been occupied by British settlers, the African peoples who followed this small group came from diverse cultures, nations, and kinship groups. Initially, some were given the status of indentured servants—people who still possessed the ability to pay off their "debts" through labor and achieve their freedom. Throughout the seventeenth and eighteenth centuries, whites arrived in numbers from Europe who also carried the status of indentured servitude. As the plantation economies of colonial America developed, however, African slaves and their descendants confronted legal systems designed more and more to strip African captives and their descendants of any legal or political rights or any hope of freedom under that legal order.

By the time Virginia's government fully codified the status of slaves in the eighteenth century, "no black, free or slave, could own arms, strike a white man, or employ a white servant. Any white person could apprehend any black to demand a certificate of freedom or a pass from the owner giving permission to be off the plantation."[38] Like the indigenous peoples, slaves and their descendants struggled to maintain their ways of life, spiritual and cultural traditions, kinship networks, families, and dignity over the coming centuries.

As colonial America moved toward a revolution based on individual liberty, it was far from an equal society. To many Europeans, the prospect of individual advancement made America more equal than their class-stratified societies, with the exception of the almost feudal southern plantation societies.[39] In New England, working-class colonials had achieved a political status that few of their counterparts in Great Britain could. However, wealth was rapidly accumulating in the hands of a small number of colonial elites.[40]

The revolutionary philosophy of colonial America did not include African Americans—nor women, many religious minorities, nor indigenous peoples—in the register of those capable of full citizenship and the rights associated with it. At times, slaves in Virginia and other slaveholding colonies organized and rose up against their oppression. In at least one uprising, slaves seized on the language of the American revolutionaries, shouting "Liberty!" while they rebelled.[41] Armed uprisings by slaves, however, were put down mercilessly with the goal of sending a message to any who would challenge the white order.[42]

The willingness of the majority of white colonial Americans to attack Great Britain for assaults on their liberty while allowing the enslavement of Africans did not go unnoticed by British officials and some white colonists. Thomas Hutchinson, governor of Massachusetts before the war, questioned how the American revolutionaries could "justify the depriving of more than a hundred thousand Africans of their rights to liberty, and the same *pursuit of happiness*, and in some degree to their lives, if these rights are so absolutely inalienable."[43] Pamphleteer Thomas Paine was one of only a relatively small number of white pamphleteers to point out the contradiction of calling for liberty in a society that allowed slavery. In a 1775 newspaper article, he wondered how the colonists could "complain so loudly of attempts to enslave them, while they hold so many hundred thousand in slavery."[44]

This contradiction did not go unnoticed by slaves and free peoples of African descent either. Nor did some of these individuals ignore the potential social and political gains that might be made by pointing out the unfulfilled expression of liberty. In April 1773, a group of African Americans in Massachusetts petitioned the government for a redress of their grievances, drawing "a straight line between their own condition as chattel slaves and the conditions colonists were then objecting to as virtual slavery."[45] They asked that the same principles be applied to their own condition in colonial America.

"We expect great things," they wrote, "from men who have made such a noble stand against the designs of their *fellow men* to enslave them. . . . As the people of this province seem to be actuated by the principles of equity and justice, we cannot but expect your house will again take our deplorable case into serious consideration, and give us that ample relief which, *as men*, we have a natural right to."[46]

In 1776 Lemuel Haynes, a Massachusetts minister, wrote an unpublished pamphlet titled *Liberty Further Extended*. The son of an African father and a white mother, Haynes became a servant to a religious white farming family in the backcountry of Massachusetts. Haynes educated himself in Puritan theology and on the pamphlets of colonial America. He volunteered as a minuteman in Boston in 1774 and for the Continental Army in 1776. In his pamphlet, Haynes anchored his arguments about the injustice of slavery in the principle of natural rights and the Christian theology with which he and colonials were very familiar:

> Liberty is a Jewel which was handed Down to man from the cabinet of heaven, and is Coaeval with his Existence. And as it proceed from the Supreme Legislature of the univers, so it is he which hath a sole right to take away; therefore, he that would take away a mans Liberty assumes a prerogative that Belongs to another, and acts out of his own domain.[47]

Revolutionary Women, Though Excluded, Did Build Institutions of Their Own

In many ways, women in revolutionary America were legally and politically invisible. In spite of commonalities in their legal standing, however, *colonial women* as an all-encompassing term fails to capture significant differences in the status, economic class, and religious orientation of the women in question.[48] Women who were slaves, of African descent, or of Native American ancestry struggled against multiple forms of oppression. While sexual and physical abuse was a danger for all colonial women, those who were slaves or indentured servants faced a higher risk.[49] War only heightened these risks; during the conflict, sexual assault was sometimes practiced systematically. In 1776 in Staten Island, New York, and New Jersey, British troops repeatedly raped women in the area.[50]

White women, unless they had acquired property through widowhood, generally had no legal identity or ability to secure their personal and economic rights in a court of law. For those women who did not struggle against the destruction of their families, traditions, and ways of life—either as slaves or members of Native American communities—theirs was a "protective oppression," designed to keep them out of involvement in government and public life. Because of more restricted educational opportunities and, therefore, lower literacy rates than men, fewer women's voices were expressed in print. In spite of these challenges, however, many women did speak, write, and act against the restrictions on their own rights and liberties in colonial America.

Because of their general exclusion from public life, women had fewer opportunities to adopt leadership roles in revolutionary America. Religious organizations proved an important exception as women could act as leaders in them without the same risk of social approbation as they would face if acting in the male-dominated political space. Maintaining the boycotts of British goods in the years before revolution also "politicized women and the domestic arena," especially in the production of substitutes for those goods.[51] The replacement of British textiles, in particular, brought many colonial women together as **Daughters of Liberty** in spinning events. While these meetings still remained in the "acceptable" realm of home production in the view of the male-dominated white colonial society, they did provide an experience in collective organization—an act of public "joining" that was itself a departure from and challenge to traditional gendered roles.[52]

A portrait of Esther de Berdt Reed by Charles Wilson Peale done sometime before 1780. The Print Collector/Getty Images

Efforts to support the Revolutionary War effort led Esther de Berdt Reed, Sarah Franklin Bache (daughter of Benjamin Franklin), and other colonial women to work to create a women's organization across, not just within, the United States. The Ladies Association was "the biggest domestic fundraising campaign of the war,"[53] in part because women and girls who were not wealthy could still participate.[54]

Reed's pamphlet, *The Sentiments of an American Woman*, published in June 1780, laid out the necessity for colonial women to organize to aid the revolutionary cause. The collection, accounting, and delivery of these donations required the development of an organizational and administrative structure. These fund-raising efforts were extremely successful, and this was perhaps the first truly national American women's organization. Though the members focused on activities considered acceptable for white women in colonial America, the act of organizing and institution building was itself revolutionary.

Indigenous Peoples in North America Challenged Colonization

To the millions of indigenous peoples spread out across two continents, the arrival of the European colonists proved utterly destructive to their societies. Throughout this centuries-long process, however, indigenous peoples challenged this disruption, either outright through diplomacy or armed conflict or less visibly by trying to maintain centuries-old traditions in the face of constant threats to them.

The indigenous peoples, called Indians by the Europeans, were not passive inhabitants of a wild paradise. They had already shaped many North American ecologies and landscapes to suit their own diverse social and economic systems, often with significant environmental impact. The British colonists, in turn, attempted to reshape the landscapes of North America to suit their own purposes and lifestyles, which caused profound disruption of the traditional ways of life of the indigenous peoples.

The social, cultural, and linguistic diversity of the native peoples in North America was staggering. At the time of first contact with the European invaders, perhaps a quarter of "all human languages in the world were North American Indian."[55] Initially, British colonists depended on the adaptive technologies and agricultural advances of the native peoples for their own survival. As the British colonies grew in size and confidence, however, they began to assert their ideas about land ownership more aggressively, provoking resistance by native peoples who had not agreed to such terms. The violence that this clash led to was often horrific, including massacres of entire indigenous local communities and reprisals against individual British colonials.

By the time Thomas Jefferson sat down to draft the Declaration of Independence, the population of the indigenous peoples in the thirteen British colonies had been reduced to a fraction of its level before first contact with the Europeans. Diseases, against which indigenous peoples had little or no immunity, were the largest factor. Death from armed conflict also played a role. However, the disruption in the traditional ways of life of native peoples that arose from European settlement, including the cascading effects of losing their land—which upset agreements and boundaries between other native peoples—also had an effect. The impact of British colonization on traditional native ways of life was comprehensive and total. The habitats upon which the indigenous peoples depended were altered and depleted. The traditional social and economic systems that had been developed before the British colonists arrived often broke down.

Indigenous peoples, however, did not sit idly by and allow this to happen. They resisted—at times militarily, and often quite successfully. Many indigenous peoples also practiced diplomacy among and between European powers and other native peoples. Sometimes this approach bore fruit, but sometimes it had disastrous outcomes, especially as the European powers were often quite willing to abandon their promises to their "allies" among the native peoples once European objectives had been met. Resistance for most indigenous peoples probably took personal, nonviolent, and largely unrecorded and unremembered forms as they tried to maintain the survival of their families and kinship networks, their spiritual traditions, and their economic and social structures in the presence of powerfully destabilizing forces.[56]

Independence Becomes Institutionalized

By the time the delegates to the Second Continental Congress convened in Philadelphia in May 1775, the "war of pamphlets and protests was giving way to the war of rifles and cannon."[57] In April British general Thomas Gage ordered troops to move on Lexington, Massachusetts—to arrest some radical leaders, including Sam Adams—and on Concord, Massachusetts, to seize some weapons. He failed to do both, and the battles of Lexington and Concord, though small, handed the radical pamphleteers the best ammunition that they could hope for. They immediately published exaggerated reports of British atrocities against colonial citizens, especially women and children. Individual colonies began to organize or expand colonial militias and organize their manufacturers for war.

Though few could probably have imagined it that May, the **Second Continental Congress** remained the government of the United States until 1781, when a new American government, one designed by the Congress, took its place.[58] The Second Continental Congress was perpetually in crisis, trying to fight a war in the face of what seemed like unending military defeats, inadequate supplies, troops, and hard money. Its capital even had to be moved in the face of advancing British troops.

When the Second Continental Congress first assembled, the colonies were not yet united in the cause of war. A group of wealthy elites with personal, political, or financial ties to Great Britain opposed independence. A second group, the radicals, set their sights on armed conflict with Great Britain. A third group, the moderates, agreed that a show of force might be necessary but only to serve the ultimate end of a negotiated solution. There were other divisions, between slave and non slaveholding states, large and small colonies, and urban and rural colonists. These divisions would become more important once independence had actually been achieved.

In the early months of 1776, events began to accelerate toward independence. *Common Sense* had given a clear voice to the cause, and British actions had given ammunition to the radicals. Individual colonies began to pass resolutions authorizing their delegates in Congress (often at the request of those delegates) to move for independence from Great Britain. On June 7, Richard Henry Lee of Virginia offered a motion in Congress declaring "that these united colonies are, and of right ought to be, free and independent states, that they are absolved from all allegiance to the British Crown, and that all political connection between them and the state of Great Britain is, and ought to be, totally dissolved."[59]

Congress was not quite ready to act on the Lee Resolution. The vote was postponed for three weeks in order to allow for more instructions to arrive from some of the colonies and to coerce reluctant colonies and their delegates on board. In the meantime, a committee was appointed to draft a basic structure for a government in the event of independence. A second committee was charged with trying to secure foreign aid. Another committee, consisting of Thomas Jefferson, John Adams, Benjamin Franklin, Roger Sherman, and Robert R. Livingston, was charged with writing a declaration, a justification, for American independence. On July 2, 1776, the Second Continental Congress approved the Lee Resolution, marking, perhaps, the actual date of America's formal declaration of independence from Great Britain. Two days later, on July 4, Congress approved Thomas Jefferson's revised Declaration of Independence, which justified its previous actions to the colonies and to the world, though the Congress had modified Jefferson's original draft.

Of all of the changes that members of the Second Continental Congress made to Jefferson's first draft, none were more significant than the deletion of his charges against the king on the issue of slavery. The first section of the deleted charges accused the king of violating natural rights by allowing the slave trade to continue. Thomas Jefferson was a slave owner, one of the largest in Virginia. His lifestyle depended on the capture, sale, and oppression of other human beings. The second deleted section, in which Jefferson charged the king with trying to incite slave rebellions in the colonies, spoke directly to the fears of many southern plantation owners. British officials had recently made offers of freedom to colonial slaves who would join the British against the American revolutionaries. Many eventually did.

In the end, Jefferson's charges against the king on the issue of slavery were deleted, partly due to opposition from southern state delegates. The contradiction—of a new nation announcing its birth on the foundation of freedom while holding hundreds of thousands of people in slavery—remained.

A Revolution Still under Construction

From the start, the Revolutionary War went poorly for the Americans. Successive defeats, disease, and logistical problems all plagued the colonials and their general, George Washington. By adapting their tactics to suit their strengths—knowledge of the terrain and support among many of the locals—the colonials managed to use hit and run tactics to harass Britain and attack its long supply lines. With the help of Britain's rivals, especially France and its powerful navy, the Americans defeated Great Britain at the Battle of Yorktown in 1781. The Treaty of Paris, signed in 1783 and ratified by Congress in 1784, secured the independence of the United States of America.

Militarily and politically, the American Revolution wasn't technically a revolution. King George III was not overthrown; the British Empire remained intact. George would go on to become the longest reigning British monarch until Queen Victoria in the nineteenth century. The conflict in America is more properly called a secession, in which a group of citizens break off from the larger government to form one of their own. In the backcountry, it was frequently a civil war, with members of the same communities fighting each other, often brutally.

It was, however, very much a revolution of ideas. Though imperfectly and incompletely, the idea of a government based upon natural rights and individual liberty had been given political and institutional form. Later American revolutionaries would undertake their own wars of ideas and political strategies to try to make the government live up to its promises. As part of their efforts, they would build, rebuild, and reshape the political institutions that protect and express Americans' natural rights in a representative democracy.

WHAT HAVE I LEARNED?

1. The Seven Years' War resulted in a change in British policy that involved ____.

   a. A large transfer of British land claims to France
   b. The decision to be more assertive in its policy toward colonists
   c. The immediate granting of independence to the colonies
   d. Widespread religious persecution

2. The Albany Plan called for ____.

   a. Closer cooperation between colonies
   b. Independence from Great Britain
   c. New forms of taxation
   d. Trade policy reform

3. Many colonial American elites worried about some of the actions of the Sons of Liberty because they ____.

   a. Were supporting Great Britain and its policies
   b. Failed to repeal the Stamp Act
   c. Were advocating for the rights of indigenous peoples
   d. Threatened mob rule

4. Why was opposition to the Stamp Act on the part of residents of the British colonies in North America so strong?

5. What contradictions were inherent in colonialists' claims to independence on the basis of natural rights?

6. What political institutions did women in revolutionary America help build? Why does this matter?

Answer Key: 1. b; 2. a; 3. d; 4. Answers might include the fact that it was a direct tax and fears of what other forms of commerce might be taxed at a later date; 5. Answers should include the fact that African Americans, indigenous people, women, and religious minorities were excluded given that their basic rights were denied or restricted; 6. Answers should focus on the transcolonial nature of women's cooperation.

THE STRUCTURE OF INSTITUTIONS AFFECTS HOW CITIZENS PARTICIPATE

- Describe the core features of American political institutions.

As we have seen in the stories that have already been mentioned, while the actions of people and their ideas matter to American government, the **political institutions** that structure how citizens may be involved matter as well. To a great extent, institutions determine how conflicts over political power are resolved, and they can also shape the ideas of people acting within them.

In devising a system of government, two basic questions need to be resolved: how much power that government will claim and how political power will be distributed or withheld. Different forms of governments distribute power in very different ways. Totalitarian governments admit no limitations on their own power or competing centers of political power. Similarly, authoritarian governments suppress the voices of their citizens to maintain a grip on power; however, unlike totalitarian systems, authoritarian systems may have some economic or social institutions not under governmental control that may serve to moderate the government's power. Governments that admit no external challenge to their claims on power might be monarchies, ruled by royal figures; theocracies, ruled by religious elites; or oligarchies, ruled by a small group of powerful elites. At the other end of the spectrum of power is a **direct democracy**, in which citizens vote directly on public policies. (See Figure 1.2.)

The United States is none of these extremes. While the nation does have elements of direct democracy—in, for example, local votes to approve or reject

FIGURE 1.2

Types of Governments

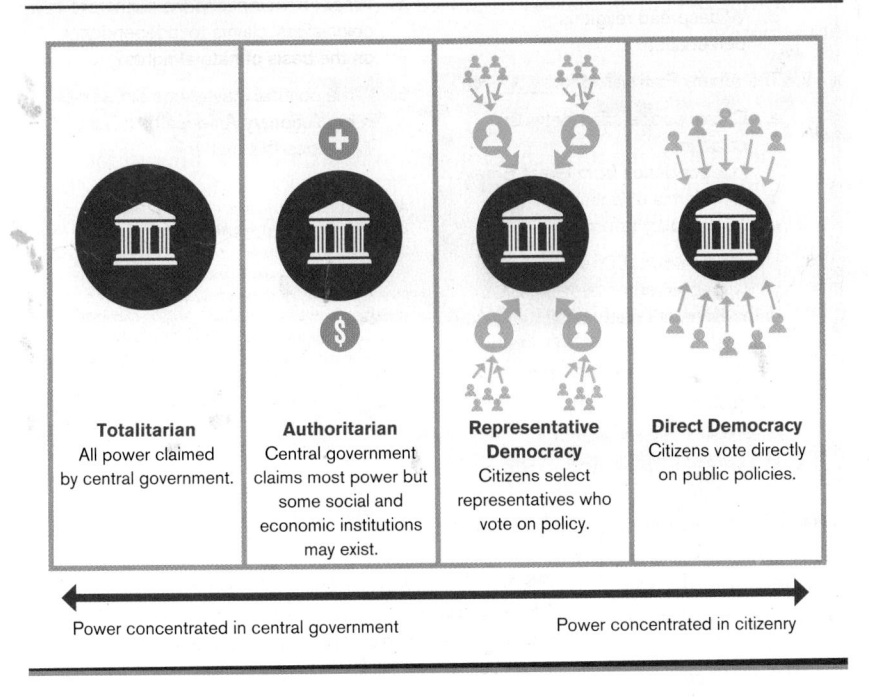

Totalitarian	Authoritarian	Representative Democracy	Direct Democracy
All power claimed by central government.	Central government claims most power but some social and economic institutions may exist.	Citizens select representatives who vote on policy.	Citizens vote directly on public policies.

Power concentrated in central government　　　　　Power concentrated in citizenry public school budgets or property tax increases—the vast majority of conflicts over power in America are handled through a system of **representative democracy**, in which voters select representatives who then vote on matters of public policy. In doing so, voters in a representative democracy are confronted with a serious challenge: How can they be sure that their representatives are carrying out their wishes? This is a question that we will examine in some detail in this book.

The number of political institutions in America today is almost too long to list, composed of bodies at the local, state, and national levels. The most important institution in American political life, however, is the U.S. Constitution. This document forms the basis of the nation's government and, in turn, creates a host of political institutions through which conflicts over political power are resolved. It places textual limits on the power of the national government in order to protect Americans' fundamental rights. It also constitutes, or creates, a people with its first seven words: "We the People of the United States."

How does a society structure political institutions in such a way that the social contract is upheld? By ceding some of the expression of their natural rights to a government, Americans have tried to create institutions that ensure an orderly and prosperous society. In doing so, however, they run the risk of creating institutions that oppress instead of uplift. The United States of America is, institutionally and fundamentally, a **constitutional republic**. In it, Americans elect representatives to make most of the laws and policies in the nation, rather than voting on them directly, which would be unwieldy in a nation of more than 300 million people. In addition, and crucially, limits are placed upon the power of government to infringe upon people's rights in a constituting document that is recognized as the highest and most supreme law of the nation.

The institutions and rules of a government do not only structure the politics of a nation but they also may serve to structure its **economy** or the ways in which goods and services are produced and distributed within a society.

When comparing different economic systems, the key thing to focus on is how much power a government has to regulate the production and distribution of goods and services. In a **communist system**, a government acting on behalf of all workers in a society controls the means of production and distribution. In a **socialist system**, private firms are allowed to operate but with significant intervention by the government, which may include governmental control of sectors of the economy, in the service of ensuring economic equality. In a **capitalist system**, private ownership of the means of production and distribution of a society's resources is emphasized and protected under the laws of that society. Capitalism emphasizes the efficiency of the marketplace in optimally allocating a society's resources. A completely unregulated capitalist system is called *laissez-faire* (from the French "let go," or "let be") and allows individuals and private firms to operate without regulation or oversight. No representative democracies currently practice laissez-faire capitalism. Instead, even nations like the United States that emphasize private economic action practice regulated capitalism, in which firms are allowed to control much of their own decision making but are also subject to governmental rules and regulations (see Figure 1.3).

FIGURE 1.3

Types of Economic Systems

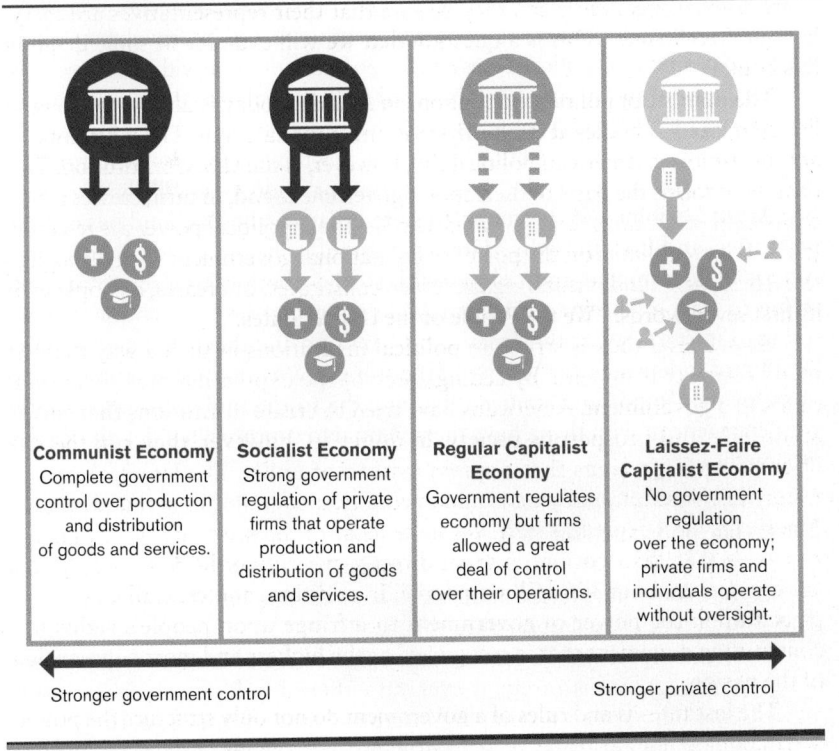

Communist Economy	Socialist Economy	Regular Capitalist Economy	Laissez-Faire Capitalist Economy
Complete government control over production and distribution of goods and services.	Strong government regulation of private firms that operate production and distribution of goods and services.	Government regulates economy but firms allowed a great deal of control over their operations.	No government regulation over the economy; private firms and individuals operate without oversight.

Stronger government control ←——————————————→ Stronger private control

CONCLUSION

The American Experiment, Continued, and You Are Part of It

A study of American government requires understanding the ideas upon which it is based. It requires an understanding of the ways in which political institutions promote, shape, or hinder the fulfilment of these fundamental ideas. It requires a study of the past and the present. However, and most importantly, a deep study of American government requires that you think, and perhaps act, as a strategic player in the political space, which is rarely, if ever, neat and clean.

Should you choose to act in American politics—should you choose to stake your own claims for your rights—you will want to be well informed, both about your own positions on critical issues and the positions of those with whom you disagree. You will want to have developed your skills in analyzing the words, images, and data that will serve as your tools along the way. And you will need to question. What is American political culture? Is there such a thing? How do the institutions of American government make "good government" more or less likely?

At the beginning of the chapter, I stated that this book would be centered on stories, and it is. But why? How is it useful to begin a book that teaches American government and politics with stories about a high school student trying to start a Christian Bible study club, a group of high school students trying to start a GSA, or the American Revolution and the drafting of the Declaration of Independence? Why read the stories? Why not just skim the definitions for the "important" content? Because the stories and, most importantly, your engagement with them, have the potential to capture what definitions and lists might not:

- The understanding that American political institutions did not fall out of the sky; they were created through conscious action and contestation, sometimes based upon success, sometimes based upon failure, and sometimes based upon pure chance
- The comprehension that in the world of American government and politics, there is rarely, if ever, an either-or solution to major problems but instead a complex interplay between ideals, actions, time, and place
- The understanding that the development of American government and politics has always involved the experiences of individuals and groups whose lives were written out of conventional narratives
- The realization that people matter, even if they did not succeed
- The knowledge that your own voices matter—that your own opinions, thoughtfully constructed and respectfully offered, matter, even if these ideas and opinions may seem to be outside of some perception of what you are supposed to think or what others tell you to think

Want a better grade?

Get the tools you need to sharpen your study skills. **SAGE edge** offers a robust online environment featuring an impressive array of free tools and resources. Access practice quizzes, eFlashcards, video, and multimedia at **edge.sagepub.com/abernathybrief1e.**

As you read, engage with, and discuss the material in this book and in your courses, there are only two things of which I will try to convince you: People like you matter. And your stories matter as well, even if nobody ever retells them in a book.

The American experiment always was a complicated and incomplete thing. It still is. At its heart, it poses one difficult and basic question: Can a people design and maintain a government that uplifts and energizes its citizens rather than oppressing them? The answer to that question is not up to other people. It is up to you.

CHAPTER REVIEW

This chapter's main ideas are reflected in the Learning Objectives. By reviewing them here you should be able to **remember** the key points and **know** these terms that are central to the topic.

1.1 Define the key elements of American political culture.

REMEMBER...

- Jefferson drew on ideas of democracy, natural rights, the social contract, separation of powers, and institutional design in drafting the Declaration of Independence, ideas that shape American political culture today.

KNOW...

- *American dream*: the idea that individuals should be able to achieve prosperity through hard work, sacrifice, and their own talents (p. 8)

- *American exceptionalism*: the belief in the special character of the United States as a uniquely free nation based on its history and its commitment to democratic ideals and personal liberty (p.10)

- *American political culture*: a shared set of beliefs, customs, traditions, and values that define the relationship of Americans to their government and to other American citizens (p. 7)

- *democracy*: a system of government where power is held and political decisions made by the people in that society (p. 6)

- *economic equality*: when wealth is relatively evenly distributed across society (p. 7)

- *government*: a system of rules and institutions that defines and shapes the contours of public action (p. 2)

- *inalienable rights*: rights that exist before and above any government or its power (p. 8)

- *liberty*: social, political, and economic freedoms (p. 8)

- *natural rights*: rights that people have inherently that are not granted by any government (p. 7)

- *political equality*: when members of a society possess the same rights under the laws of the nation (p. 7)

- *political ideology*: a set of beliefs about the desired goals and outcomes of a process of governance (p. 10)

- *politics*: the process of influencing the actions of officials and the policies of a nation, state, locality, or community (p. 2)

- *social contract*: an agreement in which people give to their governments the ability to rule over them to ensure an orderly and functioning society (p. 7)

- *social equality*: when no individual's social status is inherently higher than another's (p. 7)

1.2 Identify the political, social, and economic events and institutions that gave rise to the American Revolution.

REMEMBER...

- Colonists established forms of government, political institutions, and social practices that allowed them to increasingly assert their autonomy from Great Britain.

- Economic factors also played a part in shaping the movement toward independence.

- Slaves, the descendants of slaves, and native peoples were not extended rights under the Declaration of Independence.

- Women played a role in the economy and affairs of the colonies but were not extended full rights.

KNOW...

- *Albany Plan*: A proposal for a union of British colonies in North America in which colonial legislatures would choose delegates to form an assembly under the leadership of a chief executive appointed by Great Britain (p. 12)

- *Daughters of Liberty*: a group of colonial-era women who participated in the boycotting of British goods (p. 20)

- *Intolerable Acts*: a term used in the American colonies to refer to a series of laws enacted by Great Britain in response to the Boston Tea Party (p. 18)

- *political propaganda*: attempts to shape governmental actions and laws by changing people's beliefs and opinions (p. 15)

- *Second Continental Congress*: an assembly of delegates from the thirteen British colonies in America that drafted and approved the Declaration of Independence, conducted the Revolutionary War, and created the governmental structure that followed the war (p. 22)

- *Seven Years' War*: a war principally between France and Great Britain and other European nations that was fought across the globe (p. 12)

- *Sons of Liberty*: a group initially formed of merchants and workingmen in response to the Stamp Act that resisted Great Britain and its tax policies (p. 16)

REMEMBER...

- In the American model of representative democracy, the forms our political institutions take affect how people are represented.

- The institutional structure of the United States is that of a constitutional republic wherein the people elect representatives to make the most of the laws and policies in the nation rather than voting on them directly.

- Institutions can both protect and restrict rights, and people may use and change them to protect their own rights or those of others.

- America's political institutions also structure the country's economy.

KNOW...

- *capitalist system*: a way of structuring economic activity in which private firms are allowed to make most or all of the decisions involving the production and distribution of goods and services (p. 26)

- *communist system*: a way of structuring economic activity in which a government exerts complete control over the production and distribution of goods and services (p. 26)

- *constitutional republic*: a form of government in which people vote for elected representatives to make laws and policies and in which limits on the ability of that government to restrict individual rights are placed in a constituting document that is recognized as the highest law of the land (p. 26)

- *direct democracy*: a political system in which citizens vote directly on public policies (p. 25)

- *economy*: the systems and organizations through which a society produces and distributes goods and services (p. 26)

- *political institutions*: the rules, laws, and structures that channel and shape political action (p. 24)

- *representative democracy*: a political system in which voters select representatives who then vote on matters of public policy (p. 26)

- *socialist system*: a way of structuring economic activity in which private firms are allowed to operate and make decisions over production and distribution but with significant governmental involvement to ensure economic equality (p. 26)

2 THE CONSTITUTION OF THE UNITED STATES
A New Vision of Representative Government

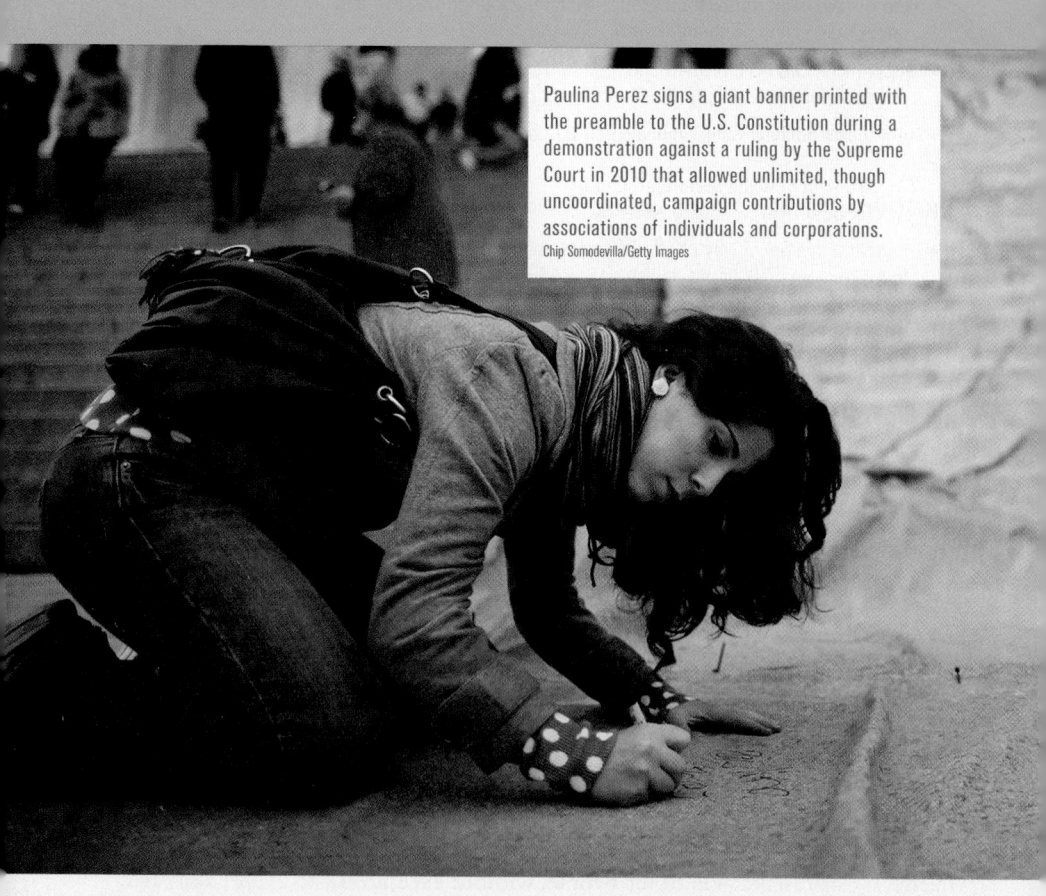

Paulina Perez signs a giant banner printed with the preamble to the U.S. Constitution during a demonstration against a ruling by the Supreme Court in 2010 that allowed unlimited, though uncoordinated, campaign contributions by associations of individuals and corporations.
Chip Somodevilla/Getty Images

In the years following the Revolution, the American states and the government that they had collectively agreed to form struggled against the realities of financial crises, the possibility of foreign invasion, and the threat of internal discord and even revolution. Against this backdrop, a group of delegates convened in Philadelphia in 1787 to create a new government—a new *kind* of government—although they were not technically authorized to do so.

The delegates to the Constitutional Convention drafted and then tried to sell to skeptical individuals in the thirteen American states a blueprint for a new government, though the delegates themselves were often divided about what this government should be, how it should be structured, and how much power it should have. In spite of all of these divisions and challenges, they produced a **constitution**, a document that simultaneously creates a people, sets out fundamental principles on which these people agree to be governed, and establishes the rules and institutions through which this governing will take place.

In this chapter, we will explore the stories of the events leading up to the Constitutional Convention, the political debates within the convention, and the debates surrounding the ratification process. We will focus primarily on one person: James Madison of Virginia. Though he was hardly the most powerful political figure of the time, Madison's efforts were instrumental in shaping the Constitution of the United States.

After reading this chapter, you will be able to do the following:

2.1 Explain how the historical context of post–Revolutionary America led to the proposal for a new, stronger national government.

2.2 Describe how the Constitution was shaped by the strategic political choices of those involved in its drafting.

2.3 Identify the ideas behind the structure of the government under the Constitution.

2.4 Compare and contrast the arguments put forth by the Federalists and Anti-Federalists during the ratification debates.

JAMES MADISON PLANS FOR A REPUBLIC THAT WILL LAST

In the spring of 1786 James Madison Jr. settled into his home in Montpelier, Virginia, with two trunks full of books. Madison was one of America's first political scientists, an avid researcher of the most pressing political questions of his era. The subject of his studies was the unspringlike topic of death, specifically the death of governments. Kingdoms and empires had endured, sometimes for centuries, under the rule of monarchs and emperors. But **republics**, governments ruled by representatives of the people, without exception had eventually died. Madison wanted to know how a people could create a republic that lasted: one that could avoid being taken over by a small group of men or descending into civil war or anarchy, one that was strong enough to govern effectively but yet not trample the rights of its citizens.

In 1786, America was in a precarious position. In the tumultuous years that followed independence, the young nation had been plagued by economic disruption, the threat of European powers, and the dangers of rebellion within the thirteen states. The country needed a clear path forward if it were to survive—a new American government. It needed someone who could sell such a plan to a skeptical public, too.[1] Madison poured himself into this project systematically, scientifically, and with a great deal of energy.

Though he was shy, often sick, and a quiet public speaker, Madison was well educated, and he did his homework. In 1786, as the American government of the time came under increasingly harsh criticism and calls to fix or replace it grew louder, Madison's years of preparation allowed him to help shape the agenda of the debates taking place in his newly independent country and to get others to talk about his ideas, whether they agreed with him or not.

Madison's immediate concern that spring was to prepare for the Annapolis Convention, a conference scheduled for later that fall that had been called to address trade and navigation disputes between states. Madison and others who shared his views hoped that the outcome of the convention might lead to significant changes in the fundamental structure of the government of the United States. However, he was not optimistic about the prospect for real change. His lack of optimism turned out to be well founded. Only five of the thirteen states sent representatives to the convention; the other states either did not appoint anyone or did not do so in time to make it to the meeting. Despite the poor attendance, however, delegates to the convention kept the dialogue of reform moving by calling for a convention in Philadelphia the following spring to discuss how to make the American government more effective in dealing with issues of trade and other pressing needs of the nation.

An engraving of James Madison, American statesman and political theorist. His study of republics led him to investigate how to create a form of people-led government that was capable of enduring. Ipsumpix/Corbis via Getty Images

Madison showed up a year later in Philadelphia having once again done his homework. Together with a group of similarly practical men, he attempted to create a republic that would last, one that would be strong enough to govern but not so strong as to trample on the rights and liberties of its citizens. Madison and his compatriots sought practical, institutional solutions for the seemingly timeless tendency of political leaders to pursue power, prestige, and riches even when this meant the downfall of their own republics. Madison and his comrades had already been involved in the real-world politics of their own colonies and, later, states. Writing in 1923, Robert Livingston Schuyler captured this essential fact about the Founders, writing, "The Fathers," he declared, "were practical men."[2] Ideas and ideals are certainly part of America's constitutional heritage, but so are politics. Yet as we will see, not all Americans wanted changes, and political leaders and citizens in several states, especially the smaller ones, did not trust what Madison and many of his fellow delegates might be up to.

Madison's research, preparation, intellect, and understated political skill played perhaps the most important role in the creation of the Constitution of the United States. The American Republic that he helped shape was based on the premise that liberty is something with which people are born, something that cannot be given or taken away by governments. This concept was expressed powerfully in the Declaration of Independence in its timeless affirmation, "We hold these truths to be self-evident, that all men are created equal." As we have explored in Chapter 1, however, this American liberty was not originally meant for all.

However, like Jefferson and George Washington—the most respected person in America during this period—Madison owned slaves. Though his own writings show that Madison struggled personally against the institution of slavery and that he realized how the practice had corrupted past republics, Madison's Virginia plantation had more than one hundred slaves. Under Virginia's laws of the time, Madison, or any other slave owner, could "correct" a slave for any offense. If that slave died under such a correction, the master would likely not be punished at all. He could take a child from his or her family and sell the child into an unknown future for profit.[3] As the delegates convened in Philadelphia, they had to struggle with these contradictions.

THE CONFEDERAL SYSTEM MADE COORDINATION BETWEEN THE STATES DIFFICULT

The government that Madison and his like-minded colleagues hoped to change was the first government of the United States. It was a confederation: a union of thirteen sovereign states in which the states, not the union, were supreme.

- Identify the challenges involved with creating a government that is strong enough to rule effectively but not so strong as to oppress the rights of Americans.

It had been created by the **Articles of Confederation and Perpetual Union.** Adopted by the Second Continental Congress in 1777 and formally ratified in 1781, the articles created a union of sovereign states that depended on cooperation for its survival. While they had successfully guided the country through war and the accompanying economic and material devastation, the articles had few carrots or sticks to make member states work together to make and carry out national policy. By 1786 the American confederation was showing its limitations, at least in the minds of those who wanted a stronger union.

The Articles of Confederation Attempted to Unite the States while Preserving Their Authority

When they created the Articles of Confederation, the delegates to the Second Continental Congress had debated two related issues. Both involved mistrust. Colonists in one state did not always trust the motives of the governments of the other states. They also did not trust any government that would rule over them from far away, whether it be that of Great Britain before the war or of the new American nation after victory had been achieved.

Though it may be difficult now to imagine a United States in which states were strong and the nation was weak, the idea that the states were the real centers of power was not at all unnatural for Americans at the time. Long after the Constitution was ratified, many Americans still referred to "these United States" instead of "the United States." Since their inception as business enterprises, plantations, or religious communities, the British colonies were used to being self-sufficient and left alone to govern themselves. Colonists often viewed members of other colonies as foreigners. They also reacted strongly against Britain's tardy attempt to create a more centralized colonial policy in the decades before the American Revolution.[4]

During the debates over the Articles of Confederation, mistrust of other colonies crystallized in conflicts over land, representation, and sovereignty. Some colonies had land claims on parts of other colonies. Small coastal colonies, such as Delaware and Rhode Island, whose size was fixed by their location, viewed the western states' claims on Native American land with worry and suspicion. How big would Virginia, whose charter had land claims extending to the "South Sea," eventually become?[5] "The most acrimonious disagreements," according to one historian, "were over control of western lands."[6] The views of the indigenous peoples on questions of ownership did not factor into these calculations.

Under the Confederal System, States Had Sovereignty and Equal Representation

Because of concerns over land rights, the Articles of Confederation provided states with protections against the possibility of any other state claiming disputed

FIGURE 2.1

The Original Thirteen Colonies and the Western Territories

HUDSON'S BAY COMPANY 49°

(SPAIN)

PROVINCE OF QUEBEC

WEST FLORIDA

INDIAN RESERVE

EAST FLORIDA

Proclamation Line of 1763

GA

SC

NC

VA

PA

MD

DE

NJ

NY

CT

MA

RI

NH

VT

(to Mass.)

Colonial Period: 1775

Original thirteen colonies

Other British territories

Boundary between Mississippi River and 49th parallel uncertain due to misconception that source of Mississippi River lay further north

(SPAIN)

Territory Northwest of Ohio River 1787

Territory South of Ohio River 1787

(to Spain)

CONN RESERVE

GA 1788

SC 1788

NC 1789

VA 1788

PA 1787

MD 1788

DE 1787

NJ 1787

NY 1788

CT 1788

MA 1788

RI 1790

NH 1788

VT

(to Mass.)

United States: 1790

States

State claims

Special status areas

Territories

Claimed areas

Foreign areas

1788 Dates for the 13 Original States refer to the year of ratification of the Constitution

1787 Dates of initial territorial organization

Erie triangle ceded by New York to U.S. 1781; sold to Pennsylvania in 1792

East and West Florida retroceded by Great Britain in 1783

Vermont extralegally self-governing 1777–1791

These two maps show the original thirteen British colonies in 1775 and the American states and territories in 1790. Note the vast areas of land bordered by powerful states such as Virginia. Smaller coastal states feared the growth in size and power of these larger states.

territory on its own, without the approval of the confederal government. In the face of the prospect of large, populous, and ever-growing neighbors, smaller states demanded, and received, equal representation in the new government. Each state had one vote in the new Congress. This Confederation Congress was unicameral, meaning it had only one chamber. States selected their representatives to the legislature and could choose the number of representatives that they sent, though each state's delegation had to agree on these decisions, and each state received only one vote. Finally, states and not the new union would be sovereign, a right that was firmly established in the document.[7]

Leading up to the Revolutionary War, the relationship between the colonies and Great Britain was one of a mutual lack of understanding and mistrust. The colonies failed to see how they played a part in Britain's role in global politics and struggles against other empires. For its part, Great Britain failed to understand that what had been plantations, business enterprises, and religious outposts "had grown up and become states in the making."[8] This did not, however, mean naturally united colonies or, later, naturally united states. Each state had its own interests, and each worried that it might lose control over its future to other states or to a national government with its own agendas and desires.

The Confederal Government Was Designed to Be Weak

The confederal government under the Articles of Confederation was intentionally made to be weak. Colonists were experiencing the tyranny of British rule, and they did not want to re-create it in a new American version. The confederal government could not tax its citizens, and it could not force states to carry out its policies. States could recall their representatives at will, and limits were placed on how long a representative could serve.[9] There was no independent judicial branch; one existed primarily to resolve differences between states but had no real way of enforcing these decisions. The president of the Confederation Congress was even less powerful than the delegates and was there mostly to keep order and count votes.

The confederal government did have certain powers. Only it could declare war and conduct foreign policy, though it had to rely on states to pay for these activities. In practice, the confederal government continually faced the challenge of getting states to contribute to the national effort. Sometimes the states had good reason not to comply with these requests. During the war, colonies had been reluctant to send away scarce troops or supplies when they might be desperately needed close to home.

Lack of money was a constant problem, and the Continental Army was continuously without adequate supplies and occasionally faced starvation. Due to the difficulties of collecting contributions from the states or getting loans from European governments, Congress made its own currency, called the continental, which was backed only by the promise of the government to make good on its debts, assuming it won and survived the war intact. The currency later collapsed, creating financial chaos, which only added to calls for reform.

The Prospect of Changes to the Systems
of Slavery and Representation Sowed Unrest

To ensure that the agreements made during their creation would hold, the Articles of Confederation placed a tall hurdle in the path of potential reformers: changing or amending the articles required the approval of all thirteen of the states. In spite of what many saw as problems with the Articles, many Americans did not want to amend, much less replace, them.

Some in the southern states feared that slavery, which was allowed and unregulated under the confederal government, might be restricted or outlawed. Citizens of smaller states feared losing their equal representation in Congress and seeing it replaced by representation based on population, a change that would drastically weaken their position. And many worried that something worse than the problems with the articles might come out of a process of revising them. When a small group of people takes it upon themselves to overturn a political order, there is no guarantee that what they create will not be worse, maybe much worse, than what came before.

Politicians in many states were still mistrustful of the actions and motives of their counterparts in other states. Many were also still nervous about the idea of a strong national government. Since the American Revolution, the political landscape had altered, the balance of political power shifted.[10] State legislative elections in 1786 and 1787 handed strong victories to nationalist candidates, who were in favor of a stronger national government. These nationalist-controlled legislatures would be selecting the delegates to the Philadelphia convention.

Crisis and Fears of Tyranny

Shays's Rebellion, named after Daniel Shays, one of its military leaders, was a grassroots popular uprising against a state government that, in the minds of many of its citizens, had grown too powerful, too distant, too much like that of Great Britain. The rebellion took place in Massachusetts, but the conditions that caused it and the popular anger that fueled it were also present in other states. This crisis added to the sense of urgency in the American confederation, and it provided ammunition to those who tried to replace the structure of government under the articles. Some, like James Madison, wanted a stronger nation, a different kind of republic than had ever been tried before. Others sought a return to monarchy and the British Empire.

The roots of Shays's Rebellion were both economic and political. In the difficult economic times that followed the Revolutionary War, there was a shortage of "hard money," of gold and silver and money backed by gold and silver. What there was no shortage of was debt. Citizens and governments throughout the confederation found themselves unable to pay debts that had been incurred during the war or during the tough economic times that followed. Shopkeepers and cash-strapped state governments alike demanded that their customers and citizens pay debts and taxes in hard currency. Foreclosures—the taking of property to pay outstanding debts backed by that property—were widespread.

The first responses of citizens in Massachusetts and other states were political. Towns asked state governments to issue paper money to help citizens settle their debts. Local citizens petitioned their governments to take action to help them. Some towns in Massachusetts called for a new state constitutional convention. Much of the debt, however, was owed to wealthy elites, and those elites wanted to be paid back in real money, not paper promises. Some states were sympathetic to the people's demands. The government of Rhode Island issued paper money, and the state did not see widespread civil unrest, though many elites came to view the "paper money" politicians as dangerous and undependable. Rhode Islanders, for their part, refused to send delegates to the Constitutional Convention and continued to resist the push for a stronger national government.

The government of Massachusetts held the line, siding with the banking interests. Many of the state's citizens began to feel that they had successfully broken with an oppressive government in London only to replace it with one nearly as bad in Boston. When their attempts at political solutions failed, citizens—especially in the western part of the state—began to take the kind of action they had against King George III and the British Parliament. They rebelled.

Rebellion Begins

To each other, the members of Shays's Rebellion were "Regulators," a label used by the American rebels in the struggle against Great Britain.[11] Many were Revolutionary War veterans with sufficient military skills and popular support to provide a genuine challenge to the Massachusetts government. The Regulators organized themselves by town and family, and they made a point of trying not to antagonize the local population. Instead, they focused on the courts, as had been done before the Revolution, closing them down in the hopes of stalling the foreclosure process until a solution to the debt crisis could be achieved in the state legislature. Although many were committed by rebels carrying weapons, some of these closures "were peaceful, even jocular."[12]

The rebellion and Massachusetts's response to it began to follow a script similar to that of the American Revolution. Citizens took action. The government (this time of Massachusetts, not Great Britain) clamped down, which only made the population more radical. In October 1786, the Massachusetts legislature passed the Riot Act, which absolved sheriffs and other officials from prosecution for killing rioters. With fears of standing armies fresh in the minds of its members, the resistance grew and became more radical, though never as radical as it was portrayed in the Boston newspapers, which accused the Regulators of wanting to redistribute private property[13] or hoping to reunite with Great Britain.[14] Both claims were untrue but served to increase the level of fear and concern within and beyond the state's borders.

The Massachusetts state militia was unable to put down the rebellion. Many militia members, themselves Revolutionary War veterans, sided with the rebels. The government of the United States, the Confederation Congress, could not raise an army; its requests to the states for money were refused by every state except Virginia. The wealthy elites in Boston ultimately paid for an army on their own, loaning money to Massachusetts for the purposes of suppressing the rebellion.

Daniel Shays, a former captain in the Revolutionary War, joined the Regulators later than many but became a commander of its largest regiment, partly due to his notable service in the war. In January 1787, Shays's regiment and two others moved on the state armory at Springfield. Major General William Shepard, commanding the newly raised state militia and in possession of artillery that the Regulators

An engraving depicts the British colonial governor of North Carolina, center, suppressing the Regulators' revolt in 1771. Daniel Shays and other members of the rebellion in Massachusetts patterned their protests against the state government on the actions of the Revolutionary War Regulators. The Granger Collection, New York

lacked, defeated Shays and the rebels, who were forced to withdraw. Two rebel leaders were hanged, and most of the other rebels eventually returned to their farms and towns. Shays escaped to Vermont and was later pardoned, though he never returned to Massachusetts. With the help of the Boston newspapers, Daniel Shays became the personification of anarchy in the United States. In reality, most of the Regulators only wanted to keep their farms and keep their family and friends out of foreclosure or debtors' jail.

From Shays's Rebellion Comes New Opportunity

After the Revolutionary War, George Washington had, as promised, stayed away from public life and retired to his slaveholding plantation in Mount Vernon. But upon receiving what turned out to be exaggerated reports of the strength of Shays's militia from one of his most trusted former generals, Washington grew fearful of what would become of the country. In a letter to James Madison in November of 1786, Washington identified precisely what was needed to "check . . . these disorders": a strong and "energetic Constitution."[15]

Madison may have sensed that Shays's Rebellion would be enough to lure Washington out of retirement and place his unequaled status among Americans behind the effort to create a new political order. Though initially reluctant to attend the Philadelphia conference, Washington eventually agreed; the Philadelphia convention would have the most famous and respected American there to give it legitimacy.[16]

Rebellion was not the only worry among the new states. Great Britain had been defeated but hardly destroyed. The nation had merely been pushed back into Canada, and that was only due to the help of Great Britain's other rivals, who themselves might not always be helpful to the young United States. As states sent their delegates to Philadelphia in the spring of 1787, the world powers were watching, expecting, and perhaps hoping for failure.

1. The Articles of Confederation produced a national government that was supreme to those of the states.

   a. True
   b. False

2. Key provisions in the articles designed to protect states against the power of other states included _____.

   a. A requirement that states could change their boundaries without approval
   b. A supreme court to adjudicate claims between states

   c. A unicameral legislature that gave each state one vote
   d. All of the above

3. What problems in the new nation did Shays's Rebellion highlight? How did people like James Madison capitalize on the crisis to pursue their political goals?

Answer Key: 1. b; 2. c; 3. Answers should discuss the inability of the national government to suppress the rebellion as well as how those in favor of a stronger national government highlighted this weakness.

DELEGATES REACH A COMPROMISE AT THE CONSTITUTIONAL CONVENTION

In May 1787, fifty-five delegates from twelve of the thirteen states began to arrive in Philadelphia. Rhode Island and its paper money men had refused to participate. Though it was by some reports a hot, humid summer, the windows of the Pennsylvania State House where delegates met were shut to ensure secrecy. This secrecy was partly to allow the delegates to say what they wanted, partly because none were sure how citizens in the various states would react to their deliberations. At the time, the meeting was called the Grand Convention or the Federal Convention, not the **Constitutional Convention** as it is called today. The delegates had not been sent to Philadelphia to write a new constitution, only to fix the Articles of Confederation as necessary. Writing a new constitution would have been thought of as a revolutionary act, which it was.

James Madison arrived eleven days early with his research in hand. Though he would become perhaps the most influential person at the convention, Madison was not the only delegate who shaped the final document. And he was certainly not the most famous person there. George Washington served as the president of the proceedings. Most delegates expected that he would be the leader of whatever government emerged, if the convention could agree on one. Benjamin Franklin, possibly the second most famous person in America, was also present, but because of poor health, four prisoners from a city jail carried him through the streets of Philadelphia in a chair on his way to and from the convention. He remained a shrewd politician, however, and used his many skills at important moments in the debate.

Other delegates also guided and shaped the debates and outcomes. Alexander Hamilton, who had served as Washington's aide in the war, emerged as one of the leading proponents of a strong national government. James Wilson of Pennsylvania made important, often unheralded, intellectual contributions to the convention. Wilson served as an intellectual ally of Madison's during and after the convention. Also from Pennsylvania, Gouverneur Morris assembled the various resolutions passed by the convention into a whole document, adding his own literary style and crafting the declaration at its beginning, "We the People, of the United States."

Many important leaders from the Revolution could not or would not attend. Thomas Jefferson and John Adams, both future presidents and supporters of the Constitution, were out of the country in service of the American government. Others, like Samuel Adams and Patrick Henry, both vocal revolutionaries and opponents of a national constitution, were not selected as delegates or refused to go, sensing that the delegates planned to do much more than merely revise the Articles of Confederation. Their suspicions were correct. Samuel Adams was skeptical of what might emerge from the convention, wary of the dangers to liberty that a strong central government might pose and concerned that such a government could not adequately address the diverse needs of the states.[17] Patrick Henry became one of the most effective opponents to the document once it had been submitted to the states. "Here is a revolution as radical as that which separated us from Great Britain," he wrote.[18]

The delegates who assembled in Philadelphia certainly did not represent a snapshot of the people living in the thirteen states. All were men. Most were well educated. None were slaves, former slaves, or Native Americans. Roughly one-third were slave owners. Not all were wealthy, but they were all elites. Unlike the revolutionaries who would soon lead France into chaos in the name of democracy, however, most of the Founders of the American Republic had previous practical political experience to guide them and temper their revolutionary ideals—Madison included. The solutions that the delegates came up with were pragmatic, political, and strategic, for better and for worse.

Delegates Looked to America's State Constitutions for Models, Good and Bad

In the time between the Declaration of Independence and the Philadelphia convention, individual states had drafted their own constitutions. They were often very different from each other. Pennsylvania's state constitution was the most democratic. All real power rested in a unicameral legislature whose legislators served one-year terms. To many elites, the Pennsylvania constitution represented nothing more than institutionalized mob rule,[19] sometimes at the expense of religious minorities. Massachusetts's constitution was much less democratic, with a much more powerful governor and property requirements to serve in the government. To the Regulators and those who sympathized with them, Massachusetts had replaced Great Britain's royal aristocracy with Boston's constitutional aristocracy. As they convened in Philadelphia, the delegates drew from the experiences of the various states as they tried to fashion a new form of government. Some worried about democracy, others about aristocracy. Most worried about failure.

Delegates Debated Forms of Representation and the Powers of the National Government

By Friday, May 25, 1787, enough delegates had made it over the muddy Pennsylvania roads to begin the deliberations. Their first order of business was to unanimously select Washington as president of the convention. Madison, though not selected as the official reporter for the convention, took a seat up front and assumed the role informally. The other delegates were agreeable to this and made sure he got copies of their speeches to be entered into this unofficial record.[20] Much of what we know about what happened in Philadelphia comes from his notes.

The delegates adopted a set of rules to guide themselves, calling for absolute secrecy about their deliberations.[21] They knew that the enormous task of coming to an agreement would be made more difficult if the details of their discussions were leaked. It was said that a member of the convention was assigned to attend dinners with Franklin, who was fond of alcoholic beverages, to change the conversation if Franklin began to talk too loosely.[22] The delegates agreed not to record their individual votes so that they would not feel bound by previous votes if the same issues came up again, giving themselves the ability to compromise and change their positions as needed.

As the proceedings began, the Delaware delegation put the issue of how states were to be represented in the new government on the table—the most contentious issue of the convention and the one that determined so many other outcomes. No other question so dominated the convention during the early

George Washington presiding at the Constitutional Convention at Philadelphia in 1787. Considerable measures were taken to ensure the secrecy of the proceedings at the convention. The Granger Collection, New York

weeks and months of deliberations or threatened to tear it apart. How would states be represented in a new government? Would it be the same one state, one vote formula as under the Articles of Confederation? Or would states be represented on the basis of their population or wealth?

The Virginia Plan Outlined a System of Proportional Representation for the States

On the third day of the convention, the delegation from Virginia presented a set of proposals for the rest of the members to consider. The ideas behind what came to be known as the **Virginia Plan** were James Madison's. Madison had been building their foundations for more than a year and had coached the rest of the Virginia delegation in the days before their presentation.[23] The Virginia Plan was much more than a modification of the Articles of Confederation. Its proposals described a new, national form of government, although Madison and his allies used the less controversial word *federal* when presenting and defending it.

The Virginia Plan laid out the failures of the American confederation—weakness in national defense and the conduct of foreign policy, conflicts between states, and the failure to suppress internal rebellion—and stepped out an answer to those defects: The national government would be strong. Its constitution would be "paramount to the state constitutions."[24] It would consist of three branches: a legislative branch to make laws, an executive branch to carry the laws out, and a judicial branch to resolve disputes between the states and between the national government and the states. The national legislature would be bicameral, consisting of two houses. Members of the lower house would be elected directly by the people. The upper house would consist of representatives nominated by state legislatures and chosen by members of the lower house. The executive and some members of the judiciary would have the power to veto—or overturn—acts of the legislature, which could, in turn, override that veto. The supremacy of the national government would be unmistakable. It could make laws as needed to govern the country as a whole and use military force against states if necessary.

Many details were vague or literally left blank, such as the length of terms of members of Congress, the frequency of elections, and the number of votes needed to override a veto by the Council of Revision. The change in representation of states, however, was clear. The Virginia Plan proposed to overturn the one state, one vote structure of the Articles of Confederation. Instead there would be a system of proportional representation in which more populous states would have more members in both houses of the legislature. The answer to the question, "Proportional to what?" was left somewhat vague, however: Would population counts include slaves? The Virginia Plan was not clear.

Delegates from smaller states reacted immediately and strongly to the Virginia Plan's suggestion of proportional representation. They had successfully fought it off in the Second Continental Congress, when the articles were drafted, and they continued to fight against it. Under the Virginia Plan, Virginia would have sixteen votes to South Carolina's one, plus all there knew that Virginia's boundaries were far from settled. They seemed limitless. New Jersey's William

Paterson vowed never to approve the plan, saying that New Jersey "would be swallowed up."[25]

For the next two weeks, however, the convention discussed the Virginia Plan and little else. Within days of its introduction, several provisions of the plan—a government of three branches and a bicameral legislature—had already been approved. Madison and his fellow nationalists had won the first victory in the strategic political struggle over the Constitution. They had set the agenda. They had forced the opposition to respond to their ideas.

The New Jersey Plan Maintained Equal Votes in the Legislature

Two weeks later, Paterson presented the small states' response to the Virginia Plan. Known as the **New Jersey Plan**, it proposed to strengthen the power of the confederal government but make relatively few changes to the Articles of Confederation. There would be only one house in the legislature, just as under the Articles. Each state delegation (chosen by state legislatures) would still get one equal vote in that legislature. That legislature would get new powers, mostly over taxation and the economy, though it would still depend on the states for some revenue. The executive and judicial branches were much less well envisioned than under the Virginia Plan. Paterson correctly argued that his state's plan was consistent with the purpose of the meeting in Philadelphia; the idea of only making some changes to the articles was the original mandate of the convention. However, delegates had already been debating almost nothing except the Virginia Plan, the framework of which centered on a strong national government and provisions that would essentially replace the current form of government.

After Paterson had presented his plan, Madison proceeded to "tear the New Jersey plan to pieces."[26] Madison argued the New Jersey Plan would leave the nation with all of the problems that motivated the convention in the first place: tax collection would remain a disaster and rebellions such as the one Massachusetts had just barely put down would continue to plague the Republic.[27]

Madison and James Wilson grew frustrated over the less populous states' objections to the Virginia Plan. To these two men, neither the states nor the national government were or should be supreme; the people were supreme to both. How their numbers were apportioned was beside the point. To allow equal representation in Congress for states would allow the political divisions between and within states to infect national politics. Delegates from smaller states did not see it this way. To them, equal representation was not open for negotiation; it was essential to their sovereignty. At one point, Gunning Bedford from Delaware threatened that the small states might have to break off, form their own union, possibly even ally with a foreign power.[28] This was, in modern political terms, the "nuclear option" for the small states. There would be no going back if it were used. All knew it was a possibility, even if unlikely, but to have the idea raised so boldly and so publicly shocked the convention and highlighted for all present the stakes with which they were playing and the possible consequences should they fail to reach an agreement.

The Great Compromise Called for a Bicameral Legislature with Different Methods of Representation in Each Chamber

With the issue of how states would be represented threatening to break apart the convention, the question was sent to a committee. While the young nation celebrated the Fourth of July, delegates to the convention were unsure if their work would succeed, or even continue. The stakes were very high. Elbridge Gerry of Massachusetts warned, "If we do nothing, it appears we must have war and confusion."[29] On July 5, the committee responded with a proposal to give something to each side. The new national legislature would be bicameral; it would have two chambers. Representation in the lower house would follow the Virginia Plan and representation in the upper house, the New Jersey Plan. Compromise having been put on the table, the mood of the convention began to shift. Bedford

TABLE 2.1 Legislative Structures under the Virginia Plan, New Jersey Plan, and the Great Compromise

	Virginia Plan	New Jersey Plan	Great Compromise
Structure of Legislature	Bicameral (two chamber)	Unicameral (single chamber)	Bicameral (two chamber)
Apportionment	**Lower House** • Number of seats apportioned by state population • Members directly elected by citizens	**Legislature** • Equal representation for states regardless of state population • Members appointed by the states	**House of Representatives** • States represented according to population • Members directly elected by citizens
	Upper House • Number of seats apportioned by state population • Members elected by lower house (from list supplied by state legislatures)		**Senate** • States represented equally (two senators per state) • Members appointed by state legislatures
Powers	• Legislature has strong powers	• Legislature has similar power as under the Articles of Confederation but can also levy taxes and regulate commerce	• Legislature has broad powers over commerce and the ability to make laws as necessary • House of Representatives has power to levy taxes

of Delaware—who had threatened the possibility that small states might seek an alliance with a foreign power—insisted that he had been misunderstood.[30]

On July 16, by a vote of 5–4, the delegates agreed to what would be called the **Great Compromise**.[31] Under this agreement, much like the committee's recommendations, the national legislature would be bicameral. States would be represented in the House of Representatives according to their populations. The people would directly elect these representatives. States would be represented equally in the upper chamber, the Senate. Two senators would be chosen from each state by their state legislatures. Not all of the small-state delegates were satisfied with the agreement; two left in protest. But the rest felt that having the Senate was protection enough, and they became much more cooperative in the weeks that followed. Delaware, for all its threats and opposition early in the convention, was the first state to later ratify the Constitution, which was being hammered out in Philadelphia. See Table 2.1.

That the question of representation in Congress was settled first is important as this shaped the political strategies of the delegates going forward. Having secured equal representation in the Senate, small states offered less opposition to a strong national government. They were now less afraid of Congress, even seeing it as a defense against the power of their larger neighbors. Madison, who had wanted popular representation in both houses, began to push to strengthen the other two branches to act as a counter to the Congress that he had proposed but now mistrusted due to the equal state representation in the Senate.[32] The Constitution did not fall out of the sky. It was the result of compromise. But it was also the result of adaptation to earlier compromises and to changes in the political landscape in which the delegates pursued their goals and those of the states that they had been chosen to represent.

WHAT HAVE I LEARNED?

1. Delegates to the Constitutional Convention were sent to Philadelphia with the intention of fixing the Articles of Confederation, not to write a new constitution.

   a. True
   b. False

2. According to the Virginia Plan, _____.

   a. There would be a unicameral legislature with members appointed by state legislatures, and with equal representation for states regardless of population
   b. The bicameral legislature would have equal representation for all states, and all members would be directly elected
   c. There would be a bicameral legislature with members apportioned by state population; lower house seats would be directly elected, and upper house seats would be elected by members of the lower house
   d. Members of the unicameral legislature would all be selected by state legislatures

3. Which aspects of the Virginia and New Jersey Plans were retained in the Great Compromise, and why?

....

Answers: 1. a; 2. c; 3. Answers should reference the bicameral legislature, proportional representation system in the lower chamber (House), and direct election of the lower house members, which was part of the Virginia Plan. From the New Jersey Plan, states would have equal representation in the upper house (Senate). The Great Compromise, in combining two systems of representation in Congress, balanced the preferences of small and large population states and allowed the Convention to move forward.

DELEGATES WORKED OUT DETAILS OF THE NEW GOVERNMENT

With the bicameral legislature having resolved the first and largest issue of the convention—the distribution of representation between the states—the convention moved on to the structure of the rest of the government and the specific powers of each branch. In doing so, it confronted the second major issue of the convention: the question of national power. Many of the details of the new government were worked out in two committees over the rest of the summer and then presented to the full convention for approval. The Committee of Detail presented its recommendations on the structure of government and the relationships between the three branches. The Committee on Unfinished Parts took up issues that had not been resolved and generally tried to tie up loose ends in the structure of the new government.

> • Explain the distribution of power across and within the branches of government as set out in the Constitution.

The Legislative Branch Was Made the Most Powerful

While representation in Congress had been settled, its powers still had to be worked out. To do so, delegates looked to the powers of the Confederation Congress under the Articles of Confederation as well as to state legislatures under the various state constitutions. As the **legislative branch** of government, Congress's purpose was to legislate—to make laws. Both houses had to work together to pass laws, but because of how congressional members were chosen, each house had a slightly different purpose. Members of the House of Representatives, who were elected directly by the people and had to run for reelection every two years, were meant to be more responsive to the people, to directly represent their constituents. Senators, who were chosen by state legislatures and served six-year terms, were there to check the passions of the people. Senators' terms were staggered in two-year shifts so that only about one-third of senators would be up for reelection in any given election year, making it more difficult for any swift change in mood among citizens to quickly affect national policy.

Congress, as expected, was made more powerful than the unicameral legislature under the Articles of Confederation, especially with regard to issues of money and the economy. Congress was given the power to borrow money, collect taxes, and "regulate Commerce with foreign Nations, and among the several states." This commerce clause has enabled Congress to become involved in large areas of the American economy, even within states. Debates over the power of and limits to the commerce clause continue today, especially between states and the federal government.

In order to preserve its flexibility, Congress was also given the ability "to make all Laws which shall be necessary and proper for carrying into Execution the foregoing Powers, and all the other Powers vested by this Constitution in the Government of the United States." The necessary and proper clause, combined with the commerce clause, paved the way for a dramatic expansion in Congress's power over national policy in the centuries following ratification.

The Executive Branch Was Initially Less Thoroughly Planned Out

Shown here arriving at Congress Hall in Philadelphia on March 4, 1793, for his second inauguration, George Washington chose to retire after his second term despite the fact that the Constitution would have permitted him to run for reelection for an unlimited number of terms. The Granger Collection, New York

Neither the Virginia nor the New Jersey Plan had been very specific about the **executive branch** of government. Madison had not given it as much thought as he had Congress—at least until he decided he needed to build in more protections against equal state representation in the Senate. Initially there was not even a consensus over how many chief executives the country should have, much less over how powerful the branch should be. Alexander Hamilton, young, ambitious, self-made, and not trusted by many delegates, proposed a powerful president who would be elected for life. His plan made the Virginia Plan look moderate. Though it was not voted on, Hamilton's suggestion of an "American king"[33] followed him for the rest of his political career. Most delegates expected Washington would serve as an, if not *the*, executive of the country. Some wrote that confidence in Washington reduced anxiety about how powerful the executive would become.

In the end, the delegates settled on a single executive—a president—who would serve for four-year terms. As head of the executive branch, the president was there to "execute," or carry out, the laws that had been passed by Congress. The president was given some, but not unlimited, power over Congress with the ability to veto a piece of legislation that Congress had passed. Congress could, however, override the veto with a two-thirds vote in each of the two houses. The president was named commander in chief of the army and navy. Again, though, power was to be shared. Congress, not the president, was given the power to declare (and raise money for) war. Presidents were given power to oversee the people working in the executive branch and to obtain from them the information needed to govern the country, which has led to the growth of a large and influential federal bureaucracy. Finally, the president was given the power to make foreign policy; though, again, this responsibility was to be shared with the Senate.

More controversial than what powers the executive would have was how the president would be elected, raising once again the question of how states would be represented in the new government. In the end, delegates settled on a complicated compromise for electing the president, one that is still not fully understood by many Americans. Citizens would not vote directly for the president. Instead, an Electoral College consisting of electors awarded to states based on their representation in Congress would select the president. Each state received two electors (for their senators) plus one each for their members of the House of Representatives. States would decide how these electors were to be chosen, and successful candidates would need to win a majority of electors to become president. The system of the Electoral College continues to incite criticism and suggestions for reform. In the minds of the delegates, however, the complicated structure managed to avoid reigniting the disagreements between small and large states over representation.

The Judiciary Was Designed to Interpret Constitutional Conflicts

The Virginia and New Jersey Plans were even less specific about the **judicial branch** of the government, the system of federal courts. Delegates decided on one supreme court to be the highest in the land and a system of lower federal courts whose structure and composition would be determined by Congress. Unlike the judiciary under the articles, the federal courts would have jurisdiction—the authority to hear and decide cases—over all disputes between states and the national government, between two or more states, and between citizens of different states. Combined with the supremacy clause of the Constitution, which declared that national treaties and laws "shall be the supreme law of the Land," the federal court emerged as superior to state courts.

Not included in the Constitution was an explicit description of the power of judicial review, which gives the judicial branch of government the authority to determine if a law, part of a law, or an act of government is or is not in violation of the highest law of the land and, if it *is* in conflict, if it is thus invalid. In the United States, that supreme law is the Constitution, and the power of judicial review rests ultimately with the U.S. Supreme Court. While state supreme courts may exercise judicial review on state laws and actions, the supremacy clause of the Constitution ensures that the exercise of judicial review by the Supreme Court includes the authority to use that power over both national and state laws and actions.

In exercising this power, the Supreme Court does not claim to be above the executive or legislative branch. Instead, the Constitution and the people are above all three branches, and it is the role of the Court to act as the interpreter of conflict between the Constitution and governmental action. This power has been retained throughout history by shrewd political action and the conscious preservation of it by Supreme Court justices. We will examine the concept of judicial review, its foundations, and controversies surrounding its use in much more detail in our chapter on the judiciary.

The power of judicial review, combined with the supremacy clause (Chapter 3), became crucial in later battles to protect civil liberties and secure civil rights, many were waged by citizens who because of their identity had been ignored by the original document or had their rights restricted by it. As with the other two branches, the judiciary was not to exist in isolation. Congress, not the Supreme Court, had the authority to create the lower federal courts. Congress would determine the number of Supreme Court justices, and the Senate had the power to confirm justices (with a majority vote), who first had to be nominated by the president.

Separation of Powers Allowed for Checks and Balances on Government

In drawing up the powers of each of the three branches, the delegates tried to make sure that no one branch could become too powerful on its own. The idea of **separation of powers** was widely supported by delegates at the convention and well known to those who had studied the writings of Baron de Montesquieu. Under this system, branches are not meant to preside over their own spheres. Rather, a system of "separated institutions sharing power" was created.[34] Each branch, whose members tended to represent a different group of people, has to work with the other branches to make things happen, though not on every issue all of the time (see Table 2.2). This was the central blueprint around which the national government was structured. Popularly known as the system of checks and balances, the idea of overlapping (but not perfectly overlapping) spheres of influence also applies to relations between the states and the federal government. Federalism, or the sharing of power over some aspects

TABLE 2.2 Separated Institutions Sharing Powers

	INSTITUTIONS		
	Executive Branch	Legislative Branch	Judicial Branch
Lawmaking Authority	• Executes laws • Has veto power • Nominates judges to the federal judiciary and key executive branch officials • Shapes legislative agenda	• Writes nation's laws • Has veto override • Senate confirms judicial nominees and key executive branch officials • Determines number of Supreme Court justices • Creates lower courts	• Interprets contested laws • Can declare both federal and state laws unconstitutional
National Security and Foreign Policy Responsibilities	• President acts as commander in chief of the military • Sets foreign policy agenda	• Declares war • Senate ratifies treaties with other nations	
Oversight Responsibilities	• Oversees federal bureaucracy	• Holds power of impeachment • Budget authority and oversight over executive branch agencies	• May declare laws or executive branch actions in conflict with the Constitution
Sovereignty	Sovereignty rests with the people. The Constitution is the supreme law of the nation.		

of governance between the states and the nation, is as central to American government as checks and balances, and it has been the source of much conflict and controversy throughout its history.

Delegates Addressed the "Unfinished Parts" but Left the Problem of Slavery Behind

At the beginning of September 1787, the Committee on Unfinished Parts[35] reported back to the convention on its efforts to address issues that had been left unresolved. Not all of these issues were ironed out, and the question of slavery threatened to break up the proceedings.

In an attempt to clear up commercial relationships between states, the delegates decided that "full faith and credit shall be given in each State to the public Acts, Records, and judicial Proceedings of every other State." The full faith and credit clause was designed to ensure that each state recognized contracts and other legal proceedings from other states. It has become an important constitutional element in the question of same-sex marriage and marriage equality in the United States (see Chapter 4). The structure of the Electoral College was finalized, as was the office of vice president of the United States, whose constitutional powers are quite limited but who plays an important role in presidential elections.

In important ways, however, the Constitution remained unfinished even after the delegates completed their deliberations in September. This was partly by design, partly due to political compromises made during the convention itself. By making provisions for changing the Constitution through a process of **amendment**, the Framers acknowledged that it would always be unfinished, that it would need to be adaptable if it were to endure. By *adaptable*, however, the delegates did not mean easily changed. They purposefully designed a system for amending the Constitution that made this very difficult to achieve. Once again, divisions over representation of states emerged, with small states arguing that states should have the power to approve amendments and the nationalists arguing that it should be left to the people to decide.

In the end, another complicated compromise emerged, with both the people—through official proposal in Congress—and the states—through the process of final ratification—necessary to alter the Constitution. Amending the document is a two-stage process, with two possible routes to completion of each of the two stages needed for amendment. First, the amendment has to be officially proposed, which involves much more than someone just suggesting an idea. Proposal can happen in one of two ways, only the first of which has ever been used: (1) passage by a two-thirds vote in both the House and the Senate or (2) passage in a national convention called at the request of two-thirds of the states. After formal proposal, the proposed amendment must be ratified by one of two ways: by (1) a majority vote in three-fourths of the state legislatures or (2) acceptance by ratifying conventions in three-fourths of the states. The second method for ratification has been used only once.

Of the thousands of suggestions for amending the Constitution presented in Congress since its founding, only twenty-seven amendments have been formally ratified. The first ten of these, which make up the Bill of Rights, became part of the debate over ratification itself and are often thought of as part of the "original" Constitution. Two others—an amendment prohibiting the sale and consumption of alcoholic beverages and one repealing that prohibition—cancelled each other out. Since the passage of the Bill of Rights, therefore, the Constitution has only had fifteen lasting changes. Though the Constitution has rarely been amended, some scholars argue that important decisions by the Supreme Court and major changes in how the American people view themselves have at critical times in history led to changes in government just as significant as formal amendments.[36]

The Founders Reached a Fateful Compromise on Slavery

At the time of the convention, nearly one out of every six individuals living in the thirteen states was a slave. Most, but not all, lived in the southern states. Southern plantation owners, many of whom were politically powerful in their state legislatures and some of whom were delegates to the Philadelphia convention, had no intention of seeing their institution outlawed or heavily regulated. Plantation owners were not the only interests who benefited from slavery. The slave trade and the trade in goods made by slaves benefited some powerful shipping interests as well, especially in the Northeast. About one-third of the delegates to the convention, including Madison and Washington, were slave owners. A few others, however, saw the preservation of slavery as a moral failure and spoke out at the convention about the hypocrisy of trying to preserve liberty in a document that allowed slavery.

In spite of a few speeches on the floor of the convention, however, the question of slavery was not generally debated in terms of morality or of liberty but rather in terms of states' representation, the same issue that affected so many others at the convention: Would slaves count when it came time to tally a state's population? In the end, the question of slavery was settled on practical, political considerations.

The final document dealt with slavery in three ways. The word *slavery* never appears—a minor tactical victory for those who did not want the Constitution to appear to approve of it. On the question of slavery and representation in Congress, the **Three-Fifths Compromise** ensured that a slave—called an "other person" in the Constitution—would count as three-fifths of a person for a state's representation.[37] Slaves could not vote or be represented, but their numbers would boost the influence of the slave states in which they were held because since slaves were counted among the population, slaveholding states would be allotted more members of Congress. In a second facet of the compromise, Congress would not be allowed to restrict the slave trade until 1808 at the earliest. Third, slaves who had successfully escaped would have to be returned to their owners, regardless of the laws of individual states.

Historians and political scientists have debated how the delegates could have agreed to preserve slavery when some observed that it went against the very idea of natural rights upon which the Constitution is based and at a time when some states were beginning to restrict or outlaw it on their own. There are several reasons, and they are not mutually exclusive.

Slavery, Population, and the Balance of Power between Southern and Northern States

One of the most important divisions between the states during the Constitutional Convention was on the issue of slavery. In addition to being a moral issue, how slavery was handled during the proceedings, as all delegates knew, would have serious implications for the balance of political power in the federal government, especially in the House of Representatives. While states would be equally represented in the Senate, their representation in the House would depend upon their population. Did that population include slaves?

Figure A shows the percentage of each state's population that was enslaved in 1790, three years after the drafting of the Constitution. The divisions between northern and southern states are striking. What might this mean for representation in the House?

Figure B presents the same data, but it does so in a way that breaks down the population—free, slave, and total—of each state and the two regions. Note the light blue bars, which represent the total population of the states and regions. Looked at this way, the balance of population between the northern and southern states is roughly equal, with just under two million individuals in each region. However, when one separates out the slave population (the green bars), the northern states have a population advantage of more than six hundred thousand people (the dark blue bars). It was this math that drove much of the bargaining over slavery and representation in the convention.

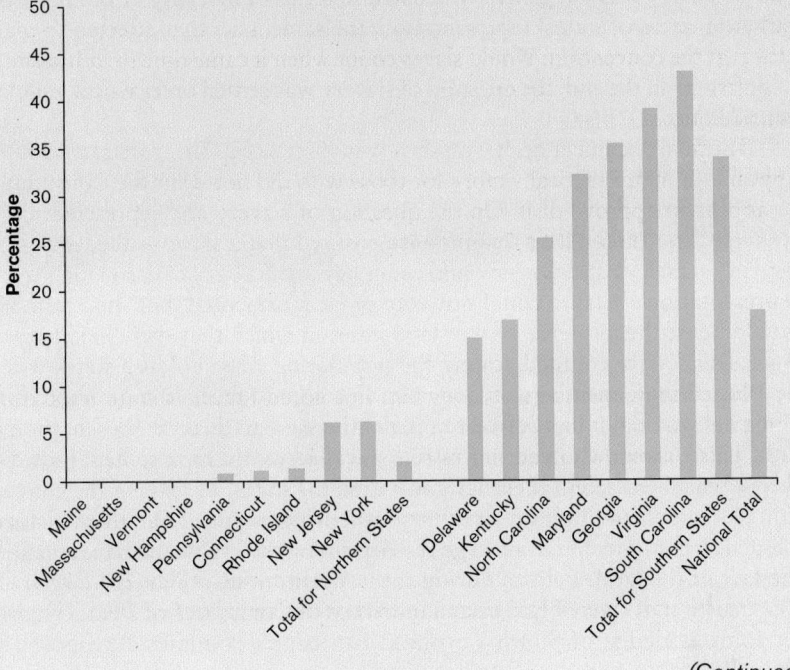

Figure A: Percentage Slave Population by State

(Continued)

(Continued)

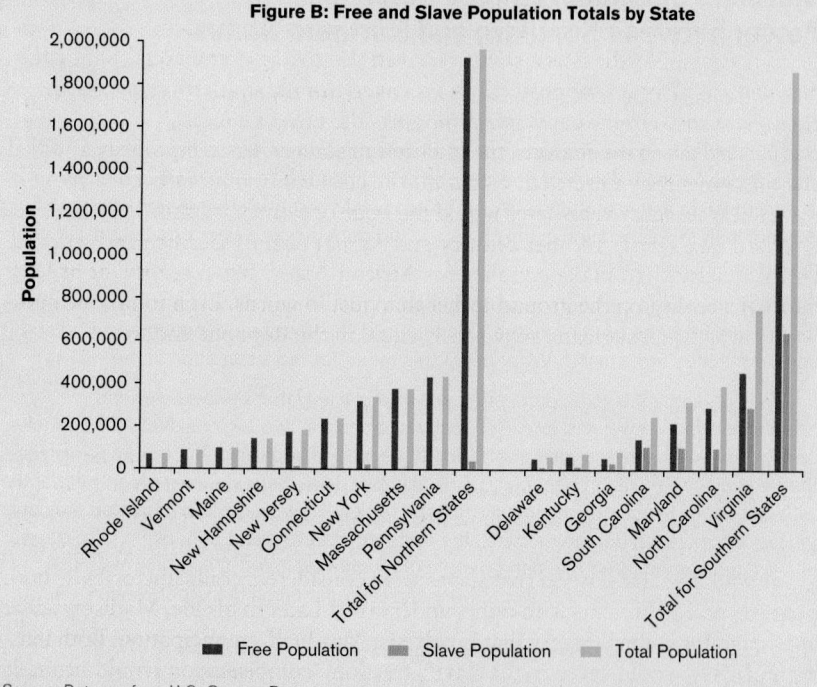

Figure B: Free and Slave Population Totals by State

Source: Data are from U.S. Census Bureau, www.census.gov/census-sis/index/teach/history-activities/American-Revolution/1790-census-and-apportionment—-analyzing-the-three-fifths-compr.html.

WHAT DO YOU THINK?

What information does Figure B convey that Figure A does not? Have you encountered different charts and tables that present the same or similar data in different ways, thus allowing you to draw different conclusions?

The first reason is that slaves had not voted for their state legislators. Some delegates did oppose slavery, but slaves had no direct representation in the Constitutional Convention. While slaves were not represented, however, slave owners were, and their delegates used the threat of leaving the convention to secure their interests. Had the southern states pulled out, the Articles of Confederation, which contained no restrictions on slavery, would have remained the law of the land. Politics during the convention also played a large role. The question of slavery had been handed to the Committee of Detail, chaired by John Rutledge of South Carolina. Rutledge's committee proposed to give the slave states everything that they demanded. In his notes, Madison commented on the political implications of this slave-state delegate being in charge of the committee that would set the agenda for debate on the issue of slavery.

Others have argued that the preservation of slavery was the result of a **logroll,** or a trading of votes, between the slave states and the northeastern commercial states. Northeastern states received the strong commercial policy that they wanted in return for protections on slavery for the southern states. Evidence from the records of the convention supports the idea of a logroll.

Regardless of the reasons, the question of slavery was temporarily handled but fundamentally unsettled. Not until the country was literally torn apart in the Civil War eighty years later would the issue of slavery be ultimately decided. It would take nearly another century and a great deal of sacrifice and strategic political activity to make equality for African Americans a reality, or at least more of a reality, on the ground rather than just in words. Even today, the question of whether Americans are all truly equal in the Republic endures.

James Madison Held Contradictory Views on Slavery

Although his views on slavery evolved over time, James Madison was never able to completely resolve the contradictions inherent in a Constitution and government that, although based on natural rights and liberties, permitted slavery. Some of his writings dating from the time of the drafting of the Constitution indicate that he understood that slaves were considered, contradictorily, as both property and as humans with rights under law.[38] Later in his life, Madison wrote out a plan for ending slavery that involved a "gradual" emancipation. Both master and slave would agree to the slave's freedom, compensation would be made to the master for his "loss," the slave would explicitly acknowledge preferring freedom to bondage, and all former slaves would be relocated to a region not "occupied by or allotted to a White population."[39]

Madison never did free his own slaves or provide for their freedom upon his death, as his colleague George Washington would do.

The Constitution Was Finished but Not Yet Made the Law of the Land

By proposing a system of amendments, the Framers ensured that the Constitution would always be unfinished so that it could adapt over time. More immediately, however, the Constitution was unfinished because the states had yet to approve it. The document that emerged from Philadelphia was just a proposal. It carried no force until the states chose to adopt it. That would be determined by the battle over ratification.

A skillful move by Benjamin Franklin at the convention's conclusion required only that delegates sign their names as witnesses to their states' endorsement, which allowed some delegates to sign the Constitution even knowing that they would soon speak out against it. Franklin's move, and the departure over the summer of delegates who did not approve of the outcomes, made the delegates appear to be in greater agreement than they really were. In fact, many did have strong reservations, and three refused to sign.

The delegates also used a bit of trickery to get around another issue. The Articles of Confederation stipulated that amendments to the articles required the approval of all thirteen state delegations in Congress. This, members of the Constitutional Convention knew, was going to be very difficult. Rhode Island never sent any delegates, and many states were closely divided. So the delegates declared that the Constitution would become the law of the land if ratifying conventions in nine out of thirteen states approved it, bypassing the state legislatures. Even with this somewhat unconventional ploy—breaking the spirit if not the law of the articles—it was still far from certain that the Constitution would be adopted.

WHAT HAVE I LEARNED?

1. The Framers of the Constitution intended for the three branches of government to operate completely independently.

   a. True
   b. False

2. Of the three branches of government, the Constitution makes _____ branch(es) the most powerful.

   a. The legislative
   b. The executive
   c. The judicial
   d. All three are coequal

3. The Committee on Unfinished Parts addressed which of the following issues?

   a. Separation of powers and the system of representation in the legislature
   b. Slavery and ratification

   c. Full faith and credit, the amendment system, the Electoral College, and the office of the vice president
   d. All of the above

4. The process of amending the Constitution requires _____.

   a. Either two-thirds of the members of Congress or three-fourths of the states to agree
   b. A unanimous vote in Congress
   c. The approval of all states
   d. A two-stage process involving proposal and ratification

5. Who do you think were the winners in the Constitutional Convention? Who were the losers?

Answer Key: 1. b; 2. a; 3. c; 4. d; 5. Answers will vary. Students may focus on small states versus large states, slaves, or other individuals excluded from the political process.

FEDERALISTS AND ANTI-FEDERALISTS FOUGHT OVER RATIFICATION

The fight between those in favor of the Constitution and those opposed to it was America's first national—and first *negative*—political campaign. Both sides issued dire premonitions of what might happen if the Constitution was or was not ratified. The debate was carried out through the printing presses, which had become widespread enough to allow both sides to carry their messages to the people.

- Explain the major differences between Federalists and Anti-Federalists in their views of the proposed constitution.

The supporters of the proposed Constitution scored the first tactical victory by claiming the name **Federalists** for their group. That was ironic because the proposed government was actually strongly national, whereas the term *federalist* generally meant more of a balance between the power of states and the national government. That forced those arguing against the document to be tagged as **Anti-Federalists** despite the fact that their position was in reality more federalist.

The Anti-Federalists were therefore put in the difficult position of having to argue against a proposal, and basing their argument only on what was good about the Articles of Confederation was a tough sell. So they turned negative. They raised fears in the minds of Americans about what this potentially radical change in the government would bring. Mostly, they argued, it would trample on the rights of the people and the states in which they lived.

For their part, the Federalists pointed to the problems that plagued the government under the articles—the inability to deal with foreign powers; economic challenges; and, especially, the threat of anarchy—and warned citizens that the only way to avoid these dangers was through the new Constitution. The Federalists had celebrity on their side in the figures of Washington and Franklin. The Anti-Federalists, with the exception of a few misguided attempts to counter the celebrity endorsements of Washington and Franklin, stayed away from the issue of famous endorsements.

In some ways, the Federalists and Anti-Federalists split along distinctions of class (see Table 2.3). Many wealthy merchants favored the strong economic policy that the Constitution would allow, and many wealthy southern plantation owners supported the agreements that had been struck. On the other side, a large number of Anti-Federalists came from rural areas and mistrusted powerful elites in their states' capitals. To say that the Federalists were wealthy elites and the Anti-Federalists small farmers and shopkeepers is, however, too strong a simplification. Many Anti-Federalist leaders were educated elites; some of the most prominent had been heroes in the Revolutionary War, delegates to the convention itself, or important members in state politics.

Though the Federalists tried to associate the threat of anarchy and Shays's Rebellion with their opponents, the Anti-Federalists were just as concerned as their opponents with securing a stable future for the country. Instead, the divisions between the two sides represented fundamentally different visions for how to do so. Three main issues divided the Anti-Federalists and the Federalists on a vision of this future: (1) the very possibility of creating a workable republic in such a large nation that would protect individual liberties against **tyranny** (the suppression of the rights of a people by those holding power), (2) the relative power of states and the nation, and (3) the lack of a bill of rights (a list of rights and liberties that people possess and that governments cannot take away) in the Constitution. Each of these issues was closely related to the others.

The fate of the Constitution was decided in the state ratifying conventions (nine states had to ratify for the Constitution to take effect), but it was the subject of intense debates everywhere—in homes, taverns, coffeehouses, and newspapers. The Granger Collection, New York

TABLE 2.3 Federalists and Anti-Federalists

Both Federalists and Anti-Federalists were interested in a politically and economically secure nation, but they differed in how they thought that would best be achieved.

Differed in Terms of ...	Federalists	Anti-Federalists
View of Proposed Constitution	Supporters	Opponents
Proponents of ...	A strong national government	Stronger state government
Concerned about ...	The tyranny of the majority	The tyranny of the minority
Proposed ...	The idea of an extended republic to limit the problem of faction and help to resolve the tyranny of the majority	Strong restrictions be placed on branches of government to help solve the problem of too-strong national government
Supporters Included ...	Wealthy merchants and southern plantation owners	People in rural areas, more farmers and shopkeepers
	George Washington, Benjamin Franklin, Alexander Hamilton, James Madison, John Jay	Fewer well-known supporters but leadership included educated elites, Revolutionary War heroes, and convention delegates

Federalists and Anti-Federalists Debate the Dangers of Power in a Large Republic

As the debate over ratification got under way, the factions for and against the Constitution disagreed on the very possibility of a republic in a country as large as the United States. Many of the Enlightenment writers that Madison had drawn his ideas from had argued republics had to be small to work properly, and all expected this one to grow even larger over time, making the challenges even worse. Anti-Federalists argued that the national government would grow more distant from the people over time and would eventually begin to oppress them. Congress having the power to tax would only make this danger greater, they claimed. Therefore, the Anti-Federalists asserted, more restrictions needed to be placed on the national government and more power reserved for the states.

These challenges required more than a tactical shift on the part of the Federalists—they went positive. The Federalists made their case for the Constitution in a collection of eighty-five essays written primarily for the New York papers from the fall of 1787 to the spring of 1788. Published under the collective name *Publius*, ***The Federalist Papers***, which were actually written by Alexander Hamilton, James Madison, and John Jay, are now considered some of the most important writings in American political history. They laid out the theory behind the Constitution (which itself does not directly speak to the reasons behind its own provisions), showing how a large republic could be constructed in a way that would prevent it from growing so self-interested and powerful that it would trample on the rights of states and their citizens.

Many of Madison's essays are now considered to be the most important in the collection. Two essays in particular, *Federalist* No. 10 and No. 51 (see Appendix), tackle Anti-Federalist critiques by laying out the reasons behind the proposed constitutional republic. From his research, Madison knew that in a republic one must not assume that people will always act in noble ways, putting their own needs behind what is best for the republic. Instead, a republic must be constructed to account for self-interest and selfish motives.[40]

A Republic Must Be Able to Handle the Problem of Faction

The danger was not only that people would act according to their self-interest but it was that they might join forces with others who had the same motives. Collectively, this group of people, however large or small, could try to use the government to get what it wanted, trampling the rights of others in the process. Such a group of self-interested individuals would constitute what Madison called a **faction**, the most dangerous challenge to a republic.

Long before Karl Marx wrote about the inevitability of class conflict in capitalist societies, Madison made it clear in *Federalist* No. 10 that inequality of wealth is the primary driver of factionalization, asserting that "those who hold and those who are without property have ever formed distinct interests in society."[41] Madison included slave ownership as a source of faction, as slaves were considered a form of property during the discussions in the Constitutional Convention. However, this issue was not addressed in *Federalist* No. 10.

Madison saw several ways to solve the problem of faction. The first was tyranny—factions emerge under conditions of liberty, not tyranny—but tyranny was an unacceptable option. The second was to create a totally unified, factionless society where everyone has "the same opinions, the same passions, and the same interests."[42] This second solution was unrealistic, especially in a large republic like the United States. Indeed, the American Republic has had factions since its origin. Political parties can be thought of as factions, as can interest groups. The question is how a republic can keep them in check.

The superior way to check their power, Madison argued in *Federalist* No. 10, is through an **extended republic**: a republic so large and diverse, with so many factions vying for power, that no one faction is able to assert its will over all of the others. Tactically, this was a clever argument. The Anti-Federalists had claimed that the American Republic would be too large to govern effectively, whereas Madison argued that the only solution to the dangers of faction was precisely to have such a large republic. Madison, however, was no populist; his design for government placed brakes on popular passions, insulating representatives from the desires of their citizens.

Federalists and Anti-Federalists Feared Different Forms of Tyranny

Federalists and Anti-Federalists did not disagree in their mistrust of government and the harm that could be inflicted by a self-interested few. Rather, both sides acknowledged that tyranny could take two forms. In a **tyranny of the minority**, a small number of citizens trample on the rights of the rest of the larger population. In a **tyranny of the majority**, a large number of citizens use the power of their majority to trample on the rights of a smaller group. The two sides disagreed on which was the greater danger and, therefore, on how a republic should be structured.

The Anti-Federalists focused more on the dangers of a tyranny of the minority. The Regulators had viewed the government of Massachusetts as becoming dangerously disconnected from the people and controlled by wealthy elites; the Anti-Federalists feared the government of the United States would follow a similar path. While acknowledging the dangers of minority tyranny, Madison and the Federalists focused more on the dangers of majority rule and its necessary counters. A majority of people, if in control of all of the levers of power, might use that power to oppress a minority of citizens. Slavery could be thought of as a tyranny of the majority, though in fact slaves outnumbered whites in many areas of the country.

Given Madison's earlier observations about property and the panic associated with Shays's Rebellion, one of the dangers the Federalists saw was a majority of poorer people using their power to redistribute wealth in a more equal way. In *Federalist* No. 10, Madison did not argue for direct democracy, in which citizens vote directly on policies, because he saw that form of government as too instable, with too few protections for personal security or private property.[43] Instead he argued for the delegation of power to representatives by the people and for power to be divided across government institutions. In *Federalist* No. 51, Madison laid out the blueprints of such a structure. Separation of powers is the guiding principle, with power divided and parsed between the states and nation, among the three branches of the national government, and within each branch.

Federalists and Anti-Federalists Debate Where Power Should Be Concentrated

Debates over the relative power of the states and the nation were central to the political battles over ratification of the Constitution. The Federalists tried to convince American citizens that the proposed form of government was necessary to preserve their rights and liberties. The Anti-Federalists argued against the proposed increase in national power and warned Americans of what might come to pass over time as the advantages given to the national government in the Constitution might allow it to infringe more and more on the authority of the states.

Federalists Argue for a Strong National Government

In their campaign to defend the proposed Constitution, the Federalists highlighted the problems and dangers of a government in which the states were strong and the nation was weak, pointing out failures of past republics as well as the problems experienced under the Articles of Confederation.[44] In *Federalist* No. 16, Hamilton argued that, for instance, if the national government in a confederacy were ever forced to use military might against one of its members, it would surely result in the "violent death of the confederacy."[45]

In his contributions to *The Federalist Papers*, Madison took a more moderate approach, emphasizing the balance between state and national power in the proposed Constitution. Across numerous papers, Madison argued that the Constitution divided the people's sovereignty in such a way as to preserve the integrity of both states and nation and to guard against the dangers of faction, with checks and balances built into both the legislature and executive.

Anti-Federalists Feared Losing Representation at the National Level

The Anti-Federalists were not convinced by the arguments in *The Federalist Papers*. They feared what they saw as a radical increase in national power, not only in the proposed Constitution but in how the government might evolve over time. They feared the distant future as much as the immediate present. They were, in many ways, conservative, trying to preserve the power of the states as enjoyed under the Articles of Confederation. In American political history, there is no one work that encapsulates Anti-Federalist thought in the same way that *The Federalist Papers* did for Federalists. There are no *Anti-Federalist Papers*; rather, as scholars have pointed out, "the Antifederalist literature is immense and heterogeneous, encompassing speeches, pamphlets, essays and letters."[46]

Many Anti-Federalist concerns centered on how representation of the people's interests could be maintained as the country grew in size, population, and power. They "feared that, once elected and comfortable in their jobs, the representatives would not relinquish power," creating the possibility of a new, elected, American aristocracy.[47] This "democratic" aristocracy, an Anti-Federalist essay warned, would be accompanied by an irresistible trend toward a large and complex national government, driven by the demands of a growing nation, ending in "despotism."[48]

The economic power of the national government to tax and regulate interstate commerce was one of the Anti-Federalists' greatest worries, and it was only made worse by the necessary and proper clause of the proposed constitution. In one Anti-Federalist essay, the author argued that "this power, given [to] the federal legislature, directly annihilates all the powers of the state legislatures."[49]

A Bill of Rights Was a Key Issue in the Ratification Debates

Strategically, the most effective Anti-Federalist charge against the Constitution was that it lacked a bill of rights—a list of rights and liberties with which people are born and which governments cannot take away. Many state constitutions already had them. Motions to include these statements were raised during the convention, but they did not pass. To Madison and other opponents of a bill of rights, such a statement was simply not necessary. In the republic that the delegates had fashioned, the people were already sovereign, and the government was already limited. There was no need to limit Congress's power over things that the Constitution gave it no control over in the first place. Some questioned if it was possible or even desirable to try to make a complete list of rights and liberties. What about the ones that were left out? Would Congress respect rights if they were not part of the official list?

Some, however, both during the convention and after, remained strongly in favor of a bill of rights. A bill of rights, they argued, was necessary to check the tendency of government to infringe on the rights and liberties of citizens over time. They pointed out that one should be concerned with what the government might become in the future, not just what it was in the present, as the prospect of tyranny loomed large in their minds. In addition, the Anti-Federalists argued that a bill of rights served an important educational function in a republic.[50] It would serve to remind citizens of their natural rights and remind them to assert those rights when governments might, often slowly, try to take them away.

One proponent of including a bill of rights was Anti-Federalist Mercy Otis Warren. Before and during the American Revolution, she had displayed her strong support for independence through her plays, pamphlets, and poems.[51] Publishing anonymously—and therefore assumed to be a man by many who read her essays—she corresponded with many revolutionary leaders, who were well-aware of her contributions. Later, during the ratification debates, Warren warned that there was "no provision by a bill of rights to guard against dangerous enchroachments of power in too many instances to be named."[52]

A nineteenth-century steel engraving depicting Mercy Otis Warren. The Granger Collection, New York

In the final days of the Constitutional Convention, two delegates proposed a clause that would guarantee liberty of the press. Their motion lost but by only one vote—a potential harbinger of future political realities of which, according to one political scientist, the nationalists should have taken heed.[53] As it turned out, the lack of a bill of rights proved to be the most effective argument that the Anti-Federalists would make in the ratification campaign. Many Americans were suspicious of centralized power and wanted specific protections against it.

In February 1788, the Federalists won a narrow victory in Massachusetts, the sixth of nine states needed for ratification, but only after the proconstitutional forces agreed to propose a bill of rights once the original document had itself been ratified. Three months later, South Carolina also ratified, also contingent on a set of amendments that would be offered in the first national Congress. On June 21, 1788, with the help of some shrewd procedural tactics on the part of Federalists in the state convention, New Hampshire became the ninth state to ratify.[54] The Constitution of the United States would become the supreme law of the land the following year.

Even after New Hampshire, James Madison continued to worry. It was not North Carolina's reluctance or Rhode Island's rejection that worried him. If Virginia and New York failed to ratify, it might lead to deep divisions within the new country. Virginia ratified in June, and New York followed in July. North Carolina and, finally, Rhode Island ratified within a year. During the campaign, sensing the realities of the political landscape, Madison had shifted course and promised to introduce a bill of rights as proposed amendments during the first session of the new Congress once the Constitution had been ratified. Madison kept his word, and in 1791 ten of the amendments that he proposed became part of the Constitution.

CONCLUSION

The Motives of the Framers and the Effects of the Constitution Are Still Being Debated

While the delegates to the Constitutional Convention were debating and negotiating behind the closed windows of the Pennsylvania State House, many Americans wondered what they were really up to. And we still do.

To some scholars, constitutions give order to disorder. They make progress in a society possible but only if the people place in them credible, enforceable restrictions on the power of those who would abuse such power.[55] The Constitution drew from the religious traditions and individual constitutions of the colonies. It is a document that creates—or constitutes—a people.[56] It sets out who those people are and why they are doing what they are doing.

To other scholars, the American reverence for the Constitution is a dangerous thing. Faith in the Constitution as a symbol of liberty misdirects citizens from the fact that some persons, past and present, have been able to enrich themselves under its protections at the expense of others.[57] Inequality in all of its forms has survived, and at times thrived, in the American Republic. Is the Constitution antidemocratic? Does it go against or restrain the will of the majority of the people? Yes, sometimes it is, and sometimes it does. The Constitution was intentionally designed to put brakes on popular desire to change public policy quickly. The result—incrementalism in public policy development whereby policy changes tend to be small and come slowly—has important implications for the United States.

James Madison's studies of the untimely deaths of republics helped to shape the longest-lived written national constitution in the history of human experience. That document did not ban slavery or the trade in slaves. It did not affirm or institutionalize the natural-born rights and liberties of women, Native Americans, slaves, former slaves, or many others. It did, however, affirm the rights of citizens to worship as they saw fit, to speak out and organize against tyranny, and to expect that their government would exist to protect and promote their rights and liberties. It created mechanisms to enforce these expectations, should those in power forget whom they were there to represent. And, intentionally or not, it provided a platform and a path for those ignored or oppressed by the original document to change it, to make it acknowledge their natural rights and liberties as well.

The Founders of the American Republic were practical, tactical, strategic men. Their compromises may have been necessary, but they had enormous consequences for people's lives. The document that emerged from the Pennsylvania State House was unfinished and imperfect. Would it allow for a remedy of its defects? Would it create, as Madison had hoped, a republic that would last? The answers to these questions cannot be found in studies of the motives of the Founders or even of the document itself. The answers have come not from words penned in quill and ink but from the efforts of political actors—sometimes generations later—using their own skills in strategic politics, developing their own ideas, and making their own compromises and mistakes. And having done their own homework.

CHAPTER REVIEW

This chapter's main ideas are reflected in the Learning Objectives. By reviewing them here you should be able to **remember** the key points and **know** these terms that are central to the topic.

2.1 Explain how the historical context of post-Revolutionary America led to the proposal for a new, stronger national government.

REMEMBER...

- James Madison wanted to form a republic that would last. He and other delegates to the Constitutional Convention met and debated how best to strengthen their union and avoid significant political and economic problems.

KNOW...

- *constitution*: a document that defines and creates a people politically, sets out the fundamental principles of governance, and creates the rules and institutions through which a people choose to self-govern (p. 33)

- *republics*: governments ruled by representatives of the people (p. 33)

2.2 Describe how the Constitution was shaped by the strategic political choices of those involved in its drafting.

REMEMBER...

- The delegates to the Constitutional Convention were not charged with drafting a new Constitution but only with proposing possible changes to the Articles of Confederation.

KNOW...

- *Articles of Confederation and Perpetual Union*: a constituting document calling for the creation of a union of thirteen sovereign states in which the states, not the union, were supreme (p. 36)

- *Constitutional Convention*: a meeting held in Philadelphia in 1787 at which state delegates met to fix the Articles of Confederation (p. 42)

- *Great Compromise*: an agreement for a plan of government that drew upon both the Virginia and New Jersey Plans; it settled issues of state representation by calling for a bicameral legislature with a House of Representatives apportioned proportionately and a Senate apportioned equally (p. 48)

- *New Jersey Plan*: a plan of government that preserved many of the provisions in the Articles of Confederation, including the unicameral legislature with equal votes for each states, but that strengthened the confederal government (p. 46)

- *Shays's Rebellion*: a grassroots popular uprising against the government of Massachusetts (p. 39)
- *Virginia Plan:* a plan of government calling for a strong national government with three branches of government and a bicameral legislature, with legislators elected using proportional representation (p. 45)

2.3 Identify the ideas behind the structure of the government under the Constitution.

REMEMBER...

- The idea of separation of powers influenced the decision to create three separate but connected branches of the federal government.

KNOW...

- *amendment*: a constitutional provision for a process by which changes may be made to the Constitution (p. 53)
- *executive branch*: the institution responsible for carrying out laws passed by the legislative branch (p. 50)
- *judicial branch*: the institution responsible for hearing and deciding cases via a system of federal courts (p. 51)
- *legislative branch*: in a divided government, the institution responsible for making laws (p. 49)
- *logroll:* an exchange of political favors, such as when legislators trade votes to support one another's proposed legislation (p. 57)
- *separation of powers*: a design of government that distributes powers across institutions in order to avoid making one branch too powerful on its own (p. 52)
- *Three-Fifths Compromise*: an agreement reached by delegates at the Constitutional Convention that ensured that a slave would count as three-fifths of a person for a state's representation (p. 54)

2.4 Compare and contrast the arguments put forth by the Federalists and the Anti-Federalists during the ratification debates.

REMEMBER...

- The proposed Constitution had to be ratified by nine of the thirteen states in order to replace the Articles of Confederation
- Proponents and opponents of the Constitution tried to rally others to their side and convince individuals of their position

KNOW...

- *Anti-Federalists*: the name taken by those opposed to the proposed Constitution; the Anti-Federalists favored stronger state governments (p. 59)

- *extended republic*: a republic so large and diverse, with so many factions vying for power, that no one faction is able to assert its will over all of the others (p. 61)

- *faction*: a group of self-interested people who use the government to get what they want, trampling the rights of others in the process (p. 61)

- *Federalists*: the name taken by supporters of the proposed Constitution; the Federalists called for a strong national government (p. 58)

- *The Federalist Papers*: a series of eighty-five essays written by Alexander Hamilton, James Madison, and John Jay and published between 1787 and 1788 that lay out the theory behind the Constitution (p. 60)

- *tyranny*: the suppression of the rights of a people by those holding power (p. 59)

- *tyranny of the majority*: when a small number of citizens trample on the rights of the larger population (p. 62)

- *tyranny of the minority*: when a large number of citizens use the power of their majority to trample on the rights of a smaller group (p. 62)

3 FEDERALISM
The Changing Boundaries between the Nation and the States

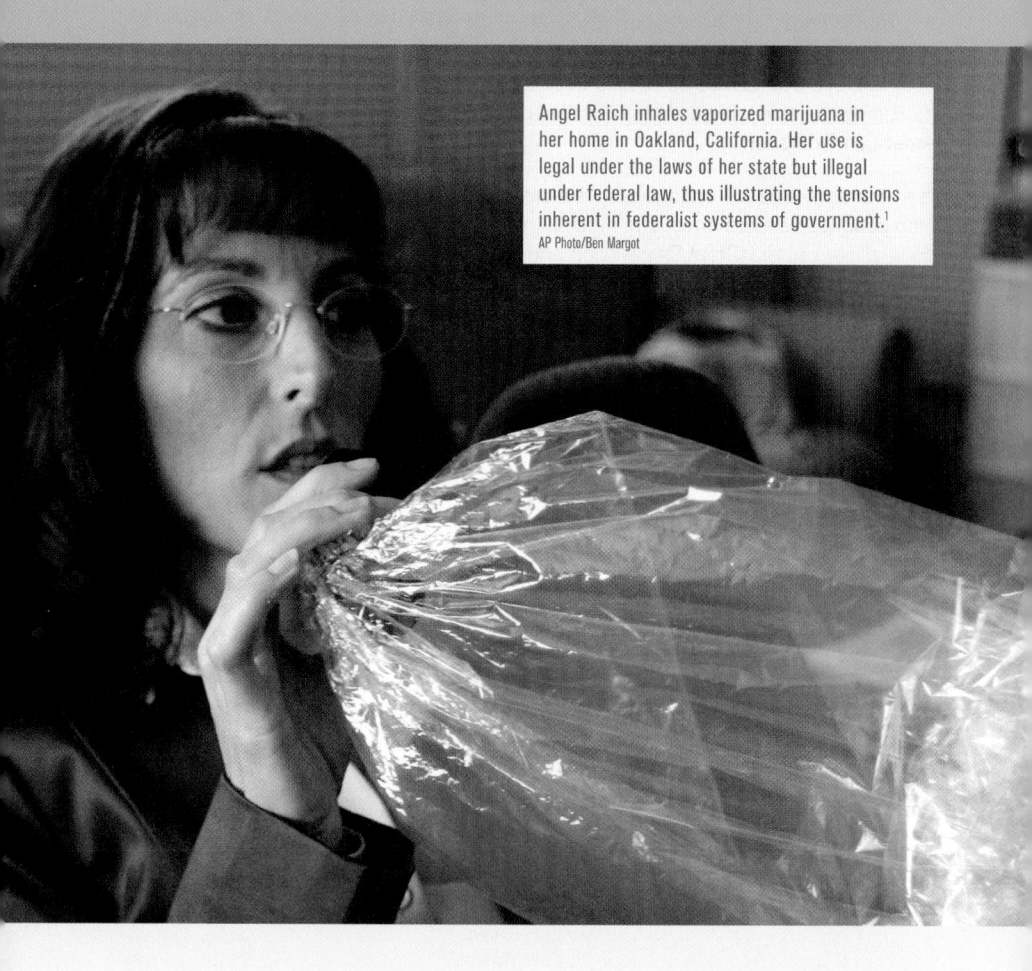

Angel Raich inhales vaporized marijuana in her home in Oakland, California. Her use is legal under the laws of her state but illegal under federal law, thus illustrating the tensions inherent in federalist systems of government.[1]
AP Photo/Ben Margot

On one fundamental issue the Constitution of the United States is absolutely clear: In its opening words, "We the People of the United States," it establishes that ultimate political authority rests with the people. We, and not the government, are sovereign and have supreme political authority.

What the Constitution is less clear on are the precise mechanisms and structures through which this supreme authority is vested in the government Americans chose to create and maintain. Under the Articles of Confederation, the vast majority of the people's authority had been placed in state governments, which left the Confederation Congress constantly struggling to secure cooperation from these multiple governments. That changed with the ratification of the Constitution, but the issue was not settled once and for all. The new system of government divided the people's authority between two levels of government—the nation and the states—with some powers exercised by one level alone, some powers denied to both levels, and some powers shared by both levels. In doing so, a system of **federalism** was created.

As we will explore, the Constitution created much of the basic framework of this division but did not delineate the boundaries between the specific powers of the national government and those of the state governments. The process of setting these boundaries continues even today. Many of the most important and controversial issues in our representative democracy involve difficult questions of American federalism.

In this chapter, we will engage with the stories of Angel Raich and Diane Monson, who sought to secure access to medical marijuana, tracing the roots of their conflict back to the Great Depression and Roosevelt's New Deal. In doing so, we will explore the tensions inherent in American federalism, how this federalism has changed over time, and where it stands in the twenty-first century.

After reading this chapter, you will be able to do the following:

3.1 Explain the tension in American federalism between state and federal laws.

3.2 Identify the elements of the U.S. Constitution that shape American federalism and evaluate arguments about the proper limits of congressional power under their authority.

3.3 Describe the development of American federalism over time.

3.4 List changes to American federalism in the post–New Deal era.

3.5 Discuss the current status of American federalism and how it might continue to evolve.

LEARNING OBJECTIVES

THE FIGHT FOR ACCESS TO MEDICAL MARIJUANA REVEALS TENSIONS BETWEEN STATE AND FEDERAL LAW

In 2002 Angel Raich and Diane Monson filed suit in a California federal court against the government of the United States. They argued that their use of medical marijuana, which was legal under the laws of California and eight other states at the time but illegal under federal law, was protected by the laws of their state and by the Constitution of the United States.

Both women were trying to cope with significant health issues, the treatment of which, they argued, was helped by the use of cannabis. Raich was struggling against an "inoperable brain tumor, seizures, endometriosis, scoliosis and a wasting disorder. She [weighed] only 97 pounds and said without pot she'd starve to death."[2] "I am not a criminal," Raich declared. "I do not deserve to be behind bars."[3] Monson used cannabis as part of her treatment for chronic back pain and spasms and grew her own plants to provide her medication: "Without cannabis, these spasms would be tortuous and unbearable no matter what other medications were available," she testified in federal court.[4]

Both women were using marijuana under the supervision of their doctors and in compliance with a California state law, the Compassionate Use Act of 1996. This act made the use and cultivation of marijuana for medical purposes legal if undertaken under the supervision of a licensed physician and in accordance with state regulations. However, Raich and Monson feared that the federal government might restrict their future ability to obtain medical cannabis. The reason for their fears was the fact that the use, cultivation, or possession of marijuana was illegal under a federal law, the Controlled Substances Act (CSA) (1970).[5] Under that law, marijuana was classified as a Schedule I drug, among the most dangerous substances, such as heroin and LSD. Raich and Monson were caught between the laws of their state and those of the nation. As such, they found themselves front and center in one of the most enduring debates in American political life—that of federalism.

In August 2002, "county deputy sheriffs and agents from the federal Drug Enforcement Administration (DEA) came to Monson's home. After a thorough investigation, the county officials concluded that her cultivation and use of marijuana was entirely lawful as a matter of California law. Nevertheless, after a three-hour standoff, the federal agents seized and destroyed all six of her cannabis plants."[6] "As I stood by and watched," Monson later testified, "the DEA agents chopped down my medicinal plants. I was crying and my back began to tighten up; for the rest of the week I experienced debilitating back spasms. . . . We do not feel safe; we have had our civil rights and our rights under California law taken from us in our own back yard."[7]

Facing a threat to their continued access to medical marijuana, the two women filed suit, and their case eventually made its way to the U.S. Supreme Court. In their case, Raich and Monson based their claims upon the laws of California and the Constitution of the United States. In restricting access to marijuana, they argued, the federal government was in violation of several amendments to the Constitution as well as of certain specific powers granted to Congress in the founding document.

For their part, representatives of the federal government and the DEA insisted that they were rightfully upholding federal law and federal authority. "Everything we're doing is according to the law," said Richard Meyer, a San Francisco–based DEA spokesman.[8] By enforcing federal law, however, the DEA agents were restricting actions that were legal under California state laws, which begs the central question, when it comes to pot and patients, does federal or state law rule?[9]

How did the federal government claim the authority to override the laws of a state? The short answer is the Constitution. To understand that more fully, we begin our exploration of American federalism with an examination of medical marijuana. At the center of Raich and Monson's challenge is one basic question: Where, precisely, does the boundary between the powers of the federal government and those of the states lie?

Diane Monson at her California home with her marijuana plants on the day that the Supreme Court ruled the federal government does have the authority to prohibit marijuana, despite state laws allowing it.

AP Photo/Max Whittaker

WHAT HAVE I LEARNED?

1. The American federalist system _____.

   a. Places the people's power in the national government
   b. Places the people's power in the state governments
   c. Divides power among national, state, and local governments
   d. Divides power between national and state governments

2. What laws were in conflict in the case of Angel Raich and Diane Monson?

3. What deeper challenges to the placement of Americans' sovereignty does their case highlight?

Answer Key: 1. d; 2. Answers should focus on the conflict between California law and those of the nation; 3. Answers should discuss the challenge of defining boundaries in the American federalist system.

THE CONSTITUTION DIVIDES POWER BETWEEN THE NATION AND THE STATES

One of the most important innovations of the U.S. Constitution was the division of the people's sovereignty between two levels of government: the national government and the states. Each level retained some exclusive powers and had some powers denied to it, and in some areas both levels were empowered to act on behalf of the people.

- Describe the different systems of federalism.

- Explain the constitutional clauses that shape American federalism and the powers belonging to the nation and the states.

There Is More Than One Way to Divide Power between Levels of Government

The American Republic created by the Constitution is only one of several possible ways of working out the relationship between different levels of government. The difference between these models is the way in which the people's sovereignty is divided between different governmental units (see Figure 3.1). In **unitary systems**, citizens place their power in one central government that then exercises authority over the subnational governments (such as states and provinces). Most policies are then actually carried out by these subnational governments that derive their power from the national government. Great Britain, France, and Japan are examples of democratic governments operating as unitary systems.

At the opposite end of the spectrum are **confederal systems.** Here, citizens limit the authority of the national government, instead placing most of their sovereignty in the subnational governments, such as states, which then grant power and authority to the national government. In confederal systems, national governments are heavily dependent upon the states to carry out and pay for public policies. The United States under the Articles of Confederation was an example of a confederal system.

Finally, in **federal systems**, citizens divide their sovereignty between two or more levels of government, each of which may have exclusive authority to act in certain areas of policy, be denied from acting in an area of policy, or be required

FIGURE 3.1

The Division of Power under Different Systems of Governance

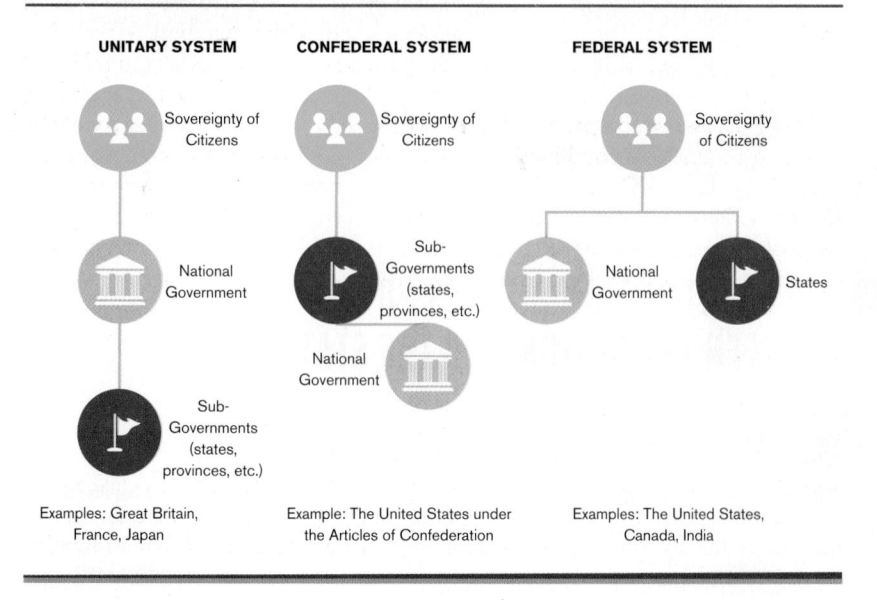

UNITARY SYSTEM

Sovereignty of Citizens

National Government

Sub-Governments (states, provinces, etc.)

Examples: Great Britain, France, Japan

CONFEDERAL SYSTEM

Sovereignty of Citizens

Sub-Governments (states, provinces, etc.)

National Government

Example: The United States under the Articles of Confederation

FEDERAL SYSTEM

Sovereignty of Citizens

National Government

States

Examples: The United States, Canada, India

to share authority with another level in some areas. Key to a true federal system is the existence of constitutional protections for each level against encroachment on its powers by the other level(s). The United States, Canada, and India are examples of countries with federal systems.

The Constitution contains a set of provisions—the supremacy, necessary and proper, and commerce clauses—that shape the relative authority of the state and national governments. At the same time, however, it does not outline a perfectly clear vision of how the system of federalism would actually work.

The Supremacy, Necessary and Proper, and Commerce Clauses Are the Keys to American Federalism

One of the Constitution's most important statements about where the people's sovereignty is located is the **supremacy clause**, which reads, "This Constitution, and the Laws of the United States . . . shall be the supreme Law of the Land."[10] The supremacy clause is a powerful statement of national power. It means that the laws that Congress passes must be executed by the states, even if state constitutional provisions conflict with them. It means that states must abide by national treaties, and it also binds state courts to the Constitution.

In another key clause, Congress is given the power to "make all Laws which shall be necessary and proper for carrying into Execution . . . Powers vested by this Constitution in the Government of the United States."[11] This **necessary and proper clause**, also called the elastic clause, is a critical source of power for the national government, granting Congress the authority to legislate as necessary for carrying out constitutionally granted powers.

In addition to these two clauses, there is a third that powerfully shapes modern American federalism: the **commerce clause**. In the language of the Constitution, this clause grants Congress the power to "regulate Commerce with foreign Nations, and among the several States, and with the Indian Tribes."[12]

Vagueness in the language regarding the specific powers of the national government has contributed to the growth of national power when combined with the necessary and proper clause. For example, under the authority of the commerce clause—in combination with the necessary and proper clause and the supremacy clause—Congress has claimed the authority to define nearly any productive activity as "Commerce . . . among the several States." Even though Diane Monson's homegrown marijuana was never sold or left her home state, the federal government claimed the authority to regulate it as interstate commerce.

The Constitution Describes the Powers Belonging to the Nation and the States

The word *federalism* does not appear in the Constitution. Nor is there any one section that clearly lays out how the Framers intended the people's sovereignty to be divided between the states and the national government. Instead, in various sections in the document, powers are given or denied to each level or allowed to be shared by both.

Most Powers of the National Government Are Explicit

In general, the powers of the national government are explicitly listed and described by the Constitution. With a few exceptions, those of the state governments are assumed to encompass those powers not explicitly given to the national government. **Enumerated powers** refer to those powers granted to the national, or federal, government in the Constitution, and especially to Congress. These include the power to tax, coin money, declare war, raise and support an army and navy, make treaties, provide for the naturalization of American citizens, and to "regulate Commerce with foreign Nations, and among the several States, and with Indian Tribes."[13] Most of the enumerated powers in the Constitution are granted to the legislative branch.

Implied powers are those not textually granted to the federal government but that are assumed to be given to it as a result of its need to make all laws "necessary and proper." For example, the Constitution does not give the national government the authority to create an air force (though the world had witnessed the first hot air balloon flight by the time of the drafting of the Constitution so might have anticipated combat in the air). That authority, however, is assumed as part of its power to raise and support a military.

In addition to describing the enumerated and implied (or delegated) powers of the national government, the Constitution denies certain powers to it, especially if consent has not been given by the residents of the states, who usually act through their own state legislatures. The national government may not pass laws that violate the rights and liberties expressed in the Bill of Rights (or other later amendments). The national government may not admit new states to the Union, nor can it change state boundaries without the consent of the state's citizens. It also cannot impose taxes on goods and services exported and imported between states.

The Powers of State Governments Are Less Explicit

The Constitution is much less specific on the powers allocated to the states. Much of the protection for state authority comes from the Tenth Amendment to the Constitution, which states, "The powers not delegated to the United States by the Constitution, nor prohibited by it to the States, are reserved to the States respectively, or to the people."

Called **reserved powers** because of the text of the Tenth Amendment, these are powers that were not given to the national government and are, therefore, reserved to the states. Among the most important of these are **police powers**, which state governments use to protect residents and provide for their safety, health, and general welfare. States are also authorized to conduct elections, including those for national office.[14] No amendments may be made to the Constitution without the consent of three-fourths of the states, either by their legislatures or by ratification conventions in the states.[15] States are also empowered to establish local, town, county, and regional governmental bodies.

The Constitution also denies certain powers to state governments. States are prevented from entering into treaties or alliances with foreign powers—a real concern to the Framers who saw the potential for the European powers to divide the states for their own economic or political gain. States may not print their own money, tax imports or exports, or declare war.[16]

Finally, both the nation and the states are given the authority to act in certain areas of public policy. These **concurrent powers** allow national and state authority to overlap—an example of the concept of "separated institutions sharing power".[17] The power to tax, already given to states under the Articles of Confederation, was extended to the new national government. Both levels are allowed to borrow money, though states have more restrictions on their own ability to go into debt than the federal government has. The nation and the states may both pass and enforce laws, create and operate a system of courts, and charter banks and corporations (see Figure 3.2).

Graduates celebrate at the U.S. Air Force Academy in 2015. The Constitution gives the national government the implied power to create such an institution as the U.S. Air Force as part of its power to raise and support a military. RJ Sangosti/The Denver Post via Getty Images

Regional and Local Governments Have No Explicit Constitutional Powers

The Constitution does not describe the powers of the levels of government below the states—the cities, towns, counties, and districts. Generally, relationships between American states and their subgovernments are unitary, with the authority of the smaller units dependent upon and subordinate to the power and authority of the states. For example, state governments can change the boundaries of school districts or combine two school districts into one larger one if they choose to. If the relationship between these two levels of government were truly federal, this would not be possible without the consent of both the state and its school districts.

Therefore, while we often talk about three levels of government in the United States—national, state, and local—from the point of view of American federalism there are only two—national and state. Dependence upon state authority is often a source of frustration for mayors, school board members, and other local officials, who have sometimes argued for something more like a three-level federalist system. Local officials are not powerless, however. According to political scientist Daniel Elazar, "The largest metropolitan centers, the so-called 'big city bloc,' do possess the political power needed to go directly to Washington."[18]

As Angel Raich and Diane Monson pursued their claims through the American legal system, they did so against a politically murky background. The boundaries between states and the nation were not clearly and definitively

FIGURE 3.2

Enumerated, Concurrent, and Reserved Powers in American Federalism

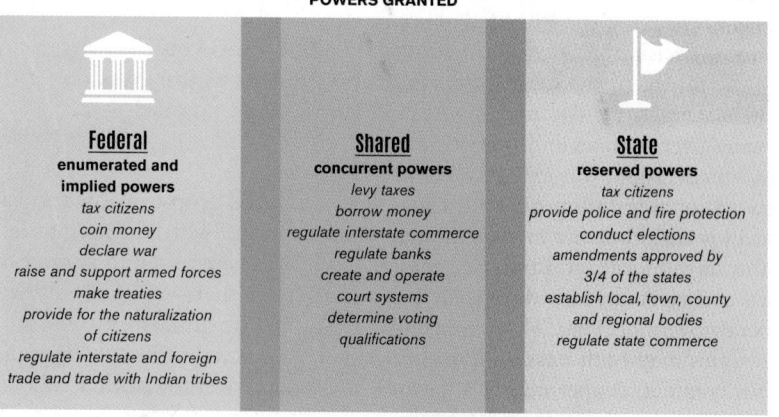

POWERS GRANTED

Federal
enumerated and
implied powers
tax citizens
coin money
declare war
raise and support armed forces
make treaties
provide for the naturalization
of citizens
regulate interstate and foreign
trade and trade with Indian tribes

Shared
concurrent powers
levy taxes
borrow money
regulate interstate commerce
regulate banks
create and operate
court systems
determine voting
qualifications

State
reserved powers
tax citizens
provide police and fire protection
conduct elections
amendments approved by
3/4 of the states
establish local, town, county
and regional bodies
regulate state commerce

POWERS DENIED

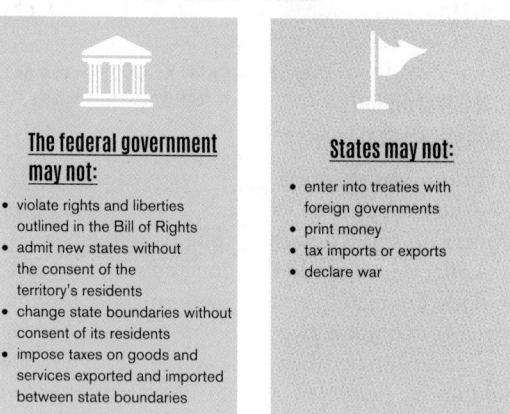

The federal government may not:

- violate rights and liberties outlined in the Bill of Rights
- admit new states without the consent of the territory's residents
- change state boundaries without consent of its residents
- impose taxes on goods and services exported and imported between state boundaries

States may not:

- enter into treaties with foreign governments
- print money
- tax imports or exports
- declare war

settled, and local governments—though not explicitly part of the federalist structure—might also act in the political space to protect their own interests.

Gonzales v. Raich Highlights the Tensions Inherent in Federalism

In 2005, the Supreme Court decided to take up the case of Angel Raich and Diane Monson, weighing their rights against the authority of the federal government under the CSA and the commerce clause of the Constitution.

In his skeptical questioning of the women's attorneys, Justice Antonin Scalia, a conservative, challenged their assertion that growing and distributing cannabis—even if it stayed within California's borders—would not contribute to the nationally problematic underground market in marijuana. Justice Stephen Breyer, considered one of the liberal members of the Court, suggested that a better course of action for medical cannabis advocates was to change federal law itself, as California had done with the Compassionate Use Act, rather than use a state referendum to challenge federal policy.[19]

In its decision in *Gonzales v. Raich* (2005), by a 6–3 vote the Court sided with the power of the federal government—and that of Congress under the commerce and supremacy clauses of the Constitution—and ruled against Raich and Monson. The majority opinion explaining the Court's logic reached back to the case of *Wickard v. Filburn* (1942).[20] In that case, an Ohio dairy and cattle farmer, Roscoe Filburn, happened to cultivate a small crop of winter wheat, some of which he used to feed his livestock and some of which he used to feed his family. Under federal laws of the time, Filburn was required to restrict his wheat acreage. Filburn, however, cultivated much more than was legally allowed by quota but, according to his testimony, only for use on his farm, not for sale.

Filburn argued that the federal government was exceeding its constitutional authority under the commerce clause since his activities were local, limited to his farm, and "their effects upon interstate commerce [were], at most, 'indirect.'"[21] The Supreme Court, in a unanimous decision in *Wickard v. Filburn*, disagreed. The Court found that even though the wheat never left the farm or the state, the quotas were a constitutional use of Congress's power under the commerce clause. According to one scholar of American federalism, "With such a definition of interstate commerce, nothing was local."[22]

If a product grown on a local farm for local consumption or marijuana grown at home for use in the home can be considered interstate commerce, then what *can't* be? In the debates over American federalism, defining the proper limits of the commerce clause remains a hotly contested issue.

Today, the landscape has changed from the time of *Gonzales v. Raich*. More than half of the states have passed laws allowing the use of marijuana for certain medical conditions, though these laws vary considerably both in terms of the medical conditions covered and in the restrictions placed upon its use. Others have decriminalized the possession of small amounts of marijuana, substituting civil fines for criminal penalties. In addition, eight states and the District of Columbia have legalized marijuana for recreational use. Federal law, however, has not changed, nor has the Supreme Court reversed its upholding of Congress's power to prohibit the growth, use, or possession of marijuana under the authority of the commerce clause.

This has put recent administrations in a very difficult spot. During President Barack Obama's second term in office, fully enforcing the CSA in the states had become impossible. In December 2015, in a federal suit brought by neighboring states against Colorado (one of the four states in which recreational use had been made legal), Obama's solicitor general argued in a brief presented to the Supreme Court that it should not decide to hear the case. To some observers, the administration's position, though based on specific legal grounds, implied a position "that marijuana should be federally legalized—even for recreational use."[23]

The Justice Department, under the president's direction, however, retained authority to prosecute the CSA, though it was to focus on drug trafficking and not on prosecuting "individuals who were in 'unambiguous compliance with existing state laws.'"[24]

With the election of Republican Donald Trump as president in 2016, many observers thought that federal policy might shift toward letting the states regulate medical and recreational marijuana use, possibly reclassifying or even removing marijuana from the list of controlled substances under the federal law. By fall of 2017, Attorney General Sessions remained staunchly opposed to legalized medical or recreational marijuana, helping to kill a congressional amendment that would prohibit the Justice Department from prosecuting marijuana businesses that were in compliance with their states' laws.[25]

WHAT HAVE I LEARNED?

1. The Constitution structures the relationship between the national government and the states in a section known as the federalism clause.

    a. True
    b. False

2. The necessary and proper clause _____.

    a. Preserves necessary powers at the state level
    b. Allows Congress to pass laws needed to carry out enumerated powers
    c. Has since been ruled unconstitutional
    d. Reserves unenumerated powers for the federal government

3. A key constitutional provision on which the Supreme Court based its decision in the case of Angel Raich and Diane Monson was _____.

    a. The commerce clause
    b. The Tenth Amendment
    c. Separation of powers
    d. The Three-Fifths Compromise

4. What are reserved powers?

5. On what grounds did the Supreme Court rule against Angel Raich and Diane Monson in *Gonzales v. Raich*?

Answer Key: 1. b; 2. b; 3. a; 4. Answers should address the Tenth Amendment and discuss the lack of enumeration of most state powers; 5. Answers should focus on the history of interpretation of the commerce clause and cases such as *Wickard v. Filburn*.

THE AMERICAN FEDERAL SYSTEM HAS DEVELOPED OVER TIME

- Describe the development of federalism in the United States.

Federalism is not one clean and unchanging concept, and there is no one set way to divide the people's sovereignty between levels of government. Defining the relative power of the two levels, as well as deciding how closely they will be intertwined, happens through the political process, and this has changed over the course of American history. In this section we will look at different types of federalism up through the early twentieth century and see how those relate to specific eras of American political history.

Early Supreme Court Decisions Shape the Division between State and National Power

The void left by the Framers of the Constitution in precisely defining the boundaries of American federalism was quickly filled by the Supreme Court—a role that it continues to pursue actively today. Perhaps the most important figure in shaping American federalism after the ratification of the Constitution was John Marshall, chief justice of the United States from 1801 to 1835 and the longest-serving chief justice in American history. During his tenure as chief justice, Marshall secured and issued several of the most important decisions in the area of American federalism.

McCulloch v. Maryland Relied on the Necessary Proper Clause to Assert the Power of Congress

The first of these major decisions was in *McCulloch v. Maryland* (1819).[26] The case involved the Second Bank of the United States, a national bank chartered by Congress. Several states, including Maryland, passed laws to tax the state branches of the Second Bank for various reasons, such as to try to kill the branches, to defend their own state's banks, or just to raise money. The case centered on two questions: Did Congress have the authority to establish the bank in the first place? And did individual states have the authority to tax the bank's branches operating within their borders? Marshall, speaking for a unanimous Supreme Court, came down firmly on the side of the authority of the national government in both questions. Citing the necessary and proper clause of the Constitution, Marshall affirmed the right of Congress to establish the bank and denied the right of Maryland and other states to tax the bank's state branches.

Gibbons v. Ogden Used the Commerce Clause to Affirm the Power of Congress to Regulate Trade

In *Gibbons v. Ogden* (1824), the Marshall Court weighed in on the powers of Congress under the commerce clause of the Constitution.[27] As with the *McCulloch* decision, in *Gibbons* the Court affirmed national power.

Chief Justice John Marshall's decisions are widely held to be among the most important for shaping the powers and limits of federalism even today. The Granger Collection, New York

Known as the "steamboat monopoly case," *Gibbons v. Ogden* arose from a battle between two powerful businessmen in the steamboat industry in New York and New Jersey. Aaron Ogden had been granted a monopoly by a New York state law that protected his routes within New York and between New York and New Jersey. Thomas Gibbons filed suit to block the monopoly.

Marshall's decision in the case reaffirmed national power but on a different constitutional principle. While *McCulloch* involved the necessary and proper clause, *Gibbons* focused on the power of Congress to regulate trade "among the several States" as part of its authority under the commerce clause. Marshall also cited the power of the national government under the supremacy clause of the Constitution. Marshall and the Court, again unanimously, struck down the steamboat monopoly between the two states and the part of the New York law that had made the monopoly possible. In doing so, Marshall affirmed the exclusive authority of Congress to regulate interstate commerce, defining commerce "among the several States" as including "the deep streams which penetrate our country in every direction [and] pass through the interior of almost every state in the Union."[28]

Barron v. Baltimore Ruled That the Due Process Clause Applied Only to the National Government

The third major federalism case decided by the Marshall Court was *Barron v. Baltimore* (1833).[29] *Barron* dealt with yet another part of the Constitution, in this case the portion of the Fifth Amendment's protections called the due process clause, which states, "No person shall . . . be deprived of life, liberty, or property, without due process of law; nor shall private property be taken for public use, without just compensation." John Barron, the owner of a wharf in Baltimore, sued the city for the cost to his business caused by sand that had accumulated in the waters off his wharf as a result of the city's development policies, thus depriving him of property without "just compensation." The Marshall Court issued another unanimous decision; however, in this case, it limited rather than expanded the power of the national government. The court ruled that the Fifth Amendment's protections were aimed exclusively at restraining the power of the national government and were not intended to apply to the states.[30]

The Marshall Court affirmed national power, especially in relation to the necessary and proper clause and the commerce clause. However, Marshall handed down his decisions with an eye toward public opinion and tempered the expansion of national authority with an acknowledgement of state authority.

Lurking in the background during this time were the interconnected and unresolved problems of slavery, states' rights, and American federalism. The delegates to the Constitutional Convention had given in to the demands of the slave states to preserve their institution, in spite of the fact that slavery violated the essential principles of natural rights upon which the Constitution was based. In the nineteenth century, as the American Republic expanded to fill the continent, the question of slavery and its implications for the relationship between the nation and the states could no longer be ignored.

The Era of Dual Federalism Separated the Powers of the Nation and the States

For much of the history of the American Republic the model of the relationship between states and the nation was one of **dual federalism**, which divided the people's sovereignty between the nation and the states. Dual federalism presumes a distinct, though not complete, separation between the two levels of authority, as if both operate side by side with relatively little interaction between the two. Dual federalism, according to an observer of American government in 1888, "is like a great factory wherein two sets of machinery are at work, their revolving wheels apparently intermixed, their bands crossing one another, yet each set doing its own work without touching or hampering the other."[31] (See Figure 3.3.)

The Supreme Court drew a similar image of two separate systems in the nineteenth century: "The government of the United States and the government of a state are distinct and independent of each other within their respective spheres of action, although existing and exercising their powers within the same territorial limits. Neither government can intrude within the jurisdiction, or authorize any interference therein by its judicial officers with the action of the other."[32] In fact, however, the division of authority between the nation and the states has never been this clean and neat. Even in areas of public policy that have been traditionally handled by the states, such as education, the federal government has been involved.[33] Driving much of the politics in the first half of the nineteenth century and heightening tensions between the states and the national government was the institution of slavery and the fears of southerners that it might be restricted or banned outright.

FIGURE 3.3

Dual Federalism

The state and federal levels of government operated under an arrangement of dual federalism for much of the history of the American Republic. In this model, federal and state government have distinct powers and function independently of one another, addressing their own areas of policy.

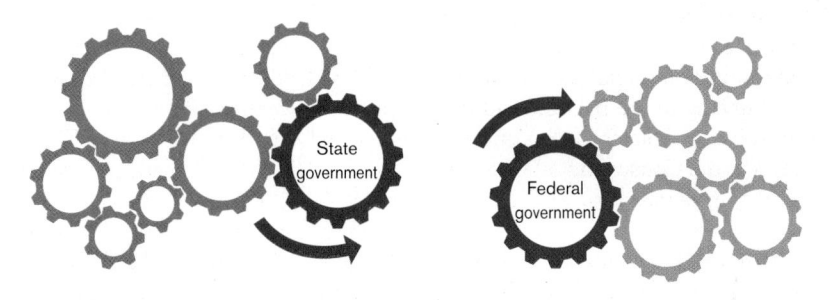

States' Rights Grew during the Civil War and Reconstruction

The expansion of national power under the Marshall Court did not mean that this new balance of power would be permanent or go unchallenged. Efforts to assert the authority of states continued during the middle decades of the nineteenth century. As the original Federalist justices retired or passed away, many of their replacements held a stronger view of state authority. Increasingly, the question of federalism also became linked with the issues of slavery, **states' rights**, and the threat of secession. In the 1830s, South Carolina senator John Calhoun argued for the right of states to "nullify" federal laws that were in conflict with those of the states.

In December 1860, South Carolina seceded from the nation. Within six months, eleven southern states had followed to form the Confederate States of America. When the American Civil War finally ended in 1865, more than six hundred thousand soldiers had died, and an unknown number of civilians had been killed.

The Civil War and the process of Reconstruction had settled the issues of secession and of legalized slavery; however, the question of how forcefully the national government would act to preserve the civil rights (the personal rights guaranteed to citizens or residents) of former slaves and their descendants was far from decided. As the government of the United States began to turn its attention to the expansion of the nation's empire toward the Pacific Ocean, the rights of African Americans received less and less consideration and protection.

Under Dual Federalism, the Supreme Court Restricted African Americans' Rights after the Civil War

Following the Civil War, the Supreme Court did not emerge as a defender of African American civil rights, a move that would have provided uniform protection for African Americans at the national level. Instead, it affirmed a vision of federalism that recognized state authority, even if that authority was used to restrict the rights of state citizens based only on their racial identity.

African American school children at a segregated school in 1896 following the "separate but equal" ruling in *Plessy v. Ferguson*. Afro American Newspapers/Gado/Getty Images

In the *Slaughterhouse Cases* (1873), the Supreme Court weighed in for the first time on the protections offered by the Fourteenth Amendment.[34] Like *Gibbons v. Ogden*, these cases involved a monopoly, this time of the slaughter of animals under a Louisiana state law. Butchers had challenged the monopoly as a violation of their rights under the Fourteenth Amendment. Ruling against the butchers, a closely divided Supreme Court drew a sharp distinction between the rights guaranteed under state and national citizenship.

Narrowly interpreting the equal protection clause of the Fourteenth Amendment to restrict discrimination only against African Americans (the butchers were white), the Court also placed limits on the privileges and immunities clause of the same amendment, stating that its protections apply only to national, not state, citizenship. In doing so, the Court upheld the authority of states to exercise their police powers.[35]

Plessy v. Ferguson (1896) was another landmark case in restricting the rights of African Americans following the Civil War and asserting states' rights. In this case, the Supreme Court upheld the constitutionality of legalized racial segregation (the separation of individuals based on their racial identity) and the ability of states to pass such laws.[36] *Plessy* was a test case, organized by the African American community in New Orleans to challenge Louisiana's segregation laws. Homer Plessy, "a light-skinned man who described himself as 'seven-eighths Caucasian,'" had been arrested and fined for violating a state law requiring separate railroad facilities for whites and African Americans.[37]

In the decision in *Plessy*, Justice Henry Billings Brown declared that Louisiana's law did not violate the Fourteenth Amendment. Arguing that "social prejudices cannot be overcome by legislation," Brown upheld Plessy's conviction and declared that "separate but equal" did not violate the Constitution. Justice John Marshall Harlan, the lone dissenter on the Court, countered, "Our Constitution is color-blind, and neither knows nor tolerates classes among citizens. In respect of civil rights, all citizens are equal before the law." Harlan, correctly, as it would turn out, saw *Plessy* as a dangerous and damaging ruling. Brown's majority opinion, however, set policy. The ruling that racial segregation could be constitutionally permissible endured for almost sixty years. We will explore the efforts—first in the states, later in the Supreme Court—of individuals to overturn this doctrine in detail in Chapter 5.

In the Age of Industry and National Expansion, Cooperative Federalism Emerged

During the latter part of the nineteenth century and the early decades of the twentieth, the Supreme Court adopted a complex role toward the growing economy. The Court generally tried not to interfere with American business interests; however, many state governments, facing challenges by powerful corporations, asked the federal government for help.

In many cases, states were happy to have the federal government take more of a leading role in regulating increasingly large and powerful corporations. As American corporations grew in size and power, states began to realize that they could not, on their own, "mobilize sufficient power to regulate wealthy railroads that could cut them off from the rest of the country in retaliation [for regulations], or deal with great industrial combines that could pull up and go elsewhere."[38]

Confronting the challenges and opportunities of economic growth together, the nation and the states began to forge what is called **cooperative federalism**, in which both levels work together in the same areas of public policy. Under this type of federalism, the two levels do not generally play the same roles. Instead, the national government tends to be "responsible for raising revenues and setting standards," while state and local governments remain "primarily responsible for administering the programs."[39] (See Figure 3.4.)

While both national and state governments began to build the foundations for cooperative federalism in the late nineteenth century, the dominant theme was one of not interfering with American business and the economy, at either the national or state level. Under this approach, government took little action to regulate or restrain private economic activity, even if it resulted in serious inequalities. In decisions that restricted the ability of the national government to regulate economic activity, the Supreme Court supported the philosophy of noninterference in the economy.[40]

While some of the seeds of the later growth in national power were planted during the era of big business, it would take a massive economic crisis, the inability of state governments to cope with the crisis, and the response of the national government to the crisis's challenges to fully realize this growth. To fully understand how major these changes would be, we need to understand the crisis itself: the Great Depression.

President Franklin Roosevelt's Response to the Great Depression Sparked a Revolution in American Federalism

In the 1920s, plentiful rains across America's Great Plains region had enticed many farmers to cultivate lands that their parents and grandparents had left

FIGURE 3.4

Cooperative Federalism

Beginning in the late nineteenth century and extending into the early twentieth, state and federal governments forged a relationship of cooperative federalism in which they worked together to shape public policy. Notice that in cooperative federalism the gears are more closely interlinked, while they work more separately in the dual federalism system.

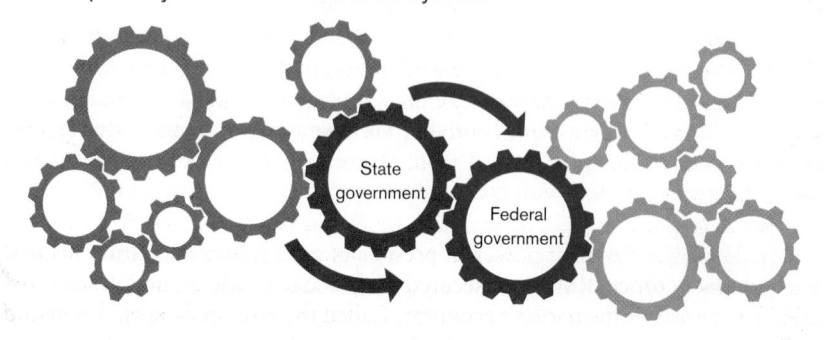

untilled because they were too dry, too risky. But in the 1930s, droughts came and the newly plowed topsoil turned into dust, which was swept up into great dust storms that turned day into night.[41]

The boom times of the 1920s—wherein plentiful crops meant cheap and easy credit as well as the ability to borrow money to buy farmland or homes—dried up along with the land. So did the ability to speculate in stocks and bonds or to invest in the financial markets thousands of miles away.

But the debts taken on during the boom times remained. Prolonged deflation meant that money became scarce, loans were hard to come by or pay back, and prices fell. Faced with the simultaneous disasters of drought, falling prices, and unpayable debts, millions of farmers faced foreclosure. The collapse in farm prices was especially hard on tenant farmers, many of whom were racial and ethnic minorities and whose for-hire labor was no longer needed. In one of the largest migrations in American history, millions of displaced farmers and their families abandoned the "Dust Bowl" and headed West in search of whatever work that they could find.

The hardship that began with massive dust clouds over American's heartland would soon extend to the entire country. In October 1929, America's stock market crashed, a very visible signal of an industrial economy grinding to a halt. This signaled the start of the **Great Depression**, the most significant economic crisis in the nation's history. The nation's banking system nearly failed. Industrial production collapsed. Workers were laid off or had their wages cut. Foreclosures swept through cities, driving families into homelessness and hunger. The most vulnerable members of the American economy—children, women, and members of racial and ethnic minorities—often suffered the most.

The crisis of the Great Depression strained American federalism. During the boom times of the 1920s, states had increased their spending, especially to expand the highways for the nation's growing fleet of automobiles. To do so, states had borrowed large amounts of money. When the economic crisis took hold, many state governments themselves faced shortfalls and were unable to respond to their residents' needs. Local governments were similarly overwhelmed, unable to care for millions of unemployed workers. Faced with challenges that they could not meet and citizens whose needs they could not assist, state and local governments appealed to the national government for help.

President Roosevelt Greatly Expanded the Role of the National Government

At his inaugural address in 1933, President Franklin Delano Roosevelt made it clear that he was prepared to bring the full power of the executive branch to bear on the Great Depression. Should Congress not take proper action to assist, he said "I shall ask Congress for . . . broad Executive power to wage a war against the emergency, as great as the power that would be given to me if we were in fact invaded by a foreign foe."[42]

Roosevelt meant what he said, and he would back up those promises and threats as one of the most powerful presidents in U.S. history. Within his first few months in office, Roosevelt secured the passage of fifteen major laws covering large areas of the nation's economy. Called the Hundred Days, this period in Roosevelt's administration resulted in the creation of a host of agencies;

Franklin Delano Roosevelt's inaugural address, March 4, 1933. In the address, President Roosevelt asserted, "This great Nation will endure as it has endured, will revive and will prosper. So, first of all, let me assert my firm belief that the only thing we have to fear is fear itself—nameless, unreasoning, unjustified terror which paralyzes needed efforts to convert retreat into advance." Franklin D. Roosevelt Presidential Library & Museum

thousands of pages of regulations and rules; and a new, stronger role for the national government. It was part of the **New Deal**, Roosevelt's plan for tackling the Great Depression.

Roosevelt was able to use his uncanny sensibilities as a strategic political actor to exert a powerful influence on the country in a short amount of time. Roosevelt knew that state governments simply did not have the resources to handle the massive problems they faced. They were in no position to refuse the massive amount of federal aid that Roosevelt offered, even if accepting the aid meant trading away some state authority. This dynamic fundamentally changed the relationship between the states and the national government, dramatically strengthening the role of the national government in the economy. In terms of American federalism, it was a true revolution.

Roosevelt's first priority was the nation's crumbling banking system.[43] He officially closed the country's banks and introduced a series of bills to regulate the nation's economy and create a set of federal organizations to carry out and enforce these policies.[44] One of the most important, and controversial, results of the Hundred Days was the National Industrial Recovery Act (NIRA). Its purpose was to "drive prices up and put people back to work."[45] To do so, the act created an administrative agency, the National Recovery Administration (NRA), which became involved in regulating the American economy in ways few would have thought possible before the economic crisis hit. The primary tool of the NRA was a code (or set of rules) created by the NIRA governing prices, outputs, wages, working hours and conditions, management-labor relations, and the employment of children that American businesses pledged to follow.

The code was detailed. It "determined the precise components of macaroni; [it] determined what tailors could and could not sew. In the poultry industry the relevant line of code had banned customers from picking their own chickens."[46] The implementation of the code created political opposition both from business owners who were frustrated by their inability to raise prices and by workers and labor leaders who felt that the law's protections for workers' rights did not go far enough.[47] The complexity of the code also entangled government in the smallest of details of businesses, about which individual code inspectors often had little or no knowledge. Roosevelt was himself said to be nervous about wading so forcefully into workers' rights, but he later became more enthusiastic "in part because it strengthened workers' loyalty to the New Deal and the Democratic Party."[48]

The Supreme Court Pushed Back against President Roosevelt's New Deal Expansions

In 1934 Martin Schechter and his three brothers, operators of two kosher Jewish butcheries in New York, found themselves the target of the federal government's NRA regulators. The Schechter brothers' butcheries followed a set of practices that were "both a matter of religious observance and good business."[49]

One of the practices in which the Schechter brothers engaged was ensuring that their slaughtered chickens were "glatt kosher," meaning that the lungs of the carcasses were smooth and, therefore, free of tuberculosis, a very serious health issue in America at the time. As part of their observance of kosher practices, the Schechter brothers allowed customers to select and inspect poultry prior to sale. The Schechter brothers had followed those practices for years, earning them a loyal customer base.[50]

Those same practices placed the Schechter brothers at odds with the administration of President Franklin Delano Roosevelt. The brothers were charged with violating the NIRA federal code, including one charge that centered on the sale of "unfit chickens" not suitable for human consumption. All four brothers were indicted for violating the new laws, and all four were convicted and imprisoned. Instead of backing down, however, the Schechter brothers sued, and their case made it all the way to the Supreme Court. Their case, *Schechter Poultry Corp. v. United States* (1935), shook the foundations of Roosevelt's plan to fight the Great Depression.

The policy at the center of the battle was the code that the NIRA created and that the NRA was tasked to implement. The power of the NRA, its code inspectors, and the federal government seemed to the Schechter brothers and others overbearing and relentless. As they put it, "the NRA code did not make sense."[51] Their lawyers argued that the federal government overstepped its powers in granting Congress and the president authority over commerce that neither had possessed under the Constitution.

By the time the Schechter brothers' case made it to the Supreme Court, even members of Roosevelt's administration had begun to realize that such regulation could only produce political opposition without any larger political benefit. The "top-down culture of the

The Schechter brothers celebrate with their attorney, Joseph Heller, center, in his law offices in New York on May 27, 1935, upon learning of the Supreme Court's ruling in their favor in the case of *Schechter Poultry Corp. v. United States*. In this case, the National Industrial Recovery Act (NIRA) was determined to be unconstitutional. The Granger Collection, New York

NRA" began to take political fire,[52] and even the mainstream political establishment began to turn against it.

So did the Supreme Court.[53] In the early years of the New Deal, the Supreme Court was in no mood to allow the new president to expand federal authority in such an unprecedented way. In its opinion in *Schechter Poultry Corp. v. United States* (1935), the Supreme Court struck at the heart of Roosevelt's New Deal, arguing that his administration's policies had gone far beyond the authority granted by the Constitution and especially by the commerce clause. How, a majority of justices asked critically, could the butchery of chickens in New York City be considered "Commerce . . . among the several States?"

In his arguments before the Supreme Court, Joseph Heller, the chief litigator on behalf of the Schechter brothers, argued that the federal government had exceeded its delegated, or implied, powers in its expansion of the commerce clause. In its regulation of the slaughter and sale of chickens in Brooklyn, the federal government, Heller asserted, had gone far beyond any reasonable interpretation of the word *among*. Almost all of the chickens, he argued, had been purchased in New York, processed in New York, and sold in New York. Since no state boundary was crossed, the commerce clause could not have been violated.

In a unanimous opinion, the court sided with the Schechter brothers. Chief Justice Charles Evans Hughes argued that in enacting and enforcing the code, the NRA had exceeded its constitutional authority: "When the poultry had reached the defendants' slaughterhouses, the interstate commerce had ended."[54] Hughes wrote in his opinion that the actions of Congress and the Roosevelt administration consisted of "assertions of extra constitutional authority," a breach of the Tenth Amendment to the Constitution, which states that "the powers not delegated to the United States by the Constitution, nor prohibited to it by the States, are reserved to the States respective, or to the people."[55]

On both of these counts—exceeding the delegated power of the commerce clause and the excessive delegation of power to the president by Congress to formulate and enforce the code—the Supreme Court overturned the convictions of the Schechter brothers and, by implication, the NIRA and perhaps the entire New Deal. As Hughes put it, "the authority of the federal government may not be pushed to such an extreme as to destroy the distinction, which the commerce clause itself establishes, between commerce 'among the Several' states' and the internal concerns of a State."[56] The code-making and enforcing authority of the NRA, the Court found, violated the commerce clause and was therefore invalid. Without such authority, the NIRA was powerless.

The *Schechter* case was just the beginning. Justice Hughes was far from done, and "between 1933 and 1936, the Court overturned acts of Congress at ten times the traditional rate," actions that "created an atmosphere of crisis in Washington."[57]

President Roosevelt Struck Back with a Court-Packing Plan

The challenge to the president's authority would not go unanswered, however. In the months surrounding the Supreme Court's invalidation of the core of his New Deal, Roosevelt pushed ahead with his legislative agenda, called the Second New Deal. This period in Roosevelt's presidency saw passage of some of the most important New Deal programs.

The Social Security Act of 1935 created a set of programs to support vulnerable groups of Americans. It established unemployment insurance for American workers. It set up old-age insurance and elderly assistance programs, which were later supplemented with disability insurance. In addition, it established Aid to Dependent Children.[58] These programs were designed to be self-funding so as not to force the government to raise taxes and further depress the economy.

Passing more laws was not Roosevelt's only response to the Supreme Court's challenge to his power. Following his landslide reelection in 1936, in a move that alarmed even his closest advisers, Roosevelt decided to take on the Supreme Court directly. The president sought to use Congress's constitutional authority to increase the number of justices on the Court from nine to as many as fifteen, thus allowing him to appoint enough pro–New Deal justices to tip the balance of power decisively in his favor. Known as the "Court-packing plan," Roosevelt's gambit was constitutional but very bold and very risky.[59]

In the end, Roosevelt's bill died in the Democratic Congress. The Court-packing plan ultimately divided his own party, driving many conservative Democrats to side with Republicans in Congress, especially over issues of civil rights for African Americans. Roosevelt eventually nominated replacements for most of the justices but only because his unprecedented four terms in office allowed him to outlast the tenure of most of them.

In the New Deal, Cooperative Federalism Replaced Dual Federalism

In the end, the Court did change its opinions, reversing in several key rulings its previous opposition to the constitutionality of Roosevelt's New Deal and similar state measures to regulate businesses and the economy. The New Deal survived, and it fundamentally altered the boundaries between the activities of the federal government and those of the states.

The expansion of national power under Roosevelt's New Deal—especially Congress's authority to regulate interstate commerce—permanently altered the relationship between the states and the nation. Cooperative federalism, in which both levels of government are involved in setting policy, firmly replaced earlier models of dual federalism and made the national government at least a coequal in many areas of public policy traditionally handled by the states.

This change did not just happen. Nor was it necessarily inevitable. Roosevelt's popularity, political skill, and miscalculations all played a role. So did the decisions and the shifting opinions of the members of the Supreme Court. However, the revolution was also made possible by the severe economic crisis facing the nation and the inability of states to handle its fallout. States did not always fight Roosevelt's policies, desperate as they were for help in handling the impact of the Great Depression.

1. Dual federalism is so named because it refers to the fact that both the House of Representatives and the Senate work to shape it.

   a. True
   b. False

2. In *Plessy v. Ferguson*, the Supreme Court ruled that _____.

   a. Legal segregation based on racial identity was constitutionally permissible
   b. All powers not granted to the nation are reserved to the states
   c. The federal government had the authority to forbid racial segregation
   d. Railroad corporations should be free to pursue westward expansion

3. Roosevelt's Hundred Days refers to _____.

   a. The opening months of World War II
   b. President Roosevelt's political campaign
   c. A period of the creation of bureaucratic agencies
   d. The Supreme Court's challenge to Roosevelt's policies

4. In writing the opinion in *Schechter Poultry Corp. v. United States*, Justice Hughes focused especially on _____.

   a. The Second Amendment
   b. The First Amendment
   c. The Tenth Amendment
   d. The Fourteenth Amendment

5. What is cooperative federalism?

....

Answer Key: 1. b; 2. a; 3. c; 4. c; 5. Answers should discuss the sharing of power between states and the nation.

MODERN AMERICAN FEDERALISM REMAINS COOPERATIVE BUT FACES CHALLENGES

- Understand how cooperative federalism has expanded up to the present day, including the policymaking tools that allow for coordination between the levels of government.

During the second half of the twentieth century, the expansion of national involvement in the American economy initiated by Roosevelt continued and was in fact strengthened and expanded. Many federal agencies created during the New Deal stayed in place, and some grew larger. As the American economy recovered from the Great Depression and World War II, the conclusion of which left the United States as a global superpower, cooperative federalism remained the dominant model. The dual federalism of the nineteenth and early twentieth centuries was long gone—and, barring a major economic or social crisis, it is not coming back.

One of the primary tools that the federal government can use to achieve its policy objectives within the states is the **grant-in-aid**, money provided to states by the federal government in order to carry out a policy that the national government has decided is important. Though the use of grants-in-aid goes back to the early days of the Republic—especially in grants of land to support public education in the states and territories—they became a common tool in a variety of policy areas during and after the New Deal.

The main form of a grant-in-aid during this period was the **categorical grant**, a grant provided to states or to local or regional governments for specific policy objectives and with certain conditions attached to receiving or spending the funds. (See the left-hand column of Figure 3.5.) These conditions might involve the requirement that the state, local, or regional authority provide matching funds in order to receive the federal monies. They might also include specific instructions on how the grant funds are to be used. Sometimes categorical grants are awarded based on formulas that allocate federal money according to factors such as population, income, and need.

Categorical grants-in-aid are an important source of national power. Though state, local, and regional governmental authorities are often not required to accept these funds, once they do they accept the national regulation that goes along with taking the money. Once a state establishes a program based on the receipt of a categorical grant-in-aid, it depends on the continued provision of those funds by the national government, along with any attached strings, to avoid a potentially serious disruption of the provision of services to its citizens and residents.

In this way, categorical grants act as both a carrot—to encourage states to carry out national policy objectives—and as a stick—to threaten states with the withholding of funds if they fail to carry out the federal government's policy

FIGURE 3.5

Grants-in-Aid

Categorical Grant

Money provided by the national government to state, local, or regional governments that is tied to specific policy objectives and that carries certain conditions for receipt or expenditure.

- National government controls purse strings.
- Once a program is established, states depend upon national government for continuation of that program
- Can mean that wealthier states "subsidize" poorer ones; but can also mean that inequalities between states are reduced and citizens in poorer states have access to benefits they might not otherwise have.
- Can make it harder for states to control their own budgets.
- Can lead to expansion in size of national and state government.

Block Grant

Money proved to state, local, or regional governments over which sub-national governments have greater control.

- State, local, or regional governments have greater say in how funds are spent.
- Sub-national governments given greater flexibility in long term budget planning.
- States can have more authority in setting and enforcing welfare rules.
- Can mean that states decide what priorities to select for their population and are more "in touch" with their needs; but also can mean that federal oversight is reduced and the ability to compare outcomes across states is more limited.
- Can mean that localities with greater need lose out to localities with greater political clout in the allocation of funds.

objectives. According to critics of national power, categorical grants pose several problems for American federalism. They may act as "bribes to induce subnational governments to execute national policies" at the expense of their own authority.[60] Officials and citizens of wealthier states may feel that their taxes are being used to subsidize lower-spending state governments. The uncertainty surrounding the continued provision of the grants can make it harder for states to plan their own budgets. Finally, the administration of these programs requires a further expansion of the size of both national and state government.

Those who argue in favor of the use of categorical grants as a tool of national policymaking emphasize the degree to which the redistribution of monies between states can act to reduce inequality between the states. Also, these monies can help state, local, and regional governments improve the lives of their citizens in ways that might not be possible without the help of the federal government.[61]

President Lyndon Johnson's Great Society Expanded Cooperative Federalism

The most significant expansion of national power through the use of categorical grants-in-aid in the post–New Deal era occurred during the presidency of Lyndon Baines Johnson. His Great Society program created a new set of administrative agencies aimed at improving social welfare in the United States. Social welfare involves the health, safety, education, and opportunities for citizens. Under the old system of dual federalism, social welfare policies were typically thought of as lying within the scope of the police powers of the states and, therefore, mostly under state control.

Although Roosevelt's policies had already involved the federal government in the provision of social welfare policy—for example, by addressing working conditions, unemployment relief, and income security—Johnson's policies expanded this role, aided by strong Democratic Party majorities in both the House and the Senate. Most of his initiatives were grants-in aid to states and communities.

Pediatrician Lanre Falusi examining an infant patient in a Maryland community health clinic in 2015. With powerful lobbying efforts behind them, members of the American Medical Association pressured Congress to revamp physician reimbursement under Medicare. Andrew Harrer/Bloomberg via Getty Images

The Medicare program (1965) supplemented the Social Security program by providing health insurance coverage to individuals aged sixty-five and older. The Medicaid program (1965) provided health care assistance to individuals receiving other forms of aid as well as to those "who were medically indigent but not on welfare."[62] As with many Great Society programs, Medicaid was set up to be funded partly by the federal government and partly by the states. The Elementary and Secondary Education Act of 1965 (ESEA) "provided for the first time, general federal support for public elementary and secondary education."[63] Title I of the ESEA provided federal assistance to children from low-income families in both public and private schools.

With New Federalism Came Devolution and Attempts to Roll Back National Power

Some backlash followed on the heels of Johnson's Great Society programs and the expansion of national authority that they produced. When Richard Nixon was elected president in 1968, he promised to roll back the expansion of national authority and return at least some of the power back to the states. He called his project "new federalism."

One of Nixon's main tools to try to reduce national authority was the **block grant**. Though they are still a type of grant-in-aid, block grants provide federal money for public policies in a way that tries to increase state, local, and regional authority in how that money is spent and decrease national authority in deciding which states, localities, or regions receive those funds.

Efforts to restore more authority to the states continued under the presidency of Ronald Reagan, who, in his speech accepting the Republican Party's nomination in 1980, promised, "Everything that can be run more effectively by state and local government we shall turn over to state and local government, along with the funding sources to pay for it. We are going to put an end to the money merry-go-round where our money becomes Washington's money, to be spent by the states and cities exactly the way the federal bureaucrats tell them to."[64] As part of his program, Reagan reduced funding for several social welfare programs and increased the use of block grants for those that continued to be funded.

The goal of returning authority for federal programs back to the states is called **devolution**, in the sense that authority is devolved, or returned to, the states. Efforts at devolution involved trying to increase states' autonomy in economic and social policy by decentralizing control and administration of programs. One of the most important of these efforts focused on social welfare policies. Democratic president Bill Clinton signed into law the Personal Responsibility and Work Opportunity Reconciliation Act of 1996 (PRWORA). PRWORA replaced a Roosevelt-era aid program with Temporary Assistance for Needy Families (TANF), which placed time limits on receipt of welfare assistance and added work requirements. In addition, block grants and other changes to the administration of the program gave states more authority in setting and enforcing the rules of welfare programs.

Johnson's Great Society expanded the role of the national government and the vision of cooperative federalism that had been firmly established during Roosevelt's New Deal. The Republican administrations of Nixon and Reagan attempted to roll back some of the growth in national power that had occurred during and after the New Deal. Democratic president Clinton—confronted with firm Republican Party control in Congress—applied the principle of devolution to social welfare policy.

In terms of returning America to the dual federalism of its early history, however, none of the policies of the twentieth-century presidents even came close. At this point in American political history, there has been no going back to the stricter separation between state and national authority that operated prior to Roosevelt's revolution. However, as the United States confronts a new set of challenges in the twenty-first century, calls for a fundamental reexamination of American federalism have gained more and more attention.

Where Is American Federalism Headed Today?

In spite of efforts to restrain the power of the national government during the periods of new federalism and devolution, the New Deal legacy of national involvement in state policy has not fundamentally changed, nor is it likely to. For states to opt out of the involvement of the federal government that comes with accepting federal funds would require opting out of the funds themselves and either replacing them or explaining to that state's citizens why certain services will no longer be provided. While individual states may do this in regard to individual programs, a national, wholesale withdrawal is almost unthinkable.

State and local governments, however, have not necessarily been passive players in cooperative federalism, and strategic political actors at the various levels have played a role in trying to shape the balance of power between the two levels of the American federalist system. That is likely to continue and may result in an increased use of tools to assert state power, even confrontationally. States have a handful of tools they can use to shape how they participate in cooperative federalism.

Taxation

One area where states are beginning to try to set policy in the absence of a comprehensive federal policy is e-commerce taxation. When state residents are able to purchase items over the Internet from companies outside of their states, state governments can lose out on sales tax revenue for those products. In many ways, the e-commerce giants, such as eBay and Amazon.com, present similar challenges to state governments as did the railroads of the nineteenth century, with individual states facing difficulties in regulating businesses that transcend state boundaries. In response, states are increasingly setting policies to collect tax revenues from products purchased online and are coordinating their policies with other state governments.

Lobbying

Another tactic that state and local governments use is to try to influence the content of federal legislation as it is being written and voted on. **Intergovernmental lobbying**, which is often carried out by state or local governmental staff in Washington, involves attempts to influence the national policymaking process to protect state and local interests. In this way, these governments themselves become part of the national legislative process. Examples of intergovernmental lobbying organizations include the National Governors Association, the National Conference of State Legislatures, and the National League of Cities.

Implementation

Even when the federal government passes laws that govern state actions, the state governments are typically responsible for implementing these policies, giving them the opportunity to use the process of implementation "to enforce federal policies in a way that promotes their interests."[65] Although the federal government often has considerable power in crafting laws and creating administrative agencies, the fact that states actually carry out many of these policies provides an important source of state power. In *Federalist No. 46*, James Madison argued that states would have considerable power to resist the carrying out of an "unwarrantable measure of the federal government" by making it difficult, if not impossible, for those unpopular policies to actually be carried out.[66] In fact, according to one scholar of American federalism, "state governments have indeed succeeded tremendously in resisting, delaying, or altering the implementation of federal policies at the state level."[67]

Challenges to Cooperation

While the modern system of cooperative federalism allows states opportunities to try to preserve their authority and influence over policymaking, the relationship between states and the national government is not always cooperative. At times, state governments have objected to federal regulations that, from the point of view of the states, are attempts to make the states pay for federal policies. Such unpaid, or underpaid, requirements are called **unfunded mandates** or, sometimes, underfunded mandates.

From the point of view of Congress, there are strong incentives to make policies whose costs have to be carried by the states: "The legislator gets the credit for benefitting

Store owner Justin Wilson III and his son in Wilson's store in Virginia in 2014. Wilson was supporting state tax legislation that would tax online sales similar to how sales at his TennisServ shop were taxed. Like many retail business owners, Wilson expressed concerns that individuals would browse merchandise in his store and then order it more cheaply online, without having to pay state sales tax. Linda Davidson / The Washington Post via Getty Images needy constituents, but the cost is paid by a lower governmental tier."[68] State, local, and regional governments have complained to Washington about the imposition of unfunded mandates in a variety of policy areas, including environmental policy, education policy, and the provision of health and social welfare benefits for low-income and disabled Americans. In March 2008, the governor of Montana complained, "We are putting up with the federal government on so many fronts, and nearly every month they come up with another harebrained scheme, an unfunded mandate to tell us that our life is going to be better if we'll just buckle under on some other kind of rule or regulation."[69]

One strategy that states use to try to reduce the impact of unfunded mandates is to pressure the federal government for waivers from certain provisions of a given law. Coordinated state pressure on the federal government can lead to exemptions from implementing—and paying for—certain unpopular provisions of a law.

As the American Republic enters the first decades of the twenty-first century, new state challenges to federal authority are emerging. One tool that many states have used to do this is the **sovereignty resolution**. Passed by state legislatures, sovereignty resolutions affirm the sovereignty of states under the Tenth Amendment to the Constitution. Variations of these resolutions have been passed or considered in response to a variety of federal laws, including those covering education, immigration, and health care. They are often a result of state claims of unfunded mandates. They are typically only statements of protest, stopping short of actually nullifying a law but asserting the rights of states to do so in the future if necessary.

Though sovereignty resolutions are largely symbolic, the Tenth Amendment has become a more prominent tool in asserting state authority in recent decades, especially in the area of gun control, as several Supreme Court decisions have cited the amendment in the logic of their decisions. In 1995, in *United States v. Lopez*, the court struck down a federal law banning the carrying of firearms near schools.[70] In 1997, in *Printz v. United States*, the Court again cited the Tenth Amendment when it struck down portions of a federal law that required local law enforcement officers to perform background checks on prospective handgun purchasers.[71]

Another tactic that states have occasionally used, and may continue to use in the future, is to pass a state law that is in direct violation of a federal law or policy, perhaps amending the state constitution in order to do so. During the election of 2012, several states passed laws or amendments to their constitutions that placed state policy in direct violation of federal policy. Three states—Montana, Alabama, and Wyoming—passed initiatives exempting state citizens from some of the provisions or penalties under President Obama's health care overhaul, the Patient Protection and Affordable Care Act of 2010. And, as we have explored, more than half of the states have now passed laws legalizing the medical or even recreational use of marijuana, in violation of federal law.

1. The term *devolution* refers to returning powers over social welfare policy back to the states.

   a. True
   b. False

2. Categorical grants _____.

   a. Are provided with specific provisions on their distribution
   b. Allow state governments great flexibility in their use
   c. Have been nullified as they support a policy of "separate but equal"
   d. Require state constitutional amendments to accept

3. An example of a way that state governments try to assert their own authority is _____.

   a. Nullification
   b. Intergovernmental lobbying
   c. Secession
   d. All of the above

4. How would you describe the current state of American federalism?

Answer Key: 1. a; 2. a; 3. c; 4. Answers will vary and should be backed up with arguments. Some may focus on national power. Others may focus on cooperative federalism. Still, others may point to increasing state resistance.

CONCLUSION

The Evolution of Federalism Continues

Today, Angel Raich is "living very happily with her loving husband" and working as a consultant and advocate for individuals' rights to use medical cannabis.[72] Raich, with the help of medical marijuana, has been able to maintain her health, pursue her goals, and express her voice as a political advocate.

However, the issue of the boundary between state and federal laws governing medical and recreational marijuana use remains far from settled. By 2016 more than half of the states had passed legislation legalizing medical cannabis. Eight other states and Washington, D.C., had also passed ballot initiatives legalizing the recreational use of marijuana.[73] However, the CSA still controlled federal law and policy.

According to the Office of National Drug Control Policy, "It is important to recognize that these state marijuana laws do not change the fact that using marijuana continues to be an offense under federal law. Nor do these state laws change the criteria or process for FDA [U.S. Food and Drug Administration] approval of safe and effective medications."[74] By federal law, any current user of marijuana, even if legal under their own state laws, is violating the CSA and is subject to federal prosecution.

There is no possible—or practical—way that this situation can continue. By 2016 the CSA could not be effectively and totally enforced as federal law since that would have entailed putting more than a million, perhaps millions, of state-law-abiding citizens in federal prison, not to mention the unimaginable political fallout from fully executing the law.[75] Officials with the federal government and the Obama administration were well aware of this situation. In a 2013 memorandum, the Department of Justice affirmed the legality and supremacy of the

CSA but also acknowledged the impossibility of enforcing the law in the states in totality. It stated, "The Department is also committed to using its limited investigative and executorial resources to address the most significant threats in the most effective, consistent and rational way."[76] In the memorandum, the Justice Department declared that instead it would focus on preventing access to marijuana by youths, transport of marijuana from a state in which it is legal to states in which it is not, and the use of firearms in connection with the production or distribution of marijuana.

How to deal with the fact that an individual might be complying with the laws of her or his state but at the same time breaking federal law is a fundamental question of federalism that is still unanswered. American federalism has never been a well-defined thing. In the twenty-first century, it remains just as contested as it been for most of the nation's history.

Want a better grade?

Get the tools you need to sharpen your study skills. **SAGE edge** offers a robust online environment featuring an impressive array of free tools and resources. Access practice quizzes, eFlashcards, video, and multimedia at **edge.sagepub.com/abernathybrief1e.**

CHAPTER REVIEW

This chapter's main ideas are reflected in the Learning Objectives. By reviewing them here you should be able to **remember** the key points and **know** these terms that are central to the topic.

3.1 Explain the tension in American federalism between state and federal laws.

REMEMBER ...

- The ultimate political authority in the American representative democracy rests with the people, but this authority is divided between two levels of government: the nation and the states.

KNOW ...

- *federalism*: a structure of governance that places the people's authority in two or more levels of government (p. 71)

3.2 Identify the elements of the U.S. Constitution that shape American federalism and evaluate arguments about the proper limits of congressional power under their authority.

REMEMBER...

- The Constitution lays out much of the framework of American federalism but not in one clear, neatly defined section. Instead, multiple clauses and sections attempt to define its basic boundaries.

KNOW...

- *commerce clause*: a part of the Constitution that grants Congress the authority to regulate business and commercial activity (p. 75)

- *concurrent powers*: powers granted to both states and the federal government in the Constitution (p. 77)

- *confederal systems*: structures of governance in which the subnational governments retain the majority of the granted authority (p. 74)

- *enumerated powers*: powers explicitly granted to the government via the Constitution (p. 76)

- *federal systems*: structures of governance that divide a people's sovereignty between two or more levels of government (p. 74)

- *implied powers*: powers not textually granted to a government but considered valid in order to carry out the enumerated powers (p. 76)

- *necessary and proper clause*: a part of the Constitution that grants the federal government the authority to pass laws required to carry out its enumerated powers; also called the elastic clause (p. 75)

- *police powers*: a category of reserved powers that includes the protection of people's health, safety, and welfare (p. 76)

- *reserved powers*: powers reserved to the states if not textually granted to the federal government (p. 76)

- *supremacy clause*: a part of the Constitution that establishes the Constitution and the laws of the nation passed under its authority as the highest laws of the nation (p. 75)

- *unitary systems*: structures of governance that place the people's sovereignty in a national government, with subnational governments deriving their authority from it (p. 74)

3.3 Describe the development of American federalism over time.

REMEMBER...

- The boundaries between the authority of national and state governments have changed over time. Many of these changes have come about as a result of Supreme Court decisions in interpreting the Constitution.

- The New Deal fundamentally reshaped American federalism, but the program was not without challenges, especially by the Supreme Court.

KNOW...

- *cooperative federalism*: a vision of American federalism in which the states and the national government work together to shape public policy (p. 85)

- *dual federalism*: a view of American federalism in which the states and the nation operate independently in their own areas of public policy (p. 83)

- *Great Depression*: a period defined by the most significant economic crisis in American history (p. 87)

- *New Deal*: a set of policies passed during the administration of President Franklin Roosevelt in order to combat the Great Depression (p. 88)

- *states' rights*: the idea that American states have the authority to self-govern, even when in conflict with national laws (p. 84)

3.4 List changes to American federalism in the post-New Deal era.

REMEMBER ...

- Subsequent administrations, especially that of President Lyndon Johnson, expanded upon the promises and programs of the New Deal. However, later presidents, such as Ronald Reagan, attempted to restrict the power of the federal government and turn over more administrative authority to the states.

KNOW...

- *block grant*: a type of grant-in-aid that gives state officials more authority in the disbursement of the federal funds (p. 95)

- *categorical grant*: grant-in-aid provided to states with specific provisions on its use (p. 92)

- *devolution*: a national policy goal of returning more authority to state or local governments (p. 95)

- *grant-in-aid*: federal money provided to states to implement public policy objectives (p. 92)

3.5 Discuss the current status of American federalism and how it might continue to evolve.

REMEMBER...

- State and local governments continue to be active in asserting their governmental authority.

KNOW...

- *intergovernmental lobbying*: efforts by state and local governments to act in Washington on behalf of their own interests (p. 96)

- *sovereignty resolution*: state legislative measure that affirms the sovereignty of states under the Tenth Amendment (p. 98)

- *unfunded mandates*: federal regulations that must be followed by the states but whose costs must also be shouldered by the states (p. 97)

4 CIVIL LIBERTIES AND CIVIL RIGHTS
Building and Defending Fences

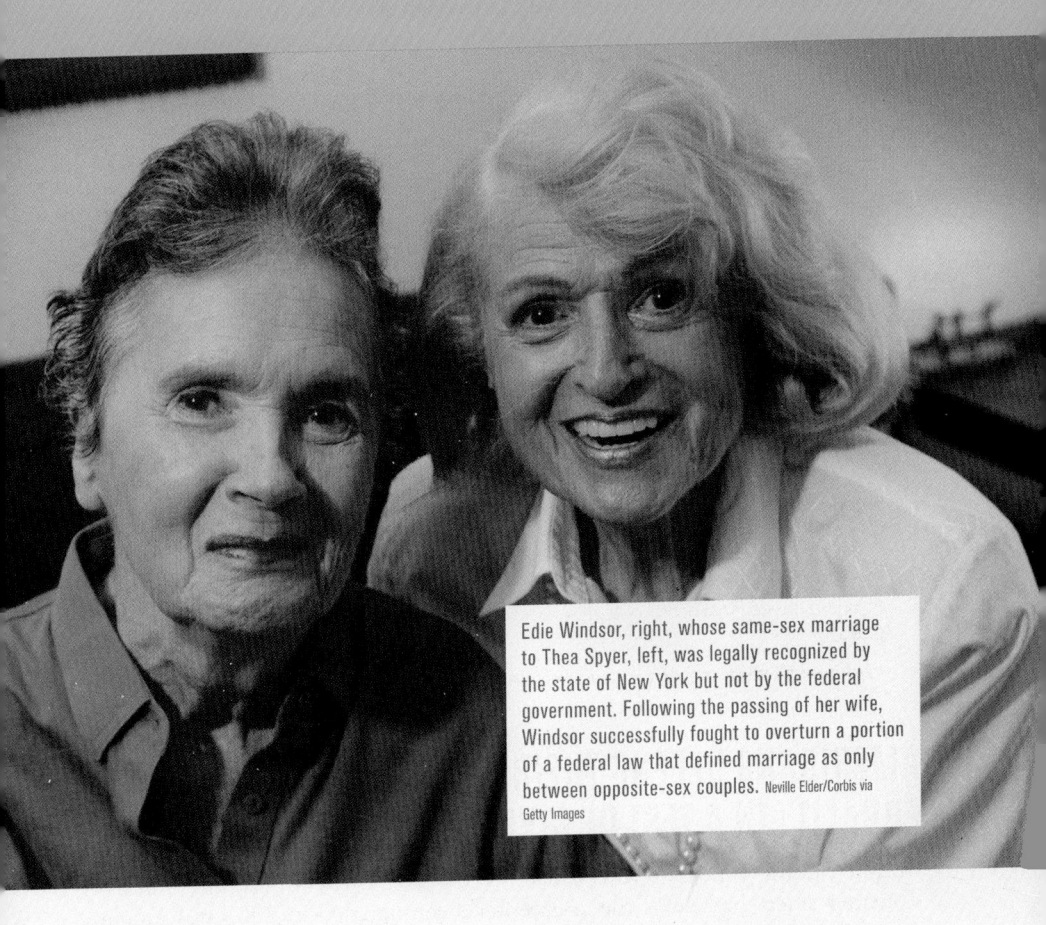

Edie Windsor, right, whose same-sex marriage to Thea Spyer, left, was legally recognized by the state of New York but not by the federal government. Following the passing of her wife, Windsor successfully fought to overturn a portion of a federal law that defined marriage as only between opposite-sex couples. Neville Elder/Corbis via Getty Images

In this book, we have heard stories featuring diverse American voices making claims to their rights and freedoms from the founding of the country up to the present day. The types of rights they've claimed, however, take distinctly different forms. The rights citizens possess that are protected from unreasonable governmental restriction are referred to as **civil liberties**. In contrast, **civil rights** refers to the fundamental rights of individuals to be treated equally under the laws and policies of governments, regardless of their identities and lived experiences.

Civil liberties are often called **negative freedoms** because protecting them involves restricting—*not* allowing—government actions. The First Amendment to the

Constitution begins, "Congress shall make no law. . . ." It is this affirmation of the *limits* on the proper powers of government that defines the fundamental freedoms of Americans. In contrast, civil rights are often referred to as **positive freedoms** since their protection generally implies positive action, either on the part of citizens to exercise them or on the part of a government to secure them.

The main challenge with civil liberties has to do with struggles to build fences to define, protect, and defend those fundamental liberties. The stories of Edie Windsor and James Obergefell are two such stories we will explore, in this regard, as they fought to have their same-sex marriages recognized. The main challenge with civil rights, by contrast, comes from deciding how vigorously a government should act to protect them. How much action does a government need to take? How equal is equal? Our story of the struggles of African Americans to overcome legal and de facto segregation and of women to secure voting rights and other legal protections illustrates those efforts.

After reading this chapter, you will be able to do the following:

4.1 Describe the civil liberties protected by the Constitution, the amendments to it, and the process by which they were incorporated in order to restrict state actions.

4.2 Explain the first amendment protections granted to religion and political speech.

4.3 Identify the civil liberties extended to the accused in the Bill of Rights.

4.4 Trace the efforts to secure civil rights for African Americans.

4.5 Describe the challenges women faced in securing their civil rights.

AMERICANS DEFEND THEIR RIGHT TO MARRIAGE EQUALITY IN A TEST OF CIVIL LIBERTIES

In 2009, Edith Windsor's wife, Thea Spyer, passed away after a long illness. Together since the 1960s, the couple had been married in 2007 in Canada wherein same-sex marriage is legal. Their marriage had also been recognized as valid by New York, their state of residence at the time of Spyer's passing. Their marriage, however, was not considered legal under U.S. federal law. As such, after her wife's passing, Windsor was not entitled to the same tax protections granted to surviving spouses in opposite-sex, federally recognized marriages. Therefore, Windsor had to pay more than $350,000 in federal estate taxes. With help from gay rights organizations, Windsor sued the federal government, claiming her right to have her marriage recognized as legal under federal law, and her case went all the way to the Supreme Court.

Testing DOMA and the Full Faith and Credit Clause

At the heart of Windsor's case lay a federal law, the Defense of Marriage Act (DOMA). DOMA had been passed in 1996 by opponents of same-sex marriage in Congress who believed that some states were likely to legalize same-sex marriages in the coming years. The act had two substantive sections. One section stated that for purposes of federal law, marriage meant a legal union between a man and a woman. Another section reaffirmed the power of the states to make their own decisions about marriage, essentially saying that no state needed to honor a same-sex marriage license issued by another state. This section of DOMA tried to clarify, or delimit, the Constitution, specifically the **full faith and credit clause**, which states, "Full faith and credit shall be given in each state to the public acts, records, and judicial proceedings of every other state."[1] Under the full faith and credit clause, a state is required to recognize and honor the public laws of other states unless those laws are contrary to the strong public policy of that state. Full faith and credit is why, for example, you only need a driver's license from one state.

In a 5–4 decision in *United States v. Windsor* (2013), the Supreme Court ruled that the first section of DOMA, the one classifying only opposite-sex marriages as legal under federal law, was unconstitutional.[2] In a later interview after Windsor had made constitutional history, she stated, "Honey, you've got to be loud and proud."[3] The Supreme Court had validated state-recognized same-sex marriages for federal purposes.

However, the Court did not strike down the other key clause of DOMA, which allowed states not to give full faith and credit to same-sex marriage licenses from other states. Nor had it legalized same-sex marriages generally. Defending that civil liberty would be left to James Obergefell. The facts of his case were, sadly, somewhat similar to those of Edith Windsor's.

In 2011, after a decades-long commitment to each other, Obergefell married John Arthur on the tarmac of a Maryland airport. The two men were Ohio residents, a state that did not recognize marriage equality, so they flew to Maryland, which did. Arthur was struggling with a terminal illness. The two men flew to Maryland in a medical transport plane, seeking to get married while they still could. Obergefell described their ceremony: "We landed at Baltimore, sat on the tarmac for a little bit, said 'I do,' and 10 minutes later were in the air on the way home."[4] John Arthur passed away in 2013.

Obergefell and Arthur's state of residence did not recognize their marriage, and the state of Ohio did not allow Obergefell to be listed as Arthur's surviving spouse. Rather than accept Ohio's refusal to recognize their marriage, Obergefell sued. "This case," he said, "was another way to take care of [Arthur] and to respect him and to respect our relationship."[5] In 2015, in its decision in *Obergefell v. Hodges*, the Supreme Court in yet another 5–4 vote affirmed the legality of Obergefell and Arthur's marriage and guaranteed the right of all couples to marry. Justice Kennedy, in his majority opinion, affirmed that "the right to marry is a fundamental right inherent in the liberty of the person." The second major section of DOMA had been declared unconstitutional. More fundamentally, marriage equality had become the law of both the nation and the states.

Reflecting on his case in an interview with *USA Today* two months before the Court's decision, Obergefell recalled how he felt about having to fly, given his husband's serious medical issues, to another state just to get married: "All I thought was, 'This isn't right, I'm p——ed off.'"[6]

James Obergefell in 2015, two and a half months prior to the Supreme Court decision that would guarantee marriage equality for all Americans. Maddie McGarvey/For The Washington Post via Getty Images

Testing the Right to Privacy

Another aspect of both Windsor and Obergefell's constitutional claims rested on a right not enumerated in the Bill of Rights: **privacy**. That meant their cases depended upon previous cases in American constitutional law and the precedent they set. In its decisions in these cases, the Supreme Court had affirmed the right to privacy and applied it to several areas of Americans' private lives, such as birth control, abortion, and sexuality.

The foundational case regarding privacy was *Griswold v. Connecticut* (1965).[7] In it, the Court overturned a Connecticut law that prohibited the provision of contraceptives and medical advice about contraceptive techniques to married couples. In striking down the law, the Court affirmed the right of privacy as a protection against government intrusion. The precedent set in that case was later extended to other cases involving sexual practices and other "private" acts beyond contraception.

In 2003, in *Lawrence v. Texas*, the Court struck down a Texas law making same-sex sexual conduct illegal, affirming the right of consenting adults to express their sexuality.[8] The Court has also affirmed and upheld the right of a woman to terminate a pregnancy. In *Roe v. Wade* (1973), the Court struck down a Texas law that made abortion illegal.[9] In that case, Justice Harry Blackmun drew on the Court's previous ruling in *Griswold*, stating, "This right of privacy, whether it be founded in the . . .concept of personal liberty and restrictions upon state action, as we feel it is, or . . . in the . . . reservation of rights to the people, is broad enough to encompass a woman's decision whether or not to terminate her pregnancy."[10]

Abortion remains a contentious issue. Since *Roe v. Wade*, trying to assess a nominee's future rulings on abortion has become a key factor in the Senate's application of its power of advice and consent in confirming justices to the Supreme Court and judges to the lower levels of the federal judiciary.

Windsor and Obergefell's cases highlight complex questions involving the expression and protection of civil liberties: What exactly are the fundamental rights and freedoms that individuals possess? How did they come to have those rights? Under what circumstances can a government legitimately restrict the expression of these rights and freedoms? As we will explore, the Supreme Court plays a pivotal role in attempting to answer these questions. In doing so, it undertakes the difficult task of defining where liberties began and end.

1. Civil liberties are called negative freedoms because they _____.
   a. Are not good things
   b. Reject elements of the Declaration of Independence
   c. Place restrictions upon governmental action
   d. Place restrictions upon individual action

2. Civil rights are called positive freedoms because they _____.
   a. Are good things
   b. Rely on a set of freedoms outlined in the Bill of Rights
   c. Typically require citizens to take action to exercise them or the government to work to secure them
   d. Apply only to individuals and not to the government

3. What role did the full faith and credit clause play in the *Windsor* and *Obergefell* cases?

4. What role did the right to privacy play in those cases?

Answer Key: 1. c; 2. c; 3. Answers should include the idea that DOMA attempted to restrict the application of the full faith and credit clause to same-sex marriages. One substantive part of DOMA was ultimately ruled unconstitutional as a result in *Obergefell*; 4. Answers should mention that both cases claimed that same-sex marriage was covered by the right to privacy.

CIVIL LIBERTIES LIMIT GOVERNMENT INTRUSTION

One of the main concerns the delegates to the Constitutional Convention in 1787 brought with them was how they would secure the protection of individual rights. Following independence, most of the state governments had included some protections for individual rights in their own constitutions.[11] However, those protections varied considerably and often lacked key components that Americans today typically think of as fundamental rights, such as freedom of the press or religion. Well aware of the need to protect individual rights, the delegates agreed to place within the original document certain protections, such as a strict limit on the definition of treason as well as restrictions on punishments available for those convicted of it.[12] The delegates did not, however, include a **bill of rights**—a list of fundamental individual rights that a government cannot restrict or intrude upon except under specific circumstances.

- Describe the civil liberties outlined in the Constitution and the amendments to it.
- Understand the process of selective incorporation of the Bill of Rights.

The Bill of Rights Takes Center Stage in the Ratification Debate

During the ratification campaign following the Constitutional Convention, the Anti-Federalists seized upon the lack of a bill of rights in the proposed document as a way to reject the proposed Constitution or to negotiate for a better outcome. Their motives for highlighting the issue were diverse. Some used the lack of a bill of rights as a tactical weapon, hoping to defeat the Constitution entirely. Some were opposed to the federal powers of taxation and regulation of commerce and wanted to see more protections for the rights of states in such a bill.[13] Others argued that such a list of fundamental rights was a necessary protection against the inevitable growth of centralized power in what was sure to become a large republic.

Against the Anti-Federalists' charges, the Federalists offered several counterarguments. In *Federalist* No. 84, Alexander Hamilton argued first that a bill of rights was unnecessary. The proposed document, he argued, already contained provisions guaranteeing specific rights.[14] Second, Hamilton argued that including a bill of rights would be dangerous to individual liberty, not supportive of it. His central concern was that any list of individual rights would necessarily be incomplete. What about those rights not enumerated? Might the lack of their textual protections encourage a tyrant to deny them? As we will discuss later in the chapter, the question of protections for rights not specifically enumerated remains one of the most important topics in the study and application of American civil liberties today.

The Anti-Federalists' strategy proved to be the winning one. On Monday, June 8, 1789, during the first session of Congress, James Madison introduced a draft of the Bill of Rights.[15] After reworking and revising his proposed list, Congress proposed twelve amendments to the Constitution and sent them to the states for ratification. Of these, ten were formally ratified on December 15, 1791.[16] The Bill of Rights had become part of the Constitution.

The list of rights was carefully crafted, covering a wide swath of issues. The First Amendment prevents the legislative branch from passing laws restricting a variety of individual rights, including religion, speech, the press, and assembly. The next two amendments deal with powers generally under the authority of the executive branch involving firearms, state militias, and the quartering of soldiers in people's homes and on their property.

The Fourth through Eighth Amendments guarantee rights of Americans involved with the judicial system: those accused of, arrested for, tried for, and convicted of crimes as well as certain noncriminal cases. The Ninth Amendment arose from concerns that any list of individual rights might be thought of as exhaustive. Therefore, it specifies that the list in the Bill of Rights does not presume or imply the protection of rights not enumerated. Finally, the Tenth Amendment declares that those powers not specifically delegated to the federal government are "reserved to the States" or, in a confounding addendum, "to the people." We will explore specific amendments in detail below. Table 4.1 summarizes the main provisions of the Bill of Rights.

Selective Incorporation Applies the Bill of Rights to State Laws and Actions

The text of the Bill of Rights does not declare restrictions upon the actions of state governments. Instead, it acts to restrain the powers of the federal government. For example, the First Amendment begins, "Congress shall make no law" and not "Congress and the Legislatures of the several States shall make no laws."

So, for much of the nation's history, the explicit protections contained within the Bill of Rights did not apply to state laws and actions, and the Supreme Court upheld this strict, textual reading of the Constitution. That changed with the ratification of the Fourteenth Amendment in 1868. The Fourteenth Amendment (often called the **due process clause**) says that no state may deprive an individual of "life, liberty, or property without due process of law." It laid the foundation

TABLE 4.1 An Overview of Protections Contained within the Bill of Rights

AMENDMENT	PROTECTION
First Amendment	Restricts the lawmaking powers of Congress in the areas of religion, speech, the press, assembly, and petitioning the government
Second Amendment	The right to keep and bear arms
Third Amendment	No forced quartering of troops in homes
Fourth Amendment	Protects against unreasonable search and seizure and establishes the right to have warrants issued prior to arrest or search
Fifth Amendment	Right to a grand jury indictment in criminal cases, protection against double jeopardy and self-incrimination, the right to due process of law, and the right to just compensation when private property is taken for public use
Sixth Amendment	Protections during criminal prosecutions for a speedy and public trial by an impartial jury, the right to confront witnesses, the right to compel favorable witnesses to testify in one's defense, and the right to the assistance of defense counsel
Seventh Amendment	Right to a trial by jury in certain civil suits
Eighth Amendment	Protections against excessive bail, excessive fines, and cruel and unusual punishment
Ninth Amendment	Nonexclusion of rights not listed in the Constitution
Tenth Amendment	Powers not delegated to the federal government, nor prohibited by it to the states, are reserved to the states or to the people.

for extending the protections of the Bill of Rights to state laws and actions, a process called **selective incorporation** because of its selective, piecemeal development, is still ongoing.

The Supreme Court has, over time, used the due process clause of the Fourteenth Amendment to expand the protections within the Bill of Rights to also cover state laws and actions. Initially, however, the Court refused to do so when given the chance. It was not until 1925 with *Gitlow v. New York* that the Court began to make use of the due process clause to incorporate protections contained within the Bill of Rights.[17] In *Gitlow,* the Court formally incorporated the First Amendment, signaling to the states that there were limits on their ability to restrict expression, and that the freedoms of speech and the press constituted *fundamental freedoms* that were beyond the legitimate restriction by state actions in the absence of a compelling reason to do so.[18]

Over the next two decades the Supreme Court began to issue a series of decisions incorporating most of the First Amendment's protections for speech, the press, assembly, and religion. Several decades later, in another burst of activity, the Court incorporated the protections for those accused of, arrested for, tried for, and convicted of crimes under state laws. Most recently in 2010 the Court incorporated the Second Amendment's affirmation of the right "to keep and bear arms" through the due process clause of the Fourteenth Amendment.[19] As of today, most, but not all, of the protections within the Bill of Rights had been incorporated.

Next we will consider specific amendments, the protections that they affirm, and the tensions and controversies arising from trying to delimit the boundaries of their promises. The process of selective incorporation has cleared up one question about civil liberties: Are state governments also restricted in their ability to infringe upon Americans' fundamental rights and freedoms? They are. Within the long list of protections contained within the Bill of Rights are many other questions, however, all revolving around where the boundaries of these protections lie. To investigate these issues, we will consider the amendments and the liberties affirmed within them in turn.

THE FIRST AMENDMENT PROTECTS RELIGIOUS FREEDOM

- Describe the first amendment protections granted to religion.

The First Amendment restricts the power of what most delegates to the Constitutional Convention thought would be the most powerful entity of the government: Congress, the legislative branch.

The Establishment and Free Exercise Clauses Ensure Separation of Church and State

The first two civil liberties affirmed and protected in the Bill of Rights involve religion. The First Amendment begins, "Congress shall make no law respecting an establishment of religion, or prohibiting the free exercise thereof." These two statements, or clauses, form the constitutional bases for protections of religious freedom and expression. The first is called the **establishment clause** as it protects individuals from governmental establishment of, or support for, religion. The second statement is referred to as the **free exercise clause** because it guards the rights of individuals to exercise and express their religious beliefs.

Any attempt by the federal government or one of the states to declare an official religion would be a clear violation of the establishment clause. Similarly, any attempt to prohibit Americans' expressions of their religious faiths in their own homes, provided they did not violate others' fundamental rights and freedoms, would also be unconstitutional. What about the more difficult cases, however? Consider a student who wants to say a prayer in her valedictory address at her public high school's graduation ceremonies. For the school to appear to condone her prayer implies a violation of the establishment clause. For it to restrict her right to say a prayer, however, implies a violation of the free exercise clause. How should this situation be handled? It is in difficult cases like this one that the Supreme Court has had to decide what is and what is not constitutionally permissible.

Courts Have Tested the Establishment Clause over School Funding and Prayer

Selective incorporation of civil liberties in the area of religious freedoms occurred over several decades in the twentieth century. With respect to establishment questions, some of the important cases have involved the allocation of public taxpayer funds for private religious schools. In both *Everson v. Board of Education* (1947) and *Board of Education v. Allen* (1968), the Court found that there were some permissible forms of taxpayer support for private religious schools. In *Allen*, however, justices cautioned that "the clause against establishment of religion by law was intended to erect 'a wall of separation between Church and State.'"[20]

Prayer in public schools has also tested the establishment clause issue. In two cases, *Engel v. Vitale* (1962) and *Abington School District v. Schempp* (1963), the Court ruled unconstitutional the reading of prayers in schools. In the latter case, Justice Tom C. Clark quoted Madison's warnings about the dangers of enmeshing government and religion, even in seemingly small ways, noting that "it is proper to take alarm at the first experiment on our liberties."[21] Today, the U.S. Department of Education provides a set of guidelines based on the Court's establishment rulings. Among other things, the guidelines state that students may not pray during instructional time but may do so (on their own volition) during noninstructional time, such as before school or during lunch.

Students at Royal High School in Simi Valley, California–a public school–in prayer during a lunchtime meeting. As long as such meetings occur outside of instructional time and are both initiated and led by students, they are constitutionally permissible. Anne Cusack/Los Angeles Times via Getty Images

Courts Have Addressed the Boundaries of the Free Exercise of Religion

While Americans are free to hold any religious beliefs, they are not always free to act on them. As is the case with the establishment clause, the Supreme Court has had to wrestle with the boundaries of free exercise.

The free exercise clause was incorporated through the due process clause of the Fourteenth Amendment in *Cantwell v. Connecticut* (1940). The case involved the distribution of religious materials and playing of religious messages on a phonograph by two members of the Jehovah's Witnesses in a predominantly Catholic neighborhood. In its decision, the Supreme Court distinguished between "freedom to believe and freedom to act. The first is absolute, but, in the nature of things, the second cannot be."[22] While the Court upheld the principal that the state might have a valid interest in restricting the actions involved in religious expression—to maintain safety and public order, for example—in this case the Cantwells' actions posed no threat other than being offensive to some.

THE FIRST AMENDMENT PROTECTS FREE EXPRESSION OF POLITICAL BELIEFS

- Describe the first amendment protections granted to political speech

Although they come after the two clauses about religion in the text, those parts of the First Amendment that deal with **freedom of expression** are often considered the most fundamental affirmations of Americans' rights and liberties. They involve the expression of political beliefs and opinions. The right to express one's thoughts, especially in being critical of those in power, is one of the cornerstones of American civil liberties.

Shortly after the new nation was founded it was confronted with the question of how far a government could go to restrict these rights. The **Alien and Sedition Acts**, a set of laws passed by a Federalist-controlled Congress and signed by Federalist president John Adams, authorized severe restrictions on the rights of free speech and the free press.[23] Under the power of these acts, newspaper editors opposing Adams and the Federalists "were quickly indicted, and ten were brought to trial and convicted by juries under the influence of Federalist judges."[24]

Courts Have Attempted to Balance Political Expression against the Needs of National Security

One of the most difficult issues in the protection of political expression is balancing that fundamental right with the needs of national security. In 1917 Charles Schenck and Elizabeth Baer oversaw the printing and distribution of antiwar leaflets encouraging young men not to comply with the military draft. They were convicted under the Espionage Act of 1917, which made it a crime to interfere with military recruiting. In *Schenck v. United States* (1919), a unanimous Court ruled against the defendants, arguing that the restrictions on expression under the Espionage Act were permissible.

In its decision, the Court established the **clear and present danger test** to evaluate legitimate and illegitimate restrictions on political speech in which the context of that expression must be taken into account. The danger, so to speak, with the clear and present danger test is its subjectivity. If a government can restrict urgings not to comply with a draft, then the scope of restricted speech might be interpreted quite widely.

Several cases in the early twentieth century upheld the right of government to restrict such speech in the national interest. However, in a dissent in one of those cases, Supreme Court justice Oliver Wendell Holmes would go on to establish the idea that ideas should compete, as in a marketplace. He wrote, "The best test of truth is the power of the thought to get itself accepted in the competition of the market."[25] Holmes's words did not reflect the mindset of the majority, but his language has been cited by justices in subsequent Courts as they wrestled with the need to balance free political expression with national security.

The modern standard for restrictions on political speech was set in 1969 in *Brandenburg v. Ohio*. At a Ku Klux Klan rally, Klan leader Clarence Brandenburg made a speech threatening that "if our President, our Congress, our Supreme Court, continues to suppress the white, Caucasian race, it's possible that there might have to be some vengeance taken."[26] The Supreme Court ruled for Brandenburg, establishing a two-pronged test of acceptable restrictions on such political speech: It must be "directed to inciting or producing imminent lawless action and [must be] likely to incite or produce such action."[27] The test that the Court developed placed a much higher standard on permissible restrictions of political speech, even speech which advocates for the legitimacy of violent action, though it must not actually organize for it.

Courts Have Weighed Press Freedoms against National Security

The tension between national security and limits on free expression also applies to the press. One of the goals of the Alien and Sedition Acts was to restrict the ability of the press to criticize the federal government. When such restriction happens before an article is published—as opposed to after the fact—it is known as **prior restraint**. The Alien and Sedition Acts were eventually repealed or expired, but the Supreme Court did not weigh in on the issue of prior restraint until the twentieth century.

The question of the permissibility of prior restraint during wartime came up during the Vietnam conflict and centered on attempts by the Nixon administration to prevent the *New York Times* and the *Washington Post* from publishing classified materials describing—often unflatteringly—high-level decision making on the part of U.S. officials in conducting the war. In *New York Times v. United States* (1971), the Supreme Court, in a highly divided opinion, ruled that the government did not demonstrate a sufficiently pressing interest to justify such prior restraint; this set a very high bar for the ability of government to prevent publication.[28]

Symbolic Speech Is Protected as a Form of Political Expression

The Supreme Court has extended its protection of political expression to **symbolic speech**, such as images, signs, and symbols used as forms of political expression. In 1968, in *United States v. O'Brien*, the Court ruled against David Paul O'Brien and three other individuals in Boston who had burned their draft cards and encouraged others to do so as well in protest against the Vietnam War. In doing so, it set out a three-pronged test of acceptable restriction of symbolic speech under such circumstances: (1) the government must have a substantial interest in doing do, (2) the restriction must not be for the purposes of restricting speech, and (3) the "incidental restriction" of the First Amendment rights should be "no greater than is essential to the furtherance of that interest."[29] In this case, the Supreme Court held that the government's need to have young men register for the selective service passed such a test.

In a closely divided opinion, the Court ruled in *Morse v. Frederick* (2007) that school officials can restrict students' rights of expression if that conduct occurs on school grounds or under school supervision and if it violates or disrupts the mission of the school. The case involved a banner displayed by a group of students in Alaska during a school-supervised event featuring the carrying of the Olympic torch through Juneau. The banner read, "BONG HITS 4 JESUS," which school officials concluded promoted drug use, which was a violation of school rules and conduct.[30] The Court agreed.

The burning, alteration, or destruction of the American flag in protest has also received Supreme Court protection as a form of symbolic political expression. In *Texas v. Johnson* (1989), the Court overturned the conviction of a man who had burned the American flag in protest during the 1984 Republican National Convention. "The Government," the Court held, "may not prohibit the verbal or nonverbal expression of an idea merely because society finds the idea offensive or disagreeable, even where our flag is involved."[31]

Protesters burn an American flag in Central Park in opposition to the Vietnam War in 1967. The Supreme Court has made the symbolic act of flag burning a form of protected speech. Leonard Detrick/NY Daily News Archive via Getty Images

Other Forms of Expression Have More Limited Protection

While political expression (in speech, writing, symbols, and of the press) has secured considerable protection, the Supreme Court has ruled that other types and forms of speech and publications do not have the same privilege, though it has often set a high bar for restrictions on them.

Expression that defames a person's character, whether in writing or similarly published media (**libel**) or in spoken form (**slander**), is not protected in the same way as political expression and may leave the actor responsible for such statements in legal trouble.[32] To win a case based on libel or slander in the United States, an aggrieved party must show that the statements or publications were made with the knowledge that they were untrue, which is rather difficult to prove. For public figures, the standard is even higher, though there is often an unclear line dividing those who qualify as public figures from those who do not.

Hate speech is another form of damaging expression upon which limits have been placed and for which the Court has struggled to define the proper boundaries. Hate speech is speech that has no other purpose but to express hatred, particularly toward members of a group identified by racial or ethnic identity, gender, or sexual orientation. One of the most charged forms of hate speech is the burning of crosses—sometimes even in people's yards—by white supremacist groups such as the Ku Klux Klan. In response to these acts, many communities have passed ordinances prohibiting such expression.

Another form of expression that receives weaker protection under the First Amendment is the issuance of fighting words—expression (spoken, written, or symbolic) that is likely to incite violence or disrupt the peace. In *Chaplinsky v. New Hampshire* (1942), the Court upheld restrictions on words that "by their very utterance, inflict injury or tend to incite an immediate breach of the peace," but it also affirmed that such restrictions must be narrowly targeted so as not to constitute an undue restriction of First Amendment rights.[33]

Finally, the Supreme Court has upheld restrictions on **obscenity and pornography**, though it has not always been clear just what constitutes an obscene statement or publication. In *Roth v. United States* (1957), the Court defined the standard for judging obscenity—and, therefore, constitutionally permissible restrictions on its expression—as "whether, to the average person, applying contemporary community standards, the dominant theme of the material, taken as a whole, appeals to prurient interest."[34] Marking the boundaries this way raises another challenge, however. What, exactly, are "contemporary community standards," and who gets to delimit them?

In *Miller v. California* (1973), the Supreme Court attempted to present a clearer definition of obscenity. It set out three criteria that all must be met for material to be considered obscene and, therefore, legitimately subject to restriction. First, the material must be "patently offensive." It must also be "utterly without redeeming social value." Finally, in determining the applicability of the first two parts of the test, "contemporary community standards" must be applied, meaning that different locales may have different standards.[35]

When one considers material published over the Internet, things become even more challenging. For example, how does one define *community* when considering online material? In 1997 the Court struck down provisions of the Communications Decency Act of 1996, which had been designed to protect minors from viewing obscene or pornographic material on the Internet. The Court held that the restrictions in the act were too vague and restrictive and that they carried the danger of having a "chilling effect on free speech."[36] Depictions of sexual material involving minors, however, have carried no similar First Amendment protections and are subject to full restriction and criminalization.

Freedom of Assembly Is Broadly Protected

The final two rights within the First Amendment—the right to peaceably assemble and to petition the government—have received relatively little Supreme Court attention. When the Court has ruled on them, however, it has generally done so in a way similar to how it has treated political expression, regarding them as cornerstones of civil liberties and rights that should be broadly protected.

The right to peacefully assemble was incorporated in 1937 in *De Jonge v. Oregon*. In that case, the Court overturned an Oregon law under which a member of the Communist Party had been convicted and sentenced to seven years in prison for holding a public meeting. In his opinion, quoting an earlier case, Chief Justice Charles Hughes noted, "The very idea of a government, republican in form, implies a right on the part of citizens to meet peaceably for consultation in respect to public affairs and to petition for a redress of grievances."[37]

As is probably clear by now, there has been a great deal of struggle, controversy, and Supreme Court action throughout American history with regard to freedom of religion, speech, the press, and assembly—and these all involve only the First Amendment.[38] In the Bill of Rights, there are nine other liberties that are also addressed.

WHAT HAVE I LEARNED?

1. The establishment clause of the First Amendment protects Americans against federal governmental support of religion.

   a. True
   b. False

2. Forms of political expression have generally received stronger protection than forms of commercial expression.

   a. True
   b. False

3. Prior restraint enables the government to _____.

   a. Arrest protesters who burn the American flag
   b. Combat the distribution of pornography

   c. Suppress a newspaper article
   d. Sue individuals for questioning the character of a government official

4. Why is prayer in America's public schools such a contentious and constitutionally tricky issue?

5. What test has the Supreme Court used to evaluate legitimate and illegitimate restrictions upon the press in the area of national security?

6. What controversies surrounding freedom of speech do you observe in American society today?

Answer Key: 1. a; 2. a; 3. c; 4. Answers should include a discussion of the tension between establishment and free exercise; 5. The clear and present danger test; 6. Answers might discuss current controversies over political expression, perhaps in issues involving racial, ethnic, or sexual identities.

THE SECOND AMENDMENT TODAY APPLIES TO PERSONAL POSSESSION OF FIREARMS

Although firearms ownership by Americans has become a highly charged topic of debate in politics today, for most of its history the Supreme Court said very little about the issue. In 1939 the Court upheld restrictions on private ownership of certain types of weapons—sawed-off shotguns and machine guns—as a result of gangland violence during the era of prohibition.[39] In his opinion in *United States v. Miller*, Justice James McReynolds stated that "in the absence of any evidence tending to show that possession or use of a 'shotgun having a barrel of less than eighteen inches in length' at this time has some reasonable relationship to the preservation or efficiency of a well regulated militia, we cannot say that the Second Amendment guarantees the right to keep and bear such an instrument."[40]

- Explain how the interpretation of the Second Amendment has changed over time.

Not until 2008 did the Court rule directly on laws prohibiting personal possession of firearms generally, as opposed to specific types of them. In a 5–4 decision in *District of Columbia v. Heller*, the Court overturned a District of Columbia ban on handgun ownership for the purpose of self-defense within an individual's home.[41] As the *Heller* case involved Washington, D.C., and not a state, it was decided based on the Second Amendment directly. Incorporation, however, happened two years later, in *McDonald v. Chicago*. In this case, the Court—again splitting 5–4—overturned a Chicago ban on handgun ownership.[42]

CRIMINAL RIGHTS ARE SECURED THROUGH PROCEDURAL JUSTICE

As its defenders pointed out during the ratification debates, one area in which the proposed Constitution (prior to the adding of the Bill of Rights) did address civil liberties was in protecting the rights of the accused and convicted. Article 1, which lays out the powers of Congress, prohibits that branch from passing laws that make illegal, and therefore punishable, conduct that was legal prior to the passage of a new law. It also prohibits bills of attainder, which are acts that punish individuals without a trial.[43]

- Describe the civil liberties that are extended to the accused in the Bill of Rights.

Article 1 also establishes the right of an individual to demand a **writ of habeas corpus** upon his or her arrest or detention (except in the case of rebellion or invasion). Such a writ, if granted by a court, demands that authorities in charge of the person's detention establish the reasons for that detention. If the authorities fail to do so, the person is free to go. This has become one of the central issues in defining and debating the limits on presidential power as America engages in the war on terror in the twenty-first century (see Chapter 10).

All these protections, however, were not sufficient for many of the opponents of the proposed Constitution, who feared that the federal government would use its power to upend, violate, or ignore the actions of the courts within the states or of the individuals residing in the states. Ultimately, fully half of the ten amendments in the Bill of Rights set boundaries for federal governmental action in dealing with the breaking of and enforcing of the laws. Central to the protections for those accused, tried, and/or convicted of a crime is the idea of **procedural justice**, in which the standard of fairness is applied to all participants equally.[44]

Most, but not all, of these standards have since been applied to the actions of the states themselves through the process of incorporation.

The Fourth Amendment Protects against Unlawful Search and Seizure

Under British rule, the American colonists had gained a vivid understanding of the potential dangers of allowing a government to stop or inspect individuals or to search citizens' homes without oversight or procedural protections for those who were targeted. Under what conditions can a government legitimately search a person or persons? Even at the time of the adoption of the Bill of Rights, this was not an easy question to answer. With the development of modern technology, the question has only grown more complicated.

In *Katz v. United States* (1967), the Supreme Court established a standard for procedures for obtaining evidence of a crime and wrestled with the challenges that technology poses to setting such boundaries.[45] The case involved an individual, Katz, who had been convicted of operating a gambling operation based on evidence obtained from a police wiretap. While the Court found there was ample reason for a judge to issue a **warrant**—a writ issued by a judge authorizing some activity, such as tapping a phone line or searching an apartment—the officers had not done so in this case. The Court overturned Katz's conviction and established the need for officers to obtain a warrant from a judge based on **probable cause,** or reasonable suspicion that a crime has been committed or that there is evidence indicating so.[46]

A closely related issue is whether or not evidence that has been obtained without following proper procedures can be used in a trial. The **exclusionary rule** governs the inadmissibility of evidence obtained without a proper warrant.

The case through which the Fourth Amendment's protections were extended to the states, *Mapp v. Ohio* (1961), dealt with just such an issue. While investigating a different crime, police obtained in the dwelling of Dollree Mapp—without possessing a warrant—"certain lewd and lascivious books, pictures, and photographs," placing her in violation of an Ohio anti-obscenity law.[47] The Court threw out her conviction and declared, "All evidence obtained by searches and seizures in violation of the Federal Constitution is inadmissible in a criminal trial in a state court."

As it has wrestled with the trickier issues in interpreting the exclusionary rule, such as electronic communications and transportation, the Court has ruled that the Fourth Amendment's protections are not absolute. In 1989

Dollree Mapp at the time of her arrest in 1957. The case of *Mapp v. Ohio* extended Fourth Amendment protections to the states by establishing that evidence gathered via illegal search and seizure is inadmissible in criminal trials in a state court. AP Photo the Court upheld the conviction of a suspected drug dealer whose luggage had been searched without a warrant based on his behavior—he had paid cash for his ticket, checked no bags, and appeared nervous, among other "tells." The Court found that the Drug Enforcement Administration (DEA) agents conducting the search had "reasonable suspicion" of criminal activity "based on the totality of circumstances."[48]

The Court has also upheld the use of evidence connected with a crime (such as a weapon) that was not named in the warrant but that was discovered in plain sight while lawfully searching for a different type of evidence (the stolen property).[49] However, the Court has placed some restrictions on the use of evidence when modern surveillance or communications technologies are involved.

The Fifth Amendment Guarantees the Accused Certain Procedures for Their Defense

The Fifth Amendment also provides protections for those accused of crimes, especially in guaranteeing processes and procedures for their defense. Those suspected of having committed serious crimes must have an indictment handed down by a **grand jury**—a group of citizens who, based on the evidence presented to them, conclude whether or not the person is to be indicted and subsequently tried in a court of law. It also establishes protections against **double jeopardy**, which is the prosecution of an individual more than once for the same crime. However, while an individual cannot be acquitted of a crime and then convicted in a court in the same jurisdiction, individuals can be acquitted for an offense in a state court but then tried and convicted for the same incident in a federal court but this time under federal charges.

Some of the most sweeping and important protections described in the Fifth Amendment involve the right not to have to testify or bear witness against oneself in a criminal case (called self-incrimination) either during the trial itself or during the introduction of testimony obtained prior to a criminal trial. These protections have been extended and strengthened by the Court over time.

One of the most important cases in delineating the protections of those accused of crimes was *Miranda v. Arizona* (1966). In that case, Ernesto Miranda had been convicted of kidnapping and rape, based partly on evidence obtained while he was being questioned by officers without an attorney present. During this questioning, he signed a confession. In its ruling, the Supreme Court overturned Miranda's conviction, declaring, "Prior to any questioning, the person must be warned that he has a right to remain silent, that any statement he does make may be used as evidence against him, and that he has a right to the presence of an attorney, either retained or appointed. The defendant may waive effectuation of these rights, provided the waiver is made voluntarily, knowingly and intelligently."[50] Police officers now routinely inform individuals suspected of criminal activity that they have the right not to speak and to have an attorney present during questioning; these rights are commonly referred to as **Miranda rights**.

The Sixth Amendment Guarantees the Accused Certain Rights to Trials and Representation

The Bill of Rights guarantees those accused of committing crimes the right to a speedy trial—a right that was extended to the states in 1963.[51] It also ensures the right to be tried in front of an impartial jury, which is more and more of a challenge given the instantaneous spread of news and opinion with modern technology. These protections, however, may not be of much use to a defendant if he or she does not have access to a qualified attorney during the complex legal process. While the Sixth Amendment guarantees the right to have counsel present at trial, for most of the nation's history that meant the right to hire an attorney only if you could afford one.

In 1932 the Court extended this right to include the provision of attorneys in federal capital murder cases that carried the possibility of the death penalty if conviction was reached.[52] In 1938 the Court extended these protections to all federal criminal cases.[53] It was not until 1963—in one of the most famous cases in Supreme Court history—that the Court extended the guarantee of counsel for those unable to afford it to state criminal cases. That decision, in *Gideon V. Wainwright*, involved the conviction for robbery of Clarence Gideon, who had resorted to defending himself in a Florida court when his request to the judge for an attorney was denied.[54] More recently, the Court has strengthened these protections to try to ensure that criminal defendants receive "effective" legal representation and not just legal representation.[55]

The Eighth Amendment Guards against Cruel and Unusual Punishment

While a criminal defendant is awaiting a speedy trial before a jury, he or she may be able to post **bail**—an amount of money posted as a security to allow the charged individual to be freed while awaiting trial. Although the Eighth Amendment protects against "excessive bail," not every criminal defendant is entitled to bail at all. Those who are deemed to pose a sufficient risk of flight or further criminal activity may legitimately be denied the ability to post bail.

Much more contentious is the question of "cruel and unusual punishment," especially as it applies to the imposition of the death penalty. The death penalty was allowed at the time of ratification of the Constitution and the Bill of Rights, and the Fifth Amendment to the Constitution refers to circumstances in which individuals are "deprived of life." Proponents of its use argue that the death penalty can be an effective deterrent against the most heinous crimes. Opponents point to the potential for errors in conviction, discriminatory sentencing, and the movement away from its use in other democracies. While the Supreme Court has not declared the death penalty to be inherently in violation of the Eighth Amendment, it has imposed restrictions on its imposition.[56] For example, the Court has prohibited its use on convicted defendants with significant cognitive disabilities[57] and on juveniles.[58]

THE NINTH AND TENTH AMENDMENTS SET LIMITS TO FEDERAL POWER

Each of the first eight amendments in the Bill of Rights places literal, textual limits on the power of the federal government. The final two do not. Instead, the Ninth and Tenth Amendments more broadly structure the inclusion and exclusion of rights as well as powers of national and state governments.

- Explain the purpose of the Ninth and Tenth Amendments.

The Ninth Amendment Guards Rights Not Specified

One of the concerns raised by opponents of including a list of rights in the Constitution was that such a list would be necessarily incomplete. What about those rights assumed but not specified? Would future federal government officials recognize or try to restrict them? The Ninth Amendment was included to address these fears as well as general concerns by Anti-Federalists about the future growth of federal governmental power. Its purpose was to put into writing one of the main worries about a bill of rights expressed during the ratification debates: that those fundamental rights and freedoms not textually listed might not be protected. The Ninth Amendment was ratified to make sure that American governments in the future would not be able to take advantage of the incompleteness of the listing of fundamental rights and freedoms to encroach on Americans' civil liberties.

The Tenth Amendment Was Intended to Protect State Powers

The inclusion of the Tenth Amendment was a direct response to the fears and demands of the Anti-Federalists during the ratification debates. Many of them wanted a direct statement of the limitation of national power to those powers textually listed, those enumerated, in the original document. All other powers were to be reserved to the several states, which is why we call most state powers under the Constitution "reserved powers." As it has turned out, however, and as we have already explored in our discussion of the development of American federalism, the Tenth Amendment has not proven to be as strong a protector of state power as some might have thought. That is not to say that it is irrelevant, however. States and their legislatures are increasingly protesting the power of the federal government—especially when they feel that it is requiring them to enact policies without fully funding their implementation—using the Tenth Amendment as their constitutional justification for doing so.

WHAT HAVE I LEARNED?

1. A writ of habeas corpus is a statement demanding authorities to produce justification for a person's detention.
   a. True
   b. False

2. Miranda rights offer protections _____.
   a. For protest
   b. During arrest
   c. Against being tried twice for the same incident

   d. In carrying out the death penalty

3. For what groups of individuals has the Supreme Court prohibited the use of the death penalty?

4. How are the Ninth and Tenth Amendments different from the first eight?

CIVIL RIGHTS SECURE AMERICANS' EQUALITY UNDER LAW

- Describe the challenges African Americans have faced in securing civil rights.

Americans' efforts to secure their civil rights (the rights of individuals to be treated equally under the laws and policies of governments, regardless of their identities) began nearly as soon as the nation was founded. Though the Declaration of Independence argued that all people enjoyed a set of natural rights and the Constitution and Bill of Rights later defined what those rights were more precisely, in practice, not all Americans were treated equally. As we have explored earlier, the unequal status of enslaved people and later of all African Americans has been the most egregious exception. The civil rights struggle for African Americans to be treated equally under law has laid the groundwork for the civil rights of many other Americans.

In the landmark 1857 case, *Dred Scott v. Sandford*, the Supreme Court ruled that former slaves and the descendants of slaves were not citizens of the United States, even if they were residents of free states or territories. The natural rights proclaimed in the Declaration of Independence and protected in the Constitution, Justice Roger Taney wrote in his opinion, did not extend to individuals "whose ancestors were negroes of the African race."[59] Natural rights, according to the Court, had been selectively bestowed.

The Court's decision served to further polarize public opinion on the question of slavery and galvanize both proslavery and antislavery forces in the United States, deepening the threat of secession. In December 1860, South Carolina made that threat a reality. Within six months, eleven Southern states had seceded from the United States to form the Confederate States of America. The following April they fired on a federal fort in Charleston Harbor. To reunite the Union, President Abraham Lincoln had to take what remained of the American Republic to war.

During the Civil War, President Lincoln had signed the Emancipation Proclamation, which in 1863 declared that all slaves in the states under rebellion were "henceforward and forever free." However, it took the actions of Union troops and slaves themselves to make that proclamation a reality on the ground. Excluded from the proclamation were slaves in the border states still loyal to the Union and territories in the South already under federal control. This was a political move, designed to preserve the loyalty of the border states while also putting pressure on Europe not to come to the aid of the Confederacy.

Three Amendments Shore Up Equal Protection under Law

Members of Company E, 4th U.S. Colored Infantry in Washington, D.C., in 1865. Many African American veterans followed their service in the Civil War with political activism after its conclusion. The Granger Collection, New York

Within five years of the conclusion of the Civil War, three amendments had been added to the Constitution, although not without considerable opposition. In 1865 the **Thirteenth Amendment** to the Constitution prohibited slavery within the United States. To ensure the power of the national government to make this provision a reality and to prevent a Supreme Court from overturning antislavery laws at it had done in *Dred Scott*, section 2 of the amendment stated that "Congress shall have the power to enforce this article by appropriate legislation." In 1868 the **Fourteenth Amendment** affirmed the citizenship of all persons "born or naturalized in the United States" and, for the first time in the history of the Constitution, placed explicit restrictions on the laws of states: "No State shall make or enforce any law which shall abridge the privileges and immunities of citizens of the United States; nor shall any State deprive any person of life, liberty, or property, without due process of law; nor deny to any person within its jurisdiction the equal protection of the laws."

The **equal protection clause** of the Fourteenth Amendment served as the constitutional basis for the assault on educational segregation in the courts and for the assertion of civil rights for Americans of many different identities in many different areas of public and private life. The Fourteenth Amendment also overturned the three-fifths rule for representation in the original Constitution.

Faced with Southern resistance to the Fourteenth Amendment—Southern states rejected or ratified modified versions of it—the Republican Congress, having won major victories in the 1866 elections, passed the First Reconstruction Act of 1867. This act disbanded Southern governments, thus voiding their rejection of the Fourteenth Amendment, and replaced them with military rule. It gave freedmen the right to vote and took that right away from Confederate veterans, and it made ratification of the Fourteenth Amendment a necessary condition of readmission to the United States.

The **Fifteenth Amendment**, ratified in 1870, went beyond threats against states for restricting voting rights and affirmed the voting rights of all freedmen, again giving Congress the power to make necessary laws: "The right of citizens of the United States to vote shall not be denied or abridged by the United States or by any State on account of race, color, or previous condition of servitude."

Jim Crow Laws Roll Back Civil Rights

These efforts did not go unopposed. As the Democratic Party gained political power in the southern states and the will of the Republican Party to make civil rights a reality on the ground faded, the early gains made by African Americans began to disappear. Southern states passed laws to preserve segregation and prevent African American men from exercising their Fifteenth Amendment right to vote. Known as Jim Crow laws, these efforts enforced segregation across all aspects of daily life, including transportation, entertainment, business, and education. While legal segregation had been enforced in the North before the Civil War, by the time of Reconstruction it had largely disappeared there but remained deeply entrenched in the post–Civil War South. Selective enforcement of poll taxes, which required voters to pay a tax at the polling place, and literacy tests, which were used by registrars to determine whether voters were "qualified" to vote, combined to prevent African American men from voting.

Separate but Equal Becomes the Law of the Land

In the decades following the Civil War, the Supreme Court proved to be an enabler of racial oppression rather than a protector against it. In 1896 it upheld the constitutionality of legalized racial segregation, dealing a further blow to fading reconstructionist dreams. As we discussed in Chapter 3, in *Plessy v. Ferguson*, justices argued that "social prejudices cannot be overcome by legislation," and that laws creating "**separate but equal**" spaces for blacks and whites did not violate the Constitution. Justice John Marshall Harlan, the lone dissenter on the Court, countered, "Our Constitution is color-blind, and neither knows nor tolerates classes among citizens. In respect of civil rights, all citizens are equal before the law." Harlan, correctly, as it turned out, saw *Plessy* as a dangerous and damaging ruling, one that would "prove to be quite as pernicious as the decision made by this tribunal in the *Dred Scott* case."[60] His charge, however, was only a dissent; Brown's majority opinion set policy. The doctrine of separate but equal remained constitutional for almost sixty years.

African Americans Fight to End Separate but Equal

With the establishment of the principle of separate but equal, **legal segregation**, the separation by law of African Americans and whites based only on their race, was constitutionally permissible. The precedent set by the Supreme Court made fighting against segregation deeply challenging.

Thirteen years after *Plessy*, the African Americans and whites who formed the National Association for the Advancement of Colored People (NAACP) in 1909 did so largely in response to white violence against African Americans. However, the organization's founders did not always share the same vision of how to most effectively confront white racism. Its decision to push for integrated schools as a main effort in the first half of the twentieth century came about only after serious discussions and disagreements within the organization itself.

A central question centered on strategy. Given that legal segregation was made possible by laws passed by state legislatures, one option was to focus on getting the laws changed by electing African Americans and allied opponents of segregation to the state governments. However, those efforts proved not to be durable. Segregationists countermobilized to undo these legislative gains. A second tactic, initiated in the 1930s, was to focus on the courts. Although it entailed its own risks, being able to secure judicial rulings against legal segregation offered the promise of more enduring gains. Leading that second strategy and focused specifically on school segregation was lawyer and former dean of the Howard University School of Law, Charles Hamilton Houston, joined later by his former student Thurgood Marshall. Through the 1950s, Houston and Marshall were able to win partial victories in some cases.

It was the case involving Oliver Brown, a Topeka, Kansas, railroad welder and part-time minister that would ultimately break through. Brown had attempted to enroll his daughter, Linda, in an all-white elementary school that was both closer to their house than the all-black school and that did not require Linda to cross through a dangerous railroad yard in order to get there. Brown's request was denied, so, with the help of the local NAACP, he and seven other parents sued. After losing in the state courts, they appealed all the way to the Supreme Court. Their Kansas case was joined with four others, and they collectively bore the name *Brown v. Board of Education*.[61]

Arguing the case, Marshall got to the heart of the NAACP's arguments. All evidence, including evidence that had been accepted by the Court in the NAACP's earlier cases, had showed that black and white children were equal in their educational potential. Educational segregation, therefore, had no legitimate basis. Moreover, it violated the Fourteenth Amendment to the Constitution, which had been made part of the Constitution specifically to protect freed slaves from violations of the state legislatures.

One piece of critical evidence introduced was a set of research findings by psychologists Kenneth Clark and Mamie Clark. In those studies, the Clarks presented young African American and white children with a set of brown and white dolls. A majority of children stated that they preferred the white dolls over the brown dolls, and many had negative comments about the brown dolls. The Clarks' evidence of psychological damage from segregation was introduced into three of the five cases in *Brown*. After Marshall had presented his arguments, John W. Davis presented South Carolina's side, highlighting the importance of local control in education.[62]

Hearing the case was Chief Justice Earl Warren, who was recently appointed. Warren's record on civil rights was not promising. As attorney

Thurgood Marshall, center, special counsel for the NAACP in *Brown v. Board of Education*, and two other members of his legal team in front of the Supreme Court following their landmark victory in 1954. Bettmann / Contributor

general of California, he had supported the internment of Japanese Americans during World War II. He had never served as a judge. Warren was, however, a skillful politician, and he used those skills to wrangle some of the most important votes in American constitutional history: those of the nine justices on the U.S. Supreme Court.

On May 17, 1954, the last day of the Supreme Court's term, Warren read the Court's decision on *Brown*, years after the case first came before the Court: "Does segregation in public schools solely on the basis of race, even though the physical facilities and other 'tangible' factors may be equal, deprive the children of the minority groups of equal educational opportunities? We believe that it does."[63] Arguing that the premise of *Plessy*—that separation based on race caused no harm in those so separated—was flawed, Warren overturned the 1896 decision, saying, "We conclude that in the field of public education the doctrine of 'separate but equal' has no place. Separate educational facilities are inherently unequal. . . . We have now announced that such segregation is a denial of the equal protection of the laws." The Court was unanimous.[64] It had to be; a deeply divided Court would not have had the legitimacy that it needed to take on segregation.

The reaction of the nation was strong and immediate. Many cheered the moral stance the Court had taken. Many voices in the African American community were supportive but measured; history had shown that white support for their cause had not always been sustained. "As Charles [Hamilton] Houston had said years earlier, 'Nobody needs to explain to a Negro the difference between the law in books and the law in action.'"[65] In the South, there was discussion among moderates on how to make the required adjustments. The Court, after all, had not set a firm date for when separate but equal had to be abolished. But there was also anger. Mobs blocked schools and universities. South Carolina governor James F. Byrnes proclaimed, "Ending segregation [will] mark the beginning of the end of civilization in the South as we have known it."[66]

Legal segregation began to disappear in the border states. Southern states, however, actively resisted. Several southern state legislatures forbade their state officials from enforcing **desegregation**—the intentional reversal of segregated educational facilities based on children's race or ethnicity. The Court's decision in *Brown* had intentionally avoided setting a strict timeline on achieving integration, but given the resistance to its efforts, the Court issued a follow-up decision the next year, in 1955, urging compliance with the law "with all deliberate speed." Nonetheless, compliance across the South was slow at best. In 1964, ten years after the Court's ruling in *Brown v. Board of Education*, 98 percent of African American children still attended completely segregated schools.

Citizens Take Action to End Segregation

Citizens themselves took increasingly strong action to end segregation in schools, workplaces, and the community. African American community leaders organized boycotts, in which people refused to buy services or products from an organization in order to force policy changes. Notable among these protests and acts of **civil disobedience** was the 1955 Montgomery bus boycott, which

Can the Supreme Court Effect Social Change?

Alexander Hamilton, in *Federalist* No. 78, argued that the Supreme Court had little power acting on its own "and must ultimately depend upon the aid of the executive" to effect change. One scholar has collected data on the pace of integration in the South following *Brown v. Board* to make a similar argument: The Supreme Court cannot, acting on its own, produce social change on the ground. His data are displayed in the chart that follows this section.

It was not until 1970 that more than half of African American children in the South were attending integrated schools (and many of these were far from fully integrated). During this period, citizens took action through events such as the Montgomery bus boycott, in which African Americans in Montgomery, Alabama, refused to ride city buses in protest over segregated seating; the executive and legislative branches became more involved in the desegregation process; and the Court issued more related rulings. The data in the graph indicate that the decision of *Brown v. Board* did not immediately result in desegregation of schools in the South. To say that the Supreme Court is powerless, however, might be too strong a statement to make based on these data alone.

First, the branches were not designed to act alone but in concert with (and sometimes in opposition to) each other. This is the principle of separation of powers discussed

Percentage of African American Children Attending Integrated Schools in the South

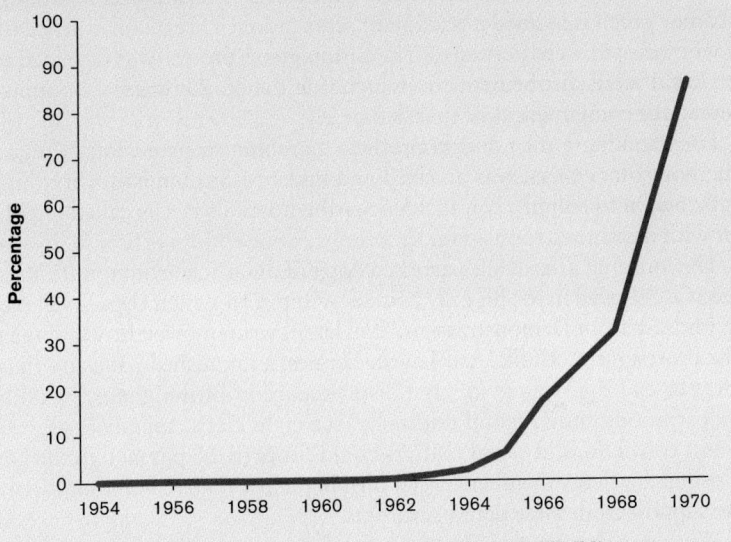

Source: Data are from Table 2.1 in Gerald N. Rosenberg, *The Hollow Hope* (Chicago: University of Chicago Press: 2008), 50–51.

(Continued)

(Continued)

in Chapter 2. Second, *Brown* was only the first of a string of decisions on school desegregation handed down by the Court—decisions that became stronger and stronger during the time period covered in the graph.

WHAT DO YOU THINK?

For ten years after *Brown*, southern public schools remained segregated. Considering all that you have read so far, why might this have been unsurprising? Do these data confirm that the Supreme Court cannot effect social change? Was the NAACP's decision to adopt a judicial strategy a wise one? Why or why not?

sought to put economic pressure on the city of Montgomery, Alabama, to end its policy of segregating bus passengers based on their race. In separate protests, Claudette Colvin, Rosa Parks, and several other African American women activists refused to move to the "Negro section" of Montgomery buses. Their case drew national attention, attracted the efforts of movement leaders like Dr. Martin Luther King Jr., and eventually resulted in the bus segregation law being declared unconstitutional.[67] Not only had they won in the Court but it was a public victory—a citizens' victory.

Protests continued over the next decade, with much activity focused on the South. In 1963, Dr. Martin Luther King Jr. traveled to march in Birmingham, Alabama, which remained a bastion of segregation. Threats of violence to anyone who resisted were pervasive. The Birmingham protest was designed to feature acts of civil disobedience in which one defied a law seen as unjust and accepted the consequences of that defiance.

For breaking a prohibition on their marching or protesting, King, along with about fifty others, was arrested and taken to Birmingham City Jail. King was thrown into solitary confinement—"the hole," as it was called—with only a cot with metal slats to sleep on.[68]

The morning after King's arrest, a copy of an article from the *Birmingham News* was "slipped in to" his cell.[69] Titled "White Clergymen Urge Local Negroes to Withdraw from Demonstrations," the letter, written by eight white members of the Protestant, Catholic, and Jewish clergies, admonished King and the other leaders to end the strategy of civil disobedience in Birmingham.[70] Calling the demonstrations "unwise and untimely," the eight clergy members argued that "honest convictions in racial matters could properly be pursued in the courts." In closing, the clergy members urged Birmingham's "Negro community to withdraw support from these demonstrations."

Writing in the margins of the smuggled newspaper, King penned a response to the clergymen.[71] His notes were smuggled out of the jail, typed up, and eventually published by a group of Quakers as the "Letter from Birmingham Jail."

In the letter, King argued the case for his and his movement's tactics on the basis of natural rights, drawing a distinction between just and unjust laws: "A just law is a man-made code that squares with the moral law or the law of God. An unjust law is a code that is out of harmony with the natural law." Racial oppression, he asserted, in all of its legal manifestations, is unjust. Individuals, therefore, have the right to break these unjust laws, but, he added, "One who breaks an unjust law must do so openly, lovingly."

Politically, one of the most important passages in the letter pointed to the white moderate as a severe obstacle to justice: "I have almost reached the regrettable conclusion that the Negro's great stumbling block in the stride toward freedom is not the White citizens' 'Councilor' or the Ku Klux Klanner, but the white moderate who is more devoted to 'order' than justice; who prefers a negative peace which is the absence of tension to a positive peace which is the presence of justice."

The actions of these activists—and their often harsh treatment at the hands of local law enforcement, which was broadcast to Americans on their televisions—began to change public opinion toward the civil rights struggle. By voting in larger and larger numbers, African Americans also began to make their presence felt in Washington, D.C. Close elections during the period highlighted to politicians the importance of securing the African American vote, which might tip an election in their favor.

Aware of changing political realities, Congress, under intense pressure from President Johnson, passed two major pieces of civil rights legislation, finally giving its support to efforts that had begun in the Supreme Court and on the streets. The Civil Rights Act of 1964 authorized the federal government to withhold grants from districts that did not integrate their schools. It outlawed racial segregation in schools and public places and authorized the federal government to sue individual school districts that failed to desegregate. In addition, the act outlawed employment discrimination based on race or ethnicity and also on religion, national origin, or gender. The provisions of the Civil Rights Act of 1964 proved to be as valuable to women and members of other minority groups in their efforts as the civil rights decisions in the Supreme Court. The Voting Rights Act of 1965 outlawed literacy tests for voters and authorized the Justice Department to send federal officers to register voters in uncooperative cities, counties, and states. The effects on African American voter registration were immediate and significant.

Southern Christian Leadership Conference leaders marching in Birmingham, Alabama, in April 1963. Fred Shuttlesworth, left, is not carrying a coat. The plan was for Shuttlesworth to join in the march to show solidarity but then break off to organize and raise funds for the conference. However, he was arrested with the others. Reverend Ralph Abernathy, center, with an extra layer of clothing and a coat in preparation for imprisonment, appears relaxed. Reverend Martin Luther King Jr., right, also clothed in preparation for arrest, appears to be much more concerned and contemplative. Birmingham, Ala. Public Library Archives

The Supreme Court Tests the Limits of Equal Protection for African Americans

The southern segregation that Thurgood Marshall and the NAACP had challenged in the courts was written into law—sometimes even into state constitutions. In many cases, these laws did not just allow segregation, they required it. This type of segregation is called **de jure segregation**, meaning that it is written into law. The efforts of activists and citizens had largely eliminated racially based de jure segregation by the end of the 1960s. Attention now focused on **de facto segregation**—segregation based not on law but on private choices, sometimes-private acts of discrimination, or the lingering social consequences of legal segregation even after those laws were no longer on the books. Addressing de facto segregation has proven to be even more complicated than addressing de jure segregation.

The Supreme Court has been more cautious in addressing de facto segregation than legal segregation. In 1974, in *Milliken v. Bradley*, the question was about how to address the de facto segregation of whole school districts in areas affected by "white flight" where neighborhoods had become almost entirely African American. How much action should be taken to integrate those districts, and who should be required to take it when there was no law to point to? In this case, the Court ruled that there was no requirement to try to desegregate the region's schools since the district boundaries had not been drawn up to segregate them in the first place. The suburban districts did not have to participate in a plan that would move students across school district boundaries. Limits on busing or any other remedy that required action between school districts had been set.

Questions about how far the Court is willing to go to secure equality in the absence of discriminatory laws have arisen in other aspects of political and economic life as well. **Affirmative action**—a policy designed to address the consequences of previous discrimination by providing advantages to individuals based upon their identities—continues to be a subject of debate in American political life. The Court has issued a much less clear set of guidelines on the use of affirmative action than it has with legal segregation. Many of these cases have involved admissions practices at American colleges and universities that have sought to boost the enrollment of African Americans and members of other racial and ethnic minorities.

A 1978 Supreme Court decision in *Regents of the University of California v. Bakke* concerned the use of quotas, or the setting aside of a number of school slots, contracts with the government, or job opportunities for groups who have suffered past discrimination.[72] In the case, Allan Bakke, who identified himself as white, had sued the regents of the University of California, Davis after having been denied admission to its medical school. Bakke argued that his academic record was superior to the group of sixteen minority applicants for whom seats had been set aside. In its ruling, the Court agreed that the quota system had violated Bakke's rights and those of other white applicants and instructed the school to admit him. However, the Court also affirmed the worthiness of the goal of increasing minority student enrollment, leaving open the possibility for plans that did not involve strict quotas.

In the years after *Bakke*, the Court issued several rulings that attempted to define the limits of permissible affirmative action. In 2003 the Court issued two rulings on the same day that tried to clarify its position. In *Gratz v. Bollinger*, the Court considered the use of a points system in undergraduate admissions decisions.[73] Rather than using a strict quota system, the university ranked applicants on a points system, much of which focused on academics. Some points, however, were awarded for having parents who attended the University of Michigan, being a state resident, having shown a commitment to public service, or having strong athletic ability. Forty of the 150 points were awarded on the basis of "other factors." One of these factors was membership in a traditionally underrepresented racial or ethnic group. The university argued that having a diverse student body was of educational benefit to the entire learning community. In *Gratz*, the Court ruled that the points system was unconstitutional, but it did not strike down the use of racial or ethnic identity as a consideration for admissions decisions.

In *Grutter v. Bollinger*, also decided in 2003, the Court affirmed the possibility of using racial and ethnic identity in admissions decisions.[74] Unlike the admissions system at the undergraduate level, the law school did not use a points system, but it did include racial identity in a group of factors considered in the application decision. By a 5–4 vote, the Court ruled that the university could use race as a factor as long as it could show that it had a "compelling interest" to do so. Ensuring a diverse student body, the Court concluded, does demonstrate such an interest. In June 2016, the Court, in a 4–3 ruling in *Fisher v. University of Texas at Austin*, upheld the constitutionality of considering racial identity in college admissions.

1. The Supreme Court's decision in *Brown v. Board of Education* was met with widespread resistance.

   a. True
   b. False

2. *Dred Scott v. Sandford* (1857) negated _____.

   a. The Fourteenth Amendment
   b. Equal protection of the laws
   c. The citizenship rights of African Americans
   d. Slavery

3. The Thirteenth Amendment _____.

   a. Abolished slavery
   b. Affirmed equal protection of the laws
   c. Guaranteed the right of African American men to vote
   d. Guaranteed the right of women to vote

4. In *Plessy v. Ferguson* (1896), the Supreme Court _____.

   a. Overturned legal segregation
   b. Upheld legal segregation
   c. Overturned restrictions on voting
   d. Upheld restrictions on voting

5. The Civil Rights Act of 1964 _____.

   a. Authorized the Justice Department to sue segregated school districts
   b. Outlawed employment discrimination based on racial identity
   c. Outlawed employment discrimination based on gender
   d. All of the above

6. Do you think the National Association for the Advancement of Colored People (NAACP) decision to focus much of its energy and resources on using the judiciary to end legal segregation was the correct one?

Answer Key: 1. a; 2. c; 3. a; 4. b; 5. d; 6. Answers should discuss the power of the federal judiciary in making broader social change as well as limitations on that power.

SECURING CIVIL RIGHTS FOR AMERICAN WOMEN

- Describe the efforts made to secure civil rights for women.

Though they constitute a slight majority of the American population, women have also struggled to secure their civil rights throughout the nation's history. Scholars often frame these efforts as having taken place in two waves. The first wave, the effort to secure the right to vote, was closely tied to the efforts of nineteenth-century American women to secure their rights in education and to end the practice of slavery. The second wave, which began in the middle of the twentieth century, extended the scope of civil rights protections to women's participation in the classroom and the workplace, their freedom from sexual harassment, and their control over their bodies and their sexuality.

Women's Early Civil Rights Efforts Focused on Enfranchisement

Early efforts by women to secure their rights often focused on education, which was considered an acceptable political space for a nineteenth-century white woman to inhabit. Many early activists for women's rights were also active in the **abolitionist movement**—the movement to end the practice of slavery.

Prudence Crandall was a white educator whose political activism in the 1830s demonstrates the close link between education, opposition to slavery, and political activism on the part of early advocates for women's rights. In 1832 Crandall admitted Sarah Harris, an African American girl, to her school for ladies in Canterbury, Connecticut, so that Harris might herself become a teacher.[75] At a time when "progressive" white thinking on race generally involved plans to recolonize African Americans to the West Indies or Africa, the actions of Crandall and Harris were considered extraordinarily radical. Many in Canterbury voiced their disapproval of the situation.

Rather than cave in to the strong community pressure that she was facing to expel Harris, Crandall closed her school. Two months later, she opened another school exclusively for African American girls and soon had seventeen students. Crandall was arrested and briefly jailed, her school vandalized, students and teachers attacked and ostracized.[76] Masked men attacked and vandalized the school using battering rams and attempted to burn it to the ground. Crandall feared for the physical safety of her students and closed her school for good in 1834.

The suppression of women's rights was often justified by claims that women needed to be protected from—and therefore shut out of—elements of public life. This "protection" had legal aspects. Rights of women were severely restricted in the public space, and married women had no legal identity outside of their marriage. For the purposes of the courts, they did not exist. The restriction of women's rights was as much social as it was legal. Part of the effort to secure women's rights, therefore, involved redefining what was considered acceptable behavior for a woman. Taking action in the public space—by speaking out, organizing, and mobilizing public opinion—was as political in its challenge to the boundaries of acceptable behavior as was the act of actually changing laws.

An engraving depicting an attack on Prudence Crandall's school for "young ladies of color" in Connecticut in 1834. This and previous threats against students and teachers forced Crandall to close her school.
The Granger Collection, New York

The efforts of sisters Sarah and Angelina Grimké to organize and speak out against slavery in the 1830s challenged both the institution of slavery and the less visible institution of protection of women from public life. Daughters of a prominent South Carolina slaveholding family, the Grimké sisters set out in 1837 on an antislavery speaking tour in New England. In doing so, they helped to change public perception about a woman's proper role in public life. Their audiences included women and men, African Americans and whites. Their speeches highlighted the cruelty at the heart of the institution of slavery, and they expressed solidarity with women slaves.

Many urged the Grimké sisters and other advocates to drop their push for "a woman's rights," as it was called, fearful that the controversy might detract from the goal of abolition, but the proponents refused. Shut out of prominent antislavery conventions in the mid-nineteenth century, abolitionist women organized their own. Lucretia Mott and Elizabeth Cady Stanton met at an antislavery convention in London in 1840 and began to plan a separate conference on women's rights. The conference met in Seneca Falls, New York, over two days in July 1848. On the first day, Stanton read a list of eleven resolutions, known as the Declaration of Sentiments. These resolutions derived their legitimacy from an appeal to higher law, just as the Declaration of Independence had done seventy-two years earlier and Dr. Martin Luther King Jr.'s "Letter from Birmingham Jail" would do 115 years later. In the years following Seneca Falls, "a cascade of women's rights conventions . . . carried the movement into towns and villages throughout the Northeast and the Midwest."[77]

Unlike the efforts to secure the civil rights of African Americans, women's rights activists, especially in the first wave, pursued a mostly legislative strategy, attempting to change state and federal laws to guarantee they received equal protection in them. After the Civil War, when giving the right to vote to freed African American men came onto the national agenda, some women's rights activists wanted to include suffrage for women in the Fifteenth Amendment.

Others feared that trying to obtain the right to vote for African Americans and women at the same time might stir up too much opposition. According to one historian, the issue of suffrage was often portrayed as "a choice between black men and educated white women."[78]

In 1869 Stanton and Susan B. Anthony formed the National Woman's Suffrage Association to try to secure civil rights for women beyond only the right to vote. Also in 1869, Lucy Stone helped to organize the American Woman Suffrage Association, which focused on suffrage, pursuing its goals at the level of state and territory. Wyoming Territory granted women the right to vote in 1869. By 1918 fifteen states had passed laws allowing women's suffrage. The right was secured at the national level in 1920 with the ratification of the **Nineteenth Amendment** to the Constitution, which had been drafted by Anthony and Stanton more than forty years earlier. The amendment stated, "The right of citizens of the United States to vote shall not be denied or abridged by the United States or by any State on account of sex."

Though the constitutional right to vote came later for women than it did for African American men, women did not face the same kind of tactics of resistance aimed to keep the legal right from becoming a practical right. As they began to exercise their right to vote, however, the broader vision of equality that many of the pioneers in the American women's movement hoped for was far from secured.

The Second Wave Focused on Ongoing Inequalities

The second wave of the movement to secure the civil rights of women in the United States began in the 1960s. Like the first wave, much of the strategy involved changing laws. However, the focus went far beyond the voting booth and addressed inequalities at work and in the home as well as protection from violence and sexual harassment.

Crucial to these legislative and legal efforts was the Civil Rights Act of 1964. Title VII of the act prohibits discrimination in employment based on race, color, religion, national origin, or sex. Title VII has proved to be an important element of equal rights for women and the basis for several rulings about gender discrimination by the Supreme Court.

One of the early leaders of this second wave was Betty Friedan, whose 1963 book *The Feminine Mystique* argued for a "dramatic reshaping of the cultural image of femininity that will permit women to reach maturity, identity, completeness of self, without conflict with sexual fulfillment."[79] Friedan also served as the first president of the National Organization for Women (NOW), a women's rights advocacy group that pushed for change in both the legislature and the Supreme Court. NOW initially organized largely to pressure the federal government to enforce the antidiscrimination provisions of Title VII. The organization's goals, however, became much more sweeping: "The purpose of NOW is to take action to bring women into full participation in the mainstream of American society now, exercising all the privileges and responsibilities thereof in truly equal partnership with men."[80]

In the 1960s and 1970s, women's rights activists secured several important pieces of legislation, including the legal right to receive equal pay for equal work in the same workplace as well as protections against discrimination based on gender, pregnancy, or childbirth. They also lobbied to ensure that these laws were vigorously enforced—to make sure that equal meant equal in the workplaces and schools and not just in the laws.

One of the most important elements of the legislative campaign for women's rights was an attempt to secure ratification of the **equal rights amendment (ERA)** to the U.S. Constitution. The proposed amendment read, "Equality of rights under the law shall not be denied or abridged by the United States or by any state on account of sex." The proposed amendment easily cleared the two-thirds vote requirement of the House of Representatives in 1971 and the Senate in 1972. Submitted to the states for ratification, the ERA got off to a quick and successful beginning, outpacing other recent amendments with its speed of state ratifications. By 1977, thirty-five of the needed thirty-eight states had ratified the ERA.

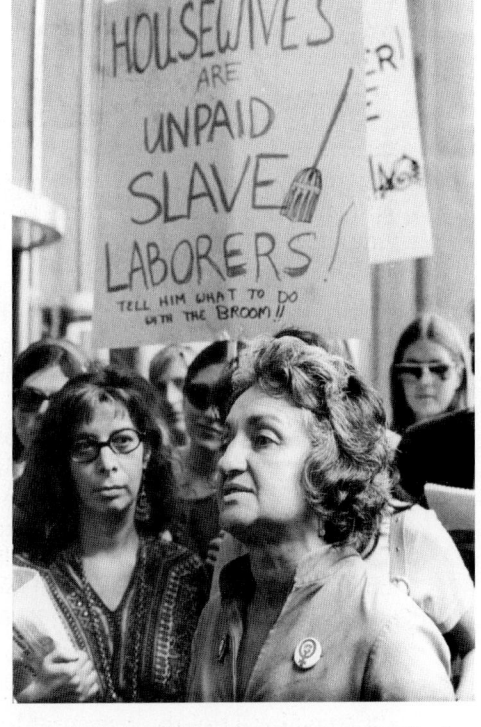

Betty Friedan in a 1970 protest march commemorating the fiftieth anniversary of the ratification of the Nineteenth Amendment. Friedan was a writer, an activist in efforts to secure equal rights for American women, and the first president of the National Organization for Women (NOW).
Fred W. McDarrah/Getty Images

No more states, however, would ratify. In spite of having its ratification deadline extended by Congress, the clock ran out on the ERA in 1982, and the amendment died.

Though the ERA was not ratified, the debate over its ratification did help increase the visibility of women's rights issues and place them on the national agenda. And, as it turns out, the Fourteenth Amendment to the Constitution and Title VII of the Civil Rights Act of 1964 provided a sufficient basis for the Supreme Court to act in the absence of the ERA.

Supreme Court Uses Different Standards of Scrutiny on Gender Discrimination and Sexual Harassment

Although part of the strategy for women's rights advocates was to use the Supreme Court, as African American rights activists had done, they did so under a slightly different standard. Due to the nation's history of slavery, the Court has treated protection of civil rights based on race and ethnicity differently than protection for other groups. Historically, the Court has used three different standards to decide if a law or policy that treats people differently based on some aspect of their identity is allowable or not. Race has been considered a "suspect" classification for the purposes of this decision. It's not the people who are suspect, or their race. It's the treatment of people differently on the basis of race that is suspect. In cases involving racial identity, the Court applies a standard of **strict scrutiny** to any attempt to provide different or separate treatment. Under such scrutiny, a government has to show a "compelling interest" to justify the unequal treatment, a high standard that is difficult to meet.

At the other end of the spectrum is the **reasonableness standard**, in which differential treatment must be shown to be reasonable and not arbitrary. It is also called the rational basis standard as one merely has to show that there is a rational reason for the distinction.[81] This is a much lower bar legally. Under the application of the reasonableness standard, for example, government may tax people at different rates based on their incomes or impose a curfew on minors that does not apply to adults.

Cases involving the rights of women have generally been considered by applying a standard in between these two extremes, one of **intermediate scrutiny**. While the Court has not yet placed gender on the same level as race in its critical view of justifications for differential treatment, it has placed gender on a higher standard than, for example, age or disability. In general, the Court has found most forms of differential treatment for men and women to be unconstitutional, except when such treatment can be justified as serving important objectives or necessities. This standard has evolved in recent years and continues to be a source of conflict and disagreement between the justices themselves.

Other Groups Have Acted to Secure Civil Rights

In this chapter, we have focused on efforts to secure civil rights and liberties for lesbians and gays, African Americans, and women, showing how their efforts to protect or defend their fundamental rights came about. Their efforts have been cumulative and crosscutting, with precedents building over time and involving long and complex legal and political battles, resulting in rights that have been affirmed and in some cases limited or denied. Many other groups in the United States have struggled similarly—people with disabilities, Latinos, Asians, Native Americans, religious minorities, transgendered people, and others. To give proper attention to all of these efforts would require an entire book at least; the guiding principle of their necessary omission here is that we cover many of these issues in other parts of this book.

In the United States in the twenty-first century, the concept of racial, ethnic, and gender identity is becoming complicated as well. As their numbers have grown, multiracial Americans, or those with more than one distinctive racial heritage, have increasingly been carving out a space for themselves in discourse and policies involving race and ethnicity. Traditional racial and ethnic identifications have been used as the basis for evaluating compliance with Title VII of the Civil Rights Act of 1964, the Voting Rights Act, and educational desegregation policies. Broadening the categories will impact all of these regulations, and some African American rights advocates have expressed concern that it might take away from gains in equality that have been achieved since the civil rights era.[82]

1. Early activities by women to secure their own civil rights were also linked to the abolition of slavery.

   a. True
   b. False

2. The Nineteenth Amendment allowed states to grant the right of suffrage to women.

   a. True
   b. False

3. The equal rights amendment (ERA)
   _____.

a. Guaranteed the right to vote regardless of gender
b. Was never ratified
c. Focused on reducing racial discrimination in the workplace
d. All of the above

4. How has the Supreme Court treated gender equality differently than it has treated racial equality?

Answer Key: 1. a; 2. b; 3. b; 4. Answers should include a discussion of suspect classification, strict scrutiny, and the reasonableness standard.

CONCLUSION

Fences Still under Construction

The stories regarding civil liberties and rights in the United States are stories about tensions—tensions between one individual's fundamental rights and freedoms and those of another and between individual freedoms and the evolving needs of a society. They are stories about courage and political action. They are also evolving, as generations of activists, Supreme Court justices, and politicians have weighed in on the proper boundaries of American rights and freedoms. While initially the restrictions upon governmental action found in the Bill of Rights applied only to the federal government, through the process of selective incorporation, most now apply to state governments as well. Not all of the civil liberties enumerated in the Bill of Rights have received the same level of protection, however. Political speech and expression, for example, has been privileged as fundamental to the ability to secure all other rights and freedoms. The extraordinary efforts people have made to secure civil rights protections have resulted in significant gains for many, though they experienced significant resistance then and even today.

During the ratification debates, one of the most powerful arguments that the Federalists made against a bill of rights was that it would be necessarily incomplete, which might provide the federal government with an excuse to restrict those fundamental freedoms not enumerated. While the Ninth Amendment explicitly states that Americans possess fundamental freedoms not listed in the other amendments, protecting those freedoms has been left to the Supreme Court and to individuals willing to fight for them.

$SAGE edge™

Want a better grade?

Get the tools you need to sharpen your study skills. **SAGE edge** offers a robust online environment featuring an impressive array of free tools and resources. Access practice quizzes, eFlashcards, video, and multimedia at **edge.sagepub.com/abernathybrief1e**.

The people whose stories we have heard about in this chapter may not have known where their actions would finally lead, but it is very likely that each knew the controversy that his or her actions would stir up and the risks being taken. In American democracy, defining and defending one's civil liberties, claiming and protesting for one's rights has always been and will always be controversial and challenging; that is why it is so essential to the nation.

CHAPTER REVIEW

This chapter's main ideas are reflected in the Learning Objectives. By reviewing them here you should be able to **remember** the key points and **know** these terms that are central to the topic.

4.1 Describe the civil liberties protected by the Constitution, the amendments to it, and the process by which they were incorporated in order to restrict state actions.

REMEMBER...

- Protecting civil liberties involves placing restrictions upon the ability of government to limit them.

- Securing civil rights requires action both on the part of individuals to advocate for their rights and on the part of government to secure and protect those rights.

- The Bill of Rights enumerates a list of fundamental freedoms that the federal government cannot infringe upon.

- The protections set out in the Bill of Rights as written applied to the actions of the federal government and not of the state governments. A decades-long process, in which the Supreme Court played a key role, changed this.

KNOW...

- *bill of rights*: a list of fundamental rights and freedoms that individuals possess; the first ten amendments to the U.S. Constitution are referred to as the Bill of Rights (p. 107)

- *civil liberties*: fundamental rights and freedoms of citizens the protection of which involves restricting the power of a government (p. 103)

- *civil rights*: fundamental guarantees ensuring equal treatment and protecting against discrimination under the laws of a nation (p. 103)

- *due process clause*: the clause in the Fourteenth Amendment that restricts state governments from denying their citizens the right to due process of law (p. 108)

- *full faith and credit clause*: a portion of the Constitution that generally requires states to honor licenses and judicial outcomes of other states (p. 105)

- *negative freedoms*: fundamental liberties the protection of which is ensured by restricting governmental action and authority (p. 103)

- *positive freedoms*: fundamental rights and freedoms that require action by individuals to express and by governments to secure (p. 104)

- *privacy*: a right not enumerated in the Constitution but affirmed by Supreme Court decisions that covers individuals' decisions in their private lives, including decisions regarding reproductive rights and sexuality (p. 106)

- *selective incorporation:* the piecemeal process through which the Supreme Court has affirmed that almost all of the protections within the Bill of Rights also apply to state governments (p. 109)

4.2 Explain the first amendment protections granted to religion and political speech.

REMEMBER...

- The first two clauses in the First Amendment to the Constitution involve religion; they prevent the federal government from establishing religion and protect Americans' rights to exercise their religious freedoms.

KNOW...

- *Alien and Sedition Acts*: four separate laws passed under the administration of President John Adams that, among other things, restricted the freedom of speech and the press (p. 112)

- *clear and present danger test*: a Supreme Court tool to evaluate whether or not forms of political expression constitute such a threat to national security as to warrant restriction (p. 113)

- *establishment clause*: a first amendment clause protecting individuals from governmental establishment of, or support for, religion (p. 111)

- *free exercise clause*: a first amendment clause guarding the rights of individuals to exercise and express their religious beliefs (p. 111)

- *freedom of expression*: a fundamental right affirmed in the First Amendment to speak, publish, and act in the political space (p. 112)

- *hate speech*: speech that has no other purpose but to express hatred, particularly toward members of a group identified by racial or ethnic identity, gender, or sexual orientation (p. 115)

- *libel*: expression in written form or similarly published media that defames a person's character (p. 114)

- *obscenity and pornography*: text, images, or video that depicts sexual activity in ways offensive to the broader community and that lacks any artistic merit (p. 115)

- *prior restraint*: the suppression of material prior to publication on the grounds that it might endanger national security (p. 113)

- *slander*: expression in spoken form that defames a person's character (p. 114)

- *symbolic speech*: protected expression in the form of images, signs, and other symbols (p. 114)

4.3 Identify the civil liberties extended to the accused in the Bill of Rights.

REMEMBER...

- The Bill of Rights guarantees a set of protections for those accused of, investigated for, tried for, and convicted of crimes.

KNOW...

- *bail*: an amount of money posted as a security to allow the charged individual to be freed while awaiting trial (p. 120)

- *double jeopardy*: the prosecution of an individual more than once for the same crime (p. 119)

- *exclusionary rule*: a rule governing the inadmissibility of evidence obtained without a proper warrant (p. 118)

- *grand jury*: a group of citizens who, based on the evidence presented to them, conclude whether or not a person is to be indicted and subsequently tried in a court of law (p. 119)

- *Miranda rights*: the right not to speak and to have an attorney present during questioning; these rights must be given by police to individuals suspected of criminal activity (p. 119)

- *probable cause*: reasonable belief that a crime has been committed or that there is evidence indicating so (p. 118)

- *procedural justice*: a judicial standard requiring that fairness be applied to all participants equally (p. 117)

- *warrant*: a writ issued by a judge authorizing some activity (p. 118)

- *writ of habeas corpus*: a statement demanding that authorities in charge of a person's detention establish the reasons for that detention (p. 117)

4.4 Trace the efforts to secure civil rights for African Americans.

REMEMBER...

- While the conclusion of the Civil War settled the question of secession, struggles to secure rights for African Americans continued, often under threats of economic and physical violence.

- The NAACP focused its efforts on ending legal segregation by using the courts.

KNOW...

- *affirmative action*: a policy designed to address the consequences of previous discrimination by providing advantages to individuals based upon their identities (p. 130)

- Brown v. Board of Education: a landmark 1954 Supreme Court ruling that overturned *Plessy v. Ferguson* and declared legal segregation in public education to be in conflict with the equal protection clause of the Fourteenth Amendment (p. 125)

- *civil disobedience*: the intentional refusal to obey a law in order to call attention to its injustice (p. 126)

- *de facto segregation*: a separation of individuals based on identity that arises not by law but because of other factors, such as residential housing patterns (p. 130)

- *de jure segregation:* the separation of individuals based on their characteristics, such as race, intentionally, and by law (p. 130)

- *desegregation*: the act of eliminating laws or practices that separate individuals based upon racial identity (p. 126)

- *equal protection clause*: a clause of the Fourteenth Amendment that serves as the constitutional basis for the assault on educational segregation in the courts and for the assertion of civil rights for Americans of many different identities in many different areas of public and private life (p. 123)

- *Fifteenth Amendment*: an amendment to the Constitution passed in 1870 affirming the voting rights of all freedmen (p. 123)

- *Fourteenth Amendment*: an amendment to the Constitution passed in 1868 affirming the citizenship of all persons born or naturalized in the United States and, for the first time in the history of the Constitution, placing explicit restrictions on the laws of states that sought to abridge the privileges and immunities of citizens of the United States (p. 123)

- *legal segregation*: the separation by law of individuals based upon their racial identities (p. 124)

- Plessy v. Ferguson: a Supreme Court case in 1896 that upheld legal racial segregation (p. 124)

- *separate but equal*: the doctrine that racial segregation was constitutional so long as the facilities for blacks and whites were roughly equal (p. 124)

- *Thirteenth Amendment*: an amendment to the Constitution passed in 1865 prohibiting slavery within the United States (p. 123)

4.5 Describe the challenges women faced in securing their civil rights.

REMEMBER...

- Early efforts to secure civil rights for African Americans and those to secure civil rights for American women often overlapped but with differences in their goals and tactics.

KNOW...

- *abolitionist movement*: a political struggle to end slavery and free all slaves (p. 132)

- *equal rights amendment (ERA)*: a proposed but not ratified amendment to the Constitution that sought to guarantee equality of rights based upon sex (p. 135)

- *intermediate scrutiny*: a middle-ground standard for determining whether differential treatment is allowable (p. 136)

- *Nineteenth Amendment*: a 1920 amendment to the Constitution that prevented states from denying the right to vote based on sex (p. 134)

- *reasonableness standard*: a more relaxed judicial standard in which differential treatment must be shown to be reasonable and not arbitrary (p. 136)

- *strict scrutiny*: the most stringent judicial standard applied for deciding whether a law or policy is allowed to treat people differently (p. 136)

5 PUBLIC OPINION
How Are Americans' Voices Measured, and Do They Matter?

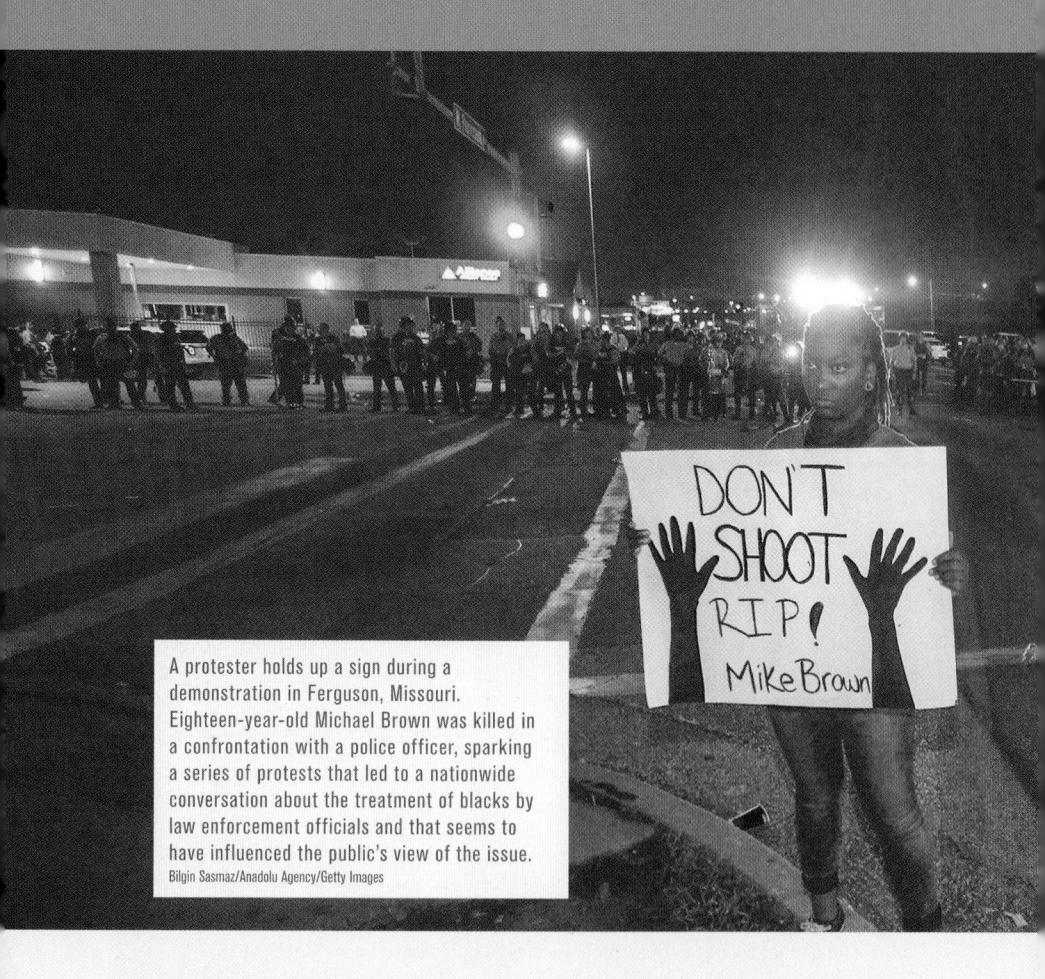

A protester holds up a sign during a demonstration in Ferguson, Missouri. Eighteen-year-old Michael Brown was killed in a confrontation with a police officer, sparking a series of protests that led to a nationwide conversation about the treatment of blacks by law enforcement officials and that seems to have influenced the public's view of the issue.
Bilgin Sasmaz/Anadolu Agency/Getty Images

In a representative government, citizens must have some knowledge of what their elected representatives are up to in order to keep watch on their activities, hold them accountable, and punish them at the voting booth if those representatives are no longer serving their interests. Conversely, elected representatives need to know what citizens' preferences are in order to appeal effectively to voters and to carry out their wishes once in office.

Nothing about that exchange of information can be taken for granted. Why? For starters, the act of conveying opinions to candidates or elected officials requires that people (as individuals and collectively) have preferences on issues in the first place and that these preferences are coherent and meaningful.

This is the central challenge of **public opinion**, the sum of individual attitudes about government, policies, and issues. Scholars debate the degree to which people have individually coherent and meaningful opinions about the issues with which government deals. When these individual bits of information become the collective thing that we call public opinion, they also wonder whether that produces anything meaningful or is just noise.

In this chapter, we will focus on American public opinion in one specific area: the treatment of young African American men by law enforcement officials. We will deal with the difficult story of the shooting death of Michael Brown by a police officer in Ferguson, Missouri, and the events that followed. We will question whether or not these events have produced meaningful changes in American public opinion on the topic of police-community relations.

After reading this chapter, you will be able to do the following:

5.1 Discuss differing theories about public opinion formation and expression and the degree to which it is meaningful.

5.2 Describe the issues involved in transmitting and measuring American public opinion and the construction of the instruments used to do so.

5.3 Examine the sources of individual political attitudes and preferences.

5.4 Debate the power of individuals, events, and people's interpretations of events to make lasting change in American politics.

LEARNING OBJECTIVES

PUBLIC OPINION MAY BE MOVED BY IMPORTANT EVENTS LIKE FERGUSON

On August 9, 2014, white law enforcement officer Darren Wilson killed Michael Brown, an unarmed eighteen-year-old African American man, during a police stop in Ferguson, Missouri. Some eyewitness accounts asserted that Brown had his hands raised in surrender when he was shot six times by Wilson.[1] His death sparked a massive public outcry. The day after Brown's death, protesters gathered in Ferguson. "Tension. . .flared off and on through the evening," as protesters cycled between peaceful prayer circles and candlelight vigils and more intense street demonstrations where they chanted "'We are Michael Brown' as wary police officers stood nearby with assault rifles."[2] By nightfall, there was violence: "After a candlelight vigil, people smash[ed] car windows, carr[ied] away armloads of looted goods from stores and burn[ed] down a Quick Trip."[3] By the time the first wave of violence ended, "more than two dozen businesses in Ferguson

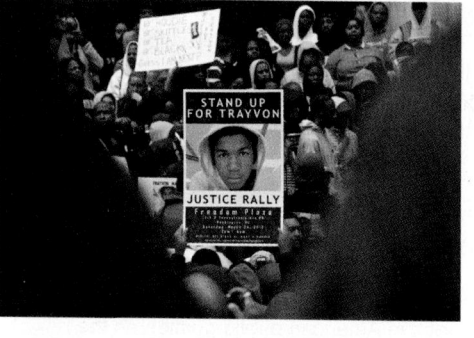

The Black Lives Matter movement began after the death of Trayvon Martin, an unarmed black Florida teenager who was shot to death by a white neighborhood watch volunteer in 2012. The group continued protesting in Ferguson after Michael Brown's death. NICHOLAS KAMM/AFP/Getty Images

and neighboring Dellwood were damaged or looted."[4] The protests, some peaceful and some violent, continued for weeks.

In the weeks following Brown's death, many of the protestors and other residents of Ferguson called for the arrest and prosecution of the officer who had shot Brown. Some chanted. One of their common refrains was "black life matters," a reference to the social movement #BlackLivesMatter, which began following the 2013 acquittal of George Zimmerman in the shooting death of Trayvon Martin in Florida. After Ferguson, however, Black Lives Matter became part of the national conversation in ways it had never been before. *Time* magazine included the protestors of Ferguson in its list of candidates for "Person of the Year."[5] The movement gained even more visibility in the public eye as numerous other unarmed African Americans were killed by police officers during the year following. In Dayton, Ohio, police shot and killed twenty-one-year-old John Crawford inside a Walmart. Crawford was handling an air rifle, which officers thought was a firearm.[6] Roughly three weeks before Brown was killed, Eric Garner "died from a police chokehold in Staten Island, N.Y., after telling the arresting officers that he could not breathe."[7]

At the same time, the views of police officers involved were also shaping the public's perception of the events. In an interview with ABC News in fall 2014, Darren Wilson, who had announced his resignation from the Ferguson Police Department, argued that he acted in self-defense in killing Brown: "I had to. If I don't, he [Brown] will kill me if he gets to me."[8] Ferguson police chief Thomas Jackson relayed to the public Wilson's suspicions that Brown and a friend were suspects in a convenience store robbery that had occurred shortly before the encounter.[9]

Less than two weeks following Brown's death, the Pew Research Center published the results of a **public opinion survey**, which is a systematic attempt to make inferences about the opinions of large numbers of individuals by carefully sampling and asking questions of a small, randomly assigned sample of the larger population. Pew was looking at Americans' responses to what Ferguson and racial identity meant in the larger national conversation. To conduct the survey, researchers had contacted a random sample of one thousand American adults, half via landlines and half via cell phones. The divisions between African Americans and whites on what Ferguson meant were clear. A full 80 percent of blacks said that Brown's shooting raised "important issues about race." But only 37 percent of white respondents agreed. A full 47 percent of whites said that "race [was] getting more

FIGURE 5.1

Opinion about Ferguson Divided by Racial Identity

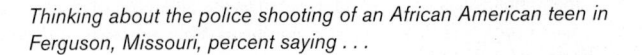

Thinking about the police shooting of an African American teen in Ferguson, Missouri, percent saying . . .

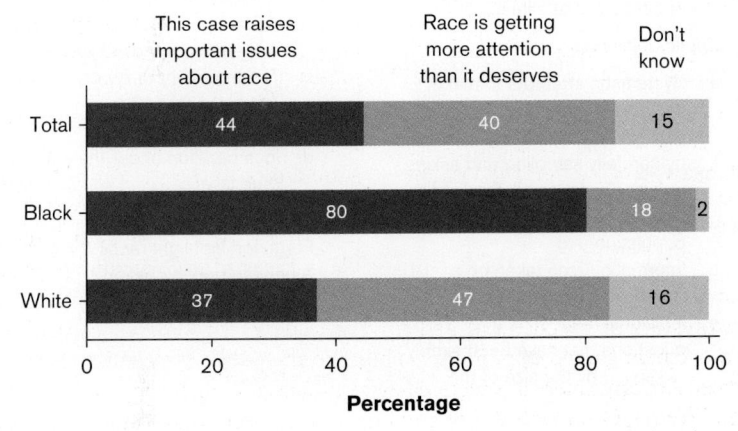

Note: Survey conducted August 14–17, 2014. Whites and blacks include only those who are not Hispanic. Figures may not add to 100% because of rounding.

Source: Pew Research Center, "Stark Racial Divisions in Reactions to Ferguson Police Shooting," August 18, 2014, www.people-press.org/2014/08/18/stark-racial-divisions-in-reactions-to-ferguson-police-shooting.

attention than it deserves" (see Figure 5.1). Clearly Americans were deeply split about whether Brown's death reflected important issues about the state of race in America. The idea that there were two Fergusons, one African American and one white, seemed to extend beyond the city limits and apply to the whole of the American public.

As we will see in the chapter, by the time a year had passed since Brown's death, the national conversation about race in America seemed to have changed. Of all the critical questions that arose from the events in Ferguson, these are the ones that we will explore: Did the events in Ferguson meaningfully shape American public opinion? If these events *did* have an impact on American public opinion, what effect did the resulting change in attitudes have on representation and the American political process? Did these changes endure, or did the national conversation go back to the way it was before, divided sharply by racial identity? Did leaders and government officials pay attention to these shifts in the opinion landscape?

1. Public opinion is _____.
   a. A set of facts only known by a subset of people
   b. The views of elites
   c. The sum of individual attitudes about government, policies, and issues
   d. Views held by the masses, as opposed to the elites

2. Public opinion surveys are _____.
   a. Systematic attempts to make inferences about the opinions of large numbers of individuals by carefully sampling and asking questions of a small, randomly assigned sample of the larger population
   b. Informal quizzes taken on social media sites like Facebook
   c. Individual responses to poll questions that have been simply multiplied by the size of the sampled population to arrive at the true opinion of a group
   d. Groups of people hired to call random respondents to find out their views on important issues

3. Central to the concerns of protesters in Ferguson, Missouri, was _____.
   a. American immigration policy
   b. A state policy related to firearms ownership by individuals
   c. The treatment of African American men by law enforcement officials
   d. Incarceration under the nation's drug laws

4. In what ways did the events in Ferguson highlight racial divisions in American public opinion?

Answer Key: 1. c; 2. a; 3. c; 4. Answers might include a discussion of racial divisions on the degree to which the events in Ferguson highlighted the need for a broader national conversation on police-community relations.

PUBLIC OPINION IS THE SUM TOTAL OF INDIVIDUAL BELIEFS AND ATTITUDES

• Understand the challenges of public opinion, including whether the opinions of Americans about political issues are actually meaningful and, if so, under what conditions; whether these opinions are coherent; and what the components of individual attitudes are.

One of the most important debates about American public opinion is whether or not there is such a thing. Of course, many Americans *have* thoughts and ideas about politics and policies, but many others do not have well-formed views on these topics. Some people might not care at all and wonder what all the fuss is about. And what do we really learn by asking Americans what they think? Recall the definition of public opinion presented previously: the sum of individual attitudes about government, policies, and issues. Public opinion, by definition, involves two components: an individual's own beliefs and attitudes as well as the accumulation of all of these individual preferences into something that we then call *public opinion*. Either of these two pieces—individual attitudes and the aggregation of individual attitudes—can make American public opinion difficult to understand. This is because individuals may not actually have meaningful preferences on any given issue, and, even if they do, the aggregation of these individual preferences might not yield meaningful and useful information.

These are more than just academic concerns. A representative democracy cannot function without meaningful public opinion. If our elected representatives do not know what we want, then how can they hope to represent us? Later in this book we will explore the role that constituents play in shaping the behavior of their elected senators and representatives. Inherent in the role of constituency, however, are two assumptions: that constituents have preferences and that they can meaningfully communicate those preferences to their members of Congress. In this chapter, we will consider both these assumptions.

There Are Competing Views about the Meaning of Public Opinion

Arguments about the meaning of public opinion in American political life fall into two general camps. One perspective holds that the average citizen either doesn't have or is unable to express meaningful opinions on the vast array of issues with which he or she is confronted. Maybe there are simply too many issues for any of us to have well-informed and meaningful opinions about all of them. Another perspective holds that even though individuals sometimes lack the information they need to form opinions, they can find ways to overcome or work around these challenges by, for example, making inferences based on their attitudes about other policies and questions, responding to messages from political parties, and/or relying on friends. Perhaps these shortcuts and cues help us arrive at an opinion. Aggregating individual opinions—even if they are individually unclear or inconsistent—can send a useful and impactful signal to elected representatives and government officials.

The Minimalist Paradigm Holds That Most People's Opinions Consist of Stereotypes and Nonattitudes

Proponents of what political scientists have called the **minimalist paradigm** emphasize how most people fall short of what we expect them to know, think about, and pay attention to in the complicated world of politics and policy.[10] Most people, according to this perspective, pay minimum attention to issues and have minimal information about them. Additionally, the opinions that they *do* have are minimally stable; they change over time or in response to attempts to control or shape them.

One of the earliest and most influential expressions of the minimalist argument was Walter Lippmann's *Public Opinion* (1922). A prominent journalist and political observer, Lippmann was concerned about how malleable (or flexible) and receptive Americans' attitudes appeared to be under the pressure of political propaganda leading up to the nation's involvement in World War I. If, in the mind of many observers of American public opinion, a nation could be led to a war most felt had nothing to do with American interests, then what *couldn't* the American people be talked into?

For Lippmann, a key concept was the **stereotype**, a preconceived, often oversimplified idea about something that people apply as a filter to the world. Stereotypes do not filter based upon a rational consideration of the issues but upon emotions, and in the world of politics they are easily manipulated by those who seek to shape American public opinion for their own political purposes.

Lippmann described a public that is dangerously unreflective and vulnerable to attempts to shape its opinions. To him, part of the reason why the Framers of the Constitution instituted so many checks and balances in the federal government, so many roadblocks to making major policy change, was mistrust of individuals' haphazard, shifting, and malleable stereotypes.

Inherent in the minimalist critique is the idea that not all Americans have the same amount of political information. A small number of individuals, the **elites**, may have well-informed and well-reasoned opinions, but the majority of individuals, the **masses**, do not. In an early study using large sample surveys, a group of researchers painted a grim picture of the majority of American voters. Most are not politically involved and have only a limited awareness of political events.[11] Instead, voters often rely on their identification with a political party—an identification that itself might not be the result of careful, thoughtful, conscious deliberation.

In 1964 political scientist Philip Converse extended this critique to question whether masses can and do learn from elites, become more informed and produce responses to surveys that are stable over time. Generally, Converse found, masses do not learn from elites.[12] Instead, most voters have **nonattitudes**. The opinions that most people express in, for example, a public opinion survey, might be vulnerable to the efforts of propagandists, as Lippmann feared, and, frankly, might just be random.

Concerns about a lack of coherent opinions in the American electorate and the challenges that this poses to American representative democracy have not gone away. Recently, two researchers found that significant percentages of Americans were not able to answer basic questions about American government, such as being able to name one or more branches of the federal government or name constitutional protections in the Bill of Rights.[13] At least as troubling was their finding that political knowledge was predictably and unequally distributed. Younger Americans, women, lower-income Americans, and members of racial and ethnic minorities consistently fared worse in their answers to such factual political knowledge questions. These gaps have remained consistent over the past few decades. Researchers with the Pew Research Center periodically administer a "News IQ" quiz to a random sample of Americans. The test contains questions regarding political figures, knowledge of current issues in domestic and international politics, and geography (see Figure 5.2). While the number of Americans who can correctly answer a question varies within and across these knowledge tests, significant amounts are unable to answer the questions correctly. To what extent does this information gap matter? Can Americans with unequal knowledge of, or access to, information about American politics express their desires with voices as impactful as those of informed Americans?

Another Perspective Says That People Can Overcome Information Gaps

While more recent scholarship acknowledges the challenges posed by proponents of the minimalist paradigm, it also emphasizes the ways in which the public can still make sense of their opinions and transmit those opinions to their representatives, both collectively and individually. On the most basic point—that Americans often lack opinions on many issues in politics and policy—these

FIGURE 5.2

A Sample Question from Pew's Political Knowledge Test

The News IQ Quiz

What is the name of this person?

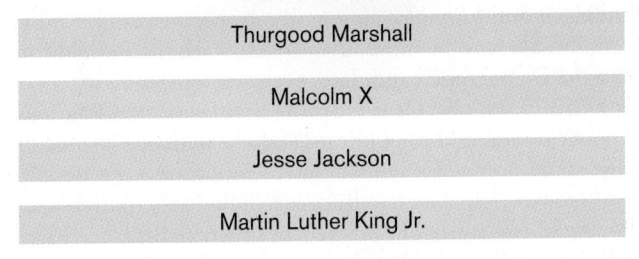

Thurgood Marshall

Malcolm X

Jesse Jackson

Martin Luther King Jr.

Ninety-one percent of respondents to Pew's "News IQ" quiz were able to correctly identify this image of Dr. Martin Luther King Jr. Far fewer were able to identify images of 2014 Nobel Peace Prize winner Malala Yousafzai or Massachusetts senator Elizabeth Warren. Only about 33 percent knew there were three female Supreme Court justices.

Source: Pew Research Center, "The News IQ Quiz," www.pewresearch.org/quiz/the-news-iq-quiz.

scholars agree. Where they disagree is on the need for any one person to have an encyclopedic set of policy preferences to be able to offer an opinion. The aggregation of individuals' opinions, according to some scholars, can produce useful information even in the presence of noise at the individual level.

How do individuals answer survey questions? Do they act as file cabinets, carrying around preformed opinions and waiting to pull out the relevant opinion when prompted? Or do they construct at least some of their opinions when asked to do so—opinions that are based on their own understandings but also perhaps shaped by the survey and the context in which they answered the survey's questions? If that is how individual opinions might be "formed," then one might reasonably expect to see changes in answers to surveys over time and in different situations since the administration of the survey will vary.

By incorporating findings from studies of cognition and political psychology, scholars have emphasized this more dynamic process and, though they acknowledge gaps in knowledge and understanding, present a more complex picture of the public's ability to make sense of the political world. For John Zaller, a basic concept in attitude construction is **consideration**, a combination of cognition and affect that contributes to any one answer to any one question or evaluation.[14] It's not as complicated a concept as it may seem. Basically, Zaller's theory says that our knowledge and our emotions both come into play when we form and express an opinion. We are not file cabinets, but we are also not the modeling clay that Lippmann worried about. We are something in between.[15]

Other research focuses on the ability of voters with low levels of specific political knowledge to make effective use of **cues and information shortcuts** to form meaningful opinions. These informational helpers may come from a variety of sources. Individuals' own personal experiences and interactions with government, accumulated over a lifetime, can help them make sense of an issue or problem. This "gut rationality" may not help on a political knowledge quiz, but it can assist people in making meaningful political choices.[16] In addition, individuals might rely on advice from friends and colleagues.[17]

Identification with a particular political party (called party identification) is another powerful informational shortcut that voters frequently use when evaluating candidates and forming opinions about specific issues.[18] If I identify as a Republican, I'm likely to be more favorable toward the Republican candidate rather than the Democratic candidate, even without knowing anything other than their party affiliations. Or if I identify as a Democrat, I am more likely to oppose a policy option that Republicans endorse than one Democrats endorse.

Finally, some political scientists have emphasized the possibility of the "wisdom of crowds"[19] in which individuals, imperfectly informed, can come up with a meaningful assessment of a problem or situation. Benjamin Page and Robert Shapiro emphasized the possibility for a public to be collectively rational even in the presence of individually inconsistent and shapeable opinions: "While we grant the rational ignorance of most individuals, and the possibility that their policy preferences are shallow and unstable, . . . public opinion as a *collective* phenomenon is nonetheless stable (though not immovable), meaningful, and indeed rational . . . : it is able to make distinctions; it is organized in coherent patterns; it is reasonable, based on the best available information; and it is adaptive to new information or changed circumstances, responding in similar ways to similar stimuli."[20]

WHAT HAVE I LEARNED?

1. According to political scientists who argue for the minimalist paradigm, information generally passes from political elites to the masses.

   a. True
   b. False

2. For political scientist John Zaller, individuals' opinions are shaped primarily by _____.

   a. Facts
   b. Political elites

   c. Political propaganda
   d. Knowledge and emotions

3. Political scientists Benjamin Page and Robert Shapiro argued that both individual and aggregated public opinion convey little useful information.

   a. True
   b. False

   Answer Key: 1. b; 2. d; 3. b.

PUBLIC OPINION IS TRANSMITTED AND MEASURED IN SEVERAL WAYS

The act of representation in a republican form of government has two basic, and crucial, informational requirements. First, voters must have opinions and preferences that can be communicated to their elected representatives. Second, elected officials must respond to, or be forced to respond to, these expressed preferences. We have already considered the debates about whether or not Americans have meaningful opinions. The second part of the equation is just as important. How can Americans effectively communicate their preferences to their government? How do elected representatives learn about the preferences of their constituents? What tools can we use to make sure we are correctly gauging their responses?

- Describe the ways that public opinion may be transmitted to elected representatives.

- Identify the problems involved with trying to accurately measure American public opinion.

Citizens' Opinions Are Transmitted to Public Officials through Direct and Indirect Channels

One method that citizens use is to directly communicate with their elected officials through phone calls or e-mails. The challenge with direct communication as a tool of representation is that elected officials know that those who call or write do not represent their constituents as a whole but only a motivated subset of people who are often unhappy about something. While direct communication can signal to an elected official the intense preferences of a small group of individuals, it does not convey a sense of the overall preferences of the citizens as a whole.

A tool that *does* give elected officials this broader knowledge is an election. While we may not often think about an election as a tool for measuring public opinion, that is precisely what it is. However, in this regard, elections have their own limitations. First, many eligible voters do not vote. The decision of whether or not to vote can be affected by efforts to mobilize potential voters, to get out the vote (see Chapter 7). In terms of measuring the preferences of constituents, the greater challenge with elections is that they tend to revolve around a small set of issues, albeit ones for which voters have intense preferences. For the majority of public policy issues with which elected officials will have to contend, elections are too broad a tool to reveal useful information.

Therefore, rather than waiting for individuals to contact them or trying to decipher the results of an election, public officials may go directly to the citizens to find out what they think and want. One tool sometimes used for this is the **focus group**, in which a small group of individuals is assembled for a directed conversation during which one hopes to uncover patterns of thinking about issues and individuals. Focus groups can be useful in understanding how individuals come to understand the political issues with which they are contending. However, by their nature, focus groups cannot paint a picture of the constituency as a whole and are therefore limited in their utility.

Another, deeper concern about focus groups and other tools for measuring public opinion comes from their origin in product marketing in which companies use these tools to try to get a sense of which products will sell best and why. This textbook, in fact, as well as most others, involved the use of focus groups in its development. The challenge for representative democracy is whether or not we want our elected officials to think of us like breakfast cereals. In one sense, we might. We want our elected representatives to care enough about our opinions to find out what they are. On the other hand, there is a danger that our elected representatives might be too concerned with taking the nation's pulse, too hesitant to make difficult decisions that might be unpopular but are necessary. The Framers most certainly did not intend for elected representatives to consistently bend to the will of voters. That is part of the reason why they set up so many roadblocks to making major and sweeping changes to American public policy.

Even so, a candidate whose eyes are on the next election will use any tools that she or he has to gauge the opinions of the voters. The most effective of these is the **scientific poll**. With this tool, pollsters try to gain an understanding of a large group of individuals by obtaining the opinions of a carefully chosen small sample of the group although they are aware of the limitations of the effort.

Scientific Polling Is Based on Efforts to Accurately Sample Representative Populations

In theory, scientific polling is simple. Given the challenges and costs of having to ask everyone in a House district, a state, or the nation what they think, pollsters instead select a smaller representative subset of that constituency and ask its members what they think. That subgroup is called the **sample**. For some political polls, the sample population may be the entire voting-age population of the United States or of an individual state or congressional district. However, there are many other possible populations of interest in a survey, such as individuals with specific racial or ethnic identities or the student population of a college or university.

A key challenge in sampling is **random selection**. For the sample to be useful, it must represent the larger population as best as possible—with no systematic errors. Some errors in sampling are not a problem. If your **respondents**, or those individuals who respond to your survey, are more likely to choose blue over green socks, that is probably not an issue. If, however, a poll systematically oversamples or undersamples individuals based on characteristics that are relevant to what the poll is trying to measure—for example, support for a presidential candidate from the Democratic or Republican Party—then you have a problem. Pollsters are well aware of these challenges. Often they may use the technique of **weighting** to adjust the results of a survey. Weighting is done based on differences between the percentages of specific groups participating in the survey and what is known about the proportion of their representation in the larger population.

Unless one can survey every single person in a population, community, or nation, no researcher can ever know what the "true" opinion of that population is. The goal is to minimize the uncertainty as much as possible while also conducting a poll that does not cost vast sums of money or take an unacceptable amount of time to conduct. When pollsters present their results, they include a measure of the **sampling error** (or margin of error) in their surveys. In larger national polls, which typically aim for about 1,500 respondents, the sampling error is often plus or minus three points, meaning that they can assert that about 95 percent of the time the true number—which is never known—lies within three points on either side of the measured number. In American politics, the number of citizens on either side of an issue might be closely divided. If, for example, an opinion survey with a margin of error of three points finds that one party's candidate for president has the support of 49 percent of Americans and the other party's candidate the support of 47 percent, then one could not confidently say that the first candidate would win in a national election. Increasing the size of the sample decreases the error, but it also increases the cost. In addition, the greater the variation in the population that one samples, the larger the sampling error.

Public Opinion Survey Reliability Varies by Type

In choosing how to administer a survey, a researcher has several options. The degree of confidence that one can place in the findings, however, depends critically upon the ways in which the sample is selected. One popular type of survey is a **straw poll**—an unofficial tally of opinion or support at a meeting or event, such as a political party meeting or caucus. While straw polls can be useful in exploring which individuals support a candidate and why, their target population is not randomly selected. The fact that people have chosen to attend the event at which the straw poll is conducted means that the sample was not randomly chosen and, therefore, cannot be relied upon to draw conclusions about general public opinion.

A **self-selected listener opinion poll** (or **SLOP**), in which respondents choose to respond to a survey prompt on their own, suffer from the same disadvantage. SLOPs are quite common. When individuals respond to a radio talk show

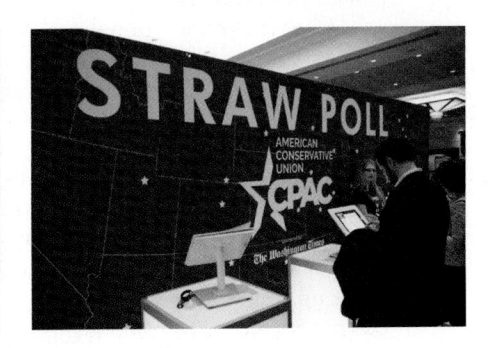

Two versions of straw polls are shown here. At left, a visitor to the 2015 Iowa State Fair casts a vote for presidential candidate Carly Fiorina with a kernel of corn. At right, attendees at the 2015 Conservative Political Action Conference (CPAC) vote in an electronic straw poll in National Harbor, Maryland.
Left Photo: AP Photo/Paul Sancya
Right Photo: AP Photo/Alex Brandon

host's requests to call in, or when a person fills out a quick survey after reading an article or watching a video on the Internet, he or she is participating in a SLOP. Because more involved and motivated individuals choose to participate—and these individuals do not represent a randomly selected subset of the overall population—one cannot confidently say that their opinions reflect the distribution of them in the larger population.

An **exit poll** is a survey conducted outside of a polling place in which individuals are asked who or what they just voted for and why. While there is much to be gained for a news organization that can call a race before other news outlets based on its exit poll results, there are risks as well. Individuals do not vote at random times, and an exit poll may unintentionally be sampling from a group that over- or underrepresents overall public opinion on an issue or candidate. Also, announcing the results of exit polls while polls are still open runs the risk of influencing an election. Learning that one candidate is supposedly winning may discourage another candidate's supporters from turning out to vote because they believe their votes would not matter. To avoid that problem, news networks have voluntarily committed to not releasing exit poll results until all of a state's polling places have closed. Exit polls can be useful, though, in understanding patterns of voting—for example, what issue was most on the minds of voters who voted for one candidate or another.

Because of the challenges posed by nonrandom selection, news organizations, media outlets, and research organizations rely primarily on the telephone when trying to gauge American public opinion. They may draw from lists of phone numbers or employ **random digit dialing** in which phone numbers are selected randomly by computer. That has the added advantage of potentially including unlisted numbers or those generally not in pollsters' (or marketers') databases, such as numbers for cell phones. Even with random digit dialing, however, there are always risks that a sample is not truly representative of the overall population. Are some of those whom one calls more likely to answer the survey than others? Might patterns of willingness or unwillingness to answer the survey bias the findings? Though pollsters are aware of and try to account for these issues, it is always a potential problem.

How Public Opinion Surveys Are Constructed Affects Their Validity

In addition to sample selection, pollsters must confront other issues that are important for informed consumers of public opinion surveys—such as the students reading this book—to note. We have explored the challenge that Americans may have nonattitudes on some issues, and there is also the risk that individuals may be unwilling to admit a lack of information or opinion and make up responses on the spot. In one survey of Americans, political scientist George Bishop asked respondents about their opinions of the Public Affairs Act of 1975. The trick was that the act never existed. In spite of this small fact, significant percentages of respondents offered an opinion on the piece of fictitious legislation, casting doubt on the reliability of results of surveys of Americans on specific public policies and policy proposals.[21] In order to try to prevent this, well-constructed survey questions should try to focus on issues with which their respondents will be familiar and have opinions about.

Even on issues for which respondents have actual preferences, other factors may shape the results of a public opinion survey. First, the **question order** might affect the results. Consider a question about whether or not individuals should be permitted to burn an American flag in protest. The same question might produce substantially different results if it were preceded by other questions that included the expressed opinions of other individuals.[22] Perhaps the flag-burning question was preceded by a question about the importance of patriotism, which might produce more opinions against allowing flag burning. Alternatively, the flag-burning question might have followed a question on the importance of free speech in American democracy, priming a different pattern of responses.

Similarly, the **question wording** might, intentionally or not, guide respondents to a specific answer. For example, in a 2003 Pew Research Center Survey about attitudes toward military action in Iraq, 68 percent of respondents said that they favored action when asked if they would "favor or oppose taking military action in Iraq to end Saddam Hussein's rule." However, when asked if they would "favor or oppose taking military action in Iraq to end Saddam Hussein's rule *even if it meant that U.S. forces might suffer thousands of casualties,*" only 43 percent of respondents favored military action.[23] Finally, the interviewers themselves may affect the results of a survey, especially one conducted in person. Political scientists have, for example, documented **race of interviewer effects**, in which the outcomes of surveys, even on questions only asking for political knowledge and information, may depend partly upon the racial identities of respondents and surveyors.[24]

Individual Opinions Vary According to Direction, Intensity, Stability, and Salience

Political scientists and scholars of political psychology and mass communication need to think not only about the various techniques and types of instruments they can use to measure public opinion but they also need language they can use to describe that individual's opinion, to break it down into distinct components. The first is the **direction** of the opinion, which is what we commonly focus on. Is the person for an issue, against it, or neutral? Does the person think favorably about a political candidate, unfavorably, or neutral? A second dimension of an opinion is the **intensity**, or strength of involvement and preference, with which an individual holds that opinion. Another component describes the **stability** of the opinion. Stable opinions tend not to change over time, in different contexts, or in response to differently worded survey questions. Some opinions, such as which political party one prefers, tend to be stable, while others, such as a preference over a specific water or transportation policy, tend to be much more variable over time and across different surveys—if the individuals have opinions at all. These two parts of an opinion are related. Intense opinions are more likely to be stable than those held with less intensity. Finally, there is the **salience** (or centrality) of an opinion in the sense that some strongly held opinions shape expressed opinions on other issues or candidate evaluations. For example, a strongly held belief about the need for an active and involved government might shape a person's opinions about specific government policies. Salient opinions tend to be more intense and stable.

One area of representation in American government that continues to evoke intense, stable, and salient opinions is the equality of treatment of individuals by law enforcement officers and the relationship between that treatment and the racial and ethnic identity of those who interact with law enforcement and the criminal justice system. As residents of Ferguson and other communities in which young men of color had been killed by law enforcement officers reacted, protested, and expressed their anger, it quickly became clear that opinions about race and treatment by law enforcement officials were often highly intense and salient. These opinions, however, were sharply divided by race, ethnicity, age, and partisan affiliation.

Polls Are Used for Commercial, Academic, and Political Purposes

Many different individuals and groups make use of public opinion polls. Media outlets work with major polling organizations when covering topics such as Americans' support or opposition to a candidate or policy proposal. Academic researchers rely on more in-depth polls to test theories about politics and public opinion. One tool that political scientists and other researchers may employ is the survey experiment, in which individuals are randomly assigned different surveys, perhaps with different question wording or framing. The goal here is not to try to measure the opinions of a larger population but to use the randomized experiments to better understand how people form opinions.

Polls also play key roles in political campaigns. The media may use tools such as exit polls to predict the outcomes of political races or to better understand why people voted one way or another in a given election. Candidates themselves may employ polls to better understand voters' interests and concerns or to gauge public support for themselves or their opponents as a campaign progresses. One controversial tool that candidates or those supporting them may employ is a **push poll**, which is not really a poll but a negative campaign tactic. Disguised as surveys, push polls try to present voters with negative or damaging portrayals of opposing candidates, sometimes with false or exaggerated information.

WHAT HAVE I LEARNED?

1. The disadvantage in measuring public opinion that self-selected listener opinion (SLOP) polls and straw polls both share is _____.

    a. They are too expensive to conduct nationally
    b. They tend to only survey conservative public opinion
    c. Their respondents are not chosen randomly
    d. They tend to only survey liberal public opinion

2. Random selection of survey respondents is challenged by _____.

    a. The communications technology used to contact potential respondents
    b. The time of day in which a respondent is contacted
    c. The decisions of potential respondents to answer or not answer the survey
    d. All of the above

3. Individually salient opinions are important because they _____.
   a. Are easily manipulated
   b. Are based on issues constructed by the media
   c. Tend to shape opinions on other issues
   d. Often change depending on the particular survey

4. If you were to try to sample American public opinion on an issue that you care about, how might you go about trying to assemble a random sample? What challenges might you face?

5. What are four components of an individual opinion?

Answer Key: 1. c; 2. d; 3. c; 4. Answers will vary but should discuss the challenges of sampling from a given population; 5. Answers should include direction, intensity, stability, and salience (or centrality).

POLITICAL ATTITUDES COME FROM A VARIETY OF SOURCES

In the days and weeks that followed the shooting death of Michael Brown, deep divisions emerged, with Americans' views on the shooting split according to racial and ethnic identity. Ferguson, Missouri, was quickly becoming many Fergusons. A *New York Times* article stated that "where once there was only one Ferguson—an anonymous suburb of St. Louis—now there is another: a small city whose name has become known for civil unrest, racial division and police harassment."[25] It was not only the shooting that caused controversy. The different "Fergusons" did not exist only in the streets of the city. The opinions of the community's reactions were as divided as the opinions over the event itself. To some, the reactions represented a justifiable expression of inequalities and injustices too long ignored; to others, they were nothing more than violence and anarchy.

To many Americans, especially whites, the protesters' anger over the events in Ferguson came as a surprise. To large percentages of African Americans, however, the death of Brown was not unique—only another tragedy in a long history of tragedies when young African American men came face-to-face with the American law enforcement system. To individuals within African American communities across the country, the only surprising thing about the fallout from Ferguson was that the issue had not been more debated, more talked about.

A political cartoon highlighting racial divisions in public opinion about the treatment of young African American men by law enforcement officials. The figure representing "Black America" is referring to the choking death of Eric Garner while in police custody in 2014. The figure representing "White America" is alleging that white Americans are not sufficiently aware of the underlying issues. Ann Telnaes Editorial Cartoon used with the permission of Ann Telnaes and the Cartoonist Group. All rights reserved. info@cartoonistgroup.com

According to Representative John Conyers of Michigan, the dean of the Congressional Black Caucus, "There are virtually no African-American males—including congressmen, actors, athletes and office workers, who have not been stopped at one time or another for driving while black."[26]

For all of us, our lived experience contributes profoundly to what we believe and the political attitudes we hold. But there are several other key factors that shape our views, including our political ideology, the groups we belong to, and other influential groups and actors. Political scientists have long studied how those attitudes are formed in the first place, how they may be altered over time, and how they are influenced by others.

The Way We Are Socialized Shapes Our Beliefs

The formation and modification of opinions and attitudes toward politics, public policy, and political figures is a lifelong process. **Political socialization** refers to the variety of experiences and factors that shape our political values, attitudes, and behaviors.

Families, Schools, and Peers Are Early Shapers of Information and Opinion

The first and most important contributor to the process of political socialization is the family, especially when it comes to shaping children's views about political figures and political authority.[27] **Party identification**—the degree to which an individual identifies with and supports a particular political party—is highly transmitted through families. Families provide, after all, the first source of political information for those who are seeking out information.[28]

Schools often intentionally play a role in political socialization through processes of **civic education** that aim to introduce students to politics and help them develop the ability to interpret and make sense of this knowledge.[29] Civic education can also transmit civic norms, such as the importance of being civically involved.[30] As spaces of learning and community, schools are also important for their ability to create a political climate, introduce students to opportunities for political participation, and introduce political learners to other students whose diverse lived experiences might reinforce or challenge the civic understandings that students bring into the classroom.[31] Families inform political learners first, then schools and educational experiences leave their mark. As such, an individual's civic education does not occur on a blank canvas but one that has already been at least partially painted by his or her upbringing.

Personal Experience and Focusing Events Affect Opinions over Time

Individual political opinions are never set in stone. While families, schools, and peers play important but different roles in our political socialization, so do later experiences in life. Our interactions in daily life may also shape our opinions on both individual and national levels, especially when we experience focusing events, like times of crisis.

We see this effect in several ways in the aftermath of Ferguson as individuals across the nation began to take a greater interest in politics and policy and became more informed and involved. One of the individuals attending a protest march at the end of August was forty-four-year-old Ian Buchanan. According to a reporter for the *St. Louis Post-Dispatch*, Buchanan, "a former principal in the St. Louis and Normandy school districts, drove to Ferguson from his home in Memphis, Tenn., to attend Saturday's march. 'I came here because I want to be part of the spirit of the movement,' he said. He spent part of the day talking to his former students about how to voice their concerns about injustice. 'The older generation usually wants to write off the younger generation, but to effect change, it comes from the young people,' Buchanan said."[32]

Sometimes the cumulative effect of a series of crises makes a difference at the national level in shifting public opinion. Commenting on the cluster of lethal shootings of young African American men in 2014, a sociologist at George Washington University claimed that while one single event might not move American public opinion, several might: "Once a critical mass of these incidents occur in real time it can certainly shift public opinion even among those . . . who might have thought the police could do no wrong."[33] Indeed, public opinion polls conducted in the weeks and months following the deaths of Michael Brown and Eric Garner found that a large majority of Americans, regardless of racial or ethnic identity or political party affiliation, expressed support for the use of body cameras by law enforcement officers to record their interactions with the public (see Figure 5.3).

American public opinion in the twenty-first century is more instanta-neously shapeable than has ever been possible. Social media allows, in theory, a national conversation between people of very different lived experiences and political attitudes.

Partisan Identification, Individual and Group Identities, and Elite Attitudes Inform Our Views

As we have seen, families, schools, and events (either over the course of a lifetime or focusing ones) play a major role in shaping public opinion. But other factors play important roles as well. How we identify politically, as well as how we define ourselves in term of gender, race, or ethnicity, can form clear, consistent, and persistent patterns of similarity and division in American public opinion.

Partisan Identification and Political Ideologies

One of the single most effective predictors of public opinion is an individual's identification with a political party. Partisan identification is closely connected to one's **political ideology**, which describes a person's beliefs about political goals, public policies, and acts to shape political choices. In the United States today, two political ideologies tend to dominate. **Liberalism**, in the modern usage of the term, refers to support for more robust governmental action to ensure equality of opportunity, particularly in regulation of the economy, as well as environmen-tal regulation. **Conservatism** highlights a reduced role for the government and an emphasis on individual liberty, again, especially in economic matters.

FIGURE 5.3

Widespread Support for the Use of Body Cameras by Law Enforcement Officers

More police officers wearing body cameras to record interactions would be a . . . (%)

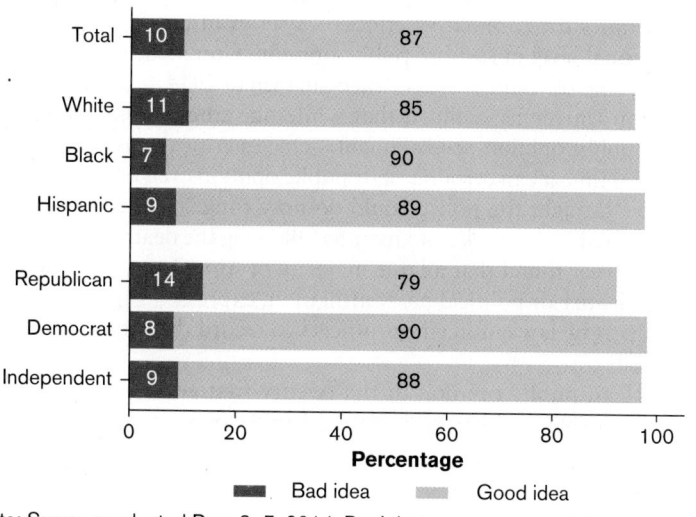

Total — 10 | 87
White — 11 | 85
Black — 7 | 90
Hispanic — 9 | 89
Republican — 14 | 79
Democrat — 8 | 90
Independent — 9 | 88

Percentage

■ Bad idea   Good idea

Note: Survey conducted Dec. 3–7, 2014. Don't know responses not shown. Whites and blacks include only non-Hispanics; Hispanics are of any race.

Source: Pew Research Center, "Sharp Racial Divisions in Reactions to Brown, Garner Decisions: Many Blacks Expect Police-Minority Relations to Worsen," December 8, 2014, www.people-press .org/2014/12/08/sharp-racial-divisions-in-reactions-to-brown-garner-decisions.

While these two political ideologies do shape much of the landscape, there are others. **Socialism,** closely related to liberalism, emphasizes an even stronger role for the government in economic matters, including advocating for governmental control over entire sectors of the economy, such as health care. **Libertarianism,** on the other hand, shares an emphasis on individual liberty with conservatism but often takes it further, arguing that governmental involvement in the lives of Americans should be as minimal as possible.

These ideologies map clearly onto partisan affiliation, with liberals, and some socialists, identifying with the Democratic Party, and conservatives and many libertarians with the Republican Party. These mappings, however, are not always neat and clear. As we will explore in our discussion of political parties later in the book, tensions *within* political parties are often as consequential as debates *between* them.

Americans' response to Ferguson was no different. On the question of whether or not local law enforcement agencies could be trusted to administer the laws of the nation impartially and without regard to racial and ethnic identity, Americans were sharply divided according to the political parties to which they attached themselves. Similar divisions emerged in polls showing that over two-thirds of Republicans thought that race was getting too much attention in the media coverage of Ferguson whereas nearly 70 percent of Democrats thought that the shooting raised important issues about race in American society (see Figure 5.4).[34]

An ongoing debate among political scientists who study American political parties and elections has been about the sources of **partisan polarization** in Congress. Members of Congress are increasingly voting with members of their

FIGURE 5.4

Partisan Divisions in Public Opinion about Ferguson

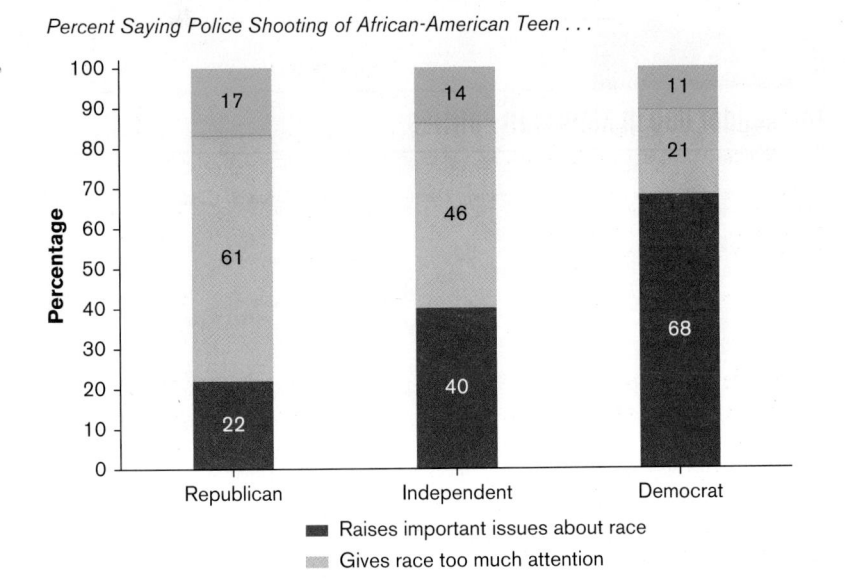

Percent Saying Police Shooting of African-American Teen . . .

■ Raises important issues about race
▨ Gives race too much attention
▨ Don't know

Source: Data are from Pew Research Center, "Stark Racial Divisions in Reactions to Ferguson Police Shooting," August 18, 2014, www.people-press.org/files/2014/08/8-18-14-Ferguson-Release.pdf.

own party. Why? It is not clear if this trend represents an increasingly polarized environment among political elites, political masses, or both, or if some other factor or factors are at play.[35]

Gender

American public opinion is also often divided along gender lines. On many issues, such as comparative levels of spending on social welfare programs versus national defense, polls have consistently found differences between men and women. These differences in opinion are translated into differences in support for American political parties. **Gender gap** refers to the fact that American women are more likely to identify with and vote for Democratic Party candidates than men, who are more likely to vote for Republican Party candidates (see Figure 5.5).

Racial and Ethnic Identity

American public opinion is also often divided on the basis of racial and ethnic identity. Members of American racial and ethnic minorities emphasize the importance of social justice and equality of opportunity more than

FIGURE 5.5

The Gender Gap in American Politics

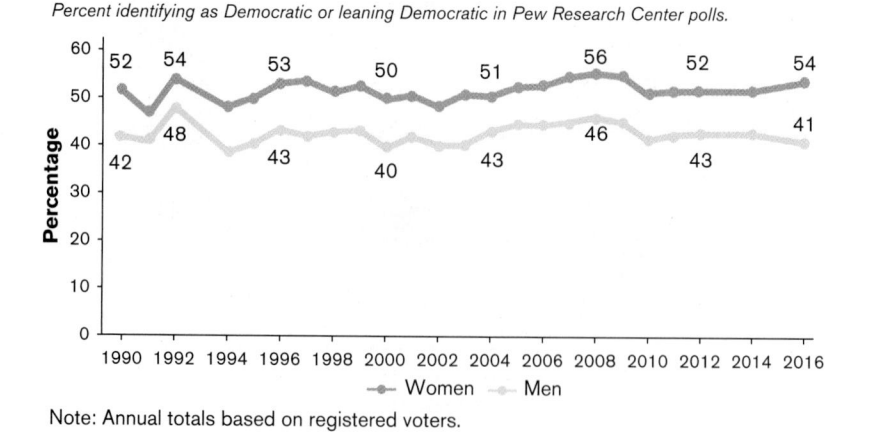

Percent identifying as Democratic or leaning Democratic in Pew Research Center polls.

Note: Annual totals based on registered voters.

Sources: Pew Research Center, "The Gender Gap: Three Decades Old, as Wide as Ever," March 29, 2012, www.people-press.org/2012/03/29/the-gender-gap-three-decades-old-as-wide-as-ever; Pew Research Center, "Party Identification Trends," 1992-2016, www.people-press.org/2016/09/13/party-identification-trends-1992-2016.

white Americans,[36] patterns that are correlated with the fact that racial and ethnic minorities are more likely to experience economic challenges and poverty.[37] In addition, scholars of race and gender in American politics have found evidence to support the notion of **linked fate**, in which individuals accept "the belief that [their own] life chances are inextricably tied to the group as a whole."[38] In the days following the shooting in Ferguson, public opinion surveys revealed sharp racial divisions on the event. African Americans overwhelmingly felt that Brown's shooting raised important racial issues and that the police response to the shooting was inappropriate or insufficient. They also expressed a lack of confidence in the subsequent investigations into the shooting (see Figure 5.6).[39]

To say that any community (as defined by the sum of their common experiences) would be united would be far too simplistic. Bernie Frazier, an African American speaker and career strategist from Ferguson, told the *New York Times*, "I've had moments where I feel violated by the protesters. To be honest, I feel violated by the media. I read a headline that said, 'Ferguson under siege.' I saw an article that described Ferguson as 'impoverished.' I've just stopped reading comments online. I'm done."[40]

FIGURE 5.6

Racial and Ethnic Divisions in Opinions of Authorities' Handling of the Ferguson Investigation

How much confidence in shooting investigations . . .

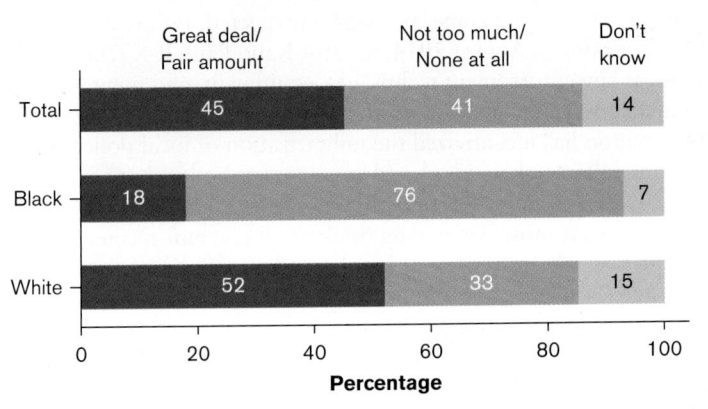

Percentage

Note: Survey conducted August 14–17, 2014. Whites and blacks include only those who are not Hispanic. Figures may not add to 100% because of rounding.

Source: Pew Research Center, "Stark Racial Divisions in Reactions to Ferguson Police Shooting," August 18, 2014, www.people-press.org/files/2014/08/8-18-14-Ferguson-Release.pdf.

Government and Media Influence Public Opinion

To many of the protesters in Ferguson, the treatment of young African American men by the American political and legal system had been a critical issue for a very long time. One of the many tasks of the president is to act as a "communicator in chief"—to focus attention on specific issues and events and to make sense of tragedies and challenges. In this role, President Barack Obama addressed the shooting of Brown in a speech at the White House, saying, "In too many communities around the country, a gulf of mistrust exists between local residents and law enforcement. . . . In too many communities, too many young men of color are left behind and seen only as objects of fear."[41]

Advancements in technology have also affected public opinion. In the next chapter, we will explore the ways that social media and online information are revolutionizing the role of the media in American political life. In the interconnected, live, and unfiltered world of social media, Ferguson made this point very clear. Following the death of Brown and the decision of the grand jury not to indict Wilson, social media lit up. According to the *Washington Post*, "'Black Twitter' . . . emerged as a powerful forum for activism and debate regarding Ferguson, helping sway public opinion by challenging racially biased interpretations of Brown's killing."[42]

Ferguson Gave Rise to Crosscutting Patterns of American Public Opinion

Much of American public opinion over the tragic events in Ferguson and the shootings of other unarmed African American men in the country was divided, whether along lines of racial and ethnic identity, gender, age, or partisan affiliation. However, there were some, perhaps unexpected, points of agreement. For example, speaking in August 2014, Senator Rand Paul, R-KY, criticized the changes in local law enforcement techniques, equipment, and mentality as surplus weapons from America's wars in the Middle East found their way back home: "Washington has incentivized the militarization of local police precincts by using federal dollars to help municipal governments build what are essentially small armies—where police departments compete to acquire military gear that goes far beyond what most Americans think of as law enforcement."[43] In his efforts to scale back the provision of surplus military equipment to local law enforcement agencies, Paul, a Republican, was joined by Representative Hank Johnson of Georgia, a Democrat.

Some surveys of American public opinion complicated the debate over police-community relations. A 2012 survey by the Pew Research Center concluded that 48 percent of Americans agreed with the following statement: "Guns do more to protect people than place them at risk." In a similar survey in December 2014, the number of Americans agreeing with that statement had increased to 57 percent. Most strikingly, "The shift [in agreement] was even more substantial among African-Americans, going from 29 percent in early 2013 to 54 percent [in 2014] (though with a margin of error of almost 10 percent due to small sample size)."[44] Critics of the poll, however, questioned the wording of the survey items, suggesting that the pollsters may have shaped their findings by the way in which they posed the questions. Reverend Kenn Blanchard, author of *Black Man with a Gun: Reloaded*, countered critiques of the Pew findings by claiming the emergence of "a generational shift in the black community, where all of the old heads say this [pro-gun] stuff is the devil [but] the new guys are, like, 'I don't think so.' . . . There's a racial divide, too, that the anti-gun people have been using to suggest that white people don't want black people to have firearms. But what I see are my white brothers, the old geezers, who are saying to the younger black generation, 'Here's a gun, I'll show you how to shoot it.'"[45] In spite of these crosscutting trends, many divisions remained. In a survey conducted in December 2014 following the grand jury decisions in the prosecutions of the police officers involved in the shooting deaths of Brown and Garner, analysts with the Pew Research Center found sharp divisions between white and African American respondents on their agreement with the assertion that race had played a factor in the grand juries' decisions not to charge the officers.[46]

WHAT HAVE I LEARNED?

1. Partisan polarization has decreased in Congress in recent decades.
   a. True
   b. False

2. The *gender gap* in American politics refers to the fact that _____.
   a. Republican Party voters outnumber Democratic Party voters
   b. The number of women representatives and senators has been decreasing in recent decades
   c. Women voters in American elections tend to support candidates from the Democratic Party in state and national elections
   d. Women voters in American elections tend to support candidates from the Republican Party in state and national elections

3. Contributors to the processes of political socialization include _____.
   a. Families
   b. Schools
   c. Lived experiences
   d. All of the above

4. When you reflect upon the events of Ferguson, what divisions in American public opinion do you observe? What might be some issues or perspectives not apparent from these divisions?

Answer Key: 1. b; 2. c; 3. d; 4. Answers will vary. Students might focus on ideas such as linked fate or differences in opinion about police-community relations.

FERGUSON AND THE EFFECTS OF PUBLIC OPINION ON DEMOCRATIC REPRESENTATION

Did Ferguson matter? Did the shooting, the protests following the shooting, and the national coverage of the controversy actually change the national conversation in a way that affected American public policy? In 2015, on the one-year anniversary of Michael Brown's death, the city of Ferguson was

- Evaluate the potential effects of focusing events on changes in public attitudes and policy in America.

once again witness to protest and then violence. New reports noted, "A peaceful day of protest and remembrance dissolved into chaos late Sunday after shots were fired and one person was hit by gunfire."[47] In that sense, the two Fergusons, the peaceful daytime and troubled nighttime Fergusons, had not changed in the year since Brown's tragic death.

Certain behaviors and attitudes *had* changed, however. For one, even though there was some violence at the protest, the police response was different. As reported by the *New York Times*, "No police officers in riot gear emerged Friday night when protesters arrived, a tactic that has drawn criticism. Rather, a small handful of officers calmly walked out and spoke with demonstrators. Many of the Ferguson police on the scene wore white polo shirts rather than their regular uniforms," an effort to deescalate potential tensions by projecting a less military-style profile.[48] Secondly, there was clear evidence that Black Lives Matter had registered their policy concerns on the national stage. Political leaders and candidates for the 2016 presidential election were paying attention to the protests. They began to talk about Ferguson and what it meant for the nation going forward. During the first Democratic Party presidential candidate debate in October 2015, one of the invited members of the public asked, "My question for the candidates is, do black lives matter, or do all lives matter?" Senator Bernie Sanders, I-VT, immediately replied, "Black lives matter," and the crowd applauded.[49] When pressed by a moderator, Maryland governor Martin O'Malley "expressed solidarity with the phrase."[50] Both Sanders and O'Malley had been confronted with public disruptions on the campaign trail challenging them to be more outspoken in their support for criminal justice reform.[51] Though moderator Anderson Cooper had changed the topic when he interacted with former secretary of state and former senator Hillary Clinton, she brought the conversation back to criminal justice reform, saying, "What we need to be doing is not only reforming criminal justice—I have talked about that at some length, including things like body cameras. . . . But I believe that the debate, and the discussion has to go further. . . . We need a New Deal for communities of color."[52] Following the debate, members of Black Lives Matter were encouraged by the attention and conversation but wanted more specifics about how each candidate would make the words a reality.

Members of Congress were paying attention as well. In January 2015, as reported by the *St. Louis Post-Dispatch*, "On the eve of the Martin Luther King holiday, leading black members of Congress squeezed into a packed Ferguson church to deliver a specific message: We've got your backs. . . . There, they vowed to push for criminal justice reform."[53] The article quoted Representative André Carson, D-IN, who said, "We're not here to tell you what to do . . . (but) just to let you know you've got some firepower in Washington, D.C. Ferguson is a clarion call. Ferguson is the new Selma."[54] In August the *St. Louis Post-Dispatch* reported that "prominent Ferguson protesters announced on Friday Campaign Zero, a policy platform to end killings by the police in the United States, and a website to help voters keep track of where political candidates stand on police brutality."[55] Political science professor Terry Jones, an expert on urban politics and policies interviewed for the article, said, "This is an effort to put some policy meat on the protest bones and say, 'We're not simply for or against that, but here's what our policies would look like.' . . . It's an appropriate evolutionary step.

Anyone who says 'I don't think the world is right as it is' should be prepared to answer the question, 'Well, what do you want to do about it?'"[56]

The question of whether individual opinions about police violence and equal rights for African Americans had shifted was a little more complex, however. On the one hand, polling did reveal an abrupt change in the patterns of opinions of both black and white responders, but it is not clear whether the events in Ferguson actually caused those changes or if there were other factors contributing to the shift. (See Telling Stories with Data: Change in American Public Opinion after Ferguson.)

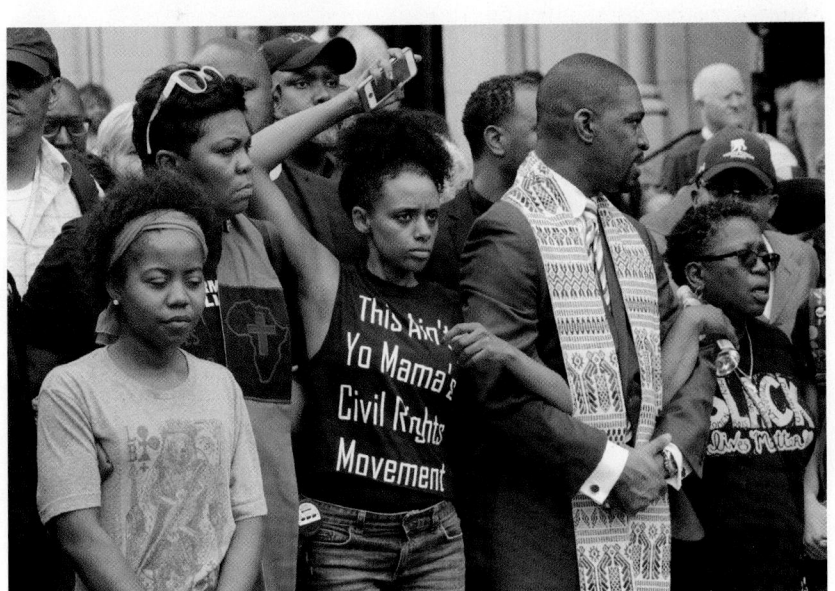

Protestors prepared to march in downtown St. Louis on August 10, 2015, to mark the one-year anniversary of Michael Brown's death. The police response to the march was markedly different from previous protests and was much more measured and low key. REUTERS/Rick Wilking

WHAT HAVE I LEARNED?

1. One year after the first protests in Ferguson, national political candidates were paying more attention to the treatment of African American men by law enforcement officials.

   a. True
   b. False

2. On the one-year anniversary of Michael Brown's death, Ferguson police responded to protests by _____.

   a. Banning further demonstrations
   b. Keeping a lower profile

   c. Trying to intimidate the crowd
   d. Refusing to keep order

3. On the one-year anniversary of Michael Brown's death, what appeared to have changed? What may not have changed?

4. What do the results of public opinion surveys tell us about these potential changes?

....

Answer Key: 1. a; 2. b; 3. Answers might emphasize the fact that the underlying issue had not gone away but that attitudes had changed and people now felt the need to pay more attention to the concerns raised by the protesters; 4. Answers should focus on an apparent break in trend, both in black and white opinion.

Change in American Public Opinion after Ferguson

In public opinion polls conducted by the Pew Research Center and the *Washington Post* in 2009, 2011, and March 2014, the percentage of Americans who agreed that the nation had "made the changes needed to give blacks equal rights with whites" did not

Divisions over the Need to Make Changes to Give Blacks Equal Rights

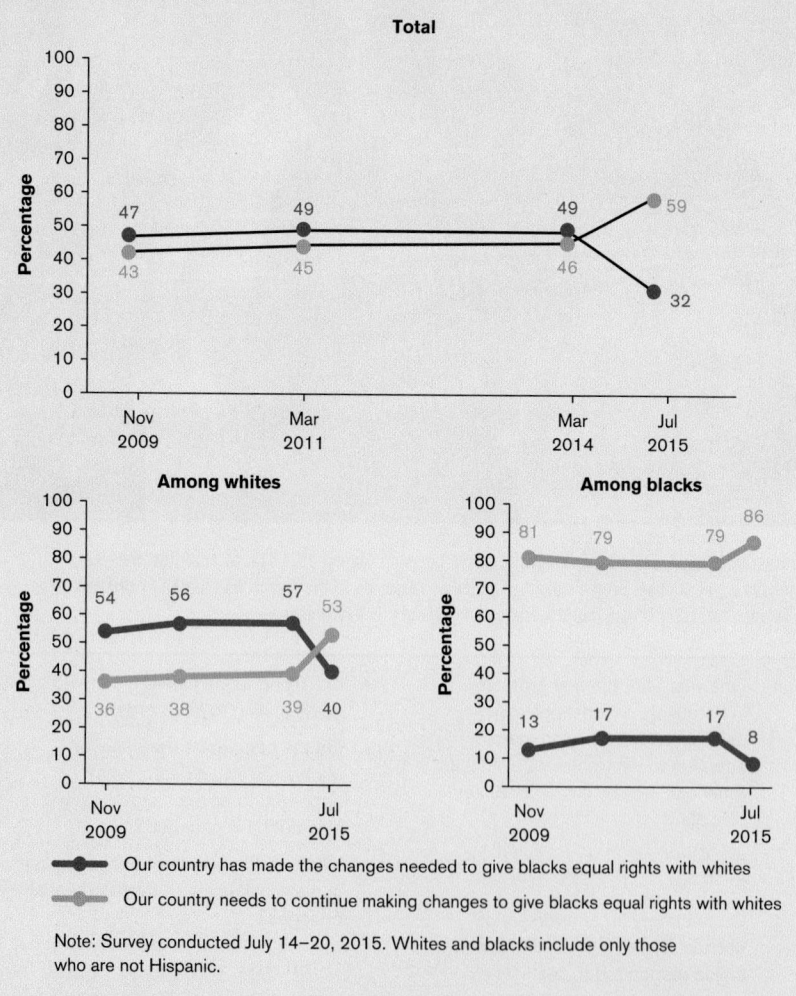

Our country has made the changes needed to give blacks equal rights with whites

Our country needs to continue making changes to give blacks equal rights with whites

Note: Survey conducted July 14–20, 2015. Whites and blacks include only those who are not Hispanic.

Source: Pew Research Center, "Across Racial Lines, More Say Nation Needs to Make Changes to Achieve Racial Equality," August 5, 2015, www.people-press.org/2015/08/05/across-racial-lines-more-say-nation-needs-to-make-changes-to-achieve-racial-equality.

change much. In each poll, roughly half of Americans overall expressed the opinion that the nation had made these changes. Individual attitudes, however, diverged sharply by racial identity. A majority of white Americans felt that the nation had made the necessary changes, but the vast majority of African American survey respondents felt that it had not.

By the late summer of 2015, however, something appeared to have changed.[57] Between the polls conducted in March 2014, six months before Brown's shooting, and July 2015, nearly a year after, there was what political scientists call a break in trend—and a sharp one at that. In the 2015 survey the percentages of Americans surveyed who felt that the nation had done enough to achieve equal rights had changed overall and for both groups of Americans.

However, when drawing conclusions about the causes of this change in public opinion—including if Ferguson caused this change—some caution is warranted. Other events between the 2014 and 2015 surveys may have contributed to the observed findings. A debate about the display of Confederate flags, for example, also made it onto the national political agenda during this time, as did more shootings and tragic events. We cannot, based on these data alone, confirm that Ferguson *caused* this change but only that there is a potentially meaningful *correlation* between the two. That said, this change in American public opinion, how quickly it happened, and how substantial it was are not things to be quickly dismissed.

WHAT DO YOU THINK?

Do these results lead you to conclude that the shooting deaths in Ferguson and other cities and the protests in response actually changed American public opinion? What other evidence might you want to make a firmer conclusion?

CONCLUSION
The Meanings of Public Opinion

Political scientist John Kingdon once asked, "But what makes an idea's time come?"[58] That is a very good question and one to which individuals must attend if they are trying to shape laws and policies to get their voices heard. In terms of public opinion, we might rephrase Professor Kingdon's question to this: But what makes *a change of public opinion's* time come? And, we might add, does it even matter if public opinion changes at all?

Reflecting upon Ferguson and other protests inspired by Black Lives Matter, one thing has changed, and that is the list of issues on the national political agenda. To that list has been added the treatment of African Americans, especially young African American men, by the American law enforcement system: "'I live in one of the poorest zip codes in Missouri,' said Ferguson protestor Tory Russell in a conference call with reporters . . . adding that fellow African-Americans in the area experience high rates of mortality and murder. 'I never heard any of my elected officials declare those things a state of emergency,' said Mr. Russell, who started the group Hands Up United after Mr. Brown's death to seek justice in Ferguson and beyond."[59] In this chapter, we have explored debates over the coherence and impact of what we call American public opinion by focusing on one tragic event. While the ultimate effects of the tragedy—as well as the protests and efforts at political mobilization that followed—are not yet certain, at the very least the nation's political conversation has been altered.

In October 2014, "Lesley McSpadden, Mr. Brown's mother, made one of her regular visits to the place where her son was killed. . . . She comes to the memorial all the time, she said, even though visits to the site of her son's death deepen her pain. . . . Gazing down at the memorial, Ms. McSpadden pondered the question of how long it should stay in place. 'Forever,' she said."[60]

CHAPTER REVIEW

This chapter's main ideas are reflected in the Learning Objectives. By reviewing them here you should be able to **remember** the key points and **know** these terms that are central to the topic.

5.1 Discuss differing theories about public opinion formation and expression and the degree to which it is meaningful.

REMEMBER . . .

- Public opinion is characterized as the aggregation of individual beliefs and attitudes.

- Representative democracy depends upon individuals having meaningful preferences on issues. Only when constituents are able to convey meaningful opinions can they be adequately represented by public officials.

- The minimalist paradigm emphasizes that most people pay minimal attention to issues and have minimal information about them. Additionally, the opinions that they *do* have are minimally stable; they change over time or in response to attempts to control or shape them.

- Other scholars emphasize the ways in which the public can still make sense of and transmit their opinions to their representatives, both collectively and individually. No single individual needs to have fully formed policy preferences and political views because when taken in the aggregate, public opinion is meaningful.

- Still others have emphasized the possibility for a public to be collectively rational even in the presence of individually inconsistent and shapeable opinions.

KNOW . . .

- *consideration*: a combination of cognition and affect that contributes to any one answer to any one question or evaluation (p. 150)

- *cues and information shortcuts*: pieces of information that individuals pick up that help them form political opinions (p. 150)

- *elites*: a small number of individuals (who tend to have well-informed and well-reasoned opinions) (p. 148)

- *masses*: the majority of individuals (who tend to be less well informed) (p. 148)

- *minimalist paradigm*: a theory of public opinion that emphasizes how most people fall short of what we expect them to know, think about, and pay attention to in the complicated world of politics and policy (p. 147)

- *nonattitudes*: a term referring to the lack of stable and coherent opinions on political issues and candidates (p. 148)

- *public opinion*: the sum of individual attitudes about government, policies, and issues (p. 143)

- *stereotype*: a preconceived, often oversimplified idea about something that people apply as a filter to the world (p. 147)

5.2 Describe the issues involved in transmitting and measuring American public opinion and constructing the instruments used to do so.

REMEMBER . . .

- Americans need to be able to communicate their preferences to government, and their representatives need mechanisms that allow them to learn what those preferences are.

- Individuals can communicate directly with representatives, but people who do so tend to represent subgroups with intense preferences rather than the constituency as a whole.

- Elections give representatives information about the public's views. But since not all eligible voters do vote, that information is imperfect.

- Sometimes elected officials solicit the public's views directly through mechanisms such as focus groups.

- Types of surveys include straw polls, SLOPs, and exit polls.

- In order to achieve random selection in polling, surveyors often reach individuals via telephone using random digit dialing.

- Even when people's opinions are well informed or when enough opinions are sampled to make them meaningful in aggregate, the instruments used to measure opinion can themselves be flawed, making survey results not meaningful.

- When poorly constructed or deliberately flawed, public opinion surveys can shape survey results and thus deliver misleading findings.

- In some cases, people are unwilling to admit a lack of information or opinion and so make up responses to survey questions.

- The way questions are ordered and worded can also affect survey results.

KNOW . . .

- *direction*: the focus of an individual's opinion (p. 155)

- *exit poll*: a survey conducted outside of a polling place in which individuals are asked who or what they just voted for and why (p. 154)

- *focus group*: a small group of individuals assembled for a directed conversation during which one hopes to uncover patterns of thinking about issues and individuals (p. 151)

- *intensity*: the strength of involvement and preference of an individual's opinion (p. 155)

- *public opinion surveys*: systematic attempts to make inferences about the opinions of large numbers of individuals by carefully sampling and asking questions of a small, randomly assigned sample of the larger population (p. 144)

- *push poll*: a negative campaign tactic disguised as a survey in which a candidate's opponent or opponents are portrayed in an unfavorable way (p. 156)

- *question order*: a concern in measuring public opinion having to do with how the sequencing of questions affects responses (p. 155)

- *question wording*: a concern in measuring public opinion having to do with how the way a question is phrased affects responses (p. 155)

- *race of interviewer effects*: the shaping of survey responses due to the racial identities of respondents and interviewers (p. 155)

- *random digit dialing*: when potential survey respondents are selected by computer-generated random numbers (p. 154)

- *random selection*: how participants are selected from the population for inclusion in the study (p. 152)

- *respondents*: individuals who answer a survey (p. 152)

- *salience*: the centrality of an individual's opinion in the sense of the opinion's ability to shape the individual's views on other issues or candidates (p. 155)

- *sample*: the subgroup of individuals from the larger population one wants to measure the opinions of (p. 152)

- *sampling error*: error in a statistical analysis arising from the unrepresentativeness of the sample taken (p. 153)

- *scientific poll*: when pollsters try to gain an understanding of a large group of individuals by obtaining the opinions of a carefully chosen small sample of the group, although they are aware of the limitations of the effort (p. 152)

- *self-selected listener opinion poll* (or *SLOP*): a survey in which respondents choose to respond to a survey prompt on their own (p. 153)

- *stability:* the degree of change over time, in different contexts, or in response to differently worded survey questions of a particular opinion (p. 155)

- *straw poll*: an unofficial tally of opinion or support at a meeting or event (p. 153)

- *weighting*: a procedure in which the observed results of a survey are adjusted according to what is known about specific proportions in the larger population (p. 152)

5.3 Examine the sources of individual political attitudes and preferences.

REMEMBER...

- Forming and changing political opinions and attitudes is a lifelong process. The process by which our experiences and other personal factors shape our attitudes toward political issues and public policies is called political socialization.

- There are many sources of political socialization.

- Families convey political attitudes and shape party identification.

- Schools deliver political information and values via civic education.

- People's personal life experiences, including focusing events, affect their views.

- Gender, race, and ethnic identity also affect people's attitudes.

- Political knowledge is predictably and unequally distributed. Younger Americans, women, lower-income Americans, and members of racial and ethnic minorities have consistently fared worse in their answers to factual political knowledge questions.

- How we identify politically as well as how we define ourselves in term of gender, race, or ethnicity can form clear, consistent, and persistent patterns of similarity and division in American public opinion.

- On some issues we see opinions that cut across identities.

KNOW...

- *civic education*: the transmission of information about the political world and civic norms to learners (p. 158)

- *gender gap*: a term that refers to the fact American women are more likely to identify with and vote for Democratic Party candidates than men, who are more likely to vote for Republican Party candidates (p. 162)

- *linked fate*: a theory of group identification that describes ways in which individuals tie their own life chances to those of a group (p. 163)

- *partisan polarization*: when an individual's stance on a given issue, policy, or person is more likely to be strictly defined by their identification with a particular political party (e.g., Democrat or Republican) or ideology (e.g., liberal or conservative) (p. 161)

- *party identification*: the degree to which an individual identifies with and supports a particular political party (p. 158)

- *political socialization*: the variety of experiences and factors that shape our political values, attitudes, and behaviors (p. 158)

5.4 Debate the power of individuals, events, and people's interpretations of events to make lasting change in American politics.

REMEMBER...

- Important events can shape public opinion.

- Individuals may filter their interpretation of these events through lenses such as partisan identification, gender, or racial or ethnic identity.

- How the media portray these events may also play a role in opinion formation and change.

KNOW...

- *conservatism*: a political ideology that focuses on limited government and emphasizes individual liberty (p. 159)

- *liberalism*: a political ideology that emphasizes a stronger role for government, especially in securing economic opportunities for Americans (p. 159)

- *libertarianism*: a political ideology that emphasizes minimal governmental involvement in peoples' economic and social lives (p. 160)

- *political ideology*: a person's beliefs about desired political goals and public policies that acts to shape peoples' political behavior (p. 159)

- *socialism*: a political ideology that emphasizes very robust governmental involvement in the economy, which may include governmental control over sectors of the economy (p. 160)

6 THE MEDIA
Truth, Power, and American Democracy

View 11 new Tweets

Ourmanintheeast · 4m

Donald J. Trump @realDonaldTrump · Now

Media reporting FAKE NEWS again. So unfair! Not nice!

RETWEETS   FAVORITES
1070   3839

1:44 PM · 27 Jan 2017 · Details

Group @TheProgressives · 4m
s a busy week! See our recap and find out what's on the agenda for next
in the S&D Times ➔socsde.ms/ZUF

edee Retweeted

elegraaf @telegraaf · 9m

ke Donald Trump tweets are shown in a Twitter
neline in February 2017. In China a site that
nerates fake tweets that look as if they were
nerated by U.S. president Donald Trump are
ing used to mock the president. Jaap Arriens/NurPhoto
Getty Images

TWEETS   FOL
34.4K

Tweets   T

Donald J. Trump ✓
@realDonaldTrump

45th President of the United States of
America

Washington, DC

Joined March 2009

Tweet to Donald J. Trump

58 Followers you know

1,940 Photos and videos

Donalc
Miami

Mian
Feari
Mayc

A mericans' political knowledge is sometimes learned directly through experiences like going to a school board meeting, talking with a political candidate, or attending a rally or protest. More often, however, it is mediated, filtered through the news outlets that inform us of political issues. Collectively, this group of news providers is called the **news media,** a broad term that includes newspapers, magazines, radio, television, Internet sources, blogs, and social media postings, all in service of informing or persuading. The word *media* is plural as it refers to a universe of venues and outlets. As we will explore, the way those news sources are produced, who their audiences are, and what technological capabilities they possess all shape the presentation, reception, effect, and even the definition of the news itself.

The American news media is in a period of radical flux. Technology-driven change, partisan politics, ownership, trustworthiness, bias, and objectivity are front and center in debates about the current, or proper, role of the American news media in our political lives. Americans are simultaneously witnessing a major decline in daily newspaper readership, the rise of social media, and increasingly divisive language in political talk shows. What do these changes in the media landscape mean for political representation and participation in the twenty-first century?

We will explore that question and others through the prism of two stories: the controversy surrounding media coverage of accusations of Russian involvement in the presidential election of 2016 and a fake radiobroadcasted invasion from Mars in 1938. Why these two stories, separated by nearly 80 years? Because they are united by two enduring questions: How effective are the news media in shaping Americans' views? Can we trust our news media sources? These are not separate questions, in fact. At their core, both point directly to Americans' role not only as receivers of the news media but as shapers of the media that they choose as their sources. This issue returns us to questions raised in our study of public opinion: How shapeable are Americans' attitudes and preferences? Are we filing cabinets with a set of predetermined and firm attitudes and opinions? Or are we pieces of clay, vulnerable to outside forces to shape as they see fit? If there was a proper test of these questions, 2017 provided it. The answers, though, are still unsettled.

LEARNING OBJECTIVES

By reading this chapter, you will be able to do the following:

6.1 Trace the historical development of the American news media.

6.2 Understand the issue of bias in the American media.

6.3 Discuss changes in the regulation of media ownership and media content.

6.4 Explain the different perspectives on the power of the media to shape political understanding and behaviors.

A FOREIGN GOVERNMENT'S EFFORTS TO INFLUENCE AN ELECTION THROUGH THE MEDIA RAISES QUESTIONS ABOUT THE MEDIA'S POWER

"Weaponized information."[1]

These were the words that Hillary Clinton used to describe what she thought contributed to her loss to Republican Donald Trump in the 2016 presidential election. Interviewed before a live audience at a May 2017 conference, Clinton and her interviewers talked about how domestic or foreign political actors might use the media, especially social media, to influence or undermine a political candidate. They returned time and again to the idea that under certain conditions news stories could be made powerful enough to become political weapons—vastly more destructive than in earlier campaign cycles.

The specific weapons Clinton was talking about were the release late in the campaign of a series of e-mails, without authorization and allegedly stolen, from the Democratic National Committee (DNC). Some of the most incendiary e-mails involved alleged exchanges between Clinton campaign chairman, John Podesta; his aides; Clinton family members; and influential donors. In those unflattering e-mails, Podesta and others talked about the perception of Secretary Clinton's close ties to Wall Street, reactions to the controversy surrounding Clinton's private e-mail server as secretary (which would later come under Federal Bureau of Investigation [FBI] review without charges), and plans to attack the policy positions and record of Senator Bernie Sanders, the other remaining Democratic nominee.

It is common for the staff involved in such a high-stakes political campaign to think of every angle, plan for every possibility. That is what they are hired to do. However, Hillary Clinton believed that the steady leak of those e-mails through the website WikiLeaks may have helped to shape the narrative of her presidential campaign and damage her political image.

Many speculated about who was behind the leaked e-mails and the news stories they generated. Clinton pointed directly to the Russian government, saying, "If you look at Facebook, the vast majority of the news items posted were fake. They were connected to, as we now know, the 1,000 Russian agents who were involved in delivering these messages."[2] Secretary Clinton noted, "I take responsibility for every decision I made, but that's not why I lost. So I think it's important that we learn the real lessons from this last campaign because the forces that we are up against are not just interested in influencing our election and our politics, they're going after our economy and they're going after our unity as a nation."[3]

Indeed, a January 2017 intelligence community assessment involving members of the Central Intelligence Agency (CIA), the FBI, and the National Security Agency (NSA) concluded that, "Russian President Vladimir Putin ordered an influence campaign in 2016 aimed at the US presidential election. Russia's goals were to undermine public faith in the US democratic process, denigrate Secretary Clinton, and harm her electability and potential presidency."[4]

Not everyone agreed, most especially President Donald Trump, who challenged the certainty of these conclusions. In a tweet from January 2016, President Trump asserted, "Julian Assange [the founder of WikiLeaks] said 'a 14 year old could have hacked Podesta' why was DNC so careless? Also said Russians did not give him the info!"[5] The presidential election of 2016 was a very close one, decided by perhaps 80,000 votes in a few key battleground states, so the idea that Russia might have used the American media to tip the election was not a welcome one and potentially undermining for a new administration. It should be noted, too, that Clinton was not the only candidate facing negative press. Candidate Trump was hardly the darling of most mainstream newspaper and television outlets and faced plenty of negative coverage of his own: "He was subject to not just relentless partisan attacks but also to overwhelmingly negative media coverage, much of it due to his own endless gaffes and scandals."[6]

Donald J. Trump ✓
@realDonaldTrump

Follow

Julian Assange said "a 14 year old could have hacked Podesta" - why was DNC so careless? Also said Russians did not give him the info!

4:22 AM - 4 Jan 2017

18,139 Retweets 61,121 Likes

💬 12K ↻ 18K ♡ 61K

President Donald J. Trump/Twitter

Investigations and debates into the source of the e-mail hacking are ongoing, and legislators, lawyers, and historians will ultimately draw their final conclusions. Our focus in this chapter, however, is not on the intent of Russian agents but more broadly on the capability of media in general: Do the media really have the power to determine the outcome of an event as important as the election of 2016?

That question speaks very much to how fair and just media sources are in their coverage and the power they wield as organizations. But it also speaks to Americans' potential vulnerability to the media's power, especially in the era of new media. As a first step in our investigation of those questions, it is useful to study the development of the American media; we will learn that the role of the American media in politics is the one story that is not really new.

Truth, trust, and power. These are the issues with which consumers of the American news media have always had to contend. Technology may have changed the medium, but the same questions endure.

THE EVOLUTION OF AMERICAN MEDIA SHOWS THAT ISSUES OF POWER AND TRUSTWORTHINESS ARE NOT NEW

The news media have played an important role in shaping American political culture and Americans' attitudes toward their political leaders and institutions from before the country's founding to today. Throughout this history, the connection between the nation's media and American politics has also been shaped in important ways by technological change, politics, and the tension between the rights of a free press and other demands, especially the desire to preserve national security.

- Explain how the news media have evolved over time and the impact those changes have had on the nature of the news, how it is produced, and how it is consumed.

Early Newspapers and Pamphlets Shaped a New Nation

The pamphlet, a loosely stitched booklet made on a hand-cranked printing press, was the first type of media to shape American attitudes, mobilizing support for the cause of independence from Great Britain. While printing had become cheaper and more widespread in the years leading up to the Revolutionary War, publishing was far from easy. The British colonial administration recognized the pamphlet for what it was, a potentially powerful and revolutionary tool. According to Patrick Novotny, the British seized some printer's presses, "while still others hid their presses or fled their homes with their families, taking their presses with them. Others closed their shops before the British could."[7]

The number of weekly and then daily newspapers grew in the years following the Revolutionary War, and the newspaper took its place as the primary source for information about American politics. First published in 1783, the *Pennsylvania Evening Post, and Daily Advertiser* was the nation's first daily newspaper; its young salesmen were instructed to shout out to passersby, "All the news for two coppers."[8] Like the pamphlets, early newspapers were a form of the print media. Like the pamphlets as well, early newspapers were hand printed, one sheet at a time, which made them expensive and restricted their access, even to those who could read them.

Four years later, the nation's second daily newspaper, the *Pennsylvania Packet, and Daily Advertiser*, published just blocks away from where the *Evening Post* had started out, was the first to print the full text of the proposed Constitution of the United States. The delegates to the Constitutional Convention had been very careful to prevent any leaks during the proceedings, thus starving the weeklies and dailies of raw materials for their stories. With the publication of the proposed Constitution, which spurred a flood of editorials for and against the document, newspapers took their place at the center of American political life in the late 1780s.

Freedom of the Press Became Enshrined in the Constitution through the Bill of Rights

With memories of British colonial suppression of freedoms of speech and of the press fresh in their minds, the delegates to the Constitutional Convention were well aware of the need to preserve and protect these freedoms. On August 20, 1787, Charles Pinckney from South Carolina proposed the inclusion of the guarantee, "The liberty of the Press shall be inviolably preserved."[9] While a guarantee of freedom of the press did not end up in the original Constitution, Pinckney's proposal signalled support for including specific rights and liberties in a constituting document. As the ratification debates began, the argument to include such a list—a Bill of Rights—became one of the most convincing arguments that the Anti-Federalists presented.

While the Bill of Rights was not part of the original document, a promise to introduce a set of amendments during the session of Congress in 1789 proved crucial to securing the ratification of the Constitution. Included in the first of the ten ratified amendments was language very close to Pinckney's initial proposal: "Congress shall make no law. . .abridging the freedom of speech, or of the press." This provided the foundation for press freedoms.

The press also played a pivotal role in the ratification debates themselves, as proponents and opponents of the document made their cases through the nation's newspapers, often writing under pseudonyms. *The Federalist Papers*, the classic statement of the theory behind the Constitution, authored by Alexander Hamilton, James Madison, and John Jay, first appeared as a series of essays written under the pseudonym "Publius" in the New York newspapers. For their part, the Anti-Federalists produced essays warning of the dangers to liberty presented by the proposed Constitution.

The Media Go "Mass" with the Penny Presses in the Eighteenth and Nineteenth Centuries

A newsboy carrying inexpensive newspapers called penny press runs along a train platform selling papers to passengers. As the cost of printing decreased with technological advances in the process, the price of newspapers also decreased, and readership dramatically increased. World History Archive / Alamy Stock Photo

In the late eighteenth and early nineteenth century, however, the dailies and weeklies reached only a relatively small part of the population, in no small part due to the fact that they were expensive and often available only through an annual subscription, which required putting down a large sum of money all at once rather than for each issue. Political and financial elites were the main consumers, not the mass public. Much of the space in newspapers was taken up by advertisements, and the stories' content was often overtly political, a fact that was hardly hidden or a point of controversy. Political parties and candidates often supported the presses financially in addition to providing them with essays, stories, and content.[10] By taking political positions and supporting candidates and parties, these papers were acting as a **partisan press**. The nation's first political parties were backed by a partisan press. James Madison and Thomas Jefferson supported the founding of the

National Gazette in 1791 in response to the partisan coverage presented by the Federalist *Gazette of the United States.*

As the cost to produce and, therefore, buy a newspaper fell during the 1830s, readership grew rapidly. The **penny press**, so labeled because an individual paper cost one penny, could be purchased on the street from newsboys hawking their products. Within just a few months of its introduction as the nation's first penny press, the *New York Sun* was the city's top-selling paper; by 1834 the *Sun* "was selling 15,000 copies a day."[11] The penny press was truly an example of the **mass media**—sources of information and entertainment (including newspapers, television and radio broadcasts, and Internet content) designed to reach large audiences.

Their content was sometimes overtly political; however, the penny papers depended far less on political parties for funding or support. They had a new boss: the public. Instead of relying on parties, candidates, or politicians for their content, the penny papers had to make their own. To do so, they hired reporters to dig up the kind of stories that would lure readers and advertisers. Newspapers depended on sales and on providing an audience for the advertisers, so they often focused on dramatic stories, of crime, riots, and scandalous behaviour.[12] **Yellow journalism**, the use of sensational headlines, cartoons and graphics, and emotional language, had a very commercial reason behind its emergence. It worked, boosting sales and profits.

Sensationalism was not confined only to stories of crime, misdeeds, and moral failures. In skilled hands, bold headlines, enticing leads, and emotional language could also be put to political purposes. William Randolph Hearst, publisher of the *New York Journal*, harnessed yellow journalism to advocate for war with Spain in the late 1890s. While the Spanish American War had many causes, Hearst's efforts helped to shape public opinion about the prospect for war. This example of the potential power of the press to influence public opinion raised the specter of a malleable American public at the mercy of presses and publishers with their own political agendas.

Journalists Became Investigators and Activists in the Nineteenth Century

A faster and cheaper printing press was not the only technological development that shaped the newspaper in the nineteenth century. The telegraph allowed news to travel instantaneously over distances that might have taken days or weeks otherwise. The papers benefited tremendously from the technology and helped to finance and spread it. In 1846, New York newspapers combined their efforts to fund a pony express route to more quickly deliver news of the Mexican War, thus creating the Associated Press.[13] Though the technology that they were originally funding ran on four legs, the Associated Press took advantage of the telegraph to create a **wire service**, an organization that gathers the news and offers it for sale to other media outlets. The nineteenth century also witnessed a new approach to news coverage, **investigative journalism**, in which journalists actively dug up and dug into stories rather than simply conveying the speeches and opinions of political leaders. During the Progressive Era, an important group of investigative reporters became known as *muckrakers*; the name was a reference to a tool used to collect manure. Muckrakers used their investigative tactics to bring to light corruption and scandal and also to shape public opinion in support of business or governmental reforms.[14]

The Twentieth Century Brought Radio and TV News Directly into Americans' Homes

Technological advances during the twentieth century brought political figures into Americans' lives and homes in a direct way, first providing their voices with the advent and widespread adoption of radio and then adding their faces and actions with television. Radio and television, which are examples of **broadcast media**, offered political news to citizens directly and immediately. Its consumption was often a shared experience, with only one radio or television set in the home or in the neighborhood, and the news could be consumed while doing other things, such as driving, doing chores, working, or eating a meal. These forms of media were also truly mass in the sense of a shared media experience by their consumers. In breaking down geographic barriers, the broadcast media were truly national in scope.

As an instrument of conveying political news, radio really came into its own in the 1930s, and no public official was more adept in its use than President Franklin Delano Roosevelt. Beginning in March 1933, Roosevelt began broadcasting speeches to the American public; these speeches became known as "fireside chats," a term coined by a bureau chief with CBS News, even though there was no fireplace.[15] The broadcasts were designed to calm anxious Americans during the depths of the Great Depression; present Roosevelt's Depression-fighting policies; and, later, guide citizens through the travails of World War II.

President Franklin Delano Roosevelt at a fireside chat in 1936. Roosevelt's broadcasts to the nation during times of crisis helped calm a worried population and enabled him to successfully pitch his policies.
Courtesy of the Library of Congress, Prints and Photographs Division

Today, the nation's radios crackle with political commentary of the views of the other side of the debate. Many of these shows lean Republican, such as *The Rush Limbaugh Show*, but there are liberal examples as well. These talk radio broadcasts have been criticized for their efforts to "provoke emotional responses (e.g., anger, fear, moral indignation) from the audience through the use of overgeneralizations, sensationalism, misleading or patently inaccurate information, ad hominem attacks, and belittling ridicule of opponents."[16]

If the 1930s signaled the emergence of radio as a powerful new force in political news, the late 1950s did the same for television. Television's version of Roosevelt was also a president: John F. Kennedy. Even though most American homes had a television by the 1950s (see Figure 6.1 in the next section), newspapers remained the primary source of news and coverage of political events. In September 1960, candidates Kennedy and Richard Nixon participated in the first of a series of the first televised presidential debates in American history. While experts and radio listeners did not declare a clear winner, Kennedy's image on television came across as robust and energetic, while Nixon, who had been fighting the flu, appeared pallid and sweaty. In 1961 Kennedy, having won the presidency, gave the first live televised news conference.

As television news broadcasts lengthened and more and more Americans relied upon the major networks for their news and coverage of political events, television news anchors became trusted figures in relaying, describing, and interpreting these events. As the Vietnam War progressed, American casualties mounted, and protests against American involvement spread and grew, trusted television journalist Walter Cronkite questioned if the war had become unwinnable. It was widely reported that President Lyndon Johnson observed, "If I've lost Cronkite, I've lost Middle America."[17] Though this response may be apocryphal, the idea that a trusted news anchor could so strongly affect American public opinion in an area as vital as foreign policy speaks to the power that many attributed to television news anchors during the heyday of network news.

The 1990s witnessed the rise of a new outlet for television and television news, and, oddly enough, its emergence as a major player came about during wartime. First broadcasting in 1980, CNN, the Cable News Network, presented Americans with twenty-four-hour coverage of the news. CNN's coverage of the Persian Gulf War, however, placed it squarely on the news media map. In 1991 CNN broadcast video coverage of the bombing of Baghdad by American and coalition forces during the Persian Gulf War live, in real-time, and unconstrained by a set news broadcast schedule typically employed by the major broadcast networks.

The American political news media had broken the clock. They had gone 24/7, and America tuned in. Later that decade, in 1996 Australian media entrepreneur Rupert Murdoch launched Fox News, which provided a self-consciously conservative interpretation of the nation's news and political events. Americans who felt that network news coverage was too liberal tuned in.

Cable television news changed more than just the schedule of coverage; it changed the form itself. Operating under looser regulatory constraints than the broadcast networks and in a time when those constraints were being relaxed (see next section), television news became more avowedly partisan, less "objective." To some, this overt partisanship seemed like a new and dangerous thing. In fact, it was not new—questions of the objectivity of network news had long been a common source of commentary and conversation. Cable television news coverage became more like what newspapers had been during much of the nation's history: unapologetically partisan.

New Media Have Reinvented the Media Landscape

Developed and deployed though a collaboration between the Defense Advanced Research Projects Agency (DARPA) and research universities, the

Internet revolutionized the media landscape in the late twentieth and early twenty-first centuries. The adoption of broadband reception, the Internet, and other communications technologies enabled Americans to receive and send text, sound, and video at increasingly fast speed and in increasingly large volume. Broadband and wireless technology has followed an accelerating pattern of adoption of new technologies not entirely different from that of radio and television (see Figure 6.1).

These new forms of media communication have revolutionized far more than the speed of delivery, or even the content, of political news available to consumers of the news and politics. In the era of 24/7 news coverage and the merging of entertainment and social media, individuals can be journalists, citizens can be editors and commentators, and members of the media can be and are often pressured to be celebrities. Throughout much of the nation's history, most Americans had a limited number of choices in their news media outlets—generally, one or two daily newspapers, several radio stations, and a few major television broadcast networks. The rise of cable television expanded the number of options, then the Internet increased these options even further.

The rise of **social media** put these trends into hyperdrive. However, the story was not only about the rise of *new* media outlets but also about the need for *old* media outlets, such as broadcast television, to stay relevant. One strategy was to create a greater presence of traditional network broadcast journalists in other venues and highlight their visibility, even celebrity, in order to reach larger audiences in an age of intense competition.

FIGURE 6.1

Patterns of Adoption of Communications Technologies

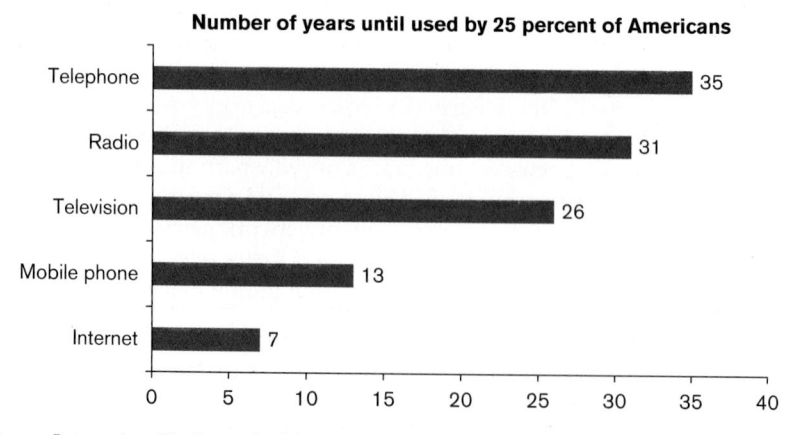

Number of years until used by 25 percent of Americans

Technology	Years
Telephone	35
Radio	31
Television	26
Mobile phone	13
Internet	7

Source: Data are from *The Economist*, "Happy Birthday, World Wide Web," March 12, 2014, www.economist.com/blogs/graphicdetail/2014/03/daily-chart-7?%3Ffsrc%3Dscn%2F=tw%2Fdc.

Much of the news content transmitted through social media is generated in traditional ways—previously produced stories, videos, and commentaries linked to on Facebook, posted on YouTube, or tweeted to members of one's social network. Other content, however, is generated by **citizen journalists**, nonprofessionals who cover events, say, through filming them on their cell phones or by providing their own commentaries and analysis. The Internet and modern communications technologies did not create the idea of citizen journalism, but they did provide the ability to capture, report on, and transmit citizen-generated news content more quickly and cheaply than has ever been possible. While citizen journalists operate in a variety of contexts, one of the most extreme is combat and military operations abroad. Some scholars of the news media point to the benefits of its democratization, but others worry about the fact that citizen journalists lack the ability to fact-check that large news organizations possess.

The term *new media* is used to refer to all of the various digital platforms through which individuals receive, share, and produce content. In one sense the new media are examples of mass media. They often reach large audiences and in many cases do so with startling speed. In another sense, however, there are also aspects to the new media that are very old. They often do not have mass appeal but cater to a group of individuals with shared perspectives, similar to many cable news channels but even more so. They shatter geographic boundaries, like the mass media, but create their own form of fragmentation, providing an

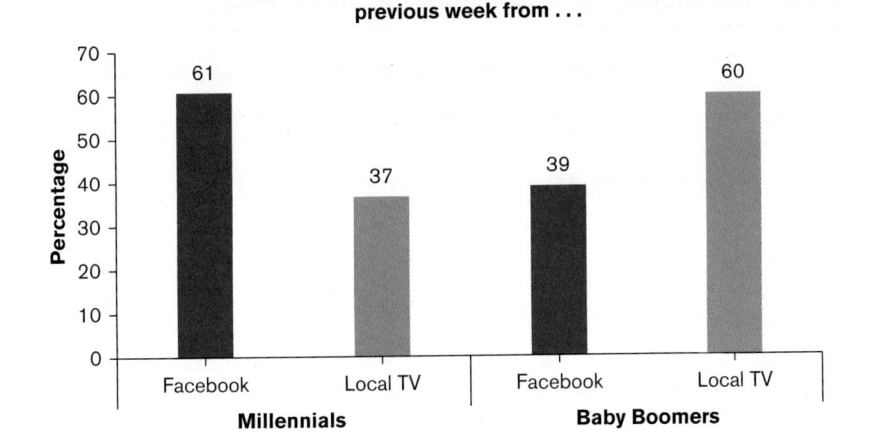

FIGURE 6.2

Generational Differences in Primary Sources for Political News

Percentage who got news about politics and government in the previous week from . . .

Source: Amy Mitchell, Jeffrey Gottfried, and Katrina Eva Matsa, "Millennials and Political News: Social Media—the Local TV for the Next Generation?," Pew Research Center, June 1, 2015, www.journalism.org/2015/06/01/millennials-political-news.

opportunity for individuals to self-select into narrow political and informational enclaves. This type of journalism is known as **niche journalism**.

One of the most important developments in the Internet age has been the rise of social media outlets, such as Facebook and Twitter. These interactive media environments allow individuals to create or share text, image, and video as well as comment on the content and forward it to other members of their own personal networks. We have already discussed the effects of new technologies in supporting citizen journalism and addressed concerns about the ability to verify such reports for accuracy. For politicians, however, there is another concern. As they are often acting and speaking amidst a sea of cell phone cameras, they must always be aware that any spontaneous, off-the-cuff remarks might find their way onto YouTube or Facebook within minutes. While the use of social media as the primary source of political news has grown tremendously in recent years, these trends are very much divided by generational differences (see Figure 6.2). Skillful political actors can take advantage of the power of social media in order to advance their own goals and policy objectives. Enter President Donald Trump.

WHAT HAVE I LEARNED?

1. The attempts of media providers to persuade Americans of a particular political point of view is a relatively new phenomenon.

   a. True
   b. False

2. The penny press was important because _____.

   a. It gave equal time to all political viewpoints
   b. It focused only on economic issues, hence the word *penny*
   c. It was financed primarily by political parties

   d. It brought the news to a much larger audience

3. In what ways did radio and television change Americans' reception of the news?

4. How have the new media changed coverage of political news?

Answer Key: 1. b; 2. d; 3. Answers might include a discussion of the role that these media played in standardizing coverage and bringing it directly into Americans' homes; 4. Answers might include the speed and immediacy of coverage but also the pressure new media has put upon broadcast media outlets to compete and survive in the new media landscape.

QUESTIONS OF BIAS CHALLENGE AMERICANS' TRUST IN THE MEDIA'S OBJECTIVITY

- Understand the issue of bias in American media

In 2017, President Donald Trump declared war. It was not on Russia but on the media covering the story about his administration's alleged ties with that nation—CNN in particular. In a series of tweets that escalated to the boiling point that summer, the President accused CNN, MSNBC, the *New York Times*, and other mainstream media outlets of broadcasting "fake news" with the goal of undermining his presidency.

In February, President Trump took on the *New York Times* and the rest of the mainstream American media directly, using his Twitter account.

The president's accusation was based upon the allegations that the *New York Times* had run an inaccurate and poorly sourced story about his ties to the Russian government.[18]

The term *fake news* is thrown about frequently today, but what does it really mean? To some, it means the intentional use of the media to support a political party, something that would have been hardly surprising to editors of nineteenth-century newspapers. To others, it means the intentional presentation of material that the news agency knows to be untrue or, at least, unverified. To others, it means the intentional use of the mass media to change political outcomes to intentionally deceive the public. In reality, it can be all of these. The challenge for consumers of the American media is to determine fact from fiction. It is not an easy task, especially in a new media environment so politically charged and one that moves at warp speed.

In June 2017, Project Veritas released what they claimed was undercover footage from an interview with a supervising producer of CNN. In it the producer allegedly claimed that the 24/7 coverage of President Trump's possible ties with Russia were all about ratings: "Trump is good for business right now."[19] Asked if the Russia story was "bullsh*t," the producer was recorded as saying, "Could be bullsh*t. I mean it's mostly bullsh*t. Like we don't have any big giant proof."[20] In another video, widely watched CNN political commentator Van Jones was recorded as saying, "The Russia thing is just a big nothing burger."[21] Later that month, three journalists resigned from CNN "after the cable news network was forced to retract and apologize for a story on its website involving a close ally of President Trump."[22]

For its part, CNN countered that Sean Spicer, President Trump's press secretary at the time, misrepresented the story. Jake Tapper from CNN reinforced the conclusions of members of the intelligence community that asserted Russian influence in the 2016 elections.[23] In the end, however, all of it—President Trump's tweets and CNN's round-the-clock coverage of the controversy—was, in spite of their starkly partisan differences, driven by the same objective: attracting an audience. In the twenty-first century, according to the fictitious character Rachel Barry in Fox's show, *Glee*, "Fame is the most important thing in our culture now." The war of words, messages, and of images in the service of attracting an audience dominate.

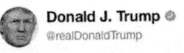

Donald J. Trump @realDonaldTrump

Follow

After being forced to apologize for its bad and inaccurate coverage of me after winning the election, the FAKE NEWS @nytimes is still lost!

5:39 AM - 4 Feb 2017

17,437 Retweets 102,728 Likes

25K 17K 103K

President Donald J. Trump/Twitter

The News Can Function as Entertainment

Commercial demands upon mainstream news providers have changed the approach with which many network executives treat not just their anchors and reporters but the news divisions themselves. According to one communications scholar, "Once upon a time, news was a money loser, but was kept separate from the other divisions of the networks so that the journalists in their employ could operate without much attention to the bottom line. No more."[24] In the run-up to the election of 2016 and in its aftermath, the cable channels CNN, Fox News, and MSNBC saw substantial increases in viewership as audiences became glued to coverage of the debates and the developments in the early months of the Trump administration.

The pressure of attracting an audience in a marketplace with so many easily accessible alternatives has led many news outlets to focus on **infotainment**, a merging of information and entertainment in a way designed to attract viewers and gain market share. This dynamic includes pressures to provide **soft news**—stories that focus on celebrities, personalities, and entertaining events rather than on events of local, national, or international political or economic significance.

Scholars continue to debate the effects of soft news on Americans' political knowledge and understanding. Candidate appearances on talk shows might engage viewers who otherwise would not have been exposed to their candidacy or the campaign in general,[25] an engagement that can increase the likelihood that voters will select candidates that more closely resemble citizens' political preferences.[26]

Soft news can act to engage individuals with foreign policy issues.[27] On the other hand, scholars have found that viewership of political comedy shows such as *The Daily Show with Trevor Noah* may decrease individuals' support for and engagement with political institutions, exposing them to political issues but increasing cynicism in the process.[28] There are also concerns that soft news may decrease the amount of knowledge about public affairs—knowledge that is necessary for effective democratic governance.[29]

Bias and the Perception of Bias Is a Problem in Media Coverage

A perennial critique of the American news media is that it is biased. Typically, the charge, especially against the nation's largest newspapers and mainstream television news outlets, is that a **partisan bias** is demonstrated and a liberal one at that. Many studies and critiques of journalists have focused on the fact that a majority of them self-identify as liberal.[30] So are the media politically biased? This is actually a very complicated question.[31] Journalists are more likely to self-identify as liberal than members of the general population, but they also tend to have higher levels of educational attainment, which may contribute to these patterns. However, journalists also operate under norms and professional expectations that reward objectivity. Finally, the perception that the media are politically biased might itself be partly shaped by certain media outlets that run stories on the "biased media," thereby encouraging their readers, listeners, or viewers to believe a bias exists.[32] Perhaps unsurprisingly, an individual's view on whether or not the news media are politically biased breaks down differently depending upon that person's own political viewpoints. The percentages of Americans who feel that there is a "great deal" of political bias in the news have risen recently (see Figure 6.3).

FIGURE 6.3

Do Americans Think the News Media Are Biased?

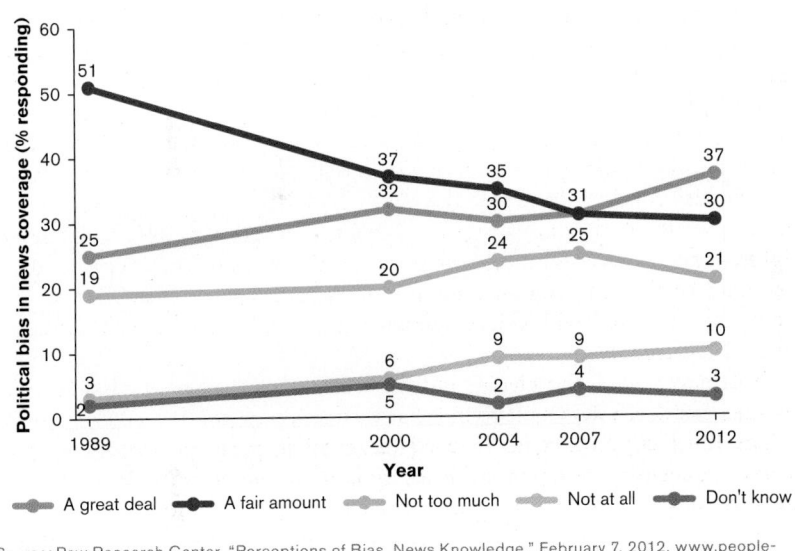

Source: Pew Research Center, "Perceptions of Bias, News Knowledge," February 7, 2012, www.people-press.org/2012/02/07/section-3-perceptions-of-bias-news-knowledge/?src=prc-number.

Concerns about bias in the media has been accompanied by a lack of trust in the news sources. Confidence in television news, in particular, has fallen dramatically (see Figure 6.4).

To the reader of a penny press publication in the nineteenth century, the idea that a particular news outlet pursued a partisan agenda would probably not have been all that surprising; it was an accepted part of the format. Factors other than the political orientation of the journalists, editors, or publishers of a specific media outlet may also shape coverage in important ways. Most mainstream news outlets employ the **beat system** in which reporters are assigned to specific types of news, policies, and events. From the point of efficiency and expertise, the beat system makes a lot of sense. Journalists can be more informed reporters if they become familiar with the lay of the land in a specific area. The worry is that certain beats are either not covered or not covered in much detail. The president, the Department of Defense, and the State Department, for example, receive much attention under this system; the Department of Transportation, not so much.

When thinking about bias in news coverage, one cannot ignore one of the most important potential sources of the problem: us. The news media—even

FIGURE 6.4

The Decline in Confidence in Television News

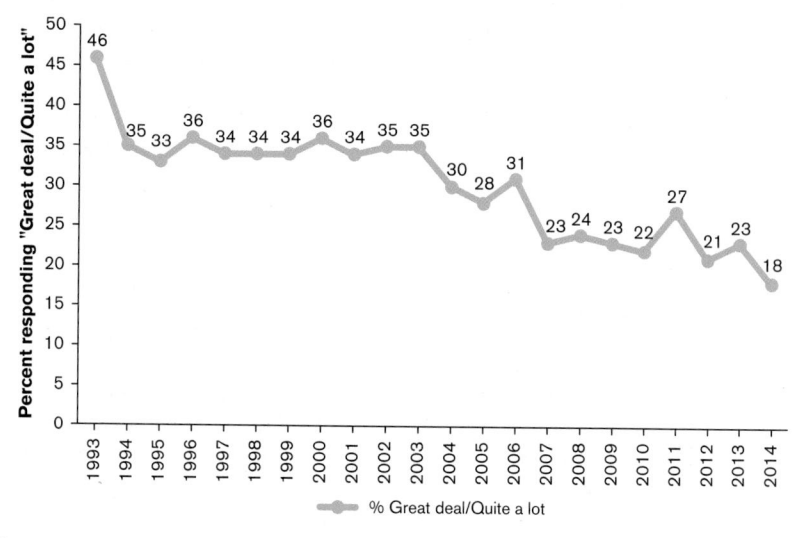

The percentage of Americans expressing a "great deal" or "quite a lot" of confidence in television news has declined dramatically over the past twenty years.

Source: Frank Newport, "Brian Williams Situation Plays Out in Context of Already Low Trust in Mass Media," Gallup, February 11, 2015, www.gallup.com/opinion/polling-matters/181544/brian-williams-situation-plays-context-already-low-trust-mass-media.aspx?g_source=trust%20media&g_medium=search&g_campaign=tiles.

outlets that are operated as nonprofit entities—need to attract an audience. They need us to consume their products, and they may shape their coverage accordingly. This creates the possibility of **commercial bias** in which some news outlets might pursue inflammatory, sensational coverage to secure their niche of the marketplace, while others might choose to play it safe for fear of upsetting their audience.

Commercial bias may shape not just *how* stories are covered but also *which* stories are covered. Stories, for example, about government regulation or public policies are often far from the compelling narratives that will attract a large audience, unless, of course, a major disaster or event shines a spotlight on some underlying problem. In a competitive marketplace, news, including political news, is based on providing compelling narratives—stories that we want to read, hear, watch, and retweet. It is easy, and often useful, to critique the American news media for failing to report on the "important stories." However, one might also ask if we would tune into the "Federal Bureaucracy Channel" with any regularity.

Contemporary Pressures Affect How the Media Covers Campaigns and Elections

The drive to attract an audience also shapes how media outlets cover political campaigns and elections, and it affects how candidates try to present themselves. When covering political campaigns, news outlets may focus on the drama of the race rather than on the policy differences between candidates, a tendency often called the **horse race phenomenon.**

Scandals also sell, as we have explored, tempting media outlets to focus on them and often crowding out discussions of policy, a pattern that political scientist Larry Sabato has called a "feeding frenzy."[33] A recent report by the Media Research Center showed that in one month's time, of all news coverage of President Trump, a full 55 percent was devoted solely to the Russia investigation, with the remainder devoted to a range of other issues.[34]

Candidates and politicians are not bystanders in the coverage of politics; they actively try to shape the news agenda and the content of the stories covered. They and members of their staff try to get their message out and shape its reception. The goal is to control the message, sometimes seemingly obsessively, by focusing on one message per news cycle, per day. Allowing or restricting access by journalists is also a strategic decision, made according to what strategy seems best able to "spin" a story in the desired way.

MEDIA OWNERSHIP AND CONTENT ARE SUBJECT TO REGULATION

Although the media serve, in part, to try to exercise control over elected officials and government employees, the media are themselves subject to regulation and control by the government. While the challenges to effective and fair regulation have often been specific to certain times, places, and technologies, the desire for elected officials to shape

- Describe the effects of regulation and deregulation on the media.

the landscape of media coverage has been present for a long time. These efforts have focused primarily on regulating two things: media ownership and media content.

Regulation Affects Who Owns the Media and How We Consume It

With the technological revolutions of radio and television in the twentieth century came demands from both citizens and content providers themselves for the federal government to regulate the broadcast media. The business logic behind these regulations was based upon the fact that the nation's radio and television frequencies were finite, like rivers, canals, and grazing lands.[35] Demands to use them, however, were not. From the point of view of publishers and broadcasters, regulations were necessary to prevent "overgrazing." Radio stations, for instance, all too often were wandering onto the electronic lands of others, given the technological reality that "the physical capacity of the available channels, or wave lengths, [were] already far exceeded by the number of stations actually in operation."[36] There were also calls to regulate the morality of the content of the material that beamed directly into American's homes. And there were calls to regulate the political content of radio and television broadcasts to ensure that multiple political viewpoints were all represented.

Regulation Affects Media Technologies and Ownership

The Radio Act of 1927 established the Federal Radio Commission and required broadcasters to obtain a license to broadcast on specific frequencies in an attempt to try to bring order to "the utter confusion within the broadcasting band."[37] The Communications Act of 1934 expanded the federal role in governing the nation's broadcast media, creating the Federal Communications Commission (FCC) to oversee its implementation. National defense was cited as one of the reasons that the FCC was needed as a matter of public policy.

In the latter half of the twentieth century, spiking demand from content providers and marketplace competition as well as changes in the ways news stories were created and distributed, forced government once again to rethink the rules governing telecommunications. New legislation was needed to help overcome what was an increasingly messy traffic jam in the nation's telecommunications systems. The Telecommunications Act of 1996 was passed by Congress in order "to let anyone enter any communications business—to let any communications business compete in any market against any other."[38] The act essentially brought deregulation to media ownership, setting in motion a process that led to massive consolidation of media ownership (see Figure 6.5). While deregulation might have been expected to increase the diversity of the nation's major news outlets, it had the opposite effect. It led to increasing consolidation as news firms tried to maximize their profits in the face of declining sales on things like printed

FIGURE 6.5

Consolidation of Media Ownership

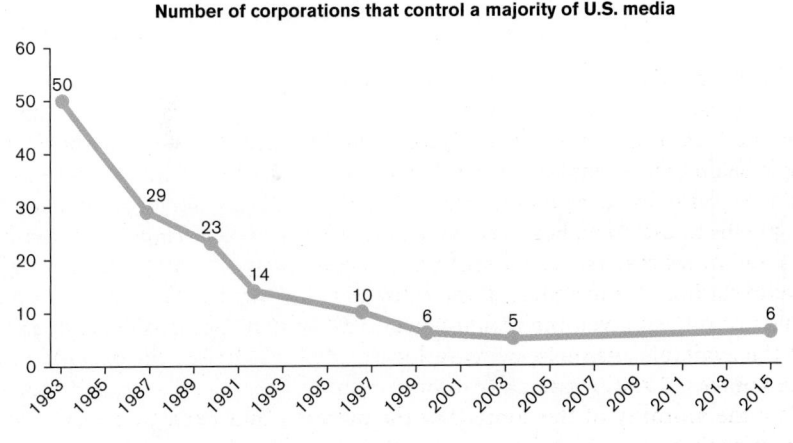

Number of corporations that control a majority of U.S. media

Source: Modified from Ben H. Bagdikan, *The New Media Monopoly* (Boston, MA: Beacon Press, 2004). Available online at www.corporations.org/media.

classified advertisements, long a mainstay of traditional newspaper revenue, made obsolete by the Internet.

The concentration of ownership of major media outlets is not only due to relaxation of regulations. There is also a logic to it. Media outlets largely fund their operations through advertising revenue. Advertisers, for their part, want to reach as many consumers as possible. Therefore, media outlets try to expand their reach as far as they can, whether by attracting the largest audiences possible or by purchasing smaller content providers. This has consequences for the content of media coverage as well. Providers may shape their coverage to attract as wide an audience as possible.

The twenty-first century has also witnessed a marked decline in consumption of printed newspapers (see Figure 6.6). Does that mean overall consumption of *news* has declined? The story is more complicated than that. Traditional papers have gone online, sometimes for free and with advertisements, sometimes behind firewalls that require registration and/or a subscription fee. Nontraditional Internet news sources often get their stories from a process called **aggregating**. In this process they still rely on the basic reporting that newspaper journalists do, but then they disseminate and comment on the original coverage.

During this era of proliferation of media outlets and the federal government's relaxation of many of the regulations first introduced during the days

FIGURE 6.6

Changes in American Political News Consumption

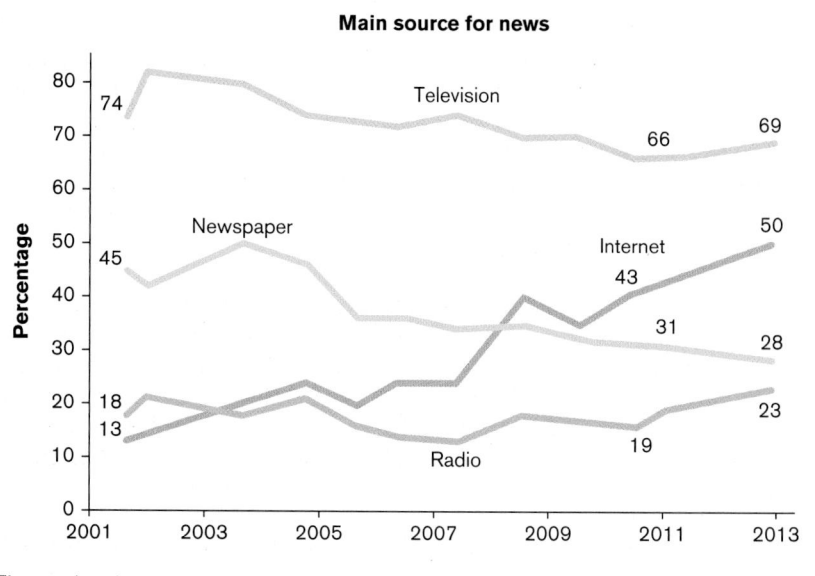

Main source for news

The results of a 2013 survey by the Pew Research Center show that for the first time more than half of Americans cited the Internet as one of their major sources for national and international news.

Source: Andrea Caumot, "12 Trends Shaping Digital News," Pew Research Center, October 16, 2013, www.pewresearch.org/fact-tank/2013/10/16/12-trends-shaping-digital-news.

of radio, and later, television, the question of "who owns the grazing lands?" has not gone away. In fact, with the issue of **net neutrality**, it is still here, only in a somewhat different form. Net neutrality is the idea that Internet service providers should treat all data and content providers equally and not discriminate based upon content or bandwidth demands. However, some feel that companies that provide the highways of the Internet and broadband age should be able to charge more to content providers whose "livestock" chew up more bandwidth. Critics who support net neutrality say that allowing firms to price discriminate based on bandwidth use will stifle the expression of multiple and diverse views.

Pro-net neutrality laws that had been advanced by the Obama administration appeared to be targets for opponents to net neutrality within the Trump administration. Under Obama, in June 2016, the D.C. Circuit Court of Appeals upheld the FCC's net neutrality rules, but several major telecommunications companies promised to appeal the decision. In 2017 President Trump nominated a series of anti-net neutrality commissioners to the FCC's board, signaling relaxed enforcement of those rules.

Regulation Also Affects Content

While the federal government plays only a small role in providing media content—with exceptions such the Corporation for Public Broadcasting, created by Congress in 1967—it has played an important role in regulating its content. The Communications Act of 1934 led to the establishment of several rules designed to shape news media content to serve the public at large. One of these, the **equal time rule**, requires licensees to guarantee political candidates equal time to present their views and opinions.

One of the more controversial aspects of the equal time provision was an implicit—and perhaps unintended—incentive for broadcasters to avoid presenting the platforms of candidates at all, for fear of running afoul of the law. According to media and politics scholar Doris Graber, the equal time provision may have acted to restrict rather than expand political information as a station may choose not to cover candidates at all, especially those in local races, wherein many candidates are vying for office. "This keeps many viable candidates off the air and has led to widespread dissatisfaction with the equal time rule and demands to abandon it."[39]

The rise of social media has also challenged the ability to ensure equal coverage. Political candidates who are also celebrities, for example, can obtain disproportionate attention based on their celebrity status alone. In the 2016 presidential campaign, Republican candidate Donald Trump used his large following on Twitter to obtain coverage without having to purchase as much airtime as other candidates.

The **fairness doctrine**, introduced in 1949, expanded regulations for American political news coverage beyond just the provision of time for candidates to the content of the coverage itself. It required "that every licensee devote a reasonable portion of broadcast time to the discussion and consideration of controversial issues of public importance" and that broadcasters must "affirmatively endeavor to make . . . facilities available for the expression of contrasting viewpoints held by responsible elements with respect to the controversial issues presented."[40] Again, scholars and broadcasters have questioned the unintended consequences of the fairness doctrine. In trying to avoid the appearance of being unfair, political news media providers might decide to play it safe, "to shy away from programs dealing with controversial public issues to avoid demands to air opposing views, in place of regular revenue-producing programs."[41] The fairness doctrine had ceased to be rigorously enforced and was largely repealed in the 1980s. In 2011, the FCC formally scrapped it. However, debates about its potential reinstatement (and how the Supreme Court would rule on such an action in the age of the Internet) continue.

WHAT HAVE I LEARNED?

1. The primary motivation behind the Radio Act of 1927 and the Communications Act of 1934 was to ensure that _____.

   a. All political viewpoints were equally represented
   b. Broadcasters could be sure that others could not encroach on their channels
   c. Americans of different racial and ethnic backgrounds were included in news coverage
   d. The federal government would receive revenue from broadcasters

2. The primary effect of the Telecommunications Act of 1996 was _____.

   a. A consolidation of ownership of media outlets
   b. The prevention of many cable television outlets from entering the marketplace
   c. Ensuring equal treatment of outlets in access to bandwidth
   d. All of the above

3. What challenges has technological change presented to the relevance and enforcement of the equal time rule and the fairness doctrine?

Answer Key: 1. b; 2. a; 3. Answers should discuss the challenges presented by cable television and the Internet to rules originally designed to cover the activities of broadcast media outlets.

THE POWER OF THE MEDIA TO AFFECT THE PUBLIC IS TESTED

- Understand the power of the media to shape public knowledge as well as the mechanisms by which that occurs.

It was fake news, intentionally so.

On Sunday, October 30, 1938, the night before Halloween, Orson Welles, who would later gain notoriety for directing movies, served up a bit of mischief to American audiences. Welles was that night directing a radio adaptation of the H. G. Wells 1897 science fiction piece *The War of the Worlds*, which centered on an invasion of England by Martians, for the CBS radio program *Mercury Theatre on the Air*.

It was a play, on radio, meant to entertain. The problem was that many Americans did not realize that fact at the time, and it caused a panic.[42]

Welles and his collaborators had decided to set their adaptation not in England but in Grover's Mill, New Jersey. During the process of creating the teleplay, a secretary who had transcribed the original novel, was reported to have remarked, "Those old Martians are just a lot of nonsense! It's all too silly!"[43] Welles, with little more than twenty-four hours before the broadcast, was worried that his play would be far from good theater.

So he made a choice: He would make it seem real, drawing on the horrific commentary and screams that accompanied the true coverage of the explosion of the airship Hindenburg the year before. Welles also decided to mimic the real "news flash" interruptions of Americans' regular comedy or music broadcasts, tapping into the fears of an already very worried nation who had become used to those kinds of announcements. At the time, the lingering gray clouds of the Great Depression seemed like they would never go away, and the ominous storm clouds of the rise of Hitler's Nazi Party cast a shadow across the globe. Reporters would often break into the entertaining radio broadcasts of that dominant medium of the day. With those trappings of "real news" in place, the broadcast went live.

During the play's climax, a fake announcer recounted, "Now the whole field's caught fire. (Explosion) The woods. . .the barns. . .the gas tanks of automobiles. . .it's spreading every-where. It's coming this way. About twenty yards to my right. . .(CRASH OF MICROPHONE. . .THEN DEAD SILENCE. . .)."[44] Six seconds of com-plete silence followed.

Another announcer followed, "Ladies and gentlemen, due to circum-stances beyond our control, we are unable to continue our broadcast from Grover's Mill. Evidently, there's some difficulty with our field transmission."[45]

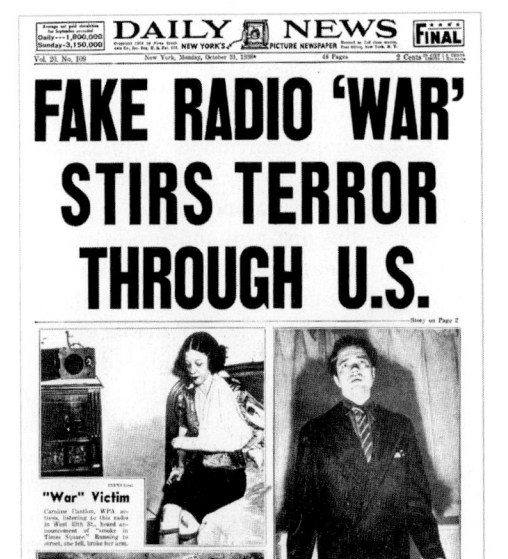

A respected newspaper coverage of the "fake news" broadcast of the "War of the Worlds." NY Daily News Archive via Getty Images

As theater, it was genius. To many listeners, the absurdities of the scenario were obvious, so it was nothing more than captivating entertainment. To an unknown number of Americans, however, it seemed real: "All they knew was that something horrible was happening on the Eastern Seaboard—and that, perhaps, it was coming their way."[46] At the conclusion of the broadcast, Orson Welles stepped out of his persona as a fake Princeton University professor and assured his audience, "This is Orson Welles, ladies and gentlemen, out of character to assure you that THE WAR OF THE WORLDS has no further significance than the holiday offering it was meant to be."[47]

Some Americans missed Welles's disclaimer. The aftermath was intense. Stories of frightened Americans were everywhere in other forms of the media, especially the newspaper on Halloween day. Welles received sharp criticism but was not accused or tried of any crime. In the sections that follow, we will explore further the debates about the media's power to influence individual and group behavior. Others have asserted that the panic over the broadcast was deliber-ately overblown by competitor newspapers "to attack their newfangled rival, the radio."[48] Perhaps it was not a *War of the Worlds* but a battle between two media outlets—newspapers and radio—for legitimacy.

In the aftermath of the *War of the Worlds*, one thing was clear: the power of the news media—whether or not they could convince Americans that they were under attack by Martians—was not fake.

Scholars Have Differed on the Media's Effects

When it comes to democratic representation, none of the topics that we have explored in this chapter matter unless one thing is true: that the media can actually shape individuals' political knowledge and understanding. Why regulate the media, for instance, unless you presume it *can* affect people's political beliefs and understanding?

But just how much power does the media have? Are they major players in the national political drama or just commentators on it? As with so much else about the American news media, the answers to these questions are evolving. Scholars' views of **media effects**—the power of the news media in shaping individuals' political knowledge, understanding, and preferences—have evolved along with the media itself.

In the early decades of the twentieth century, many observers of American political life considered the media a powerful and potentially dangerous force. The effectiveness of World War I propaganda posters and efforts, which helped to mobilize the nation in support for intervention in a European conflict about which many Americans were ambivalent, seemed to indicate that the public was like political Play-Doh: shapeable and malleable. In this view, media were thought to have a direct effect on a public.

This model of the direct effects of the media began to fall out of favor in later decades as scholars, employing empirical techniques and focusing primarily on the effects of the media in vote choices, found important but limited effects of the media on political outcomes. Though playing an important role in citizen information about candidates and their policy positions, the media were found to be only one factor in an individual's ultimate choice about which candidates to vote for in a given election.[49]

The current view of most scholars of the relationship between the media and American politics lies somewhere in between those of the direct and limited effects models. The model of subtle effects focuses not so much on how the media may or may not change—for example, the partisan affiliation or vote choice of a given individual—but on the ways in which the media may shape the overall conversation taking place in the public sphere.

How the media place a story in a larger context—the textual or visual cues that they present along with a particular story—may cause individuals to focus on particular considerations when consuming a media product, an effect known as **framing**. According to political scientists James Druckman and Kjersten Nelson, "For example, if a speaker describes a hate-group rally in terms of free speech, then the audience will subsequently base their opinions about the rally on free speech considerations and, perhaps, support the right to rally. In contrast, if the speaker uses a public-safety frame, the audience will base their opinions on public-safety considerations and oppose the rally."[50] Similarly, a particular media source's coverage of a candidate or issue may highlight specific contextual details in providing the coverage, thereby **priming** individuals to draw on those details when forming opinions.

The power of the media to select which stories are covered cannot be understated. In the choice of coverage, the media may exert an agenda-setting role by highlighting which issues are worthy of coverage and, as a consequence, worthy of the public's attention. The question of **agenda setting** gets to the very purpose of the role of the media in a representative democracy. According to political scientist Harold Lasswell, the media perform three important and interconnected functions: to survey and report on political events and outcomes, to interpret those events and outcomes to the public, and to educate citizens.[51] To these three, media and politics scholar Doris Graber added a fourth function: to deliberately manipulate the political process.[52]

Lasswell's assertion that the media survey and report on the political world is often what we think about when we consider the media's role in American representative democracy—hard-hitting journalists asking hard-hitting questions and acting as a watchdog for, or, perhaps more accurately, a watchtower over, American politics. The role of watchdog is well entrenched in Americans' understanding of the role of journalists, editors, and anchors. Objective, aggressive interviews designed to get to the truth is very much a part of the ideal of the American news media. The tricky questions, however, are these: On what issues does the watchtower shine its light? Corruption? Scandal? Infrastructure? Cats? Who controls its aim and focus? To whom does the watchtower's controller answer? Corporate interests, powerful politicians, fellow journalists, or the American consumer? They are important questions with no easy answers. A watchtower cannot, by design, focus on the entire ocean—only a very small part of it at one time. Who decides where the light is to shine, and what are the consequences of those decisions?

The challenge of interpreting the dynamics behind these findings illustrates an important concept in empirical political science research: that correlation does not, by itself, establish causation. As you consume stories that show a relationship between variables, be careful not to assume that this relationship demonstrates that one factor is causing another.

Americans May Be Separated by a Digital Divide

At first glance, the proliferation of news sources in the twenty-first century might provide scholars of the news media with a source of optimism. Perhaps, through infotainment, the diversity of perspectives on cable stations, and the spread of social media, Americans who were previously disconnected from the political process might be brought into it and prompted to think about issues and to connect friends and family in their own social networks to American politics. Again, it may not be that simple; the story might not be so neat and inspiring. All Americans do not make use of the new technologies and outlets in the same way. According to the work of political scientist Markus Prior, the new technologies and media avenues may be dividing Americans, making them more partisan.[54] We call those gaps the **digital divide.**

Americans with the skills to navigate this media landscape that contains many options and unclear editorial standards may benefit tremendously, but those who cannot, or choose not to, may be left behind. The Internet, according to Prior, "has widened gaps in news exposure, political knowledge, and turnout between those who like news and those who prefer entertainment."[55] Older, low-income, rural, Spanish-speaking, and disabled Americans are among those less likely to make use of the Internet, as are those with lower levels of educational attainment.[56]

Do the Media Make Us Smart (or Not So Smart)? Or Do We Make Them Look Good (or Not So Good)?

In a study published in 2007, the Pew Research Center reported the findings of a study of Americans' political knowledge and media usage.[53] Part of the study was a political knowledge quiz in which the roughly 1,500 respondents were asked to identify individuals and answer questions about American government. Based on how well they did answering these questions, researchers divided the respondents into three groups: high knowledge, moderate knowledge, and low knowledge.

Another part of the survey asked respondents to identify which sources of political news they regularly consumed, including print, radio, television, cable, and Internet sources. The sources themselves were then "scored" based on how knowledgeable their regular consumers were. While no one technology emerged as being more or less consumed by more or less knowledgeable individuals, there were some considerable differences between specific sources.

The Daily Show and *The Colbert Report*, along with newspaper websites, had the most knowledgeable consumers. The conservative Rush Limbaugh radio show and *O'Reilly Factor* also had relatively knowledgeable consumers. Fox News Channel and the network morning shows had the least knowledgeable consumers.

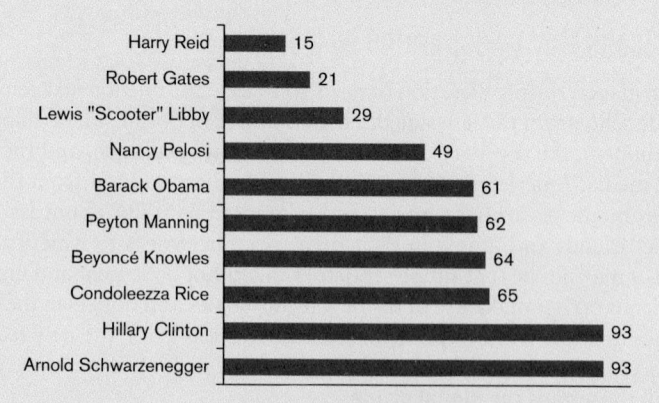

Percentage of Survey Respondents Who Can Identify...

Person	Percentage
Harry Reid	15
Robert Gates	21
Lewis "Scooter" Libby	29
Nancy Pelosi	49
Barack Obama	61
Peyton Manning	62
Beyoncé Knowles	64
Condoleezza Rice	65
Hillary Clinton	93
Arnold Schwarzenegger	93

Percentage of Survey Respondents Who Can Recall the Name of...

	Percentage
The president of Russia	36
Their state's governor	66
The vice president	69

Knowledge Levels by News Source

Nationwide
- 35
- 31
- 34

Among the regular audience of . . .

Daily Show/Colbert Report
- 52
- 25
- 21

Major newspaper websites
- 54
- 26
- 20

NewsHour with Jim Lehrer
- 53
- 19
- 28

O'Reilly Factor
- 51
- 32
- 17

National Public Radio
- 51
- 27
- 22

Rush Limbaugh's radio show
- 50
- 29
- 21

News magazines
- 48
- 27
- 25

TV news websites
- 44
- 33
- 23

Daily newspaper
- 43
- 31
- 26

CNN
- 41
- 30
- 29

News from Google, Yahoo, etc.
- 41
- 35
- 24

Network evening news
- 38
- 33
- 29

Online news discussion blogs
- 37
- 26
- 37

Local TV news
- 35
- 33
- 32

Fox News Channel
- 35
- 30
- 35

Network morning shows
- 34
- 36
- 30

■ High ■ Moderate ▢ Low

Source: "What Americans Know: 1989-2007" Pew Research Center, Washington, D.C. (April 2007) http://www.people-press.org/files/legacy-pdf/319.pdf.

WHAT DO YOU THINK?

What kind of a "story" can one write about these findings? This is where it is important to be careful. It may be that *The Daily Show* is very educational, making its consumers more informed. On the other hand, it may be that it attracts more informed consumers, as much of the show's humor is not that funny without some background information. Or it may be a combination of these two causes.

1. The question of political bias in political news has been largely settled.

   a. True
   b. False

2. Commercial bias refers to _____.

   a. The increase of commercials in television news
   b. The role that journalists play in trying to push a certain political perspective
   c. The way in which the media shape their coverage to attract an audience

   d. All of the above

3. How have scholars' views of the power of the media changed over time?

4. Why are scholars worried about an increasing digital divide?

Answer Key: 1. a; 2. c; 3., Answers should include a discussion of the direct effects, limited effects, and subtle effects models; 4. Answers should include the connection between access to news sources and individuals' identities and lived experiences.

■ CONCLUSION

Navigating the News

How powerful are American media sources in the twenty-first century?

Amidst all of the controversy surrounding allegations of Russian intervention in the presidential election of 2016, for us, no one question is as important as this one. The challenges of filtering the truth of the images, issues, and arguments with which they are bombarded is a major task for Americans. This is as true today in the multilayered media environment of the twenty-first century as it was for listeners tuning in to hear about a Martian invasion in 1938 and for pamphlet readers at the start of the nation. Because so much of our knowledge about the political world comes indirectly from the media and not from direct interaction with politicians, policymakers, or the political process, Americans are tasked with the challenge of needing to be very savvy about the media they consume. Why are we being bombarded with one set of specific issues and not others? What issues are being ignored, and why?

Want a better grade?

Get the tools you need to sharpen your study skills. **SAGE edge** offers a robust online environment featuring an impressive array of free tools and resources. Access practice quizzes, eFlashcards, video, and multimedia at **edge.sagepub.com/abernathybrief1e.**

CHAPTER REVIEW

This chapter's main ideas are reflected in the Learning Objectives. By reviewing them here you should be able to **remember** the key points and **know** these terms that are central to the topic.

6.1 Trace the historical development of the American news media.

REMEMBER...

- Since the founding, there has been tension between the constitutional right to freedom of speech and of the press and constraints on those rights.

- Pamphlets and later weekly and daily newspapers were among the first print media in the United States.

- As time went on, costs to produce newspapers decreased, making the news more affordable and available and able to reach a mass audience.

- For much of the history of the American media, the press has been partisan—funded by and disseminating the point of view of particular political factions.

- Sensationalism was also used to sell news, a practice that continues today.

- The nineteenth and twentieth centuries saw the rise of other technologies, such as the telegraph and radio and television.

KNOW...

- *broadcast media*: outlets for news and other content that rely on mass communications technology to bring stories directly into people's homes; subject to stricter content regulations than cable television outlets and alternative sources of information (p. 182)

- *citizen journalists*: nonprofessionals who cover or document news and events or offer their own analyses of them (p. 185)

- *investigative journalism*: an approach to newsgathering in which reporters dig into stories, often looking for instances of corruption or failures to uphold the interests of citizens (p. 181)

- *mass media*: sources of information that appeal to a wide audience, including newspapers, radio, television, and Internet outlets (p. 181)

- *news media*: the variety of sources providing information and covering events, including newspapers, television, radio, the Internet, and social media (p. 175)

- *niche journalism*: media that caters to fragmented and specialized audiences (p. 186)

- *partisan press*: media outlets or organizations that promote a particular political ideology or support a political party (p. 180)

- *penny press*: nineteenth-century American newspapers that sold for only one cent each, thus increasing the size of the audience that could afford to purchase them (p. 181)

- *social media*: forms of electronic communication that enable users to create and share content or to participate in social networking (p. 184)

- *wire service*: an organization that gathers and reports on news and then sells the stories to other outlets (p. 181)

- *yellow journalism*: an approach to reporting employed in the nineteenth century that relied on sensational headlines and emotional language to persuade readers and sell newspapers (p. 181)

6.2 Understand the issue of bias in the American media.

REMEMBER...

- Cable news offers round-the-clock news coverage, often with a partisan slant.

- Newer technologies, such as the Internet, broadband, and social media, have not only increased the pace and volume of news content but have also blurred the lines between information, entertainment, citizens, and journalists.

- Americans increasingly perceive the media as politically biased and less trustworthy.

- Scholars' views of the power of the media to shape political understanding and behaviors have changed over time.

- A growing digital divide separates Americans along partisan lines as well as by race, class, and ethnicity.

KNOW...

- *beat system*: a system of reporting in which journalists are assigned to specific types of news, policies, and events (p. 189)

- *commercial bias*: the shaping of the content and focus of news based upon the desire to capture news consumers (p. 190)

- *fake news*: a controversial term that is sometimes used to describe news that is in error or not factual but is also used to refer to the intentional use of political propaganda (p. 196)

- *horse race phenomenon*: coverage of political campaigns that focuses more on the drama of the campaign than on policy issues (p. 190)

- *infotainment*: the blurring of the lines between providing information and entertaining audiences when covering events (p. 188)

- *partisan bias*: the slanting of political news coverage in support of a particular political party or ideology (p. 188)

- *soft news*: stories that focus on celebrity and personality rather than political or economic issues (p. 188)

6.3 Discuss changes in the regulation of media ownership and media content.

REMEMBER...

- Some efforts to regulate the news media have focused on ownership; others have focused on its content.

- The Radio Act of 1927 established the FCC and required broadcasters to obtain licenses.

- The Telecommunications Act of 1996 modified regulations on media ownership and led to a period of consolidation.

- The principle of net neutrality calls for Internet service providers to treat data streams equally.

- The equal time rule and fairness doctrine sought to ensure a level playing field for political candidates; however, recent regulatory and technological changes have reduced their impact and raised questions about their relevance.

KNOW...

- *aggregating*: a process through which Internet and other news providers relay the news as reported by journalists and other sources (p. 193)

- *equal time rule*: a regulation that required American radio and television broadcast networks to provide equal time for political candidates to present their views on issues (p. 195)

- *fairness doctrine*: a federal rule that expanded regulations for American political news coverage beyond just the provision of time for candidates to the content of the coverage itself (p. 195)

- *net neutrality*: a Federal Communications Commission (FCC) rule that requires Internet service providers to treat all data and content providers equally and not discriminate based upon content or bandwidth demands (p. 194)

6.4 Explain the different perspectives on the power of the media to shape political understanding and behaviors.

REMEMBER...

- How has the need to attract an audience shaped the coverage of political news?

- What are possible sources of bias in coverage of political news? Which of these do you think are the most significant?

- Can the media shape Americans' political understandings?

KNOW...

- *agenda setting*: the media's ability to highlight certain issues and bring them to the attention of the public (p. 198)

- *digital divide*: divisions in society that are driven by access to and knowledge about technologies; these gaps often fall along the lines of partisanship, class, race, and ethnicity (p. 199)

- *framing*: influencing peoples' interpretations of news, events, or issues through the presentation of the context (p. 198)

- *media effects*: the power of the news media in shaping individuals' political knowledge, preferences, and political behavior (p. 198)

- *priming*: shaping individuals' interpretations of news or events by highlighting certain details or contexts (p. 198)

7 PARTIES, ELECTIONS, AND PARTICIPATION
The Insurgents versus the Establishment

Republican president Donald Trump speaking as a candidate at a rally in West Virginia in May 2016. Trump's insurgent campaign posed major challenges to his Republican Party by breaking many political rules about how candidates should pursue and win office and added to questions about whether traditional wisdom about political parties still applies. BRENDAN SMIALOWSKI/AFP/Getty Images

In a representative democracy, elections involve a lot of uncertainty. Which candidate will win? How will citizens figure out which candidates to support? How can voters be sure that they are selecting individuals who will advocate for their interests? Even the most attentive voters find it difficult to grasp all of the details about what a candidate stands for or hopes to accomplish once in office.

Enter the **political party.** By organizing and supporting candidates running for office, parties provide labels to those candidates—shortcuts for voters, really—that cut through the noise and signal to voters that this is a candidate who deserves their support. Once in office, those candidates work with the support of other party members to advance a set of policies.

Party leaders face another challenge: creating an attractive and consistent message that gets their candidates elected and maintains party cohesion. American political parties have often been successful in doing this, but every several decades or so, a party finds itself challenged by members within its own ranks who have felt that their voices are being ignored by party leaders.

In 2016 both major parties, the Democrats and the Republicans, found themselves confronting just such a situation. Bernie Sanders and Donald Trump—as far apart on the traditional American political spectrum as one could diagram—emerged as major forces in their respective parties. Both were outsiders and insurgents, and a lot of Americans responded to their campaigns. They also turned much conventional wisdom on its head, causing uproar within their parties, forcing experts in American politics to admit that they had gotten it wrong, and leading the established leaders in both parties scrambling to figure out how to respond.

The 2016 election cycle may very well be studied by future political scientists as one of the most critical in the nation's history. How did this all come to pass? Could it result in a reshaping of party politics or even the destruction of one or both of America's major political parties? How will voters respond? The 2016 election cycle provides a chance to analyze this presidential election in relation to others that have come before and also to better understand the role that parties play in American representative democracy.

LEARNING OBJECTIVES

Through an exploration of the presidential election of 2016 and the challenges that Bernie Sanders and Donald Trump posed to their own party establishment, you will be able to do the following:

7.1 Identify the roles that parties play in American representative democracy.

7.2 Explain how American party systems have evolved over time.

7.3 Understand the rules surrounding national elections and the function they serve.

7.4 Describe the structure, stages, and main challenges of presidential and legislative campaigns.

7.5 Describe the forms of political participation Americans engage in, including the factors that limit or facilitate engagement.

BERNIE SANDERS AND DONALD TRUMP SHAKE UP THE FIELD . . . AND CONVENTIONAL WISDOM ABOUT THE POWER OF PARTIES

American presidential elections are often filled with drama. Normally, most of the fireworks happen between the candidates vying to win office. To put it mildly, 2016 was different. There, the explosions were happening within the major parties themselves. Two of the leading candidates in the election—Vermont senator Bernie

Sanders, an independent running as a Democrat, and Republican multimillionaire Donald Trump—in different times would have been regarded as too extreme to pose a legitimate threat to party status quo. Trump's highly unconventional and controversial campaign in particular upended many widely accepted political rules and challenged the belief that political party leaders are powerful.

In 2016 Sanders and Trump advanced far in the electoral process due to voters' profound disgust with "politics as usual." Both made statements or adopted policy positions that were on the fringes of party platforms or far out of touch with the mainstream. And, unlike many presidential contenders, neither of them concentrated on courting the best-known activists and leaders in their parties—the so-called party establishment or party elites, who are the most powerful insiders in party politics. In fact, their campaigns seemed to go out of their way to alienate those elites.

The emphasis on criticizing elites and the establishment, generally referred to as *populism*, has a long political history. America has witnessed several powerful populist movements, many of which tied their critique of the establishment to perceptions of racial, ethnic, or cultural superiority or to strong anti-immigrant views, a charge frequently leveled against Trump. What made Sanders and Trump more noteworthy was that their criticisms struck such a deep chord with so many voters; each kept winning state nomination contests long after many political observers were certain they would fade. To the astonishment of both Republican and Democratic loyalists, Trump would eventually go on to win the general election.

The success of the campaigns of Sanders and Trump came in part because Americans have become less attached to political parties. At the same time, the country has grown increasingly polarized by political ideology. More conservatives hold strongly conservative views than in the past and more liberals strongly liberal views. The party organizations have shouldered much of the blame for creating and fostering an environment in which the two sides seem forever locked in combat. Despite this ongoing battle, the parties haven't become any stronger. According to journalist Jonathan Rauch, "Here is the reigning political paradox of our era: Partisanship is strong, but parties are weak."[1]

Both Sanders's and Trump's campaigns reflected this disjuncture. Sanders didn't even belong to the Democratic Party when he announced he was running for that party's nomination. Instead, he described himself as an "independent socialist," strongly in favor of the idea that government and society should meet the needs of the public. Sanders's message that the playing field was unacceptably tilted toward the top 1 percent of Americans resonated with many voters, especially young adults who felt the American Dream was out of their reach. Sanders said his campaign involved creating a

An attendee holds up a sign in support of Democratic presidential candidate Bernie Sanders at a rally in Brooklyn, New York, in April 2016. Sanders's call for a "political revolution" was an effective rallying cry, especially among young voters. Victor J. Blue/Bloomberg via Getty Images "political revolution" that could serve "millions of Americans, working people who have given up on the political process."[2]

But his main Democratic opponent, Hillary Clinton, and many others in the mainstream of the Democratic Party said Sanders's proposals were unrealistic. Party leaders were concerned his ideas were too radical and might drive away people who otherwise would support Democrats in other races. Many voters disagreed. "I really like Bernie Sanders for his consistency, authenticity and relative independence from corporate interests," said Anton Terrell, a recent college graduate in Austin, Texas.[3]

Like Sanders, Trump was very much an outsider in his party. Unlike Sanders and most other presidential candidates, though, he had never held elected office. That disturbed some in the GOP ("Grand Old Party" or Republican Party) as they believed those seeking the nation's highest legislative post should have at least some prior political experience. As well, between 1987 and 2012, Trump had switched political parties seven times, registering for periods of time as a Democrat, a Republican, or as an independent until he became a Republican again in 2012.[4] That made conservative Republicans question whether Trump would remain faithful to the party. Many Republicans also viewed his claim that he would use his business acumen to cut deals to benefit the U.S. economy as directly contradicting their philosophy of limited government; the conservative magazine *National Review* devoted an entire issue to arguing why its readers shouldn't support Trump for that reason.[5]

On the campaign trail, Trump did little to assuage the Republican Party that he would toe their line. Trump's extreme statements on immigration caused a further uproar. He called for building a massive wall on the U.S.-Mexican border to keep out those coming into the country illegally also and for a ban on Muslims being allowed to enter the United States. His positions enraged Hispanics and Muslims, and a number of Republicans said he had gone too far. Part of Trump's campaign theme, "Make America Great Again," involved replacing "stupid" decision makers with smart ones. His blaming of all politicians— not just Democratic ones—for what he called their inability to solve problems irked the GOP's establishment, which he bluntly described as ineffectual. He accused them of being too beholden to what he said were the party's narrow interests and unresponsive to the public's massive hostility toward government. "People are angry . . . I just know it can be turned around. It can be turned around quickly," Trump said.[6]

Trump could afford to alienate the Republican establishment because of his celebrity and his ability to command significant news media attention without buying advertisements. Unlike other Republicans, he feuded with Fox News, whose audience consisted largely of hard-core GOP loyalists. One study estimated that he had essentially been given $2 billion in free media coverage in newspapers, television, and other journalistic sources. That was two-and-a-half times more than Democratic Party candidate Hillary Clinton and many times greater that of any of his Republican rivals.[7] Trump made frequent use of Twitter, regularly condemning his opponents with tweets that drew even more media attention.

Many of Trump's supporters cared little about any of the criticisms leveled against him. He tapped into their deep frustration with politics and, in turn, the parties. They said they agreed with Trump's call to upend the entire system and described him as refreshingly authentic and blunt—qualities they said mattered more to them than his sometimes-vague policy stances. "He disrupts a broken political process and beats establishment candidates who've long ignored their interests," a lawyer in a poor, rural North Carolina town wrote in explaining Trump's widespread appeal there. "When you're earning $32,000 a year and haven't had a decent vacation in over a decade, . . . you just want to win again, whoever the victim, whatever the price."[8]

Americans asked for a disruptor, and they got one. Everything political insiders thought parties had the power to do—choose candidates, influence their messaging during the election cycle, and win voters—came apart. In the next section we look at what roles parties ordinarily can and do play in American politics in order to come to an understanding of their potential effectiveness—and their limitations. Later in the chapter we will also look at the role the political campaign structure and the factors that influence political participation and voting play in shaping electoral outcomes.

PARTIES ORGANIZE, SIGNAL, AND PROMOTE POLICY AGENDAS

Political parties have long been central to democracy and serve several functions. A healthy party serves as a credible check on the opposition, promoting ideas and candidates that differ from the other party's so that voters can choose how they want to be represented. Political scientist V. O. Key Jr. identified three primary roles that political parties play in American representative democracy:[9]

- Describe the major roles that political parties play.

1. As organizations, political parties recruit, nominate, and support candidates for political office.
2. In the electorate, parties act as labels that are provided to candidates and officeholders and that voters can use as shortcuts in identifying

candidates closer to their own political ideologies and advocating similar policy positions.

3. In government, a party enacts the policy positions of its members and acts as an opposition to the majority party when it is in the minority.

Parties Unite People as Organizations

A political party seeks to unite people under a shared banner of social, economic, and ideological goals. It finds and supports candidates to run for federal, state, and local offices, which includes mobilizing voters and potential voters to support its candidates. Parties raise money to fund campaigns and provide other forms of help to try to get their candidates elected. If those candidates win, the parties then try to make sure the politicians stay in office. The parties also come up with themes and principles that they want their candidates to follow in appealing for votes.

Political Parties Are Decentralized

When some people think of political parties, they think of big shots in Washington, D.C., commanding the armies of supporters below them. The reality is that parties are decentralized. They're basically a large collection of state organizations that, in turn, are loose collections of local groups. This is because the system of federalism dictates that power should not just be concentrated at the top. As reporter Jonathan Rauch explained it, "State parties play a key role. They recruit and cultivate political talent, building a farm team of candidates for higher office. They coordinate campaigns up and down the ballot, connecting politicians to each other and discouraging rogue behavior. They build networks of volunteers, connecting leaders with the party base. They gather voter data and make it available to all candidates, building a library of knowledge about the electorate."[10]

Today, however, many state party organizations are struggling in part because of the ability of nonparty groups to legally raise and spend large amounts of money on behalf of political causes. This has overshadowed not just state parties but the federal ones as well. Another problem facing state parties is the complexity of the campaign finance system. Its rules restrict the ability of the state parties to raise and spend money and to coordinate campaigns so that candidates of the same party can pool their expenses.

Party Leaders Are Advisers, Not Rulers

The president generally chooses the chair of his or her national party. The national party chair raises money and serves as a prominent spokesperson on television and other media. But the national party organization's power over the state and local parties is advisory; it can't tell them what to do. In fact, the state parties can put pressure on national parties. In 2014, for example, Republican Party officials at the state level began dropping party platforms and policies opposing same-sex marriage; the national committee leadership later followed their lead.

Each state has a central committee made up of people from that state's counties and legislative districts who run for office and are elected to terms just like regular politicians. They help shape the national party's governance, or how it manages its money and runs its operations.

Parties Shape Elections by Recruiting and Supporting Candidates

One way a party tries to shape elections is through **recruitment**, which is considered one of its central tasks. The parties seek candidates who best reflect the party's philosophy and who can attract the voters the parties seek to mobilize. Party officials often recruit by finding people who can appeal to specific groups with high concentrations of voters, such as African Americans or Latinos. The parties also look for people who can contrast sharply with their opponents.

In recruiting, parties also try to discourage prospective candidates within their own ranks who aren't seen as having a good chance of winning. They fear that those candidates could end up drawing votes away from their preferred choice.

Parties Help Run Political Campaigns

Parties play a key role in national, state, and local political campaigns. While we often talk about one candidate's "campaign," in fact there are several phases to a campaign, each with its own dynamics. First, candidates have to decide to run, which often involves the help of party leaders and activists. Second, parties establish a process through which they will nominate their chosen candidates. Finally, parties act to support their nominees in the elections themselves. We will examine the decision to run for national office as well as the dynamics of presidential and congressional campaigns later in this chapter. Here, the focus will be on the process of nomination.

Parties Select Candidates through the Nomination Process

After recruiting and supporting candidates, parties shape the process of **nomination** in which a party officially selects one candidate to run for one office against the nominees from other parties. In some races and in some states, the electoral process may pit members of the same party against each other in the general election.

Once the official presidential campaign process kicks off, declared candidates vie with others in their own party for that party's nomination. Beginning early in the election year, candidates seek to get the support of party **delegates**, whose votes they will later need to secure the party's nomination. While many of the rules governing the nomination process are set by federal and state laws, most of the details about *how* things actually work are hammered out by the parties themselves. There remain key differences across states and between the parties themselves.

Most states hold **presidential primary elections** wherein a state's voters choose delegates who support a particular candidate (see Figure 7.1). In some states, these elections may be **open primaries** in which all eligible voters may

FIGURE 7.1

Presidential Primary Systems by State, 2016

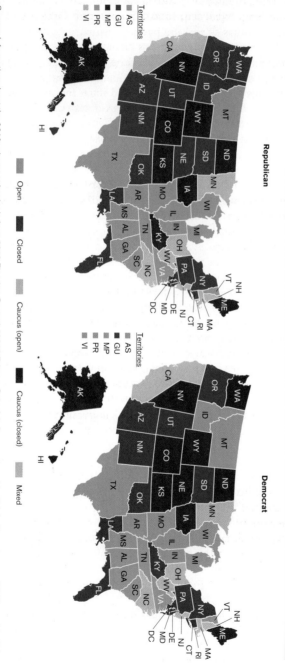

Republican

Democrat

Territories
AS
GU
MP
PR
VI

Open

Closed

Caucus (open)

Caucus (closed)

Mixed

Source: Information about the 2016 primary calendar is from 2016 Election Central, "2016 Primary Schedule," www.uspresidentialelectionnews.com/2016-presidential-primary-schedule-calendar.

vote in a party's primary election, regardless of that voter's partisan affiliation. Others may hold **closed primaries**—open only to registered voters from a particular political party. While open primaries encourage undecided and independent voters to participate in a way that closed primaries do not, they also open up the possibility for strategic voting. Feeling confident in the chances of the presumed nominee in their own party, voters may then use their votes to sabotage the candidate in the opposing party whom they see as the biggest threat to their own preferred candidate.

Some states hold caucuses wherein eligible voters gather to discuss candidates and issues and to select delegates to represent their preferences in later stages of the nomination process. Caucuses differ from primaries because the voting may be public instead of being done by secret ballot. The rules for taking part in a **caucus** also are more complicated as they involve more than simply marking a ballot to record the selection of a candidate. Because of their complexity, caucuses tend to draw fewer participants than primaries and attract those who are more committed to a candidate or cause.[11]

The schedule of primary elections and caucuses also matters to the ultimate outcomes of the nomination process. Party leaders in a state have a strong incentive to hold their primary election as early as possible in order to garner media attention as well as candidate attention. A win in an early state helps party candidates establish momentum, and issues that are important to specific states may translate later into policy attention should one of the party's candidates win the presidency. To take advantage of this, states try to engage in a process of **front-loading**—pushing their primaries or caucuses as early in the season as possible.

By tradition, the Iowa caucuses and then the New Hampshire primary have been the first two on the schedule. While neither state's nomination process results in a large number of delegates awarded, their early position creates a problem of perception and **demographics**, the grouping of individuals based on shared characteristics such as ancestry, race, ethnicity, and gender. Since both states have larger white, non-Hispanic voting populations than much of the rest of the nation, there is a concern that the diversity of American voices will not be heard until the narrative of the nomination campaign has already been established.

The final phase of the nomination process takes place in the **national conventions** held by the parties in the summer of the presidential election year. During the conventions, delegates vote to select the party's nominee. For much of American history national conventions were sources of high drama, with many rounds of delegate voting required to select a nominee, in recent decades the final outcome is already known or expected. In modern conventions, the drama comes from the selection of the vice presidential nominee—typically done by the presumptive presidential nominee.

Questions about what parties do and how they should go about it both involve a third consideration: how effective parties are in going about their activities. In 2008 four political scientists argued in an influential book titled *The Party Decides* that party leaders serve as powerful gatekeepers. The parties—whom the political scientists defined not just as senior party officials but the organized advocacy and interest groups that make them up—"scrutinize and winnow the field before voters get involved, attempt to build coalitions behind a single preferred candidate, and sway voters to ratify their choice."[12]

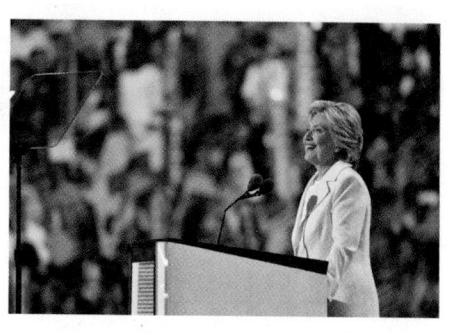

Parties typically select their nominees for president at their national conventions amidst much fanfare but without much drama. In 2016, both the Republican National Convention in Cleveland, Ohio (left), and the Democratic National Convention in Philadelphia, Pennsylvania (right), had more drama than usual. At the Republican Convention, some Republican Party leaders refused to endorse Trump, and Sanders's supporters disrupted the proceedings in Philadelphia at several points. Eventually, however, both Donald Trump and Hillary Clinton received their party's nod.
Left Photo: JIM WATSON/AFP/Getty Images
Right Photo: Ricky Carioti/The Washington Post via Getty Images

In the complicated relationship between candidates and their parties, politicians rely on their parties to help them get elected or stave off challengers, but in doing so they grant power to party leaders. According to political scientist John Aldrich, things get really interesting when candidates no longer feel that the parties and party leadership are serving their goals and may "turn elsewhere to seek the means to win."[13] Does the party decide, steering the nomination process toward selecting the most "electable" candidates in the general election, or can voters in primaries and caucuses impose their will should they feel that party leaders are not responding to the issues that voters want addressed?

The Party Connects with Voters in the Electorate

Parties shape American politics not only through their organizational capabilities but also through their ability to connect with voters. In their efforts to do this, parties rely on a variety of methods. One is **party identification**, or the degree to which voters are connected to a particular party.

One of the most important things that parties do is to signal that they will advance the agendas associated with a particular set of political beliefs, which is key to their role in providing candidates with labels and voters with cues and shortcuts. **Party ideology** refers to the consistent set of stances on major issues shaped by an underlying philosophy about the proper role of government in society and then communicated to voters.

In the United States, the two major parties identify with the key political ideologies that we discussed earlier. In recent decades, the Democratic Party has told voters that it will pursue policies connected with liberalism and the Republican Party with conservatism (see Figure 7.2). It is important to remember that party ideology and party identification are not the same thing. Parties do try to appeal to potential members by focusing on issues, policies, and solutions that might appeal to individuals with particular ideologies. Individuals' political beliefs, including partisan party identification, have many contributors and sources, including family, education, and life experiences.

FIGURE 7.2

Party Ideology: How Democrats and Republicans Differ

Democrat		Republican
Pro-choice	*Abortion*	Pro-life
Maintain race-based preferences	*Affirmative action*	Against race-based preferences
Protect the rights of the accused	*Crime*	Strong punishment for offenders and protect the rights of the victim
Increased regulation and worker protection	*Business*	Ease regulation and keep government out of business
Ban	*Death penalty*	Maintain
Decrease or maintain	*Defense spending*	Increase
More regulation	*Gun control*	Protect gun ownership
Maintain or expand the Affordable Care Act	*Health care*	Repeal the Affordable Care Act
Amnesty for undocumented immigrants, allow undocumented people to obtain drivers' licenses	*Immigration*	Prevent amnesty, no drivers' licenses, create a national ID card, add border fences
Increase	*Minimum wage*	Lower or eliminate
Legalize	*Same-sex marriage*	Ban
End	*School vouchers*	Expand
Increase taxes, especially for wealthy	*Taxes*	Cut taxes, especially for businesses

Liberalism — *Conservatism*

Since the 1980s, more people have identified themselves as Democrats than as Republicans. But one frustration for both parties is that increasingly larger numbers of people consistently have not identified with either party.[14] Instead, the percentage of Americans self-identifying as independent has grown sharply (see Figure 7.3). Why? A big part of it is Americans' deep frustration with the inability of the federal government to enact policies.

An increase in partisanship also means that voters have shown less inclination in recent decades to back candidates of different parties in a single election, a practice known as **split-ticket voting.** From 1964 until 1988, as many as one-third of House elections featured a candidate of one party winning even though a presidential candidate of the other party got the most votes in that House candidate's district. Once people identify a group to which they belong, "they are much more likely to vote for their party and less likely to split a ticket," according to political scientist Matthew Levendusky. "They are more likely to become devoted cheerleaders."[15] In 2016, despite deep divisions in the Republican Party establishment, every state that went for Trump elected a Republican senator. On the other side of the aisle, every state that went in Clinton's favor elected a Democrat to the Senate.

The Party Assists in Policy Formation and Governing

If they have been successful in mobilizing citizens to vote for the candidates they have selected and supported, a party's members take office and begin the process of governing. At the national level, during presidential nomination

FIGURE 7.3

Americans' Party Identification over Time

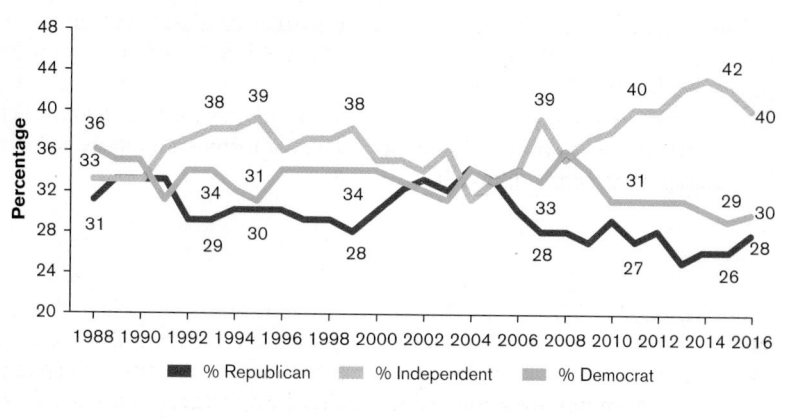

U.S. Party Identification, Yearly Averages, 1988–2016

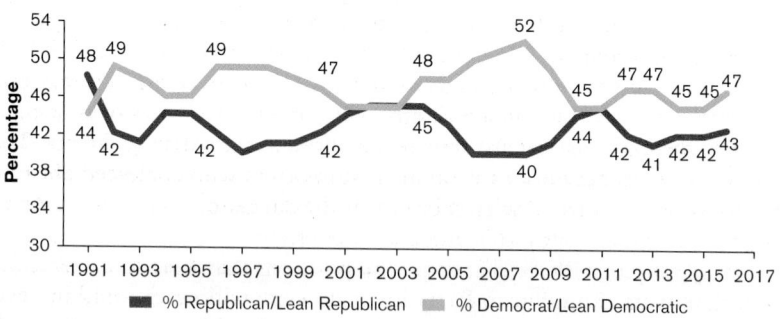

U.S. Party Identification (Including Independent Leanings), Annual Averages, Gallup Polls, 1991–2016

Note: Gallup began regularly measuring independent party leanings in 1991. Data for 2016 are current through September 18, 2016.

Sources: Jeffrey M. Jones, "Democratic, Republican Identification near Historical Lows," Gallup, January 11, 2016, www.gallup.com/poll/188096/democratic-republican-identification-near-historical-lows .aspx?g_source=Politics&g_medium=lead&g_campaign=tiles; Gallup, "Party Affiliation," www.gallup.com/ poll/15370/party-affiliation.aspx. Copyright © 2016 Gallup, Inc. All rights reserved. The content is used with permission; however, Gallup retains all rights of republication.

conventions, party members write, argue over, and agree on a **party platform**, which seeks to define the party's general stance on issues. These platforms are then voted on at the conventions.

The pressures that parties face to point out sharp differences between their positions and those of the opposition have led to increasing political **polarization**. Polarization isn't the result of a flaw in our constitutional system, but the Constitution's separation of powers has made it worse. In Washington, increased polarization has led to **gridlock**, which occurs when parties are unable to find any common ground to work together, an increasingly common occurrence over the past few decades.

All members of a political party do not hold the same beliefs. Each party contains factions within it that try to pressure the party to adopt its positions. Labor unions are one important faction within the Democratic Party; they push the party to raise the minimum wage and pass other bills aimed at improving working conditions. In the Republican Party, the House Freedom Caucus has become an influential faction within the last decade. It is not a formal party but a loosely organized collection of groups that demands steep cuts in government spending, extremely limited regulation of private companies, and more accountability from government employees.

In 2016, Both Parties Chose but at a Cost

By the time of the Democratic National Convention, it was clear that the Democratic Party's rules had worked in Hillary Clinton's favor. Even though Sanders actually won the vote in some state primaries and caucuses, the party's rules for how delegates are allocated neutralized his victory, handing Clinton the nomination. The Democratic Party had developed a specific set of rules precisely because it wanted to be able to pick presidential nominees strategically. Party members believed that long-term party members would have an interest in backing the strongest possible candidates and that giving those officials the power to switch their votes could avoid messy fights over the nomination.[16] The Democratic Party provided Clinton with other advantages over Sanders. The most obvious was that she actually belonged to the party; he did not. That gave her a broad network of prominent supporters who coalesced ahead of primary voting to warn of what they saw as the danger of a Sanders candidacy affecting other races in which Democrats were running.

In his campaign, Donald Trump took positions that were so extreme that fewer than usual Republican Party loyalists were willing to join him, even though his stances and pugnacious style attracted public support. But as he gained strength in the polls and began winning primaries, those party officials were caught in a difficult bind. Trump's candidacy exposed the Republican Party's weaknesses in several ways. Republicans leaders could not, as they had in some past elections, unify around a consensus candidate. None of the party-favorite, mainstream candidates succeeded in captivating broad swaths of voters and all eventually dropped out. Changes in party nomination rules that were brokered between conservative activists and party leaders in 2012—proportional delegate selection in the primaries and a shorter primary calendar—also ended up providing Trump with significant and unexpected institutional advantages.

For both Democrat and Republican Party elites, rules and institutions had been established to help bring order to an often chaotic process, though their nomination rules were different. For both establishments, however, things turned out differently.

1. The responsible party model focuses on the need for party leaders to be less cohesive and offer a variety of perspectives to voters.

   a. True
   b. False

2. How do state caucuses and primaries differ?

3. How has party identification by the American electorate changed in recent decades?

4. What challenge to the theory that "the party decides" did the Sanders and Trump campaigns pose?

Answer Key: 1. b; 2. Answers should focus both on the different mechanics of the processes and on the differences between participants; 3. Answers should emphasize the fact that while most Americans still identify as either Democratic or Republican, the percentage of those who identify as independents has risen; 4. Answers should focus on the candidates' different challenges to the party establishment.

AMERICAN POLITICAL PARTIES UNDERGO CYCLES OF CHANGE

- Describe how American party systems have changed over time.

For about the past 150 years, most politicians have belonged to either the Democratic or Republican Party. Since then, control of government has shifted back and forth between the parties in periods of **realignment**, which occur when public support shifts substantially from one party to the other. Periods of realignment may be ushered in by **critical elections** (or critical eras) in which, according to political scientist Aldrich, a short event or era leads to a "new period of relative stability."[17]

Party Systems Are Eras of Stable Party Control

Political scientists have drawn on the underlying idea to which Aldrich was referring—periods of stability punctuated by periods of rapid change—in their debates about the boundaries of major eras in party control and how decisive a particular election was in signaling a change in those boundaries. They call the more or less stable eras **party systems**. Political scientists often divide American political history into six party systems (see Figure 7.4).

The First Party System, 1790-1828: Factions and the Creation of America's First Political Parties

America's first president, George Washington, was not a member of a political party and indeed had warned the nation about the dangers partisanship posed to the young Republic. However, during his tenure, Washington's administration split into two factions: those like Treasury secretary Alexander Hamilton and Vice President John Adams supporting a strong federal government and those like Secretary of State Thomas Jefferson and James Madison who believed that individual states should be given more authority over their own affairs.

FIGURE 7.4

American Party Systems

FIRST PARTY SYSTEM
1790–1828
- Hamilton and Adams's Federalist Party: strong federal government
- Jefferson and Madison's Democratic-Republicans: more power to states

SECOND PARTY SYSTEM
1828–1856
- Demise of the Democratic-Republican Party, replaced largely by the Whig Party
- Decline of the Federalist Party; rise of the Democratic Party

THIRD PARTY SYSTEM
1856–1892
- Disputes about slavery precipitate realignment. Party identification becomes regionally divided
- "Free Soil" Democrats join Whigs, together form Republican Party: opposed to slavery

FOURTH PARTY SYSTEM
1892–1932
- Democrats and Republicans dominate with some third party challenges.
- Electorate divided by urban/rural splits and other policy issues

FIFTH PARTY SYSTEM
1932–1968
- Depression Era Democratic Party focuses on strong federal government
- Republican Party fights for smaller federal role

SIXTH PARTY SYSTEM
1968–present
- Democratic and Republican Parties remain divided about role of government but constituency changes with Nixon's "Southern Strategy."

As these individuals tried to gain support for their policies in Congress and in the state legislatures, they coalesced into two parties: the Democratic-Republicans (Jefferson and Madison) and the Federalists (Adams and Hamilton).

The Second Party System, 1828–1856: The Roots of Mass Politics

The Democratic-Republican Party had largely dissolved by 1824, with many of its members moving to form what became known as the Whig Party. This era also saw the decline of the Federalist Party. Due to the granting of suffrage to large numbers of white men who had previously been excluded because of their lack of wealth or property, this era saw the rise of the Democratic Party and the election of Andrew Jackson as president in 1828. The Democratic Party remained the dominant party in Congress for the next three decades. The politics of national campaigns evolved into how we now think about them, featuring broad appeals to voters and strengthening party organizations.

The Third Party System, 1856-1892:
The Issue of Slavery Upends the Party System

The unresolved issue of slavery led to a major realignment, with members of both parties divided among themselves. This led to the forming of two new parties. "Free Soil" Democrats joined with Whigs in arguing that slavery should be kept out of the rapidly expanding southwestern territories in the United States. They stressed a belief in the potential of the individual and argued against slavery on moral grounds.[18] The antislavery Whigs and Democrats formed the Republican Party. The new Republican Party won control of the House of Representatives but then lost it two years later. That led the party to broaden its appeal to owners of small farms and businesses, and it succeeded in recapturing control of the House in 1858. Two years later, it also took control of the Senate and elected Abraham Lincoln as president.[19] After the Civil War, the United States entered the period of two-party dominance by the Democratic and Republicans. Party identification became sharply regional, with Republicans dominating the Northeast and Democrats the South. Support for the parties was divided in the midwestern states.

The Fourth Party System, 1892-1932:
New Divisions in the American Party System

During this era, Democrats and Republicans continued to dominate national politics, though not without occasional challenges by third parties. Slavery had ended, but the two parties were divided by the politics of Reconstruction and differences of opinion about how strongly the federal government should act to secure civil rights. In addition, divisions between urban and rural voters as well as debates over immigration and federal policy in an era of massive industrialization shaped politics and party success and failure.

The Fifth Party System, 1932-1968:
Economic Crisis and a New Party System

In 1932 the Great Depression ushered in another major change in the party system. The election of Franklin Roosevelt in 1932 and in three subsequent elections led to a period of Democratic Party dominance. Between 1930 and 1994, the Democrats lost their majority in the House just twice, in 1946 and 1952, and they quickly regained control two years later both times.[20] The Democratic Party emphasized a commitment to a strong federal government in the service of social welfare policies. Republicans emphasized a smaller role for the federal government and less involvement in and regulation of the economy.

The Sixth Party System, 1968-Present Day: Shaping Modern Contours of American Party Politics

During the sixth party system, the Democratic Party remained focused on a vigorous federal government in the service of securing civil rights and support for affirmative action and a woman's right to choose. Republicans remained focused on a smaller federal government, advocating conservative views on social issues, lower taxes, and fewer restrictions on American businesses. What changed were the coalitions of voters supporting the parties, especially with regard to the geography of partisan support in the nation.

The underpinnings of today's Republican Party were laid in 1964 when its presidential nominee, Barry Goldwater, was roundly defeated by incumbent Democratic president Lyndon B. Johnson. The Republican Party's conservative base, frustrated by Goldwater's loss but still animated by his opposition to civil rights legislation, began shifting away from the Northeast and toward the rapidly growing South and West, enabling Nixon to win the presidency. Much of this had been driven by the realignment of large numbers of southern white voters from the Democratic Party to the Republican Party during the civil rights era. Nixon strategist Kevin Phillips had urged the president to pursue a "southern strategy" and play on whites' negative reaction to the Civil Rights Act of 1964.[21]

The Republican Party's fortunes declined temporarily as a result of the Watergate scandal, which led to Nixon's resignation in 1974. But Ronald Reagan reinvigorated the party with his landslide critical election win in 1980 against Democrat Jimmy Carter. Reagan's message of lower taxes, smaller government, and a strong defense remains highly influential in the GOP today.

In 1992 Democrat Bill Clinton prodded his party toward the ideological center after years of being depicted as being too captive to its most liberal factions. But two years later, Republican representative Newt Gingrich emerged with a sharply partisan approach that focused on intensifying public resentment of Washington politicians. Gingrich's moves helped his party break the Democrats' forty-year hold on the House and also regain control of the Senate. But continued warring between the parties helped propel Clinton to reelection in 1996.

With Republicans in search of someone who could unite the party, Texas governor George W. Bush campaigned in 2000 as a "compassionate conservative." He lost the popular vote to Vice President Al Gore but carried every southern state while drawing 83 percent of the evangelical Christian vote.[22]

At the state level, the Republican Party began using the congressional redistricting process to redraw districts to move greater numbers of Democrats into cities, making the Republican Party more competitive in suburban areas. Meanwhile, northeastern states became less Republican as large numbers of people migrated to the South and West and the mostly moderate and liberal Republicans who remained were overshadowed by what had become a southern-anchored party.

In 2008 Republicans hoped that Arizona senator John McCain could muster enthusiasm among voters with his national security credentials and heroic story of survival as a prisoner of war in Vietnam. Nonetheless, he lost to Barack Obama, who took 53 percent of the popular vote, the best Democratic percentage since 1964. Democrats also kept control of the House and Senate and eventually had a sixty-vote majority in the latter chamber to give them even more clout.

FIGURE 7.5

Changes in Party Control, 2000-2016

Election	Presidency	House	Senate
2000	Republican George W. Bush	Republican	Democrat
2002		Republican	Republican
2004	Republican George W. Bush	Republican	Republican
2006		Democrat	Democrat
2008	Democrat Barack Obama	Democrat	Democrat
2010		Republican	Democrat
2012	Democrat Barack Obama	Republican	Democrat
2014		Republican	Republican
2016	Republican Donald Trump	Republican	Republican

The party's dominance was extremely short-lived. President Obama pushed several pieces of economic- and health care-related legislation that led to a political backlash that gave rise to the Tea Party movement. The Tea Party was credited with helping Republicans regain control of the House in the 2010 elections. The weakened economy, with an unemployment rate stuck at around 8 percent, led Republicans to confidently predict they could recapture the White House in 2012. But the party did not coalesce quickly around its candidate, Mitt Romney. Romney and other Republicans sought to make the elections a referendum on the president's handling of the economy, but Democrats portrayed Romney as a wealthy corporate executive with an inability to understand average Americans. Not only did Obama win but Democrats kept their majority status in the Senate.

As we have seen, the 2016 election did not go as either the Republican or the Democratic Parties planned. Both have been forced to take a hard look at how they might please their party bases while at the same time appealing to other groups to form a winning electoral and governing strategy. See Figure 7.5.

A Seventh Party System?

The sixth party system has been one of the longest in the nation's history. However, it is unclear how much longer it will last. The Democratic and Republican Parties are trying to stay relevant in an age of intense and increasing polarization. That polarization has led some voters to become engaged not just because they support their party but out of an intense dislike of the other side.

It remains to be seen what this means for the parties. Robert Reich, an economist and liberal activist who served as secretary of labor under President Clinton, predicted an antiestablishment "People's Party" made up of disaffected Democrats and Republicans could take root as soon as 2020.[23] Others say such a shift could occur but that it's also possible the parties could absorb elements that are currently in the other party.

The Democratic Party, however, has had its own problems. Democrats were unable to translate the support Obama enjoyed into broader enthusiasm for the party in general and unable to recruit successful candidates for many lower political offices. As a result, during Obama's two terms, the Democrats lost many seats in the House, Senate, and state legislatures as well as more state governorships. Part of the reason was Republicans' ability in many states to redraw congressional districts after the 2010 census to make it easier for members of their party to win and remain in office. Another reason was the continued inability of Democrats to turn out their most loyal supporters in midterm elections, when a presidential candidate isn't on the ballot.

In the cases of both the Democratic and Republican Parties, many experts agree that they are institutions formed in a different era; they now must deal with a host of obstacles to maintain the social conditions that help parties thrive.[24]

America's Electoral System Leads to Two-Party Dominance

There is no law requiring that American national politics be dominated by two major political parties. Other countries have none, one, two, or many political parties dominating national politics with the existence of more than two being the norm. With a few very important exceptions, a two-party system has been dominant for most of America's political history. Why?

Scholars usually point to institutional explanations for America's two-party dominance, specifically the ways in which candidates are elected to national office, especially Congress. The U.S. method of voting—a **single-member plurality system** in which voters have a single vote for one candidate and the candidate with the votes wins—encourages this. Other countries have **proportional representation systems** in which the rules discourage a two-party system. Although there are many differences between nations in the details, proportional representation systems award party representation in legislative bodies based upon percentage of votes overall.

In the American winner-take-all single-member plurality system, the candidate who gets the most votes in a state or congressional district wins the election. In presidential elections, with the exceptions of Maine and Nebraska, the candidate who wins the popular vote in a state wins all of that state's electoral votes.

The winner-take-all system allows the largest politically cohesive groups—the Democrats or Republicans—to elect almost every office in a jurisdiction. Proponents of the system say this promotes stability; if people are happy with the job that a representative from one of those parties is doing, they can keep voting for that representative's party even after he or she leaves office.

Critics say it doesn't do much to help people who are stuck in an area in which one party dominates, such as Republicans in cities and Democrats in rural states. They say that this can be a significant barrier to encouraging greater numbers of people, including minority groups and young people, to take part in politics. Instead, candidates can run divisive campaigns aimed at turning out only the most partisan voters since the winner-take-all system provides little incentive to reach out to opponents.

Minor Parties May Challenge the Two Major Parties

The Democratic and Republican Parties have occasionally had some competition. **Third-party candidates** usually focus on a single issue that they don't think the major parties are emphasizing enough. "What happens is, third parties act as a gadfly," said Sean Wilentz, director of the American Studies program at Princeton University. "There'll be an issue that's being neglected or that is being purposely excluded from national debate because neither party wants to face the political criticism that it would bring."[25]

Third-party candidates do sometimes make fairly big splashes. In the 2000 election, consumer activist Ralph Nader captivated many liberals when he ran for president under the Green Party banner. He won 2.74 percent of the popular vote—just enough, many Democrats continue to believe, to deny the presidency to Al Gore.[26] The tendency among some voters to conclude that a vote for a third-party candidate essentially is a vote helping someone they oppose has made it difficult for third-party candidates to win national elections.

The Democratic and Republican Parties have worked to discourage third-party candidacies. One way is to prevent those candidates from taking part in presidential debates. Another is having local officials set stringent requirements for candidates to collect a certain number of signatures before they can appear on a ballot, which can be difficult for many third-party hopefuls.

During the general election in 2016, as the Clinton and Trump campaigns both struggled against heavily negative perceptions, third-party challengers emerged, drawing votes from both. Gary Johnson, candidate for the Libertarian Party; Jill Stein, the Green Party candidate; and Evan McMullin, an independent candidate, all vied to establish their respective parties as credible challengers to the Democratic and Republican Parties. Many observers originally expected third-party presidential candidates to do well, Johnson and Stein in particular; ultimately none presented a serious challenge to Hillary Clinton or Donald Trump.[27]

WHAT HAVE I LEARNED?

1. The primary reason for two-party dominance in American political history is ____.
   a. The Constitution of the United States
   b. U.S. Supreme Court decisions
   c. The method of electing individuals to national office
   d. All of the above

2. What issues have led to major transitions between American party systems?

3. Why might the election of 2016 usher in a new party system?

Answer Key: 1. c; 2. Answers might focus on crises and perceived failures by the parties to address them or the parties' failure to adequately incorporate Americans' concerns; 3. Answers should emphasize cleavages between party members and supporters.

ELECTIONS AND CAMPAIGNS HAVE MANY MOVING PARTS

As we explored previously, political parties ordinarily do strongly affect the outcomes of elections. Next we look more closely at the electoral process that brings candidates to office. National elections are the tools with which the American political system chooses its presidents and members of Congress. National campaigns are the tools that would-be representatives use to connect to American voters.

- Understand the rules surrounding national elections and campaigns and the function of those rules.

Campaigns and elections are both composed of many moving parts. The rules governing them, the people who choose to run, and the composition of the electorate all may shift over time, sometimes with profound and long-lasting consequences. Candidates, even those who have been in elected office for years, need to be aware and adaptable, ready to change message or strategy if necessary.

The Framers of the Constitution did not want the system they created to be *too* democratic; they feared the potential mischief of faction and the dangers of tyranny of the majority. Therefore, they built in roadblocks to slow down the transmission of the "passions of the people" into public policy. Senators, for example, were originally chosen by state legislatures rather than by the people.

Another safeguard against faction is the system of American federalism, which divides sovereignty between the nation and the states. The Constitution requires that "The Times, Places and Manner of holding Elections for Senators and Representatives, shall be prescribed in each State by the Legislature thereof."[28] The effects of this clause have been consequential. Today its language ensures that states can devise their own voting technologies, whether electronic or paper based, and have different policies on whether or not those convicted of felonies are allowed to vote.

American elections are also notable for the fact that they occur on fixed and predictable schedules. Unlike in parliamentary systems in which the chief national executive has the choice of when to "call" an election (subject to specific rules and constraints), in the United States, voters weigh in on their president every four years, regardless of what is happening in the nation or world, through economic depressions and even war.

Elections Help Hold Elected Officials Accountable

In a representative democracy, elections serve other important purposes besides selecting individuals for a specific office or position in government. Elections are the key way Americans can keep their elected officials in line. Voters achieve this by using the threat of voting an **incumbent** out of office and voting in a **challenger** if they decide the incumbent's performance has not been in line with their goals and policy preferences. This reflecting back on an incumbent's past performance in an election is called **retrospective voting**.[29] Elections also serve as a signal—a way of transmitting information to elected officials about voters' preferences and priorities.

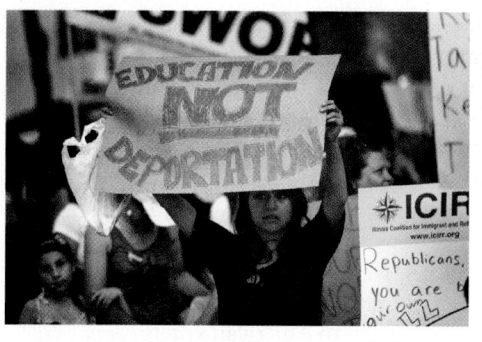

Protestors outside Republican Party headquarters in Chicago, Illinois, hold signs calling for immigration reform and a new focus on domestic policies such as education, which is one of the most important issues to many Latino voters. Scott Olson/Getty Images

Elections help define or change the national agenda, especially when candidates respond to the growing electoral and political power of voters whose agenda-setting preferences may not have been well-addressed in the past. For instance, trying to assess the top issues for Latino voters, one of the fastest-growing demographic groups in the United States, is not always an easy task. It is a diverse group, and many surveys are not conducted in Spanish. However, a 2014 Pew Research Center survey concluded that the top five issues for Latino registered voters were—in order of perceived importance—education, jobs and the economy, health care, immigration, and conflicts in the Middle East.[30]

Elections also confer legitimacy on the laws and public policies enacted. Finally, participation in the electoral system may serve to remind Americans of their rights and liberties and the need to protect those rights; thus, they are educative.

Elections Are Expensive

In the 2016 presidential campaign, roughly $1.5 billion in total was spent in support of each of the campaigns of Democratic candidate Hillary Clinton and Republican candidate Donald Trump and the other minor party candidates, a figure that includes candidate spending, national party spending, and money spent by others in support of their respective campaigns.[31]

Adding in total candidate and outside spending on the other national elections that year, the total spent was about $6.8 billion. According to CBS News, "That's more than what consumers spend on cereal ($6 billion), pet grooming ($5.4 billion) and legal marijuana ($5.4 billion)."[32]

What Money Buys

What do candidates get for all of this money? Where does it go? First and foremost, money buys media time on television and radio, in print, and in social media outlets. Some campaign advertisements focus on the candidate's qualities and creating a positive image. Others focus on policy differences between the candidate and his or her opponents. **Negative campaign advertisements** attack an opponent or opponents and try to raise doubts in voters' minds about them. While negative campaigning is pervasive and often uncomfortable, not all scholars agree that it is a bad thing. Political scientist John Geer has argued that negative campaign ads may actually "increase the quality of information available to voters as they make choices in elections."[33]

Money also allows a candidate to hire campaign staff, help manage the campaign message, coordinate a campaign and media strategy, arrange public appearances, and conduct public opinion polls. Efforts to mobilize voters or potential voters, called **get out the vote (GOTV)** efforts, also cost money. Finally, having a sizable war chest, especially early in a campaign, might discourage potential challengers from entering a race in the first place. In this way, money is also a strategic weapon. For all of these reasons, the cost of winning the presidency has only gone up.

Can Campaign Contributions Be Effectively Regulated?

Given the power of money, several sources, including activists, the Supreme Court, and the federal government, have long struggled to control the dangers of campaign finance. In the 1970s, following the Watergate scandal, Congress passed the Federal Election Campaign Act, which created the Federal Election Commission (FEC), a bureaucratic entity charged with overseeing and implementing national campaign finance laws. The act also set rules for the disclosure of the source of campaign funds, placed limits on campaign contributions, and instituted a system for public financing of presidential elections. In 1976, in *Buckley v. Valeo*, the Supreme Court upheld the constitutionality of restrictions on campaign contributions by individuals, though not on monies spent independently, monies spent by the candidates themselves, or the total amount of contributions.[34]

When it comes to money and elections, however, controlling the influence of money has often been like handling a balloon—squeeze it in one place and it seems to pop up somewhere else. In 2002, in an effort to more effectively control the balloon, Congress passed the Bipartisan Campaign Reform Act (BCRA), which placed stricter limits on campaign contributions. Since then, however, the Supreme Court has limited these regulations. In *Citizens United v. Federal Election Commission* (2010), in a divided 5–4 decision, the Court struck down portions of the BCRA, ruling that independent, uncoordinated political contributions by corporations during political campaigns is protected by the First Amendment.[35]

The "new world" of campaign finance in the United States is thorny. Although limits on individual campaign donations remain in place, groups of individuals may contribute, but the rules are complicated. **Political action committees (PACs)** are groups of at least fifty individuals who seek to raise money to elect and defeat candidates. PACs may contribute higher dollar amounts than individuals; though, again, there are limits. In the wake of the Court's decision in *Citizens United*, certain types of PACs called **super PACs** are allowed to spend unlimited amounts on a political campaign; however, that spending must not be coordinated with that campaign. These contributions raise a tricky issue. Even if there is no contact between a super PAC and members of a campaign, if the super PAC, for example, runs a series of campaign advertisements that work, candidates will take notice. Information will still change hands, even if this transfer is uncoordinated and legal.

1. American representative democracy is designed to provide as many opportunities as possible for voters to weigh in on public policy directly.

   a. True
   b. False

2. In a political campaign, money buys a candidate _____.

   a. Media coverage
   b. Get out the vote (GOTV) efforts
   c. The possibility of scaring off potential challengers
   d. All of the above

3. A super PAC _____.

   a. Can spend unlimited amounts of money but must not coordinate with a campaign

   b. Has strict limits placed on its allowable contributions
   c. Can spend unlimited amounts of money in coordination with a campaign
   d. Can no longer make campaign contributions

4. In a debate about the degree to which contributions to political campaigns should be restricted or regulated, what might some arguments be for each side?

Answer Key: 1. b; 2. d; 3. a; 4. Answers for restrictions may focus on wealth inequality or factions. Answers against might focus on free speech and the First Amendment.

PRESIDENTIAL AND CONGRESSIONAL ELECTIONS: THE SAME BUT DIFFERENT

The basics of both presidential and legislative elections are, unsurprisingly, laid out in the U.S. Constitution and subsequent amendments. For the presidency, that includes the frequency of these elections (every four years) and the general rules defining what it takes to run for the presidency. Much of the structure of the congressional electoral process is the same as it is for presidential elections. For example, states still structure the nuts and bolts of the process. Would-be national legislators also seek out their party's nomination, just as aspirants to the presidency must do. And they must then win in the general election, just as presidential nominees must do. Many important structures and processes are also influenced by two other sets of actors: the states and the political parties.

- Understand the stages and rules governing presidential elections.
- Explain the issues affecting congressional campaigns, including the roles of constituency and incumbency.

Presidential Campaigns Are Divided into Different Phases

Presidential elections have two official campaign phases: the nomination campaign in which candidates try to secure the nomination of their political party and the general election campaign in which successful nominees compete for the presidency. While the ways in which parties structure their nomination processes have changed, the general trend in modern campaigns has been one of increasing openness, of taking some of the power away from party elites and placing it in the hands of party activists and average Americans. This is not to say that party leaders do not matter, however. They still have more power to shape the nomination than the average American voter.

Before the Official Campaign

Nomination campaigns begin long before the actual events through which the nominees are picked. Presidential hopefuls may work on laying the foundations for their bids years before the official process begins. They begin raising money and set up an **exploratory committee**, which is subject to different federal campaign finance rules than a campaign committee. An exploratory committee allows a potential candidate to "test the waters," to travel around the country in order to conduct public opinion polls, make outreach phone calls, and raise money to pay for all of this. In addition, a candidate's announcement that he or she has formed an exploratory committee may gain a bit of a bump in media coverage.

If a candidate decides to press ahead, his or her campaign will become official, a status that can be triggered through a potential candidate's statements and fund-raising or other activities.

The Nomination Process

Once the official campaign process kicks off, declared candidates vie with others in their own party for that party's nomination. Beginning early in the election year, candidates seek to get the support of party delegates, whose votes they will later need to secure the party's nomination. While many of the rules governing the nomination process are set by federal and state laws, most of the details about *how* things actually work are hammered out by the parties themselves. Key differences exist across states and between the parties themselves. As we discussed earlier in the chapter, most states hold presidential primary elections in which a state's voters choose delegates who support a particular candidate. The concluding phase of the nomination process takes place in the national conventions held by the parties late in the summer of the presidential election year.

The General Election

Once selected by their parties, the nominees then proceed to the general election campaign. At this point, candidates need to pivot from speaking mainly to their base of core supporters and begin

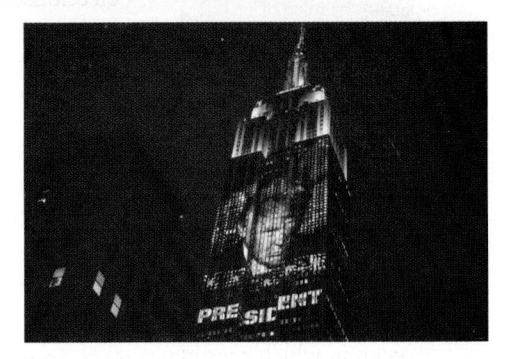

Donald Trump's 2016 electoral victory is announced against the backdrop of the Empire State Building. Vanessa Carvalho/Brazil Photo Press/LatinContent/Getty Images

to try to appeal to independent and undecided voters. This can be a trap. Voters who participate during the nomination campaigns trend toward the wings of their parties, and there are not often enough of them to win a general election.

Maintaining the energy of core party voters while also appealing to the undecided middle is a challenge. If core partisan voters think their nominee has moved too far to the center and abandoned core party goals, they will not help mobilize undecided voters to join their nominee's side. On the other hand, if a candidate has survived the nomination campaign by appealing primarily to the extremes of the party, then he or she may be seen as too far left or too far right to be the best person for governing the nation in the views of independents and undecided voters.

The Rules of the Electoral College Decide the Presidency

The dynamics of the **Electoral College** system presents another significant challenge. Technically speaking, American voters do not vote for the president. Instead, they vote for a slate of electors pledged to vote for a nominee in the presidential election. These electors are chosen by party leaders within their respective states in a system called the Electoral College. It is their vote that actually chooses the president. Established in the original Constitution and modified since the founding, its roots lie partly in the Framers' mistrust of direct democracy but also in concerns of convention delegates from less populous states who feared Virginians would always be elected since theirs was the most populous and powerful state at the time.

Presidential candidates need to clear 270 Electoral College votes in order to win. Each of the fifty states is allocated one electoral vote for each of its two senators and one for each of its members of the House of Representatives, guaranteeing each state at least three electoral votes. Adding the three electoral votes allocated to the District of Columbia brings the total to 538. In all but two states, Maine and Nebraska, electoral votes are awarded in a winner-take-all system.

Electors are chosen from party leaders and loyal activists. Although they have pledged to vote for their party's candidate, there is a risk that they may become **faithless electors**, changing their minds in between the general election and the electors' vote.

This system has significant consequences. Theoretically, it is possible to become president by winning in only the eleven most populous states. More significantly, a presidential candidate can win the presidency without actually winning the popular vote. That can happen when a third-party candidate poses a serious challenge, which contributed to President Bill Clinton's victory in 1992, or when a candidate wins a majority of the popular vote but loses in the Electoral College, which happened in 2000 when George W. Bush defeated Al Gore, and again in 2016 when Donald Trump defeated Hillary Clinton (see Figure 7.6).

The system of electors shapes candidate strategies. Given that all but two states award their electoral votes in a block, candidates tend to focus their campaigns on states with a large number of electoral votes and those whose electoral votes seem to be in play, largely ignoring other states.

FIGURE 7.6

Electoral College Results, 2016

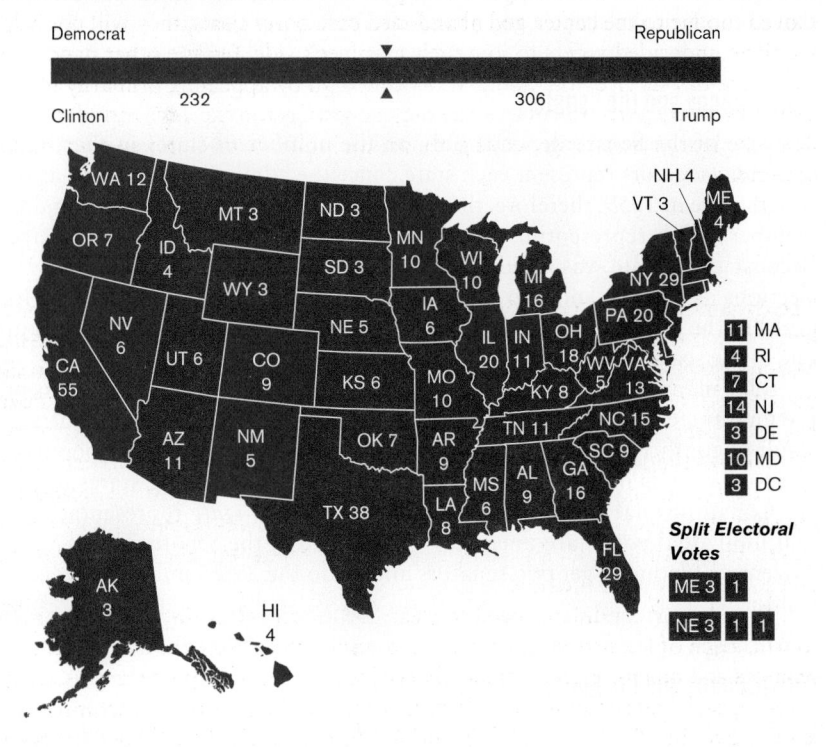

Note: Voting outcomes as of November 29, 2016.

In Congressional Elections Constituency Is Key

The most important difference between legislative and presidential elections is defining whom the legislative candidate hopes to represent. States differ on where the bar is set for congressional nominees in the general elections. In most states, a candidate needs a **plurality** of votes in the primaries or general election, meaning that the candidate receives more votes than any other candidate. In other states, a candidate needs a **majority** of votes (more than 50 percent), which may lead to a **runoff election** between the two with the highest total if no one candidate scores a majority.

At the most basic level, the rules governing the division of voters into **constituencies**—bodies of voters in a given area who elect a representative or senator—are laid out in the Constitution. However, the process of this division, especially for the House of Representatives, is often controversial. Even the

Supreme Court has had to weigh in on the process in the past. The ways in which incumbent members of Congress use their incumbency to enhance their chances of getting reelected have significant effects on the behavior of all candidates in an election. Finally, every election is unique. Local, state, and national conditions during a given election matter as well, and there are always unanticipated events that can powerfully shape a given candidate's electoral chances.

Constituency and the Senate

The size of the Senate depends only on the number of states in the Union since two senators represent each state. Since the admission of Hawaii as the fiftieth state in 1959, therefore, the Senate has been composed of one hundred members, each representing the entire state from which they were elected. Because the Senate was divided into three "classes" in order to stagger the elections of senators, no two senate seats from the same state will be up for grabs in the same election unless a retirement or other event has opened up one of the seats.

Like many other aspects of the basic structure of the federal government, the guarantee of equal state representation in the Senate came about as a result of conflicts and bargaining between less populous and more populous states as well as between slaveholding and non-slaveholding states during the Constitutional Convention. The result of equal *state* representation is that individual *voters* are unequally represented in the Senate. The 585,501 citizens of Wyoming get two senators and so do the 39.25 million citizens of California.

Constituency and the House of Representatives

In spite of the potential repercussions of equal state representation in the Senate, determining one's potential constituents is a very simple matter for that chamber. When it comes to the House of Representatives, however, things are a bit more complicated—and political.

Apportionment

While initially the size of the House was allowed to grow with the population, it is now fixed at 435 members.[36] The size of a state's representation in the House depends upon its population. The process of determining the number of representatives for each state is called **apportionment**; through this process the number of representatives is allocated based on the results of the census that is conducted every ten years. As part of the process of apportionment, each state is divided into one or more congressional districts with one seat in the House representing each district and each state guaranteed one representative, no matter how small its population.

Given the fact that the size of the House is capped, changes in population can produce "winners and losers" among the states following each census. Trends in population growth and distribution in recent decades have produced a clear pattern of gains in House seats for states in the South and the West and losses for states in the Northeast and Midwest.

Redistricting and Gerrymandering

While the process of apportionment has important consequences for the representation of states in the House, it also has important consequences for the boundaries of constituency. Following each census, states enter into the process of **redistricting** in which they redraw the electoral district boundaries. Seven states have only one representative; therefore, their district boundaries are the same as the boundaries of the state. Some states have undertaken redistricting *between* censuses, especially when a political party gains control over the state's legislative and executive branches, though many states have constitutional or legislative prohibitions against this practice.

The stakes involved in redistricting are high, and the process is often very political and controversial. In most states, the legislature appoints the members of a commission to draw the district boundaries. In others, a bipartisan or nonpartisan commission handles the process to try to make it less political, though the state legislatures typically still have to approve these plans.

The intentional use of redistricting to benefit a specific interest or group of voters is referred to as **gerrymandering**. The term comes from state legislative districts that were oddly drawn in 1812 under Massachusetts governor Elbridge Gerry to benefit his Democratic-Republican Party. Federalists complained that one district looked like a monster or a salamander, and the term created by the fusion of salamander with the governor's last name stuck. There are three types of gerrymandering: partisan, racial and ethnic, and incumbent.

Partisan Gerrymandering

Partisan gerrymandering aims to increase the representation of one political party at the expense of another. The idea is to concentrate the opposing party's supporters in a small number of districts, which that party will win easily. The party in control then tries to maximize the number of districts that its candidates will win comfortably but not by huge margins. By doing so, the party in charge of redistricting is able to "waste" many of the votes of its opposition since there is no more of an advantage—in terms of the number of House seats a party has—of winning 90 percent of the votes in any one district than there is by winning 55 percent. Redistricting can put incumbents at risk by changing the composition of their constituencies or by forcing two incumbents to run for the same seat.

Racial and Ethnic Gerrymandering

A second form of gerrymandering aims to increase the likelihood of electing members of racial and ethnic minorities as representatives by concentrating voters of minority ethnicity within specific congressional districts. Racial and ethnic gerrymandering results in **majority-minority districts** in which voters of minority ethnicity constitute an electoral *majority* within the electoral district. Racial and ethnic gerrymandering has led to some oddly shaped congressional districts—some of the most notable of which were drawn after the 1990 census. The Twelfth Congressional District in North Carolina, for example, "stitched together African American communities in several of the state's larger cities, using Interstate 85 . . . as the thread."[37]

Incumbent Gerrymandering

The third form of strategic redistricting is incumbent gerrymandering wherein district lines are drawn to protect the reelection prospects of an incumbent representative. It is often less compelling for a party in power in state government to undertake incumbent gerrymandering, as it does not necessarily improve the prospects of the party overall. In addition, ambitious members of a state legislature may themselves be eyeing a seat in the House, giving them a strong incentive to ensure their party's victory in their home district but few incentives to protect the electoral fortunes of a potential rival.

The Supreme Court and Congressional District Boundaries

In recent decades, the Supreme Court has become more active in ruling on congressional district boundaries, the drawing of which had generally been left up to the states and the political process. Affirming the "one person, one vote" rule of representation, the Court in two cases ruled that **malapportionment**—where the population is distributed in uneven numbers between legislative districts—is unconstitutional as it violates the equal protection clause of the Fourteenth Amendment.[38]

While the Court has highlighted potential problems with partisan gerrymandering in several recent cases, it has not gone so far as to declare the practice inherently unconstitutional. The Court has held that voters in these districts are still represented but by members from different political parties. *Davis v. Bandemer* (1986) involved an Indiana redistricting plan. The Court upheld the plan, ruling that the partisan gerrymander did not violate the Fourteenth Amendment's equal protection clause.[39] *Vieth v. Jubelirer* (2004) involved a Pennsylvania partisan gerrymander. In this case, the Court overturned the Republican-controlled gerrymander, but it did so on the grounds that the plan created districts with unequal numbers of voters, not because it was an attempt to favor one political party.[40] In 2006, in *League of United Latin American Citizens v. Perry*, the Court upheld most of the Texas redistricting plan from 2003 but required that one district's lines be redrawn to protect the voting rights of Hispanic Americans.[41] In June 2017, the Court, as its session ended, declared that it would consider revisiting the constitutionality of partisan gerrymandering in its session that would begin in October.[42] Given the nature of the Court in 2017, should it do so, whatever decision is made will no doubt be sharply divided.

The Court has also weighed in on the proper role of racial and ethnic considerations in drawing district boundaries. In *Thornburg v. Gingles* (1986), the

The Representational Consequences of the Great Compromise

Number of U.S. Residents per Senator

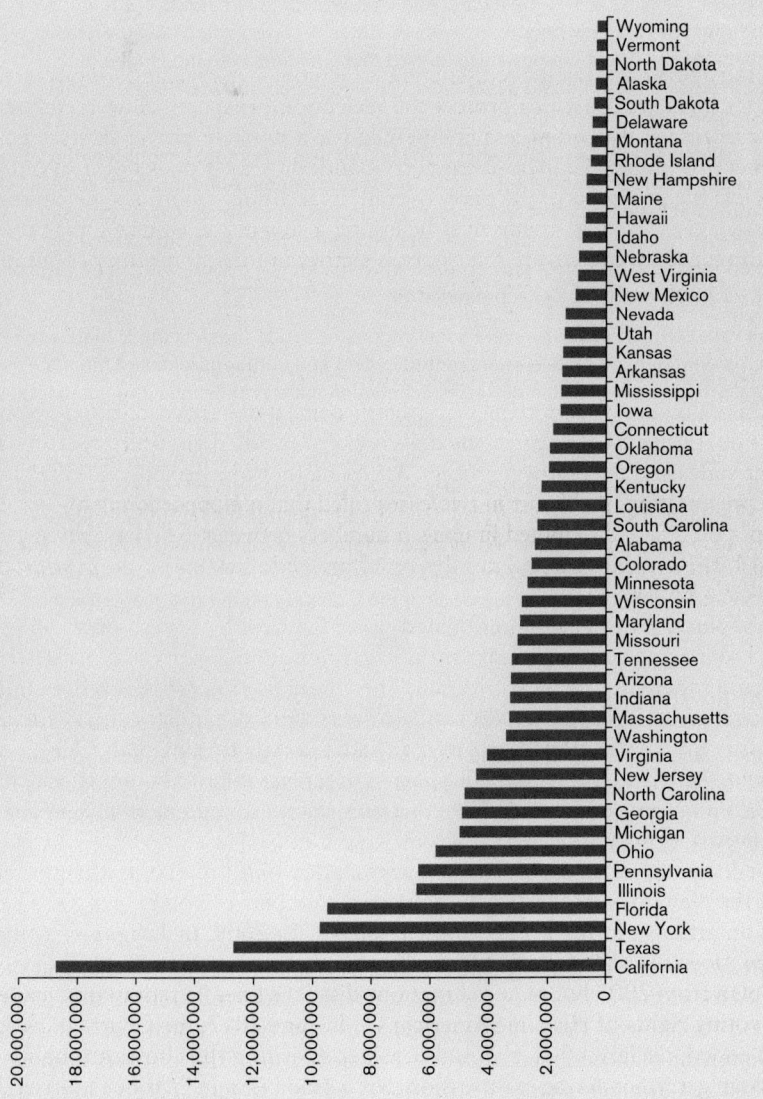

Source: Data are from "2012–2020 Federal Representation by People per House Seat, Senate Seat, and Electors," The Green Papers, January 5, 2011, www.thegreenpapers.com/Census10/FedRep.phtml?sort=Sena#table.

(Continued)

(Continued)

One of the most contentious battles in the Constitutional Convention was over changing the "one state, one vote" structure of state representation in the Confederation Congress (under the Articles of Confederation). Less populous states, such as New Jersey, Delaware, and Connecticut, were not about to consent to the formation of a new congress in which states received votes based on their populations. The Great Compromise settled this question, with the House of Representatives apportioning seats based on population and the Senate allotting seats equally, two to each state.

While the compromise avoided what many feared was a fight that might tear the young nation apart, it did so with representational consequences. Although each state is guaranteed at least one representative in the House, there are variations between states in the number of representatives per resident, which range from about six hundred thousand residents per representative to nearly a million, with an average of about 710,000 residents per representative.

These variations, however, are very small in comparison to those in the Senate wherein each resident of each state is represented by two senators regardless of the state's population. Given the sizable differences between state populations, the number of state residents per senator varies dramatically.

As they come from the most populous state in the Union, each of California's two senators must represent more than sixty-five times the number of citizens as a senator from Wyoming, the nation's least populous state.[45] This means California's senators are spread much more thinly when trying to address the concerns of individual constituents. There is also evidence that the least populous states benefit more from congressional spending than they would if the Constitution did not guarantee them equal representation in the Senate.[46]

WHAT DO YOU THINK?

Say that you are a researcher exploring whether or not citizens from less populous states receive better senatorial representation than those from the most populous states. How might you define *better*? What evidence would you look for to form your hypothesis?

Court overturned a state's legislative district boundaries on the basis that they diluted the electoral power of African American voters and violated their voting rights.[43] In *Shaw v. Reno* (1993), the Court rejected a North Carolina reapportionment plan designed to produce majority-minority districts because it resulted in a bizarrely shaped district and used race to such a degree in drawing these boundaries that it could "only be understood as an effort to segregate voters into separate districts on the basis of race."[44] Since *Shaw v. Reno*, states are allowed to use race as a consideration but not as the predominant factor in drawing district boundaries.

Congressional Incumbents Have Significant Institutional Advantages

In congressional elections, the most important determinant of who will win is incumbency. Stated simply, incumbents usually win, and those with serious aspirations to enter Congress are often, and wisely, very wary of challenging an incumbent representative or senator. Making full use of the resources available to them, incumbent representatives and senators possess many advantages over any candidate who might challenge them. This **incumbency advantage** has only grown stronger in recent decades.

The vast majority of congressional incumbents who seek reelection succeed. Incumbent senators and members of the house have reelection rates of 80 to 90 percent.[47] Given the fact that incumbents enjoy such an advantage, "nearly everything pertaining to candidates and campaigns for Congress is profoundly influenced by whether a candidate is already an incumbent, is challenging an incumbent, or is pursuing an open seat."[48]

The Logic of Incumbency

Political scientist David Mayhew explained the strategic logic of incumbents and how they use their institutional advantages to maximize their chances of reelection. For Mayhew, legislators are "single-minded seekers of re-election" who make the most of their institutional advantages.[49] These advantages include using their franking privileges, the free use of the mail for communication with constituents, to advertise their campaigns. Incumbents usually enjoy higher levels of name recognition than their challengers, which is increased by more media coverage than any potential challengers. In media coverage and public events, incumbents claim credit for what they have done in Washington and announce their positions on key pieces of legislation of interest to their constituents.[50] Finally, incumbents perform casework for individual constituents, especially in helping them deal with the federal and state bureaucracy.

If incumbents are usually in no danger, then why do they spend so much time and energy trying to secure reelection? Another strategic explanation involves decisions made by potential challengers. Not all challengers are equally credible, and incumbents maximize their resources to try to ensure that they will not face qualified challengers. Knowing the odds, credible challengers often wait for their chance to run in an **open seat election** in which there is no incumbent to face.

What makes for a high-quality challenger? Successful challengers are skillful with the media and public events. They also are knowledgeable about the issues and where their constituents stand on those issues. But they need two things above all else: experience and money. Experience is usually gained by moving up through the layers of local and state politics to become professional, polished, and respected. Money buys more than airtime, advertising, and campaign events—it also buys information, by, for instance, hiring pollsters to help them better understand their constituents' preferences. Money can help scare off potential opponents and signal to other potential donors that this is a campaign with a legitimate shot at success. Most challengers lack the financial resources to wage effective campaigns.[51]

1. Party leaders choose the timing of presidential general elections.

   a. True
   b. False

2. Apportionment refers to _____.

   a. The allocation of seats in the House of Representatives
   b. The allocation of seats in the Senate
   c. Congressional committee assignments
   d. The number of candidates who may run in a congressional election

3. Partisan gerrymandering is designed to _____.

   a. Spread your own party's voters out as much as possible
   b. Encourage the representation of members of minority groups

   c. Protect incumbents in the House of Representatives
   d. Concentrate the opposing party's voters in a small number of districts

4. What are some of the potential problems raised by the Electoral College?

5. Why do incumbents have such an advantage in congressional elections? Do you think that the nation should consider any electoral reforms to give challengers a better chance? If so, what might these be?

Answer Key: 1. b; 2. a; 3. d; 4. Answers may include the possibility, which happened again in 2016, of winning the popular vote but failing to secure the presidency. Answers might also include how the system alters presidential campaign strategies; 5. Answers should describe specific characteristics of theories of the incumbency advantage.

POLITICAL PARTICIPATION TAKES MANY FORMS

Everyday Americans are also involved in many ways in the political process—and not simply as the receivers of political messages from parties and candidates. Casting a ballot in an election is the form of **political participation** most think of when they consider participation, but other forms of participation can influence the choices of those in office and the attitudes and actions of other citizens. Efforts to work to make society better through political and nonpolitical action is called **civic engagement**. In their foundational study of American political participation, Sidney Verba and Norman H. Nie sorted acts of civic engagement into four categories: (1) voting, (2) supporting or participating in political campaigns, (3) contacting or pressuring politicians in office, and (4) acting outside of the electoral process—for example, by volunteering or organizing in concert with fellow citizens.[52] The first two of these forms of participation take place within the electoral process; the second two take place after its outcomes have been determined or outside of it.

- Describe the forms of political participation Americans engage in, including the factors that limit or facilitate engagement.

Within the electoral process, individuals may choose to vote. They may also act to support the candidacies of those vying for political office whether through working on campaigns, donating money, or convincing others to support their chosen candidate.

Once the elections are over, citizens have many ways to connect with their elected representatives if they want to make their preferences known about issues being discussed in government. They might join together to work cooperatively for a shared set of political goals by organizing members of their community or working with members of their religious communities. While Americans participate at the voting booth at lower rates than individuals in other democracies, their rates of nonelectoral participation are equal to or higher than their counterparts in other nations (see Figure 7.7).[53]

Individuals might also take part in a social movement, which occurs when a group of people come together to make social and political change and place ideas and issues on the political agenda. People in social movements participate in political protests, attend political meetings, contact elected officials, or reach out to other citizens to educate them on issues. Whether acting as a member of a social movement or on their own, individuals may also work on political campaigns, donate time and money to candidates, work in their communities, or contact their elected representatives. In all of these activities, individuals try to make their voices heard.

FIGURE 7.7

Americans' Participation in Elections Outside of the Voting Booth

Percent of respondents who reported having been involved in the following activities during the past year.

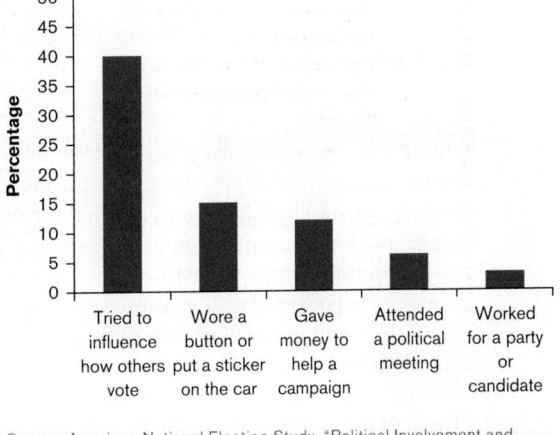

Source: American National Election Study, "Political Involvement and Participation in Politics," 2012, http://electionstudies.org/nesguide/gd-index.htm.

Voting Decisions Are Influenced by Institutional, Circumstantial, and Individual Factors

Participation in the electoral process is an essential component of a representative democracy, yet very large percentages of Americans do not vote. In 2016, only an estimated 58 percent of eligible voters showed up at the polls, placing the United States near the bottom of democratic nations based on **voter turnout**. Americans' relative lack of voting participation raises two immediate questions: Why? And, does it matter?

Anthony Downs has argued that the decision not to vote might very well be a rational one, given the costs of voting in terms of an individual's time and intellectual effort and the infinitesimally small probability that any one vote will prove to be decisive, especially in national elections.[54] In the view of democratic theorists, however, should all potential voters make a rational calculation not to vote, then the mechanism of representation would be endangered.

Many factors shape a person's decision of whether or not to vote. Some contributors to voter turnout are institutional, shaped by the laws and procedures surrounding the electoral process. Others depend upon the particulars of an election—for example, whether or not it takes place during a presidential election year. A third category of contributors centers on the potential voters themselves, their characteristics and lived experiences. Elsewhere in the book we have examined how individual characteristics impact *how* people vote and *who* they choose to support. Now, we will consider how these characteristics shape *whether or not* people vote. Political scientists count a set of individual factors as among the most important determinants for voting: level of economic status, level of education, political efficacy, age, race or ethnicity, gender, and partisan attachment.

Socioeconomic Status and Educational Attainment

Voting is costly. It takes time, commitment, and intellectual engagement. Not all voting-eligible Americans have the same resources with which to engage in the process of voting.[55] A key factor in voter turnout is an individual's **socioeconomic status (SES)**, which is a measure of an individual's wealth, income, occupation, and educational attainment.

A clear and consistent pattern in electoral participation is that Americans with higher levels of SES participate in electoral activities, likely because individuals with higher incomes have more money to donate to a political campaign. Also, certain occupations might be associated with networks in which political issues are more likely to be discussed and acted upon.

The most important contributor to the measure of an individual's SES, and one of the most important determinants of the decision to vote is the level of educational attainment by a potential voter. Not only are higher levels of educational attainment associated with higher incomes but they also reduce the "costs" of voting by making it easier to navigate the issues involved in an election and the process of becoming a voter itself.

Political Efficacy

Education also plays a role in shaping how individuals think about themselves as political actors and potential voters. The intellectual resources and skills that higher levels of education produce also increase an individual's sense of **political efficacy**, or one's confidence that she or he can make effective political change.

Age

Another trend is also clear: Young adult voting-eligible Americans vote at lower rates than members of older generations.[56] Again, like income and education, age is connected to many other factors. Older Americans are more likely to have higher levels of income and wealth. Another factor may be the challenges of learning about voter registration requirements, especially if the young adult voter is in college or has recently moved to a new state. For college students living in a different state, voter identification laws may add another hurdle to their decision to participate at the polling place. While a 1979 Supreme Court ruling affirmed the right of college students to vote in their states of school attendance,[57] state voting laws and local practices "often make students travel a rocky road."[58]

Racial and Ethnic Identities

The turnout of voting-age Americans is also highly correlated with racial and ethnic identity, which, again, is often connected to SES. While turnout rates between white and African American potential voters have narrowed in recent years, Latino American turnout rates lag far behind those of Americans with other racial and ethnic identities. While some Latino Americans are undocumented immigrants and therefore ineligible to vote, they are also as a group younger, and as we have discussed, younger voting-eligible Americans vote in far fewer numbers than their older counterparts. As Latino eligible voters grow older and grow in numbers, the political landscape is going to shift dramatically.

Gender and Voter Turnout

Since the presidential election of 1980, women have voted at a slightly higher rate than men—typically a difference of a few percentage points.[59] Prior to 1980, voting-eligible men voted at higher rates than women. The differences between men's and women's modern voting patterns hold true across racial and ethnic identities with the largest percentage difference between black men and women, which was more than 9 percent in the 2102 presidential election. Differences in voter turnout in recent elections between men and women are also connected with age, as a higher percentage of women ages eighteen to forty-four voted than men in the same age cohort, while men seventy-five and up voted at higher rates than women within the same age group.

Partisan Attachment

Individuals with a stronger attachment to a political party are more likely to vote than those without one.[60] Efforts by members of American political parties to turn out the vote matter as well, and individuals with strong partisan attachment may find themselves more likely to be on the receiving end of party activities. **Political mobilization**, such as efforts to GOTV, can be decisive in an election. These efforts may be direct—recruitment, sponsorship of meetings, or requests for contributions—or indirect, such as in the building of social networks through which potential voters engage with their friends and associates.[61]

Legal and Institutional Factors Enable and Constrain Voter Turnout

Other factors that affect voter turnout are not individual but rather systemic or institutional. Since the ratification of the Twenty-Sixth Amendment to the Constitution in 1971, all American citizens eighteen years old or older are guaranteed the right of **suffrage**. The practical exercise of this basic right, however, is complicated. Undocumented American immigrants are not granted the right of suffrage, and in most states, otherwise eligible voters who have been convicted of felonies are also denied the right to vote in what is called **felon disenfranchisement**, though the time of their loss of this right varies according to state laws.

State **registration requirements** may also help or hinder the ability of voting-age Americans to participate in the electoral process. Voting actually involves two actions. The second is the casting of a ballot on an election day. But the first is the act of registering to vote. In some states, a voter may register on election day. In most states, however, would-be voters need to register prior to the election, often as much as thirty days before, otherwise they will not be allowed to vote.[62]

The scheduling of national presidential and congressional elections, by tradition held on the first Tuesday after the first Monday of November, may also serve to discourage participation as work schedules may make it more challenging for some Americans to make it to the polling place. Although states are increasingly allowing voters to cast **absentee ballots**, some reformers have proposed that national elections be held on weekends or that election day be declared a national holiday.

Finally, some advocates of electoral reform have focused on the process of registration itself, hoping to make it easier and less costly in terms of time and energy. In contrast to most modern representative democracies, in the United States the burden of registering to vote falls entirely on the potential voter, and there is no governmental action to register them automatically. The National Voter Registration Act of 1993, commonly called the **Motor Voter Law**, tried to make voter registration less difficult by allowing Americans to register to vote when applying for or renewing their driver's licenses and making it easier for Americans with disabilities to register to vote. As of 2016, thirty-one states and the District of Columbia had established systems of online voter registration, with six more having passed but not yet fully implemented them.[63] While effective online registration requires efforts to make the process secure and free from fraud, it offers the promise of increasing turnout.

Election-Specific Factors

Also contributing to the level of voter turnout in a given election are factors surrounding the election itself. If it is a presidential election year, then voters will turn out in higher numbers than if it is not.

Finally, an "election" is not really one election. It is many. When Americans go to the polls, they are often confronted with a long list of choices that, depending on the election parameters, can include the president, members of Congress, state legislature positions, state judges, county supervisors, and members of a water resource board. **Ballot roll-off** refers to the fact that voters may often not complete the entire ballot; they may stop once they reach a set of races with which they are not familiar and for which they may not have traditional cues, such as partisan affiliation.

1. Political participation refers only to voting.

   a. True
   b. False

2. Factors that contribute to Americans' relatively lower levels of voter turnout among representative democracies include _____.

   a. Felon disenfranchisement
   b. Registration requirements
   c. Mobilization
   d. All of the above

3. Election-specific factors that affect voter turnout include _____.

   a. Presidential or nonpresidential election years
   b. Age
   c. Level of education
   d. All of the above

4. Why do you think Americans choose to vote or not vote?

Answer Key: 1. b; 2. d; 3. a; 4. Answers might focus on demographic characteristics, election-specific factors, or thoughts about why people might feel that their voices do not matter.

CONCLUSION

The Fallout

There is a somewhat obscure 1950s science fiction movie called *Attack of the Crab Monsters*. Thanks to, I think, radiation, giant mutant crabs on an island evolve, eat people, and absorb their unfortunate victims' voices, personalities, and knowledge to grow stronger, more powerful, and more dangerous. The mutant crabs use the voices and identities they've stolen to lure other unsuspecting humans to their doom. In the "words" of one of the crab monsters, impersonating a human and trying to lure a group of people into the caves, "It is almost exhilarating! Will you come?"[64]

This is what the two dominant American political parties in American political history have always tried to do with insurgents—without the eating people part, of course. An internal revolution is often a signal that the party has to adapt; to bring the voices of those insurgents back into the fold; to keep the party viable, relevant, and strong. Or, if that fails, it is to put an end to the insurgency, once and for all.

While political scientists will no doubt be talking about the election of 2016 for years, one of the main questions will be this: What impact will the candidacies of Bernie Sanders and Donald Trump have on their respective political parties? And how will voters act in subsequent elections? Sanders attempted to push the Democratic Party to embrace the need to address economic inequality, issues that nominee Clinton

$SAGE edge™

Want a better grade?

Get the tools you need to sharpen your study skills. **SAGE edge** offers a robust online environment featuring an impressive array of free tools and resources. Access practice quizzes, eFlashcards, video, and multimedia at **edge.sagepub.com/abernathybrief1e.**

began to address more frequently as her campaign progressed. Will Democrats continue to prosecute that argument? Donald Trump's populist rhetoric alienated many Republican leaders, yet after the election the Republican Party controlled the White House, Congress, and the majority of state governorships and legislatures. Is that message going to continue to appeal to and mobilize voters?

In this chapter, we have explored the challenge that Bernie Sanders and Donald Trump presented to their own parties' establishment. That turned out to be very true; however, the larger story about the election of 2016 may not be only about divisions within political parties but about deeper divisions within the American republic itself.

CHAPTER REVIEW

This chapter's main ideas are reflected in the Learning Objectives. By reviewing them here you should be able to **remember** the key points and **know** these terms that are central to the topic.

7.1 Identify the roles that parties play in American representative democracy.

REMEMBER...

- In their ideal form, parties are organizations with leaders who work to promote the candidates and issues they support, uniting people under a set of common ideas and goals. They are reflected in the electorate by citizens who express solidarity with their views. In government, elected officials work to enact their parties' policies.

- Political scientists have argued that parties often play the deciding role in candidate selection.

KNOW...

- *caucus*: a process through which a state's eligible voters gather to discuss candidates and issues and select delegates to represent their preferences in later stages of the nomination process (p. 215)

- *closed primaries*: primary elections in which only registered voters from a particular political party may vote (p. 215)

- *delegates*: people who act as voters' representatives at a convention to select their party's presidential nominee (p. 213)

- *demographics*: the grouping of individuals based on shared characteristics, such as ancestry, race, ethnicity, and gender (p. 215)

- *front-loading*: when a state pushes its primary or caucus to a date as early in the season as possible to become more instrumental in the nomination process (p. 215)

- *gridlock*: an inability to compromise and enact legislation that is driven by political polarization (p. 219)

- *national conventions*: meetings where delegates officially select their party's nominee for the presidency (p. 215)

- *nomination*: the formal process through which parties choose their candidates for political office (p. 213)

- *open primaries*: primary elections in which all eligible voters may vote, regardless of their partisan affiliation (p. 213)

- *party identification*: an individual's attachment to a particular party (p. 216)

- *party ideology*: a set of stances shaped by an underlying philosophy about key issues and the proper role of government in society and then communicated to voters (p. 216)

- *party platform*: a set of positions and policy objectives that members of a political party agree to (p. 218)

- *polarization*: a sharp ideological distance between political parties (p. 218)

- *political party*: an organized group of candidates, officeholders, voters, and activists that work together to elect candidates to political office (p. 207)

- *presidential primary elections*: elections in which a state's voters choose delegates who support a particular candidate for nomination (p. 213)

- *recruitment*: the process through which political parties identify potential candidates (p. 213)

- *split-ticket voting*: when a voter chooses a candidate from one party for one office and a candidate from a different party for another position on the ballot (p. 217)

7.2 Explain how American party systems have evolved over time.

REMEMBER...

- Control of government has shifted back and forth between the parties during periods of realignment, which occur when public support shifts substantially from one party to the other, often following critical elections.

KNOW...

- *critical elections*: major national elections that signal change either in the balance of power between two major parties or the emergence of a new party system (p. 220)

- *party systems*: periods of stability of the composition of political parties and the issues around which they coalesce, brought on by shorter periods of intense change (p. 220)

- *proportional representation systems*: structures of electoral representation in which parties are represented in government according to their candidates' overall share of the vote (p. 225)

- *realignment*: a major shift in allegiance to the political parties that is often driven by changes in the issues that unite or divide voters (p. 220)

- *single-member plurality system*: a structure of electoral representation in which a candidate and the party that he or she represents must win the most votes in a state or district in order to be represented in government (p. 225)

- *third-party candidates*: members of a political party that operates over a limited period of time in competition with two other major parties (p. 226)

7.3 Understand the rules surrounding national elections and the function they serve.

REMEMBER...

- American national elections are somewhat unique among democratic nations in that they occur on fixed and regular schedules.

KNOW...

- *challenger*: a candidate for office who does not currently hold office (p. 227)

- *get out the vote (GOTV)*: efforts to mobilize voters or potential voters (p. 229)

- *incumbent*: a current officeholder (p. 227)

- *negative campaign advertisements*: campaign ads that attack an opponent or opponents and try to raise doubts in voters' minds about them (p. 228)

- *political action committees (PACs)*: organizations that raise money to support chosen candidates and defeat others (p. 230)

- *retrospective voting*: reflecting back on an incumbent's past performance in an election (p. 227)

- *super PACs*: PACs permitted to spend unlimited amounts of money in a campaign, though these actions must not be coordinated with that campaign (p. 230)

7.4 Describe the structure, stages, and main challenges of presidential and legislative campaigns.

REMEMBER...

- The presidential campaign involves two formal stages: the nomination campaign and the general elections. Presidents are elected by the Electoral College.

- Challenging entrenched congressional incumbents is extremely difficult; credible challengers often wait for an open seat election.

KNOW...

- *apportionment*: the process of determining the number of representatives for each state using census data; states are divided into congressional districts that have at least one representative each (p. 234)

- *constituencies*: bodies of voters in a given area who elect a representative or senator (p. 233)

- *Electoral College*: a process for electing the president that involves the voting population choosing a slate of electors who are pledged to vote for a nominee in the presidential election (p. 232)

- *exploratory committee*: a group that helps determine whether a potential candidate should run for office and that helps lay the groundwork for the campaign (p. 231)

- *faithless electors*: party electors who change their minds in between the general election and the Electoral College vote (p. 232)

- *gerrymandering*: the intentional use of redistricting to benefit a specific interest or group of voters (p. 235)

- *incumbency advantage*: institutional advantages held by those already in office who are trying to fend off challengers in an election (p. 239)

- *majority-minority districts*: districts in which voters of a minority ethnicity constitute an electoral majority within those electoral districts (p. 236)

- *majority*: when a candidate receives more than 50 percent of the vote (p. 233)

- *malapportionment:* the uneven distribution of the population between legislative districts (p. 236)

- *open seat election*: an election in which no incumbent is seeking reelection (p. 239)

- *plurality*: when a candidate receives more votes than any other candidate (p. 233)

- *redistricting*: states' redrawing of the electoral district boundaries following each census (p. 235)

- *runoff election*: an election that is held between the two candidates with the highest total votes if no one candidate scores a majority (p. 233)

7.5 Describe the forms of political participation Americans engage in, including the factors that limit or facilitate engagement.

REMEMBER...

- By participating politically, either in traditional or nontraditional ways, Americans express their commitment to civic engagement.

KNOW...

- *absentee ballots*: ballots completed and submitted by a voter prior to the day of an election (p. 244)

- *ballot roll-off:* when voters do not cast votes for a set of races with which they are not familiar and for which they may not have traditional cues (p. 244)

- *civic engagement*: working to improve society through political and nonpolitical action (p. 240)

- *felon disenfranchisement*: the denial of voting rights to Americans who have been convicted of felonies (p. 244)

- *Motor Voter Law*: law allowing Americans to register to vote when applying for or renewing their driver's licenses and making it easier for Americans with disabilities to register to vote (p. 244)

- *political efficacy*: a person's belief that she or he can make effective political change (p. 242)

- *political mobilization*: efforts by members of American political parties to turn out the vote and encourage their members to get others to do so (p. 243)

- *political participation*: the different ways in which individuals take action to shape the laws and policies of a government (p. 240)

- *registration requirements*: the set of rules that govern who can vote and how, when, and where they vote (p. 244)

- *socioeconomic status (SES)*: a measure that captures an individual's wealth, income, occupation, and educational attainment (p. 242)

- *suffrage*: the right to vote in political elections (p. 244)

- *voter turnout*: the number of eligible voters who actually participate in an election versus the total number of eligible voters (p. 241)

8 INTEREST GROUPS AND SOCIAL MOVEMENTS
Collective Action, Power, and Representation

Former senator Trent Lott, now senior counsel at lobbying firm Squire Patton Boggs in downtown Washington, D.C., meets with Senator Bill Nelson, D-FL, at the Capitol. Between 2008 and 2011, financial firm Goldman Sachs spent over $15 million lobbying Congress on its behalf. Squire Patton Boggs was among the lobbying firms hired by Goldman in the wake of the financial collapse of 2008. Bill Clark/CQ Roll Call

When we think of the people who represent the interests of citizens in government we tend to think of the leaders that those citizens have elected. Elected officials, however, are not the only people who try to represent American interests. The people themselves come together to shape policy or to call attention to issues as well. They form voluntary associations—groups and communities who join with each other in pursuit of collective interests and common goals.

In this chapter, we will dive into two related stories: the first is of lobbyists acting on behalf of America's banks and financial firms following the financial collapse of 2007–2008 and the other of a group of protesters who came together a few years later under the name Occupy Wall Street (OWS) to call attention to the issue of income inequality. Both groups were acting on behalf of someone and representing that someone's interests. However, the financial firms and their representatives in Washington acted as **interest groups**, voluntary associations of people who come together with an agreed-upon set of political and policy objectives and who attempt to pull the levers of political power in service of these defined goals. By contrast, OWS attempted to spark a **social movement**. Social movements (sometimes referred to as political movements) are associations of individuals who also come together to change things or keep things from changing, but they often do so by calling attention to a set of injustices in order to get policymakers to act. They also work to educate the public about a set of issues. As we will see, members of interest groups and social movements use different tactics to achieve their goals as both have different organizational capabilities and tools at their disposal. We will also see that the problem of faction is inherent in both: How can one be sure that a group or movement does not trample on the rights of others? As the stories you will explore show, some voices do get heard more clearly than others.

LEARNING OBJECTIVES

After reading this chapter, you will be able to do the following:

8.1 Identify the constitutional foundations of voluntary association in the American political process.

8.2 Summarize the challenges interest groups and social movements confront in recruiting, mobilizing, and organizing the activities of their members.

8.3 Discuss the types of interest groups in the American political landscape and the different tactics that they use.

8.4 Analyze and contrast the tactics that interest groups and social movements use in order to advocate on their members' behalf.

A HOUSING BUBBLE BURSTS. . . AND INTEREST GROUPS POP OUT

In the early 2000s, a very small number of individuals started getting unimaginably rich selling what had once been a very ordinary product: the home mortgage, a type of loan issued by a financial firm to cover the purchase of a home. They did so by turning the humble home loan into a financial monster that nearly wiped out the global economy. How that happened, and what happened in the aftermath, give us important insight into the power of interest groups.

In the economic boom years of the 2000s, lenders had started to issue loans to people who would not have qualified for them under older rules and with terms that were very dicey. Even Americans with very low incomes enjoyed much easier access to home loans, envisioning them as springboards for sending their children to college and moving their families a few rungs up the economic ladder. Banks at the time issued these subprime mortgages with full confidence that the government would cover for them if things went south.

As lenders got busy lending, prominent banks and investment firms also started creating remarkable new investment products based on those risky mortgages. Local banks would sell their subprime and other mortgages to larger financial firms, who would then chop the loans into little bits (the process is really complicated) and reconstitute them into financial products called mortgage-backed securities (MBS). By the time they were sufficiently chopped, those MBS couldn't be traced back to the assets that secured them in the first place, so their real value was unclear, and the relationship between the borrower and the holder of the loan was by that point totally disconnected. While MBS had been invented decades prior, during the housing boom of the early 2000s firms began to find ever more creative, lucrative, and riskier variations on them, and investors gobbled them up. MBS ultimately became so complex that the banks themselves did not fully understand the risks they posed. What they *did* know was that there was a lot of money to be made from buying and selling these new financial Frankenfoods. Banks started to take bigger and bigger risks and issue more and more loans. Between 2000 and 2005, those risks seemed to be paying off for investors who got very, very rich.

For all of this to keep going, however, home prices had to keep going up, and homeowners had to keep making their payments. That was not to be the case. In 2006 home sales peaked and prices began to decline; foreclosure rates began to spike as the people who were the least likely to be able to repay their loans *did not* repay those loans. The market began to crash. The housing bubble was popping.

By 2007 one of the main lenders, Freddie Mac, announced that it was going to stop buying the riskiest subprime mortgages and MBS, sending shock waves through the markets. Other banks that had issued those loans started failing. Some analysts started to suspect that the party was about to end. Others saw less cause for concern. Ben Bernanke, then chair of the Federal Reserve, reassured a congressional committee in March 2007 that things would not get out of hand, saying, "At this juncture . . . the impact on the broader economy and financial markets of the problems in the subprime market seems likely to be contained."[1]

Bernanke was wrong. By late 2008, a total of nine major U.S. banks were teetering on the brink of ruin, and nearly $20 trillion of Americans' wealth had been vaporized.[2] The Wall Street bankers and investment firms behind the mess plunged into a panic as global markets imploded.

Powerful interest groups stepped in immediately. Wall Street insiders and the interest groups acting on their behalf quickly realized that it was time to scramble for seats on whatever financial lifeboat the U.S. government might launch. Henry ("Hank") Paulson, then Treasury secretary, recounted the steps he took when things began breaking badly: "I immediately started making phone calls to see how Wall Street was responding: Dick Fuld at Lehman, Stan O'Neal at Merrill Lynch, Steve Schwarzman at Blackstone, and Lloyd Blankfein at Goldman Sachs. All these CEOs were on edge."[3] The financial firms wanted a bailout—a big one. Appearing on the Sunday morning political news talk shows that month, Paulson warned the public "of an economic doomsday if Congress [did not] immediately okay a colossal Wall Street bailout."[4]

Privately, behind closed doors in Washington, D.C., Paulson and Bernanke together spoke to members of Congress "in such apocalyptic terms that lawmakers were struck dumb with horror."[5] They argued that the only way to stop the collapse was with taxpayer money—$700 billion, to be exact—and it needed to be delivered *immediately*. Such a transaction would transfer these riskiest loans out of the hands of the suddenly imperiled financial giants and place them firmly in the hands of American taxpayers.

Under fire from skeptical members of Congress who objected both to the price tag and the time frame, Paulson and his supporters pointed to Paulson's previous experience on and connections to Wall Street as a plus. This was no place for amateurs, they argued, in safeguarding Americans' interests. Paulson had firsthand insight into how things worked in the industry and the kinds of personal connections necessary to make things happen as he ran this enormous, unprecedented, one-man ATM. Prior to leading the Department of the Treasury, Paulson had served as chair and chief executive officer of the investment-banking titan Goldman Sachs & Co. Indeed, he had led Goldman during "the Gold Rush that [had] brought the global financial system to the brink of collapse."[6]

As the Senate considered how, or whether, to bail out financial firms and homeowners, lobbyists from America's financial firms were hard at work. Representatives of major banks spent days on Capitol Hill in private conversation with members of Congress and their staffs, and their efforts appeared to pay off.[7] The Bush administration's originally more limited plans to bail out the financial firms evolved in short order into a situation where Wall Street was effectively dictating the terms. The "Securities Industry and Financial Markets Association, Wall Street's main trade and lobbying group, [was by then holding] conference calls to discuss 'your firms' views and priorities related to Treasury's proposal,' according to an e-mail message sent to members."[8]

House Speaker Nancy Pelosi of California, center right, and House Democratic leaders meet with Treasury secretary Henry Paulson, center left, and Federal Reserve chair Ben Bernanke, second from left, in Pelosi's office on Capitol Hill to discuss the financial crisis. AP Photo/Manuel Balce Ceneta

At the same time, opposition to a Wall Street bailout was emerging from other groups, and some wondered just how well Americans' interests were being represented by Paulson and other financial insiders. Messages from Americans to their members of Congress were clear and came in heavy volume. "The phone calls into the district office are about 75 percent saying: Don't do this. They think this is about Wall Street" and not about helping average homeowners, reported a Republican member of the House.[9] In addition to average Americans, organized interest groups joined the chorus of voices expressing concerns about the possible effects of the proposals on struggling

Americans. Groups representing farmers, senior citizens, and undocumented Americans as well as civil rights advocates began to put pressure on Washington.[10]

In October, 2008 the Senate passed a bailout bill. Included in the bill were tax breaks for consumers to purchase energy-efficient appliances, $500 million in tax breaks for film producers, breaks for rum producers and Alaskan fishermen, and a "$10 million credit to help employers defray the costs of storing the bicycles of their employees who commute to work."[11] The strategy, which was designed to peel off enough of the no votes in the House so that the bill could proceed to the Senate, worked. The bailout bill ultimately made it to President George W. Bush's desk wherein it became law. Along the way, however, the tab had grown to $850 billion, inflated by lawmakers' efforts to extract concessions for their constituents and for interest groups important to their electoral fortunes.

Wall Street breathed a sigh of relief; the stock market stabilized. But there would be more to come.

AMERICANS FACE CHALLENGES IN ACTING COLLECTIVELY IN A REPRESENTATIVE DEMOCRACY

As we have seen with our story about the Wall Street bailout, groups of people acting on behalf of different interests engaged in efforts to get the policies they preferred adopted and to make their points of view heard. Their efforts require massive coordination, however. How do such groups form in the first place? On what basis may they make their claims? Regardless of their differences members of voluntary associations do share some common traits. Their rights to organize and press their claims upon government are protected in the Constitution, specifically in the First Amendment's restrictions

- Describe the constitutional foundations of voluntary association in the American political process.

- Explain the theories behind how interest groups form and the obstacles posed to their formation.

on Congress's ability to impinge upon free expression: "Congress shall make no law . . . abridging the freedom of speech . . . or the right of the people peaceably to assemble, and to petition the Government for a redress of grievances."

In exercising these fundamental rights, people create what James Madison described in *Federalist* No. 10 as a faction: a group of individuals, large or small, who come together to get what they want out of the political process. Madison recognized that factions were potentially dangerous. Their actions risk trampling upon the rights of others or damaging the political community as a whole. Yet, paradoxically, the freedoms protected under the Constitution virtually guarantee the formation of factions. We can eliminate faction at its source, Madison argued, but only by preventing individuals from coming together, speaking, writing, and pressing their government to address their concerns. While effective, such restrictions upon liberty go against the very principles of a representative democracy. If you have freedom, Madison concluded, you will have faction. The challenge is not how to eliminate it but how to make sure that no one faction can do too much damage.

Pursuing that challenge, Madison developed a theory as to how the effects of faction would be moderated in an extended republic. He believed many factions would compete with each other in the large political space of the American Republic, making any one faction less of a danger to the nation as a whole. Given that so many competing factions would all fight to achieve their goals in a system that allowed each a voice, the most dangerous consequences of their inevitable formation could be contained.

But . . . can they *really* be contained? In the history of the American Republic and, for certain, with regard to the financial crisis of the twenty-first century and the federal government's response to it, no question has been more important or more controversial.

Theories of Interest Group Formation Focus on Overcoming Faction

In Frenchman Alexis de Tocqueville's *Democracy in America*, his book recounting his observations while traveling the country from 1831 to 1832, Tocqueville famously called America a "nation of joiners," so struck was he by the passion with which Americans made use of the "powerful instrument" of association.[12] His idea of a nation of joiners is a compelling one, provoking us to address some key questions. Who joins? What does it mean to join? What do people get from joining? And, most crucially, are the opportunities to join—and the results of doing so—equally effective for all Americans?[13]

One of the primary and enduring causes of faction is inequality of wealth. James Madison wrote, "the most common and durable source of factions, has been the various and unequal distribution of property. Those who hold, and those who are without property, have ever formed distinct interests in society."[14] Nearly two centuries later, political scientist Robert Dahl confronted the same basic problem: "How does a 'democratic' system work amid an inequality of resources?"[15] Drawing upon Madison's theory of the extended republic, Dahl explored the theory of **pluralism**, in which the distribution of political power—unequal as it may be—among many competing groups serves to keep any one of them in check. Such a widely contested and competitive political space also gives groups that might otherwise be excluded an entry into the political process, helping to ensure the representation of the interests of the less powerful—although not their success.

Not all of Dahl's contemporaries agreed with his pluralist framework or its optimistic conclusion that democratic societies can function effectively despite the presence of inequality of resources and wealth. The debate continues today. In contrast to pluralist perspectives, **elitist theory** focuses on the advantages that certain interests have in the political process based on the unequal distribution of economic and political power. For C. Wright Mills, writing in 1956, a **power elite** composed of the top echelons of people in the business world, government, and military could "look down upon . . . and by their decisions mightily affect, the everyday worlds of ordinary men and women."[16] To Mills, the nation's defense industry and its allies in government posed the greatest danger. Many Americans in the twenty-first century would add the nation's financial firms to a list of power elites.

In his study, Mills also noted that the exercise of power may be seen not only in those actions that are taken but also in inaction or in preventing actions to which the elites are opposed. A few years later, E. E. Schattschneider explored the ways in which elites used power to shut down opposition, including preventing organization from happening in the first place, preventing ideas from being discussed at all, and exercising power to keep certain ideas off of the **policy agenda**, which is the set of issues to which policymakers attend.[17] These debates were not settled in the 1960s, and they still have not been. While some scholars point to the dominance of business- and corporate-focused interest groups in campaign contributions (as we will see below), others point out that elite-oriented interest groups are often competing against each other.

Groups Must Overcome the Challenges of Collective Action

David Truman's *The Governmental Process* is one of the most important early works that systematically explored the dynamics of interest groups in American political life.[18] While exploring the pluralist theory of interest group operation, Truman's study also highlighted the fact that interest groups can wield a considerable amount of power in American political life. How each group wields that power—and how much power it has—depends upon organization within the group itself. Interest groups, after all, are not monolithic

This political cartoon depicts the perception that Wall Street's contributions to the federal government give its "elite" members undue political influence. The title "Occupy D.C." is a reference to the Occupy Wall Street (OWS) movement.

entities but collections of individuals, each with his or her own goals and desires. Successful interest groups harness those energies and direct them toward the group's goals. In trying to do so, however, leaders and members of voluntary associations—interest groups and social movements alike—have to overcome challenges to successful organization and coordination.

In getting organized and acting for the interests of their members, advocates for American financial firms and (as we shall see) the members of OWS both had to contend with one similar basic challenge, that of **collective action**—getting individuals to contribute their energy, time, or money to a larger group goal. However, the members of these two voluntary associations did not necessarily solve this problem in the same way. Differences in size, wealth, and political power all shape the strategies available to the leaders of voluntary associations as they try to overcome the challenges of collective action.

Economist Mancur Olson developed one of the most influential theories of the logic of interest group participation, or, more precisely, the logic of choosing *not* to participate. According to Olson, "Rational, self-interested individuals will not act to achieve their common or group interests . . . unless there is coercion to force them to do so, or unless some separate incentive, distinct from the achievement of the common or group interest, is offered to the members of the group individually on the condition that they help bear the costs or burdens involved in the achievement of group objectives."[19]

A key concept in this framework is the **collective good** (also called a public good), which is some benefit or desirable outcome that individuals can enjoy or profit from even if they do not help achieve or secure it.[20] The problem with collective goods comes from the fact that people can enjoy their benefits without contributing to their provision. Since, in this framework, individuals are completely rational with how they allocate their time, energy, and resources, there is no incentive for them to help out as they know they will receive the benefits of others' efforts. A strong national defense, clean air, or a really nice fireworks display may all be thought of as examples of collective goods. Those individuals who enjoy collective goods without help to secure them are called **free riders**, and they pose a serious challenge to the efforts of any voluntary association to work toward collective goals. Note that free riders are acting rationally in this framework. Based upon a pure cost-benefit logic, individuals should "free ride" and devote their energies elsewhere, knowing that others will make up for their inaction.

In the absence of some way to force individuals to contribute, therefore, public goods will be underprovided. Taxes, laws, and other forms of coercion are tools that governments use to overcome the challenges of public goods provision.[21] Voluntary associations of individuals, however, do not generally have the coercive power of government behind them, yet people still join and contribute, even at great personal cost and risk. Why? One explanation, which Olson discussed, is that a given group might be small and homogenous enough that the payoffs for individual participation and the collective risks of nonparticipation are obviously clear and compelling.

Other explanations for how interest groups can overcome the challenges of collective action focus on the incentives such groups offer to individuals to join or contribute.[22] These inducements may include **selective benefits**, which are made available only to those who join or contribute to the group. One set of selective benefits are **material rewards**, which may include discounts on goods and services, access to group publications and information, special offers, travel opportunities, or a host of other tangible benefits available only to members and contributors. AARP (formerly known as the American Association of Retired Persons) is widely known for the material benefits that it provides for its members. Professional associations or trade unions may provide their members with the credentials needed to operate in their profession, as is the case for state bar associations and regulation of the practice of law, or achieve for their members higher wages or better benefits, as may be the case for trade unions.

Other rewards that may be available only as a result of participation are **social benefits**, which might allow members to network with other individuals with similar interests and goals. Social benefits may come in the form of personal relationships and the benefits individuals attach to forming such relationships for their own sake, or they may take the form of job opportunities and other avenues for personal advancement. A third set of selective benefits arises from the satisfaction of working with others to achieve a common goal or purpose. For this reason, these inducements are referred to as **purposive benefits**.

INTEREST GROUPS VARY BY TYPE AND TACTIC

Following the Wall Street bailout, many Americans clamored for financial reforms to make sure that what many saw as a taxpayer-backed reward for excessive risk-taking by financial firms would not be repeated. They had reason to be concerned. The

- Understand the terms and concepts that describe lobbying and its tactics, goals, and controversies.

very firms that had been involved in the greatest risk-taking leading up to the crisis were among the most active in lobbying for the bailout program Congress passed and benefitted the most from it.[23] The influence of those lobbyists was pervasive: ". . .[N]early 1,500 former federal employees and 73 former members of Congress . . . have been deployed during debate on financial reform legislation."[24] This "army" included "former Speaker of the House Dennis Hastert (R-Ill.), former Senate Majority Leaders Bob Dole (R-Kan.) and Trent Lott (R-Miss.) and former House Majority Leaders Dick Armey (R-Texas) and Dick Gephardt (D-Mo.) . . . 'Wall Street hires former members of Congress and their staff for a reason,' said Public Citizen Congress Watch Director David Arkush, 'These people are influential because they have personal relationships with current members and staff. It's hard to say no to your friends.'"[25]

While representatives from Wall Street firms mobilized in force during and after the financial crisis, they were not the only ones acting. Other interest groups advocated as well, although many of their members were less connected to the corridors of political power than the titans of the American financial services industry. AARP, for example, argued that in the wake of the crisis, "the social safety net needs to be strengthened and extended. Workers should not have to worry about losing their health and pension benefits when they lose a job."[26] In this section, we will explore the landscape of interest groups in the United States and the varied tactics that they use in order to advance their members' goals.

Americans with a wide variety of political goals join, hire, or support interest groups in order to make their wishes known. Interest groups are often categorized and analyzed according to the broader goals that they set out to achieve and for whom they are advocating. Though scholars differ on specific classification schemes, the central idea is to examine what kinds of benefits the groups are seeking.

Economic interest groups, as their name implies, advocate on behalf of the economic interests of their members. These groups form the largest category of interest groups and are responsible for the largest amount of campaign donations. Within the category of economic interest groups, the largest and generally most influential subcategory consists of business groups, which advocate for the policies that favor their particular firms or industries. Labor groups, such as trade unions, advocate on behalf of the workers that they represent. Finally, farm groups have a long historical tradition of acting in American politics on behalf of farmers.

In contrast, **public interest groups** act on behalf of the collective interests of a broad group of individuals—many of whom may not be members or contributors to the organization. Groups advocating in the areas of civil rights, civil liberties, social welfare, education, or the environment are all examples of public interest groups. Many of these associations focus on one specific area of public policy and are, therefore, often called single-issue groups. A key subcategory of public interest groups advocate for their members with regard to issues of identity and lived experiences. The actions of the National Association for the Advancement of Colored People (NAACP) in challenging legal segregation, of the National Organization for Women (NOW) on behalf of gender equality, and of groups acting to secure marriage equality are all examples of public interest groups whose efforts you may be familiar with.

Finally, **governmental interest groups** act on behalf of state, regional, local, or even foreign governments to keep their members apprised of policy discussions; weigh in on the regulatory process; and generally act on behalf of the relevant government, especially during the appropriations process in Congress.

"Inside" Interest Groups Lobby to Influence Policymaking

All interest groups share the same ultimate goal: to influence public policy on the ground. To do so, they may try to influence any one stage of the policymaking process at the federal, state, or local level.

When one pictures organized interest group activity, one of the first things that often comes to mind is the act of **lobbying,** or interacting with government officials in order to advance a group's goals in the area of public policy. Lobbying in America is as old as the Republic itself. The stereotypical idea of lobbying is often of powerful interest group members contacting members of Congress and pressuring them to act on the group's behalf. Though that may be part of the story, lobbying is actually a much more complex and nuanced process. In the first place, interest group members lobby all three branches of the federal government, not just Congress, though the tactics that they use may vary depending on which branch is being lobbied. Second, even when they do approach Congress, lobbyists' tactics are varied and complicated and often focus as much on providing information to representatives, senators, and congressional staff members as they do on pushing for a specific position directly.

Rather than as a single effort, lobbying is most accurately thought of as an ongoing process, in which a lobbyist "seldom does only one specific thing at one specific time . . . but multiple things over a period of time."[27] It may involve efforts to shape policy across all three branches; legislative lobbying seeks to influence how legislation is written, executive branch lobbying focuses on how these laws are implemented, and judicial lobbying centers on how the laws are interpreted.

Who Lobbyists Are

The First Amendment to the Constitution guarantees the right of any citizen to lobby—"to petition the Government for a redress of grievances." Modern lobbying, however, is very much a professional undertaking. It involves large numbers of people and a lot of money. The Center for Responsive Politics calculated that in 2016 more than 11,166 paid lobbyists spent a total of $3.15 billion lobbying Congress and federal agencies.[28] As these figures are based only on registered lobbyist activities, however, they understate the actual numbers of total activity, both in the number of lobbyists and the amount of money they spent (see Figure 8.1).

Successful lobbyists must be able to provide a service to their clients, the people and firms that hire and pay them. To do so effectively, lobbyists need solid, useful knowledge about the particular policy area and the ability to be heard by those in government. For this reason, former government officials are often in high demand by lobbying firms. And government agencies themselves may recruit individuals from lobbying firms and the private sector for their experience and expertise. The movement of individuals between government and lobbying positions is called the **revolving door phenomenon.** Those who argue that the revolving door is a good thing point to benefits that agencies receive from the experience of former lobbyists and argue that effective lobbying depends on the kind of knowledge and experience that former government officials can bring to

FIGURE 8.1

Lobbying by the Numbers

Total Lobbying Spending (in billions of U.S. dollars)		Number of Lobbyists	
1998	$1.45	1998	10,405
1999	$1.44	1999	12,926
2000	$1.57	2000	12,541
2001	$1.63	2001	11,826
2002	$1.83	2002	12,118
2003	$2.06	2003	12,919
2004	$2.19	2004	13,168
2005	$2.44	2005	14,074
2006	$2.63	2006	14,482
2007	$2.87	2007	14,827
2008	$3.30	2008	14,157
2009	$3.50	2009	13,751
2010	$3.52	2010	12,932
2011	$3.33	2011	12,622
2012	$3.31	2012	12,185
2013	$3.24	2013	12,116
2014	$3.25	2014	11,824
2015	$3.22	2015	11,520
2016	$3.15	2016	11,166

Source: Center for Responsive Politics, Lobbying Database, OpenSecrets.org, https://www.opensecrets .org/lobby.

the table. Others, however, have raised concerns about the degree to which those groups capable of paying high prices for well-connected lobbyists tilt public policy in favor of the wealthy and powerful.

Members of interest groups know that their organizations are not all created equally with regard to their wealth, political clout, and access to powerful governmental officials. As such, they may modify their particular lobbying strategies to make the best use of the resources and advantages that they have. Consideration of whether or not all these strategies are equally effective, however, also raises questions about the degree to which Americans are fairly and competently represented . . . or represented at all.

Lobbyists Influence Legislation in Congress

Because it writes the nation's laws, Congress is a natural target for lobbyists, who employ several strategies in their efforts to influence legislation. One method, and the one that many people think of when they think of the term *lobbying*, is when lobbyists contact members of Congress or their staff directly to advocate for their group's position. This kind of direct contact is an example of **inside lobbying**, and it takes many forms, which is not surprising given how complex the legislative process is.

In addition to direct contact with representatives, senators, and congressional staff members, lobbyists may prepare research reports and briefs, work to shape the legislative agenda by bringing more attention to their issues of interest, or help coordinate a legislative strategy on an issue.[29] These efforts may focus on the content of a piece of legislation and also on the levels of funding for agencies and programs though the appropriations process. Lobbyists may try to influence the total amount of funding available to an agency, spending priorities within that agency, earmarks for specific projects, or riders to appropriations bills, which may specify how money *cannot* be spent and are often a powerful weapon in shaping the implementation of the laws that Congress passes.[30]

Successful inside lobbying often depends on personal relationships, access to decision makers, and financial resources—something not all interest groups possess. Much of the power of inside lobbying, however, also relies on the provision of useful and timely information, such as research that might save a congressional staff valuable time, specific language or wording that may shape or find its way into a bill, or studies that convincingly portray the group's position as one that a member's constituents care about and agree with. Testifying at committee or subcommittee hearings and providing members of Congress with research reports and summaries are two common ways interest groups use information to try to advance their positions.

Lobbyists Influence Executive Branch Implementation

From the point of view of interest groups and their lobbyists, winning or losing the battle in Congress is only part of the war. As it is tasked with executing the laws that Congress writes—shaping legislation through the process of implementation—the executive branch also finds itself the target of lobbying efforts. Congress cannot account for every detail within the policy areas covered by its laws. Some flexibility needs to be built in to allow for effective implementation, and legislators eyeing reelection may prefer not to specify certain provisions in too much detail. In trying to influence the appropriations process in Congress, members of organized interest groups try to shape the implementation of the laws by the executive branch. In some cases, they do so directly by lobbying the president (or, more realistically, members of his or her executive staff) or members of the federal bureaucracy.

Federal law requires executive branch agencies to notify the public and solicit its input when establishing rules and procedures, an opening into which organized interests happily step.[31] The detailed nature of most proposed legislation provides an advantage to interest groups armed with data and knowledge of the minutia of the legislation and the affected policy.[32] Interest groups may work to increase the prominence of their goals in the executive branch agenda, and they may also use the courts to challenge federal rules to which they are opposed.

Closely connected to the idea of the revolving door is the risk of **agency capture** (also called regulatory capture), in which those agencies tasked with regulating businesses, industries, or other interest groups are populated by individuals with close ties to the very firms that they are supposed to regulate. This can result in ineffective oversight or regulatory actions that favor the firms over the general interests of society or those not so strongly represented.[33]

Lobbyists Influence Judicial Interpretation

Interest groups and their lobbyists may also try to shape how the nation's laws are interpreted by targeting the federal judiciary. As the thought of a lobbyist badgering an individual member of the Supreme Court about a group's position seems somehow unseemly and, depending on the justice, might actually backfire, groups generally use other methods to try to shape the activities of the federal judiciary, especially the Supreme Court.

Interest groups may try to influence judicial appointments, either through the presidential nomination or Senate confirmation process. Given the importance of the federal judiciary and its influence over a host of issues, interest groups often have a very strong desire to shape the appointment process. In 2016, as Judge Merrick Garland—President Obama's nominee to fill the Supreme Court seat left vacant by the passing of Justice Antonin Scalia—awaited Senate action that, as it turned out, never came, interest groups such as the National Federation of Independent Business, the National Rifle Association, Planned Parenthood, and many others acted to support or oppose his confirmation.

The Supreme Court has two decisions to make on each case that comes before it: whether or not to hear the case and how to rule should it decide to hear it. Interest groups may try to influence each of these decisions, typically by filing amicus curiae briefs, which describe a group's position and the arguments for it. As one scholar put it, "Although they were originally envisioned as a 'friend of the Court' and neutral toward the parties, amici are now more appropriately viewed as friends of the participants to the litigation."[34] There is evidence that a high number of amici can increase the chances that justices will hear a case,[35] though some scholars have pointed out that this does not necessarily mean that interest groups have any particular advantage when it comes time for the Court to rule on the merits of the case.[36]

Interest groups may sponsor litigation, guiding a case through the judiciary, but this is an expensive and time-consuming task, even when it goes well. In the 1950s, the Legal Defense Fund of the NAACP undertook a lengthy, expensive, and risky strategy in trying to use the federal judiciary to bring an end to legal segregation in the United States. To do so, the group had to find individuals willing to bring suits in court, which could, and did, subject many of them to physical and economic violence. The litigators and staff of the Legal Defense Fund also had to conduct the research and legal analysis that formed the bases of these lawsuits, which was also a personally risky undertaking.

Lobbying Activities Are Regulated

Given the potential influence of lobbyists on shaping public policy, it is not surprising that attempts have been made over the years to regulate their activities. This is not, however, a simple task. First, the Constitution protects the fundamental rights of interest groups to act on their members' behalf, which includes lobbying activities. Second, there are incentives for members of Congress not to overregulate these activities since representatives and senators may benefit from the information and campaign support that interest groups provide. Most recent efforts to regulate lobbying have focused on making the process more transparent.

Interest Groups Exert Influence through Webs and Networks

One of the classic, and worrisome, depictions of the connections between interest groups and government is the **iron triangle** (see Figure 8.2). As the term suggests, the iron triangle consists of three parts—interest groups, Congress, and the bureaucracy—each of which works with the other two to achieve their shared policy goals, even if achieving those goals runs counter to the general interests of society or specific groups within it. In doing so, the members of the triangle act as factions, each helping the other two members and receiving benefits from doing so.

Interest groups provide electoral support to members of Congress, who use their influence, especially on committees and subcommittees, to advance legislation favorable to the interest groups and reduce oversight of interest group activities. These same interest groups lobby on behalf of the relevant bureaucratic agencies to secure the agencies' desired funding and policy goals. In return, the agencies conduct their job of regulation in ways favorable to

The Iron Triangle

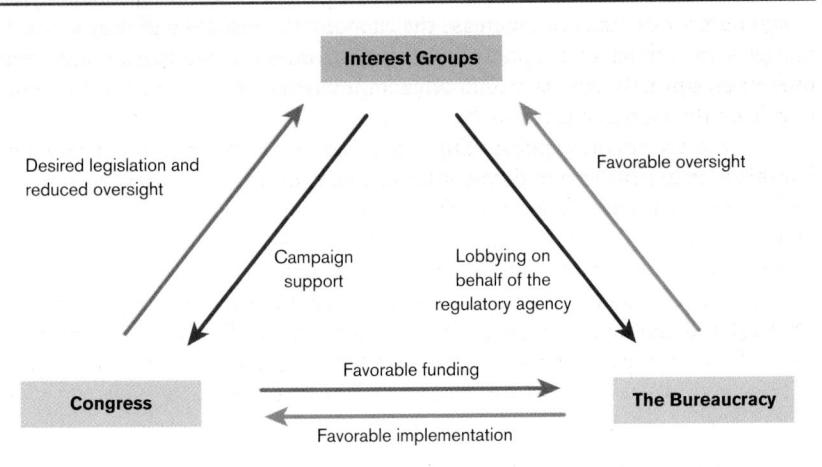

The iron triangle illustrates the linkage of benefits that each of the three members provide to the other two. While all members help each other, it is their common interest in the overall policy goal that drives individual decisions.

interest group objectives. Finally, members of Congress determine funding levels and pass legislation desired by the bureaucratic agencies, which, in turn, implement the laws passed by Congress in ways desired by those members of Congress.

Due to the growth in the number of interest groups and an increasingly fluid and complex policy landscape in recent decades, political scientists have employed the concept of the **issue network** to describe the webs of influence between interest groups, policymakers, and policy advocates. In contrast to iron triangles, issue networks are often temporary, arising to address a specific policy problem. Any one issue may give rise to competing issue networks, each of which advocates on a different side of the issue. In this way, issue networks are closer to the idea of pluralism than iron triangles.

Interest Groups Are Involved in Election-Related Activities

Interest groups are often heavily involved in the electoral process. First, and perhaps foremost, their participation revolves around the targeted distribution of financial resources. Money is a powerful strategic tool as it can fund media coverage, a solid ground campaign, and research. Money can also act as a weapon to discourage others from even running for election. Campaigns are often won or lost long before the actual vote. If a candidate can signal to potential opponents that they will be facing a formidable and well-funded foe, then savvy would-be competitors may very well wait until conditions are more favorable for a realistic run; no serious potential challenger wants to wage a hopeless campaign. Serious challengers are smart and patient; they wait if they have to.

How and under what conditions interest groups contribute to political campaigns is often determined by the status under which they file with the Internal Revenue Service (IRS). Those classified, for example, as 501(c)(3) organizations, whose contributions are tax deductible, face defined rules on the amounts that they may contribute and on the activities toward which those funds may be deployed. Political action committees (PACs) may spend more money on campaigns than individuals and may solicit funds from their members to do so, but they also operate with limits. Following an important Supreme Court decision in 2010, American politics has seen the emergence and rapid rise of the so-called super PAC, which is allowed to raise and spend money without financial limits but only in ways that are uncoordinated with a campaign itself.[37]

Efforts to regulate interest group spending on campaigns and elections are ongoing and not always successful. In addition to financial contributions and spending, interest groups also try to influence electoral outcomes by mobilizing voters through get out the vote (GOTV) campaigns and by recruiting and endorsing candidates.

Grassroots Lobbying and Political Protesters Act from "Outside" to Influence Policy

Interest groups that attempt to represent less powerful constituencies often have to use a different set of tactics than those available to the more well-funded and well-connected groups. They also aim to change public policy, but they often face

Reportable Campaign Contributions by Economic Sector, 2016

Rank	Sector	Amount	To Cands/Parties	Dems	Repubs	
1	Finance/Insur/RealEst	$912,350,256	$465,411,328	42.20%	57.60%	
2	Other	$593,872,619	$494,067,188	58.30%	41.30%	
3	Ideology/Single-Issue	$411,670,519	$271,757,477	61.20%	38.70%	
4	Misc Business	$374,585,616	$267,396,042	43.20%	56.50%	
5	Communic/Electronics	$254,271,572	$159,533,487	67.30%	32.50%	
6	Health	$222,951,892	$165,365,804	49.70%	50.10%	
7	Lawyers & Lobbyists	$198,008,151	$184,822,173	68.40%	31.30%	
8	Energy/Nat Resource	$149,794,510	$97,886,669	22.20%	77.70%	
9	Labor	$142,121,291	$63,252,831	86.90%	12.90%	
10	Agribusiness	$93,418,018	$68,528,589	26.70%	72.80%	
11	Construction	$88,793,884	$66,993,474	31.20%	68.50%	
12	Transportation	$79,237,183	$63,393,786	30.10%	69.70%	
13	Defense	$25,873,898	$25,605,610	38.20%	61.60%	

Source: Center for Responsive Politics, "Totals by Sector," OpenSecrets.org, https://www.opensecrets.org/overview/sectors.php?cycle=2016, accessed November 14, 2016.

Note: Percentages may not add up to 100 percent as money can be given to third party candidates and party committees.

2016 Campaign Contributions by Economic Sector

Legend: ■ To DEMS ■ To REPUBS

(Continued)

(Continued)

The OpenSecrets.org project by the independent nonprofit Center for Responsive Politics collects, analyzes, and shares data on money, lobbying, politics, and elections. The center focuses a considerable amount of its efforts on tracking reportable campaign contributions. The figure that follows presents the total amounts of campaign contributions in the 2016 election cycle reported to the Federal Election Commission (FEC) as of June 21, 2016, broken down by sector of the economy. It includes contributions from individuals (of $200 or more) and PACs as well as contributions given to super PACs and other groups.

As is clear in the figure, the finance/insurance/real estate sector accounted for the single largest group of contributions. Contributions were dominated by economic sectors; however, interest groups and individuals within the labor sector as well as those representing single-issue groups also made significant campaign contributions. Note also that the relative allocation of sector donations to Democratic and Republican candidates varied considerably.

WHAT DO YOU THINK?

Why might these groups and individuals have allocated their contributions across the two major political parties in the way that they did? What strategic choices might have been involved in these decisions? What other campaign contribution data would you like to analyze in order to assess the landscape of interest group involvement in American campaigns and elections?

different challenges and have to adjust accordingly. Their members generally consist of a diverse group of previously immobilized and possibly unorganized individuals. Problems associated with collective action and the dangers of free riding are often of more concern to such groups.

These less powerful groups may engage in **outside lobbying**, which focuses on reaching constituents and mobilizing them to pressure their representatives rather than pressuring the representatives directly. A group may decide that outside lobbying is its best course of action, or it may have no other choice and have to use this tactic "out of desperation when an 'inside' strategy has failed."[38] Using outside lobbying tactics is also referred to as grassroots lobbying.

In some cases, when grassroots support does not really exist, or would not exist if it hadn't been "purchased" by a lobbying firm, an interest group will present the facade of grassroots support. This is referred to as **Astroturf lobbying**; the term alludes to the fact that the "grassroots" drawn upon are made out of fake grass and thus do not reflect genuine public support. While Astroturf lobbying is widely criticized, the lines between genuine grassroots support and Astroturf lobbying may not always be entirely clear. As political scientist Ken Kollman has questioned, "If two interest groups mobilize the same number of people to contact Congress, but one of them relies on volunteers and its own members and the other pays a consulting house to generate telephone calls and letters, who is to say which is real and which is artificial?"[39] Astroturf lobbying can be effective, and according to political scientist Kenneth Goldstein, its increasing use may be contributing to a new wave of citizen participation that would not exist if not for the fact that "interest groups and lobbying firms inside the beltway are increasingly utilizing new and sophisticated techniques to water the grass roots outside the beltway."[40]

Interest Groups Face Challenges in Representation

Writing in the 1960s, Grant McConnell pointed out that corporations and private interest groups do not rule themselves democratically and that there are far fewer protections provided within them that are afforded to citizens.[41] McConnell's critique of the exercise of power within interest groups also raises questions about representation within social movements themselves—even those that attempt to speak for the less powerful.

In recent decades, political scientists have come back to the questions of power and representation raised by scholars such as Robert Dahl, C. Wright Mills, and E. E. Schattschneider. They have done so often empirically, using the tools of quantitative analysis to get a better understanding of the dynamics of representation among and within interest groups. In general, in spite of a proliferation of groups and movements devoted to the less well-represented members of society, such as minorities, women, and the elderly, much of the evidence points to a continuation of overrepresentation of the elite, powerful, and wealthy.

Exploring data involving nearly seven thousand interest groups, political scientist Kay Lehman Schlozman concluded that in spite of the growth of public interest groups since the 1960s, business and commerce interest groups still account for the majority of associations, a fact that she attributes to their staying power in the face of all of the pressures on a group to maintain its membership and influence.[42] Political scientist Dara Strolovitch concluded that even in interest groups devoted to representing more marginalized members of American society, the relatively better-advantaged members within those groups receive more attention and political effort.[43]

---

1. Different types of interest groups include _____.

   a. Economic interest groups
   b. Public interest groups
   c. Labor groups
   d. All of the above

2. Lobbying is _____.

   a. Interacting with government officials to secure a group's objectives

   b. Something that only happens in Congress
   c. Rarely a successful strategy
   d. A new development in American politics

3. The "revolving door phenomenon" refers to _____.

   a. Public protests
   b. Individuals moving between government and lobbying positions

(Continued)

WHAT HAVE I LEARNED?

(Continued)

c. Being reelected to Congress

d. Restrictions on campaign contributions

4. Astroturf lobbying is _____.

   a. The same thing as grassroots lobbying

   b. Conducted by owners of major professional sports teams

   c. When lobbyists go door to door to drum up support for their goals

d. When firms posing as grassroots groups pay individuals to generate calls and letters

5. The concept of the iron triangle is often illustrated using defense spending and the defense industry. If you were to apply the concept to the financial industry in the twenty-first century, what might the three parts of the triangle be?

Answer Key: 1. d; 2. a; 3. b; 4. d; 5. Answers might include financial firms, members of Congress, and officials with the Department of the Treasury.

OCCUPY WALL STREET ILLUSTRATES THE STRUGGLES, SUCCESSES, AND FAILURES OF SOCIAL MOVEMENTS

- Understand the strategies used by social movements, and consider how they differ from interest groups.

American political history teaches us that social movements can achieve major policy changes over time: the civil rights movement and the struggle for the rights of women; disabled Americans; and lesbian, gay, bisexual, and transgender (LGBT) Americans are all widely acknowledged as social movements that have had significant impact. Though their specific goals were different, those groups often employed similar tactics.

They used **protest**, a public demonstration designed to call attention to the need for action or change. As part of these protests, some members engaged in **civil disobedience**, the intentional breaking of a law for the purpose of calling attention to an injustice. Protest and civil disobedience can be powerful and effective tactics, especially in altering the political agenda—placing an injustice front and center on the national stage and forcing people to confront it. Both of these tactics are risky, however, not only for the individuals involved but also for the movement itself.

In leading or joining an act of protest or civil disobedience, individuals may endanger their freedom, jobs, physical safety, or even their lives. For the movement itself, there is a chance that these activities may alienate rather than mobilize—that they may further isolate the movement from those who its members hope to convince of the importance of the cause. There is also

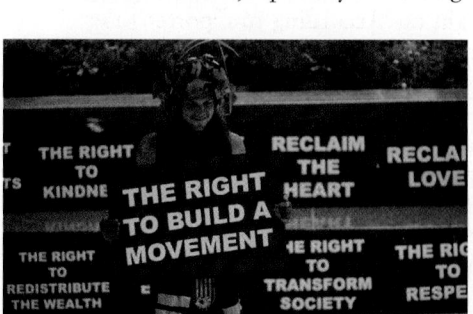

An Occupy Wall Street (OWS) activist takes part in a protest at Zuccotti Park on July 11, 2012, advocating for the right to form a social movement. REUTERS/Eduardo Munoz

the risk that the protesters will be ignored. The story of OWS illustrates the power and effectiveness of protest and civil disobedience but also the challenges such movements face.

Occupy Wall Street Catches Fire

In September 2011, almost three years after the financial collapse, about 1,000 people gathered in New York's Zuccotti Park, just blocks from Wall Street and the New York Stock Exchange in lower Manhattan, to protest against the concentration of wealth at the very top of American society and what they saw as a deep and structural lack of fairness, made far worse by the bailout of Wall Street. This disparate and evolving group of protesters became known as Occupy Wall Street, or OWS; the movement's message, one fueled by disillusionment and frustration, eventually spread around the globe via strategic use of social media.

Many observers attribute the origins of OWS to a blog entry posted in July 2011 by the Canadian activist group Adbusters.[44] The founder of Adbusters, Kalle Lasn, told the press that "his group originally proposed one demand—to separate money from politics." According to an article in the *Christian Science Monitor*, "When asked . . . why it was such a slow burn for people to finally protest the financial crisis, Mr. Lasn said that it took some time for people to realize that President Obama," who was by then president, "was not handling the meltdown effectively, going so far as to call him a 'gutless wonder.'"[45]

At that first protest in Zuccotti Park, about eighty individuals were arrested, mostly on charges for blocking traffic, a relatively minor offense. However, in some cases arrests were accompanied by charges of police brutality. Videos that seemed to support those charges went viral on platforms like YouTube. A few weeks later, OWS protesters marched across the Brooklyn Bridge, again leading to many arrests, hundreds this time. By this point, however, people were more aware of the movement's existence.

Those who joined OWS did so for a variety of reasons; they were not united by self-interest, as the Wall Street financial firms had been. However, their message that a small faction of the wealthiest Americans was working against the interests of everyone else caught on. According to reporter John Ennis, "'WE ARE THE 99 PERCENT' became the rallying cry of a generation. The simplicity and inclusivity of that message was worthy of the advertising gurus on Madison Avenue."[46]

Early efforts of OWS barely received a mention in the nation's press. What coverage they did get was condescending and dismissive. Though protesters were generally united behind a message of income inequality, OWS as a whole struggled to further define what that message was, a common challenge for those who would start a social movement. It is a particular challenge to successfully mobilize Americans to respond to political and economic inequalities since this depends upon communicating to them an understanding of the messy details of the workings of government. "What do you say about a financial crisis where the villains are obscure and the solutions are obscure," wondered one critic.[47] While the media may have had a hard time figuring out what OWS was all about, the movement's members felt it was clear that something had gone wrong in the nation. The rich were getting richer, and everyone else seemed to be getting left behind. Change was needed, and Americans needed to be woken up. As Rachel Pletz, a participant in the Zuccotti Park protests who helped to organize similar efforts in Philadelphia, put it, "This is about solidarity. This is about getting people together and figuring it out. We just know something's wrong."[48]

OWS protesters did find a way to make strategic use of social media and other creative protest methods to coordinate and communicate and ultimately got attention from some high-profile celebrity activists who also helped spread word of the cause. The OWS movement quickly went national, even international. In the first week of October, "smaller-scale protests spread . . . to Los Angeles, Chicago, Boston, Denver, Washington, Albuquerque, Portland, Maine, and several other cities. An 'Occupy Toronto' protest [was] planned in Canada."[49]

As the protests gained momentum, some critics claimed not only did the movement fail to represent the diverse interests of its members but also that it was actively discriminatory, especially toward the American Jewish community. In October 2011, the Republican National Committee issued a memo that "included three videos showing anti-Semitic outbursts by purported Wall Street protestors," though a spokesperson for the Anti-Defamation League countered that these outbursts were "isolated incidents."[50]

The movement was also criticized for failing to sufficiently empower members from traditionally marginalized groups or address their concerns. An article in the *New York Times* in late October 2011, for example, described a sense of alienation felt by a group of organizers from the South Bronx, an area with a high concentration of low-income individuals and those of minority ethnicity. "'Nobody looked like us,' said Rodrigo Venegas, 31, 'It was white, liberal, young people who for the first time in their life are feeling a small percentage of what black and brown communities have been feeling for hundreds of years.'"[51]

Other members of minority groups concluded that a unity of voices—based not on identity but a shared struggle against those in power—might make the social movement stronger. One journalist's account is telling: "Frank Diamond, a 26-year-old-Haitian-American from Jamaica, Queens, who was holding an

John Hector, one of the relatively few people of color amongst Occupy Wall Street (OWS) protesters, wraps himself in a blanket against cold temperatures at the group's protest in Zuccotti Park in November 2011. "My concern is the economic situation and particularly police brutality and stop-and-frisk policies in Black and Latino communities," said Hector. AP Photo/Bebeto Matthews

'Occupy the Hood' sign at a recent rally, said that many working-class blacks who had originally watched the protests from a distance, were starting to realize they should join. 'It takes a wave to realize that the boat you have been riding is too small,' he said. 'We need to be represented here too. This is about us, too.'"[52]

By November 2011, New York City authorities began to clamp down, stripping the demonstrators in Zuccotti Park of their generators and fuel just as a snowstorm and cold wave hit the city. Less than two weeks later, Mayor Michael Bloomberg and city authorities evicted the protestors from Zuccotti Park. Other cities removed protestors as well. The few encampments that lingered through the winter in New York, Boston, Los Angeles, and other cities had mostly disappeared by the spring of 2012. Protests continued but without the same level of media coverage. Some debated what had been accomplished. Some noted that the OWS protests had served an important purpose, spurring more Americans to recognize that "our system of capitalism and free markets, the electoral system and tax policies . . . has been distorted by moneyed interests. Our challenge is to revive America as a land of equal opportunity."[53]

Other observers had a very different set of suggestions for the movement's leaders. According to one reporter, "Many pundits suggest that it's time for the activists to hire political consultants and assemble a list of demands—in short, to become much more involved in electoral politics."[54] It was time, in other words, for OWS to stop trying to form a social movement and become an interest group.

The Success of Social Movements Is Difficult to Measure

As we have explored, small, homogenous, and economically powerful interest groups have many advantages in overcoming the challenges of collective action. When broad, diverse, voluntary associations of individuals come together to create a social movement, they lack many of the advantages of the more powerful groups. According to Olson, there is a logic to the idea that social movements should not come together at all. Yet some do. Why?

This is not an easy question to answer, either for scholars or for participants in the social movements themselves.[55] Part of the problem lies in the inherent differences in observing success and failure between interest groups and social movements.[56] When an interest group tries to influence legislation in Congress, for example, it is much easier to see if its efforts pay off or if they do not. However, what does it mean for a social movement to succeed, and how would we know if it did or did not? Those social movements that fail are difficult to study, like the proverbial tree that falls in the forest with nobody there to observe. To dive a bit deeper into this question, we have to incorporate insights from both political science and sociology, which is a close relative of political science but which focuses more on social processes than on political institutions, processes, and outcomes.

For social movements, success or failure may be best determined not by the final public policy outcomes or by laws that were or were not passed but by the fact that the movement came together at all—that it managed to overcome the problems of collective action and engaged others in its efforts to challenge the political dynamics, that it persuaded the uninvolved to become involved, to mobilize, infuriate, and educate. These efforts do not go unopposed, whether by governments, other powerful political players, or the inertia of a public confronted with a new cause or call to combat an injustice.[57] For sociologist Edwin Amenta, some answers, and a better framing of the question itself, may lie in the uneven power relationships that define interest groups and social movements. He argued, "Asking why social movements fail is a little like asking why children do not have backyards full of ponies. Most social movements fail most of the time because they embody a recipe for failure: they combine ambitious goals with severe power deficits."[58]

By some accounts, and not without cause, it is not even clear if OWS had created a social movement at all. By the three-year anniversary of the first Zuccotti Park protests, the movement seemed to be over. In comparison to widely acknowledged twenty-first century movements such as Black Lives Matter, OWS did not appear to have the same staying power or have built the necessary infrastructure to sustain it over the long haul.

However, in our exploration of political parties, we studied the insurgent candidacy of Senator Bernie Sanders, I-VT, who most certainly highlighted American economic inequality in his campaign. The efforts of Sanders and others to call attention to this issue illustrate one of the primary tools that social movements have: changing the conversation in an effort to influence the political agenda.

Trying to determine whether or not a social movement has been successful by focusing only on what laws were or were not passed might miss this key contribution.[59] The policy agenda is a shifting and evolving thing; nothing is ever settled, and those who wish to influence political outcomes can never let their guard down.[60] The outcome of any one social movement may teach the members of future movements important lessons about what has worked and what has not. The activities of individuals involved with the civil rights movement, for example, served as lessons to members of future movements that sought to call attention to other forms of injustice.[61]

CONCLUSION
Organizing for Change or to Prevent Change

Separated in space only by city blocks and in time by only three years, the activities of powerful and well-connected American financial firms in 2008 and the protests of OWS in 2011 might seem as far apart as the citizens that they tried to represent. In many ways, they were. The tactics used in these two situations were, to be sure, very different. Insiders—the CEOs of financial institutions and their well-paid lobbyists—worked the levers of the American political system to ensure the survival of the firms that they represented. Outsiders—students, opponents of the American capitalist system, advocates for economic equality, and many others without a well-defined agenda—tried to come together and use tools of protest and action to bring about social change.

These two groups, as different as they were, shared more in common than even they may have realized. Their leaders and members had to assess where they stood strategically in the real world of American economic and political power, and they had to adjust their strategies accordingly. They had to motivate and coerce members to join and contribute. Most fundamentally, they had to decide exactly whose interests they were trying to represent.

The twinned stories of the financial bailout and OWS are united by two strong and interconnected threads: power and inequality. Even within a social movement that hopes to represent the interests of outsiders, the disconnected, and the less powerful, there is no guarantee that all voices within that movement will be heard. When one compares the activities of interest groups and social movements, the challenges are even greater. The concentration of wealth at the very top of the economic strata is as great as it has ever been in the nation's history.

From these two stories one could draw a simple, neat conclusion: One faction ended up tipping the balance of power in its favor, and the other failed—end of story. However, the complex ways in which social movements have been involved in the American political space are better thought of as seeds. Political seeds—sometimes derided, attacked, or ignored from their beginnings—need two key ingredients: their own potential and the soil upon which that potential falls. Whether or not OWS had a consistent, clear, salable message and what effect that message had on the political process in 2011 or in the years since is not the main concern in this view. What matters is whether or not the efforts of OWS sowed the seeds for a true challenge to the power structure of the American political system in the twenty-first century. And did these efforts fall upon a receptive and fertile soil? Did the political dynamics of Americans' confrontation with the inevitable challenge of faction— and the inevitable contribution of economic inequality to the formation of faction in republican forms of government—change? The verdict is still out.

Want a better grade?

Get the tools you need to sharpen your study skills. **SAGE edge** offers a robust online environment featuring an impressive array of free tools and resources. Access practice quizzes, eFlashcards, video, and multimedia at **edge.sagepub.com/abernathybrief1e.**

CHAPTER REVIEW

This chapter's main ideas are reflected in the Learning Objectives. By reviewing them here you should be able to **remember** the key points and **know** these terms that are central to the topic.

8.1 Identify the constitutional foundations of voluntary association in the American political process.

REMEMBER...

- The Constitution of the United States ensures the ability of Americans to form voluntary associations and make their wishes known.

KNOW...

- *elitist theory*: a theory of governmental influence that focuses on the advantages that certain interests have in the political process based on the unequal distribution of economic and political power (p. 257)

- *interest groups*: voluntary associations of people who come together with an agreed-upon set of political and policy objectives and who attempt to pull the levers of political power in service of these defined goals (p. 252)

- *pluralism*: a theory of governmental influence that views the distribution of political power among many competing groups as serving to keep any one of them in check (p. 256)

- *policy agenda*: the set of issues to which government officials, voters, and the public attend (p. 257)

- *power elite*: a group composed of the top echelons of people in the business world, government, and military (p. 257)

- *social movement*: voluntary associations of individuals who come together to change things or keep things from changing, but they often do so by calling attention to a set of injustices or wrongs in order to get policymakers to act and to educate the public about the issue (p. 252)

8.2 Summarize the challenges interest groups and social movements confront in recruiting, mobilizing, and organizing the activities of their members.

REMEMBER...

- Political scientists have offered a variety of explanations for why Americans choose to join or not join voluntary associations in political life.

- When acting collectively, there are often rational incentives for individuals to allow others to carry the burdens of doing so.

KNOW ...

- *collective action*: political action that occurs when individuals contribute their energy, time, or money to a larger group goal (p. 258)

- *collective good (public good)*: some benefit or desirable outcome that individuals can enjoy or profit from even if they do not help achieve or secure it (p. 258)

- *free riders*: individuals who enjoy collective goods without help to secure them (p. 258)

- *material rewards*: a type of tangible benefit made available to members and contributors of a group (p. 259)

- *purposive benefits*: rewards in the form of satisfaction from working with others to achieve a common goal or purpose (p. 259)

- *selective benefits*: goods that are made available only to those who join or contribute to a group (p. 258)

- *social benefits*: rewards in the form of new connections or access to networks that members of a group receive through their participation (p. 259)

8.3 Discuss the types of interest groups in the American political landscape and the different tactics that they use.

REMEMBER ...

- Interest groups may form to advocate for a variety of goals, including those focused on business and the economy, public issues, and the interests of governmental units.

- Interest groups lobby all levels and all branches of government.

- Interest groups also act to influence campaigns and elections.

KNOW ...

- *agency capture*: when agencies tasked with regulating businesses, industries, or other interest groups are populated by individuals with close ties to the very firms that they are supposed to regulate (p. 263)

- *Astroturf lobbying*: when a group presents the facade of grassroots support that does not exist on its own or would not exist without the "purchase" of support by the lobbying firm itself (p. 268)

- *economic interest groups*: groups that organize to advocate on behalf of the economic interests of their members (p. 260)

- *governmental interest groups*: organizations that act to secure the interests of local, state, or foreign governments in the political process (p. 260)

- *inside lobbying*: when lobbyists contact members of Congress or their staffs directly to advocate for their group's positions (p. 263)

- *iron triangle*: the coordinated (and mutually beneficial) activities of interest groups, Congress, and the bureaucracy to achieve shared policy goals, sometimes against the general interests of society or specific groups within it (p. 265)

- *issue network*: the webs of influence between interest groups, policymakers, and policy advocates (p. 266)

- *lobbying*: interacting with government officials in order to advance a group's goals in the area of public policy (p. 261)

- *outside (or grassroots) lobbying*: a type of lobbying that focuses on reaching constituents and mobilizing them to pressure their representatives rather than pressuring the representatives directly (p. 268)

- *public interest groups*: groups that act on behalf of the collective interests of a broad group of individuals, many of who may not be members or contributors to the organization (p. 260)

- *revolving door phenomenon*: the movement of individuals between government and lobbying positions (p. 261)

8.4 Analyze and contrast the tactics that interest groups and social movements use in order to advocate on their members' behalf.

REMEMBER...

- Close ties between interest groups and governments continue to worry political scientists and observers.

- Interest groups often choose different tactics depending on how well financed or well-connected they are.

KNOW...

- *civil disobedience*: an intentional breaking of a law for the purpose of calling attention to an injustice (p. 270)

- *protest*: public demonstration designed to call attention to the need for action or change (p. 270)

Senator Maria Cantwell, D-WA, left, and Senator Lisa Murkowski, R-AK, talk before the start of a Senate Energy and Natural Resources Committee hearing in early 2016. Compared to just a few decades ago, many more women and people from traditionally underrepresented groups currently serve in Congress. Bill Clark/CQ Roll Call

SEN. CANTWELL

SEN. MURKOW
CHAIRMAN

Congress is in some ways a story of division. Members are divided into two chambers: the House and the Senate. They are increasingly divided along lines of political partisanship. They sort themselves into various committees and subcommittees to do the actual work of their institution.

In spite of those divisions, however, all members of U.S. Congress are united in one thing. They are there to **represent**, to stand for, the interests of the voters who sent them there.[1] Americans cannot all fit into the Capitol—at least not without computer-generated graphics. Therefore, Americans elect people to make the laws, raise and spend the nation's money, and watch over other institutions in the federal government, along with a host of activities that shape American public policy in a profound way.

The stories we tell in this chapter are focused primarily on one particular group in Congress: women in the Senate. We will look back on what has been accomplished and ahead to what still needs to be done to achieve more equal representation for women in Congress. We will also learn that their experience as legislators is, like their colleagues', shaped by the institution itself. The ways that their stories are both similar to and different than other members of Congress allows us to get at the heart of what representation means in American democracy.

LEARNING OBJECTIVES

After reading this chapter, you will be able to do the following:

9.1 Describe how Congress is designed, including its various constitutional powers and the differences between the two chambers.

9.2 Identify the obstacles to winning a seat in Congress, the factors that influence an individual's decision to run, and the resources and skills that successful candidates need.

9.3 List the primary organizational features of Congress, including the role of chamber leaders, political parties, committees, and congressional norms.

9.4 Explain the steps of the legislative process and how it can diverge from traditional "textbook" descriptions.

9.5 Connect the issues surrounding the representation of women in Congress to the challenges involving representation of other individuals in America.

THE EXPERIENCE OF WOMEN IN CONGRESS RAISES ISSUES OF REPRESENTATION

Winter storm "Snowzilla" slammed into the East Coast of the United States on January 22, 2016, forcing nearly a dozen governors to declare states of emergency, airlines to cancel more than ten thousand flights, and transportation and commerce to grind to a halt.[2] Buried in snow, Washington, D.C., shut down. In the aftermath, its citizens, including some members of Congress, began to dig out. Senator Susan Collins, R-ME, no stranger to snow, got out her shovel and posted a photo to her Twitter account.

The next morning, a Tuesday, the Senate convened for a brief morning session. Not much was on the agenda; too many senators could not make it to Capitol Hill. As Senator Lisa Murkowski, R-AK, opened the session, she looked around the chamber and noticed something very different: There were no men to be seen. Not one. The chamber was 100 percent female. As Murkowski put it, "You look around . . . and the presiding officer is female, all of our parliamentarians are female, our floor managers are female, all of our pages are female. . . . We came in this morning, looked around and thought, something is different this morning. Different in a good way, I might add."[3]

The next day, Murkowski introduced a bipartisan energy policy bill cosponsored by Maria Cantwell, D-WA. The men were filing back in, and when full attendance was achieved, male senators outnumbered women in the Senate five to one. The women Senators were back to being just 20 percent of the chamber.

The numbers that snowstorm produced are part of a larger story. At the time of Snowzilla, the 114th session of Congress was the most diverse in the nation's history. Across both houses, there were 96 members of racial or ethnic minorities, and 104 women. The 115th, which began in January 2017, is more diverse still.[4] Despite those gains, women represent only a fraction of Congress even though they make up just over half of the voting-eligible population.

The changes occurring in Congress point beyond quantity to qualitative differences: members of historically underrepresented groups have also moved up the chain of power within the institution. Attaining key assignments in congressional leadership depends upon talent, political skill, and seniority. In 2013, Patty Murray, D-WA, became the first woman to chair the powerful Senate Budget Committee, and Barbara Mikulski, D-MD, served as chair of the Senate Appropriations Committee, one of the most important committees in Congress from 2012 to 2015. Susan Collins and Lisa Murkowski, both Republicans, today both sit on the Senate Appropriations Committee and so help control the nation's purse strings. How did they arrive at their positions of power? Why did they choose to run for office in the first place? How were their chances affected by the structure of congressional elections? How have the rules and organization of Congress itself shaped how much power they have within the institution?

In order to answer these questions, the stories in this chapter will first take us back in time to 1992. That year, many of these women began their journeys as congressional representatives, joining the lone two women senators then on the Hill.[5] Many thought it was about time. In the run-up to the elections, Dianne Feinstein, then a candidate for a Senate seat for California, famously remarked, "Two percent may be good for fat in milk, but it's bad for women in the U.S. Senate."[6] Their collective electoral success meant that 1992 would go down as "the Year of the Woman," with a record fifty-three women in total elected to Congress.[7] As these new senators embarked on their new jobs, each had to learn the spoken and unspoken rules that governed the U.S. Congress, figure out how to make their voices heard, and find mentors to show them the way. To understand how that group of new members of Congress went about doing that, we turn first to the institution of Congress itself and the Constitutional principles in which it is grounded.

Sen. Susan Collins ✓
@SenatorCollins

Stuck in DC due to blizzard. A real storm. Tough for DC to handle; Maine could!

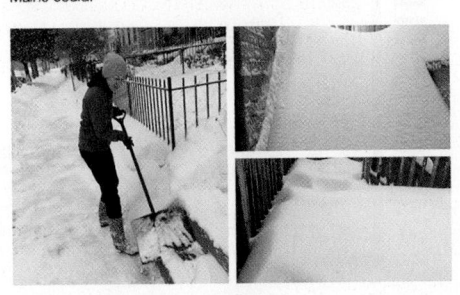

Jan 23, 2016, 1:53 PM

43 RETWEETS **83** LIKES

Maine senator Susan Collins tweeted a photo of herself digging out after "Snowzilla" in January of 2016.
Senator Susan Collins/Twitter

1. Men and women have been represented in Congress in about equal numbers for the past twenty-five years.

    a. True
    b. **False**

2. Representation in Congress means _____.

    a. Advancing one's personal agenda
    b. Running first for a seat in the House and then advancing to the Senate
    c. The act of "standing for" one's constituents in government
    d. Voting according to the majority view

3. What do you think it means for members of Congress to represent the voters' interests?

....

Answer Key: 1. b; 2. c; 3. Answers might include various aspects of congressional activity and/or speaking for the people.

THE CONSTITUTION DEFINES CONGRESS'S SHAPE AND POWERS

The U.S. Congress is called the *first branch* of government for good reason: the Constitution deals with its powers and procedures first, in more detail, and at greater length than those dealing with the executive and judicial branches.

- Explain the major differences between the House of Representatives and the Senate as laid out in the Constitution.
- Identify the constitutional powers of Congress.

The House and Senate Serve Different Roles

The Great Compromise that emerged from the Constitutional Convention in 1787 called for the creation of a **bicameral** legislature composed of two chambers, the House of Representatives and the Senate. While both the House and the Senate are involved in the legislative process, the Framers of the Constitution saw their roles differently.

These differences were designed partly to add checks and balances *within* Congress and not just between Congress and the other branches. In *The Federalist Papers*, James Madison emphasized the dangers of faction, in which a group of individuals could damage the rights and liberties of others or the interests of the Republic itself. Federalism and the separation of powers between the three branches were two ways in which the Framers tried to contain the dangers of faction. Separating legislative authority within Congress itself was another.

The House of Representatives Is Designed for Greater Accountability

Members of the House of Representatives are meant to be close to the people and their wishes. At the Constitutional Convention, delegates agreed upon two-year terms for each representative, believing this would keep them close and accountable to the people while also giving them enough time to become competent in their work and familiar with all of the relevant laws and issues.

Today, 435 representatives serve in the House, each directly elected by eligible voters in state districts that have been apportioned by population. The Constitution requires that representatives be at least twenty-five years old, a resident of his or her state, and a citizen of the United States for seven years.[8]

The Constitution did not include property ownership or affiliation in a particular religion as restrictions, because the Framers believed that the requirements for legislative service in the House should be "open to merit of every description."[9] While the Constitution did not explicitly bar women from holding office, the states did, excluding all but a few from participating in public life. Slaves and indigenous peoples were barred from public service, one of many restrictions upon their natural rights and liberties.

The Senate Is Designed for Greater Stability

Senators, in contrast, are meant to be more insulated from the whims of the public, adding stability to the legislative branch. Elected for six-year terms, the classes of senators are staggered so that about only one-third are up for reelection in a given cycle.

Today, one hundred senators serve in the Senate, two for each state. Senatorial candidates have to be older than representatives—at least thirty years old—and citizens for at least nine years, and they must live in the state that they seek to represent. Missing from the Constitution was any mention of **term limits**—limitations on how many terms a given representative or senator could serve—and today the idea is often debated.

TABLE 9.1 The House of Representatives and the Senate Compared

	House of Representatives	Senate
Requirements for Membership	At least twenty-five years old	At least thirty years old
	Seven years of citizenship	Nine years of citizenship
	Resident of the state	Resident of the state
Service	Two-year terms, with unlimited number of terms	Six-year terms, divided into three classes, with unlimited number of terms
Constituency	District, apportioned to states by population	Entire state
Organization	More governed by rules, more institutionally structured, more power to individual leadership positions	Less governed by rules, more power to individual members, more informal
Goals	To be closer to voters' preferences	To be more insulated from voters' preferences

Congress Has Three Key Powers: Lawmaking, Budgeting, and Oversight

The powers of Congress fall into three broad areas: those related to its role as the main lawmaking body, those related to its position at the center of the budgeting process, and those it exerts when exercising oversight of the federal bureaucracy and other public officials.

Legislative Authority

The most important power of Congress is its legislative authority—the ability to pass laws in areas of national policy. The body of law that Congress creates is called statutory law as it is written down in the **statutes** that Congress passes.

Among legislative bodies in the world's democracies, the U.S. Congress is the most active and independent in terms of its ability to make national policy. The list of the enumerated powers of Congress is substantial; Congress is authorized to legislate in economic policy, national security, foreign policy, and other policy areas (see Table 9.2).

The Budgeting Process

The second major role of Congress involves its central position in setting a federal budget. Creating a bureaucratic agency requires two steps: First, congressional action authorizes the department or agency. Second, through the process of **appropriation**, Congress funds the agency's activities. Many of the rules governing the budgetary process were first set out in the Congressional Budget Act of 1974.[10] The Budget Act created the Congressional Budget Office (CBO), whose role is to provide information and estimates of the likely budgetary consequences of funding the agencies and programs created by Congress. The Budget Act also established the process of reconciliation, whereby congressional committees work out how federal spending will align with the overall congressional budget. Reconciliation bills are passed using a more streamlined process than other bills in Congress. This can make them harder to stop.

One controversial way in which members of Congress have been involved in the budgetary process has been through **earmarks**, through which members direct monies to projects within their districts or states. Popular with constituents, earmarks have been criticized for putting particular interests ahead of those of the nation's voters as a whole. In 2011 the House of Representatives, led by Republicans, instituted a ban on earmarks.

Oversight

The third major role of Congress in national policymaking is that of **oversight**; Congress uses its authority to ensure that laws are implemented in the way that Congress intended when it passed them. Given the growth in the size and complexity of the federal government, this is not an easy task.

TABLE 9.2 Legislative Powers of Congress in the Constitution

The constitution grants Congress the power to legislate in the following areas.

Enumerated Powers			
	Both Chambers	**House**	**Senate**
Economic Policy	Create and collect taxes, coin money, borrow money, regulate the value of currency, borrow money, and regulate commerce.	All bills to raise revenue must be generated in the House.	In practice, the Senate has become a coequal partner in setting national revenue policy.
Foreign Policy	Regulate trade with other nations.		Ratify treaties entered into by a president.
National Security	Declare war, raise and support armies and a naval force and make rules for their governance and regulation, power to call up the military, and define and punish piracies and felonies committed on the high seas.		
Other Powers Involving the Executive Branch		Impeach the president, vice president, and other executive branch officers.	Confirm presidential nominations of executive branch officers, and try members of the executive branch impeached by the House.
Powers Involving the Judicial Branch	Create levels of the judicial branch below the Supreme Court, and establish the number of Supreme Court justices.	Impeach members of the federal judiciary.	Confirm by majority vote presidential nominees to the federal judiciary, try members of the federal judiciary who have been impeached.
Via Necessary and Proper Clause			
	"To make all Laws which shall be necessary and proper for carrying into Execution the foregoing Powers, and all other Powers vested by this Constitution in the Government of the United States."		
Via Subsequent Amendments			
	Individual amendments (such as the Thirteenth, Fourteenth, and Fifteenth) grant Congress "the power to enforce, by appropriate legislation," those amendments.		

Congress has oversight responsibilities over the federal bureaucracy as well as over other branches of government and elected and appointed officials. Congressional committees and subcommittees may conduct hearings and investigations into the actions of executive agencies to try to ensure that funds appropriated for programs are being spent efficiently and in accordance with the law's intent and that agents are not abusing their powers. While many committee hearings are routine, some may be called in the event of a perceived breakdown or failure by an executive branch agency.

In 2017, congressional committees were investigating many aspects of the 2016 presidential election, including accusations of Russian interference into the elections, communications between current and former officials in the administration of President Donald Trump with that nation, and alleged efforts of members of the prior administration of President Barack Obama to shape the narrative of the investigation into the use of an unsecured server by former secretary of state Hillary Clinton.

The calling of hearings in response to a visible crisis is called **fire alarm oversight**, with oversight being triggered only by an alarm call. This kind of oversight is different from **police patrol oversight**, in which Congress continually monitors the actions of a bureaucracy. Because of the difficulty in continuously monitoring the immense federal bureaucracy, fire alarm oversight is more commonly used than police patrol oversight.[11]

In implementing the idea of checks and balances, the Constitution gave each of the branches shared authority over some aspects of governance, which allows a kind of oversight of one branch over the other two. As discussed earlier, Congress is given the authority to declare war and the Senate to ratify treaties, thus forcing the executive and legislative branches to work together in important aspects of foreign and national security policy.

Other Congressional Powers Involve Advice and Consent, Senatorial Courtesy, and Impeachment

Using its power of advice and consent, the Senate confirms presidential nominees to the federal courts by a simple majority. The norm of **senatorial courtesy** generally allows senators to nominate lower-level federal judges to serve in their states with the expectation that they will be confirmed without significant opposition. Also with respect to the judiciary, both the House and Senate have a role in the nation's court system as they have the power "to constitute Tribunals inferior to [below] the Supreme Court" (Article 1, section 8) and set the number of justices on the Supreme Court.

In addition to the confirmation of presidential nominees to the federal judiciary, the Senate also exercises the same role of advice and consent in the confirmation of most presidential nominees to important posts in the federal bureaucracy.

Congress is also given the authority to remove federal officials—including the president, vice president, government officials, and federal judges—through the process of **impeachment**. The House of Representatives votes to impeach if a majority of its members feel that an official has committed "Treason, Bribery, or other high Crimes and Misdemeanors" (Article 2, section 4). The vagueness of this language has resulted in debates about just what constitutes an impeachable offense.

If a majority of the members of the House votes to impeach, the trial takes place in the Senate, with a two-thirds majority needed to convict (Article 1, section 3).[12] Impeachment is a power that has been used rarely.

Two presidents have faced successful House resolutions to impeach, but neither was removed from office. Andrew Johnson—impeached during the Reconstruction era following the Civil War—survived by a single vote in the Senate. Bill Clinton—charged with lying during and obstructing an investigation into his relationship with intern Monica Lewinsky—was acquitted by a vote of 55–45.

These fundamental structural features, grounded in the Constitution, are the framework in which all members of Congress operate once they are in Congress. Getting to Congress, however, involves factors that are constitutionally based and others that are based in pure politics and personal experience, as we will see in the next section.

GETTING TO CONGRESS INVOLVES PERSONAL, PROFESSIONAL, ELECTORAL, AND FINANCIAL FACTORS

Like all members of Congress, the pathways that ultimately led the women who ran for office in 1992 to Congress were as diverse as they were and involved factors like their personal motivations,

- Understand the various factors that contribute to success in congressional elections.

their professional experience, the way congressional elections work, and whether they had basic supports like money and staff. So, how did this particular group get to Washington? And why did they run?

For many of the women who ran in that fateful election, one moment in congressional history crystalized their commitment to bring about change in Congress: the Senate confirmation hearings of Clarence Thomas to the U.S. Supreme Court.

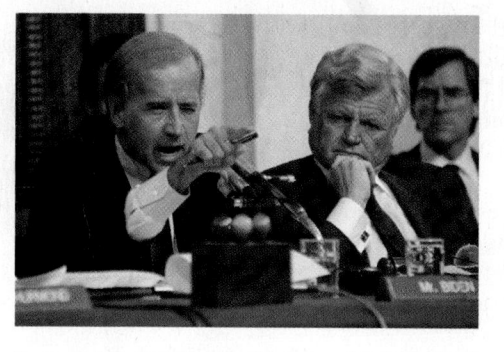

Senate Judiciary Committee members Joseph R. Biden, D-DE, presiding, and Senator Ted Kennedy, D-MA, right, ask pointed and skeptical questions of Anita Hill during the Clarence Thomas confirmation hearings, 1991. AP Photo/Greg Gibson, File

Federal judicial confirmations are often very politically charged since appointments have profound and long-lasting consequences. Given Thomas's conservative views, the confirmation proceedings were bound to be heated. However, an unusual point of controversy emerged during Thomas's hearings. Thomas's former aide, Professor Anita Hill, asserted that Thomas had sexually harassed her while the two were serving in the federal government.

Though many women were concerned about the specific charges of sexual harassment, it was the skepticism displayed by the members of the all-white, male Senate Judiciary Committee to Hill's testimony—dismissive and condescending in the eyes of many—that galvanized women around the country by "symbolizing the lack of representation for women and their interests on Capitol Hill."[13] In response, "Many voters decided that if given the chance they would vote for a woman candidate, in part because she was a woman. . . .[P]arty and grassroots organizations redoubled their efforts to find and fund women candidates. And . . . a number of women decided that they would put themselves on the line and run for local, state, and national office."[14]

Across the country in Washington State, Patty Murray, then a state legislator, "watched in disbelief as the committee members questioned Hill's veracity about Thomas' sexual advances and innuendo. Murray found herself asking 'Who's saying what I would say if I were there?'"[15] That evening, at a neighborhood party, as others expressed similar frustration, Murray announced, "You know what? I'm going to run for the Senate."[16]

Political Ambition Launches Careers

Murray exemplifies a characteristic that, according to political scientists Linda Fowler and Robert McClure, sets declared candidates apart from "the unseen candidates—the men and women who could have run for Congress but chose not to." That is, she had **political ambition**.[17] Only those with the strongest personal desire to act in politics decide to face the long odds against success, especially if such a bid would mean facing a well-resourced incumbent. Where does political ambition come from? The answers are not always neatly categorized by gender, racial or ethnic identity, or any one simple category. As Murray's example shows, political ambition is as unique to a potential candidate as it is to the constituents she or he hopes to represent.

The decision to stand for national legislative office, though a monumental one, is only the first step in the long journey toward membership in the U.S. Congress. The next step is to actually get elected. For first-timers, this involves a very steep climb. The odds are stacked against them. In this process, the first thing a candidate has to assess is whose votes she or he is trying to win.

Constituency, Incumbency, and Other Electoral Factors Lay the Groundwork

The Constitution sets the framework for the boundaries of **constituency**. Would-be senators hope to represent the voters of their states. Hopeful candidates for the House strive to secure the votes of the constituents in their congressional districts, the boundaries of which can and do change in response to fluctuations in state population and the often intensely political process of redistricting.

The power of incumbency—running for reelection as opposed to running for the first time—strongly affects the outcomes of congressional elections. Congressional incumbents possess so many advantages, such as media coverage, a record of providing beneficial service and legislation to a state or district, and name recognition, that qualified challengers often rationally wait until they can run in an open seat election after an incumbent has retired or moved on to another office.

In the 1992 elections, there was an important crack in the normal power of incumbency. For a variety of reasons, there were a record high number of open congressional seats, and potential challengers who had been waiting for their chance pounced. The advantages that incumbent candidates would normally have enjoyed were gone. According to government professor Clyde Wilcox, "For experienced women politicians who lived in the open districts, 1992 was likely to be their best shot for many years at a House seat."[18]

Moreover, the end of the Cold War focused voters' attention away from issues of national security and onto issues of domestic policy, issues on which a number of women candidates had strong track records. Finally, with Democrat Bill Clinton's presidential victory that year, the electoral strength of the Democratic Party helped other Democratic candidates. Of the twenty-four women elected to the House for the first time in 1992, twenty were Democrats. All five of the newly elected or successfully reelected women in the Senate were Democrats as well.

Experience and Money Legitimize Candidates

When challengers do decide to stand for office, they need many things; however, above all else, they need experience and money. Experience is hard earned, usually gained by moving up through the layers of local and state politics and becoming professional, polished, and respected. Congressional elections are usually no place for amateurs, who often lack the knowledge, political organization, and well-honed political skills prerequisite to success in the high-stakes enterprise of a national campaign.

Looking back on her successful campaign for the U.S. Senate in 1992, Senator Dianne Feinstein, D-CA, advised congressional hopefuls, especially young women,

Carol Moseley Braun greets constituents in her hometown of Chicago, Illinois. Steve Kagan/The LIFE Images Collection/Getty Images

to "earn your spurs" by starting locally on the school board or town council and building a coherent portfolio that reflects a set of consistent policies "so that people will turn to you."[19] Money is inseparable from congressional elections. It buys media spots, funds a ground campaign, and acts to scare off potential opponents. The pressures of fund-raising in the modern Congress are relentless.

The opportunity presented in 1992 would not have translated into electoral success without a slate of experienced and well-funded candidates. Women candidates were able to recruit individuals and organizations who were willing to contribute money and time to their political campaigns and to organize and mobilize voters on their behalf.

For Carol Moseley Braun, who had previously served in the Illinois House of Representatives, the Thomas confirmation hearings were most certainly a contributor to her decision to run for the Senate in 1992. However, her path to the chamber was also paved by the hard-earned experience of Chicago politics—as tough a venue as there is in American government. Moseley Braun would go on to defeat in the primary the incumbent Democrat from Illinois who had voted to confirm Clarence Thomas and then also beat the Republican challenger in the general election.

For candidates like Moseley Braun and Murray, the Thomas confirmation hearings and the increased national attention on issues of concern to American women voters brought money to the table. Organizations called political action committees (PACs) that raise and spend money on behalf of candidates that year contributed large amounts of money to their campaigns. In particular, PACs that were focused on financing and advising women candidates played a major role. Patty Murray's campaign received critical early support from one of the largest, EMILY's List, a pro-choice Democratic women's PAC. As political scientist Candice Nelson put it, "Early money enables candidates to do the things necessary to establish credibility: hire a pollster, develop a campaign plan, and be prepared for challenges to her credibility when they occur."[20] EMILY's List was founded in 1985, and by 1992, it was the largest of all PACs in the election.[21] The group's membership grew from 3,000 from before the Thomas-Hill hearings to 24,000 after the election.[22]

All congressional candidates are driven to run for office to advance and advocate for a set of policy goals—to change the congressional conversation. Each has a set of issues they want to focus on. Having succeeded in winning office, the next step is for them to figure out how to translate those goals into actual laws in order to make their voices, and those of their constituents, heard in Congress.

1. The term *political ambition* refers to
   _____.

   a. The need for potential candidates to have the commitment necessary to overcome the long odds faced by a challenger running against an incumbent
   b. A willingness on the part of first-time candidates to skirt campaign fund-raising laws
   c. A desire to use a seat in Congress as a springboard to the presidency
   d. The willingness of congressional incumbents to use their advantages to prevent credible challengers

2. Open seat elections tend to attract more first-time challengers in congressional elections.

   a. True
   b. False

3. What were some of the reasons why a record number of women candidates decided to run for Congress in 1992?

4. What qualities do successful first-time candidates for Congress generally need?

Answer Key: 1. a; 2. a; 3. Answers should include the fallout from the Thomas confirmation hearings, the number of open seat elections, and campaign support from outside groups; 4. Answers should include experience and money and may discuss the challenges of running against incumbents.

CONGRESS IS ORGANIZED AROUND FORMAL AND INFORMAL RULES

In 1992 the political stars had aligned to make it possible for newcomers to alter the face of the Congress. As the 103rd Congress convened in Washington in January 1993, these newcomers would quickly need to learn the complicated rules, procedures, and processes of Congress if they hoped to make their viewpoints manifest in American public policy.

The Constitution is much more specific on what Congress does than on how it is supposed to do it. With a few exceptions, the Constitution does not describe most of the day-to-day processes and procedures of Congress. These rules and details have been created by the chambers themselves; important modifications have been made over time. Congress includes both formal and informal organizational features. Formally, political parties, party leaders, and the committee system shape much of what happens in the House and Senate. Congressional staff and the congressional bureaucracy are involved as well. Informally, norms and traditional ways of doing things also play a role.

Members of Congress must be very familiar with the organizational structure of Congress if they are to succeed in advancing their agenda. Groups may form around a shared set of lived experiences, a shared set of policy goals, or a shared desire to reform how Congress works. In addition, members gain power

- Explain how the structure of Congress can help or hinder members of congress as they try to act on behalf their constituencies.

- Describe the role political parties play in achieving congressional success.

and influence as their congressional careers develop and they establish seniority within the institution.

While rules and procedures may seem like a dry subject of study, they matter a great deal to what legislation does or does not emerge from Congress. Battles over organization or congressional procedure are often just as heated and consequential as battles over specific policies.

Representative Paul Ryan, R-WI, stands next to outgoing House Speaker John Boehner, R-OH, in the House Chamber on Capitol Hill in October 2015. Now the House Speaker, Ryan, like Boehner before him, has had trouble unifying a fractured Republican House. AP Photo/Andrew Harnik

Political Parties Shape How Congress Is Structured

Much of the formal structure of Congress revolves around the role of political parties and party leaders. The majority party, which is the party with the most members in each chamber, and the minority party, which has the second-highest number of members, each control important leadership positions and organize congressional behavior—both to advocate for their preferred policies and to help individual members in their reelection efforts.

In contrast to most modern representative assemblies, party leaders in the U.S. Congress often struggle to make sure that their own members act and vote in support of party positions, especially when a member's constituent preferences clash with those of the member's political party. Leaders, however, are not powerless and have a variety of carrots and sticks with which to steer their members in the desired direction. Party leaders work through party caucuses (Democratic Party) and party conferences (Republican Party), in which members of a party meet, set up goals, choose leaders, assign members to committees, and try to present a unified voice to the American electorate through the media.

Party Leadership in the House of Representatives

Larger than the Senate since the founding of Congress, the House of Representatives is, by necessity, more formally structured than the Senate, with rank-and-file House members individually less powerful than their Senate colleagues. The **Speaker of the House**—the only House leadership position described in the Constitution—wields a considerable amount of power, though that power has changed over time in response to demands on the House and strategic political action on the part of its members.

At the beginning of each new Congress (every two years), members of the House elect the Speaker, who has almost always been a member of the majority party. A long history of successful service in the House is usually a prerequisite. Increasingly, the ability to raise money for other members of one's party is considered in selecting a Speaker. These leadership PACs "are designed for two things: to make money and to make friends," and representatives use that money to assist fellow party members' campaigns.[23] The Speaker is second in the line of succession (behind the vice president) to the presidency in the event of death, resignation, removal from office, or inability to conduct the office's duties. In Congress, the Speaker has considerable power over the House agenda and committee assignments.

Assisting the Speaker is the House **majority leader**, the majority **whip** (and other members of the whip system), and various caucus and conference chairs and vice chairs. Members of the whip system collect information about how individual members are planning to vote, corralling their support on key votes and setting party strategy in Congress. The term comes from British hunting; the "whipper-in" tried to keep the hounds in some sort of a coherent group. The House **minority leader** has far less structural influence in the House than the Speaker but works to coordinate minority party activity, opposition to the majority party, and overall strategy. House minority party leadership also includes its own whips and whip systems.

Party Leadership in the Senate

Constitutionally, the official leader of the Senate is the vice president of the United States, though he or she can cast a vote only in the event of a tie. The president pro tempore presides over the chamber's proceedings when the vice president is not present (which is almost all of the time) but wields no real power. Typically, junior senators fill in to oversee the day-to-day proceedings.

The most powerful position in the Senate is the Senate majority leader, who is chosen from the majority party by its members in caucus or conference. As individual senators retain more power than their colleagues in the House, the Senate majority leader is not as powerful as the Speaker; however, she or he plays a key role in shaping the legislative agenda. The Senate minority leader—chosen by the minority party members—acts as the leader of the opposition in the Senate. Assisting both party leaders are party whips, leadership committees, and party caucuses and conferences. See Figure 9.1.

The Work of Congress Is Done through the Committee System

The work that Congress deals with is considerable and complex. There is no way any one member could be directly involved in each piece of legislation. To divide the workload, both the House and the Senate have established the committee system, a system of committees and subcommittees that do most of the work of Congress.

FIGURE 9.1

The Structure of Leadership in Congress

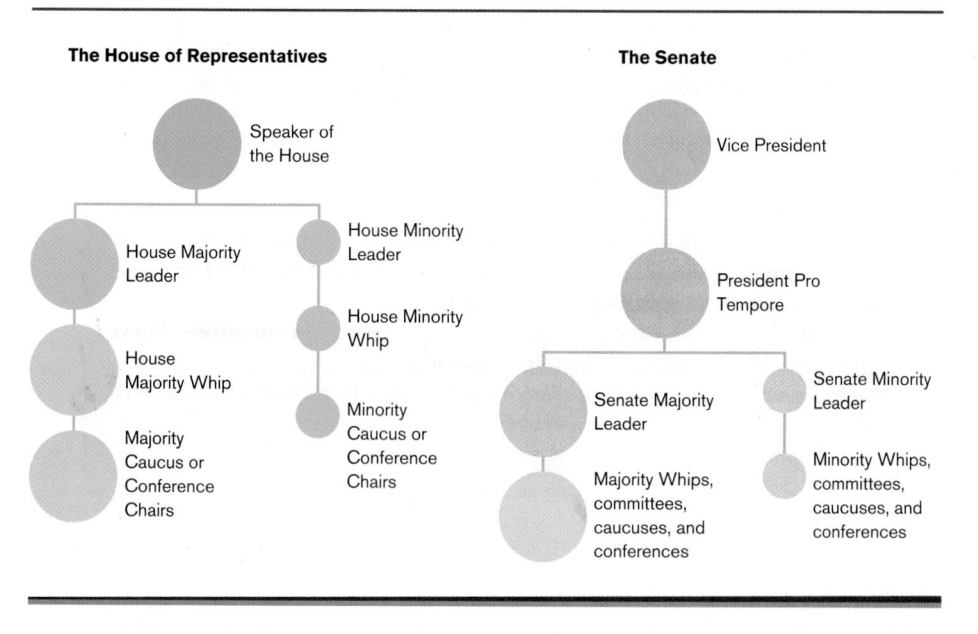

The House of Representatives

- Speaker of the House
- House Majority Leader
- House Minority Leader
- House Minority Whip
- House Majority Whip
- Minority Caucus or Conference Chairs
- Majority Caucus or Conference Chairs

The Senate

- Vice President
- President Pro Tempore
- Senate Majority Leader
- Senate Minority Leader
- Majority Whips, committees, caucuses, and conferences
- Minority Whips, committees, caucuses, and conferences

Committee Membership and Leadership

Committee membership is determined and negotiated by party leaders and generally reflects the ratio of party membership in each chamber. Seniority, or the length of consecutive service on the committee, plays a major role in determining **committee chairs**. These chairs have considerable influence over committee processes, especially in setting the committee's agenda. Because of the differences in the size of the chambers, House committees tend to have more members than Senate committees, while individual senators tend to serve on more committees than their colleagues in the House.

New representatives and senators often try to get appointed to committees that deal with issues of interest to their constituents or that provide benefits to their districts and states. That has the added advantage of helping their prospects for reelection along the way. Requests for committee membership, though, may also be driven by genuine policy interests on the part of members of Congress.[24]

Types of Committees

Congress has four types of committees: standing, joint, conference, and select. **Standing committees** are where most of the work of Congress gets done. They are so named because they continue across Congresses, and members tend to serve on them for multiple terms, developing expertise and working to bring benefits to their districts and states. Standing committees consider legislation and exercise oversight of bureaucratic agencies, usually recommend funding levels for them. They are divided by policy areas, with a given committee having jurisdiction over its area of specialization. Standing committees are divided into subcommittees, which specialize even further, usually considering parts of legislation under instructions from their parent committees.

Joint committees contain members of both the House and the Senate. In general they do not have a great deal of power but are used to focus public attention on an issue, gather information for Congress, or help party leaders speed things along in the legislative process.

The **conference committee** is a temporary joint committee that resolves differences between the House and Senate versions of a bill, which is required by the Constitution before a president can sign the bill into law. Party leaders determine conference committee membership, though members who have been centrally involved in a bill are usually included.

The fourth type of committee is the **select or special committee**. These temporary bodies are usually called upon to investigate an issue, sometimes in response to a crisis or a scandal. Select committees may be given the authority to report legislation, but their role is usually informational only.

Congressional Staff and the Congressional Bureaucracy Help Members Represent Their Constituents

The third component of the formal organization of Congress consists of the people and institutions developed to help members represent their constituents. Congressional staff assist representatives and senators in providing casework and give members information about policies, legislation, and constituent preferences. Staff often work closely with members in drafting bills. As the size of the American Republic and the complexity of issues before Congress have both grown, so has the size of the congressional staff.

Congress has also developed bureaucratic organizations to assist its members' efforts. These nonpartisan institutions provide members with estimates of the likely impact of laws on the national budget and keep them informed about how well agencies are performing the tasks Congress intended of them. For instance, the Government Accountability Office (GAO) keeps track of agencies created and funded by Congress.

Norms Are Informal Contributors to Congressional Organization

In addition to the formal structures, less formal processes also play a role in congressional action. Norms are unwritten expectations of how members are supposed to act and help members balance representing their constituents and contributing to the smooth functioning of the House and Senate. Members are expected to be respectful toward their colleagues, to reciprocate help from other members, and to specialize in one or more policy areas to assist the overall level of information and expertise in Congress. Animosity between members of the two political parties has challenged the role of norms in constraining member behavior in recent years.

THE LEGISLATIVE PROCESS IS COMPLEX BY DESIGN

By design, the legislative process is complicated and multistepped, with each stage offering another chance to kill a prospective law. Having seen the passions of the people sweep through state legislatures and sometimes trample on minority rights, the Framers of the Constitution intentionally placed many hurdles in the path of legislation.

- Understand the legislative process, including both the formal and "unorthodox" paths a bill may take.

- Identify the actors that play a role in influencing whether a bill is passed.

What's more, the modern legislative process rarely follows the traditional, linear "textbook" way that it is described, especially when it comes to major legislation. Political scientist Barbara Sinclair used the term *unorthodox lawmaking* to describe the realities of the modern legislative process: whereas "the route to enactment used to be linear and predictable; now it is flexible and varied."[25]

This reality does not mean that legislators are bypassing constitutional provisions, only that the process is much more fluid, complex, and political than any flowchart can adequately describe (see Figure 9.2).

The First Step Is Bill Introduction

The first stage of the legislative process is the formal introduction of a **bill**, a draft of a proposed law, into either the House or the Senate. Any member may introduce a bill, but only members of Congress may do so. Even here we see evidence of unorthodox lawmaking, as other actors often play a role in shaping a bill or encouraging a member to introduce it. For instance, the president, for all of her or his tremendous power, cannot literally walk into the House of Representatives and place a bill into "the hopper" for consideration; only a member of the House can do that. However, presidents can encourage, cajole, and press members of either chamber to get a major piece of legislation on the

FIGURE 9.2

The Legislative Process

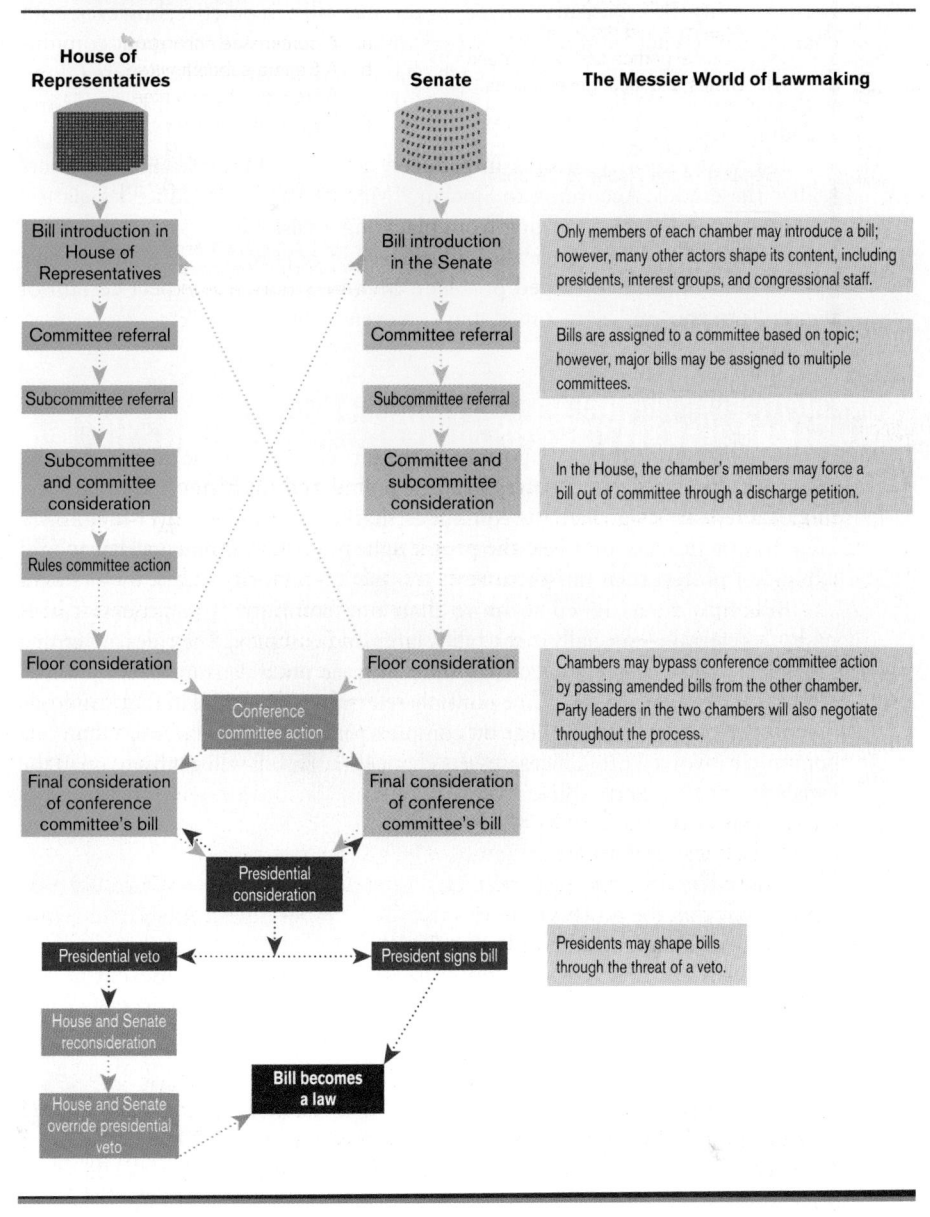

House of Representatives

Senate

The Messier World of Lawmaking

Bill introduction in House of Representatives

Bill introduction in the Senate

Only members of each chamber may introduce a bill; however, many other actors shape its content, including presidents, interest groups, and congressional staff.

Committee referral

Committee referral

Bills are assigned to a committee based on topic; however, major bills may be assigned to multiple committees.

Subcommittee referral

Subcommittee referral

Subcommittee and committee consideration

Committee and subcommittee consideration

In the House, the chamber's members may force a bill out of committee through a discharge petition.

Rules committee action

Floor consideration

Floor consideration

Chambers may bypass conference committee action by passing amended bills from the other chamber. Party leaders in the two chambers will also negotiate throughout the process.

Conference committee action

Final consideration of conference committee's bill

Final consideration of conference committee's bill

Presidential consideration

Presidential veto

President signs bill

Presidents may shape bills through the threat of a veto.

House and Senate reconsideration

House and Senate override presidential veto

Bill becomes a law

legislative agenda, whether through discussions with party leaders or though appeals to the American public.

Once introduced, a particular bill must wind its way through the originating chamber and then proceed to the other chamber to begin the process anew. Formally, only the House may introduce revenue bills. In practice, however, both chambers often act simultaneously on similar policies, with frequent communication between party leaders in each chamber. In addition, the Senate (along with the president) has become a coequal partner in the overall revenue and spending process.

The vast majority of bills introduced never become law, and members realize these odds. According to Sinclair, "Members may introduce legislation for a variety of reasons, ranging from placating a pesky interest group in their home state or district to publicizing a little recognized problem or an innovative approach to an acknowledged problem. Members may not expect certain of their bills to pass and, sometimes, may not even want them to."[26]

Referral to Committee Involves Political Strategy

Because committees are so important to the ultimate success or failure of a bill, assignment to committee involves strategic political calculations. In the textbook model, a bill simply goes to the committee that has jurisdiction over that policy area. In practice, committees sometimes fight for bill assignments that would expand or protect their jurisdiction.

Bills may be assigned to more than one committee—a process called multiple referral—especially if the bill is large and complex. The rules governing multiple referral have changed over time, and the practice is more common in the House than the Senate. While multiple referral can be useful in that "multiple perspectives are brought to bear on complex problems," having more than one committee involved often increases the chances that a bill will get hung up in the legislative process and expire.[27]

Bills Are Altered–and Die–Due to Committee and Subcommittee Action

Once referred to one or more committees, legislation is usually sent to one or more subcommittees—more narrowly focused groups of legislators operating under the guidance of the parent committee of which they are a part. Committees and subcommittees hold hearings to gather information about a bill or issue. Outside experts may be brought in to testify. The **markup** session allows committee members to make changes to a bill before the committee reports it to the floor. The committee report follows the bill from committee to the floor. It acts as a history of the bill and offers guidance to administrative agencies and (if necessary) courts about the committee's intent regarding the bill. Sometimes early cost estimates of the bill's provisions are included in the conference report.

Congressional committees are the graveyards of most bills. In committee, bills can die from a committee's refusal to report the bill to the full chamber, changes made to them to make them impassable on the House or Senate floor, or simple neglect.

The committee may reject the bill by vote, or it may table the bill with no further action. In the House, a member may file a discharge petition to free a bill from an unfriendly committee and move it to the House floor for a vote if this is agreed to by a majority of representatives. Discharge efforts are rarely successfully used, but they can serve to "pressure a committee and the majority party leadership to bring to the floor measures that they would rather not consider."[28] Often the mere threat of using a procedural maneuver can shape legislative outcomes by signaling to other members that they may face opposition from members of the minority party.

Voting Takes Place during Floor Consideration

Once they have successfully passed out of committee, bills proceed to consideration on the floors of the House and Senate.

Consideration in the House of Representatives

An important difference between the House and the Senate is the role of the **House Rules Committee** in the legislative process, which has no equally powerful analogue in the Senate. A majority of the House Rules Committee's members are chosen by the Speaker. This committee determines when a bill will be subject to debate and vote on the House floor, how long the debate will last, and whether amendments will be allowed on the floor. These special rules can play a major role in whether the bill passes the House or not.

Open rules allow all relevant amendments while closed rules prohibit amendments other than those reported by committee. Most bills are considered under rules that fall in between these extremes, with modified open or modified closed rules. The rules about amendments are important because adding amendments to a bill is yet one more way to kill a piece of legislation. Killer amendments are designed to do just that by peeling away support for a bill by adding unpalatable or indefensible language or provisions. Closed rules can occasionally be used to kill a bill as well, if there are only enough members who would support a bill if key amendments were added, which is not allowed under closed rules.

If the House approves the rules governing a bill, then floor debate on the bill begins under those rules. A vote to accept or reject the rules reported out of the Rules Committee can be just as consequential to the fate of a piece of legislation as an actual vote on a bill—though in ways that are less visibly clear to most American voters. If allowed, amendments may be offered and, perhaps, amendments to amendments. The time allowed for debate and who controls that time will also have been set by the Rules Committee.

A **roll-call vote** is a vote in which each member of the chamber debating a bill indicates "yea," "nay," or "present." In the House, most votes are electronic. Many interest groups keep track of key votes on issues relevant to them, scoring individual members on how friendly or unfriendly their votes have been to the members of that interest group.

Consideration in the Senate

In the Senate, individual senators have more ability to shape outcomes on the floor than their House colleagues. Party leadership still matters, however, and the Senate majority leaders schedule the agenda. While the House was first to adopt more formal procedures for bill consideration, the Senate has also become more formalized—though not to the same degree as the House. In the Senate, most procedures are governed by unanimous consent, in which all senators agree to let a motion proceed to a vote. A simple unanimous consent request may be used on noncontroversial measures. A more complex unanimous consent agreement will be worked out between the parties on major legislation to govern the length of debate and the rules governing amendments.

If an individual senator objects to a bill or part of a bill, that senator may place a hold on the legislation and communicate to the majority leader her or his reservations about the bill. In their ability to place holds, offer amendments, and debate issues on the floor, individual senators have the ability to consume Congress's scarcest resource: time. As Sinclair reported, "A single dissatisfied senator, even if she is junior and a minority party member, can cause a great deal of trouble."[29] While the majority leader does not have to honor the hold request, a hold indicates the possibility of a filibuster on the bill.

A **filibuster** is the use of the power of individual senators to continue to debate issues in order to delay a motion or vote on the floor.[30] Only a successful vote of **cloture**, which requires three-fifths of senators (60), can shut down debate and end a filibuster, allowing the Senate to move on to a vote. Therefore, a determined minority party, provided they have at least forty-one seats and are able to maintain party unity, can delay or kill legislation through the use of the filibuster.

The filibuster has a long and controversial history in the Senate. In 1917, under the urging of President Woodrow Wilson, the Senate adopted the rule of cloture. At the time, ending a filibuster required a two-thirds majority; it was changed to three-fifths in 1975. The placing of holds and threats of a filibuster are increasingly common in a closely split but deeply divided Senate. Because of the increased use of the filibuster threat, votes of cloture have become much more numerous as well. Senators have not only threatened to filibuster a bill that they object to, they have also at times held up an unrelated vote or confirmation of a presidential nominee in order to extract concessions on something else, a process referred to as **hostage-taking**.[31]

By 2017, Senate processes had been changed to prevent filibusters of executive branch nominees and lower-level federal judges (by the Democratic-controlled Senate in 2013) and of Supreme Court nominees (by the Republican-controlled Senate in 2017). The ability to filibuster most bills in the Senate, however, remained. During debates over the budget bill in the spring of 2017, President Trump called for the elimination of the filibuster entirely in a set of Twitter posts. "Either elect more Republican Senators in 2018 or change the rules now to 51%," he tweeted. "Our country needs a good 'shutdown' in September to fix this mess!"[32] In a rare bipartisan response to his comments, "Sixty-one senators signed a letter circulated by Senators Chris Coons, Democrat of Delaware, and Susan Collins, Republican of Maine, backing the 60-vote threshold on legislation."[33]

The House and Senate Resolve Differences between Their Bills

The next step in the legislative process is to resolve differences between House and Senate versions of a bill prior to presidential action. The formal structure for reconciling differences between two versions of a bill is the conference committee. Traditionally bipartisan, the Speaker of the House chooses that chamber's members. Because the Senate operates under unanimous consent, leaders from both parties choose its members to conference. Key players on a bill's progress through Congress are usually included as well.

When the differences are over spending amounts, negotiation is usually more straightforward. When they involve major policy differences—especially if one party controls the House and another the Senate—negotiations may be much more difficult. Because the process of sending a bill to conference from the Senate requires several procedural votes, which are subject to filibuster threat, the modern Congress often bypasses conference, though it still has to produce identical language.

On minor bills, or when the differences are small, one chamber may avoid going to conference by simply accepting the other chamber's version of the bill. This especially happens late in a session when time is scarce and can be used by the political opposition as a weapon.[34] Party leaders may also negotiate informally behind the scenes, with the results of these negotiations offered as amendments. The strategy of ping-ponging (also called amendment exchange) is also designed to avoid having to go to conference. House and Senate versions are amended and sent back and forth between the two chambers until the process has produced a single text.

Bills Go Back to the Floor for Reconsideration

Once differences between the two versions have been resolved, the single bill goes back to each chamber for reconsideration, without the possibility of amendment. By this point, on major bills, party leaders have already engaged in lengthy negotiations with their counterparts in the other chamber to avoid any surprises.

The President Takes Action

Following successful passage in each chamber, the bill goes to the president for action. The president then has three choices for each bill that lands on her or his desk. The president may sign it, in which case the bill becomes a law. She or he may **veto** it, sending it back to Congress with the objections noted. Bills that are vetoed can still become law if two-thirds of both chambers vote to override the president's veto. Veto overrides are not common and signal a deep disconnect between a president and Congress.

Just as is the case with a filibuster in the Senate, the power of a presidential veto lies as much with the *threat* of its use as with the actual veto. Veto-bargaining is a negotiation tactic used by presidents to shape the legislation before it lands on his or her desk by using the threat of an eventual veto to gain desired concessions or amendments.[35] The president's third option is to do nothing, though what happens next depends on how much time is left in that session of Congress. If the president does nothing and there are ten or more days left in session (Sundays excluded), the bill becomes law anyway. This quiet veto does not change the outcome, but it might signal to American voters presidential displeasure with all or part of the law. If Congress has adjourned that year's session during the ten-day period and the president has not signed it, then the law is vetoed, an outcome that is called a pocket veto. A controversial tactic for Congress to avoid a pocket veto is to leave one or more members behind while everyone else goes home.

MEMBERS REPRESENT CONSTITUTENTS BY HOW THEY ACT AND WHO THEY ARE

- Explain the different forms of congressional representation.

- Describe the constitutional barriers that slow the translation of electoral success into policy change.

- Explain why the exclusion of certain groups from Congress has had long-term consequences for representation.

The most difficult question in the study of Congress is what may seem to be the simplest: What does it mean to represent one's constituents in Congress? Political theorist Hannah Pitkin has written about the multiple meanings of representation in Congress, noting for starters that "representation means . . . *re-presentation*, a making present again."[36] What are constituents asking their representatives to "make present" in Washington that was not there before? Part of the answer lies in *acting*—in the sense of what representatives do. In a representative democracy, citizens choose representatives, with senators included in this broader conception of "representatives," to act on their behalf—to vote on the floor and in committee, to sponsor legislation, to negotiate, and to lead. Another part of the answer lays in *being*—in the sense of who the representatives are.

When voters select representatives, they are choosing people who may or may not reflect and share their policy preferences, identities, interests, and lived experiences. They ask that their representatives transmit information about them—the constituents—to the other members of Congress by adding their voices to the debates and deliberations within the institution. In doing so, according to political scientist Richard Fenno, voters are in a sense asking their representatives to take on sometimes competing roles, which he used the term *home style* to denote. Voters want their political representatives to be effective in Washington, which takes them away from home. However, voters also want their members to come home, to present themselves and explain to voters what they have been up to and what they are going to accomplish.[37] More time at home connects representatives and senators to their constituents, while effective representation necessarily involves spending time operating in the intricate machinery of Congress.

Acting in Congress Involves Visible and Invisible Legislative Work

Passing laws—the legislative function—is Congress's most important task, and voting on the House and Senate floor is the most public legislative act members undertake. However, the process of legislation involves many stages and many less visible acts, such as committee work, bill sponsorship, and negotiation, which can pose a challenge to constituents trying to keep tabs on their elected representatives.

Legislators' Voting Decisions Are Affected by Constituents' Interests and Political Parties

When approaching a vote in Congress, members have several factors to consider.[38] First, they must always at least consider their constituents' interests. Though a senator or representative may ultimately decide to vote against the wishes of those who sent her or him to Washington, no member can ignore voters repeatedly without facing a constituent backlash. If, however, a senator or representative has earned a level of trust from constituents through long and successful service to them then she or he may be more willing to act against constituent interests if it feels like the right course of action.[39]

A member's political party also influences how that member will vote. Members may seek input from their colleagues, especially if those colleagues are policy specialists and are known to have a particular expertise relevant to a bill. Input from a member's congressional staff may play a role, as may signals from interest groups, especially if individuals within the interest groups can convince the representative that his or her constituents agree with the group's position. Finally, the president may try to convince representatives to vote a certain way, especially if they are in the same political party.

Representatives' Actions Are Shaped by Level of Constituent Knowledge

Elections are the primary tool that voters have to shape the actions of their elected representatives. Voters can pressure candidates to make certain promises during campaigns in exchange for their vote and also threaten backlash in the future if those promises are not kept.[40] Both of these mechanisms, however, require some basic level of information on the part of constituents and representatives. Constituents must have policy preferences to begin with and must communicate those preferences to their representatives. They must also have some basic level of information about the actions of their representatives in Congress to know whether to reward or punish those representatives in the next election.

Unfortunately, a long tradition of research in political science has shown that on most issues the majority of constituents are poorly informed, uninterested, or lack any coherent policy preferences. Some constituents are far better informed than others, especially if they have formed themselves into an interest group for the purpose of influencing congressional action. This inequality of information runs the risk of tilting Congress in the direction of acting only in the interests of its most informed and involved constituents to the detriment of the majority of uninformed ones.

Political scientist R. Douglas Arnold's research explored the ways in which Congress might pass laws that benefit the many even if they impose costs on a well-informed and involved few. But this is not easy.[41] First, representatives must shield themselves as much as possible from the backlash of powerful interests, with as few easily traceable votes as possible. Their leaders must frame failure to act as an unacceptable alternative, making it easier for members to explain individually costly votes.

In addition, there must be a real threat that voters who are not currently paying attention might become aware of and involved in an issue in the future. Interest groups may perform the role of "auditing" on behalf of less informed and less aware voters.[42] Congressional challengers may also play a role, bringing up issues in a campaign that incumbents incorporate into their own agendas.[43] Even the most secure incumbents worry about an issue that might cause their constituents alarm or concern. Successfully worrying about what might happen is part of what has kept them in office in the first place.

Key Aspects of Lawmaking Happen Outside of the Public Eye

There is another challenge to the ability of constituents to control or influence representatives' actions. While votes on the floor or in committee can usually be traced to a particular member, much of the actual work on legislation happens outside of the public eye. The choices that representatives make in allocating their time and energy can have important consequences for the fate of legislation, whether these choices determine how much effort to undertake to steer a bill through the constitutional obstacle course that is Congress or how much energy to devote to blocking a bill's progress.[44] The challenge for constituents is that these individual choices are difficult to observe and, therefore, reward or punish.

Yet members do act, even when the reelectoral math does not add up. Why? Sometimes the decision to act comes from personal motivations and experiences. Senators Feinstein and Moseley Braun both were involved in one of the most important pieces of legislation taken up by the 103rd Congress: a comprehensive effort to reduce crime and reshape criminal justice policy. Following their elections in 1992, both joined the powerful Senate Judiciary Committee and used their experience and qualifications to translate their influence into legislation. According to one article, in the Senate, "Moseley-Braun . . . highlighted racial concerns while Feinstein led a successful floor fight to add an assault weapons ban to the Senate crime bill."[45] Feinstein had personally witnessed the assassinations of San Francisco mayor George Moscone and supervisor Harvey Milk, becoming acting mayor in the aftermath of their shooting deaths. Moseley Braun summed up her colleague's efforts: "I'd say that the assault weapons ban is a testimony to her hard work and just doggedness, because at a time when I and every other member of the Committee had concluded that this was a symbolic thing and there was no way we were going to get the votes, Dianne went out and worked and got the votes."[46]

Partisan Polarization Strongly Affects Voting and Cooperation

Representatives do not act in a vacuum. Their behavior is influenced both by the rules and procedures in Congress and by political parties. Political scientists, congressional observers, and some members themselves have become increasingly concerned about trends in partisan polarization in which members of parties vote and act strongly with their own party and become less likely to cross the aisle and cooperate with each other. While scholars disagree about the causes of polarization in Congress, voting records on the House and Senate floor show a clear trend toward intraparty cohesion (see Figure 9.3).[47]

Intense partisanship can lead to more than ill feelings between members. It may contribute to **gridlock**, a situation in which Congress's ability to legislate is slowed or stopped by its inability to overcome divisions, especially those based on partisanship. Gridlock is made more likely in a period of **divided government**, which occurs when control of the presidency and one or both chambers of Congress is split between the two major parties.

Mentorship Is Another Form of Representation

One important, but not frequently discussed, way that legislators can represent their own constituents—as well as those in other states and districts—is to act as mentors to newly elected colleagues. Mentorship builds the kinds of personal connections that a legislator needs to advance the interests of her or his constituents and also helps build a more effective legislative body.

After successfully defending her Senate seat in 1992, Barbara Mikulski took it upon herself to mentor her four new women colleagues, a practice she continued up to her retirement in 2017.

Descriptive Representation Is about Who Members Are

Many of the Framers and supporters of the U.S. Constitution expected that Congress would be a reflection or "portrait" of the people in the Republic, though the definition of who had the right to be a represented person was highly restrictive.

FIGURE 9.3

Visualizing Partisan Polarization

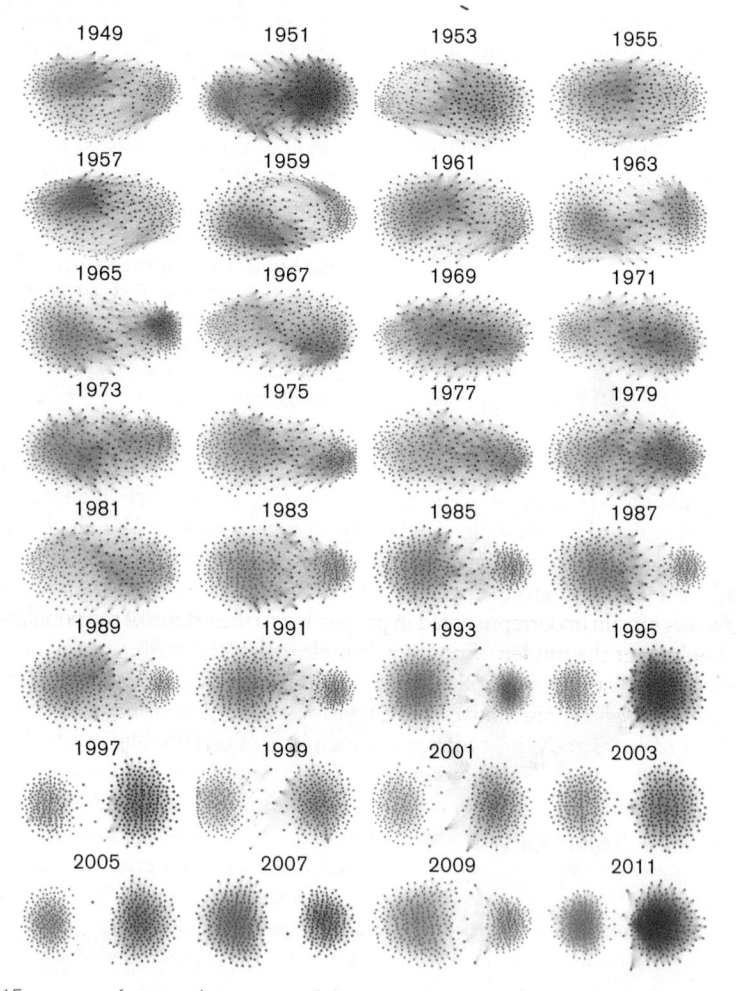

In 2015 a group of researchers mapped the networks of members of the House of Representatives from 1949 to 2011, identifying points of agreement between members on significant issues based on political party. Democratic members are identified in blue and Republicans in red. Each dot represents an individual. The connections represent points of agreement above a specific threshold. Note that over time, the dots have increasingly separated into red and blue groups and are increasingly tightly clustered.

Source: Clio Andris et al., "The Rise of Partisanship and Super-Cooperators in the U.S. House of Representatives," *PloS One* 10, no. 4 (2015), http://journals.plos.org/plosone/article?id=10.1371/journal.pone.0123507.

Several issues and challenges arise when attempting to view Congress as a portrait of America. The first is that no single member can represent each of his or her constituents' diverse identities, experiences, and interests. Even if somehow possible, this might not be desirable in the extreme. Constituents, for example, might want their legislators to be more knowledgeable about, experienced in, and motivated to act in the messy space of politics than the average American voter.

Senator Barbara Mikulski, D-MD, right, was well known for her mentoring of other women in the Senate. Here, Mikulski plays host to fellow women senators, including new senator-elect Joni Ernst, R-IA, left, at a meeting at the U.S. Capitol in Washington on November 13, 2014. Also pictured are Senator Patty Murray, D-WA, second from left; Senator Jeanne Shaheen, D-NH; and Senator Kirsten Gillibrand, D-NY. REUTERS/Jonathan Ernst

Descriptive Representation in Congress

Instead, when scholars and observers talk about making Congress a more accurate reflection of America, they are referring to increasing **descriptive representation**: Members of Congress "mirror some of the more frequent experiences and outward manifestations of belonging to the group."[48] Usually the goal of increasing descriptive representation in Congress is to selectively increase the membership of a particular group or groups who because of other historical and contextual factors remain underrepresented in proportion to their share of the population.[49]

Looking at the modern Congress, it is clear that the members do not come close to presenting a mirror of the American electorate. While Congress has grown more descriptively representative in recent years, women, lower-income Americans; members of racial and ethnic minorities; members of certain religious faiths; and lesbian, gay, bisexual, and transgender (LGBT) Americans remain underrepresented in proportion to their percentage of the American voting-age population.

As a whole, members of Congress tend to be older, whiter, wealthier, and more educated than the American electorate. The lack of descriptive representation raises a complicated set of related questions: Does it matter? Is it necessary for a member of Congress to share the lived experiences of the constituents whom she or he hopes to represent? Can a man represent a woman? Can a wealthy person represent a lower-income person?

Some scholars have argued that there may be benefits to having a descriptively representative legislature apart from what it actually does in Congress. Seeing a diversity of faces in Congress may, in the eyes of the American electorate, confer greater legitimacy to the institution and the policies that it passes. Others have pointed out that legislators who do not descriptively represent groups of their constituents are still under the reelectoral threat of ignoring those constitutents' concerns.

Another challenge to descriptive representation is that any given legislator may share key attributes with some of her or his constituents but not others. Does a wealthy African American legislator from an urban district reflect her constituents? In terms of racial and ethnic identity, quite possibly. In terms of

Representing Representation

The U.S. Congress remains descriptively unrepresentative. Women and members of most minority groups remain underrepresented in Congress in proportion to their numbers in the American voting-age population.

There has been improvement in recent elections, however. Telling the story of this improvement in pictures and graphs is subject to the way in which these data are presented. As with all data stories told with graphs, how one draws the *scale* of the chart, the vertical or *y*-axis here, can convey very different impressions using the same data. Consider this graph of the percentages of women in the Senate over the past twenty-five Congresses (fifty years). In this chart, the gains made by women in recent elections look quite impressive.

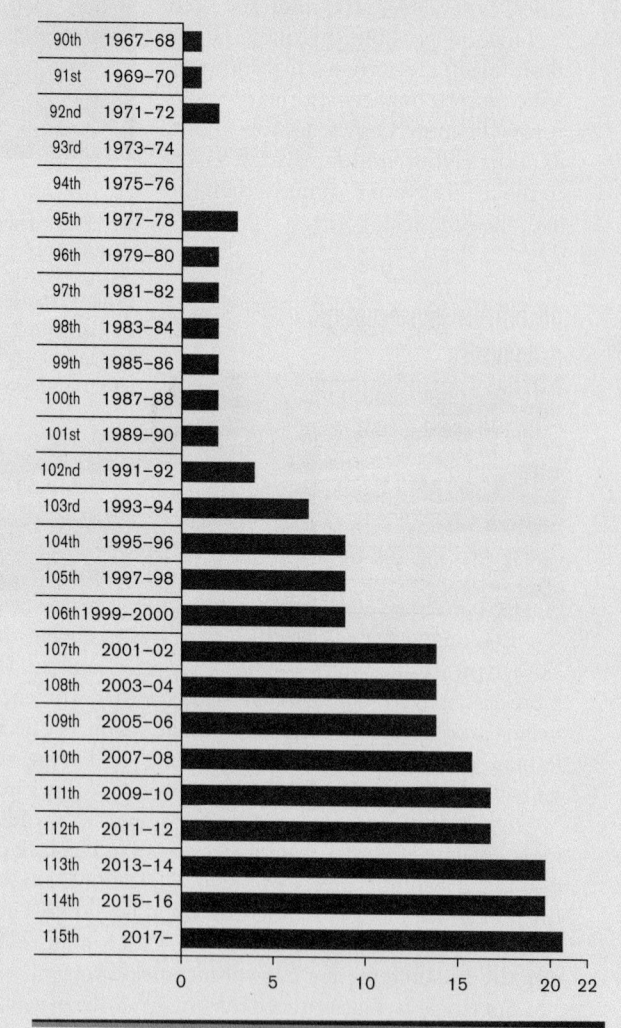

Women Senators in the U.S. Congress

Consider the same data but showing the full range of the number of senators that might be categorized on the basis of gender, from zero to one hundred.

This presentation of the same data in the second graph tells a very different story. With the full scale changed from zero to one hundred, recent gains in the descriptive representation of women in the Senate do not look so impressive. The tactic of cutting off, or truncating, the scale of a graph can be used to either present a pessimistic or an optimistic portrait, depending on the data storyteller's objective.

Women Senators Scaled by the Full Senate Numbers

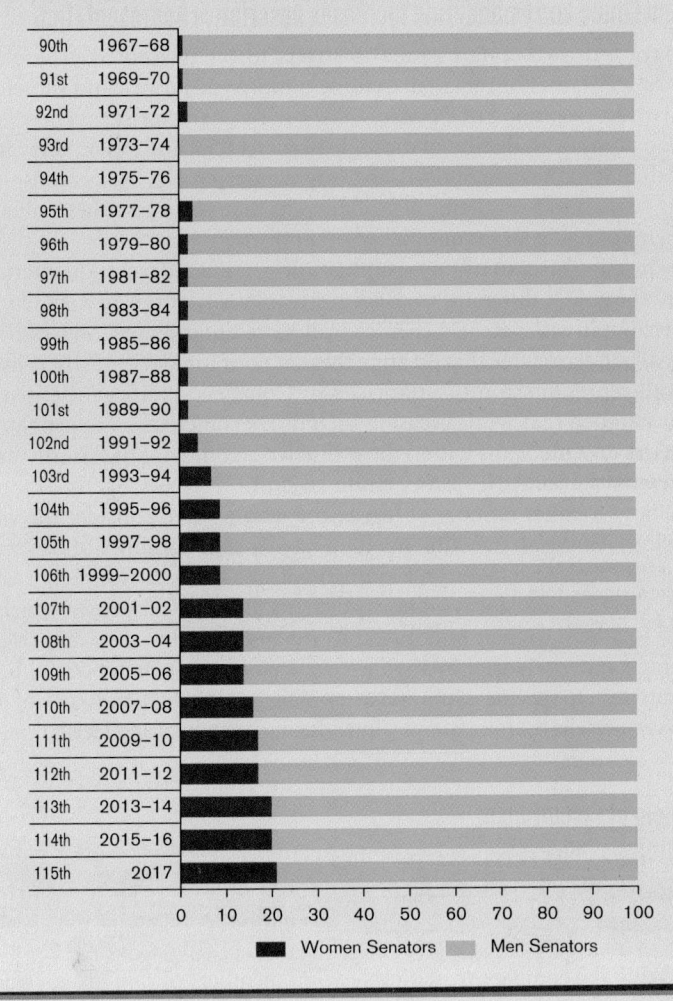

90th	1967–68	
91st	1969–70	
92nd	1971–72	
93rd	1973–74	
94th	1975–76	
95th	1977–78	
96th	1979–80	
97th	1981–82	
98th	1983–84	
99th	1985–86	
100th	1987–88	
101st	1989–90	
102nd	1991–92	
103rd	1993–94	
104th	1995–96	
105th	1997–98	
106th	1999–2000	
107th	2001–02	
108th	2003–04	
109th	2005–06	
110th	2007–08	
111th	2009–10	
112th	2011–12	
113th	2013–14	
114th	2015–16	
115th	2017	

0 10 20 30 40 50 60 70 80 90 100

■ Women Senators ▨ Men Senators

In the first presentation of the data, the election of 1992 appears to mark the beginning of a major wave of change, which it did. Looking at the same data in the second figure, however, tells a somewhat different story; there were gains, to be sure, but much less revolutionary ones.

When reading a graph and the story it's telling, pay attention to the ways in which different presentations of the same set of data—in this case the scale—can portray very different narratives depending on which one the data storyteller wishes to present. The presentation of data can be just as political as that of word stories.

income and wealth, perhaps not so much. Similarly, does a white legislator from a midwestern agricultural district with little experience in farming describe his constituents? Again, in some ways, probably, but maybe not in others.

Racial and Ethnic Gerrymandering Increases Descriptive Representation

States have redrawn congressional districts to try to improve the electoral chances of legislators of racial and ethnic minority identities and therefore the descriptive representation of Congress along these characteristics. There is, however, a potential contradiction in the logic of such racial and ethnic gerrymandering. Recall that in the case of partisan gerrymandering, the logic is to isolate the opposing party into a small number of districts that you know they will win but dilute their votes in a larger number of other districts—to "waste" the opposing party's votes. In the case of racial and ethnic gerrymandering, the tactic is the same, but the goal is different: to concentrate minority voters in a small number of districts but in order to help their overall representation in Congress.

Not all scholars agree that creating these majority-minority districts increases the overall representation of minorities in Congress. Political scientist Carol Swain has argued that while creating such districts increases the probability of electing African Americans within those districts, it does not necessarily improve the representation of African Americans overall.[50] Perhaps, Swain argued, it is better to have a larger number of legislators who have to consider the views of their African American constituents than have a small number of descriptively representative legislators who lack enough votes to advocate for their positions.

If the creation of majority-minority districts dilutes the degree to which members have to attend to their minority constituents' interests, then that risk might need to be counterbalanced by the importance of having members who have a close connection to specific issues and are willing to undertake the work of making those voices present by, for example, introducing or sponsoring legislation.

The Problem of Essentialism

Thinking about constituents in terms of specific characteristics poses another challenge, that of **essentialism**, which political theorist Jane Mansbridge defined as "the assumption that members of certain groups have an essential identity that all members of that group share and of which no others can partake."[51] Essentialism risks masking the complexity of views *within* members of that group, sidelining policy disagreements between them in the name of some shared "women's interest" or "African American interest." Second, it also risks cordoning off members' efforts into a few predefined acceptable issues: the idea that women should only talk about "women's issues" or that black people should only talk about "black issues."

Substantive Representation Connects How Members Act and Who They Are

Both the acts that members of Congress undertake and the degree to which they share the lived experiences of their constituents shape representation. It is the connection between acting and reflecting that holds the promise of sorting out some of the contradictions and challenges in each. While it very well may be important for American voters to feel that their Congress is a legitimate portrait of the nation, what really matters is, according to Hanna Pitkin, "the nature of the activity itself, what goes on during representation, the substance of the content of acting for others."[52] Pitkin calls this **substantive representation**.

Substantive representation is important because it holds the promise of linking constituents' lived experiences not just to the actions of their own legislators but to the actions of the institution itself, to the way that the institution works. It has the potential to improve the way that Congress deliberates by expanding the congressional agenda and by facilitating representation across geographical and partisan boundaries.

Deliberation May Be Improved by Substantive Representation

As imagined by those who designed it, Congress is supposed to be much more than just a place to count predecided votes and hear preformed arguments. It is also supposed to be a place for **legislative deliberation**, the considered argument and discussion of the issues. Deliberation is discussion of "which policies are good for the polity as a whole, which policies are good for representatives' constituents, and when the interests of various groups within the policy and constituency conflict."[53]

Deliberation is itself a complicated thing. For viewpoints to be discussed, they must first capture the attention of a large enough number of legislators. Second, deliberation is personal, as often are its politics. Individual relationships between members who share interests and experiences can make for a more effective deliberative body. When this occurs, members who share common experiences can work with colleagues in the other party, thereby helping to counter trends in partisan polarization.

In any given session of Congress, there are only so many issues that can be dealt with and discussed, the list of which constitutes the legislative agenda. Why some issues seem to rocket toward the top of the agenda and others languish at the bottom or are ignored is sometimes easily explained—for example, in times of national crisis some concerns are seen as more urgent than others. However, the setting of the congressional agenda is often unpredictable.[54] By bringing unconsidered issues to Congress's table and making them salient, legislators who share common lived experiences with underrepresented constituents may enlarge the institution's agenda. In doing so, members are acting (in political theorist Jane Mansbridge's analysis) as surrogate representatives—they are representing people who may not live in their district or state but with whom they share common concerns.[55]

Presenting information to one's legislative colleagues is an important part of representation. After the 2000 election, a reporter asked Senator Kay Bailey Hutchinson, R-TX, "Why can't a male senator do everything a woman senator can do?" Hutchinson's reply was, "Sometimes, from our experience there are issues that men just haven't thought about. . . . Most of the time our colleagues are supportive once we've made the case."[56] In 1993 Carol Moseley Braun, D-IL—the only African American senator serving at the time—brought to the chamber's attention the larger implications of an issue that may have seemed trivial to many members, if it was on their radar at all. Senator Jesse Helms,

R-NC, had offered as an amendment a renewal of the patent for the design of the symbol of the United Daughters of the Confederacy, which included the Confederate flag—an image the national sanctioning of which many African Americans find problematic. Had Moseley Braun been focused only on her reelectoral prospects, this was probably not a battle that needed to be fought. Yet Moseley Braun successfully killed the amendment and in doing so signaled to her own constituents as well as to African American voters across the nation that she intended to voice their shared concerns in the Senate.

Rarely, however, can one legislator reshape the congressional agenda on his or her own. It requires enough members to join in advocating minority positions. And, as we have seen, the importance of committee action suggests that effective substantive representation requires enough members with shared experiences to make present these voices not just on the floor but behind closed doors in committees. Equally important is going beyond just getting a "woman's issue" or an "African American issue" on the congressional agenda—having enough voices to reveal the conflicts and tensions *within* members of these groups and presenting the full range of opinion on the issues.

CONCLUSION

The Complexity of Representation

Today, representation in the Senate involves the same issues it always has: standing for constituents, bringing voices and energy to its deliberations and outcomes, and operating within an institution intentionally designed by the Framers of the Constitution to place brakes on the pace of political change. But much has changed since the 103rd Congress, too. The 115th Congress, which convened in January of 2017, includes 21 women, one more than the outgoing 114th Congress. One of these senators, Catherine Cortez Masto, D-NV, is the first Latina senator in U.S.

history. She joins Tammy Baldwin, D-WI, who came to Congress in 2012 as the first openly LGBT member of the Senate. Mazie Hirono, D-HI, had been the first Asian American women elected to Congress when she won a House seat in 2006, and in 2012 she became the first Asian American woman, as well as the first Buddhist, to serve in the Senate. Patty Murray, who, due to her political skills and her survivorship in Congress, now holds one of the most powerful positions in the Senate hierarchy and will likely "move up in leadership," having "garnered the respect of Democrats and Republicans."[57]

The Framers of the Constitution did not intend for Congress to be purely and perfectly representative. They mistrusted the ability of *citizens* to avoid the dangers of faction. In recent decades, however, Congress has come to more accurately reflect the American electorate, though it is still far from being perfectly descriptive. These gains have not come about by chance; they are mostly due to the strategic actions of citizens to reshape Congress to better portray the diversity of the nation.

Representation and lawmaking in Congress is complicated, messy, and often uncomfortable. Though the legislative branch is the first branch of government—and viewed as the most powerful by the Framers—it is still only one of three. Over the course of American history, strategic political actors in the other two branches—the executive and judicial—have also tried to shape the power of their institutions, to present their own views of representation in the United States, and to stand for the people.

$SAGE edge™

Want a better grade?

Get the tools you need to sharpen your study skills. **SAGE edge** offers a robust online environment featuring an impressive array of free tools and resources. Access practice quizzes, eFlashcards, video, and multimedia at **edge.sagepub.com/abernathybrief1e.**

CHAPTER REVIEW

This chapter's main ideas are reflected in the Learning Objectives below. By reviewing them here you should be able to **remember** the key points and **know** these terms that are central to the topic.

9.1 Describe how Congress is designed, including its various constitutional powers and the differences between the two chambers.

REMEMBER...

- Congress is a bicameral legislature: the House of Representatives and the Senate are divided to establish a set of checks and balances within Congress.

- Members of the House are meant to be closer to the people. Senators are meant to be more insulated from the public to ensure greater stability.

- The House and Senate have legislative authority as well as budgetary and oversight powers.

KNOW...

- *appropriation*: the process through which congressional committees allocate funds to executive branch agencies, bureaus, and departments (p. 284)

- *bicameral*: a legislature composed of two chambers (p. 282)

- *earmarks*: an addition to a piece of legislation that directs specific funds to projects within districts or states (p. 284)

- *fire alarm oversight*: a term that describes congressional oversight procedures primarily in response to problems or complaints (p. 286)

- *impeachment*: a process for removing federal officials granted by the Constitution to Congress (p. 286)

- *oversight*: efforts by Congress to ensure that executive branch agencies, bureaus, and cabinet departments, as well as their officials, are acting legally and in accordance with congressional goals (p. 284)

- *police patrol oversight*: a term that describes congressional oversight as a process of constant monitoring rather than responding to specific crises (p. 286)

- *represent*: "standing for" one's constituents in government (p. 279)

- *senatorial courtesy*: a traditional norm in which presidents consult with senators from the states when considering potential nominees to the lower levels of the federal judiciary (p. 286)

- *statutes*: written laws established by a legislative body (p. 284)

- *term limits*: restrictions on the length of time an officeholder may serve (p. 286)

9.2 Identify the obstacles to winning a seat in Congress, the factors that influence an individual's decision to run, and the resources and skills that successful candidates need.

REMEMBER...

- Factors that contribute to a decision to run for election include election-specific ones: adequate funding resources and personal ambition.

- Factors that contribute to winning a seat in Congress include incumbency, understanding one's constituency, experience, and money.

KNOW...

- *constituency*: the population to whom a member of Congress is accountable (p. 289)

- *political ambition*: the willingness of congressional incumbents to use their advantages to prevent credible challengers (p. 288)

9.3 List the primary organizational features of Congress, including the role of chamber leaders, political parties, committees, and congressional norms.

REMEMBER...

- Political parties exert a good deal of influence in Congress, especially over key leadership positions.

- Congressional committees do most of the work of Congress.

- Norms and traditional ways of doing things also play a role—albeit a more informal one—in the smooth functioning of Congress.

KNOW...

- *committee chairs*: leaders of the subunits of congressional committees who have authority over the committee's agenda (p. 294)

- *conference committee*: a temporary committee that resolves differences between the House and Senate versions of a bill as required by the Constitution before a president can sign the bill into law (p. 295)

- *joint committees*: temporary committees used to focus public attention on an issue, gather information for Congress, or help party leaders speed things along in the legislative process (p. 295)

- *majority leader*: the head of the party with the most seats in Congress, chosen by the party's members (p. 293)

- *minority leader*: the head of the party with the second-highest number of seats in Congress, chosen by the party's members (p. 293)

- *select or special committee*: temporary committees with limited power formed to investigate an issue, sometimes in response to a crisis or a scandal (p. 295)

- *Speaker of the House*: the leader of the House of Representatives, chosen by an election of its members (p. 292)

- *standing committees*: long-standing committees divided by policy area that consider legislation, exercise oversight of bureaucratic agencies, and usually recommend funding levels for them (p. 294)

- *whip*: an individual in the House or Senate, chosen by his or her party members, whose job is to ensure party unity and discipline (p. 293)

9.4 Explain the steps of the legislative process and how it can diverge from traditional "textbook" descriptions.

REMEMBER...

- Before they can become law, bills must be passed by both the House and Senate and then approved by the president.

- Actors other than members of Congress may play a role in influencing whether a bill gets introduced.

- Most bills are never passed.

KNOW...

- *bill*: a draft of a proposed bill introduced into Congress (p. 296)

- *cloture*: a procedure through which senators can end debate on a bill and proceed to action, provided three-fifths of senators agree to it (p. 300)

- *filibuster*: a tactic through which an individual senator may postpone action on a piece of legislation (p. 300)

- *hostage-taking*: when a member of congress threatens to hold up an unrelated vote or confirmation of a presidential nominee in order to extract concessions on something else (p. 300)

- *House Rules Committee*: a powerful committee that determines when a bill will be subject to debate and vote on the House floor, how long the debate will last, and whether amendments will be allowed on the floor (p. 299)

- *markup*: a process during which a bill is revised prior to a final vote in Congress (p. 298)

- *roll-call vote*: a recorded vote on a bill (p. 299)

- *unorthodox lawmaking*: a term that refers to ways in which legislative activity, especially on major bills, is often more fluid than described in a traditional textbook description (p. 296)

- *veto*: The constitutional power of a president to prevent a bill from becoming a law though subject to an override by a two-thirds vote by both chambers (p. 301)

9.5 Connect the issues surrounding the representation of women in Congress to the challenges involving representation of other individuals in America.

REMEMBER...

- When taking action in Congress, members must consider the preferences of their constituents, their party, and other influencers.

- Representation in Congress may be descriptive or substantive.

KNOW...

- *descriptive representation*: the degree to which a body of representatives in a legislature does or does not reflect the diversity of that nation's identities and lived experiences (p. 307)

- *divided government*: a situation that occurs when control of the presidency and one or both chambers of Congress is split between the two major parties (p. 305)

- *essentialism*: the risks posed by linking individuals' lived experiences to policy preferences, whether by identifying those individuals by those policies or excluding them from advocating different policy objectives (p. 310)

- *gridlock*: a situation in which Congress's ability to legislate is slowed or stopped by its inability to overcome divisions, especially those based on partisanship (p. 305)

- *legislative deliberation*: the considered argument and discussion of the issues by congressional representatives (p. 311)

- *substantive representation*: the degree to which elected representatives or senators represent the interests and policy preferences of their constituents (p. 311)

10 THE AMERICAN PRESIDENCY
Individuals, Institutions, and Executive Power

Speaking from the White House in April 2015, President Barack Obama spoke about a U.S. drone strike that targeted a suspected al-Qaeda compound in Pakistan. The decision to exercise the powers of the presidency to authorize drone strikes has been hotly contested, raising issues of executive overreach. Mark Wilson/ Getty Images

As, arguably, the most powerful officeholder in the world, the American president stands alone—and not just at a podium or a press conference but also in comparison to leaders of other democratic nations. However, he or she does not *operate* alone, which is as the Framers of the Constitution intended. The president sits atop a massive collection of organizations, agencies, and bureaus. He or she must contend with a Congress whose members have their own political goals, even if the majority of those members are from the president's own political party. If the majority of one or both chambers in Congress is not from the president's party, then things get even tougher. And then there are the American people, to whom a president speaks directly. With the American people on his or her side, a president can be very powerful, especially when dealing with members of Congress. Without this support, presidents are vulnerable. In the American political system, the president acts as the head of the **executive branch** of government, which is charged with executing, or putting into effect, the laws of the nation.

In the stories in this chapter, we will focus primarily on one aspect of presidential power: the making of war. There are many others. Presidents act to shape policy in all areas—economic, social, domestic, and foreign. However, by focusing on this one facet of presidential power, you will confront a fundamental question in American politics: In American representative democracy, how much power should any one person have, even if he or she is the elected president?

After reading this chapter, you will be able to do the following:

10.1 Describe the powers of the presidency as defined in the Constitution, the tensions inherent in those descriptions, and constitutional limitations on presidential power.

10.2 Evaluate how presidents have tested the limits of the power of the office during wartime and national crises.

10.3 Discuss institutional and informal sources of presidential power.

THE KILLING OF AN AMERICAN CITIZEN TESTS THE LIMITS OF PRESIDENTIAL POWERS

On a September morning in 2011, a group of men had just finished eating breakfast in a remote desert in the country of Yemen. One of them was Anwar al-Awlaki, an American citizen who was, to counterterrorism officials, "a rock star propagandist for al-Qaeda's arm in Yemen who recruited followers over the Internet."[1] Patrolling the Yemeni skies that day were American drones launched from an airstrip in Saudi Arabia and remotely piloted from far away. Noticing the drones, the men "scrambled to get to their trucks."[2]

They were too late. Two Predator drones marked the men's trucks with lasers, and larger Reaper drones launched three Hellfire missiles. Al-Awlaki's vehicle "was totally torn up into pieces" according to reports from unidentified witnesses to the strike, the men reduced to "small human parts."[3]

For more than a year and a half following the strike, the administration of President Barack Obama remained officially silent on the targets. Under pressure from members of Congress, including some key Democrats, Attorney General Eric Holder formally acknowledged in May 2013 that the 2011 strike had targeted an American citizen: al-Awlaki. According to the *New York Times*, "For what was apparently the first time since the Civil War, the United States government had carried out the deliberate killing of an American citizen as a wartime enemy and without a trial."[4] Al-Awlaki's name had been placed at the top of the Central Intelligence Agency (CIA) list of individuals to be captured if possible or killed if not. Many of the details about how individuals made this list were secret, but reporters learned that the target list was vetted and approved in secret by the National Security Council and others on the administration's legal team.[5]

It was the "secret" part of the administration's decision to target al-Awlaki that made many uncomfortable. In a public speech in 2012, Obama's top counter-terrorism adviser, John Brennan, reassured his audience that individuals, including Americans, were only targeted for killing if capture was not a realistic option and only after a careful and thorough review.[6]

Some of the details surrounding why and how Anwar al-Awlaki was targeted are known: Born in New Mexico in 1971 but later raised in Yemen, al-Awlaki returned to the United States for undergraduate and graduate education. He was serving as imam of a mosque near Washington, D.C., in 2001 at the time of the 9/11 attacks. In the weeks following, al-Awlaki presented a moderate face to Americans trying to understand what had happened and to many Muslim Americans worried about a backlash against members of their faith. However, according to the *New York Times*, "Nine years later, from his hide-out in Yemen, [he had] declared war on the United States," his primary weapon, the Internet.[7] His "website became a favorite for English-speaking Muslims who were curious about jihad."[8] With his command of the English language and ability to draw on American social and cultural references in his posts and videos, al-Awlaki became a very effective "recruiter and propagandist."[9]

By al-Awlaki's own account, it was U.S. intervention in countries like Iraq, Afghanistan, Pakistan, and Yemen that drove him to follow "the religious obligation to defend his faith."[10] Interviews with others who knew him cited al-Awlaki's eighteen months in a Yemeni prison—much of it in solitary confinement—as the driving force behind his radicalization. He blamed the United States for allowing his detention, and there is some evidence that this was the case. The *New York Times* reported that "John D. Negroponte, then director of national intelligence, told Yemeni officials that the United States did not object to his detention."[11]

Expanding on the comments of other administration officials, in a May 22, 2013, memo informing congressional leaders of the administration's 2011 decision to target and kill al-Awlaki, Attorney General Holder laid out the

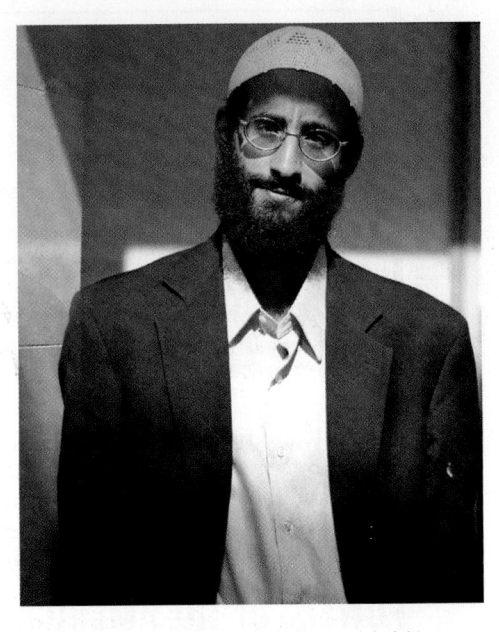

American citizen and Muslim cleric Anwar al-Awlaki poses for a photo at Dar Al-Hijrah mosque in October 2001 in Falls Church, Virginia. Ten years later, al-Awlaki was killed in a targeted drone strike by the United States in Yemen. Tracy Woodward/The Washington Post via Getty Images

administration's case for why such measures had been necessary. He based the justification not on al-Awlaki's inflammatory rhetoric but on intelligence that al-Awlaki had moved from the role of terrorist propagandist to one of senior leadership in al-Qaeda in the Arabian Peninsula (AQAP). Holder said the decision to target and kill al-Awlaki had been taken only after an extensive review process and only after the conclusion that he could not feasibly be captured alive and brought to a court for a hearing.[12]

In its justification for the targeted killing of al-Awlaki, the Obama administration argued that it was left with no other options to protect national security. Al-Awlaki had, in the estimation of officials, become a clear and present danger to the United States. As one anonymous counterterrorism official in the Obama administration told the *New York Times*, "American citizenship doesn't give you carte blanche to wage war against your own country."[13]

The targeted killing of al-Awlaki and other American citizens in the war on terror is a hotly debated issue in the nation's politics. In this chapter we will use the targeted killing and imprisonment of Americans without trial as a lens to focus on what is probably the most powerful job in the world: the American presidency. In doing so, the goal will not be to debate the use of drones or the targeted assassination of Americans in other nations. Instead, the goal will be to gain a deeper understanding of the power that American presidents have and reflect upon the proper limits to the exercise of that power in the twenty-first century.

WHAT HAVE I LEARNED?

1. The executive branch of government is charged with putting the nation's laws into effect.

   a. True
   b. False

2. Obama administration officials conceded that for the first time since the Civil War, the U.S. government had ____.

   a. Carried out the deliberate killing of an American citizen as a wartime enemy and without a trial
   b. Found an American citizen guilty of treason and revoked his citizenship

   c. Found a foreign national guilty of being a terrorist and sentenced him to life in prison in the United States
   d. None of the above

3. What justifications did the Obama administration offer for its action against al-Awlaki? What criticisms did it receive?

Answer Key: 1. a; 2. a; 3. Answers might include a discussion of how the administration argued that al-Awlaki had become a member of the organization's leadership as well as concerns that he was an American citizen who was targeted and killed without trial.

THE CONSTITUTION OUTLINES THE POWERS OF THE AMERICAN PRESIDENCY

James Madison had given more thought to creating a new type of republic than any of the other delegates to the Constitutional Convention. Even so, even he hadn't been able to come up with the specifics for what would become the

executive office. Like so many other details involving the office, the agreement that there would be
one president was worked out later in the convention. Some provisions, especially the method of
electing presidents, were sources of intense conflict. One reason was that the
job that the delegates ended up creating had no real precedent.

- Identify the constitutional powers of the presidency and the tensions inherent in them.

Delegates to the convention were in general agreement that the new
government would have to be more powerful than that under the Articles of
Confederation. That confederal government had been in perpetual financial
crisis, often unable to coerce individual states to contribute sufficient funds to
allow it to operate effectively. While the Framers of the Constitution knew that
the executive needed to be powerful enough to lead, they also feared that the
office might become too powerful. They were in no mood to recreate the tyranny
of the British monarchy with an elected one on American shores.

Delegates Settle Questions of Selection, Qualifications for Office, and Length of Terms

Once they settled on a single president, the most contentious issue facing the
delegates was how this person was going to be selected. The factionalized
debate between less populous and more populous states that had resulted in
the bicameral Congress reared its head once again. Less populous states feared
that direct popular election of the president would see their states' interests
swallowed up by their more populous neighbors. Most delegates assumed that
voters would pick candidates from their own states. Many delegates also mistrusted Americans' ability to responsibly directly elect a president. In the end,
the delegates agreed to a method of presidential selection that did not involve
direct popular election. Instead, electors, chosen by state legislatures and
apportioned to states based on congressional representation, were to choose
the president.

Delegates also settled on a term of four years with the possibility of reelection. No limits were placed on the number of times a person could be elected
president. The nation's first president, George Washington (1789–1797), chose
not to seek a third term, however, establishing a precedent that held until
Franklin Roosevelt (1933–1945) was elected four times.[14] Ratified largely in
response to Roosevelt's multiple terms, the Twenty-Second Amendment (1951)
prohibited future presidents from being elected more than twice and only once if
that person had assumed the office (due to a death, resignation, or impeachment)
more than two years prior to the end of that partial term.

Delegates set out a number of conditions for eligibility for the office of
the presidency. A candidate had to be "a natural born Citizen, or a Citizen
of the United States at the time of the Adoption of this Constitution," be
thirty-five years old or older, and have been a resident of the United States for
at least fourteen years (Article 2, section 1). The Constitution did not explicitly
prohibit women from holding the office; however, at the time of ratification,
women were generally denied the right to vote or hold political office within
their states.[15]

The President Is Granted Considerable Powers

One of the main reasons that the method of selecting the president caused so much debate was that as the summer of 1787 progressed, the office grew in power and scope. The expectation that Washington, trusted and admired throughout the nation, would be the first president may have allayed delegates' concerns about the powerful office that they were creating. Although the convention settled on the simple title of president of the United States, Washington was said to have preferred, "His High Mightiness, the President of the United States and Protector of their Liberties."[16]

When the delegates hammered out the framework of the American presidency, they created an institution that had never been seen on a national scale. In some ways there is still no exact equivalent to its scope and complexity in modern democracies. The powers placed in the president's hands are threefold. Expressed (or enumerated) powers are those given to the president explicitly in the Constitution. Implied powers, though not laid out in the text, are assumed as part of the president's expressed powers as they are necessary to carry out the expressed powers. Delegated powers are those that Congress grants to the president in order to execute, or carry out, the laws that Congress has passed (hence the name the *executive branch*). In wielding these three types of powers, the American president assumes a variety of roles.[17]

As Chief Executive the President Carries Out the Nation's Laws

As the head of the executive branch, the president is responsible for carrying out the laws of the nation. He or she oversees what has become a large and complex system of agencies and bureaucracies in order to do so. The Constitution, however, does not offer many specifics as to what it means to execute the laws. Article 2, which is devoted to the presidency, begins, "The executive Power shall be vested in a President of the United States of America."[18] When taking the oath of office, the president promises to "faithfully execute the Office of the President of the United States" and is later instructed to "take Care that the Laws be faithfully executed."[19] Other than that, the Constitution does not give much detail on *how* the president is supposed to run the federal government.

Presidents *are* given some help, however. They are authorized to "require the Opinion, in writing, of the principal Office in each of the executive Departments, upon any Subject relating to the Duties of their respective Offices."[20] Though not mentioned by name, the president's cabinet has evolved into a powerful source of information and a point of contact with the nation's sprawling federal bureaucracy. It also provides a way to reward individuals and members of important interest groups for past (and future) support through their appointment to positions within the cabinet.

Modern presidents have the authority to appoint individuals to thousands of administrative positions, from his or her closest advisers and heads of large agencies to lower level administrative staff. Roughly one thousand of these appointments require Senate confirmation. Presidents also nominate individuals to serve as judges in the federal judiciary; each nomination also requires Senate confirmation. A president may make a **recess appointment** without Senate confirmation while Congress is not in session, but the term of the recess appointment ends at the conclusion of that congressional term.

As Chief Diplomat the President Guides Foreign Policy

The president is also responsible for guiding U.S. foreign policy and interacting with the heads of other nations. The president is authorized "to make Treaties," to "appoint Ambassadors," and to "receive Ambassadors and other public Ministers."[21] This diplomatic power is partly symbolic and ceremonial; events like state dinners and parties showcase the power and prestige of the office.

The diplomatic power of the president helps to shape national foreign policy. While Congress, particularly the Senate, plays a major role in foreign affairs, the fact that the president is one person—and not 100 or 435, as is the case for the Senate and House—gives him or her an advantage over Congress in the ability to act quickly and decisively on the international stage.

As Chief Legislator the President Influences Policy

In devising a system where power was to be shared between the three branches, the Framers gave the president a limited and mostly negative role in the legislative process. However, this role has since been extended quite far.

The president is directed to "from time to time give Congress Information of the State of the Union" (Article 2, section 3). For much of the nation's history, presidents sent written reports to Congress without actually addressing the legislative branch in person. Today, no president would pass on the opportunity provided by the **State of the Union Address** to speak live on television before Congress; members of the Supreme Court; the military; and, most importantly, the entire nation. In the address, a president encourages or cajoles Congress to pass key pieces of his or her legislative agenda. The real audience, however, is the American people, and presidents use the address to try to mobilize support and pressure members of Congress to act.

The president is also expected to "recommend to their [Congress's] Consideration such Measures as he shall judge necessary and expedient."[22] While, as we saw in Chapter 9, only members of Congress can formally introduce bills, presidents work with party leaders in both chambers to shape the legislative agenda. Finally, the president is given the power to veto legislation, although this veto is subject to a potential override by a two-thirds vote in both chambers. Individual presidents have varied considerably in the use (and successful use) of the veto. Overrides are rare; marshaling the required two-thirds vote in both chambers is usually very difficult to do. The mere threat of a presidential veto is often enough to shape a piece of legislation more to a president's liking.[23] Vetoes are more likely during periods of divided government, when one or both chambers of Congress are under the control of a party other than that of the president.

As Commander in Chief the President Is Responsible for the Nation's Security

Perhaps the most fateful role that the Constitution creates for the president is his or her authority as "Commander in Chief of the Army and Navy of the United States, and of the Militia of the several States."[24] The president is at the top of the entire military chain of command, including the strategic nuclear forces of the nation, an awesome responsibility.

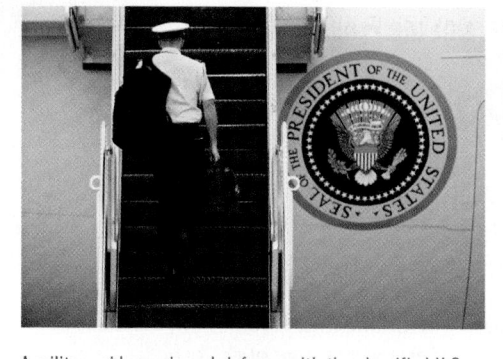

A military aide carries a briefcase with the classified U.S. nuclear war plan aboard Air Force One to join the president. No president is ever intentionally far from the so-called nuclear football; the contents of this heavy briefcase are classified but have traditionally included communications equipment and strategic plans and codes for a variety of nuclear combat scenarios. AP Photo/Cliff Owen

Originally, the constitutional warmaking power of the presidency was a limited one; it was designed so the president could efficiently lead the American armed forces during a time of war and to allow for quick response to threats when Congress was not in session. Therefore, the president was also given a role in national war making, though "the Commander-in-chief clause remained 'the forgotten clause' of the Constitution for the early decades of the nation's history."[25] That would change, however.

Presidents Have the Power to Issue Pardons

Another power the Constitution carves out for the president is the ability to issue a **pardon**. The "Power to grant Reprieves and Pardons for Offenses against the United States, except in Cases of Impeachment," allows the president to release individuals convicted of federal crimes from all legal consequences and restore their benefits of citizenship.[26] Presidents often grant pardons in the final days and weeks of office. In cases where it appears that pardoned individuals have close personal or professional ties to the president, this practice can be quite controversial.

The Powers of the Presidency Are Constitutionally Limited

The Framers also placed limitations on the power of the office, primarily by granting specific powers to Congress and the federal judiciary.[27] In most circumstances, the judicial branch has little involvement with presidential actions and responsibilities. Congress, however, is a different story. Presidents cannot accomplish most of their objectives without at the very least a lack of opposition by Congress, as the Constitution places in Congress's hands several negative checks on presidential action. Presidents need majority support in Congress to pass the laws, create and fund the programs, and confirm the presidential appointments that are necessary to fully realize their policy objectives. The president must obtain from the Senate majority approval to confirm

TABLE 10.1 Powers and Limits to Powers of the President

Enumerated, Implied, and Delegated Powers	Limits to Powers
The President may. . . .	*Congress may. . .*
Execute the nation's laws	Investigate or impeach the president
Submit the annual federal budget	Pass the budget
Appoint and seek the advice of cabinet departments	Confirm, delay, or block nominations
Shape foreign policy by enacting treaties, appointing ambassadors, and conducting diplomacy	Ratify treaties
Provide information and make policy recommendations to Congress; veto congressional legislation	Override vetoes
Act as commander in chief of the armed forces	Declare war and fund the armed forces
Deliver pardons but may not pardon individuals who have been impeached	Not override a pardon (and neither can the judiciary)

appointments to the federal judiciary as well as to many executive branch offices. Ratification of a treaty requires a two-thirds vote in the Senate.[28] With a two-thirds vote in each chamber, Congress can override a presidential veto, though veto overrides are relatively uncommon given the high vote hurdle needed to succeed. See Table 10.1.

Congress has the power to impeach the president (as well as "the Vice President and all civil Officers of the United States") for the vaguely defined transgressions of "Treason, Bribery, or other high Crimes and Misdemeanors."[29] A majority vote in the House is needed to pass articles of impeachment. Once an officeholder is impeached, the trial takes place in the Senate. The chief justice of the United States presides over a presidential impeachment and a two-thirds vote is necessary to convict.[30]

Only two presidents have been impeached, and none have been removed from office. Andrew Johnson barely survived a Senate vote over political battles following the Civil War in 1868, and Bill Clinton avoided conviction over charges of perjury and obstruction of justice during an investigation into his involvement with a White House intern, Monica Lewinsky, in 1998. President Richard Nixon would almost certainly have been impeached and convicted for his role in covering up a break-in at the Democratic Party national headquarters (the so-called Watergate affair) in 1972. He resigned from office in 1974 before a House vote took place, however, and received a pardon from his successor, President Gerald R. Ford, later that year.

1. The delegates to the Constitutional Convention were in general agreement on the basic structure of the American presidency when they convened.

   a. True
   b. False

2. George Washington's role in the Constitutional Convention helped to shape the American presidency because _____.

   a. He was a forceful advocate for a strong national executive
   b. Most delegates agreed that he would be the first individual to fill the post
   c. He wrote the sections of the Constitution dealing with warmaking authority
   d. All of the above

3. The American president serves as the nation's _____.

   a. Chief executive
   b. Chief diplomat
   c. Commander in chief
   d. All of the above

4. Why did the Framers divide warmaking authority between the president and Congress?

Answer Key: 1. b; 2. b; 3. d; 4. Answers should discuss issues of expediency and separation of powers.

▬ THE POWERS OF THE PRESIDENCY HAVE EVOLVED OVER TIME

- Understand how presidents have tested the limits of executive power during wartime and other crises.

When President Obama ordered the targeted killing of Anwar al-Awlaki, he did so with the conviction that he was acting within his constitutional powers as the commander in chief of the United States. Some questioned whether this was in fact true. What is not up for debate, however, is that Obama was neither the first American president to challenge the boundaries of warmaking authority in the name of national security nor was he the last. President Donald Trump ordered missile strikes in Syria without Congress's consent early in his term.[31] As we discussed previously, the Framers originally viewed the war powers of the president as more limited, relative to Congress's powers. How and why have those powers expanded?

Since George Washington was inaugurated as the nation's first president in 1789, the institution of the American presidency has undergone a major transformation, one that would likely seem remarkable to the Framers of the Constitution. The office has grown in power, prestige, and complexity, "not smoothly but with great leaps, periods of dormancy, and occasional setbacks."[32] These changes have been affected by the actions, choices, and strategic behavior of the individuals who have held the nation's highest office. Most significantly, individual presidents have, whether out of opportunity or necessity, seized upon crises and key turning points in American political development to redefine the boundaries of their power and influence. In this section we examine some of the most important of those moments, beginning with a watershed moment in the history of presidential power: Abraham Lincoln's detention of John Merryman during the American Civil War.

Abraham Lincoln Suspends Habeas Corpus during the Civil War

In April 1861, at the outset of the Civil War, a mob attacked a group of Union soldiers in Baltimore, Maryland, en route to Washington, D.C.[33] According to one observer, a local police officer assaulted one of the Union soldiers, "crying, 'You black son of a bitch you came here to fight us white men.'"[34] Someone fired a pistol into the group of soldiers, and the soldiers—frightened and disorganized—fired upon the mob.[35] Four Union soldiers and twelve civilians died in the violence.

Four days later, John Merryman, a prominent and well-to-do Marylander and member of a Southern secessionist group operating in that state, oversaw and led the burning of at least six railroad bridges and the toppling of some telegraph lines that formed one of the key military links between Washington, D.C., and the Union states of the North. Merryman claimed he was acting on orders from a former U.S. Army captain. According to witnesses, "Barking orders, repeatedly citing his 'authority,' Merryman proclaimed his intention to stop Northern troops from invading Maryland. 'God damn them,' he shouted at one place, 'We'll stop them from coming down and stealing our slaves.'"[36]

President Lincoln (1861–1865) knew that keeping the border states from joining the South was key to any hope of winning the war and reconstituting the Union, and Maryland was one of the most important of these states (see Figure 10.1). If Maryland were lost, then the Union's capital in Washington, D.C., would be nearly impossible to defend as it would be cut off from supplies and reinforcements by land. Lincoln used the full force of his presidency to ensure the border states remained in the Union: He called up state militias, blockaded southern ports, expanded the army and the navy, spent $2 million from the U.S. Treasury, "closed the Post Office, and . . . suspended the writ of habeas corpus in certain localities, [and] caused the arrest and detention of persons who were 'represented to him as being engaged in treasonable practices.'"[37] Calling up the state militias was within his executive authority. All of his other actions, including suspending habeas corpus, were "without any statutory authorization."[38]

On the morning of May 25, 1861, federal troops roused Merryman from his bed and took him to Fort McHenry in Baltimore Harbor where he was imprisoned. As he was from a prominent family and had powerful political connections in Maryland, Merryman's detention did not go unnoticed. Within hours of his internment at the federal fort, Merryman's lawyers arrived and prepared a petition for his release.[39] Supreme Court chief justice Robert Brooke Taney received Merryman's petition and issued a writ of habeas corpus on his behalf. Taney noted that Merryman had been "imprisoned by the commanding officer, without warrant from any lawful authority . . . upon charges of treason and rebellion, without proof and without giving the names of the witnesses, or specifying the acts which, in the judgment of the military officer, constituted these crimes."[40] Taney called on the Union general in charge of the fort to produce "the body of John Merryman"[41] so the charges against him could be examined. Habeas corpus—from the Latin "you [shall] have the body"—defines a procedure through which a person can challenge what they see as unlawful detention. If Taney's writ of habeas corpus in the case of Merryman was honored, either an arrest warrant would be issued for Merryman or Merryman would be free to go.

FIGURE 10.1

The United States at the Start of the Civil War

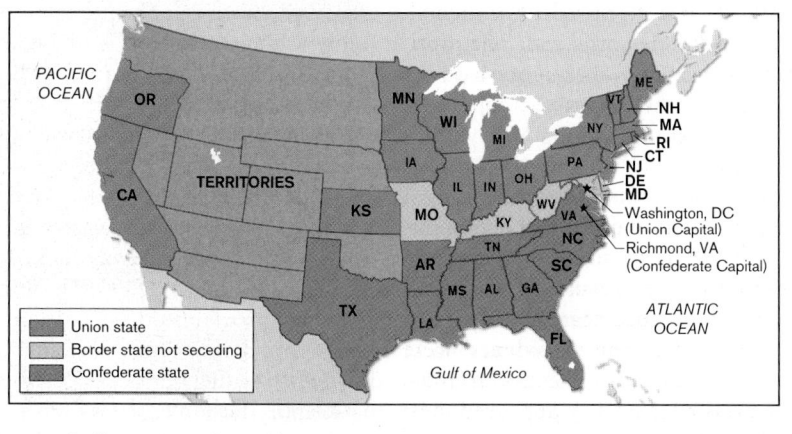

The map in Figure 13.1 shows Union states to the north and Confederate states to the south. Lincoln knew that ensuring the border states (shown in yellow) did not secede was key to winning the war. Maryland, where John Merryman was jailed for treason, was one of the most important of these states: if it joined the Confederacy, the Union's capital in Washington, D.C., would be nearly impossible to defend.

The Union commander refused to honor the writ. Instead, he sent an aide, who showed up in Taney's courtroom without Merryman. It became clear to Justice Taney that Merryman was being held under the authority of President Lincoln and was not to be released, not even upon Taney's direct demand. According to Baltimore mayor George William Brown, "A more important question could hardly have occurred. Where did the president acquire such a power? Was it true that a citizen held his liberty subject to the arbitrary will of any man? In what part of the Constitution could such a power be found?"[42]

Taney pushed back, threatening to arrest the fort's commander if his orders were not followed and directed the aide to have the commander produce Merryman by noon the next day, Tuesday, May 28. Taney's demand was again refused, and Merryman remained imprisoned, without a trial or an arrest warrant, under the authority of the president of the United States.

On Tuesday morning, having been twice rebuffed, Taney prepared to confront the president. He wrote and swiftly delivered an opinion, *Ex parte Merryman* (1861), in which he challenged the president's authority to suspend writs of habeas corpus, even in times of war and rebellion.[43] "The President, under the Constitution and laws of the United States," Taney declared, "cannot suspend the privilege of the writ of *habeas corpus*, nor authorize any military officer to do so."[44]

In his opinion, Taney acknowledged that the Constitution does grant the federal government the power to suspend the writ of habeas corpus during times of rebellion or invasion.[45] However, Taney noted, Article 1 gives that power to Congress, not the executive branch. And, Taney continued, the judicial branch has the power to issue arrest warrants, not the president or the military under his command. The president, therefore, "has exercised a power which he does not possess under the Constitution."[46]

For his part, Lincoln justified to members of Congress and the Union "these actions of dubious constitutionality by reference to the 'war powers' granted to the executive."[47] In other words, he argued that the war powers granted to the presidency were sufficient grounds for his actions. Congress retroactively approved most of Lincoln's actions taken that year. However, it did not approve the suspension of habeas corpus (with some limits) until 1863 after the president had issued a broader suspension of the privilege the year before.[48]

Abraham Lincoln, left, shown here with Chief Justice Roger Brooke Taney at Lincoln's inauguration on March 4, 1861. Ex parte Merryman pitted the two men against one another in a watershed case that tested the limits of executive power.
ullstein bild via Getty Images

Such drastic unilateral presidential action in times of war and national crisis led political scientist Edward Corwin to conclude that "the Constitution is an easily dispensable factor of our war effort—perhaps one might say 'expendable' factor," transforming it, during wartime, "from a *Constitution of Rights* into a *Constitution of Powers*."[49]

Taney expected to be impeached or even arrested over his confrontation with Lincoln, and Lincoln is said to have contemplated it. In the end, however, the president simply ignored Taney, prosecuting the war with whatever means he saw necessary in order to restore the Union. Lincoln continued to defend his suspension of habeas corpus and other measures as valid uses of the constitutional power of the government "when in cases of Rebellion or Invasion the public Safety may require it."[50]

Lincoln believed that the powers that he had to assume during the war would no longer be necessary once the crisis of the Civil War was successfully resolved. In this prediction, he proved to be correct. Presidential power did recede in the decades following the Union victory, and Congress once again assumed its position as the strongest of the three branches. As America has confronted wars, major crises, and other extraordinary circumstances, many presidents have also tested the limits of executive branch power or impacted the office through their actions. As well, changes in the political landscape and to political institutions themselves have affected the powers of the presidency.

Other Presidents Develop and Test the Power of the Office

George Washington (1789-1797). As he was the first president, everything Washington did set a precedent for his successors, and intentionally or not, his decisions cast a shadow over their terms in office. By establishing regular meetings with heads of executive branch departments, Washington laid the foundations of the modern cabinet system. His tours of the country linked the office to the people of the entire nation. His suppression of the Whiskey Rebellion in 1794 "helped establish both the idea of the supremacy of federal law and the power of the federal government to levy and collect taxes."[51]

Washington retired from office after two terms, though he was not obligated to do so, thus setting a two-term precedent that was followed for over 140 years.

Thomas Jefferson (1801-1809). Jefferson came to office riding the wave of a major victory of his Democratic-Republic Party over the Federalist Party in the election of 1800. Using this power, Jefferson was "the first president to govern through personal leadership of a political party."[52] In his two terms in office, Jefferson did not veto a single bill. He did not have to. Since his party controlled Congress the president was able to use his influence to shape or kill legislation before it arrived on his desk. Possibly pushing the boundaries of his powers beyond their intended limits, Jefferson doubled—in one deal—the size of the nation with the Louisiana Purchase in 1803.

Andrew Jackson (1829-1837). Andrew Jackson was a rough and quick-tempered frontier man and a wealthy land and slave owner. Jackson gained the presidency during a period in which the presidential nominating process became more democratic and less under the control of powerful party men. With a power base among the American people—or, more precisely, among white workers, backwoodsmen, Irish immigrants, and farmers—Jackson was able to challenge both Congress and the Supreme Court.

The legacy of Jackson's connection to the people was a double-edged sword. "The electoral changes made the presidency more powerful vis-à-vis other branches, and also yet more dependent upon—and controlled by—the public."[53] To a president, Congress may be frustrating and seem obstinate. Party leaders may have their own power bases from which to challenge the chief executive. To rely on popular support for one's power, however, risks seeing that power erode quickly with the shifting and often unpredictable opinions of the American people.

Theodore Roosevelt (1901-1909). "Teddy" Roosevelt took office during a breathtaking period of growth in American industrial power and all of the social upheaval that this transformation brought about. He carried a "big stick" in foreign affairs, using the navy to demonstrate the nation's growing industrial might to both European powers and nations in the Western hemisphere. He intervened in Central and South American political affairs in order to promote and preserve American interests as he saw them. Roosevelt was also a national celebrity, by design: "He went on bear-hunting trips in the west, played tennis and took jujitsu lessons in the White House, and went horseback riding in the afternoon."[54] To Roosevelt, the presidency was a "bully pulpit" that he could use to shape and mobilize public opinion in support of his administration's objectives.

Woodrow Wilson (1913-1921). Woodrow Wilson was, in character and demeanor, as far from Teddy Roosevelt as one could get. To many, he came off as intolerant and arrogant. He was also firmly convinced that his presidency was part of a divine plan. After he was elected president, he told the chair of the Democratic National Committee (DNC) (who helped get him there), *"God ordained that I should be the next President of the United States.* Neither you nor any other mortal could have prevented that!"[55]

Wilson took office with the goal of increasing the president's role in legislative affairs. He both succeeded and failed spectacularly in this. A skilled speaker, Wilson was the first president since John Adams (1797–1801) to deliver the State of the Union address in person. His greatest legislative success was securing from Congress unprecedented control over the nation's economy during America's involvement in World War I (1914–1918).[56] These powers included the authority to "allocate food and fuel, to license trade with the enemy, to censor the mail, to regulate the foreign language press of the country, and to operate railroads, water transportation systems, and telegraph and telephone facilities."[57]

However, Wilson also saw the defeat in the Senate of the Treaty of Versailles—a treaty that he had helped write. The treaty included the League of Nations, which was his vision for an international governing body to prevent future catastrophes like World War I. Many scholars attribute the failed ratification at least partly to Wilson's stubbornness and refusal to compromise. Even though the country's president designed it, the League of Nations would not count the United States among its members.

Franklin Delano Roosevelt (1933-1945). Roosevelt responded to the economic crisis of the Great Depression by greatly expanding the size, scope, and power of the federal government as well as that of the executive branch within it. He sponsored a variety of programs and policies, collectively known as the New Deal, aimed at helping those suffering from the Depression. Responding to the military crisis of World War II (1939–1945), Roosevelt "carried the wartime Presidency to breath-taking heights of authority of the American economy and social order."[58] He created an alphabet of bureaucratic organizations to oversee the mobilization of the American economy in pursuit of military victory. The agencies, which the president claimed were advisory only, "rested on no statutory foundation" but instead on the "President simply by virtue of power which he claimed as Commander-in-Chief."[59] Roosevelt used the power of his voice—carried via the radio into living rooms for his "fireside chats"—to rally support for the war effort. He encouraged Americans to buy war bonds to finance the war and to remain committed to the cause and confident of a victorious outcome.

Lyndon Baines Johnson (1963-1969). Johnson was able to use his perhaps unequalled skill in working with, cajoling, and arm-twisting members of Congress in pursuit of his vision of a Great Society, in which the power of the federal government was put to work in order to eradicate poverty and racial and social injustice. He was an excellent, if sometimes crude, storyteller and a tireless campaigner. In spite of his achievements in domestic policy, however, Johnson's

President Richard Nixon and Chinese premier Zhou Enlai toast during Nixon's unprecedented trip to China in 1972.
AFP/Getty Images

dramatic expansion of the conflict in Vietnam eclipsed all else. The war was becoming increasingly unpopular, and more and more people were saying that it could not be won. Johnson chose not to run for a second term in 1968.[60]

Richard Milhous Nixon (1969-1974).

Nixon's presidency is considered one of the most troubled in American history. He is the only president to have resigned from office. He did so because he was facing near-certain impeachment and conviction for his role in covering up illegal activities, including a break-in at the Democratic Party headquarters at the Watergate office complex in 1972. The break-in was part of a misguided and illegal set of strategies for a reelection that Nixon would have won easily. However, Nixon's efforts to build relations with China, which included a visit to that country in 1972, have been credited as an important step in U.S.-Chinese relations. These efforts were important as the United States sought to drive a wedge between China and the Soviet Union during the Cold War.

The **War Powers Resolution of 1973**, passed despite Nixon's veto, has been one of the most enduring and controversial legacies of his presidency.[61] Initially intended by its sponsors to reassert congressional authority over the introduction of American armed forces into combat, the resolution is credited by some scholars as being "the high-water mark of congressional reassertion in national security affairs."[62] Passed during the weakening of Nixon's authority as the Watergate investigations unfolded, the resolution was the product of widespread public and congressional dissatisfaction with the prosecution and expansion of the Vietnam conflict as well as unilateral presidential actions carried out by Johnson and Nixon.

Drawing on Congress's authority under the necessary and proper clause of the Constitution, the resolution's purpose was to re-center warmaking authority.[63] Under the terms of the War Powers Resolution, a president may only introduce armed forces into conflict or likely conflict if one of the three following conditions is present:

1. "a declaration of war [by Congress]," a
2. "specific statutory authorization [by Congress]," or
3. "a national emergency created by an attack on the United States, its territories or possessions, or its armed forces"[64]

Once introduced, the president is required within forty-eight hours to notify Congress of "the circumstances necessitating the introduction of United States Armed Forces; . . . the constitutional and legislative authority under which such introduction took place; and . . . the estimated scope and duration of the hostilities or involvement."[65] Unless Congress has declared war, passed specific authorization, extended the notification deadline, or is physically unable to meet, the president must withdraw those forces within sixty days, with a thirty-day extension allowed if necessary to withdraw those forces safely.[66]

The last war officially declared by Congress was World War II in 1941. Since that time, American armed forces have been stationed in more than one hundred countries, though many of these are allies or military partners. Presidents have often held that the War Powers Resolution unconstitutionally restricts their war power; though they have also routinely pursued congressional authorization of the use of military force consistent with the resolution. Some critics of the resolution argue that it actually makes the president more powerful since he or she may feel less constrained during those sixty or ninety days than they would if the resolution did not exist.[67]

Chief of Staff Andrew Card whispers into the ear of President George W. Bush on the morning of the September 11, 2001, attacks during a visit to an elementary school in Sarasota, Florida. AP Photo/Doug Mills

Ronald Reagan (1981-1989). Reagan, who earned the nickname the "Great Communicator," drew on his experience in film, television, and radio to connect to the American people and encourage their support of his initiatives, often to the dismay of Congress. Reagan did not only rely on his public voice and personality, however. He assembled an effective communications staff devoted to "managing the message" and controlling the media agenda to shape the national conversation in support of his policy objectives.

George W. Bush (2001-2009). On the morning of September 11, 2001, Bush was reading to a second-grade classroom in Sarasota, Florida, when Chief of Staff Andrew Card whispered into his ear, "America is under attack." That morning, nearly three thousand people died in a series of terrorist attacks in New York, Washington, D.C., and Pennsylvania. National security and military officials concluded that the attacks had been planned and carried out by al-Qaeda, a radical Islamic terrorist organization. Its leader, Osama bin Laden, later claimed responsibility.

On that day, George W. Bush became a wartime president, serving as commander in chief in two wars, one in Afghanistan (2001) and the other in Iraq (2002). Neither involved an official declaration of war, though both had congressional authorization.[68]

The resolution that authorized the president to use force in Afghanistan stated "that the President is authorized to use all necessary and appropriate force against those nations, organizations, or persons he determines planned, authorized, committed, or aided the terrorist attacks that occurred on September 11, 2001, or harbored such organizations or persons, in order to prevent any future acts of international terrorism against the United States by such nations, organizations, or persons."[69]

The war on terror had begun. By including "organizations or persons" and not just nations as acceptable targets, the boundaries of this twenty-first century war were much less defined and restricted than those in previous conflicts. The consequences for presidential power of that authorization are still being determined and debated.

WHAT HAVE I LEARNED?

1. As the example of John Merryman illustrates, the Framers intended to grant the executive branch extensive wartime powers—in particular the power to both make and declare war.

   a. True
   b. False

2. Justice Taney issued a writ of habeas corpus on behalf of John Merryman, but Abraham Lincoln intervened, suspending all writs. Lincoln did so because _____.

   a. He believed that Merryman and others had committed acts of treason against the government of the United States and were a direct threat to national security
   b. He wanted to protect Merryman from charges of treason
   c. He believed that Taney was overstepping his role as chief justice of the United States

   d. He saw it as way to appeal to Union voters and ensure his reelection

3. The War Powers Resolution _____.

   a. Outlines specific rules that must be followed by Congress and the president in declaring war in attempt to restore warmaking authority to Congress
   b. Attempted to restrict congressional power in warmaking activities
   c. Has never been formally subject to judicial review
   d. All of the above

4. What challenges does the war on terror in the twenty-first century pose to properly delimiting the powers of presidents in wartime?

....

Answer Key: 1. b; 2. a; 3. a; 4. Answers should mention the War Powers Resolution and the potential lack of boundaries in its prosecution.

INSTITUTIONS AND OTHER INFORMAL SOURCES OF POWER SHAPE THE MODERN EXECUTIVE BRANCH

• Understand the institutional and informal sources of executive power.

While the American presidency must feel at times like the loneliest job in the world, no president truly acts alone. Instead, the president operates at the center of multiple organizations and institutions. As with many aspects of the presidency, the size and complexity of the presidential establishment is both a source of presidential power and a constraint on it. The machinery of the presidential establishment allows the president to act in many areas of domestic and foreign policy and provides him or her with large amounts of information, which is an important commodity in dealing with other nations, Congress, and the many actors in American politics. However, the size and complexity of the executive branch establishment—especially the federal

The Problem of Small Numbers in the Study of the Presidency

How much do the personal characteristics of an individual president matter to his or her performance in office? Can we say anything systematic about the relationship between character and performance?[70]

Originally published in 1972, James David Barber's *The Presidential Character: Predicting Performance in the White House* applied understandings from psychology to try to predict how presidents would behave—and how successful they would be—by categorizing them into four types, based on two separate personality traits: (1) how active or passive they were, in the sense of the energy and innovation that they brought to the office and (2) how positively or negatively they approached their duties, in the sense of the enjoyment they displayed in managing the ship of state.

Based on these determinations, George Washington, for example, was a passive-negative president in that he reluctantly led the nation and preferred stability over dramatic change. Thomas Jefferson, on the other hand, was an active-positive president who actively engaged in the give-and-take of politics in the service of a grand vision for the young nation.

Though it has been highly influential in political science, Barber's approach has not escaped criticism. Some have argued that the many institutional and political limitations on presidential action overwhelm the ability to define a president's actions. Others have critiqued the validity of the two underlying measures themselves.

There is another challenge in drawing systematic conclusions about individual presidents that goes beyond the issue of character. The reality is that there have not been that many presidents; thus, the question is one of sample size. To demonstrate empirical relationships with confidence we need a certain number of observations to better ensure that the patterns we observe are indeed representative of the group under study.

WHAT DO YOU THINK?

How might political scientists get around the problem of the limited number of presidents in making social scientific claims about executive branch politics? One option might be to look at executives across nations, giving us more observations. The problem here is that other systems are typically very different from that of the United States. Another approach might be to look at state governors. The challenge here, though, is that the American federalist system defines very different roles for state and federal executives. This is not to say that such an approach might not be useful—only that we should be careful in using it. What might we learn from examining the behavior of state governors that could translate into a better understanding of the American presidency?

bureaucracy—can act as a powerful brake on presidential initiatives, particularly since most lower-level federal bureaucrats keep their jobs long after any one president has come and gone.

The Vice Presidency Plays a Limited but Important Role

While the Constitution's vague language created an ambiguous but ultimately powerful presidency, it also created a very weak second in command: the office of the vice president. Delegates to the Constitutional Convention were not even sure that the nation needed a vice president. The ultimate inclusion of the position was probably driven by the need to soothe tensions between more populous and less populous states over the presidential election process.[71]

Constitutionally, the vice president has two jobs. He or she is "President of the Senate, but shall have no Vote, unless they be equally divided."[72] Rarely does the vice president actually preside over the Senate. Instead the president pro tempore of the Senate usually presides officially, but junior senators routinely fill in for this role. The logic behind the vice president's leadership role in the Senate was to ensure that no state lost its equal Senate representation by virtue of having one of its two senators serving as president of the chamber.

Second, the vice president assumes the office of the presidency should a serving president vacate the office due to death, resignation, or impeachment. The Twenty-Fifth Amendment (1967) established the modern rules of succession and also established a process for replacing a vice president who leaves office during his or her term. In this process, the president nominates a replacement and approval is required "by a majority vote of both Houses of Congress."

In addition to addressing succession, the Twenty-Fifth Amendment also established a procedure through which the vice president may temporarily assume the role of acting president in the event "that the President is unable to discharge the powers and duties of his office." During his presidency, George W. Bush twice notified Congress that he would temporarily be unable to fulfill his duties as he underwent sedation for colonoscopies, making Vice President Dick Cheney acting president for about two hours each time.

Historically, most vice presidents have had little impact on national policy, but it has recently become more common for vice presidents to have a larger role in White House deliberations. Other than being ready to take over, the main job of the vice president is to help the president get elected. Vice presidential nominees have often been selected to "balance the ticket" with respect to geographical representation, connections to important blocks of voters, or experience.

The Cabinet and the Executive Branch Bureaucracy Help Advise the President

The president's cabinet consists of the heads of the fifteen major executive branch departments, the vice president, and the heads of other agencies that the president wishes to assign cabinet-level status. In addition to leading their agencies, cabinet department heads, most of whom are called secretaries, advise the president and act as the link between the president and their own bureaucracies.

Unlike the majority of people who work for the federal bureaucracy, heads of the executive branch departments typically come and go with each new administration. See Figure 10.2.

In choosing cabinet members, presidents have to juggle several considerations. Presidents need capable, experienced, and strong appointees to provide useful information and to effectively run their departments. However, assertive cabinet secretaries, who often have their own bases of power, can challenge the president or drag their heels if they disagree with a policy objective. Presidents must also consider politics and public opinion in their choices. Cabinet department heads with ties to important interest groups—teachers or members of the business community, for example—can help a president to be informed of the concerns of those groups as policy is shaped. Cabinet appointments can also signal to a diverse constituency of Americans and those who represent them that the President will advance their interests.

FIGURE 10.2

The Organization of the Executive Office

Source: WhiteHouse.gov, "The Cabinet," https://www.whitehouse.gov/administration/cabinet.

The First Spouse Can Help the President Connect

The wife or husband of a president occupies no formal role in an administration but is in a unique position to act as an adviser to the president and a public and personal link between the president and the American people.

Edith Bolling Galt Wilson, President Woodrow Wilson's wife, was probably the most powerful first lady. She helped to organize and run the White House after her husband suffered a serious stroke in 1919, becoming, to some, an acting president. Eleanor Roosevelt spoke and wrote frequently about public policy and had a successful and influential career in public life following Franklin Roosevelt's death in 1945. Modern first spouses often choose one or more policy areas and use their influence and visibility to call attention to issues in those areas and promote solutions.

The Executive Office of the President Assists the President with Policy

Established in 1939 upon the recommendation of a presidential commission that concluded "the president needs help," the **Executive Office of the President (EOP)** is a collection of agencies and offices that assist the president in both an advisory and policymaking capacity.[73] The White House chief of staff oversees the EOP and is usually a close, trusted, and politically skilled associate of the president. The chief of staff often acts as a protector of the president's scarcest resource: time. Most individuals who work for the various agencies within the EOP are appointed by a president and not expected to serve past that administration; though some of the larger offices do have permanent staff members.

The Office of Management and Budget advises and assists the president in crafting the national budget and studies various plans and initiatives designed to increase the efficiency of executive branch departments. The National Security Council advises the president on issues of national security, the military, and foreign policy.

The White House Office (part of the EOP) has grown into an important bureaucracy itself, and its most important members share offices

Marian Anderson, renowned opera singer, receives the Spingarn Medal from first lady Eleanor Roosevelt in Richmond, Virginia, in July 1939. Eleanor Roosevelt's efforts to overcome racial discrimination in the United States were among her most important achievements on behalf of her husband's administration. Keystone-France/Gamma-Keystone via Getty Images near the president's. The hundreds of staff members in this office are there to support the president in achieving his or her policy objectives. They achieve this by effectively communicating the president's vision to the American people, building support for goals and polices, and playing the complicated and high-stakes game of Washington politics. In choosing the members of the White House staff, presidents value political skill and loyalty. Many times staff members are individuals who were involved in the campaign or with the president in previous roles. Directors and deputy directors of communication ensure that the president's message is delivered to the American people. The White House press secretary acts as the president's spokesperson to members of the media and conducts daily press briefings, partly to inform but also partly to shape the national conversation in a way that helps the president achieve his or her policy goals.

Political Parties Influence the Executive Office

The role that the president plays as "chief of party" is not mentioned in the Constitution. The Framers worried privately and publicly about the dangers of faction—of which political parties were viewed as a particularly dangerous example. Parties, however, are nearly as old as the Republic; divisions between President Washington's closest advisers gave rise to the nation's first political parties.

Modern presidents serve as the unofficial, but real, leaders of their own political parties. They often choose the official leadership of their party, or at least have a major say in it. Presidents must contend with partisan politics in Congress, especially if they serve during a period of divided government and the opposing political party is controlling one or both chambers of Congress. Periods of divided government are often associated with legislative gridlock in which Congress's ability to pass laws is diminished or grinds to a halt completely.[74]

Presidents expect to have to battle and negotiate with members of the opposing party in Congress. Even with Republican control of both chambers of Congress, President Trump has found it far from easy to achieve his policy objectives. However, support from their own party members can never be taken for granted either. Presidents and members of Congress serve different constituencies. The American people demand that their presidents keep them safe and prosperous. Demands on senators and representatives are often more local and address the unique characteristics and needs of their states or districts. No member of Congress can ignore the wishes of her or his constituents without risk, even if the president requests it. Skillful presidents are fully aware of these tensions and—working with party leaders in Congress—often try to accommodate individual defections by members of their own party with the expectation that loyalty will be shown on less locally contentious votes somewhere down the line.

The President Responds to and Shapes Public Opinion

As the power of the American presidency has evolved, so has the president's relationship to the nation's citizens. Public opinion—the distribution of people's preferences and evaluations of policies and individual political actors—has come to play an important role in expanding or constraining the power of individual presidents. When expertly harnessed, public opinion is a powerful tool in battles with Congress, the judiciary, or too-independent members of a president's own political party. If it is poorly mobilized or understood, however, the unfortunate president, in the words of Clinton Rossiter, "will find himself exposed to all those enemies who multiply like mosquitoes in a [New] Jersey August. The various institutions and centers of power that check the President are inept and often useless without public opinion—and with it are often wondrously armed."[75]

Modern communications technologies and ease of travel have significantly contributed to connecting the president to the American public. But long before the Internet, television, and even radio, individual presidents recognized and tried to harness the latent power of public opinion. Andrew Jackson, who drew on his public support in battles with Congress and the judiciary, commented, "The President must be accountable at the bar of public opinion for every act of his administration."[76] Modern presidents attempt to make full use of communications technologies and public appearances in order to mobilize American public opinion in support of their own goals and policies. Political scientist Samuel Kernell used the term *going public* to describe "a strategy whereby a president promotes himself and his policies in Washington by appealing directly to the American public for support."[77]

Perhaps no president in American history is as tied to public opinion as President Donald Trump. Without question, his use of social media has been more powerful and effective than any other candidate, or president. The question, though, is this: Does the immediacy of connection outweigh the risk of poorly timed or, perhaps, not politically savvy tweets?

Americans' Evaluations of Presidential Performance Can Affect the President's Policy Agenda

Since Franklin Roosevelt's presidency, pollsters have periodically taken the national pulse on Americans' views of how well their presidents are doing. These presidential approval ratings provide more than just a snapshot of the public's views. A president with high approval ratings is in a more powerful position in relation to Congress than one with low or sinking ratings. Sometimes unanticipated events—and the president's response to them—can produce dramatic changes in presidential approval. A national economic or military crisis, if handled successfully in the eyes of the American public, can produce a surge in presidential approval. In the months after the 9/11 attacks, President Bush's approval rating rose to 90 percent, the highest ever recorded, but it later declined as the public became increasingly skeptical of his handling of the war in Iraq and of the nation's economy.

Some patterns of presidential approval are more predictable. A president—especially after a convincing first-term victory—ordinarily enjoys a period of strong public approval, called a honeymoon period. For this reason, presidents often try to secure major legislative victories early in their first terms to capture public support and build momentum for future battles with Congress. Presidential approval, however, usually declines over time as the American public begins to assign blame to the president for things that are not going well, whether this is deserved or not. There is also typically some recovery in presidential approval as the term draws to a close.[78]

Scholars' views of the American presidency and the power of the office have, like the institution itself, changed over time and in response to the individual presidents and the times in which they have governed. Increasingly, political scientists have focused on a unilateral model of presidential action in which presidents attempt to influence both domestic and foreign policy with few or no constraints by Congress or the judiciary. It is, in other words, when presidents try to act alone. Individual presidents have often tried to defend the power of their office or even push the boundaries of that power, but the scope and frequency of unilateral presidential action in recent administrations has raised questions about the degree to which powers truly remain separated among the three branches of the U.S. government.

Presidents attempt to exercise independent control over information through the assertion of **executive privilege** in which they try to shield from Congress; the judiciary; and, ultimately, the public the details of debates, discussions, memos, and e-mails surrounding presidential decisions and actions. Since the administration of George Washington, presidents have asserted that their ability to control information is essential to their effectiveness.[79]

During the investigation of President Nixon and his role in the Watergate affair, Nixon refused to hand over to a special prosecutor audio recordings of his conversations with senior aides as well as other documents relating to the investigation, citing the power of executive privilege. In *United States v. Nixon* (1974) the Supreme Court affirmed the power of executive privilege, finding that "a President and those who assist him must be free to explore alternatives in the process of shaping policies and making decisions, and to do so in a way many would be unwilling to express except privately."[80] However, the Court also demanded that the president hand over the recordings and documents, balancing the need for executive privilege with the need for the rule of law in criminal investigations.

In the area of foreign policy, presidents may sign **executive agreements** with foreign nations without the need for Senate ratification, which is needed for treaties. Though they are not binding upon future presidents in the way that treaties are, executive agreements can give a president a way to shape foreign policy that bypasses the Senate's role of advice and consent. Their details are often kept secret from the public and Congress for reasons of national security.

In the president's role in the legislative process, the use of **signing statements** has gained increased attention recently. When a president signs a bill into law, he or she may add written comments that convey instructions to the various agencies that will actually carry out the law or that offer the president's interpretation of the law. Sometimes signing statements are far from controversial; they may be offered to try to build a public record of support for an issue, to call attention to an issue, or to offer a slightly different interpretation of a law that a president otherwise supports. However, if the president either interprets the law differently from the way Congress intended or instructs agencies to execute it selectively or differently, then concerns can be raised that the president is taking the lawmaking authority intended for Congress for himself or herself.

Executive orders are policy directives issued by presidents to the executive branch bureaucracy that do not require congressional approval. Most executive orders are issued under congressional authorization and constitute a set of instructions given by the president to the executive branch agencies informing them of how they are supposed to go about implementing a law or policy. Often they deal with routine administrative procedures. Presidents have also used executive orders, however, to make major changes in public policy (see Figure 10.3).[81]

In 1942 President Roosevelt issued Executive Order 9066, which authorized the secretary of war to declare certain areas in the United States as "military areas . . . from which any or all persons may be excluded, and with

FIGURE 10.3

Executive Orders, Washington to Trump

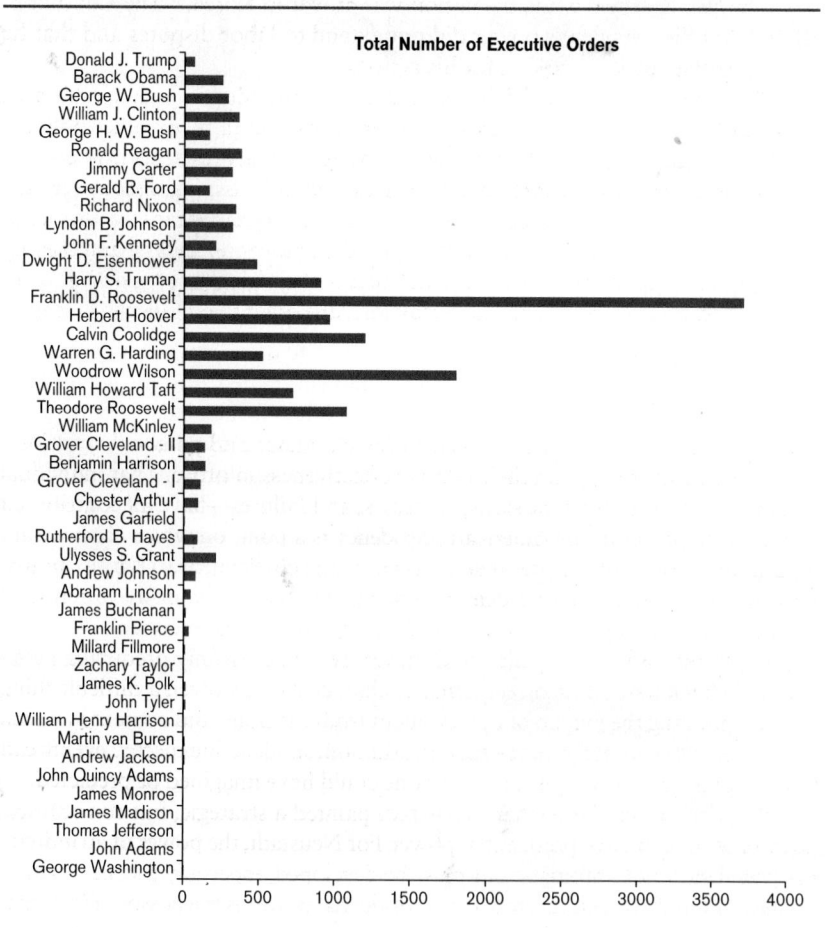

Source: Data for executive orders are from Gerhard Peters, "Executive Orders," in *The American Presidency Project*, ed. John T. Woolley and Gerhard Peters (Santa Barbara: University of California, 1999–2016). www.presidency.ucsb.edu/data/orders.php#orderlist.

Note: Data for the Trump administration are current through July 2017.

respect to which the right of any person to enter, remain in, or leave shall be subject to whatever restrictions the Secretary of War or the appropriate Military Commander may impose in his discretion."[82] Issued for the declared purpose of "protection against espionage and against sabotage to national-defense material," Roosevelt's executive order led to the internment of more than 130,000 individuals, most of whom were Japanese Americans.[83] In *Korematsu v. United States* (1944), the Supreme Court upheld Roosevelt's authority. In a dissent, however, one justice commented about the internment: "I need hardly labor the conclusion that Constitutional rights have been violated."[84]

The Supreme Court, however, has not always upheld presidential use of the executive order, even during wartime. In *Youngstown Sheet & Tube Co. v. Sawyer* (1952), the Court rejected the authority of President Harry S. Truman (1945–1953) to order the seizure of most of the nation's steel mills to avert a strike by steel workers while the nation was at war in Korea.[85] The Court concluded that the president's power did not extend to labor disputes and that he lacked legislative authorization for his actions.

While you have read primarily about unilateral presidential action in the area of national security, questions about its exercise extend to many other political fields. As political scientist William Howell has examined, presidents may act first and alone across a wide variety of policy areas, often by issuing directives to the vast federal bureaucracy without waiting for Congress to clarify the laws that it has passed (see Chapter 11). In doing so "the president moves policy first and thereby places upon Congress and the courts the burden of revising a new political landscape."[86] Acting first and acting alone may force the other two branches to react.

Presidential Character Affects the Success of a Presidency

Some political scientists have looked to the character and personality of individual presidents to explain their relative effectiveness in office. That individual presidents—their characters, skills, successes, and failures—have all contributed to the development of the American presidency is a point on which most would agree. For scholars of the presidency, however, the challenge is to figure out just how these traits matter to presidential performance. Some scholars have classified presidents based on personal and psychological characteristics as a way of gaining insight into behavior inside the Oval Office.[87] Successfully predicting presidential behavior based on assessments of character is, however, a difficult thing to do. Separating the person of the president from the times and context in which that president governed is never easy. In addition, sudden, unexpected events can thrust a president into situations that none could have imagined or predicted.

Presidential scholar Richard Neustadt painted a strategic, but constrained, portrait of the source of presidential power. For Neustadt, the power of an individual president is not automatic but must be developed, especially through skillful political action.[88] Neustadt wrote that presidential power is the power of information, of presenting a credible threat to known and potential political enemies and, finally, of convincing allies and opponents that supporting the president is in their own self-interest. According to him, "The essence of a President's persuasive task is to convince such men that what the White House wants of them is what they ought to do for their sake and on their own authority."[89]

1. The office of the vice presidency was created to be an important check on presidential power.

   a. True
   b. False

2. In choosing cabinet members, presidents consider _____.

   a. Their qualifications
   b. Politics and interest group support

   c. Public opinion
   d. All of the above

3. What tools of unilateral action do presidents have at their disposal?

4. What role does the president's character play in governing?

Answer Key: 1. b; 2. d; 3. Answers should include executive orders, executive agreements, and signing statements; 4. Answers should include the learned ability to persuade and influence others to follow his or her agenda.

CONCLUSION
The Paradox of Power

No writ of habeas corpus was ever issued for al-Awlaki. After the U.S. government had acted, there was no live person to bring to a U.S. court for a hearing. There was likely not even an intact body. Barack Obama was not the first American president to authorize a drone strike that resulted in the death of an American citizen. In 2002, under the administration of President George W. Bush, "the C.I.A. struck a car carrying a group of suspected militants, including an American citizen, who were believed to have Qaeda ties."[90] Nor was Obama or Bush the first president to refuse or negate a writ of habeas corpus for an American citizen in time of military conflict. President Abraham Lincoln never honored Chief Justice Taney's directive, though the president tried to calm a worried public by assuring that his assumption of unprecedented power would no longer be needed once the Union had been restored.

The power of the American presidency is not easily defined, nor are its roots and sources easily traced or separated. Many factors—constitutional provisions, institutional and political contexts, individual personality and skill, and responses to crises—have all played a role in its development. As scholars have observed, the office of the presidency is full of paradoxes.[91] The Framers wanted a strong and decisive office, yet they were wary of creating an elected monarch. Americans often look to their presidents for leadership above the fray of partisan politics, yet the position is, by design, political and embedded in a system of checks and balances. Americans look to their presidents for leadership yet expect them to follow the will of the people.

$SAGE edge™

Want a better grade?

Get the tools you need to sharpen your study skills. **SAGE edge** offers a robust online environment featuring an impressive array of free tools and resources. Access practice quizzes, eFlashcards, video, and multimedia at **edge.sagepub.com/abernathybrief1e.**

The modern presidency is a massively powerful office. As Americans are confronted with a global war on terror in the twenty-first century—a war that features undefined boundaries and no specific nation with which to conclude a peace treaty—the question of the proper limits of presidential power remains as vital as it did in 1861 when Abraham Lincoln expanded his authority to reconstitute a nation divided. Certainly President Trump will continue to face these questions during his term in office; these issues are not going away.

CHAPTER REVIEW

This chapter's main ideas are reflected in the Learning Objectives. By reviewing them here you should be able to **remember** the key points and **know** these terms that are central to the topic.

10.1 Describe the powers of the presidency as defined in the Constitution, the tensions inherent in those descriptions, and constitutional limitations on presidential power.

REMEMBER...

- The Framers called for a single executive, the president, with enough power to lead successfully but not so much power to make him susceptible to tyranny.

- As set out in the Constitution, the president serves a four-year term with the possibility of reelection. Candidates must be natural-born citizens, at least thirty-five years old, and a resident of the nation for fourteen years. Women were not expressly prohibited from running in the Constitution but were disenfranchised.

- The office of the presidency is granted a set of expressed, implied, and delegated powers, including the powers to carry out the laws of the nation, guide foreign policy and relations with foreign leaders, provide Congress with information, make policy recommendations to Congress, veto legislation, act as commander in chief of the military, and grant pardons.

KNOW...

- *executive branch*: the branch of government charged with putting the nation's laws into effect (p. 318)

- *pardon*: the presidential authority to forgive an individual and set aside punishment for a crime (p. 324)

- *recess appointment*: occurs when Congress is not in session and the president appoints a person to fill a position that would normally require the advice and consent of the Senate; unless the person is formally confirmed when the Senate reconvenes, the position ends at the conclusion of that session of Congress (p. 323)

- *State of the Union address*: the annual, constitutionally required transmittal of information from the president to Congress updating that branch on the state of national affairs (p. 323)

- *War Powers Resolution of 1973*: a law passed over President Nixon's veto that restricts the power of the president in committing the nation's armed forces into combat or situations of likely combat (p. 332)

10.2 Evaluate how presidents have tested the limits of the power of the office during wartime and national crises.

REMEMBER...

- The Constitution provides that the U.S. government has certain powers to suspend rights during times of rebellion or invasion. The text granting that power is within Article 1, which is devoted to the structure and powers of Congress, not the executive branch. However, presidents have sometimes pointed to the "war powers" granted to the executive as justification for their actions.

10.3 Discuss institutional and informal sources of presidential power.

REMEMBER...

- No president truly acts alone. The president operates at the center of multiple organizations and institutions within the executive branch.

- The office of the vice presidency provides stability as the vice president assumes the office of the presidency should a serving president vacate the office due to death, resignation, or impeachment. The vice president also helps the president get elected.

- The president's cabinet acts as a source of information for the president and also can communicate to the citizens a president's commitment to representing all Americans and their interests.

KNOW...

- *executive agreements*: an agreement between a president and another nation that does not have the same durability in the American system as a treaty but that may carry important foreign policy consequences (p. 341)

- *Executive Office of the President (EOP)*: a collection of offices within the White House organization designed primarily to provide information to the president (p. 338)

- *executive orders*: directions made by presidents to the executive branch departments that often contain nothing more than instructions to be carried out by agencies, bureaus, and departments but that may at times be considered to be acts of presidential lawmaking (p. 341)

- *executive privilege*: a right claimed by presidents to keep confidential certain conversations, records, and transcripts from outside scrutiny, especially that of Congress (p. 341)

- *going public*: a strategy through which presidents reach out directly to the American people with the hope that the people will, in turn, put pressure upon their representatives and senators to press for a president's policy goals (p. 340)

- *signing statements*: text written by presidents while signing a bill into law that usually consists of political statements or reasons for signing the bill but that might also include a president's interpretation of the law itself (p. 341)

11 THE FEDERAL BUREAUCRACY
Putting the Nation's Laws into Effect

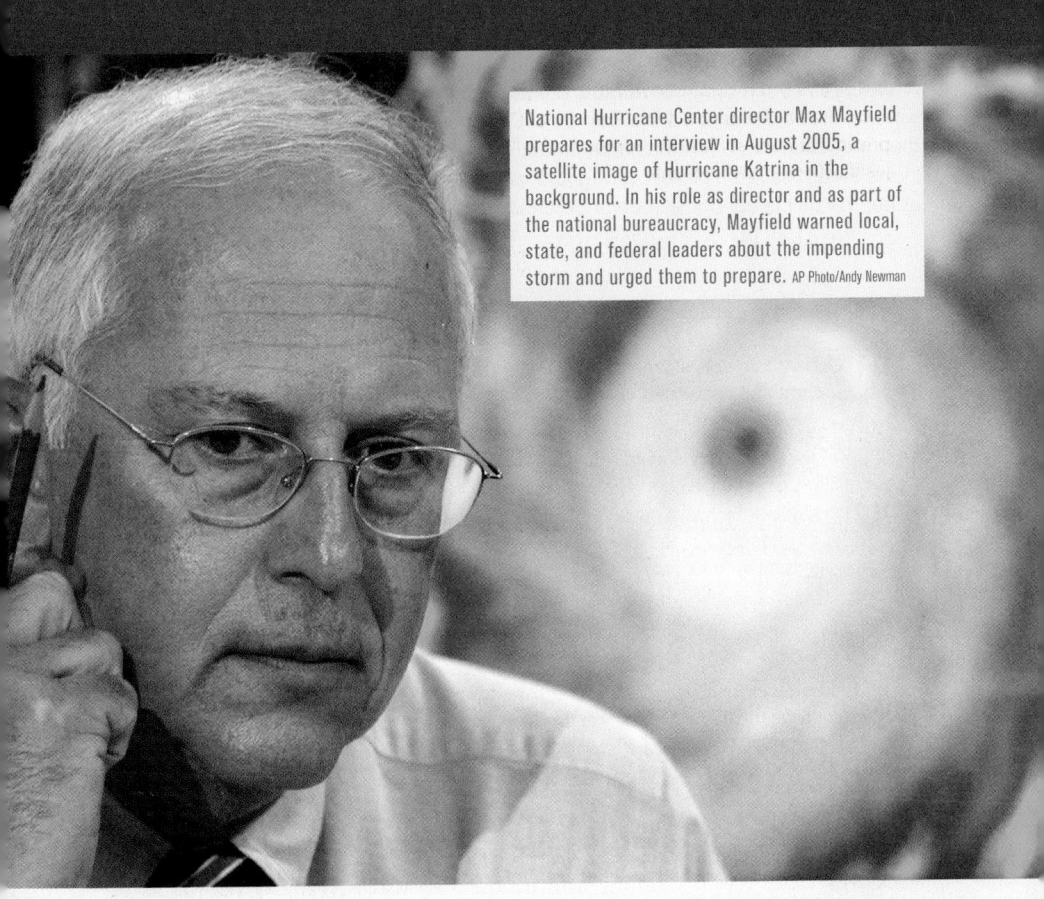

National Hurricane Center director Max Mayfield prepares for an interview in August 2005, a satellite image of Hurricane Katrina in the background. In his role as director and as part of the national bureaucracy, Mayfield warned local, state, and federal leaders about the impending storm and urged them to prepare. AP Photo/Andy Newman

To most Americans, the word *bureaucracy* refers to something that must be dealt with when necessary, complained about at times, and perhaps feared when confronted with its seemingly faceless exercise of power. Bureaucracy, however, simply describes an organization designed to carry out specific tasks according to a prescribed set of rules and procedures. In this chapter, you will learn about the **federal bureaucracy**—what it is, how it is structured, and how it works. Formally, the federal bureaucracy is part of the executive branch of the national government, charged with executing, or putting into action, the laws that Congress has written. However, the federal bureaucracy is actually a powerful player in the American political scene in its own right—though one that rarely makes the news unless something goes wrong. Whether you realize it or not, this is the part of the federal government that actually impacts your life in a more personal way than the actions of the president, Congress, or the judiciary typically do.

Americans often have contradictory views of bureaucracy and make many demands of it. At times, they complain that bureaucracy is too powerful, capable of making their lives more difficult or expensive—or even corrupt. At other times, they complain that it is powerless to help them, incompetent, wasteful, and inefficient. As you will see, these enduring tensions have spurred periods of reform and change since the nation's founding, in turn shaping the modern bureaucracy.

In this chapter, we will examine the American federal bureaucracy through the lens of one of the most destructive natural disasters in the nation's history, Hurricane Katrina, which devastated the Gulf Coast in August 2005. Though it has been more than a decade since Katrina made landfall, its effects are still being felt not only in the areas that are still recovering and rebuilding but also in an ongoing debate about the efficiency of the federal bureaucracy.

After reading this chapter, you will be able to do the following:

11.1 Name the key characteristics of bureaucratic organization and the theories that try to explain why bureaucratic organization happens.

11.2 Outline the historical development of the American federal bureaucracy.

11.3 Describe the structure of the federal bureaucracy, including executive branch agencies, cabinet departments, and regulatory bodies.

11.4 Describe the tools of bureaucratic control, oversight, and reform.

HURRICANE KATRINA TESTS THE FEDERAL BUREAUCRACY

Max Mayfield saw it coming, and he tried to warn as many people as he could. As director of the National Hurricane Center, based in Miami, Florida, Mayfield and the scientists on his team sounded the alarm on August 26, 2005, that a potentially catastrophic hurricane would make landfall on the coast of Louisiana, southeast of New Orleans. In predicting the point of impact for the hurricane's eye, they were off by a mere eighteen miles. As one reporter noted, "In the business of hurricane prediction, that's laser-beam accuracy."[1]

That storm was Hurricane Katrina, one of the deadliest, most destructive, and costliest hurricanes in the nation's history. Two days prior to landfall, "Mayfield was so worried about Hurricane Katrina that he called the governors of Louisiana and Mississippi and the mayor of New Orleans. On Sunday, he even talked about the force of Katrina during a video conference call to President George W. Bush . . . 'I just wanted to be able to go to sleep that night knowing that I did all I could do.'"[2]

As the storm approached shore, officials warned that it could make landfall with winds in excess of 130 mph, pushing ahead of it a storm surge of devastating intensity and volume. New Orleans mayor C. Ray Nagin cautioned residents to leave the city, saying, "This is the real deal. Board up your homes, make sure you have enough medicine, make sure the car has enough gas. Do all things you normally do for a hurricane but treat this one differently because it is pointed towards New Orleans."[3]

Of all of the concerns, the most worrisome was the city's system of levees and pumps, designed by the Army Corps of Engineers to keep the water at bay. With much of the city below sea level, a failure in any one section of the system would cause New Orleans "to fill up like a bathtub."[4] By the morning of Sunday, August 28, New Orleans was under evacuation orders. The roads were packed. Inbound lanes of the main highways were redirected to handle outbound traffic. Many residents, however, could not or would not leave. In a press conference, Nagin had acknowledged that the Superdome would be needed to temporarily house the one hundred thousand or more of the city's residents who lacked the transportation needed to leave the city; a disproportionate number of whom were elderly, poor, or African American.[5] When the Superdome opened to receive those unable to evacuate, "people on walkers, some with oxygen tanks, began checking in."[6]

On the morning of August 29, Hurricane Katrina's eyewall made its first Gulf Coast landfall at Plaquemines Parish, Louisiana. Initially, New Orleans and its mayor were hopeful that a disaster had been avoided. The city had been spared the storm's strongest winds and storm surge. Within hours, however, it became clear that the levee system was failing. Water overtopped the levees in some areas. In others, leaks developed, and the pumps designed to protect the city from the water that entered it began to fail. The "bathtub" that included many of the city's poorest neighborhoods began to fill up.

More than one thousand residents of Louisiana died in the storm and the flooding that followed— many of them its most vulnerable. A study of the bodies recovered following the storm concluded that "64 percent of the people who died were elderly."[7] Immediately after the scope of the devastation became clear, calls went out for donations to private relief agencies, such as the American Red Cross and the Salvation Army. Money—rather than food, blankets, or other goods—was the main request, which allowed these organizations to respond more quickly and effectively

The effects of Hurricane Katrina were felt far beyond New Orleans. New Orleans residents, including five-year-old Donte Percy, were evacuated first to the Superdome and then ultimately to places like this shelter for refugees in Houston, Texas. AP Photo/LM Otero

as they saw needs arise. Then, in the days, weeks, and months that followed, Gulf Coast residents looked to the Federal Emergency Management Agency (FEMA) to step in and lead recovery efforts. However, as refugees from New Orleans evacuated to nearby states following the storm, they shared not only stories of loss and devastation but plenty of criticism for how public officials had handled the disaster. Some of the sharpest words came from those who sheltered at the Superdome. One woman, Maia Brisco, told reporters the stadium was "a total hell hole."[8]

In the aftermath of Hurricane Katrina, the performance of local, state, and federal officials in predicting, preparing for, and responding to the storm came under intense scrutiny. Figuring prominently in this process was the federal bureaucracy, which is really a small universe of organizations operating across the country. Within this vast system are departments, agencies, and bureaus, which themselves are often divided and subdivided into smaller organizational units. The National Hurricane Center, for example, and Max Mayfield and the members of his team, are part of the National Weather Service, which is part of the National Oceanic and Atmospheric Administration, which, in turn, is part of the Department of Commerce. As the nation was confronted with scenes of devastation and loss in Katrina's wake, parts of the federal bureaucracy, such as the National Hurricane Center, were singled out for praise. Others, however, such as the Army Corps of Engineers and FEMA, received sharp criticism. How could some parts of the vast machinery of the federal government have gotten things right while others seemed to have gotten them so wrong? As Congress, the White House, and the American people asked this very question, it was concluded that the answers were complicated, just like the vast bureaucracy responsible for preparing for and responding to disasters such as Hurricane Katrina. We will begin exploring those questions by turning to the idea of bureaucracy itself to think about what it is *supposed* to do.

WHAT HAVE I LEARNED?

1. The American federal bureaucracy is ____.

   a. A specialized part of the executive branch, carrying out the orders of the president
   b. The organizations and suborganizations of people who put into effect national public policy through the use of specialization, division of labor, and standardization of administrative processes
   c. The organizations based at the state level with powers equal to the legislative, judicial, and executive branches
   d. The branch of government primarily responsible for making the nation's laws

2. What were some of the criticisms leveled at the federal bureaucracy following Hurricane Katrina?

Answer Key: 1. b; 2. Answers might include criticism of FEMA for its response or of the Army Corps of Engineers for the failed levee system.

THEORIES OF BUREAUCRATIC ORGANIZATION FOCUS ON RULES, PEOPLE, AND TASKS

Americans' ambivalence about the federal bureaucracy may be partly due to the fact that—unlike Congress, the president, or the Supreme Court—Americans actually have contact with it in their personal or professional lives. Any American-made product you consume involved federal agencies making sure that the factory was safe for its employees, that it did not discriminate in hiring, that it dealt with labor issues and complaints fairly, and that it did not degrade the environment. For anything you purchase manufactured by a foreign country, the bureaucracy acted to ensure that the country of origin was following rules of fair trade and labor practices promised in trade agreements. Driving much of this bureaucratic involvement in daily life are the demands of Americans themselves—for safe products, fair labor practices, and environmentally conscious factories. Ensuring that these demands are met involves the federal bureaucracy in many areas of the nation's economy and private life. The vast majority of the federal bureaucracy lies within the executive branch of the federal government, which is tasked with executing, or carrying out, federal laws.

> • Describe the key characteristics of bureaucratic organization and the theories that explain why that organization happens.

In addition to the federal bureaucracy, there is another category of public bureaucracies: **state and local bureaucracies**. These agencies are also involved in the lives of Americans; they make the rules that govern the construction of the house in which the citizen lives; determine the property taxes that he or she pays; provide the school, police station, and firehouse down the street; and supply the water in the glass next to the alarm clock.

What's more, the same products regulated by public bureaucracies—federal, state, and local—have been produced by another category of bureaucratic organizations: **private bureaucracies**. While corporations and companies are not usually called bureaucracies, they in fact are. They share some, though not all, of the characteristics of public bureaucracies. A common critique of public bureaucracies is that they should try to operate more like the makers of consumer products and less like the government, a topic to which we will return later in the chapter. In short, bureaucratic organization is everywhere. It is an elaborate system but not necessarily a mysterious one.

Before we begin to untangle the complex constellation of federal administrative organizations, we need to consider how bureaucracies operate. The term *bureaucracy* describes an organization or a set of organizations, but it also describes a way of organizing, a way of distributing power. Scholars have offered a variety of theoretical approaches to explaining bureaucratic organization, none of which have to be mutually exclusive. Three approaches, in particular, highlight different aspects of bureaucratic organization: rules, people, and tasks.

Weber's Theory Focuses on Rules

Max Weber (pronounced VAY-ber), a German sociologist, was among the first to define the boundaries and characteristics of bureaucratic organization. Weber saw bureaucracy as a large and complex machine. Each individual in this machine—a **bureaucrat**—was "only a single cog in an ever-moving mechanism."[9] For Weber, bureaucratic power rested upon what he called rational-legal authority in which citizens accept the authority of organizations, or, more precisely, the rules and organizational structures that define that authority and place limits upon it. Once firmly established, Weber concluded, "bureaucracy is among those social structures which are hardest to destroy."[10]

The Weberian bureaucracy is characterized by four main organizational traits. First, bureaucrats have defined tasks and rules governing how these tasks should be carried out, creating a clear *division of labor* within the organization. The sets of rules governing the behavior of bureaucrats are commonly referred to as **standard operating procedures.** Second, authority in bureaucracy is *hierarchical*, having "a clearly established system of superordination and subordination in which there is a supervision of the lower offices by the higher ones."[11] Third, individual jobs within the organization are *specialized*; workers are increasingly selected for specific jobs based on their technical competence. Finally, the modern bureaucracy is characterized by *impersonal relationships*. Weber's ideal of a bureaucracy was, by design, divorced from politics and personal relationships, its effective functioning made more likely if "it succeeds in eliminating from official business love, hatred, and all purely personal, irrational, and emotional elements which escape calculation."[12] See Figure 11.1.

Barnard's Theory Focuses on People

Chester Barnard drew on decades of experience with the American Telephone and Telegraph Company in the early twentieth century to outline a theory of the bureaucracy in which people—and not just rules and procedures—mattered to the life of a bureaucracy. For Barnard, the essence of a bureaucracy is that it involves "conscious coordination" of the activities of individuals in pursuit of a joint objective.[13]

Whenever people undertake action in pursuit of a common goal, however, they are taking a risk that others involved might not do what they are supposed to do. Political scientists often describe these risks in terms of the **principal-agent problem.** The "principal" in this model is the actor who asks the agent to carry out a task. The challenge in doing so is twofold. First, the agent may have his or her own goals, which may not be the same as the principal's. Second, the agent may have information that the principal lacks, which opens up the opportunity for the agent to behave in a way that is not in the interests of the principal.

Principal-agent relationships are everywhere. An example from politics is when voters (the principals) elect members of Congress (the agents), the voters run the risk that their elected representatives will not faithfully carry out their

FIGURE 11.1

Weber's Model Bureaucracy

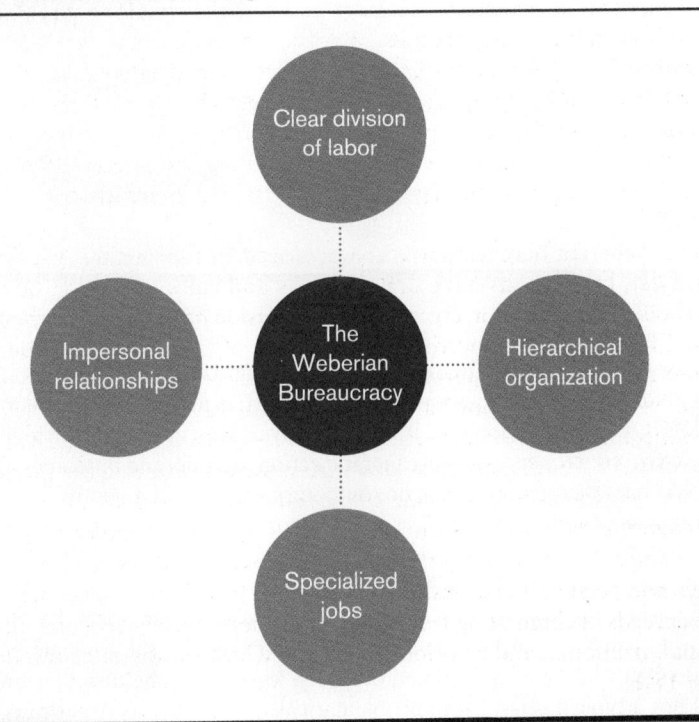

wishes, especially during the parts of the legislative process that are harder to observe and happen out of public view.

According to Barnard, bureaucratic leadership is central to the success of a bureaucracy. The job of the leader is to secure the cooperation of those within the organization.[14] In this effort, **incentives**—those inducements that the leaders of a bureaucracy can offer to their employees—are key to successful performance. Incentives do not always have to involve money. Power, prestige, a sense of accomplishment, and a shared vision of important work can also act as incentives for successful bureaucratic performance. As we will examine later, however, incentives can act the other way, sending bureaucrats off in directions that Congress, the president, or the American people did not intend for them to go. See Figure 11.2.

Wilson's Theory Focuses on Tasks

For political scientist James Wilson, rules and procedures mattered, as did individuals. However, his analysis added a third element of bureaucratic organization:

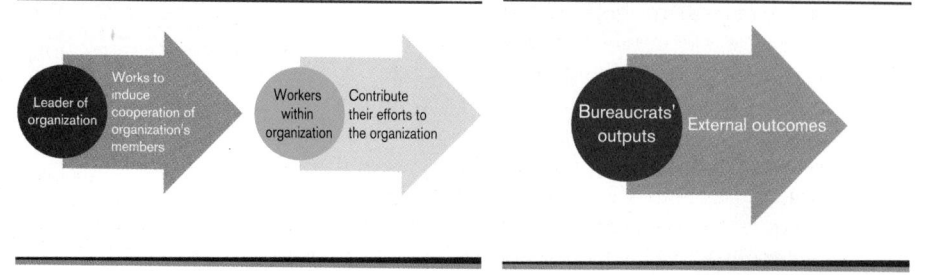

FIGURE 11.2

Barnard's People-Centered Model

Leader of organization → Works to induce cooperation of organization's members → Workers within organization → Contribute their efforts to the organization

FIGURE 11.3

Wilson's Outcomes and Outputs Model

Bureaucrats' outputs → External outcomes

tasks, or what different bureaucrats in their organizations actually do. Wilson wrote that "people matter, but organization matters also, and tasks matter most of all."[15] Of special concern in Wilson's analysis was the ability or inability to observe two consequences of bureaucratic action: outputs and outcomes. Outputs are what bureaucratic operators do; outcomes are what changes in the world as a result of their actions. When either outputs or outcomes are difficult to observe with any certainty, problems arise. When both are difficult to discern, "effective management is almost impossible."[16]

Consider the nation's public schools.[17] When a teacher closes the classroom door, that teacher's outputs are largely unseen except by the students. Sure, the principal can observe the teacher, but both know that the observation day is likely not a typical class. More problematically, especially as America is testing its students like never before, it is very difficult and expensive to try to measure a teacher's outcomes, or what a teacher is adding to the mind of one particular student.[18] In order to be effectively managed, both outputs and outcomes must be "visible." See Figure 11.3.

WHAT HAVE I LEARNED?

1. According to Max Weber, one of the key characteristics of bureaucratic organization is _____.

   a. Its highly political nature
   b. A set of standard operating procedures
   c. The highly personal nature of relationships within it
   d. The ability to vote bureaucrats out of office

2. In a people-centered model of bureaucracy, one of the most important elements is _____.

   a. Strict control of employees based on rules and procedure
   b. Incentives to encourage better performance
   c. Weak leadership
   d. Routine weekly meetings

3. What is the principal agent problem?

   ....

   Answer Key: 1. b; 2. b; 3. Answers should discuss the challenges principals face in holding their agents accountable, especially in the presence of unequal levels of information.

THE BUREAUCRACY HAS DEVELOPED IN RESPONSE TO DEMANDS AND CRISES

In the early years of its history, the American bureaucracy was absolutely tiny, reflecting the reality that the autonomous and mostly agrarian society did not place many demands on the young national government. From its beginnings as a small set of departments employing few people, the bureaucracy has grown enormously and today has nearly three million civilian employees working across the country.

- Describe the historical development of the American bureaucracy.

This growth has not been steady and gradual but—like the power of the national government itself—has experienced periods of relatively little growth and periods of intense expansion. The increase in the nation's population and boundaries, the complexity of tasks performed by the federal government, and greater demands for services by citizens have all contributed to this process. In addition, responses to crises—economic, social, and military—have produced some of the most dramatic expansions in the size, scope, and complexity of the federal bureaucracy.

The Founders Were Skeptical of, and Unclear about, the Role of the Bureaucracy

Although the delegates to the Constitutional Convention wrestled a great deal with the issue of the power and independence of the chief executive, they spent very little time discussing the administrative apparatus itself, and the "Constitution is virtually silent on the subject."[19] Much of the constitutional basis for the bureaucracy lies in Article 2, which lays out the functions and processes of the executive branch of government. In it, the president is authorized to "require the Opinion, in writing, of the principal Officer in each of the executive Departments, upon any Subject relating to the Duties of their respective Offices."[20] This section forms the basis for the executive branch departments, special organizations created by acts of Congress to assist the president in executing the laws of the nation. The heads of these departments are referred to as secretaries. Those secretaries form the president's cabinet, along with the vice president and the heads of other offices given cabinet-level status.

Delegates Aimed to Avoid Tyranny but Preserve Efficiency

The delegates to the Constitutional Convention brought with them a deep mistrust of administrative power that was born out of experiences under British colonial rule: Many of the charges against King George III in the Declaration of Independence focused on administrative abuses. The delegates were in no mood to create a homegrown swarm of officers.

On the other hand, the delegates also held the general belief, gained from hard experience, that placing administrative responsibilities entirely in the hands of the legislature would be slow and inefficient. The Continental Congress had done just that with numerous committees handling the business of fighting a revolution. This arrangement worked poorly, and individual members of the Congress were constantly overworked and overburdened.

Trying to steer a course between executive tyranny and legislative inefficiency, the delegates agreed to place in the hands of the president the authority to nominate executive branch officials rather than having a council of officers selected by Congress, which had been discussed in the convention. The Senate, though, retained the role of advice and consent in approving presidential nominees by a majority vote.[21] In addition, Congress retained the ability to impeach (in the House) and try (in the Senate) "all civil Officers of the United States" for "Treason, Bribery, or Other high Crimes and Misdemeanors."[22]

How Officers Would Be Removed Remained Unsettled

Having settled on how executive branch offers would be selected, the most contentious question facing the delegates was how these people were to be *removed*. Did the president have the authority to remove officers at will, was it Congress's job, or should there be a role for both the president and the Congress? Or were these people to serve for life with no possibility for removal? On this question—other than setting out the rarely used process of impeachment—the Constitution remained silent.

Only weeks after the first national Congress assembled, the issue of the removal of officers came before it in what has become known as the Decision of 1789. Following what became "the first major constitutional debate" in the young Republic,[23] Congress left the power of removal in the hands of the president. The question, however, reemerged with the Tenure of Office Act (1867), which—largely because of the tense politics following the Civil War—restricted the president's authority of removal. Only in 1926, in the case of *Myers v. United States*, which held the Tenure of Office Act unconstitutional, was the question settled. Presidents retained the authority to remove officials in the executive branch, a necessary ability in their role of ensuring laws are faithfully executed.[24]

Washington Formed the First Administration and the First Cabinet Departments

President George Washington's cabinet included just four men and three official departments. Secretary of State Thomas Jefferson oversaw the Department of State, handling the young nation's dealings with foreign nations as well as publishing laws and overseeing the hiring of civil officials. The Department of War (later incorporated into the Department of Defense) oversaw the nation's small military with fewer than one hundred civilian employees. Alexander Hamilton used his position as secretary of the Treasury to advance his goal of expanding the role of the federal government in the nation's economic affairs. Finally, Washington's attorney general (later made the head of the Department of Justice) acted as a legal adviser to the president and members of his cabinet. In the centuries since, Congress has created new departments and reorganized others.

In forming his first cabinet, Washington tried to reassure members of the experimental nation that his government was competent and representative of all of the thirteen states. He knew this task would not be easy. A week after his inauguration, the president wrote to a friend, "I anticipate that one of the most difficult and delicate parts of the duty of my Office will be that which relates to nominations for appointments."[25] Three of the members of his small cabinet represented diverse and powerful states: Massachusetts, New York, and Virginia.[26]

Washington was right to be worried. Within the first three years of his administration, "open warfare had broken out" between two powerful members of his cabinet: Alexander Hamilton and Thomas Jefferson.[27] With very different visions of the role of the federal government—especially in the nation's economic life—these men participated in some of the first **turf wars** in the history of the federal bureaucracy, which each tried to take duties and responsibilities away from the other's department or keep his opponent from doing so.

In choosing men to fill out his administration, Washington's primary consideration was what he referred to as "fitness of character," by which he meant integrity, a man's standing in the community, and qualities that would ensure the nation's confidence. Washington's priorities ensured that members of the upper social classes tended to be the ones to fill these positions.[28] Technical competence, except in a few positions, such as those involving legal matters, was not the primary consideration. Washington also viewed his cabinet as very much subordinate to his leadership, sometimes calling on his cabinet secretaries to take dictation.

The Jacksonian Era Saw the Rise of Political Patronage

In the early decades of the nineteenth century, most of the growth of the federal bureaucracy was a result of the geographic expansion of the nation; one particular issue that needed to be addressed was delivery of the mail across the growing territory. The bureaucratic reforms of President Andrew Jackson (1829–1837) sought to separate the person from the office. In his inaugural address, Jackson railed against the sense of "ownership" of important (and sometimes well-paying) administrative positions on the part of the officeholders, who in some cases unofficially handed the positions down to their heirs, as had been done officially in Britain and other European countries.

As part of his reforms, Jackson employed what is called **political patronage**—filling administrative positions as a reward for support, rather than solely on merit. His use of patronage is commonly referred to as the **spoils system**; the name indicates that part of the "spoils" of a successful election is the ability to clean house of one's opponents and install supporters in their place. Although politics—specifically removing political opponents and installing supporters—played a role in Jackson's reforms, so did a desire to separate a man from the office he held in order to undercut individual power bases as a challenge to Jackson's power and authority.

Ironically, one of the consequences of patronage was to make the federal bureaucracy in some ways closer to what Weber described: impartial, neutral, driven by standard operating procedures and technical expertise. If, after elections, a nation is constantly shuffling people in and out of important administrative positions—people who often have little expertise in the operations of those agencies and departments—then it becomes necessary to standardize procedures. Otherwise, little would get done, or at least done well. Thus, through his practices, Jackson and his supporters laid the foundations for the modern federal bureaucracy.

Post-Civil War, the Bureaucracy Grew Along with the Nation's Territories

As America emerged from the devastation of the Civil War, the nation found itself engaged in relentless expansion of both the nation's boundaries in the West and of agriculture and industry. In order to cope with the demands placed upon the federal government as a result of this expansion, the bureaucracy grew in size and also in the scope of its involvement with the nation's economy.

As large corporations such as the railroads outgrew the ability of individual states to control and regulate them, demands by the public for a more active federal role in supervising businesses and commerce led to the creation of **independent regulatory agencies**, which exist outside of the major cabinet departments and whose job is to monitor and regulate specific sectors of the economy. Congress created the first, the Interstate Commerce Commission, in 1887 in order to monitor price setting and other practices by the railroads.

In addition to calls for regulation, the federal bureaucracy found itself confronted with the demands of organized interests, such as farmers, who sought to use the power of the federal government to advance and promote their own endeavors. The result was the development of **clientele agencies**, which, like their name implies, act to serve and promote the interests of their clients. The Department of Agriculture (1862) served the interests of farmers—one of the most powerful clientele groups of the time—by, for example, collecting and distributing data about advancements in agricultural practices.[29]

The development and expansion of the federal bureaucracy happened relatively late in the life of the American democracy, especially when compared to European democracies of the period. For most of these nations, a well-developed bureaucracy existed before they became democracies, having developed under the rule of monarchs. For political scientist Stephen Skowronek, the fact that the American bureaucracy had to develop in the shadow of two other, already established, sets of political institutions—the court system and political parties—resulted in a federal bureaucracy that was more fragmented and decentralized than its European counterparts.[30]

Political scientist Theda Skocpol looked to the same period in state development in order to explain why America never developed the kind of comprehensive social welfare state as Europe, even though America introduced some of the earliest social welfare policies in the world with its system of pensions for

Civil War veterans and their survivors. For Skocpol, the well-developed system of federal courts was hostile to large-scale government intervention on behalf of citizens, and American political parties did not want to give up the power they gained by providing benefits in return for political patronage.[31]

Both of these studies highlight the idea of American exceptionalism, in which scholars have examined how the unique histories, paths, and development of American political institutions may have led to uniqueness in the nation's representative government itself. In doing so scholars have also stressed the importance of **path dependence** in which a set of political choices at one time produces a set of outcomes that shapes the possibilities for future politics and public policies.

Bureaucratic Expansion in the Progressive Era Focused on Labor and Eliminating Patronage

The Progressive Era (roughly from 1890 to 1920) is known for the continued expansion of the role of the federal bureaucracy in the nation's economic life and for attempts to take politics out of the bureaucracy itself. Congress created the Department of Commerce and Labor in 1903 to oversee and regulate workplaces, the rights of employees, and working conditions, which had become the focus of reform-minded journalists called muckrakers.[32] In 1913 the department was split in two with the Department of Commerce focusing on economic growth and the Department of Labor on employee-employer relations and workplace conditions.

The Progressive Era also witnessed attempts to reform the bureaucracy, especially in trying to alleviate the effects of the patronage system of appointment. The model that these reformers used was one of science and business. Their target was what they saw as a corrupt, inefficient, and too-political bureaucracy. Under President Chester A. Arthur (1881–1885), Congress passed the Civil Service Reform Act of 1883, commonly known as the **Pendleton Act** in reference to its primary Senate sponsor. The Pendleton Act created the first U.S. Civil Service Commission. Its three members, appointed by Arthur, were active reformers. Their task was to draw up and enforce rules on hiring, promotion, and tenure of office within the civil service.

Under these new rules, members of the **federal civil service** were hired and promoted on the basis of the **merit system** in which competitive testing results, educational attainment, and other qualifications formed the basis for hiring and promotion rather than politics and

A NAUSEATING JOB, BUT IT MUST BE DONE

A political cartoon depicting President Theodore Roosevelt as a muckraker taking on the meatpacking industry. Muckrakers focused on a variety of abuses in private industry, including working conditions. North Wind Picture Archives via AP Images personal connections. In the early years after the act's passage, only a small percentage of federal bureaucrats were covered by its content; by 2016, more than 90 percent were.

Twentieth-Century Crises Expanded Clientele Agencies and the Military Bureaucracy

As we discussed in Chapter 3, President Franklin Roosevelt's New Deal efforts to combat the crisis of the Great Depression resulted in an unprecedented expansion of the size of the federal bureaucracy as well as an equally startling expansion of the role of government and the bureaucracy in the American economy. Roosevelt created a host of bureaucratic agencies (despite challenges from the Supreme Court) that were primarily clientele agencies, acting on behalf of specific groups of citizens, such as the unemployed. Their purpose was to increase the provision of social services to affected Americans, including senior citizens, low-income and unemployed Americans, and individuals with disabilities.

Roosevelt and the nation faced a second struggle during his administration. As president, Roosevelt was commander in chief during most of his nation's involvement in World War II. Roosevelt and his administration oversaw a massive expansion of the military, the creation of new agencies to prosecute the war, and significant federal intervention in the American economy in order to support and supply the war effort.

That expanded bureaucracy remained in place after the war. America and its former ally, the Soviet Union, entered a decades-long period of competition for global supremacy known as the Cold War. While no full-scale global war broke out, the United States and the Soviet Union aimed thousands of nuclear weapons at each other and engaged in smaller military confrontations across the globe, supporting opposing sides without directly engaging each other's militaries on a large scale.

To fight the Cold War, the federal bureaucracy saw the creation of new agencies. President Harry S. Truman (1945–1953) signed into law the National Security Act of 1947, which created the National Security Council to advise the president on security matters and the Central Intelligence Agency (CIA) to advise the president on intelligence matters and help coordinate intelligence-gathering activities.[33] Not a formal cabinet department, the CIA is an example of an **independent executive agency**. These agencies resemble cabinet departments in many ways, such as having their top administrators appointed by and reporting to the president, but they exist outside of the cabinet structure and usually have a narrower focus of mission.

In the Mid-Twentieth Century, the Social Safety Net Grew

Postwar economic prosperity allowed the nation to fund a large expansion in the national bureaucracy in the areas of defense and the provision of social services. Under the umbrella of the Great Society, President Lyndon B. Johnson (1963–1969) proposed a series of expansions to the social safety net with the goal of securing opportunity for more Americans. Health care, education, housing, transit, job training, and urban renewal all became targets for Johnson's programs, and an increase in the size and budgets of federal departments and agencies made it possible to carry these projects out. The Department of Housing and Urban Development (HUD) was created in 1965 and the Department of Transportation in 1966. Efforts to secure civil rights for Americans and battle discrimination based on sex and race led to the passage of the Civil Rights Act of 1964.[34] The act created the Equal Employment Opportunity Commission, which today acts to enforce prohibitions on discrimination in the workplace based on racial identity, sex, religious preference, national origin, age, or disability.

The Late Twentieth Century Brought Reform and Scaling Back

When he was elected president of the United States in 1980, Ronald Reagan (1981–1989) promised to reduce the size of the federal government as well as its impact on the daily lives of Americans. As discussed in Chapter 3, efforts at devolution attempted to return power over implementing public policy back to the individual states. Efforts at deregulation aimed to reduce government oversight of and involvement with specific industries, notably transportation, banking, and utilities. Though Reagan, his Republican successor President George H. W. Bush (1989–1993), and his Democratic successor Bill Clinton (1993–2001) all promised some form of bureaucratic reform or improvement, the federal bureaucracy did not undergo a major restructuring during the period. One area in which the federal bureaucracy did see a significant reduction, however, was in defense; this was a result of the end of the Cold War with the collapse of the Soviet Union in 1991 and a reprioritizing of American military goals and strategy. After having been elected in 2016, President Donald Trump promised to shrink the American federal bureaucracy and its power over the American economy.

In the intensely divided partisan politics of Congress—and even divisions within the Republican Party, as of the fall of 2017 the realization of Trump's ambitious agenda remains uncertain.

1. Reasons for the growth of the federal bureaucracy include _____.

   a. Growth in the nation's population
   b. Demands for services
   c. The complexity of tasks performed by government
   d. All of the above

2. The cabinet includes _____.

   a. The heads of executive branch departments
   b. Members of key congressional committees
   c. Federal justices
   d. All of the above

3. The spoils system refers to _____.

   a. Ruining the chances of one's electoral competition
   b. Rewarding political supporters with political appointments

(Continued)

WHAT HAVE I LEARNED?

(Continued)

c. Restrictions on campaign contributions

d. Firing bureaucrats for incompetence

4. Clientele agencies _____.

a. Are found mostly in local bureaucracies

b. Act as independent regulators of businesses

c. Undertake mostly technical tasks, such as space exploration

d. Promote the interests of specific groups or industries

5. What is the theory of path dependence?

Answer Key: 1. d; 2. a; 3. b; 4. d; 5. Answers should describe the ways in which a set of political outcomes shapes future possibilities for political action.

A FUNCTIONING BUREAUCRACY DEPENDS UPON EFFECTIVE ORGANIZATION

Today, bureaucratic tasks have become increasingly technical and specialized. The organization of authority within the federal bureaucracy and the tasks that agencies undertake matter not just because they are complex but because both can affect how well a bureaucracy functions and how easy it can be to reform one that has gone astray. The individual parts of the federal bureaucracy are people, not bits of a machine, and they have their own priorities and competencies. Politics, competition, and even faction are as present in bureaucratic action as they are in any other endeavor in which individuals work to achieve goals.

- Describe the structure of the federal bureaucracy.

The Federal Bureaucracy Is a Web of Organizations

The American federal bureaucracy is not one structure but a complex web of organizations. As the head of the executive branch, the president is tasked to ensure that the bureaucracy faithfully executes the laws of the nation. She or he appoints (with Senate confirmation) people to the top levels of the bureaucracy and directs and advises the departments, bureaus, and agencies on how they should go about putting the laws into effect. The requirements of this task, however, are by no means only technical. They are also political. When the American people feel that the federal bureaucracy has failed, the president acts as a lightning rod for their outrage. Less than a month after Katrina, a second hurricane bore down on Texas. With the lessons of Katrina firmly in mind, President George W. Bush flew to his home state to signal to the nation that his administration was prepared and engaged. Briefings held with then-Texas governor Rick Perry, the heads of federal agencies, and Pentagon officials showed that, according to White House press secretary Scott McClellan, "[Bush] is the

The Growth of the Federal Bureaucracy

One of the common concerns about the federal bureaucracy has been its dramatic increase in size, number of regulations, and spending—especially over the last century. This growth has led to charges that the federal government is becoming too powerful, too involved in Americans' lives. Critics often imply that more power—and more money—should be found at the state and local level.

Consider Figure A, which plots the real (inflation-adjusted) per capita federal expenditures from 1947 to 2004 (with and without defense spending included).[35]

Based on that figure, one might plausibly tell a story about the massive growth in the influence of the federal government in the past fifty years. For example, in the early 1950s, real per capita federal spending was about $2,000. By the early 1980s, it had grown to $6,000 per person, three times as much, even when adjusted for inflation. When reading and interpreting graphs, however, it is often useful to also consider *data that are not presented* when making an argument—data that might complicate or counter the argument being made. Consider a similar chart that plots spending by state and local governments during roughly the same period.

Adding Figure B leads to a more complex story. The past fifty years have witnessed increased spending across all levels of the American bureaucracy—federal, state, and local. Again, note that real per capita expenditures by state and local bureaucracies

FIGURE A

Real per Capita Federal Expenditures, 1947-2004

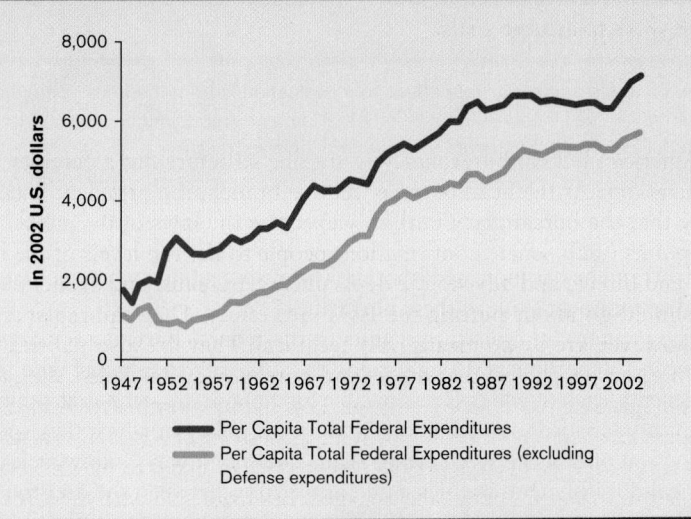

Per Capita Total Federal Expenditures
Per Capita Total Federal Expenditures (excluding Defense expenditures)

(Continued)

(Continued)

Real per Capita State and Local Government Expenditures, 1948-2004

nearly tripled in the same time period (from the early 1950s to the early 1980s), rising from about $1,000 per person to nearly $3,000 per person. While the amounts were smaller than federal spending, the rate of growth was nearly the same.

WHAT DO YOU THINK?

How might these additional data affect your evaluations about the development of bureaucracy in the United States? What other data or graphs might you want to have in order to fully evaluate the growth in the federal bureaucracy?

president, and he has indicated [that] it is his responsibility when it comes to the federal government's role in these hurricanes."[36]

The primary administrative units in the federal bureaucracy are the fifteen cabinet departments. Congress has the authority to establish and fund the departments, each of which is responsible for a major area of public policy. They are typically divided into subunits based on the policy in which they specialize. The division of tasks between departments does not always follow a clear logic; historical development, politics, and competition between the divisions of the federal bureaucracy over the authority to perform a specific task—and spend the funds Congress has allocated to do so—have all shaped the division of labor between departments.

There is considerable diversity in the size and budgets of the cabinet departments. Sizable budgets do not always mean large numbers of employees. For example, the Department of Health and Human Services (which issues payments for Social Security and Medicare) and the Department of the Treasury (which makes interest payments on the national debt) both have relatively large budgets for the number of employees in them. Prestige also varies between the departments, including one of its most visible markers: face time with the president.

Cabinet departments are headed by cabinet secretaries (or by the attorney general in the case of the Justice Department) who are nominated by the president and confirmed by a majority vote in the Senate. Cabinet secretaries formally work under the president; however, they also depend on Congress for appropriation of funds and for legislation that sets out specific goals and objectives for their departments. In addition, cabinet secretaries often have to contend with pressure from those affected by the actions of their departments, such as citizens or organized interest groups. Independent executive agencies like NASA and FEMA function similarly to departments in many ways but are usually narrower in focus and retain more independence in carrying out their goals. In the aftermath of Hurricane Katrina, both the cabinet secretary of Homeland Security Michael Chertoff and FEMA director Michael Brown took considerable heat from the public for their agencies' poor performance in responding to the disaster; Brown eventually resigned as a result of the pressure.

Independent regulatory agencies act to oversee and regulate governmental function, especially in economic affairs. Created by Congress to have enough independence to protect them from political partisanship, they are typically headed by appointed boards with fixed and staggered terms of service, making it more difficult to remove their leadership.

Government corporations act as businesses within the federal government, charging fees for their services but still subject to governmental control and possible financial subsidization. The earliest government corporation was the Federal Deposit Insurance Corporation (FDIC), established as part of the New Deal to avoid a repeat of the bank runs in the Great Depression by insuring deposits in the nation's banks.

Private contractors are not officially a part of the federal bureaucracy, but the government increasingly relies on them to provide goods and services in support of federal activity. The U.S. military, for example, relies on contractors for logistical support. Proponents of contracting argue that it allows the military and federal agencies to focus on their core missions. Opponents worry about a lack of careful oversight of contractor activities.

Bureaucratic Authority Is Hierarchical

Formally, authority across the federal bureaucracy is structured like a pyramid (see Figure 11.4).[37] At the top are the **executive political appointees**, such as cabinet secretaries and deputy secretaries, who serve at the pleasure of the president and are subject to presidential removal. Of the roughly 6,500 political appointees in the executive branch, about 1,500 require Senate confirmation. Compared to the vast majority of federal bureaucrats, these individuals are short-timers. They

FIGURE 11.4

The Hierarchy of Labor in the Federal Bureaucracy

The structure of the federal bureaucracy, including the civil service system, is in many ways similar to that described by Max Weber: hierarchical and organized, with clear divisions between the levels. This structure was intentional, designed to insulate the majority of federal bureaucrats from the ebb and flow of party control of the executive branch.

do not expect to transition from one administration to the next. Presidents must juggle several considerations in selecting who will lead their departments and agencies. Experience and competence are certainly important but so are political calculi and a desire to signal to important constituencies a willingness to work with them. The American people also expect a commitment to representing the wide diversity of their interests, experiences, and backgrounds.

Below this top level are the members of the **Senior Executive Service (SES)**. These individuals—most of who are drawn from the lower ranks of the federal bureaucracy—enjoy slightly more job security than high-level appointees and are paid and treated more like vice presidents of businesses than political figures. They are expected to use their authority to achieve concrete results.

The vast majority of employees occupy the bottom of the pyramid. They are the career civil servants, whose job ranks are clearly defined according to the General Service (GS) levels. Entrance into and advancement within the federal civil service is governed by the merit system, which relies on competitive examinations, educational qualifications, and performance reviews. Career civil servants enjoy considerable protections from termination, especially for political reasons. This job security is by design, though it presents presidents with a significant challenge. The federal bureaucracy is not a power station in which a president flips a switch and makes things happen automatically. Instead, it is a complex hierarchy of people, most of who will still have their jobs long after the president and political appointees have moved on.

The Core Tasks of the Bureaucracy Are Implementation, Rulemaking, Advising, and Representation

The primary function of the federal bureaucracy is to implement, or put into action, the laws that Congress has passed. **Implementation** is rarely, if ever, a straightforward process.[38] New policies are not enacted in isolation; they are introduced into a universe of existing policies, sometimes with competing demands.

The technical knowledge required of many federal bureaucrats in order to successfully implement public policies also acts as a brake on the ability of a president or her or his political appointees to shape bureaucrats' actions. High-level executive branch officials may lack the technical expertise necessary to evaluate or challenge the actions of their subordinates.

In addition, many frontline bureaucrats interact directly with citizens in an environment that makes it difficult to observe and control their behavior effectively. Law enforcement officers, teachers, and social workers are all examples of what are called street-level bureaucrats.[39] Because of their close contact with citizens, street-level bureaucrats may conclude that they need to "bend the rules" to do their jobs as they see them.

When Congress passes laws it often only sets general goals and targets, leaving many of the details up to the bureaucratic agencies themselves. The complexity involved with implementing policies, the technical and specialized knowledge often required to do so, and the flexibility needed to handle unforeseen circumstances all argue for giving bureaucrats the authority to flesh out parts of the laws in action. By doing so, however, Congress opens up a space for **bureaucratic discretion** in which the bureaucrats have some power to decide how a law is implemented and, at times, what Congress actually meant when it passed a given law. In addition those affected by legislation cannot go about planning how they are going to respond to a law or set of regulations until they actually know the details of it. How much will it cost to comply? What changes must be made in order to do so? The answers to these important questions more often than not come from the bureaucracy rather than Congress, the president, or the courts.

The process through which the federal bureaucracy fills in critical details of a law is called **rulemaking**. By law, agencies must follow a specific set of steps. The first is to announce a proposed set of rules and allow interested parties to weigh in; this process is called *notice and comment*. Agencies may have to notify the president or Congress about the anticipated impact of a proposed rule or set of rules. Finally, the adopted rules must be published in the *Federal Register*, which is published annually and typically runs more than seventy thousand pages. These rules matter; "they carry the same weight as congressional legislation, presidential executive orders, and judicial decisions."[40]

Part of the Framers' purpose in establishing the president's cabinet advisers and other executive branch officials was for them to share their expertise and knowledge with the president; Congress; and, increasingly, clientele groups and the public. At times the bureaucracy also acts somewhat like a court. It may settle disputes between parties that arise over the implementation of federal laws and presidential executive orders or determine which individuals or groups are covered under a regulation or program—a role called **bureaucratic adjudication.**

Finally, and perhaps surprisingly, bureaucrats can act as representatives of the American public, especially if they have the ability to act on behalf of their clients in the way that street-level bureaucrats often do.[41] While cabinet secretaries are increasingly representative of the diversity of the American people, they still do not present a complete portrait of the nation. Members of the civil service, in contrast, do represent the nation's diversity in many ways, save perhaps educational attainment (as it factors into the hiring and promotion process). In this view, having a "representative bureaucracy"—a civil service that truly reflects the diversity of the American people—may also act to legitimize its actions.[42]

One area in which federal employees are restricted from acting is the political process. Concerns about political patronage in President Roosevelt's New Deal programs led to the passage in 1939 of what is commonly known as the Hatch Act, which restricted the actions of federal workers in the political realm with exceptions for the highest-level political appointees. Federal workers were prohibited from participating in political campaigns, coercing other employees to participate, raising funds for a campaign, or holding all but a few elective offices. The Federal Employees Political Activities Act of 1993 relaxed some of the restrictions of the Hatch Act, allowing most federal employees to run in nonpartisan elections and contribute to and to participate in fund-raising for political campaigns as long as they do not use their official authority to do so.

WHAT HAVE I LEARNED?

1. Congress plays a major role in how cabinet departments function.

   a. True
   b. False

2. Implementation is usually a very straightforward process.

   a. True
   b. False

3. Independent executive agencies are different from cabinet departments because _____.

   a. Cabinet departments are responsible for fewer tasks
   b. Independent executive agencies are narrower in their focus
   c. Independent agencies charge fees for their services
   d. Cabinet heads are hired to lobby the government

4. The top of the federal bureaucratic organizational structure consists of _____.

   a. Executive political appointees
   b. Career civil servants
   c. Members of the Senior Executive Service (SES)
   d. Private contractors

5. A process through which many details of laws are filled in is _____.

   a. Rulemaking
   b. Appropriation
   c. Bureaucratic discretion
   d. Bureaucratic adjudication

6. The *Federal Register*, published annually, often runs more than seventy thousand pages. What is in this enormous publication? Why do you think it is so massive?

Answer Key: 1. a; 2. b; 3. b; 4. a; 5. a; 6. Answers should describe the vast number of rules collected in it and how they carry the same weight as acts of Congress, executive orders, and judicial decisions.

THE BUREAUCRACY IS CONSTRAINED BY OVERSIGHT AND REFORM

While complaints about the bureaucracy are as old as the institution itself, recent decades have seen a renewed focus on highlighting its failures and offering reforms to fix them. One set of critiques focuses on the inefficiency of large and complex bureaucracies. The term *red tape*, derived from "the narrow ribbons used at one time in England and America to tie up packets of legal and government documents," conjures up images of bureaucrats mindlessly following rules and standard operating procedures, whether or not it actually helps get things done.[43] Another line of critique emphasizes the tendencies of federal departments, bureaus, and agencies to be budget maximizers—that is, to seek to expand their level of appropriations beyond that necessary for the efficient provision of their services.[44]

> • Describe the tools of bureaucratic control.

Still another accusation points to problems that arise when bureaucracies stray from their established goals and devote their energies and efforts to non-essential tasks, an outcome known as **bureaucratic drift**. Worries about straying from the intended mission may apply to individual bureaucrats as well. Individuals may not do their jobs effectively or responsibly, a failing commonly referred to as shirking. Or they may actively work against the stated mission of their agency, substituting their own evaluations of a proper course of action, which is referred to as sabotage.[45] From the point of view of the bureaucrat, sabotage may be for very good reasons—for example, bending the rules to help out a client confronted with a rigid set of rules and procedures.

Another concern, especially for bureaucrats in regulatory agencies, is that individuals may undermine effective regulation if their own interests are more closely aligned with the targets of regulation than the mission of the agency, a problem known as **agency capture**. If a regulator has close ties to the industry being regulated—either through previous employment or, perhaps, expected future employment—then there may be temptations to "look the other way," instruct their subordinates to do so, or conduct their jobs in such a way as to benefit a few preferred clients.[46]

Separation of Powers Makes Overseeing the Bureaucracy Difficult

The system of separation of powers that the Framers designed poses a special challenge to controlling the bureaucracy. As authority over the federal bureaucracy is divided between different branches, federal agencies and bureaus often have to answer to more than one overseer. According

A political cartoon depicting octopus-shaped red tape from Washington, D.C., gripping the states with its tentacles.

to political scientist Joel Aberbach, "Since usually no one set of institutional actors has clear control and signals often conflict, it is difficult to hold the bureaucracy. . . reasonably to account."[47]

The President

As head of the executive branch, the president formally controls most of the federal bureaucracy.[48] He or she has the authority to appoint and remove individuals at the top layers of the bureaucracy. Presidents can also shape bureaucratic priorities in the annual budgets that they present to Congress and, with congressional approval, by reorganizing agencies. As discussed in Chapter 10, executive orders carry the force of law and typically instruct departments, agencies, and bureaus on how they are to go about implementing policy.

Presidents, however, often confront restrictions in their control over the day-to-day functions of the bureaucracy. Bureaucratic discretion and the bureaucracy's size and complexity all conspire against achieving quick results.

Congress

Congress plays a key role in controlling and guiding the bureaucracy. The Senate has power over confirmation for the higher levels of the federal service. Congress as a whole can pass legislation creating or terminating agencies and programs and, through the process of appropriation, has control over the resources that departments, bureaus, and agencies receive to carry out their tasks. Congressional committees, especially the House and Senate appropriations committees, are key players in these processes.

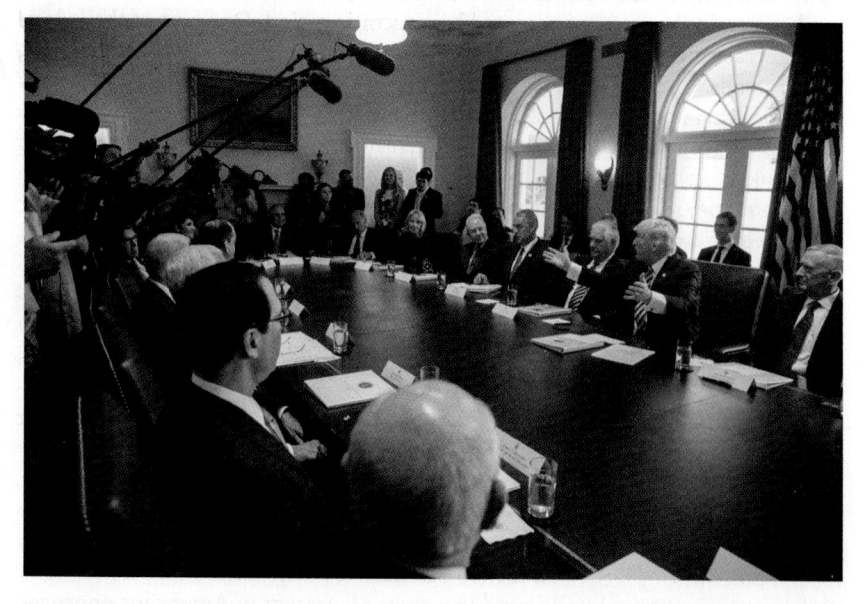

President Donald Trump, flanked by Secretary of State Rex Tillerson, left, and Defense Secretary Jim Mattis, speaks during a Cabinet meeting, Monday, June 12, 2017, in the Cabinet Room of the White House in Washington. AP Photo/Andrew Harnik

While legislation can be a proactive way to shape bureaucratic behavior by setting goals, priorities, and the overall organizational structure, Congress also has the ability to influence what happens when agencies are up and running through the process of oversight. Congress has established its own bureaucracies to keep tabs on executive branch implementation. The Government Accountability Office (GAO) is an example of this type of agency. Its work can have real bite. One GAO report investigating what had happened after Hurricane Katrina stated, "No one was designated in advance to lead the overall federal response in anticipation of the event despite clear warnings from the National Hurricane Center."[49]

When deciding how to oversee the federal bureaucracy, Congress has a choice. By doing field investigations, conducting hearings, or requiring information from the agencies, Congress may exercise police patrol oversight, analogous to a law enforcement official surveying the neighborhood to make sure all is well. The problem with police patrol oversight is that it is expensive, especially in terms of Congress's scarcest resource: time. Therefore, Congress often chooses instead to exercise fire alarm oversight, bringing the machinery of investigation and correction into action only when individuals or interest groups—some formally authorized to acquire information or bring suit in court—sound the alarm that part of the federal bureaucracy has gone astray.[50]

Other Influences: The Judiciary, the Media, and Public Opinion

Decisions by the federal judiciary can significantly impact bureaucratic behavior. Judicial control is typically negative—not in the sense that it is bad but in the sense that judicial decisions on, for example, civil liberties and civil rights, restrict and constrain the scope of accepted bureaucratic action. One part of the federal bureaucracy may also find its actions constrained by other departments, agencies, and bureaus.[51] Bureaucratic jurisdiction—the authority to act in a certain policy area—is often not clearly or cleanly defined. **Interagency rivalry** occurs when two or more agencies are charged with a similar mandate, an outcome that becomes more likely in times of budget cuts and competition for scarce or dwindling appropriations. Clientele groups and businesses affected by federal rules, whether proposed or formalized, will lobby parts of the federal bureaucracy as well as Congress to get a more favorable outcome according to their perceived interests.

As a rule, the media infrequently cover the workings of the federal bureaucracy. Most Americans are understandably not well informed of the day-to-day workings of the vast bureaucracy, and there are no doubt numerous agencies many Americans don't know even exist. Crises are exceptions to public inattention. When the machinery of government is involved in a major crisis or catastrophe that becomes highly publicized—and especially when it appears that it has failed—the federal bureaucracy might find itself center stage with a full and angry audience in attendance. Such was the case after Katrina. A year after its landfall on the Gulf Cost, thousands of residents were still waiting for federal help, and public opinion had turned against President Bush on his handling of the disaster. A national poll found that only 31 percent of Americans approved of his management of the storm, and 56 percent did not "believe that the country [was] ready for another disaster."[52]

Reform Efforts Involve Devolution, Deregulation, Reinvention, and Privatization

In addition to calls for oversight of bureaucracies and the agencies in which they operate, pushes have been made—especially in recent decades—to shrink, overhaul, or eliminate parts of the federal bureaucracy. Ronald Reagan's petitions to roll back the growth in the size and power of the bureaucracy in his successful presidential bid in 1980 focused public attention on these efforts. As discussed in Chapter 3, **devolution** aimed to transfer power over public policy back to the states and shrink the size of the federal government by allowing states to have more authority to determine how taxpayer dollars should be spent. Proponents of **deregulation** argued that the personnel rules of the civil service, along with excessive red tape, made it difficult to attract "talented energetic potential candidates" to the federal service and restrained their energies once hired.[53] As a result of deregulation efforts beginning in the 1970s, certain federal agencies saw their authority curtailed or they were abolished entirely, particularly in the areas of transportation, commerce, and the provision of utilities.

Another set of reforms sought to make the federal bureaucracy work more efficiently—more like the private sector. Under President Bill Clinton, the National Performance Review—efforts to "reinvent government"—sought to collect detailed data on bureaucratic efficiency and inefficiency and to propose measures to streamline bureaucratic operations.[54]

Other reform proposals advocate placing control over the provision of certain functions in the hands of the private sector and not the federal bureaucracy. Proponents of **privatization** argue that many tasks currently handled by the federal service can be more efficiently and more cheaply handled by private organizations and businesses. Opponents of privatization argue that reducing or eliminating governmental oversight over the provision of these services might lead to waste or fraud or might undermine the larger policy goals of the national government.

Political scientist James Q. Wilson pointed out that there might be valid reasons for the fact that public bureaucracies often act differently and less efficiently than private bureaucracies. By their very nature, public bureaucracies operate under a different set of constraints. Congress, and not the marketplace, sets the goals for, budgets of, and allocation of resources within the federal service. In addition, the American public often demands a higher standard of fairness in the actions of its public bureaucracies than it does of private ones. Public schools, for example, generally face more binding constraints over admission and expulsion of students than do the nation's private schools.[55]

Following Katrina, investigators and members of Congress questioned both the government's reliance on private contractors in relief efforts and governmental interference with private sector efforts. Concerns included a lack of competition in awarding contracts for cleanup and recovery efforts, a failure to adequately employ local businesses and contractors, and a failure on the part of FEMA to have enough "sufficiently trained procurement professionals" to effectively manage and oversee the contracting process.[56] According to a local official in Louisiana, FEMA had blocked private relief efforts as well: "We had Wal-Mart deliver three trailer trucks of water. FEMA turned them back. They said we didn't need them."[57]

1. Appropriation is one tool that Congress has to oversee the bureaucracy.
   a. True
   b. False

2. Red tape refers to _____.
   a. Overly burdensome rules and regulations
   b. Going over the budget set by Congress
   c. Rules set by the Republican Party
   d. The publication of federal rules

3. Agency capture happens when _____.
   a. Congress folds one agency into another
   b. Civil servants are fired
   c. An agency has close ties to the group it regulates
   d. An agency undertakes a different mission than it is tasked to

4. Proponents of privatization argue that the private sector can more efficiently carry out tasks than the government. Can you think of some tasks that the private sector carries out better than government? Do you think there are tasks that should not be left up to private firms to carry out?

Answer Key: 1. a; 2. a; 3. c; 4. Answers should raise questions about whether potential gains in efficiency might come at the cost of waste, fraud, or undermining larger governmental goals.

CONCLUSION

Another Devastating Hurricane, Another Federal Response

In October 2012, Hurricane Sandy spread destruction from the Caribbean to the East Coast of the United States from Florida to Maine. More than 140 people died as a direct result of the storm. In America, the devastation was the worst in New Jersey and New York, mostly due to flooding. According to the National Hurricane Center, Sandy resulted in tens of billions of dollars in damages, ranking it second behind Katrina in total economic costs in the United States from a hurricane or tropical cyclone.

In Sandy's wake, many observers praised the federal government's response, including President Barack Obama's swift action in declaring a state of emergency from Washington, D.C., to New York a day before Sandy made landfall in New Jersey. Enabled by legislation passed in Katrina's wake, Obama was able to quickly instruct FEMA to coordinate and streamline its rescue response across all responders.[58] Not all evaluations of the federal bureaucracy's response to Sandy, however, were positive. Three months after Sandy's landfall, when a blast of arctic air hit the Northeast, some critics pointed to families having to rely on space heaters to stave off the cold while still awaiting

Want a better grade?

Get the tools you need to sharpen your study skills. **SAGE edge** offers a robust online environment featuring an impressive array of free tools and resources. Access practice quizzes, eFlashcards, video, and multimedia at **edge.sagepub.com/abernathybrief1e.**

repairs and rebuilding. Others questioned whether the states, and not the federal government, should pick up more of the tab for disaster prevention and relief.

Americans want the primary instrument of national policy implementation to be effective and strong. When they feel that it is not—such as was the case with Hurricane Katrina—they demand change. However, Americans do not want the federal bureaucracy to be *too* strong. When they feel that it has become too powerful, they worry. Both the separation of powers and the realities of American federalism shape the behaviors of the federal departments, agencies, and bureaus. These organizations are not smoothly running machines but a constellation of teams operating in an often political space; they have multiple constraints on their behavior and also must contend with multiple interests and groups trying to shape that behavior. Such is the complex nature of the American federal bureaucracy.

CHAPTER REVIEW

This chapter's main ideas are reflected in the Learning Objectives. By reviewing them here you should be able to **remember** the key points and **know** these terms that are central to the topic.

11.1 Name the key characteristics of bureaucratic organization and the theories that try to explain why bureaucratic organization happens.

REMEMBER...

- Most of the federal bureaucracy lies within the executive branch. State and local bureaucracies also make rules that impact people's daily lives. Private bureaucracies are companies and corporations that also operate like federal, state, and local bureaucracies.

- Various theories of bureaucracies exist to explain how and why they are organized the way they are.

- Max Weber proposed a rules and procedures-centered organizational model in which bureaucratic power was based on rational-legal authority.

- Chester Barnard focused on overcoming problems inherent in principal-agent relationships and in organizations in general and saw bureaucratic leadership as key.

- James Wilson saw tasks—what different bureaucrats in their organizations actually do—as central to the effective functioning of a bureaucracy and to understanding the outcomes of bureaucratic actions.

KNOW...

- *bureaucrat*: an official employed within a government bureaucracy (p. 352)

- *federal bureaucracy*: the organizations and suborganizations within the executive branch that are tasked with putting the laws of the nation into effect (p. 347)

- *incentives*: inducements that leaders of a bureaucracy can offer to their employees to spur successful performance (p. 353)

- *principal-agent problem*: the challenge that arises when one actor, the principal, tasks another, the agent, to carry out the principal's wishes in the presence of uncertainty and unequal information (p. 352)

- *private bureaucracies*: privately owned corporations and companies that carry out specific tasks according to a prescribed set of rules and procedures (p. 351)

- *standard operating procedures*: the sets of rules governing the behavior of bureaucrats (p. 352)

- *state and local bureaucracies*: public organizations below the federal level designed to carry out specific tasks according to a prescribed set of rules and procedures (p. 351)

11.2 Outline the historical development of the American federal bureaucracy.

REMEMBER...

- The federal bureaucracy has grown exponentially over time, as has the complexity of the tasks it must perform and the demands for services placed upon it by the American people.

- The Constitution calls for executive branch departments to assist the president in executing the laws of the nation. To control the power of the executive, Congress was given the power to approve nominees and impeach executive officers.

KNOW...

- *clientele agencies*: organizations that act to serve and promote the interests of their clients (p. 358)

- *federal civil service*: the permanent professional branches of government concerned with administrative functions, excluding the armed forces and political appointments (p. 359)

- *independent executive agency*: agencies otherwise similar to cabinet departments but existing outside of the cabinet structure and usually having a narrower focus of mission (p. 360)

- *independent regulatory agencies*: organizations that exist outside of the major cabinet departments and whose job it is to monitor and regulate specific sectors of the economy (p. 358)

- *merit system*: a system of hiring and promotion based on competitive testing results, education, and other qualifications rather than politics and personal connections (p. 359)

- *path dependence*: the way in which a set of political outcomes shapes future possibilities for political action (p. 359)

- *Pendleton Act*: (or Civil Service Reform Act of 1883) created the first U.S. Civil Service Commission to draw up and enforce rules on hiring, promotion, and tenure of office within the civil service (p. 359)

- *political patronage*: filling administrative positions as a reward for support, rather than solely on merit (p. 357)

- *spoils system*: the practice of cleaning house of one's opponents and installing supporters in their place following a successful election (p. 357)

- *turf wars*: when bureaucrats compete to take duties and responsibilities away from one another's departments or keep their opponents from doing so (p. 357)

Describe the structure of the federal bureaucracy, including executive branch agencies, cabinet departments, and regulatory bodies.

REMEMBER...

- The federal bureaucracy is a complex web of organizations and organizations within organizations, headed by the president.
- Congress has the authority to establish and fund the departments—each of which is responsible for a major area of public policy.
- Independent regulatory agencies act to oversee and regulate governmental function, especially in economic affairs.
- At the top of the bureaucracy are executive political appointees who are often in their positions for short periods of time. Below them are SES employees with supervisory and administrative responsibilities. Career civil servants make up the bulk of the employees.
- Implementing the laws passed by Congress is one of the bureaucracy's core tasks. Bureaucrats typically have some discretion over how the laws are implemented.

KNOW...

- *bureaucratic adjudication*: when the federal bureaucracy settles disputes between parties that arise over the implementation of federal laws and presidential executive orders or determine which individuals or groups are covered under a regulation or program (p. 368)
- *bureaucratic discretion*: the power to decide how a law is implemented and, at times, what Congress actually meant when it passed a given law (p. 367)
- *executive political appointees*: employees at high levels in the federal bureaucracy who serve at the pleasure of the president and are subject to presidential removal (p. 365)
- *government corporations*: organizations that act as businesses within the federal government, charging fees for their services but still subject to governmental control and possible financial subsidization (p. 365)
- *implementation*: the bureaucracy's role in putting into action the laws that Congress has passed (p. 367)
- *private contractors*: nongovernmental workers hired by the federal bureaucracy to provide goods and services in support of federal activity (p. 365)
- *rulemaking*: the process through which the federal bureaucracy fills in critical details of a law (p. 367)
- *Senior Executive Service (SES)*: federal employees with higher-level supervisory and administrative responsibilities who are paid and treated more like vice presidents of businesses than political figures (p. 366)

Describe the tools of bureaucratic control, oversight, and reform.

REMEMBER...

- The most common complaint about the bureaucracy is its perceived inefficiency. Another has to do with bureaucratic drift, which occurs when bureaucracies stray from their established goals and devote their energies and efforts elsewhere. Agency capture—when individuals undermine effective regulation if their own interests are more closely aligned with the targets of regulation than with the mission of the agency—is also a concern.

- Control over the bureaucracy is challenging given that responsibility and power are shared across the executive, legislative, and judicial branches of government.

- Interagency rivalry occurs when two or more agencies are charged with a similar mandate, an outcome that becomes more likely in times of budget cuts and competition for scarce or dwindling appropriations.

- Efforts to reform the bureaucracy—limit its power, reduce its size, and fix inefficiencies—include devolving responsibilities to the states, deregulation, and privatizing government responsibilities to increase competitiveness.

KNOW...

- *agency capture*: a problem that occurs when a bureaucrat's own interests are more closely aligned with the targets of regulation than the mission of the agency, thus undermining effective regulation (p. 369)

- *bureaucratic drift*: when bureaucracies stray from their established goals and devote their energies and efforts to peripheral tasks (p. 369)

- *deregulation*: the reduction or elimination of government power in a particular industry, usually in order to create more competition within the industry (p. 372)

- *devolution*: the transfer of power over public policy back to the states in order to shrink the size of the federal government and allow states to have more authority to determine how taxpayer dollars should be spent (p. 372)

- *interagency rivalry*: when two or more agencies are charged with a similar mandate, an outcome that becomes more likely in times of budget cuts and competition for scarce or dwindling appropriations (p. 371)

- *privatization*: shifting control over the provision of certain governmental functions from the federal bureaucracy to the private sector (p. 372)

12 THE FEDERAL JUDICIARY
Politics, Power, and the "Least Dangerous" Branch[1]

At her confirmation hearing in July 2009, Supreme Court nominee Judge Sonia Sotomayor answered questions from Senator Jeff Sessions, R-AL. Because they are appointed to lifetime terms, Supreme Court justices are very influential and their appointment can be a challenging political process. Sotomayor would go on to become the third woman on the Court and the Court's first Hispanic justice. Alex Wong/Getty Images

What is the federal judiciary? Like with many questions you are asked to consider in this book, there are both simple answers and more complicated ones. In this chapter, we will deal with both. The definition is simple. The **federal judiciary** is one of the three branches of the nation's government. Its role is to interpret and apply the laws of the nation. Sitting atop the federal judiciary is the **U.S. Supreme Court**, which was established in the Constitution and serves as the highest court in the nation.

On a deeper level, however, more difficult questions arise. First, how different is the federal judiciary from the other two branches—or, more precisely, how *political* is it? How political should it be? Also, how *powerful* is it? As we have explored, both Congress and the president have at their disposal powerful levers to shape national public policy. Congress writes the laws; it has the power to tax and to fund. The president is the commander in chief of the armed forces and is tasked with carrying out the laws of the nation. What power does the federal judiciary have other than the authority to apply the law to the cases brought before it?

These questions are very much interconnected. The power of the federal judiciary affects how it engages as a political actor. Conversely, the degree to which the federal judiciary chooses to involve itself in political controversies has and will continue to impact its legitimacy with the American public.

In this chapter, you will engage with the stories of the confirmation of Sonia Sotomayor to the Supreme Court and John Marshall's establishment of judicial review. They are presented as "trials," though neither of the individuals were actually *on* trial. Their institution, however, was, and it still is.

After reading this chapter, you will be able to do the following:

15.1 Describe the structure and powers of the federal judiciary as laid out in the Constitution.

15.2 Explain John Marshall's development of judicial review in the Supreme Court decision in *Marbury v. Madison*.

15.3 Describe the structure of the American legal system and the federal judiciary.

15.4 Compare theories of judicial decision making as well as arguments for or against judicial restraint and activism in constitutional review.

THE "TRIAL" OF SONIA SOTOMAYOR HIGHLIGHTS THE COMPLEXITY OF JUDICIAL DECISION MAKING

In May 2009, President Barack Obama was presented with his first opportunity to nominate an individual to the U.S. Supreme Court. The retiring justice, David H. Souter, ordinarily sided with the liberal bloc of justices in his decisions, so Obama's appointment, likely a liberal, would probably not shift the ideological balance of the Court. In the intensely partisan world of the modern federal government, that lessened, if only a bit, the tensions surrounding the nomination. Even so, observers and insiders expected an intensely political battle as justices on the Supreme Court are appointed for life.

Although the nomination of a liberal justice was expected, there were other hopes pinned on the president's selection. With only one woman, one African American, and no Latino justices on the bench, many urged the president to use the opportunity to expand the diversity of the Court. On Obama's short list was Sonia Sotomayor, the daughter of Puerto Rican immigrants, a graduate of Yale Law School, a former prosecutor and litigator, and a sitting judge with the U.S. Court of Appeals for the Second Circuit. She was, however, according to the *Washington Post*, the "riskiest choice" of the likely nominees, largely because of public remarks that she had made on the importance of identity and personal history in approaching judicial decision making.[2]

When Sotomayor's nomination became official, both sides swung into campaign mode with each accusing the other of violating norms of propriety in handling a Supreme Court nomination. Although she was not *literally* on trial as the confirmation proceedings in the Senate began, Sotomayor may very well have felt like she was—and with good reason.

Republicans in the Senate painted Sotomayor as a justice who was "willing to expand constitutional rights beyond the text of the constitution."[3] Given the president's popularity at the time, and with the Senate under Democratic control, defeating Sotomayor was unlikely. Still, Republicans hoped to use the confirmation proceedings to "galvanize a movement demoralized by Republican electoral defeats."[4] Remarks made by Sotomayor at a public lecture in 2001 received particular scrutiny from Republicans during the confirmation proceedings. Sotomayor had highlighted the role that her Latina identity and life experiences played in her judicial career—a perspective that, to her, helped her make just decisions, especially in cases involving equality and discrimination. Addressing the attendees, Sotomayor said the following:

> Who am I? I am a "Newyorkrican." For those of you on the West Coast who do not know what the term means: I am a born and bred New Yorker of Puerto Rican-born parents who came to the states during World War II....
>
> No one person, judge or nominee will speak in a female or people of color voice....Yet, because I accept the proposition that, as Judge Resnik describes it, "to judge is an exercise of power" and because as, another former law school classmate, Professor Martha Minow of Harvard Law School, states "there is no objective stance but only a series of perspectives—no neutrality, no escape from choice in judging," I further accept that our experiences as women and people of color affect our decisions. The aspiration to impartiality is just that—it's an aspiration because it denies the fact that we are by our experiences making different choices than others....
>
> Justice O'Connor has often been cited as saying that a wise old man and a wise old woman will reach the same conclusions in deciding cases...I am also not so sure that I agree with the statement. First, as Professor Martha Minow has noted, there can never be a universal definition of wise. Second, I would hope that a wise Latina woman with the richness of her experiences would more often than not reach a better conclusion than a white male who hasn't lived that life.[5]

President Obama urged quick action on the nomination, but the press raised the specter of failed confirmations of the past, wondering if a similar ideological showdown was looming.[6] A leading Republican senator summed up his party's planned line of questioning: "Do I want a judge that objectively applies the law to the facts?"[7]

The Senate Judiciary Committee began its proceedings on the nomination in mid-July. Sotomayor rehearsed her testimony and her answers to expected questions in the week before the hearings. Addressing her critics, Sotomayor affirmed her judicial legacy, stating that in her seventeen years on the bench, she had "applied the law to the facts at hand."[8]

In the end, the vote in the Senate Judiciary Committee was without much drama or surprise. In a 13–6 vote, with one Republican joining the unanimous Democrats, the committee approved her nomination and sent it to the full Senate, wherein an expected filibuster-proof confirmation vote was all but certain. On August 9, the Senate confirmed Sotomayor's appointment to the Supreme Court by a vote of 68–31. Like other supporters gathered at a "vote watch" party nearby, law student Lucy Flores was jubilant, but she offered words of caution for those who might think that Sotomayor's confirmation marked an end, rather than just a step forward. "It shouldn't be a historic moment," she said. "Everyone of all races and all backgrounds should be able to get to where she is based on their ability and their desire."[9]

On Saturday, August 8, Sotomayor took the judicial oath of office, promising to "administer justice without respect to persons, and do equal right to the poor and the rich" as the nation's newest member of the Supreme Court. As a member of the Court, Sotomayor would be carrying the hopes and aspirations of many Americans on her shoulders. She would also be joining an institution that itself carries the burdens of adjudicating Americans' claims upon their rights and defining and protecting the Constitution that established a nation.

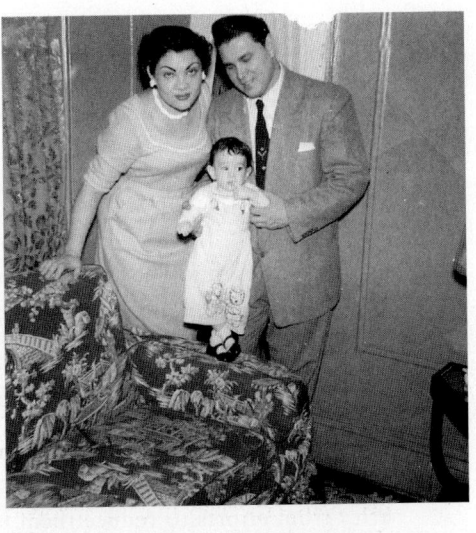

This undated family photograph shows Judge Sonia Sotomayor as a child with her mother Celina Sotomayor, left, and father Juan Luis Sotomayor, right. Both of her parents immigrated to the United States from Puerto Rico during World War II. Sonia Sotomayor was born and raised in New York. She has spoken about her experiences as a "Newyorkrican" and the role of identity in judicial decision making. The White House via Getty Images

THE CONSTITUTION CASTS THE JUDICIARY AS THE WEAKEST BRANCH

- Understand the constitutional powers and structure of the judiciary.

The delegates to the Constitutional Convention spent much less time debating the structure and powers of the federal judiciary than they did hammering out the design of the legislative and executive branches. They were in general agreement that the judicial branch would be the weakest of the three, lacking an equivalent to Congress's power of the purse and the president's power as commander in chief. Second, the delegates agreed that the judiciary should retain a degree of independence from the other two branches—especially in the processes of appointment and removal of judges—though the specific details were not worked out until the summer of 1787.[10] That federal judges should have tenure with "good Behavior" was generally agreed upon, as was the need to protect their salaries from efforts to reduce them by an unhappy or vengeful Congress.[11] Both of these protections made it into the final document.[12] The question of appointment, however, remained unresolved until late in the convention with the delegates finally approving a process through which the president would nominate federal judges and the Senate through its role of advice and consent would confirm the nominations.[13]

Finally, a diverse group of delegates agreed that the judiciary should have the power to strike down laws that were in violation of the Constitution. Unfortunately, the federal "courts were not *expressly* given the power to rule on constitutionality," an instance of "carelessness" that would have a profound impact on the court.[14]

The Constitution Grants the Federal Judiciary Supremacy over Lower State Courts

This issue of constitutionality and the judiciary is not the only instance in which the text of the Constitution is less than thorough. Only the highest level of the federal judiciary—the Supreme Court—is actually described in the document, while the establishment of lower federal courts was left in the hands of Congress: "The judicial Power of the United States, shall be vested in one supreme Court, and in such inferior Courts as the Congress may from time to time ordain and establish."[15]

On one point the Constitution was clear: the federal judiciary, and the Supreme Court in particular, was to be the highest judicial power in the land: "The judicial power shall extend to all Cases, in Law and Equity, arising under this Constitution, the laws of the United States, and Treaties made, or which shall be made, under their Authority."[16] This judicial power, when combined with the supremacy clause of the Constitution, which declared the "Constitution, and the Laws of the United States" to be "the supreme Law of the Land; and [instructed that] the Judges in every State shall be bound thereby," established the federal judiciary as supreme to those of the states.[17]

In defining the scope of the power of the federal judiciary, the Constitution also (briefly) describes one of the most fundamental characteristics of any court: its jurisdiction, or its authority to hear and decide on specific cases.[18] Although there are many types and classifications of jurisdiction, the two most relevant to the study of the American judicial system are original and appellate jurisdiction. If a court has **original jurisdiction** in a case, then that court acts as the originating court, with the authority to hear the case first and to establish the facts pertaining to it. Courts with original jurisdiction are commonly referred to as trial courts. If a court has **appellate jurisdiction** over a case, then it possesses the authority to review the decision of a lower court

Members of the U.S. Supreme Court pose for a group photograph in June 2017. In the front row, from left, Associate Justice Ruth Bader Ginsburg, Associate Justice Anthony M. Kennedy, Chief Justice of the United States John G. Roberts, Associate Justice Clarence Thomas, and Associate Justice Stephen Breyer. Standing, from left, Associate Justice Elena Kagan, Associate Justice Samuel Alito Jr., Associate Justice Sonia Sotomayor, and Associate Justice Neil Gorsuch. Olivier Douliery/picture-alliance/dpa/AP Images

and, if it so decides, to revise that decision. Courts operating under appellate jurisdiction generally focus on the lower courts' actions and procedures without finding facts on their own.

During Ratification, Concerns about Judicial Abuse of Power Were Addressed

During the ratification debates, those who opposed the Constitution, the Anti-Federalists, raised concerns about potential abuses of power by the proposed federal judiciary. Where the courts were concerned, Anti-Federalists feared the growth in the power of the national government and an associated subjugation of the rights of states and individuals by an increasingly powerful federal judiciary. In granting the power to overturn legislation to the Supreme Court, Anti-Federalists argued that the nation would run the risk of unconstrained justices imposing their own views of what is constitutional and what is not.

In *Federalist* No. 78, Alexander Hamilton sought to reassure skeptical Anti-Federalists and others that the planned federal judiciary would not trample upon their rights and liberties because it would neither want to nor be able to. In the first place, Hamilton argued, members of the federal judiciary—because of the process of their selection and their lifetime tenure—would stand apart from politics and the dangers that politics might pose to liberties and be able to "secure a steady, upright, and impartial administration of the laws."[19] Second, the federal judiciary was weak—indeed it would be "the least dangerous" branch.[20] Compared to the power of the executive branch's sword and the legislature's purse, Hamilton reassured, the federal judiciary—exercising only the power of judgment and located outside of the arena of political struggle—was not to be feared. He argued that it was in fact the judiciary that needed protection from encroachment on its limited powers by the other two branches.

Congress Filled in the Blanks with the Judiciary Act of 1789

Taking up its constitutional authority to establish "inferior Courts" in the federal judiciary, the first Congress passed the Judiciary Act of 1789 to flesh out "the nature and the organization" of the court system.[21] Only the chief justice of the United States is mentioned in the Constitution; the document does not specify the number of justices in the Court, instead leaving that decision to Congress. The Judiciary Act added five associate judges to the Supreme Court, bringing the total number of justices to six, and it instructed that the Court was to meet in session twice a year in February and August. (Although the number of justices has varied throughout the nation's history, it has been set at nine since 1869.) The act also established two lower tiers to the federal judiciary, as only the Supreme Court had been set out in the Constitution, though changes have been made to their organization since.

The Judiciary Act of 1789 also created the office of attorney general "to prosecute and conduct all suits in the Supreme Court in which the United States shall be concerned, and to give his advice and opinion upon questions of law when required to by the president of the United States."[22] Today, the office of the solicitor general represents the president in the Supreme Court, while the attorney general is head of the Justice Department. Finally, the act gave the Supreme Court the power to review and reverse actions of the state courts if it found them to be in conflict with the Constitution—a power tied to both the Constitution's description of the scope of judicial power and the supremacy clause.

WHAT HAVE I LEARNED?

1. The delegates to the Constitutional Convention spent less time debating and discussing the federal judiciary than they did the other two branches.

   a. True
   b. False

2. The combination of language in Article 3, which describes the federal judiciary, and the supremacy clause of the Constitution _____.

   a. Sets the federal judiciary as superior to the state judiciaries in all cases in the nation
   b. Sets the state judiciaries as superior to the federal judiciary in all cases in the nation
   c. Leaves the question of supremacy unresolved
   d. Establishes the Constitution as supreme with the federal judiciary superior in constitutional matters, federal laws, and treaties

3. What concerned Anti-Federalists about the proposed federal judiciary?

4. What was Alexander Hamilton's response to these concerns in *Federalist* No. 78?

....

Answer Key: 1. a; 2. d; 3. Answers should discuss fears over federal judicial power as a threat to state power; 4. Answers should include Hamilton's argument that the federal judiciary would be neither political nor powerful.

THE "TRIAL" OF JOHN MARSHALL ESTABLISHED THE PRINCIPLE OF JUDICIAL REVIEW

In 2017, perhaps no issue in American government is more important than the confirmations of Supreme Court justices. In April 2017, after Republicans in the Senate had changed the institution's rules to prevent a filibuster of a Supreme Court nominee, Neil Gorsuch joined the bench. As a replacement for the deceased, and highly conservative, Antonin Scalia, that appointment did not cause as much concern as future ones might. If President Trump, however, is able to replace a more liberal or moderate justice, however, it might have consequences for American policy for decades. But why? Aren't justices supposed to be insulated from politics? That is a very important question to which we will now turn.

- Explain how the case of *Marbury v. Madison* led to the development of judicial review.

The Election of 1800 Gave Rise to a Federalist Judicial Strategy

The election of 1800 was one of the nastiest in American history. The seeds of faction that had been planted during George Washington's presidency came into full bloom in the late 1790s as political parties took root. President John Adams, once Washington's vice president and now seeking his own second term in office, had allied with Alexander Hamilton, who had been Washington's secretary of the Treasury, under the banner of the Federalists. In Hamilton, Adams saw a partner who would help him promote a strong national government, especially in the area of economic policy and banking.[23]

They squared off against Thomas Jefferson and the Republican Party.[24] They mistrusted the Federalists' motives and the reach of Hamilton's economic policies. As each side sought support for its views in Congress and in the state legislatures, America's first political parties increasingly gained power, like new planets pulling in more and more supporters into their political gravity. Throughout the election, Republicans accused Adams and the Federalists of trying to bring a British-style monarchy to America. For their part, the Federalists accused Jefferson and his fellow Republicans of being too close to France and pointed to the chaos that had unfolded in that country in the wake of the French Revolution. Both campaigns were bitter, partisan, and personal right up to the election.

And then there was a tie: Jefferson, the Republican, had unexpectedly tied for votes in the electoral system of the time not with John Adams but with Aaron Burr.

The decision about who would become president would move from the Electoral College to the House of Representatives.

Months of post-election discord followed with accusations of voting irregularities flying and partisan rancor so intense that some feared a civil war would break out. Thomas Jefferson was finally elected president of the United States by the House on the thirty-sixth ballot. Jefferson, in his inaugural address, sought to calm tensions throughout the nation. "We are all republicans," he said. "We are all federalists."[25] Nonetheless, the Federalist Party paid dearly.

The election of 1800 had far-reaching implications. John Adams lost the election, and the Federalist Party unraveled. In addition, friendships and political alliances were fractured. Here, Alexander Hamilton and Aaron Burr, Thomas Jefferson's vice president, prepare to duel in July 1804. Hamilton was killed in the duel. Bettmann / Contributor

It had been soundly defeated in both the presidential election and in the congressional elections. Its days in power were numbered.

Trying to preserve their influence within the national government, the Federalists turned to the federal judiciary, the one branch where they might endure, given that the Constitution grants federal judges lifetime job security.[26] In the waning weeks of Adams's administration, the Federalists in the legislature and the executive branches made several changes to the federal judiciary in order to cement their power.[27]

With the Judiciary Act of 1801, Federalists in Congress changed the Supreme Court's schedule, reduced the size of the Court from six to five justices, and reorganized the lower federal courts in such a way as to create sixteen vacancies that were promptly filled by Adams's administration. The reduction in the size of the Supreme Court could not force a justice out; that would have been unconstitutional. What it did do was ensure that incoming president Jefferson would not be able to fill the next vacancy with someone the Federalists presumed would be a Republican.

Just before leaving office, Adams set about filling the vacancies created by the Judiciary Act of 1801. He also set about building up the administration of the nation's new capital in Washington, D.C. (the seat of government had been recently relocated from Philadelphia in 1800). There were many good jobs to fill there, including justices of the peace.[28] One candidate for one of these new jobs was a Mr. William Marbury.

Less than two weeks before he signed the Judiciary Act of 1801 into law, the Senate confirmed Adams's appointment of his secretary of state, John Marshall, to be the new chief justice of the United States.[29] Marshall was a Federalist and an experienced politician. For the last weeks of the Adams administration, Marshall was also both chief justice and secretary of state. He had a lot on his plate—fatefully, as it turned out, perhaps too much. In the scramble to complete the paperwork before the Republicans took the reins of government, some of the commissions Adams had signed, including one for William Marbury, had not been delivered and were still sitting on Secretary of State Marshall's desk when Adams's term expired at midnight.

Upon assuming office, President Jefferson did deliver the commissions to some of those hastily approved appointees after he took office. But William Marbury and several others did not receive theirs. Marbury, along with three other men, brought suit against Jefferson's Secretary of State James Madison, requesting that the Court issue a writ of mandamus ("we command") ordering Madison to deliver their commissions as justices of the peace.[30] The men argued that all of the required steps in their appointments had been properly taken: President Adams had nominated them, the Senate had confirmed their nominations, and the commissions had been signed and affixed with the presidential seal. Marshall's failure to deliver the commissions, they insisted, constituted a serious breach of etiquette and tradition.

Chief Justice John Marshall Confronted Politics and the Power of the Supreme Court

As he contemplated how the Court would respond to the demands of Marbury and his fellow would-be justices, Marshall confronted two powerful and related sets of questions about the role of the federal judiciary in the life of the American Republic—the same two questions with which we began this chapter: How powerful is the federal judiciary? And how political is it? In *Marbury v. Madison* (1803), the Court found itself involved in an intense partisan battle between the defeated Federalists and the victorious Republicans.[31] That Congress and the executive were highly political branches was obvious to everyone, especially after the election of 1800. The judiciary, however, was supposed to be different. It was constrained and defined by law, not politics. How should such an institution handle its role in the larger political life of the nation?

Chief Justice Marshall could not ignore either of these considerations; both had to be addressed. If his Court waded into the political battle of the time forcefully—ordering Jefferson's administration to deliver the commissions—he risked being rebuffed by the president or even impeached by the Republican-controlled Congress. Marshall *could* choose not to enter the battle. He could deny Marbury's petition, thus preventing a confrontation with Jefferson and his Republicans. However, to do so might send a message that the judiciary was weak in the face of powerful political forces, which could deal a blow to its power, prestige, and independence.[32] Marshall was in a bind and he knew it. In the decision that he ultimately delivered, Marshall noted the "peculiar delicacy of this case."[33] The way in which Marshall dealt with this dilemma continues to shape the role of the Supreme Court in American political life to this day. The two questions with which he wrestled, however, have not gone away: How political is the federal judiciary? How powerful is it?

Marbury v. Madison Led to the Establishment of Judicial Review

Because of the changes to the Supreme Court's schedule brought about by the Judiciary Act of 1801, Marbury and his associates had to wait for nearly two years before the Court heard their request to issue a writ of mandamus to Secretary of State Madison. Both of Chief Justice Marshall's apparent options in the case seemed likely to diminish the power of his judiciary. Either he could order Jefferson's administration to deliver the commissions and risk being refused or ignored or he could decide not to challenge the president and risk looking weak and timid.

Marshall chose neither option. Instead, in a tactically brilliant move, he broke the decision before him into three separate questions. First, the chief justice asked if the men were entitled to their commissions. To this first question, Marshall, in his opinion, answered "yes." The presidential signing of such commissions is the last formal act, and that had been done. Delivery of the commissions, Marshall noted, "is a practice directed by convenience, but not by law."[34] Once this part of the decision was established, Marshall considered whether or not a legal remedy involving the courts was available to Marbury and his fellow plaintiffs. To this second question, Marshall also answered in the affirmative, arguing that "the individual who considers himself [so] injured has a right to resort to the laws of the country for a remedy."[35]

So far, it seemed that Marshall was going to take on Jefferson's administration with all of the risks that such a strategy entailed. But he did not. Instead, Marshall presented a third question for his Court to consider: Were Marbury and the other plaintiffs entitled to the remedy that they sought—the writs of mandamus? To this question, Marshall answered no. The power to issue these kinds of writs in this particular instance, he declared, had been improperly given to the Court by a section of the Judiciary Act of 1789.[36] Though the reasoning is a bit technical, Marshall argued that when Congress granted the Court the authority "to issue writs of mandamus to public officers," it was attempting to expand the scope of the original jurisdiction of the Court, which Congress cannot do. Only the Constitution can. Therefore, the Court did not have the power to give Marbury the remedy he sought.

In stating the inability of his Court to legitimately provide the sought-after remedy, Marshall also found that the part of the Judiciary Act that tried to give his Court such power was in violation of the Constitution and, therefore, invalid: "[A] law repugnant to the Constitution is void, and that courts, as well as other departments, are bound by that instrument."[37]

It proved to be a bold strategic move. Madison did not have to deliver the commissions. Marshall, however, had just asserted what the Constitution had failed to lay out in its brief treatment of the third branch: The Supreme Court had the power of **judicial review**, which is the authority of a court to review laws and actions of other branches and levels of government to decide if they are in conflict with the highest law of the land—in this case, the Constitution—and, if they are, to declare those laws or actions invalid.

In establishing the precedent for judicial review over federal laws, Marshall expanded the Court's responsibility in **constitutional interpretation** in which the judiciary reviews laws and actions in light of the meaning of the Constitution. In exercising judicial review, according to Marshall's logic,

Abigail Adams, wife of President John Adams and correspondent to Thomas Jefferson. Their conversations via letters outline Jefferson's fear that Marshall's decision could make the judicial branch "despotic." The Granger Collection, New York

the Court does not place itself above the other two branches; it is coequal to them, and the Constitution is supreme to all three.

President Jefferson had been a student and practitioner of the law, and he clearly understood the implications of Marshall's decision. Jefferson argued that Marshall had set a dangerous precedent. In a letter to Abigail Adams in 1804, Jefferson worried, "But the opinion which gives to the judges the right to decide what laws are constitutional, and what not, not only for themselves in their own sphere of action, but for the legislature and executive also, in their spheres, would make the judiciary a despotic branch."[38]

Under the decades-long tenure of Marshall, the Supreme Court used the tool of judicial review to weigh in on the constitutionality of several state laws, declaring some invalid. Marshall, however, never again used the power of judicial review to strike down an act of Congress. It would be more than fifty years before the Court took such an action again, in its infamous decision in *Dred Scott v. Sandford* (1857). In this case, Justice Roger Taney and his Court overturned the Missouri Compromise, deepening national divisions over the future of slavery[39]

In the end, William Marbury and his fellow job seekers never received their commissions, and the power of judicial review and the role of the Court in constitutional interpretation remain highly debated issues to this day. Before we can explore the implications of this claimed authority, however, it is necessary to examine the structure and operation of the American judicial system.

THE AMERICAN LEGAL SYSTEM IS DEFINED BY FEDERALISM

Each of the two levels in the federalist system—the nation and the states—operates its own system of courts, with a single federal judiciary for the nation and separate state judiciaries in each of the fifty states. While the structure of American federalism defines the basic organization of the nation's legal system, the dual systems of federal and state courts share in common the tradition of the **adversarial system** of justice in which the opposing

- Describe the structure of the federal judiciary and the American legal system.

parties present their sides of a case in the most persuasive way possible. In this system, a **plaintiff** is the party bringing a complaint and the **defendant** is the party accused of wrongdoing.[40]

Cases Are Divided into Criminal and Civil Types

Whether or not a specific court has jurisdiction over a specific case may depend on whether that court is a state or a federal court, the details of the case, or where that court lies within the overall structure of the federal or state court system. Both state and federal courts have jurisdiction over two categories of law, criminal and civil (see Figure 12.1).[41] **Criminal law** covers actions determined to harm the community itself, such as committing an act of violence against another person.[42] In a criminal case, the state or federal government acts as the plaintiff and tries to prove the guilt of the defendant, the party accused of a crime. Although many acts (such as murder or assault) are considered to be criminal offenses in all of the states, some acts (such as gambling or recreational use of marijuana) are legal in some states but not in others. As of 2017, for example, an adult in several states could lawfully use marijuana recreationally according to state law (subject to certain restrictions) but in doing so be in violation of federal law, presenting a tricky issue for American federalism.[43] States may also vary in the punishments handed out for those convicted of similar crimes.

In 1992 an all-white California jury found four white Los Angeles police officers not guilty of assaulting Rodney King, an African American man, during a traffic stop and arrest, much of which was captured on videotape by a witness. That verdict was quickly followed by rioting and heightened racial tensions throughout the city. The next year, a federal jury found two of the officers guilty of violating King's civil rights through the application of excessive force or a refusal to stop the exercise of excessive force during the original incident.

Being convicted under a criminal statute leads to some form of punishment, such as fines, imprisonment, or, in some cases, the death penalty.[44] Most criminal cases are resolved through the process of **plea bargaining**. In this process, a defendant in a criminal case agrees to plead guilty to a lesser charge than the one brought by the prosecutors in order to reduce his or her punishment. Plea bargaining is also used in civil cases. As is the case with defendants during the arrest and trial phases, those ultimately convicted of crimes have constitutional protections, specifically against the imposition of "cruel and unusual punishments" (Eighth Amendment). Whether or not the death penalty—or specific methods of instituting it—constitutes a violation of the Eighth Amendment's protections continues to be debated today.

Noncriminal law, commonly referred to as **civil law**, covers cases involving private rights and relationships between individuals and groups. In a civil case, the plaintiff is the party who argues that she or he has been wronged, and the defendant is the party accused of violating a person's rights or breaking an agreement. While in criminal cases a government (state or federal) is always the plaintiff, in civil cases the plaintiff may be a government or an individual. A jury or a judge might decide civil cases, though most are settled without a formal verdict either before the case goes to trial or during the proceedings.

FIGURE 12.1

Comparing Criminal and Civil Law

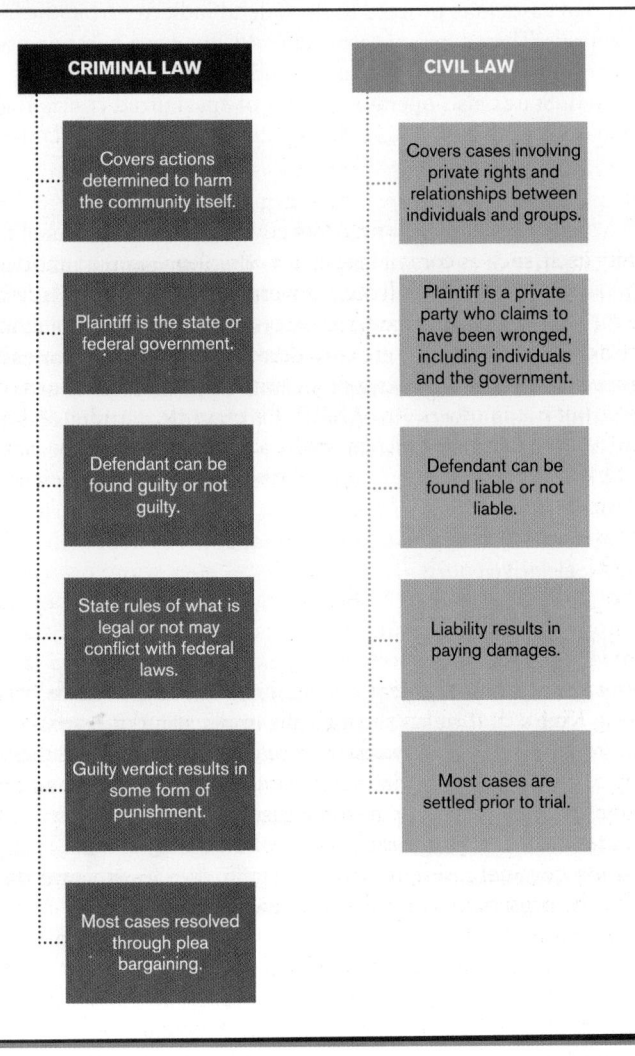

CRIMINAL LAW

Covers actions determined to harm the community itself.

Plaintiff is the state or federal government.

Defendant can be found guilty or not guilty.

State rules of what is legal or not may conflict with federal laws.

Guilty verdict results in some form of punishment.

Most cases resolved through plea bargaining.

CIVIL LAW

Covers cases involving private rights and relationships between individuals and groups.

Plaintiff is a private party who claims to have been wronged, including individuals and the government.

Defendant can be found liable or not liable.

Liability results in paying damages.

Most cases are settled prior to trial.

State Courts Handle the Majority of Cases in the United States

While our focus is on the federal judiciary, it is important to note that state courts handle the vast majority of court cases in the United States. While states may vary in how their judicial systems are structured and organized—including how judges are selected—the state court systems share a few common traits. State judicial systems handle both criminal and civil cases. Each state has a system of trial courts that does most of the work of the state's judiciary, handles cases arising under that state's laws, and possesses original jurisdiction. More than half of the states have an intermediate system of appellate courts that operate with appellate jurisdiction. Each state has at least one state supreme court, which acts as the highest court in that state's system and as the final level of appeal.[45] A select group of cases may proceed to the federal judiciary from the highest state court of appeals. These types of cases generally involve a question arising under the Constitution, such as a claim that an individual's constitutional rights have been violated. States also operate systems of specialized courts that typically handle issues like traffic violations, family disputes, and small claims.

Most of the Impactful Cases Are Handled by the Federal Judiciary

While the majority of cases are handled by the state courts, many of the most impactful happen at the federal level. The federal judiciary includes two types of courts. The term *constitutional courts* refer to the Supreme Court and the lower levels of the federal judiciary that the Constitution authorized Congress to create in Article 3. Legislative courts are specialized courts created by Congress under its authority in Article 1 to handle matters such as tax and trade law. While all federal justices must be nominated by the president and confirmed by a majority vote in the Senate, justices in the legislative courts, unlike those in the constitutional courts, serve for fixed terms. Our focus in this chapter will be on the constitutional court system rather than on the specialized legislative courts.

The Federal District Courts

The constitutional court system is structured as a three-layered pyramid (see Figure 12.2). At the bottom are the nation's **federal district courts**. Congress created the district courts in the Judiciary Act of 1789. In most federal cases, district courts act as the trial courts and possess original jurisdiction. As of 2017, there were ninety-four district courts in the United States, and each state had at least one. District court boundaries do not cut across state lines. The district courts handle most of the work of the federal courts, and their cases are heard by a single federal judge. Cases heard in a district court may or may not include a jury; the Constitution guarantees the right to a jury trial in all federal criminal cases (Sixth Amendment) and in some civil cases (Seventh Amendment).

The Appellate Courts

The **federal courts of appeals** occupy the middle level of the constitutional courts. There are thirteen courts of appeals; eleven have jurisdiction over regionally based "circuits," one has jurisdiction over the District of Columbia (which handles appeals involving federal agencies), and the thirteenth handles cases arising under international trade and patent law. The courts of appeals exercise appellate jurisdiction only, reviewing decisions made by the federal district courts and certain specialized federal courts (see Figure 12.3). The federal appellate courts have, as their name implies, appellate jurisdiction only and are staffed with justices specifically appointed to that level of the federal judiciary.

FIGURE 12.2

The Modern Court System

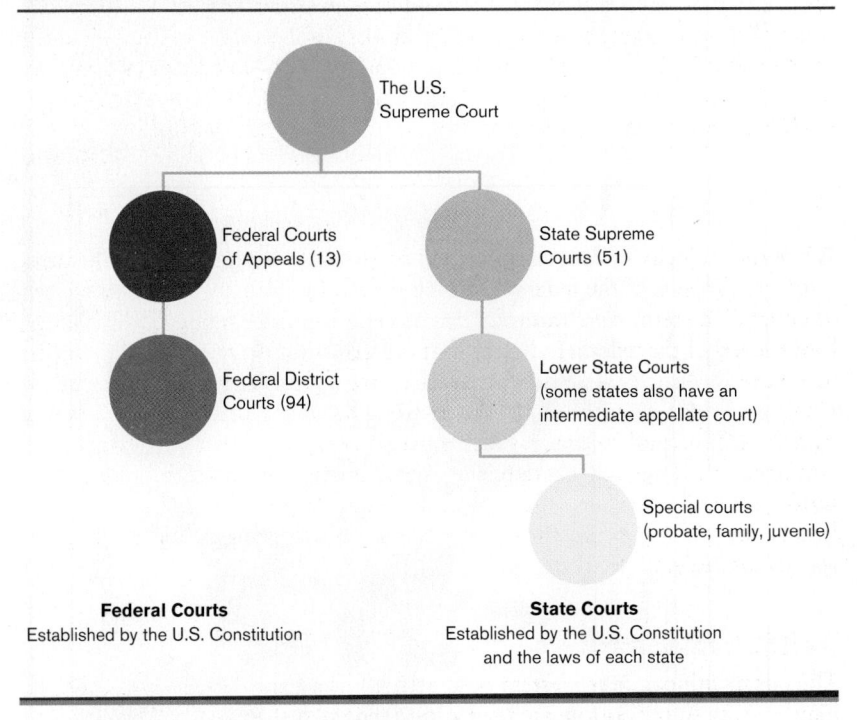

Federal Courts
Established by the U.S. Constitution

State Courts
Established by the U.S. Constitution
and the laws of each state

The Supreme Court

At the top of the federal judicial system is the U.S. Supreme Court, which, as the Constitution established, is the highest court in the nation. Part of the Court's intended purpose was to resolve differences between the states, which had not effectively been provided for in the government created by the Articles of Confederation. The Court also acts to resolve differing interpretations of the law in the lower federal courts. Each justice has a small number of clerks to assist in selecting, researching, and issuing decisions in Court cases. The Court meets in session roughly nine months out of the year, beginning on the first Monday in October. Those cases still on the docket (the schedule of cases to be heard) when a term ends continue to the next term's docket.

Cases in which the Supreme Court exercises original jurisdiction are few and are described in Article 3 of the Constitution: "In all Cases affecting Ambassadors, other public Ministers and Consuls, and those in which a State shall be a Party, the supreme Court shall have original jurisdiction."[46] In all other cases in which the federal judiciary has jurisdiction, the Court possesses appellate jurisdiction only. In addition to having appellate jurisdiction over all federal cases, the Court possesses appellate jurisdiction over certain state cases, especially those involving a federal issue.

FIGURE 12.3

Map of the District and Appellate Courts

Source: U.S. Courts, "Geographic Boundaries of United States Courts of Appeals and United States District Courts," www.uscourts.gov/uscourts/images/CircuitMap.pdf.

Cases Involving Federal Questions
Proceed through the Federal Judiciary

Those cases that begin in the federal judiciary—in which the federal courts have original jurisdiction—must fall into one of three categories. The first category is cases in which the federal government is a party in a dispute. Second, the federal judiciary possesses original jurisdiction in civil suits involving parties from two different states in which the amount of money in question is more than $75,000. Finally—and, for our purposes, most importantly—the federal judiciary possesses original jurisdiction in cases that involve a federal question, such as a case in which a party files a claim of violations of rights under the Constitution, a dispute involving a federal treaty, or a case involving a federal law. Cases involving federal questions may be either criminal or civil cases. State cases that proceed to the Supreme Court also involve federal questions. Many of the most important federal cases in American history—and most of the cases that we consider in this book—are those involving charges of violations of constitutional rights and liberties.

As the courts of original jurisdiction in most federal cases, the federal district courts act as the trial courts, finding facts and delivering opinions on the case. Litigants who lose in a district court have an option to appeal the decision to the appellate courts in which case the case moves up to the next level.[47] Most federal cases, however, go no farther than the district courts.

Appellate courts possess appellate jurisdiction only and review cases on appeal. Rather than finding facts, the appellate courts focus on how the decision of the district court was rendered and if that decision was appropriate in the context of the law. With cases typically heard by three-judge panels, an appellate court has several options. It may refuse to hear the appeal in which case the decision of the district court (or specialized federal court) holds. Litigants whose appeal is refused by the appellate court may still appeal to the Supreme Court, though their odds of receiving a hearing by the Court are very small.

If it decides to hear a case, an appeals court may choose to affirm the judgment of the lower court, confirming that court's ruling. It may reverse the decision; if this is the case, it is typically based on questions of how the lower court proceeded or applied the law. Finally, it may remand the case back to the lower court for reconsideration, again often because the appellate court judges had questions about procedure or application of the law. These options are not mutually exclusive for any one case. The court could affirm part of a lower court's decision in a particular case, reverse part of it, and remand yet another part, though this is far from a common outcome. The side that loses in an appellate court has the right to appeal to the Supreme Court, but there is no guarantee that its case will be heard. If not, the decision of the appellate court stands, though it applies only to that circuit.[48]

The Supreme Court: The Decision to Take Cases on Appeal

In exercising its authority of appellate jurisdiction, the Supreme Court is confronted with two questions, the first of which actually determines the outcome of roughly 99 percent of the appeals before it. First, the Court decides whether or not to hear the case. Second, if it does decide to hear the case, it issues its decision based on the merits of the case and applicable law. The vast majority of cases heard on appeal in the Court originate with a litigant who has lost in a lower court filing a petition to have his or her case heard. Almost all such petitions are denied, however. The modern Court receives, on average, between eight thousand and nine thousand such petitions a year but hears less than 1 percent of these cases, or about seventy to eighty. In recent decades, the Court has gained a much greater degree of control over its docket.

A petitioner who wishes to have the Court accept his or her case files an argument with the Court in a written **brief**, which presents the arguments for the appeal. Not everyone can file a legitimate brief before the Court. In addition to certain other technical requirements about the facts and merits of a case, a petitioner must demonstrate that he or she has **standing**, which involves demonstrating an actual or imminent harm from a law or action in question. As we will discuss later in the chapter, the need to establish standing acts as a limitation on the power of the Court to shape national public policy. The opposing party in a case may also file a brief with the Court laying out her or his arguments.[49]

As the Constitution offers little guidance on which cases the Court does or does not take, justices have adopted the custom of the rule of four, which simply means that it will generally hear a case if four or more justices vote to do so. If it decides to hear a case, the Court issues a **writ of certiorari** (from the Latin "to be more informed") to the lower court for the records of the case, a process that is commonly referred to as certiorari, or "granting cert." As discussed earlier, very few petitions for cert are granted. In its own rules, the Court makes it clear that the hurdle for having a case heard on appeal is high: "Review on a writ of certiorari is not a matter of right, but of judicial discretion. A petition of a writ of certiorari will be granted only for compelling reasons."[50]

The most important factor in the decision to grant or deny cert is if there is confusion about or alternate interpretations of a law or previous ruling among or between lower-level federal courts or state supreme courts. Cases presenting a federal question are also more likely to be heard. The Court does not, however, act as the corrector of all lower court mistakes in finding fact or applying the law when these errors do not present or affect important federal concerns.

Interested parties who are not plaintiffs or defendants may also try to signal to the Court their interest in the decision to grant cert or on the merits of the case should cert be granted. Plaintiffs and defendants are not the only parties that may file briefs. An interested party (such as an interest group) may also submit its opinions to the Court in what is called an amicus curiae brief (from the Latin, "friend of the court").[51] The volume, authorship, and content of these briefs can act as a signal to the Court about how the public or interest groups view an issue.[52] An especially important filer of amici curiae briefs is the **solicitor general**, who is appointed by the president to represent the federal government in the Court. An indication to the Court that the government (or the president, specifically) is interested in a case can be a powerful signal both on the question of whether or not the Court should hear a particular case and on its ruling should it decide to do so.

The preferences of the justices may also play a role in the decision to grant cert. After all, the final decision rests on the votes of the justices themselves. While scholars continue to debate the role that justices' political or policy preferences play in their decisions (which we will examine later in the chapter), a justice who supports a particular view on an issue before the Court must consider how the other justices are likely to vote on the merits of the case. Justices are well aware that the outcome of a Supreme Court case can set a **precedent**, or a judicial decision that acts as a basis for deciding similar cases in the future. An individual justice may be more or less likely to grant cert if there is a perceived likelihood that the outcome might be a precedent that the justice desires or wishes to avoid.

The Supreme Court: Considering and Deciding upon Cases

If the Supreme Court decides to grant cert to a case, it requests briefs from both sides laying out their full arguments. Court clerks will assist the justices in reviewing these briefs. The case is then scheduled for **oral argument** before the assembled justices, during which each side gets a fixed amount of time (typically half an hour) to present. In exceptional circumstances, filers of amicus curiae briefs may also be given time during oral arguments, but this is not common. During this phase, the justices are not passive but frequently interrupt and question the lawyers as they present, though some justices tend to interrupt and question more than others. Cameras are not allowed in the courtroom during oral arguments, though sketch artists and audio recordings are.

Scholars debate how influential oral arguments are in shaping justices' rulings in a case.[53] This process, however, is often of intense interest to members of the public, who analyze the content of justices' questions for clues as to how those justices will ultimately vote. As most of what follows the oral argument phase happens in secret, court watchers have few other means to try to divine the Court's decisions ahead of time. After oral argument, the case proceeds to judicial conference in which the justices meet and vote in secret; not even their clerks are present. The process can go on for months (on and off, of course), and individual justices can and do change their votes during this phase.

Finally, the Court issues its decision. The majority opinion consists of the ruling—and the logic behind it—of the majority of justices in the case. When it acts under appellate jurisdiction (which is most of the time), the Court has the same options as other appellate courts. It may affirm, reverse, or remand back to the lower court the case (or certain rulings within a case).[54] The decision and the majority opinion are binding and serve to guide lower courts and future courts in handling similar cases. If the chief justice is in the majority, then he or she selects the author of the majority opinion. If not, the most senior member of the majority does so. The power to choose the author of an opinion can be a useful strategic tool as even justices who vote together may have differences in their interpretations of certain points brought up in the case. If there is no majority, which typically occurs when many justices disagree on the logic behind a ruling, then a plurality opinion will be written that expresses the views of the largest number of justices who voted together.

A justice voting with the majority may also write a concurring opinion (often called a concurrence) explaining the reasoning behind his or her particular vote. More than one justice may collaborate on a concurrence. Concurrences are more common when a justice has some differences in logic or reasoning with the other members of the majority but not enough to cause that justice to side against them. A justice who voted with the minority may write a dissenting opinion, called a dissent, also alone or with other justices. These opinions do not carry the weight of the Court behind them (since the justice writing the dissent was on the losing side). However, if a future court should revisit a precedent with a thought to perhaps overturning it, a dissent may provide a useful record and analysis of why at least one justice thought the Court got it wrong the first time. See Figure 12.4.

Appointment to the Federal Judiciary Is Often Political

While individual states vary in how they select their judges, all federal judges must be nominated by the president and confirmed by a majority vote in the Senate. As federal judges are appointed for life—assuming "good behavior"—successfully placing individuals on the federal bench is one of the most important things that a president can do. Trying to preserve the influence of their defeated party after the election of 1800 was what drove John Adams and the Federalists to try to pack the federal judiciary with as many of their people as possible.

While most district court nominees are approved, the confirmations of appellate and Supreme Court judges have become increasingly affected by partisan political battles in recent years, though there have been many other periods in American history where this has also been the case. Part of the reason that things tend to run more smoothly at the district court level is the custom of senatorial courtesy, in which presidents (and the high-ranking members of the Justice Department who do much of the actual work of identifying candidates) consult with senators from the state in which the vacant district judgeship is located, especially if those senators are from the president's political party.

The higher two levels of the federal judiciary often witness more direct presidential involvement in the nomination process, and these nominations are more likely to be caught up in partisan battles. While most Supreme Court nominees are confirmed, their confirmation hearings can and have often involved intense scrutiny of the nominee. In addition, recent confirmation votes in the Senate have tended to be closer than those in decades prior. As with other presidential nominees subject to Senate approval, federal judicial nominees have sometimes found their paths blocked by a filibuster or the threat of one. That obstacle began to go away in 2013 when a Democrat-controlled Senate changed the chamber's rules to prevent filibusters of federal

FIGURE 12.4

How Cases Move through the Court System

1 WHERE CASES BEGIN

FEDERAL COURT SYSTEM
- Federal government is party to dispute
- Must possess original jurisdiction in civil cases with two parties from different states where more than $75,000 is in question

STATE COURT SYSTEM
- Either civil or criminal cases involving federal questions

2 DISTRICT COURT LEVEL

FEDERAL DISTRICT COURTS find facts, deliver opinions

Most cases end here

3 COURT OF APPEALS LEVEL

Litigants may move to APPELLATE COURTS

Focus is on how the decision of the district court was rendered and if that decision was appropriate in the context of the law

Case can be...
- ...refused, in which case the district court decision stands
- ...affirmed, confirming the district court decision
- ...reversed, overturning the district court decision
- ...remanded, sent back to the lower court for reconsideration
- some combination of the above

Losing side may **appeal** to the U.S. Supreme Court

4 APPEALING THE SUPREME COURT

Upon appeal, the SUPREME COURT may...
- refuse to hear the case (most common outcome)
- decide to hear the case

petitioners with standing file briefs, arguments for their appeal and deliver a decision based on merits of the case and applicable law

interested parties may file **amicus curiae** briefs

"rule of four": four or more justices must agree to hear a specific case

- if case presents a federal question
- if case would resolve conflicting interpretations of a law or discrepancies in previous rulings
- preferences of individual justices may play a role

5 THE CASE AT THE SUPREME COURT

If accepted...
Court issues **writ of certiorari**

Oral arguments presented by each side

6 THE DECISION

Judicial conference wherein justices meet and vote in secret

Court issues its **ruling and opinion**

The **majority decision** is binding

If no majority (when many justices disagree on logic of ruling), a plurality opinion is written

Concurring opinion may be written by justices agreeing with majority, to share reasoning for vote

Dissenting opinions may be written as a way to preserve a record for possible future analysis

The American Legal System Is Defined by Federalism **399**

district and appellate court judges. In 2017, a Republican-controlled Senate did the same for Supreme Court nominees.

Presidents Balance Legal and Political Considerations in Making Supreme Court Nominations

Unlike presidents and members of Congress, the Constitution places no requirements on the necessary qualifications to serve in the federal judiciary; judges do not even have to be lawyers. When vacancies occur in the Supreme Court, presidents are presented with an important, though challenging, opportunity to help shape policy for years to come. When the position of chief justice is vacant, a president may nominate a sitting member of the Court for that position and fill the newly vacant position of associate justice (which is how it usually happens), or the president may nominate an individual from outside the Court to the position of chief justice directly.

Because they are such high-profile appointments, nominees to the Court have to be weighed especially carefully. When choosing Court nominees, presidents have to balance both legal and political considerations. Experience, ethical integrity, and legal accomplishment are extremely important factors and can help smooth the confirmation process. Modern Court nominees will have typically already served in the federal judiciary or a similarly high-level position.

Presidents may also strive to nominate individuals who share their judicial philosophies and approaches to constitutional interpretation. Once confirmation occurs, however, presidents have no control over the behavior of their nominees. More than one president has successfully nominated an individual only to be surprised by some of that justice's later decisions. Political calculations come into play as well. Nominees who are considered outspoken on contentious political issues are likely to face careful scrutiny and intense questioning by senators concerned about these stances. As the Court, like Congress, still does not descriptively represent the American people, presidents may also consider nominating those with diverse backgrounds to the Court to make it more closely resemble a portrait of the nation.

WHAT HAVE I LEARNED?

1. State and federal courts consider both criminal and civil cases.
   a. True
   b. False

2. The number of levels in the federal judiciary (aside from some smaller specialized courts) is _____.
   a. 1
   b. 2
   c. 3
   d. 4

3. What considerations do Supreme Court justices take into account when deciding whether or not to grant cert?

Answer Key: 1. a; 2. c; 3. Answers should include whether or not the case involves a federal issue, the filing of briefs, conflict in the lower courts, and individual strategic considerations of justices.

JUDICIAL REVIEW RAISES QUESTIONS OF CONSTITUTIONAL INTERPRETATION AND JUDICIAL DECISION MAKING

Since its inception, the federal judiciary itself has been on trial—in the court of constitutional law, political science, and American public opinion. The chief defendant in this long and sometimes contentious history has been the Supreme Court, and the primary behavior in question has been the use of judicial review. Four main problems lie at the heart of the issue.

- Understand the different models of judicial decision making and arguments about judicial activism and restraint in constitutional interpretation.

The first, and potentially biggest, concern about judicial review arises from the fact that Supreme Court justices are not elected by the people but are appointed for life terms, removable only through the process of impeachment. In striking down state or federal laws, a small group of unelected justices can overturn acts passed by representatives who *were* elected. Alexander Bickel described the countermajoritarian difficulty in the exercise of judicial review: the worry that in striking down legislation, the Court "exercises control, not in behalf of the prevailing majority, but against it."[55]

This is precisely what President Thomas Jefferson warned about when he feared the judiciary becoming too powerful.[56]

Second, there is the concern that Americans may become less vigilant about who they elect, knowing that if they do a poor job in choosing their representatives, the Supreme Court will be there to bail them out. In modern terms, this is called the problem of moral hazard. The term comes from the concept of unwanted incentives created by having insurance. When a person is insured against bad outcomes from his or her own actions, then the person may take less care in avoiding those outcomes. By acting as a safety valve against poor, factious, or tyrannical legislation, the Court might actually make unwanted legislative outcomes more, not less, likely.

Third, the power of judicial review lies as much in its power to affirm as in its power to negate. In upholding the constitutionality of laws, the Supreme Court also exercises power over the legislative process by adding legitimacy in the minds of the American public to those laws passed by Congress.[57] In doing so, the Court risks validating laws that trample on the rights of minorities, thereby giving its stamp of approval to tyranny of the majority.

Finally, there exists the challenge inherent in interpreting and applying the Constitution to a variety of specific cases and circumstances across time and by individuals with their own opinions on what is or is not in accordance with the document, its language, and its intent. As James Thayer cautioned in an 1893 article, "Much which will seem unconstitutional to one man, or body of men, may reasonably not seem so to another; [and] that the constitution often admits of different interpretations."[58] In order to fully consider this issue, however, it is first necessary to explore in more detail how justices go about interpreting the Constitution and applying this highest law of the land to the cases brought before them.

Justices Take Several Approaches to Constitutional Interpretation

Trying to figure out why justices vote the way they do on any specific case is very difficult given all of the factors that likely contribute to an individual justice's vote. However, political scientists have identified several models that describe different approaches to judicial decision making. While a justice may emphasize one approach more than others, these models are best thought of as elements in the overall process and not as exclusive approaches that a given justice will only use. Justices themselves likely combine several considerations when approaching a case, especially difficult ones involving constitutional interpretation.

The Legal Model

The legal model focuses on applying the law to the facts of the case. In this model, justices rely on precedent—a previous decision on a similar case that serves as a basis for future decisions. When a justice follows precedent, he or she is said to be employing the doctrine of **stare decisis** (from the Latin, "to stand by things decided").[59] All justices—even the ones who emphasize their own capacity to interpret the Constitution—are bound by and employ the legal model to some extent in their decisions. There is good reason for this. It is, after all, how the legal system operates; similar cases are supposed to be decided in similar ways. To do otherwise would bring an unacceptable lack of uniformity to the legal system. There is also, however, a more strategic concern. A Supreme Court that is constantly ignoring its own precedents would likely not retain much legitimacy and authority in the eyes of the American people. While all justices employ the legal model, especially when deciding criminal cases, when it comes to those cases with significant implications for public policy—when the constitutionality of laws is at stake—other models may factor into judicial decision making as well.

Some justices applying the legal model look to the written text of the Constitution and the intent of the Framers of the document for guidance rather than to their own interpretation of the document's intent. Proponents of original understanding (or originalism) argue that the process of constitutional amendment, not Supreme Court decisions, should be the primary way to make major changes in the fundamental law of the nation.

The Attitudinal Model

The attitudinal model describes a process through which the political and policy preferences of individual justices shape their votes on cases rather than a neutral weighing of the facts and the law.[60] This model describes an overtly political approach to judicial decision making, one very far from Alexander Hamilton's reassurances about the nonpolitical federal judiciary in *Federalist* No. 78. Much of the research in this area has focused on explaining and predicting the votes of justices based on what we know about their political ideologies.[61] For scholars who emphasize the role of the individual attitudes and political ideologies of justices, the countermajoritarian difficulty can be especially worrisome. Not only can unelected justices strike down the will of the majority but they may do so in order to advance their own political and policy agendas.

The Strategic Model

Finally, the strategic model portrays individual justices as strategic political actors who, according to political scientist Walter Murphy, try to make the best use of their "resources, official and personal, to achieve a particular set of policy objectives."[62] Strategic justices do more than just vote according to their individual preferences. They consider the likely behaviors of their fellow justices; understand the national political context and the system of shared powers in which their branch of government operates; and, when deciding how to act, "compute in terms of costs and revenues whether a particular choice is worth the price which is required to attain it."[63] Strategic considerations may shape whether or not a justice votes to grant cert,[64] how justices vote on cases before them, and how justices craft their opinions.[65] See Figure 12.5.

Justices Exercise Degrees of Judicial Restraint and Judicial Activism

Related to the question of how justices make their decisions is the issue of how willing or reluctant they are to exercise the authority of judicial review. How

FIGURE 12.5

Theoretical Models of Constitutional Interpretation

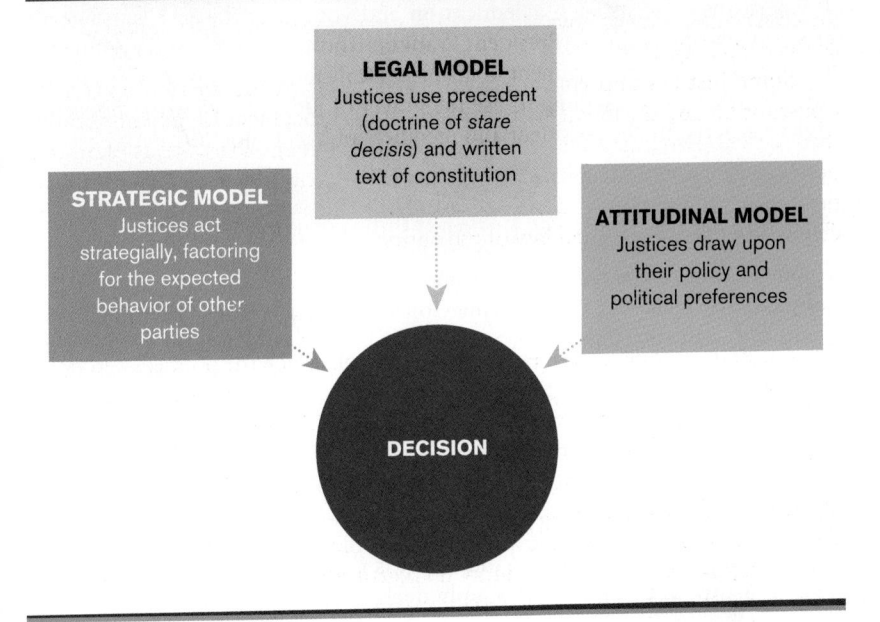

LEGAL MODEL
Justices use precedent (doctrine of *stare decisis*) and written text of constitution

STRATEGIC MODEL
Justices act strategially, factoring for the expected behavior of other parties

ATTITUDINAL MODEL
Justices draw upon their policy and political preferences

DECISION

eager, in other words, should the Court be to overturn the actions of the other two branches of government?

Proponents of **judicial restraint** argue that the Court should use this power rarely and whenever possible defer to the judgment of the legislative and executive branches on decisions that those branches have made. These proponents offer several justifications for their caution. First, they point to the dangers of the countermajoritarian difficulty and the potential antidemocratic consequences of unelected justices overturning the actions of elected representatives. In addition, the Supreme Court's voice in declaring a law to be unconstitutional is more authoritative when used sparingly, sending a clear signal in those times when it is employed. Finally, justices are legal and constitutional specialists; they are not policy specialists, nor are their clerks. The public policies that may be impacted by the use of judicial review may involve complex technical questions the details of which justices may not fully understand.

Proponents of **judicial activism**, on the other hand, argue that justices should be willing to step in and overturn laws when they see a need to do so. Sometimes the other two branches may make mistakes or, worse, trample on individual rights and liberties. The very power that fuels concerns about the countermajoritarian difficulty—that the Court can strike down the will of the majority—also gives it the power to protect the rights of minorities. Proponents of activism point to times when the other two branches act in ways damaging to rights and liberties; they also point to the fact that these branches often do not act at all. Free from the need to be concerned about the popularity of their actions, Supreme Court justices can place on the agenda issues that Congress and the president are unwilling to tackle.

Judicial activism and restraint are not inherently linked to political liberalism or conservatism. During the 1960s, an activist and liberal Court used the power of judicial review to strike down state laws restricting the civil rights of Americans in areas such as education and voting. In the 1930s, however, the strongest opposition to President Franklin Roosevelt's efforts to employ the power of the federal government in his New Deal came from an activist, conservative Supreme Court willing to use the power of judicial review to oppose the reforms enacted by the president and members of his Democratic Party.

The Supreme Court Acts as National Policymaker

No one branch of the federal government operates in a vacuum, and the federal judiciary, including the Supreme Court, is no exception. When the Court attempts to influence public policy, it does so in the face of multiple constraints on its independent use of authority, but its unique role within the system of shared powers offers it opportunities to shape policy in a way that the other two branches cannot.

Limitations on the Power of the Supreme Court

One constraint on the power of the Court is the legal process itself. A Court, no matter how activist, cannot simply declare unconstitutional a law that it

Judicial Review and the Political Ideologies of Justices

What role do the political ideologies of Supreme Court justices play in the willingness of justices to overturn federal or state laws? This is a very complex question that political scientists continue to debate. Part of the issue is actually measuring the

FIGURE A

Liberal and Conservative Uses of Judicial Review in the Warren Court, 1953-1968

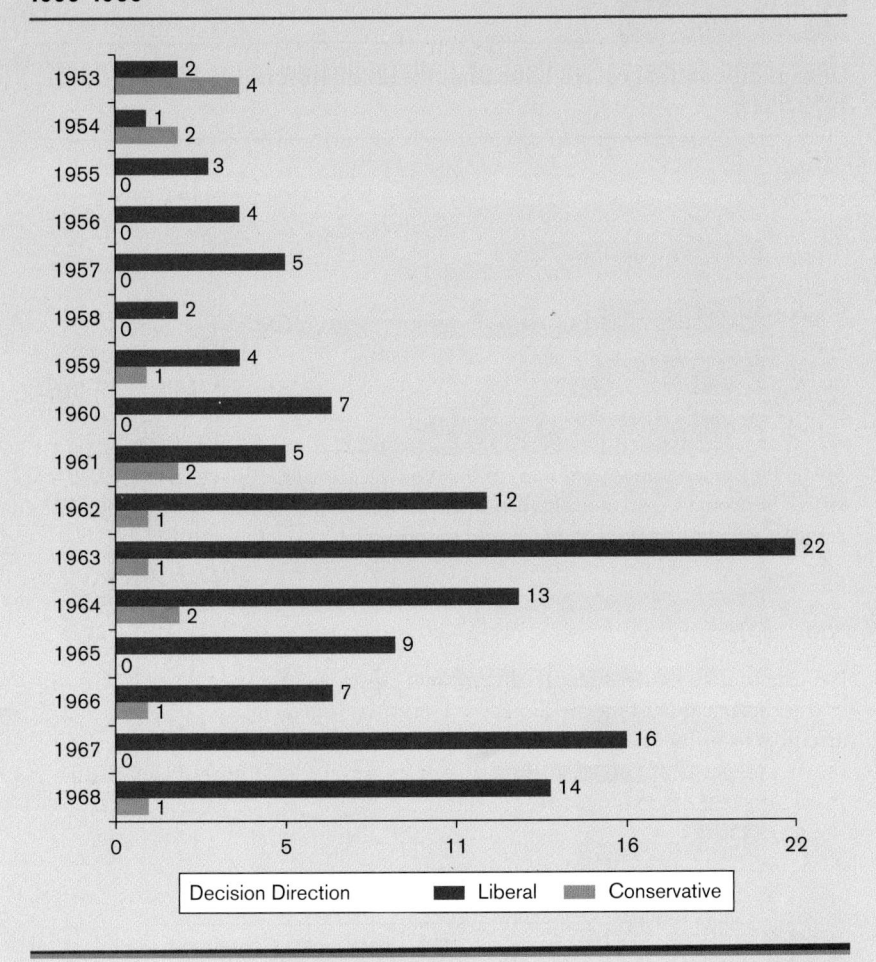

(Continued)

(Continued)

political ideologies of justices as they are not required to wear a label or announce to the world their personal politics. Many presidents are unhappily surprised to find that a justice they nominated has a different judicial philosophy than expected once the justice is on the Court and serving a lifetime term.

Using data from the Supreme Court Database—created and shared by a group of scholars—we can begin to explore this question. Figure A displays the total number of cases in which the Court declared as unconstitutional an act of Congress or a state or territorial law (or state constitutional provision) during a specific time in the

FIGURE B

Liberal and Conservative Uses of Judicial Review in the Hughes Court, 1929-1940

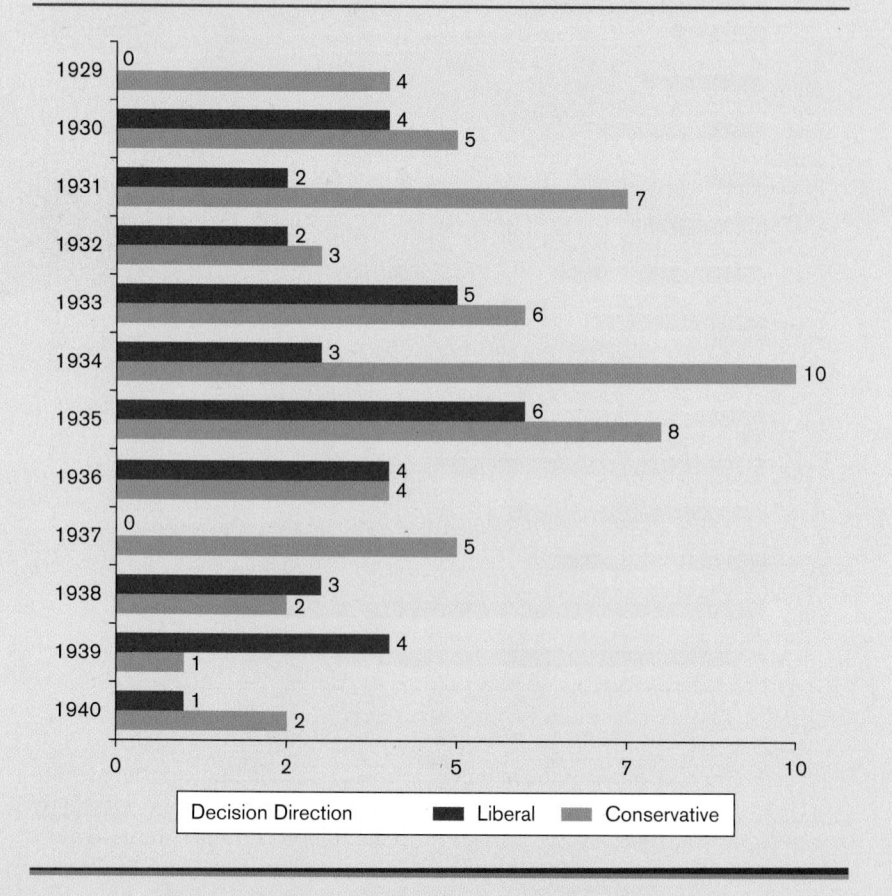

Court's history: 1953–1968. These years cover the Warren Court, in which Earl Warren served as the chief justice. The Warren Court is often considered to be one of the most liberal Courts in the nation's history. The blue bars indicate a use of judicial review to overturn a law or provision in a liberal direction as defined by the scholars, and the green bars indicate a use that overturned a law in a conservative direction. The largest group of these decisions involved questions of civil rights, followed by First Amendment concerns.

Based on Figure A, one might infer that liberal justices are more likely to overturn federal or state laws than conservative justices since nearly 90 percent of the decisions are in a liberal direction, and the Court was considered to be composed of a majority of liberal justices.

However, it is important to remember that these data are from only one Supreme Court era. Figure B presents a similar analysis; however, these data are from the tenure of Chief Justice Charles Evans Hughes when the Court was considered to be a very conservative one.[66] In contrast to the Warren Court, the majority of uses of judicial review to overturn federal or state laws in the Hughes Court era were conservative and focused primarily on economic activity and taxation policy. In terms of federal laws, many of these uses of judicial review focused on challenging President Roosevelt's New Deal, which we discussed in Chapter 3.

The data from Figure B present a more complex picture of the connection between judicial ideology and the willingness of justices to overturn federal or state laws, especially before Roosevelt began a series of appointments (some of whom served on the Warren Court) in 1937. These data challenge the assertion that liberal justices are *necessarily* more likely to exercise judicial review to overturn federal or state laws than conservative ones. However, they do support the idea that the political ideologies of the justices *can* affect patterns of the use of judicial review. This important issue is one scholars will continue to examine.

WHAT DO YOU THINK?

To what extent do you think justices should or should not bring their own political views into the use of judicial review? What responsibility should the Senate exercise in trying to ascertain the politics of Supreme Court nominees during the confirmation proceedings?

Source: All data are from Harold Spaeth et al., *"2016 Supreme Court Database,"* http://supremecourtdatabase.org.

does not like. It can only rule on a specific case that has been properly filed and brought before it. Only plaintiffs who can demonstrate standing can bring suit in court, which requires that they demonstrate that they have been wronged by a law or action and that the law in question covers the interests the plaintiff alleges to have been violated or denied. Even when everything works efficiently, the process of moving a case through the federal judiciary takes time. When a case begins in a state judiciary, the process can take even longer.

The legislative and executive branches may also act as a check on the power of the federal judiciary. We have discussed the role of the president in nominating justices and that of the Senate in confirming them. We have also examined the role of Congress in setting the size of the Supreme Court and establishing other federal courts. Congress and the states may collectively amend the Constitution, the results of which are not subject to judicial review. In addition, the Court lacks the tools for implementing public policy and often must turn to the other two branches to add force to its rulings. When a Court goes against the will of the president or Congress, the other branches may be less than supportive in implementing the decisions or even might ignore or defy the Court entirely. Even when the other two branches do not openly defy the Supreme Court, their lack of support of its rulings can limit the Court's power in setting national policy.

Finally, although justices are appointed for life and do not need to worry about being reelected, they do operate in the American political system in which public opinion plays an important role. Political scientists continue to debate the degree to which Supreme Court justices attend to public opinion in crafting specific decisions; however, scholars agree that it is not something that can completely be ignored.[67] President Washington ensured that the first Court "contained judges from Massachusetts, New York, Pennsylvania, Virginia, Maryland, and South Carolina" to demonstrate to the experimental nation his commitment to ensuring representation from all parts of the country.[68]

Since the time of John Marshall, justices have had to attend to the fact that their power in exercising judicial review is tied to Americans' views of the legitimacy of their branch of government. It is no accident that of all the branches only the federal judiciary, and the Supreme Court in particular, chooses to retain its costumes, secrecy, and traditional ways of doing things, as out of time as they may seem. The drama of the Court adds to its legitimacy in the view of the American people, and all justices—whatever their own political beliefs—know that they play a key role in preserving the story of the Court and its power.

The Agenda-Setting Power of the Supreme Court

While the Supreme Court and the rest of the federal judiciary cannot act as all-powerful, unilateral makers of public policy, their particular position in the nation and the federal government does give them a unique role in American politics: that of setting the national agenda. Because they do not face elections like members of the other two branches, Supreme Court justices are able to bring up in the national conversation issues that need to be discussed. They can act in front of public opinion—perhaps not *too* far but far enough to force debate on the national stage. Recent Court rulings on marriage equality may be perfect examples of this power. In exercising this power, the Court may not necessarily be acting against the wishes of elected representatives, or at least of all of them. A member of Congress or a president who may be afraid to weigh in on an important and controversial issue out of fear of the backlash from public opinion can point to a Court decision and tell the American people that they now have to act. Providing political cover for elected representatives who wish to act on an issue may be one of the most important powers of the unelected branch of government.

1. The major models of judicial decision making are the legal, adjudicative, and strategic models.

   a. True
   b. False

2. The term *countermajoritarian difficulty* refers to _____.

   a. The ability to impeach Supreme Court justices
   b. The fact that justices are not elected by the people
   c. Congressional oversight of the Supreme Court
   d. Presidential nominations of justices

3. What are some of the limitations on the power of the Supreme Court?

4. What are arguments made in support of judicial restraint? Of judicial activism?

Answer Key: 1. b; 2. b; 3. Answers should include the fact that the Court decides only on cases before it, executive and legislative checks on its functioning, and that it has few tools with which to implement public policy; 4. For restraint, answers should focus on the countermajoritarian difficulty, the fact that justices may not have policy expertise, and the risk of its overuse. For activism, answers should focus on the fact that Congress may not act in areas that it needs to and the danger of tyranny of the majority.

CONCLUSION
The "Trials" of Merrick Garland and Neil Gorsuch

In February 2016, Justice Antonin Scalia passed away, presenting President Barack Obama with the possibility of a third Supreme Court nomination during his tenure. While Sonia Sotomayor's confirmation had been somewhat contested, his second, that of Elena Kagan, had gone relatively smoothly. In March 2016, with ten months left in office, Obama nominated Judge Merrick Garland to fill Scalia's seat. Republicans, with a majority in Senate, refused even to consider the president's nominee, arguing that the nomination should be made by the next president, a gamble that a Republican might win the White House. As Scalia was one of the staunchest conservatives on the Court, Republicans knew that his replacement would have the potential to shift the ideological balance of the Court for years if not decades.

Both Donald Trump's win in the presidential election of 2016 and the continuing Republican control of the Senate ensured that Garland would not get his "trial." As a candidate, Trump had presented his own list of possible Supreme Court nominees. In 2017, he secured the nomination of Neil Gorsuch to the bench after Senate Republicans changed the chamber's rules to prevent a filibuster. Replacing a very conservative justice, Antonin Scalia, Gorsuch's confirmation did not shift the Court's balance of political power. In fact, three Democrats voted for his confirmation. Should one of the more liberal justices retire during the Trump administration, that confirmation process will surely be far more heated.

In this chapter, we have explored two important and closely related questions: How political is the Court? And how powerful is it? In *Federalist* No. 78, Alexander Hamilton—a proponent of a strong national government—tried to reassure a skeptical confederation during the ratification debates that the Court was neither political nor powerful. History has proven Hamilton correct and incorrect on both counts.

The justices of the Supreme Court and the federal judiciary are not political in the ways that presidents, representatives, and senators are in no small part because they do not have to worry about reelection. They must consider the facts of the case and the letter of the law when ruling on cases. Justices are, however, political people, and their personal views on issues may affect their decisions on impactful cases. They must always be strategic in understanding the role their institution plays in the system of separation of powers and in Americans' views on the legitimacy of the institution.

Theirs is a power that must be nurtured, cultivated, and protected, as John Marshall and subsequent members of the federal judiciary have had to learn. Compared to the legislative and executive branches, the power of the federal judiciary in national policymaking is much less imposing. It cannot write laws; it has no army. It has only the power of its decisions and the willingness of the people and the members of the other two branches to acquiesce to its decisions. It is not powerless; it is just different. How dangerous—or promising—this difference is continues to be a central subject of debate in American politics.

CHAPTER REVIEW

This chapter's main ideas are reflected in the Learning Objectives. By reviewing them here you should be able to **remember** the key points and **know** these terms that are central to the topic.

12.1 Describe the structure and powers of the federal judiciary as laid out in the Constitution.

REMEMBER...

- The Constitution contains less detail about the judiciary than about the legislative or executive branches, but it is clear that the Framers intended it to be the weakest of the three and also relatively independent of the other two.

- Article 3 does not expressly give the judiciary the power to strike down laws that it views as being in violation of the Constitution.

KNOW...

- *appellate jurisdiction*: the authority of a court to hear and review decisions made by lower courts in that system (p. 383)

- *federal judiciary*: the branch of the federal government that interprets and applies the laws of the nation (p. 379)

- *original jurisdiction*: the authority of a court to act as the first court to hear a case, which includes the finding of facts in the case (p. 383)

- *U.S. Supreme Court*: the highest level of the federal judiciary, which was established in the Constitution and serves as the highest court in the nation (p. 378)

12.2 Explain John Marshall's development of judicial review in the Supreme Court decision in *Marbury v. Madison*.

REMEMBER...

- In part of his ruling in *Marbury v. Madison*, Marshall found that part of the law that Marbury was basing his claim on, the Judiciary Act of 1789, was unconstitutional and thus unenforceable.

- Marshall, therefore, asserted that the Supreme Court had the power of judicial review over federal laws, which is the power to review laws and actions of other branches and levels of government to decide if they are in conflict with the Constitution. If conflict is found, the Court may declare that law or action invalid.

KNOW...

- *constitutional interpretation*: the process of applying the Constitution in assessing whether or not a law, part of a law, or an action by a governmental official is or is not in conflict with the Constitution (p. 388)

- *judicial review*: the authority of the highest court in a political system to determine if a law is or is not in conflict with a government's highest law, which in the United States is the Constitution (p. 388)

- Marbury v. Madison (1803): a Supreme Court decision that established judicial review over federal laws (p. 387)

12.3 Describe the structure of the American legal system and the federal judiciary.

REMEMBER...

- All courts in the American system are based on the adversarial system with plaintiffs and defendants arguing their opposing sides of the case in the most persuasive way possible.

- Criminal law covers actions determined to harm the community itself whereas civil law covers cases involving private rights and relationships between individuals and groups.

- The federal judiciary is composed of constitutional courts and specialized legislative courts. The constitutional courts are organized into three levels: federal district courts, the federal court of appeals, and the Supreme Court.

- Cases beginning at the state court level may be either civil or criminal cases; to move on to the federal level they must involve federal or constitutional questions. Most are resolved at the lower court level. If they move from the district court to the highest state court, the losing side may appeal to the Supreme Court.

- Cases beginning in the federal system must meet certain requirements and may involve either a civil or criminal case, but the federal government must be party to the dispute.

KNOW...

- *adversarial system*: a legal structure in which two opposing sides present their case in the most persuasive way possible (p. 389)

- *brief*: legal document presented by plaintiffs; defendants; and, at times, other interested parties outlining their arguments in a case (p. 396)

- *civil law*: a category of law covering cases involving private rights and relationships between individuals and groups (p. 390)

- *criminal law*: a category of law covering actions determined to harm the community itself (p. 390)

- *defendant*: a person or group against whom a case is brought in court (p. 390)

- *federal courts of appeals*: the middle level of the federal judiciary; these courts review and hear appeals from the federal district courts (p. 392)

- *federal district courts*: the lowest level of the federal judiciary; these courts usually possess original jurisdiction in cases that originate at the federal level (p. 392)

- *oral argument*: presentation made by plaintiffs and attorneys before the Supreme Court (p. 397)

- *plaintiff*: a person or group who brings a case in court (p. 390)

- *plea bargaining*: a legal process in which the plaintiff and defendant agree to an outcome prior to the handing out of a verdict (p. 390)

- *precedent*: a judicial decision that guides future courts in handling similar cases (p. 397)

- *solicitor general*: a presidential appointee who represents the federal government in the Supreme Court (p. 396)

- *standing:* the legal ability to bring a case in court (p. 396)

- *writ of certiorari*: the process through which most cases reach the Supreme Court; after four justices concur that the Court should hear the case, a writ of certiorari is issued to the lower court to request the relevant case records (p. 396)

12.4 Compare theories of judicial decision making as well as arguments for or against judicial restraint and activism in constitutional review.

REMEMBER...

- There are four concerns raised by use of judicial review: (1) an unelected group of justices may overturn acts that were passed by representatives who *were* elected; (2) the American people could become lax in who they elect to office, thinking that the court could bail them out if their representatives made serious errors; (3) in validating laws that trample on the rights of minorities, the Supreme Court may give its stamp of approval to tyranny of the majority; and (4) interpretation and application of the Constitution to a variety of specific cases and circumstances across time and by individuals with their own opinions on what is or is not in accordance with the document is inherently challenging.

- There are three main models of constitutional interpretation: (1) the legal model, which is based on precedent; (2) the attitudinal model, which relies on the political and policy preferences of individual justices; and (3) the strategic model, in which justices make calculations about the behavior of other actors and take context into account in their decision.

- Proponents of judicial restraint argue that the Court should use the power of judicial review rarely and whenever possible defer to the judgment of the legislative and executive branches on decisions that those branches have made. Proponents of judicial activism, on the other hand, argue that justices should be willing to step in and overturn laws when they see a need to do so.

KNOW ...

- *judicial activism*: a philosophy of constitutional interpretation that asserts justices should wield the power of judicial review when needed (p. 404)

- *judicial restraint*: a philosophy of constitutional interpretation that asserts justices should be cautious in overturning laws (p. 404)

- *stare decisis*: means "let it stand"; the doctrine that legal precedent should serve as the basis for future legal decision making in similar legal cases unless overruled (p. 402)

13 PUBLIC POLICY
Promoting the General Welfare and Advancing Americans' Interests

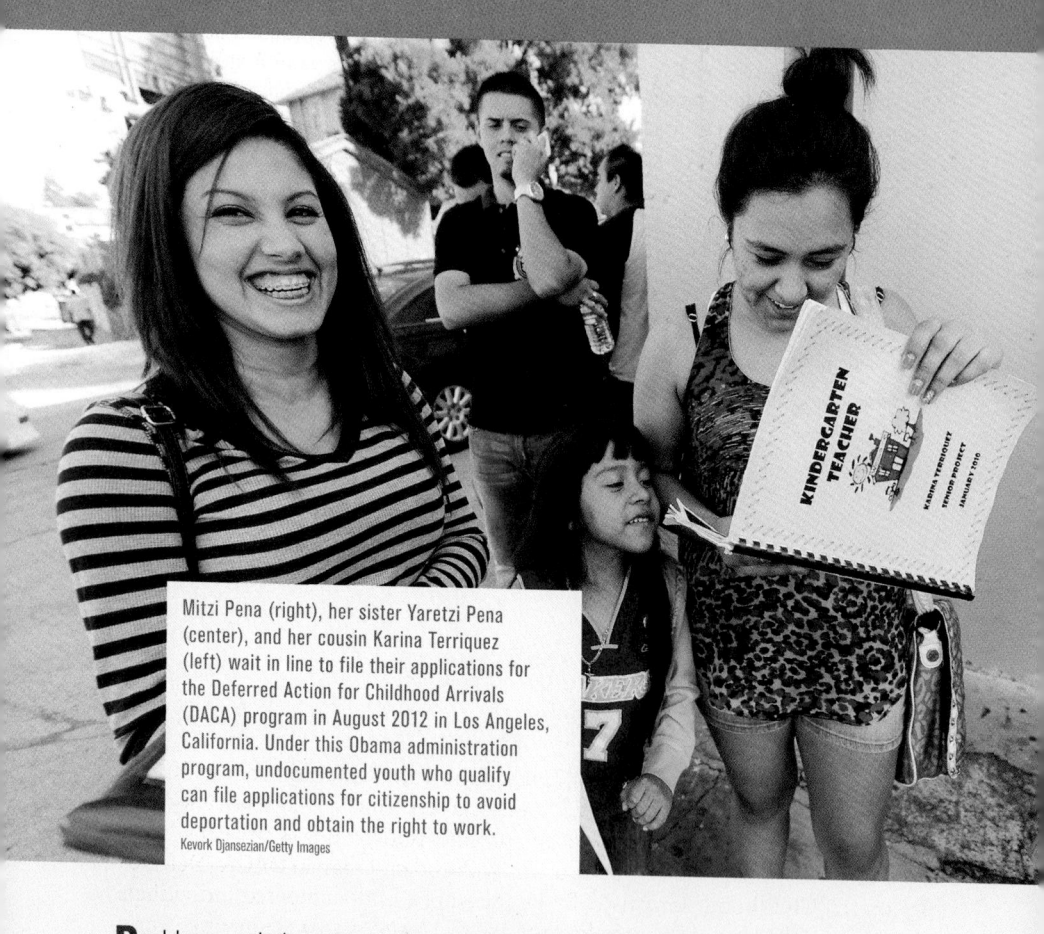

Mitzi Pena (right), her sister Yaretzi Pena (center), and her cousin Karina Terriquez (left) wait in line to file their applications for the Deferred Action for Childhood Arrivals (DACA) program in August 2012 in Los Angeles, California. Under this Obama administration program, undocumented youth who qualify can file applications for citizenship to avoid deportation and obtain the right to work.
Kevork Djansezian/Getty Images

Problems, solutions, and politics. In America, there has been no shortage of any of these things. Experts, members of Congress, presidents, and members of interest groups have all presented to the American public their analyses of problems that need to be solved and their best solutions to those problems. In doing so, all are engaged with the political process, and all must be strategic in this engagement if they hope to succeed

In this chapter, you will explore American **public policy**, which is the intentional use of governmental power to secure the health, welfare, opportunities, and national security of its citizens. The lens we will use to look through in this chapter is one of the most contentious issues in American politics today: immigration.

Governmental action involves **domestic policy** wherein policymakers aim to improve the social welfare of the American citizens. It also involves **economic policy** through which American policymakers try to ensure that all Americans can achieve their futures. Finally, it involves **foreign policy** through which policymakers try to protect Americans' interests in an uncertain world.

These issues are not separate. As you will discover, American public policy involves connections between domestic, economic, and foreign policy. Throughout this book, we have wrestled with questions of power, politics, and representation. This chapter is no different except for one thing: we move between Washington, D.C., the state capitals, and other nations as officials at all levels of the American government are tasked to meet the demands of America's citizens and those who strive to become part of the American dream.

After reading this chapter you will be able to do the following:

13.1 Understand the steps in the policymaking process and the different forms of domestic social policy in America today.

13.2 Understand the U.S. approach to fiscal policy and the tools that are used to measure and implement those policies.

13.3 Summarize the events that have shaped changes in America's approach to the world and the actors involved in formulating policy.

LEARNING OBJECTIVES

AMERICAN DREAMERS' FUTURES DEPEND UPON WHETHER A POLICY WILL CONTINUE

In an interview with the *New York Times*, Julia Verzbikis told her story. It was highlighted as part of a series called "American Dreamers."[1] The story focused on the path to inclusion and American citizenship for young Americans introduced in 2012 through an executive order by President Obama: DACA (Deferred Action for Childhood Arrivals).[2] By its measures, undocumented individuals who came to the United States before the age of 16 and who were in, or recently graduated from, school, could seek a deferment on their deportation.

Julia Verzbikis' arrival to the United States was not without many challenges, but she persevered:

"The lawyer we had turned out to be fraudulent, and as a result, my parents, my sisters and I all lost our status in the country. It was the summer before my first year of high school. The future remained unclear, but I made some choices. I chose to keep my grades up in school. I chose to give myself the opportunity at a future...The week after my twenty-first birthday, I got a notice that my DACA application had been approved...In August 2015, I started teaching...I've been teaching middle school since then, and I love it. My kids are amazing. They drive me nuts on any given day, but I love them."[3]

According to public opinion polls, most Americans believe that undocumented immigrants living in the United States who meet certain requirements should be allowed to stay in the country legally, but more Democrats support that position than Republicans, making the issue a partisan one.[4] As part of a broader effort at immigration reform, DACA was aimed at enfranchising a group of people who seemed to be both the most vulnerable and least controversial from a policy perspective—the children of undocumented immigrants. As one report put it, "DACA is an important tool for expanding economic and civic contributions from these individuals. Ultimately, these . . . initiatives will benefit places, not just individuals and families."[5]

With the arrival of the administration of President Donald Trump in 2017, however, many expected that DACA would be rescinded. A spokesperson for the Federation for American Immigration Reform, a group that supports reduced immigration, noted, "This was the crown jewel of illegal executive orders—amnesty for illegal aliens. It doesn't get any more blatant than that.'"[6] Many Republicans in Congress had critiqued President Obama's executive orders on immigration, along with other issues, as a way of sidestepping the Republican-controlled Senate and House. Many state government officials tried to force the president's hand: "Texas Attorney General Ken Paxton was joined by his counterparts in nine other states in a letter. . .warning [federal] Attorney General Jeff Sessions that if the Trump administration does not move to end the Deferred Action for Childhood Arrivals, they will file a court challenge to the program."[7]

On September 5, 2017, President Trump and Attorney General Sessions announced a phased end to the policy, calling on Congress to act if it wanted to preserve DACA. In the days that followed, the president seemed to shift, in a mixed set of tweets and statements, suggesting a potential deal to congressional Democrats—one that would include their support for a wall across the U.S-Mexican border. While the initial order provided for a two-year renewal of deferment for some individuals, the youngest, those without DACA status, could face deportation as early as March 2018. "'This is a sad day for our country,' Mark Zuckerberg, Facebook founder, wrote on his personal page. 'It is particularly cruel to offer young people the American dream, encourage them to come out of the shadows and trust our government, and then punish them for it.'"[8]

The rescinding of DACA would affect the lives of hundreds of thousands of young people. It also has the potential to have deep political reverberations for years to come, and the reason is math. By 2043, according to analysts with the U.S. Census Bureau, America will be a plural nation, with members of no single traditional racial or ethnic group constituting an absolute majority of the population. This will mark the first time in the nation's history that white non-Hispanics will not have constituted a majority of

Advocates for the Massachusetts Immigrant and Refugee Advocacy Coalition (MIRA) in Boston gather to search for news about an executive order on DACA on Jan. 23, 2017.
Jessica Rinaldi/The Boston Globe via Getty Images

Americans and eligible voters.[9] By 2060 Hispanics are projected to make up over 30 percent of the nation's population—nearly doubling the percentage of just a few decades prior. In contrast, the percentage of white non-Hispanic Americans in the nation's population is projected to decline from more than 60 percent in 2013 to roughly 43 percent. Today, lawmakers are having to account for the implications of that changing demographic in all areas of policy. Their political survival depends upon it as well; any political party that wants to remain in power must at least consider the implications of these coming demographic changes.

Public policy, as we will explore, is about real people, impacting their lives. It is also, however, about politics. Policy is where politics meets people, and the interaction has been, continues to be, and will likely always be contested.

WHAT HAVE I LEARNED?

1. Public policy is the intentional use of governmental power to secure the health, welfare, opportunities, and national security of its citizens.

   a. True
   b. False

2. The government uses _____ to take action to improve the social welfare of the American citizens.

   a. Economic policy
   b. Devolution
   c. Domestic policy
   d. Regulation

3. Policymakers use foreign policy to _____.

   a. Regulate commerce within the United States

   b. Expand social programs
   c. Protect Americans' interests abroad
   d. None of the above

4. What specific problem was the Deferred Action for Childhood Arrivals (DACA) program designed to fix? Why do opponents want to see it rescinded?

   Answer Key: 1. a; 2. c; 3. c; 4. Answers about "fixes" should include creating a pathway for the children of undocumented immigrants who meet certain criteria in order to integrate them into American society; answers about "opponents" should include mention of the perception that the Act was an overreach of executive authority.

DOMESTIC SOCIAL POLICIES SAFEGUARD AMERICANS' WELFARE

Domestic public policies are designed to improve or protect the health, safety, education, and opportunities for citizens and residents. Policies implemented with these aims are also called **social welfare policies**. Federal and state governments aren't the only sources that define and shape social welfare policies. Citizens do, too. Identifying why some policies get enacted and others do not continues to be a subject of study and debate among scholars.

- Explain the stages of the policymaking process as well as the different forms domestic social policy takes in the United States.

At its core, social welfare policy involves redistribution of resources. Providing resources to specific populations necessarily implies diverting those resources from other potential uses and raising funds—typically through taxation—to do so. As such, social policy involves contestation; therefore, citizens can play direct and indirect roles in how policies are shaped.

Policymaking Happens in Stages

Scholars of public policy often break down the process into a series of stages or steps. While it is very useful to think in these terms, it is also important to remember that the entire process is fluid; constantly changing; and, above all else, political. Nothing is ever settled, and the American political system is designed to have multiple points of access and contestation throughout.[10]

Step 1: Defining the Problem

What may seem like the simplest part of domestic policymaking may actually be the most consequential and most contested part of the entire process: defining the problem. How a problem is formulated typically means that a particular set of solutions becomes possible—some specific lines of attack are open, and others closed off. Having one's definition of the problem accepted constitutes a very effective exercise of power in the policy process.

Step 2: Getting on the Agenda

Defining a problem amounts to little if one's ideas do not get discussed or debated. Getting on the policy agenda—the necessarily limited set of issues on which policymakers focus their attention—is crucial but challenging. Getting one's concerns considered depends not only on the merits of the issue but also on the political and economic contexts in which the ideas are offered. The ways in which the public views the issue, its importance, and the "deservingness" of those targeted for public policy action also matter. As political scientist John Kingdon queried, "What makes an idea's time come? That question is actually part of a larger puzzle: What makes people in and around government attend, at any given time, to some subjects and not to others?"[11]

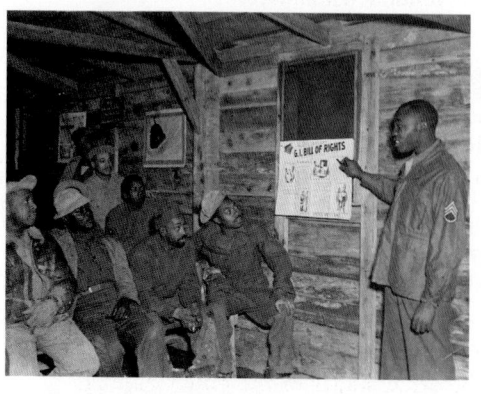

Staff Sergeant Herbert Ellison explains the G.I. Bill to the African American members of the Quartermaster Truck Company. Library of Congress/Corbis/VCG via Getty Images

Public attention and action is often more likely when the targets of the policies under discussion are perceived to be "deserving," which is a very controversial designation. The first national policies to provide assistance to a specific group of Americans targeted Civil War veterans and their surviving spouses and families in the nineteenth century.[12] In 1944 Congress passed the Servicemen's Readjustment Act, commonly called the G.I. Bill, to assist

World War II veterans in attending college or obtaining vocational training.[13] Second, when trying to get on the political agenda, the perception of a crisis surrounding the issue in question may be useful. Again, however, how a "crisis" is defined is a constructed and contested process—one that may help to get the concern on the policy agenda but that also then shapes the perception of appropriate solutions.

Finally, when considering how ideas do or do not make it onto the national or state policy agenda, we must be aware that people matter, too. **Policy entrepreneurs** are individuals operating in government, academic institutions, think tanks, interest groups, and other venues who try to shape the political agenda and get their solutions implemented on the ground.

Step 3: Creating Policy and Adopting It

Getting a policy proposal on the agenda is only the beginning. The policies have to be worked out and passed by either the state legislatures or the federal Congress and signed into law by governors and presidents.

Step 4: Budgeting: More Than Just Money

Financing an adopted policy is yet another political process. State governments have to set their budgets, and state legislatures and state executives are important players in this process. The federal government also uses the power of its purse to push its agendas into other policies generally handled by the states. In 1974, under the administration of President Richard Nixon and during the energy crisis of the time, the Emergency Highway Energy Conservation Act required states to reduce the maximum speed limits on their highways or risk losing federal transportation monies.

It is by using this financial leverage that the federal government often coerces states to comply with federal policy. When, however, members of state governments feel that the federal government is requiring them to institute a policy without offering sufficient federal funds for its implementation, they may argue that such a requirement constitutes an **unfunded mandate.**

Step 5: Implementing

After being authorized by the relevant federal or state governmental actors, policies have to be **implemented**, or enacted, in the real world.[14] Once implemented, a public policy may be very different on the ground from the idealized form created in the responsible legislative body or institution.

Step 6: Evaluating

What may seem like the least political part of the policymaking process is often far from it. Evaluation—determining if a policy is achieving its stated objectives—is just as consequential as the other stages of the policymaking process and, therefore, just as contested. Congress, state legislatures, academic institutions, federal and state courts, and policy entrepreneurs all weigh in on evaluations of different policies.

Step 7 (Maybe): Terminating

The last step in the policymaking process is one that does not always happen—at least formally—even when there is widespread agreement that a policy is not working. If the political consequences of ending the policy are high (as they most certainly would be with entitlement programs), or if the recipients of the "failed" policy are seen as deserving, a policy might endure despite poor evaluations of it.

The authority to formally terminate a policy may reside with Congress or a state legislature. There are, however, other ways in which a policy might be terminated. Courts, especially the Supreme Court, might terminate a policy through the use of judicial review.

Domestic Social Policy Takes Several Forms

While immigration is a critical issue in American domestic policy, it is only one of many. All levels of government are also involved in protecting Americans from poverty, providing access to housing, protecting the environment, and implementing many other areas of domestic policy. In this section, we will examine several of these goals and some of the most important policies enacted to achieve them.

Social Insurance

The Social Security Act of 1935 created a set of programs to support vulnerable groups of Americans. It established unemployment insurance for workers and set up the old-age insurance and old-age assistance programs, which were later supplemented with disability insurance. In addition, it established Aid to Dependent Children (see the Need-Based Public Assistance section).[15] Social Security was designed to be self-funding so as not to force the government to raise taxes and further depress the economy. Its ability to be sustained in the twenty-first century—when life spans are significantly longer than when the program was first enacted—is the subject of much current debate in American politics.

Social Security is an example of a **social insurance program**—so called because it is financed by payroll taxes paid by individuals and does not have income-based requirements to receive its benefits. While the Social Security Act created several types of insurance, the term *Social Security* is generally used to refer to old-age insurance, which protects against the loss of income in an individual's later years. The level of benefits received depends upon one's contributions during the working years, or the contributions of one's spouse in the case of survivorship. These programs are often called **entitlement programs**, meaning that if one meets the categorical requirements, such as age or a minimum number of years of payroll contributions, one is entitled to receive the benefits, regardless of income.

While projections vary, the financial reserves underlying Social Security will be out of money at some point in the coming decades. Fixing this deficit is not just a problem of mathematics; it is also a problem of politics. Reducing benefits to current recipients would produce a massive backlash from a large group of politically active Americans who would mobilize to ensure the continuation of the program as is. For this reason, Social Security is often called the "third rail" of American politics—so named for the rail in many subway systems that carries electricity and would likely cause death if touched. Raising the payroll tax on current workers is another possibility—though, again, one with significant political risk for lawmakers if enacted.

Need-Based Public Assistance

Unlike entitlement programs such as Social Security and Medicare, which are funded through payroll taxes and do not require a demonstration of need (beyond meeting certain categorical requirements such as age or disability), another major category of social welfare programs requires that individuals demonstrate specific need. As such, these programs are called **need-based assistance** programs, and they involve a means test that is usually based on income. In assessing who qualifies for need-based assistance, the federal government often employs a concept called the poverty line, which defines an income below which a family is considered poor. In 2015 the federally defined poverty threshold for a family of four was an annual family income of $24,250.[16] Need-based social welfare policies are funded through federal and/or state tax revenues rather than payroll taxes.

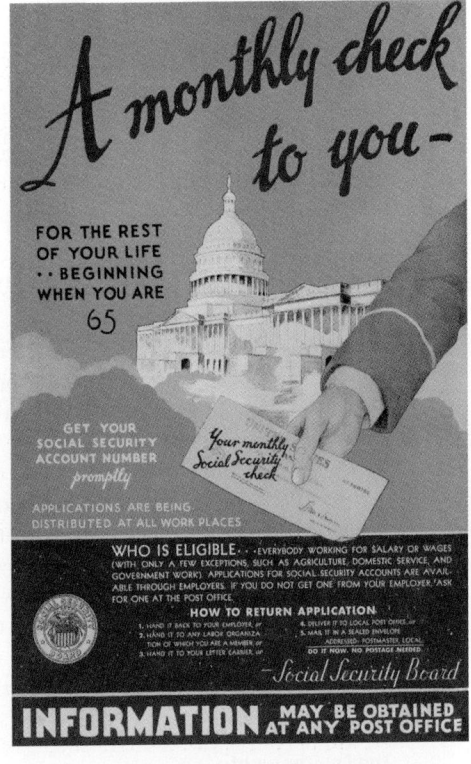

A poster from 1935 informing Americans aged sixty-five and older of their entitled benefits under the Social Security program and how to obtain them. GraphicaArtis/Getty Images

In addition to covering health services for low-income Americans, the federal government also provides other forms of need-based assistance. Aid to Families with Dependent Children (AFDC) was created in the 1930s to help families support their children in the event that a parent was deceased, disabled, unable to work, or out of work. In the decades following, AFDC was expanded to aid parents as well, increasing the number of covered individuals as well as the cost of the program. AFDC was sometimes accused of cultivating dependency among the families receiving it and creating generations of families that received its benefits.

With the Personal Responsibility and Work Opportunity Reconciliation Act of 1996 (PRWORA), Democratic president Bill Clinton signed into law the principles of devolution to social welfare programs. The outlines of PRWORA had been part of the Republican Party's "Contract with America," a set of campaign promises made during the congressional elections of 1994 in which Republicans took control of both the House and the Senate.[17] PRWORA replaced AFDC with Temporary Assistance for Needy Families (TANF), which placed time limits on receipt of welfare assistance and added work requirements for beneficiaries.

The Supplemental Nutrition Assistance Program (SNAP), formerly called the Food Stamp Program, assists the poor in meeting their needs for food. The Earned Income Tax Credit (EITC) provides a tax credit to the working poor, one that in many cases results in these Americans receiving a larger refund than the amount of federal income taxes that have been deducted from their paychecks.

Housing

Many efforts to secure adequate housing for Americans occur primarily at the state and local levels. The federal government, however, has involved itself in housing policy in several ways. One of President Roosevelt's New Deal programs was the establishment of the Federal Housing Administration (FHA) in 1934, tasked with combating widespread foreclosures as a result of the Great Depression. By regulating interest rates and home mortgage terms, the FHA sought to make homeownership more attainable. It also undertook programs to increase the availability of affordable rental units.

In 1965 the FHA was folded into the Department of Housing and Urban Development (HUD). The department administers programs to combat homelessness; oversees programs to provide housing vouchers for low-income Americans; and enforces federal laws against discrimination in housing based on racial and ethnic identity, religion, national origin, sex, disability, and family status. HUD also provides assistance in financing home mortgages, a role that was significantly increased following the housing and financial crisis of 2008.

The Environment

Another major area of federal domestic policy involves efforts to clean up and protect the environment. The Environmental Protection Agency (EPA), established in 1970 during the administration of Richard Nixon, works in coordination with state, tribal, and local governments to enforce federal laws governing environmental standards, monitor pollution and cleanup efforts, and oversee energy conservation measures. Among the federal laws that the EPA is tasked to enforce are the Clean Air Act, the Water Quality Act, and the Endangered Species Act (all of which have had subsequent extensions). While not an official cabinet department, the EPA administrator is typically given cabinet-level status.

WHAT HAVE I LEARNED?

1. Social welfare policies are types of policies whose goals are to improve or protect the health, safety, education, and opportunities for citizens and residents.

   a. True
   b. False

2. Defining the problem, getting on the agenda, creating policy and adopting it, budgeting, implementing, evaluating, and terminating are all _____.

   a. Part of unorthodox lawmaking
   b. Stages in the policymaking process
   c. Aspects of economic policy formulation
   d. Domains of foreign policymaking

3. _____ are programs that are financed by payroll taxes paid by individuals and that do not have income-based requirements to receive its benefits.

a. College tuition assistance programs
b. The Deferred Action for Childhood Arrivals (DACA) program and the Development, Relief, and Education for Alien Minors Act (DREAM Act)
c. Social insurance programs
d. Need-based assistance programs

4. Social welfare programs that require that individuals demonstrate specific need are called _____.

a. Need-based assistance programs
b. Social insurance programs
c. Social Security programs
d. DACA and the DREAM Act

5. What is the concept of "deservingness," and what role does it play in the policymaking process?

Answer Key: 1. a; 2. b; 3. c; 4. a; 5. Answers should discuss the fact that the success of a particular policy idea depends upon the perception that the recipient of that policy "deserves" the benefit.

ECONOMIC POLICY PROTECTS AMERICANS' FINANCIAL PROSPECTS

- Describe the U.S. approach to fiscal policy and the tools used to measure and implement those policies.

One of the most important jobs a president, senator, or representative does is provide Americans with economic opportunities. If a single voter loses his or her job, that voter may not necessarily blame the federal government. If, however, that unemployed worker—or even workers who are still employed—also starts to see friends, family members, or neighbors out of work or in severe financial stress, then there may be a political price to pay in the next election.

Desirable economic outcomes, though not always valued the same by different groups of voters, are not things that can be pulled out of a hat. In the first place, these objectives are often at cross-purposes. Lowering taxes might make a particular individual feel wealthier, but it also reduces the amount of money available for programs designed to spur employment and economic activity.

Policymakers cannot avoid making those thorny choices. One of the most important jobs tasked to the federal government is formulating and implementing the nation's economic policy through which it regulates economic and business activity, protects and expands Americans' individual financial prospects, and supports American businesses competing in the global marketplace.

Managing the nation's economy is not an exact science; there are too many variables at play to know for sure what all of the consequences of any one economic policy decision or set of decisions will be. In spite of these uncertainties, federal authorities can and do act to produce desirable economic outcomes. One major set of governmental activities is called **fiscal policy**.

America Has a Mixed Economic Model

Before deciding on the smaller details of any one economic policy, a society must first wrestle with the question of the proper role of government in regulating economic activity. To what degree should individuals and businesses be left alone to pursue their own economic interests? To what degree should a government intervene in order to, for example, protect workers, consumers, or the environment from excesses of economic competition and growth? While this question has never been fully settled once and for all, the relationship between markets and politics is one of the most impactful in a society.

In his foundational 1776 work *An Inquiry into the Nature and Causes of the Wealth of Nations*, Adam Smith argued that national economic prosperity can best be obtained by allowing individuals to freely pursue their own economic self-interest and bargain with others in a competitive marketplace. In a **laissez-faire** (meaning "to leave alone") **economy**, governments intrude as little as possible in the economic transactions between citizens and businesses. In reality, however, it has never been that simple. Even in the nineteenth century, for example, the federal government acted in the economy to support broad policy goals, such as the building of the transcontinental railroad.

At the other end of the fiscal policy spectrum is a **command-and-control economy** in which government dictates much of a nation's economic activity, including the amount of production and the prices of goods. Russia, for example, employs a command-and-control philosophy in its handling of fiscal policy.

America is neither a laissez-faire economy nor a command-and-control one. Rather, American fiscal policy follows a **mixed economy** approach in which many economic decisions are left to individuals and businesses, but the federal government also plays a role in shaping these decisions. In Chapter 3 we discussed American federalism and the growth of national influence across a host of policy areas, including those involving the economy.

Government Monitors the Health of the Economy

In its role in guiding the nation's fiscal policy, one of the main roles that the federal government plays is to monitor the health of the American economy. It collects and distributes data about that health and uses this information to guide future decisions in fiscal policy. To do this, federal fiscal policymakers often rely on a few key data indicators.

One of these indicators is the **gross domestic product (GDP)**, which attempts to measure the total value of goods and services produced by American economic activity. A decline or stagnation of the nation's GDP indicates that the country's economy is not firing on all cylinders and could be slipping into an economic recession in which American economic activity slows down. This is not good for American workers—or for their elected representatives should voters place the blame for the recession upon their shoulders.

Economists also focus on the nation's **unemployment rate** to gauge the health of American businesses. A rise in the unemployment rate indicates a private sector that is cutting back, not hiring, or laying off workers based on its own calculations about the health of the economy going forward.

A third key indicator of the health of the American economy is the rate of **inflation**, or the rise in the prices of goods and services purchased by individuals. A high rate of inflation, especially if not accompanied by an equal increase in wages, makes American workers poorer with all of the negative electoral consequences for government officials produced by this development. One key measure of inflation is the consumer price index (CPI). The CPI does not only effect voters' decisions; many programs that involve mandatory spending, such as Social Security payments, are tied to calculations of the nation's CPI.

Business Cycles

Definitions matter in the world of public policy. Describing the underlying issues and highlighting the problems in need of attention can open up or close off future paths of action. In the realm of economic policymaking, conflicts over defining problems and potential solutions arise, leading to very different policy proposals. Even when policymakers agree that an observed phenomenon exists, they often differ on explaining its sources or implications.

One of the most important observed patterns in economic policymaking is the fact that economies undergo shorter periods of expansion and contraction around underlying long-term trends. Economists use the term **business cycle** to describe this cyclical nature of economic activity (see Table 13.1). An economy experiencing a generally upward trend of positive GDP growth may still experience periods of contraction and expansion.

Where economists and policymakers differ, however, is on the sources of change in economic growth or contraction, of periods of rising or falling prices, or of rising or falling rates of unemployment. These differences in interpretation arise from fundamental outlooks about the drivers of economic outcomes, and they necessarily lead to different prescriptions when things go wrong.

Monetary Theory. To monetarists, the primary driver of business cycles is the supply of money in an economy, including credit markets. According to this theory, a policy of readily available money (whether through outright printing or making credit easier to obtain) will inevitably lead to price inflation with too much money chasing too few goods. Monetarists argue against government efforts to fine-tune the nation's economy through policies that stimulate it, such as large public works projects, or policies that restrict economic growth, such as increased levels of taxation. Instead, a government should try to match access to money to the growth in economic productivity.

TABLE 13.1 What Is the Best Way to Handle Business Cycles?

According to ...	The main driver of business cycles is ...	And so government should ...
Monetary Theory	The supply of money in the economy	Match the growth of money supply to the growth in economic productivity
Keynesianism	Aggregate decisions over saving and spending	Policy should be countercyclical to trends in consumer spending and saving
Supply-Side Theory	Fluctuations in the supply of money in the economy	Maintain a stable money supply and focus on low tax rates

Keynesianism. Another broad theory of business cycles comes from the work of John Maynard Keynes, whose highly influential work, *The General Theory of Employment, Interest, and Money*, was published in 1936 during the depths of the Great Depression.[18] For Keynes, the aggregation of individual decisions over saving and spending drives business cycles. During periods of expansion, individuals become overconfident about future economic conditions and may make excessive, unwise investing decisions, thus exacerbating the economic boom. In periods of economic contraction, by contrast, individuals become excessively gloomy and cut back on spending and investing, thereby exacerbating the contraction—possibly to the point of a national economic depression. For Keynes, therefore, governmental economic policy should be countercyclical, injecting more money into the economy during periods of contraction. Similarly, government should act as a brake on the economy during periods of expansion, running a budget surplus with the tax revenues received that can then be spent to prime the economic pump during the next downturn.

Supply-Side Theory. In stark contrast to Keynesian economic theory, which emphasizes the demand for goods and services, supply-side theory, as its name suggests, emphasizes the role of supply in fostering economic growth. Often called "Reaganomics" in reference to one of the theory's most influential proponents, President Ronald Reagan, supply-side theory proposes lower taxes on individuals and businesses as the most effective tool to combat economic downturns. Unlike Keynesians, who see a useful role for adjusting the supply of money in the arsenal of recession-fighting weapons, supply-side theorists argue for a stable money supply, focusing instead on a fiscal policy of low tax rates. Critics of supply-side theory often use the term *trickle-down economics* to describe it, arguing that these policies benefit the wealthy and that it is unlikely these benefits will make their way to individuals not directly impacted by lower tax rates.

Tax Policies Determine How Much Money the Government Can Spend

The federal government does not only spend; it also taxes its citizens to pay for its spending. Aside from a brief period during the Civil War, individual incomes were not taxed until 1913 and the ratification of the Sixteenth Amendment, which instituted a national tax on the incomes of Americans.

But how does the government set the national income tax rates? This has always been a politically charged issue. The debate has been about both the rates themselves and income tax deductions and exemptions. The result has been a vast and complicated system of income tax law.

Federal taxation policies, as vexing as they may be to individual taxpayers, determine the amount of money that the federal government takes in to pay for its fiscal policies. If the federal government takes in more money than it spends, then it runs a **budget surplus**. If not, it runs a **budget deficit**, forcing it to borrow from expected tax revenues and the economic activity that will produce these projected revenues. On this issue, one thing is clear: The federal

FIGURE 13.1

Federal Budget Deficits, Historical and Projected

The *y*-axis depicts the given year's surplus or deficit (*x*-axis) as a percentage of the nation's gross domestic product (GDP).

Source: Congressional Budget Office, Figure 1-1, Total Deficits or Surpluses, "An Update to the Budget and Economic Outlook: 2015 to 2025," https://www.cbo.gov/sites/default/files/114th-congress-2015-2016/reports/50724-BudEconOutlook-3.pdf.

government has been, is, and will be borrowing from future activity for the foreseeable future (see Figure 13.1).

While the federal government plays a critical role in guiding and supporting the American economy, it does not do so on its own. The decisions of corporations and other national governments may have their own effects on the nation's economic performance. Another major player is the board of governors of the **Federal Reserve System**, often referred to as the Fed.

The Fed is the most important player in charting national **monetary policy,** which regulates the amount of money in the economy (in circulation and in the deposits) and influences **interest rates**, the rates paid to borrow money. The system's primary tools involve buying and selling Treasury securities—through which the federal government borrows money—regulating the amount of deposits that banks must keep as reserves, and setting the interest rate at which banks can borrow money from the Fed. By using these three tools, the Fed also influences other interest rates in the economy since banks and credit card companies usually adjust the rates that they charge their own customers in response to the actions of the Fed.

The Federal Reserve System is not without its critics. Some question whether or not it is truly independent of politics, especially when an anxious Congress or president is urging it to take action. Others critique the Fed's stated goal of maintaining a "moderate inflation" of, say, 2 percent. While a 2 percent rise in the price of goods and services might not seem so drastic in one year, over time persistent moderate inflation undercuts the spending power of Americans if they are unable to increase their own wages. Still, others question the wisdom of giving so much power to an entity that, though governed by a nominated and confirmed board, is mostly owned by private banks.

1. The government uses fiscal policy to take action to produce desirable economic outcomes for Americans.

   a. True
   b. False

2. In a _____ economy, many economic decisions are left to individuals and businesses, but the federal government also plays a role in shaping these decisions.

   a. Command-and-control
   b. Mixed
   c. Laissez-faire
   d. Fiscal

3. Government uses the measures of gross domestic product (GDP), the unemployment rate, the inflation rate, and the consumer price index (CPI) to _____.

   a. Plan command-and-control policies

   b. Determine who will receive social benefits
   c. Set Americans' incomes
   d. Measure the health of the economy

4. Keynesianism is the business cycle theory that calls for _____.

   a. Matching the growth of money supply to the growth in economic productivity
   b. Enacting policies that are countercyclical to trends in consumer spending and saving
   c. Maintaining a stable money supply and focusing on low tax rates
   d. Buying low and selling high

Answer Key: 1. a; 2. b; 3. d; 4. b.

FOREIGN POLICY ADVANCES AMERICANS' INTERESTS ABROAD

- Describe the events and actors that have shaped American foreign policy.

On November 9, 1989, a wall came down—a wall between two hostile and nuclear-armed global superpowers. It was the Berlin Wall, which had stood, in some form, since 1961. The wall divided West and East, not just in Berlin but also across the globe. Symbolically, it divided capitalism from communism, the United States of America and its allies from the Union of Soviet Socialist Republics (USSR) and its allies and client states. That day, the leader of the East German Communist Party announced that citizens of the communist German Democratic Republic could cross the border freely, and they did. Some climbed over the wall; others took to it with hammers, pickaxes, or whatever tools they had.

The Soviet Union officially ceased to exist on December 26, 1991, the day after Soviet president Mikhail Gorbachev, one of the key architects of these changes, resigned. On the top of the Kremlin, the Soviet flag was taken down and replaced by a nearly century-old Russian flag. The fall of the wall signaled to the world the coming end of the Cold War, during which two superpowers, the United States of America and the USSR—allies during World War II—had glared at each other from opposite sides of the globe and opposite sides of the ideological spectrum, each backed, at the height of the military buildup, by tens of thousands of nuclear weapons. It was called a "cold" war because it never went "hot" in the sense that full and open warfare between the two nations never happened, though it could have. The superpowers, however, did become involved in conflicts in other countries during the time.

With the collapse of the Soviet Union and the end of the Cold War, the world collectively breathed a sigh of relief that perhaps the danger of a potentially planet-changing global war was over. What had been for decades a world characterized by bipolarity wherein two global superpowers had struggled for ideological and military dominance suddenly seemed to be defined by unipolarity wherein the United States stood alone as the unquestioned ideological, economic, and military superpower—a hyperpower, really. Nearly three decades after the fall of the Berlin Wall communism has not made a successful challenge to Western liberalism and capitalism.

U.S. secretary of state John Kerry meeting with Russian foreign minister Sergei Lavrov, left, and Russian president Vladimir Putin, right, to discuss the situation in Syria in December 2015. The United States and Russia have a long and complex foreign policy history. Kremlin Press Center /Anadolu Agency/ Getty Images

By the twenty-first century, however, the world had changed in other ways. History, it seems, has its own timetable. As a result of its breathtaking economic development, China has emerged as a global economic power and has undertaken a significant military buildup to protect its national interests. The Russian Federation, though no longer possessing the size and conventional military might of the vast former Soviet Union—but still with a massive nuclear capability—has begun to act against what it sees as a renewed and aggressive American policy of trying to restrain and contain Russian influence and an unproductive and arrogant use of its superpower status across the globe.

Has the era of American global supremacy ended? Has the world gone from unipolar to multipolar with powers such as Russia and China challenging over two decades of American unilateral supremacy and placing new limits on America's use of military, economic, and diplomatic power? The jury is still out on this issue.

What is clear, however, is that by 2015 Russia, often referred to as "the bear," had emerged from its hibernation and began to act more assertively to protect its own interests, especially its boundaries. This behavior was fueled partly by a deep mistrust of American intentions in deploying antiballistic missile technology in Europe and partly by the desire of Russia to protect its allies and security in Ukraine and in the Middle East. As 2015 turned into 2016, the United States and Russia found themselves diplomatically at odds; the potential for direct military conflict between the two nuclear powers was not 100 percent out of the question. If the old cold war, or, perhaps, a new cold war goes hot, Syria may very well be where it starts. Before we get to that, however, just a bit more of history.

Just as the United States has changed since its founding, so has its relationship to the rest of the world. And just as the national government has grown tremendously, especially in the twentieth century, so have the various parts of the foreign policy decision-making apparatus.

The Beginnings

In his Farewell Address to the nation, after declining to run for a third presidential term, George Washington presented a muted perspective of American influence. Washington's admonishments pointed in many ways to a policy of **isolationism**, wherein a nation attempts to stay out of foreign entanglements. The fact is that the United States has never been a truly isolationist nation, even in its early decades. In 1803, as president, in spite of his worries about the strength of the national government, Jefferson oversaw the successful purchase of the Louisiana Territory from Napoleon Bonaparte of France. This transaction nearly doubled the size of the nation in one $15 million deal.[19] During his administration, Jefferson also expanded and employed the U.S. Navy.[20]

American Influence in the Western Hemisphere in the Nineteenth Century

In 1812 the nation again went to war with Great Britain, partly over trade issues. In 1823 President James Monroe announced what is known as the Monroe Doctrine, a policy that asserted American interests in and primacy over actions in the Western Hemisphere. President Theodore Roosevelt expanded upon the Monroe Doctrine in 1904 by issuing the Roosevelt Corollary, which asserted that the United States was the guarantor of political, military, and economic stability in Latin America and the Caribbean. The corollary involved the use of American armed forces to back up its provisions.

Four Global Wars in the Twentieth and Twenty-First Centuries

The patterns of global involvement that had dominated America's approach for more than a century—defined by economic involvement globally but a lack of military involvement outside of the Western Hemisphere—began to change in the twentieth century and into the twenty-first. Four wars, two "hot," one "cold," and one whose boundaries are still being defined, served as the catalysts for these changes, which not only redefined America's role in the world but the nation itself.

Though the United States had, in decades prior, chosen to actively engage with other nations to protect its interests (especially in the Western Hemisphere), arguments for isolationism still shaped much of its foreign policy. In the twentieth century, however, the nation began to adopt a foreign policy defined much more by **internationalism**, an approach that emphasizes closer contact and cooperation between nations.

The first of the four wars, World War I, established the United States as a major player in global economic and military affairs. The second, World War II, which came after a period in which America had once again withdrawn to its own hemisphere, established the nation as a major military and economic superpower. The third, the Cold War, locked America into an ideological, economic, diplomatic, and occasionally military conflict with the other global superpower, the Soviet Union. The fourth, the so-called war on terror, is still being fought today. This conflict is challenging the very notion of what a national boundary is and raising questions of what the limits should be on the use of American military force.

World War I. American intervention in World War I (1914–1918) was initially opposed by large numbers of citizens who saw it as a conflict between European monarchies and autocratic governments that did not, nor should, involve the United States. Eventually, after helping convince the people through the intentional use of political propaganda, America entered the war in 1917 and allied with France and Great Britain against Germany and the Austro-Hungarian Empire. Many other nations were involved in the global conflict, including Russia and Japan on the allied side and the Ottoman Empire (which included the modern-day nation of Turkey) on the side of the Central Powers of Germany and the Austro-Hungarian Empire. It was the most global and destructive war in human history to that point; however, it would not be the last or the most horrific.

The war—and the allies' victory—changed the global map, the global balance of power, and the international system in a major way. The United States was established as a global military and economic power. American involvement had major effects at home as restrictions on civil liberties in the name of national security were put in place—restrictions that had not been seen to such an extent since the actions of President Abraham Lincoln during the Civil War.

World War II. World War II (1939–1945) surpassed World War I as the largest and most destructive war in human history. The deaths in World War II have never been accurately tallied, especially in the Soviet Union. Civilian deaths were almost certainly greater than those of combat personnel. Sixty million people is often cited as an estimate of the war's final global toll.

Many of the seeds of World War II had been sown by the consequences of World War I. As in World War I, the list of participants in World War II was long. Primarily, however, it pitted the allies (France, Great Britain, the United States, and the Soviet Union) against the axis powers (Germany, Japan, and Italy).[21] Following grinding island

A man stands amidst the ruins of Hiroshima, Japan. The United States dropped the world's first atomic bomb on that city on August 6, 1945, at the end of World War II, killing an estimated seventy thousand people instantly and completely destroying the city. Three days later, the United States dropped a second bomb on Nagasaki. Many thousands more died over the following years due to radiation; the total number of the victims is thought to be approximately 340,000. Hajime Miyatake/The Asahi Shimbun via Getty Images campaigns in the Pacific, the firebombing of cities in Germany and Japan (in which hundreds of thousands of civilians were incinerated), and a nearly unimaginably horrific block-to-block battle in Berlin, the war finally ended with two atomic bombs dropped on Japan by the United States in August 1945—the first on Hiroshima and the second on Nagasaki. World War II had ended, the atomic age had begun, and for a time the American economy produced as much industrial output as the rest of the world combined.[22]

The Cold War. The two clearly victorious powers in the aftermath of World War II, America and the Soviet Union, quickly became enemies.[23] The world had become bipolar. In the words of former British prime minister Winston Churchill, "From Stettin in the Baltic to Trieste in the Adriatic an iron curtain has descended across the continent. . . . The safety of the world, ladies and gentlemen, requires a unity in Europe, from which no nation should be permanently outcast."[24] On the Western side of this curtain were America and its allies (North Atlantic Treaty Organization [NATO] members). On the Eastern side, the Soviet Union and its client states dominated, having formed the Warsaw Pact in 1955 in response to the creation of NATO. The possibility of tanks rolling across the iron curtain was very real, as was the threat of nuclear confrontation.

Neither superpower engaged in all-out war against the other in the era of nuclear weapons, though both sponsored governments and rebels in proxy wars across the globe in order to undercut the other's influence and power. Instead, the goal of American military policy became one of **containment**, or the restriction of the expansion of Soviet ideological and military influence, using military force if necessary.

Part of America's containment strategy was to rebuild Western Europe as a bulwark against Soviet expansion into the parts of Germany and the rest of Western Europe that the United States, Great Britain, and the Soviet Union had agreed would remain under Western control. A key tool in this policy was the Marshall Plan, named after Secretary of State George Marshall, who had been instrumental in mobilizing and organizing American economic and military output during World War II. The plan involved loans and aid to the devastated nations of Western Europe and established organizations of economic cooperation that would eventually lead to the modern European Union (EU).

The American response to threats of Soviet expansion in Western Europe were not just economic; they were also diplomatic, including efforts within multinational institutions, such as the United Nations, to gather other countries in support of Soviet containment. These efforts involved military commitments. In 1949 the North Atlantic Treaty was signed, creating NATO, a mutual defense pact in which member nations agree to "settle any international dispute in which they may be involved by peaceful means in such a manner that international peace and security and justice are not endangered, and to refrain in their international relations from the threat or use of force in any manner inconsistent with the purposes of the United Nations."[25]

The **Cold War** was a very real and major conflict in which each superpower used its economic, political, and military might to influence nations across the globe. It spawned many proxy wars in which the United States and the Soviet

Union, rather than fighting each other directly, supported competing factions in places such as Southeast Asia, Africa, and Central America. One disputed area of influence during the war was Cuba, and in 1962 both nuclear powers nearly went to war over the deployment of Soviet nuclear ballistic missiles in that country. This incident is known as the Cuban missile crisis.

In the 1980s, President Ronald Reagan put into effect what is known as the Reagan Doctrine, which offered American assistance to anticommunist groups, most notably in Nicaragua and Afghanistan. This assistance included military training and weaponry. Citizens in both nations suffered the effects of the conflicts that were fueled and supported by the distant superpowers. In particular, American assistance in the resistance of Afghanis to Soviet occupation in Afghanistan had repercussions that continue today. The Afghani mujahideen, whom America armed most effectively with shoulder-fired missiles that decimated Soviet helicopters, successfully expelled the Soviet military from their nation. Years later, however, some of the mujahideen's former members and leaders, along with new recruits, turned their anger toward the United States and helped plan the 9/11 terrorist attacks.

The Cold War ended with the collapse and disintegration of the Soviet Union in 1991. What had been a bipolar world with two major powers shaping the political, military, and economic landscape of the globe suddenly became a unipolar one wherein the United States stood alone as the world's unquestioned military and economic superpower.

World War II and the Cold War that followed did not just change America's relationship with other nations; they changed America itself. These two wars resulted in a major expansion of American military, political, and diplomatic engagement across the globe in order to counter the threat of Soviet power whenever possible. They also resulted in a massive expansion of the American military and intelligence-gathering bureaucracy.

The War on Terror. The fourth war, the global war on terror, changed things yet again. This conflict drew many nations, including the United States and its allies and Russia and its partners and allies, into the cauldron of civil war in the Middle East and North Africa in a complex and contentious way.

Terrorism was not invented in the twenty-first century. The term refers to the use of extreme and inhumane violence to achieve *political* ends. It is fundamentally a political tool.

On September 11, 2001, members of the terrorist organization al-Qaeda, under the leadership of Osama bin Laden, hijacked and crashed four U.S. commercial aircraft in U.S. targets including the twin towers of the World Trade Center in New York City and the Pentagon in Washington, D.C. Nearly three thousand people died, including over four hundred firefighters, law enforcement officers, and paramedics responding to the attacks on the World Trade Center.

America's response to these attacks was immense and far-reaching. The administration of President George W. Bush declared a war on terrorism and, with congressional authorization, brought American military power to bear. Bush sent forces into combat in Afghanistan in 2001; Afghanistan was the country from which Osama bin Laden had operated, planned, and recruited individuals for the terrorist attacks.

In 2003 the United States invaded Iraq. Though Saddam Hussein's autocratic regime proved not to have been a part of the 9/11 attacks, Bush named the nation as part of an "axis of evil" (along with Iran and North Korea)—the defeat of which he argued was necessary to ensure the security of the United States. In a speech at West Point in 2002, Bush articulated a theory of **preemptive war** in which the United States would use its military might to challenge adversaries before they launched attacks upon the nation or harbored those who might do so.

Bush's decision to move against Iraq in 2003 without a formal declaration of war—but with congressional authorization—remains one of the most controversial and impactful choices in foreign policy in the nation's history. Militarily, the battle was quick and successful—though not without great effort and sacrifice by American soldiers both during combat and in the years that followed. By April 9, 2003, less than a month after the beginning of air and ground operations, America and its coalition partners had captured the nation's capital, Baghdad. In December, Iraq's former leader, Saddam Hussein, was captured, tried by an Iraqi tribunal, and hung.

The decision to go to war against Iraq and the long-term consequences of that decision, however, are still debated. Prior to the war, in February 2003, Secretary of State Colin Powell presented to the United Nations evidence that Saddam Hussein had undertaken efforts to procure weapons of mass destruction. According to Powell, "Indeed, the facts and Iraq's behavior show that Saddam Hussein and his regime are concealing their efforts to produce more weapons of mass destruction."[26] But the truth behind those accusations and the national intelligence that informed Powell's statements were later challenged.[27]

Following victory, the U.S. government chose to disband the Iraqi military, as some commentators have asserted, "without the knowledge or consent of either the Pentagon or the President."[28] Some of the Iraqi army's former officers and soldiers chose to join a radical Sunni Muslim resistance group founded by Abu Musab al-Zarqawi. The militant Islamic organization has many names: the Islamic State in Iraq and Syria (ISIS), the Islamic State in Iraq and the Levant (ISIL), and Daesh. The last is a derogatory term, and the movement's leaders threaten "to cut off the tongue of anyone heard using it."[29] Today there is not even a consensus on what to call the group, much less how to deal with it.

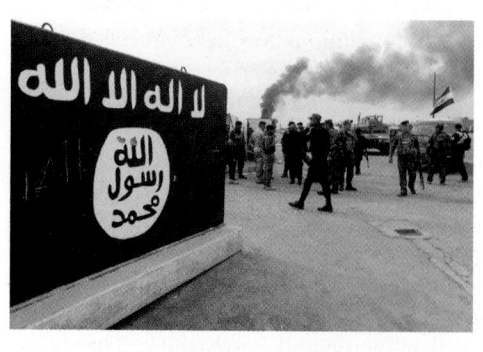

Iraqi security forces and other allies gather next to a mural depicting the emblem of the Islamic State of Iraq and Syria (ISIS) outside one of the presidential palaces in Tikrit on April 1, 2015. ISIS rose to power during the instability in Iraq and the region as a whole after the American invasion.
AHMAD AL-RUBAYE/AFP/Getty Images

The Aftermath of the War on Terror

On December 17, 2010, Mohamed Bouazizi, a street vendor in the North African nation of Tunisia, poured flammable liquid over his body and set himself on fire. He later died from his burns. By some accounts, Bouazizi made this tragic statement in protest against local police corruption and a lack of response to it by the autocratic government of Tunisian president Zine El Abidine Ben Ali.

Bouazizi's tragic death sparked a series of protests in the nation of Tunisia. Modern communications technologies played a key role in their spread. "Protesters took to the streets with 'a rock in one hand, a cell phone in the other,' according to Rochdi Horchani—a relative of Mohamed Bouazizi—who helped break through the [government-imposed] media blackout."[30]

More protests followed against authoritarian governments in North Africa and the Middle East, and the governments of some nations were overthrown. The uprisings, which became known as the **Arab Spring**, were rooted in a history of Western control over the region, autocratic governments, and centuries-old tensions between groups of individuals in the nations involved. They were sparked largely by young members of these nations who were connected to the world and to each other through modern communications technologies and social media. As it spread across the affected regions, the Arab Spring led to democratic reforms in some nations, such as Tunisia, and to hope.

In other nations, however, spring led to winter and then chaos. "Almost every Arab country is either worse off than it was in 2011 or no significant positive change has occurred, so the phase that the region is in right now is a brutal winter," said Amy Hawthorne, deputy director of research at the Project on Middle East Democracy.[31]

Particularly affected was Syria. The country's boundaries had been drawn by the victorious powers after World War I without sufficient consideration of the various factions within the area, and these cleavages resulted in an earthquake.[32] There were protests and calls for democratic reforms but also atrocities and civil war, which led to the eventual intervention of outside powers, including the United States and Russia. Though both countries had the same goal of fighting terrorist groups in Syria and other nations, they were often on opposite sides of conflicts, especially in Syria.

In 2011, according to news accounts, "peaceful protests inspired by earlier revolutions in Egypt and Tunisia rose up to challenge the dictatorship running [Syria]. The government [of Bashar al-Assad] responded—there is no getting around this—like monsters. First, security forces quietly killed activists. Then they started kidnapping, raping, torturing and killing activists and their family members, including a lot of children, dumping their mutilated bodies by the sides of roads. Then troops began simply opening fire on protests. Eventually civilians started shooting back."[33]

One of the groups fighting against the al-Assad regime was ISIS. Some of its future leaders had been imprisoned in neighboring Iraq, captured with the assistance of American forces.[34] The terrorist group's goal was clear: to establish a worldwide caliphate, an Islamic state ruled by a political and religious leader with absolute authority. Its tactics were horrific; it publicized beheadings and burning people alive through social media. ISIS members also, according to widespread reports from Syria and Iraq, sold women and girls into sexual slavery.[35]

The Syrian cauldron continued to burn. By the end of 2015, it was estimated that fully half of Syria's population of twenty-three million had been displaced, either within the country or to other nations. Jordan and Turkey received the

American Public Opinion Regarding the Diplomatic Effort over Syrian Chemical Weapons Capabilities

In a poll conducted in September 2013 in the wake of the Russian-brokered diplomatic deal to dismantle Syrian chemical weapons capabilities, a majority of Americans supported the deal but mistrusted the intentions of both Syria and Russia.[36]

The following graphs display responses to a series of questions from all Americans surveyed.

These assessments, unsurprisingly, differed based on the partisan identification of the respondents in the survey.

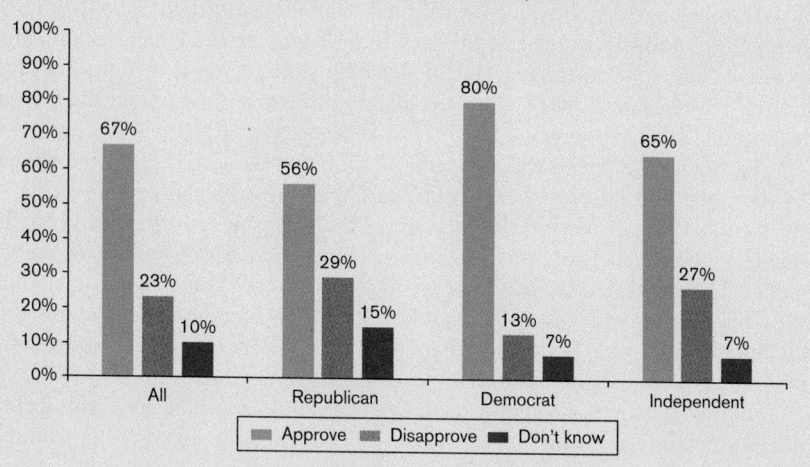

Obama's delay of airstrike decision for diplomatic efforts . . .

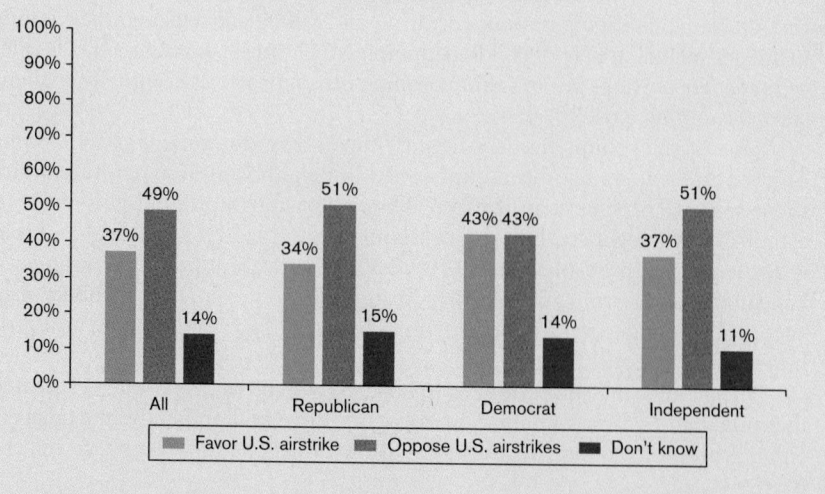

If Syria doesn't give up chemical weapons . . .

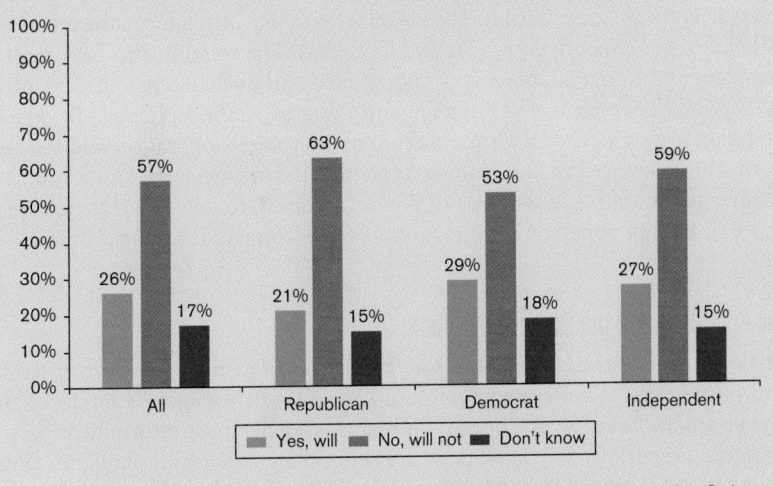

Will Syria give up chemical weapons in response to diplomacy?

Legend: Yes, will | No, will not | Don't know

All: 26%, 57%, 17%
Republican: 21%, 63%, 15%
Democrat: 29%, 53%, 18%
Independent: 27%, 59%, 15%

Source: Data for all figures are from Pew Research Center, "Public Backs Diplomatic Approach in Syria, but Distrusts Syria and Russia," September 16, 2013, www.people-press.org/2013/09/16/public-backs-diplomatic-approach-in-syria-but-distrusts-syria-and-russia.

WHAT DO YOU THINK?

Given what we have learned about the degree to which Americans are informed about political issues or actually have meaningful opinions (see Chapter 5), are you skeptical of these results? Do you think Americans have sufficient knowledge of foreign affairs to formulate meaningful opinions on specific diplomatic efforts?

largest share of refugees, but Europe also took in sizable numbers. The United States took in comparatively few Syrians.

Many Players Are Involved in the Formation of American Foreign Policy

When we think about who actually formulates and implements American foreign policy, two key actors often come to mind: (1) the president and (2) Congress. In addition, however, the president oversees multiple departments, agencies, and bureaus, each with their own foreign policy agendas. Congressional foreign policy action takes place amidst debates between party members and in the context of a committee system that subdivides their responsibilities. As you will see, conflicts *within* the two branches of government are as consequential as conflicts *between* them.

The U.S. Constitution

Political scientist Edward Corwin is often quoted as asserting that the Constitution "is an invitation to struggle for the privilege of directing American foreign policy."[37] Corwin was correct. The Framers planted the seeds for such struggle in the document itself. The key players in that struggle are the president, as head of the executive branch, and Congress. The relationship between the president and Congress, however, is not a fixed and unchanging one. According to Corwin, "The relations of President and Congress in the diplomatic field have, first and, last, presented a varied picture of alternate cooperation and tension, from which emerge two outstanding facts: first, the overwhelming importance of Presidential initiative in this area of power; secondly, the ever increasing dependence of foreign policy on Congressional cooperation and support."[38]

The President and the Executive Branch

The president of the United States is the most powerful single actor in setting and implementing American foreign policy. Two of the main sources of this power are information and speed. Though presidents must inform members of Congress, especially key leaders, of foreign policy issues and plans, no single member of Congress or any congressional committee has access to the same amount of information as the president. And Congress is slower. Deliberation, legislation, and partisan conflict all make the legislature move far slower than executive action in responding to crises, formulating policy, or rallying the American public to achieve some desired outcome.

The power of information, though important, does have limitations. The various bureaucratic organizations within the executive branch that provide information to the president may have their own agendas and may not all have the same analyses, objectives, and conclusions. And the power that presidents possess has its own challenges. Presidential action makes it very clear to the nation who is responsible for a policy decision. When things go well, a president may gain widespread support from the American people and the political power that goes with that. When things do not, the president gets blamed. As we will discuss shortly, political calculations about who might receive blame for a decision lead us to a more complex evaluation of executive and legislative relations in foreign policy, especially in cases that involve military conflict.

Executive Branch Departments. A vast array of departments, agencies, and bureaus assists the president in gathering information, formulating policy, and responding to international crises. The Department of State, led by the secretary of state, is primarily responsible for diplomatic relationships with other nations. Many of its tens of thousands of employees are posted abroad. This department is responsible for advising the president on the positions and concerns of foreign governments and the realities on the ground in those nations. State employees also negotiate with their counterparts in other countries and represent the interests of American citizens residing abroad. While ambassadors take the lead in communicating with their assigned governments, lower-level State Department employees, including foreign service officers, do much of the actual day-to-day work.

For much of American history, the Department of State was the dominant foreign policy player within the executive branch, but today many other organizations and suborganizations also exert considerable influence. Many of these changes occurred in the twentieth and twenty-first centuries in response to the wars that we have discussed.

The powerful Department of Defense was created after World War II with the combination of the War Department and the Department of the Navy. It is the dominant executive branch department in formulating and enacting American defense policy and managing the U.S. armed forces. It is the largest department by personnel, with millions of employees, including American servicemen and servicewomen. In accordance with the policy of civilian control over the military, the Department of Defense is led by a secretary of defense whose most onerous responsibility is to assist the president in devising military policy and developing options on the use of force in a given conflict.

The newest cabinet department—and one of the most influential in conducting American foreign policy—is the Department of Homeland Security. This department was originally devised through an executive order issued by President George W. Bush and then formally established by Congress following the 9/11 attacks. A combination of some previously existing agencies and some new ones, the department oversees and implements policies enacted to respond to national disasters (the Federal Emergency Management Agency [FEMA]), secure transit points to and within the United States (the Transportation Security Agency), and protect the nation's borders (the Coast Guard and Customs and Border Protection).

State, defense, and homeland security are the major cabinet departments in formulating and implementing American foreign policy. But they are not the only ones. Secretaries and members of the Department of Commerce, the Department of Agriculture, and the Department of Labor also have their own goals to pursue in advancing the objectives of their constituents and influential interest group members.

Advice and Intelligence Gathering. While the Department of State takes the lead in helping the president formulate and implement diplomatic efforts and the Department of Defense takes the same role in military matters, other agencies and groups also advise the president on the conduct of foreign policy, especially in matters concerning military policy options and those devoted to gathering, assessing, filtering, and interpreting intelligence.

Advising the president on military options are the members of the Joint Chiefs of Staff, composed of a chair, a vice chair, and leaders from the military services (army, navy, air force, and marines). Their role is not one of command but is an advisory one, and they are assisted by hundreds of officers within the armed forces.

Also assisting the president are leaders and members of organizations devoted to gathering and assessing information and intelligence. Within the White House are the members of the National Security Council, which is composed of, among others, the president; the vice president; the secretaries of state, defense, and homeland security; the chair of the Joint Chiefs of Staff; and the director of national intelligence. The council meets to provide the president with intelligence, analysis, and advice on critical matters of national security.

The intelligence community, composed of all the intelligence agencies and their members, offers its own information and advice to the president. Following the 9/11 attacks, many concerns were raised about a lack of coordination between intelligence-gathering agencies and bureaus, so Congress reorganized the intelligence-gathering structure within the national government and placed the director of national intelligence at the top of the new structure.[39] Many organizations within the intelligence community gather information and funnel it to the president, including the Central Intelligence Agency (CIA), the Defense Intelligence Agency (which provides intelligence support for the Defense Department and the Joint Chiefs of Staff), the National Reconnaissance Office (which directs spaced-based–intelligence-gathering capabilities), and the Federal Bureau of Investigation (FBI), along with specific service intelligence offices within the armed forces divisions and many other agencies and groups.

Congress and the Power to Make War

While Congress has fewer constitutionally defined responsibilities than the president, it nonetheless exerts considerable influence over American foreign policy. As we have discussed, the Senate exerts its power of advice and consent in the ratification of treaties and in the confirmation of ambassadors, cabinet secretaries, and many other leaders and deputies in executive branch departments, agencies, and bureaus.

In the spirit of "separated institutions sharing powers,"[40] Congress also plays a major role with its power to declare war. In the wake of the fallout from the American withdrawal from South Vietnam, in response to concerns by many members of Congress that America had been drawn into a major proxy war against the Soviet Union in Vietnam, Congress passed the War Powers Resolution in 1973.

Passed over President Richard Nixon's veto, the War Powers Resolution has been one of the most enduring and controversial legacies of his presidency.[41] The resolution is credited by some scholars as being "the high-water mark of congressional reassertion in national security affairs."[42] Passed during the weakening of Nixon's authority as the Watergate investigations unfolded, the War Powers Resolution was the product of widespread public and congressional dissatisfaction with the prosecution and expansion of the Vietnam conflict and unilateral presidential actions by Presidents Johnson and Nixon.

Under the terms of the War Powers Resolution, a president may only introduce armed forces into conflict or likely conflict if one of the three following conditions occurs: (1) a declaration of war by Congress, (2) a specific statutory authorization by Congress, or (3) a national emergency created by an attack on the United States, its territories or possessions, or its armed forces.[43]

Once introduced, the president is required within forty-eight hours to notify Congress of "the circumstances necessitating the introduction of United States Armed Forces; . . . the constitutional and legislative authority under which such introduction took place; and . . . the estimated scope and duration of the hostilities or involvement."[44] Unless Congress has declared war, passed specific authorization, extended the deadline, or is physically unable to meet, the president must withdraw those forces within sixty days; a thirty-day extension is allowed if necessary to withdraw those forces safely.[45]

The last war officially declared by Congress was World War II.[46] Since that time, American armed forces have been involved in conflicts across the globe, with U.S. military personnel operating in more than one hundred countries, though many of these are or were allies or military partners. American presidents have routinely held that the War Powers Resolution unconstitutionally restricts their war power, though they have also routinely pursued congressional authorization of the use of military force consistent with the resolution. Some critics of the resolution argue that it actually makes the president more powerful, as the president may feel less constrained during those sixty or ninety days than he or she would if the resolution did not exist.[47]

In the twenty-first century, these issues are even more complicated. Acting against stateless actors, such as transnational terrorist organizations, challenges the very definition of a declaration of war. On whom does one declare war upon? With whom would one sign a peace treaty? The technological development of military assets only makes things trickier. Does, for example, the use of American drones (remote-controlled aircraft), whether to observe or fire upon enemies, constitute a "commitment" of American forces to combat? Questions such as this continue to be debated.

In August 2013, Obama went to Congress, asking it to authorize military force against the regime of al-Assad in Syria based on disputed reports that the Syrian government had used chemical weapons in its efforts to suppress an internal revolt. "While I believe I have the authority to carry out this military action without specific congressional authorization, I know that the country will be stronger if we take this course, and our actions will be even more effective," Obama said. "We should have this debate, because the issues are too big for business as usual."[48]

In the end, neither the debate nor the attack happened. In September, the United States and Russia reached an agreement to oversee the dismantling of Syrian chemical weapons and the capabilities to produce them. The diplomatic effort was spearheaded by Russia and gained steam amidst the ambivalence of American allies, including Great Britain, and congressional opposition in the United States. Obama decided to pursue the diplomatic track.

American-supported rebels in Syria were furious. "Gen Salim Idris, the head of the Supreme Military Council of the rebel Free Syrian Army denounced the agreement. 'All of this initiative does not interest us. Russia is a partner with the regime in killing the Syrian people,' he told reporters in Istanbul [Turkey]. 'A crime against humanity has been committed, and there is not any mention of accountability.'"[49]

U.S. president Donald Trump (right) meets with Russian president Vladimir Putin at the G20 Summit in Hamburg in July 2017. A separate U.S.-Russia–brokered truce for southern Syria is meant to help allay growing concerns by neighboring Jordan and Israel about Iranian military ambitions in the area. AP Photo/Evan Vucci, File

By the fall of 2017, the fate of the people of Syria remained uncertain, and the crisis continued.

The president, the rest of the executive branch foreign policy apparatus, and Congress do not act in a vacuum. Members of interest groups—whether acting on behalf of their members' economic self-interest or to promote human rights or global environmental policy—pressure members of the national government to adopt their policy objectives. American public opinion may also influence the formation of foreign policy—though generally only in the aftermath of wars and conflicts that bring the consequences of battle home. The polarized atmosphere of partisan politics in Washington, D.C., also has consequences for the formulation and implementation of American foreign policy.

Economics and American Foreign Policy

In advancing American interests, diplomacy and military capabilities are important, but they are not the only tools available to the national government. Economic policy also factors into foreign policy calculations in a major way. This, too, is often tricky. Adopting a policy of **protectionism**—restricting access by foreign producers to the nation's markets in order to benefit specific domestic agricultural, industrial, and service providers—can shield certain American individuals and organizations from foreign competition. However, these efforts can restrict overall global economic activity and prosperity.

Most current American efforts to coordinate international economic policy focus instead on fostering **free trade**, which offers few restrictions on the flow of goods and services across national borders. While overall global economic prosperity may benefit from free trade, those domestic producers who suffer from these policies—and the interest groups that represent them—will most certainly voice their concerns in Washington. When the free flow of goods and services involves nations with less-than-stellar support for workers' rights or environmental protections, these trade relationships may come at a political cost for an administration that supports or encourages them.

Trade agreements may be bilateral, which means they are struck between the United States and only one other nation. Increasingly, however, foreign economic policy actors have focused on regional trade agreements, which bring a group of nations into an overall agreement. In 1993 the United States entered into the North American Free Trade Agreement (NAFTA) with Canada and Mexico, increasing trade between the nations but also costing Americans jobs, an outcome that remains highly debated. In the fall of 2016, Obama continued to push for congressional support for the Trans-Pacific Partnership (TPP), a regional trade agreement struck between twelve nations in the Pacific Rim, including Mexico, Australia, and East Asian and South American nations. In his campaign, President-elect Donald Trump had promised to kill the TPP. After his election, President Trump ended that initiative.

Soft power can be used to promote American interests in other countries. Soft power refers to advancing a nation's interests by exporting its values and culture abroad.[50] American has, and continues to be, a major player in the use of soft power through its universities, athletic teams, music, movies, and restaurants.

The exportation of soft power, however, may cause resistance from members of other nations, who might resent or resist what they see as an undermining of their own cultural or religious traditions.

1. Isolationism is a foreign policy orientation in which a nation actively engages in foreign problems.
   a. True
   b. False

2. During the Cold War, the United States attempted to restrict of the expansion of Soviet ideological and military influence, using military force if necessary, through a strategy of _____.
   a. Protectionism
   b. Preemption
   c. Unipolarity
   d. Containment

3. The term *preventive war* is often used to describe actions undertaken to prevent future terrorist attacks. What do you think are the key challenges and controversies that might arise from the adoption of this strategy?

4. There has always been conflict between American presidents and Congress over the conduct of American foreign policy. Why do think this is so?

Answer Key: 1. b; 2. d; 3. Answers may include the justification for such actions, international opposition to them, and the possibility of inflaming local or regional conflicts; 4. Answers should include a discussion of separation of powers and the overlapping roles that the president and Congress play.

FROM SYRIA TO NORTH TEXAS

From War and Chaos to the Pursuit of the American Dream

According to many accounts, Daraa, Syria, is where the nation's civil war started, after antiregime graffiti was painted on a wall by teenagers in February 2011 in support of the Arab Spring.[51] The Syrian government's response was reportedly brutal: "In a gloomy interrogation room the children were beaten and bloodied, burned and had their fingernails pulled out."[52] Syrian citizens in Daraa, Damascus, and other cities began to protest. In March, Syrian forces opened fire against protesters in Daraa, killing at least four. By April the Syrian government laid siege to Daraa. CNN reported, "Mass arrests unfolded and tales of torture spread across the country. The protest movement grew and solidified into an opposition."[53]

By 2013 Daraa had become a living nightmare, caught between rebel fighters from the Free Syrian Army (FSA) and government forces. One of the residents of Daraa trying to survive was Faez al Sharaa. He had worked in the health insurance industry in Syria before the chaos; his wife, Shaza, had been a schoolteacher. In March he ran into soldiers from the Syrian Army. The following was reported in *Time* magazine:

> Faez al Sharaa was sure he was going to die.... On that Tuesday morning in late March Faez was confronted by a group of Syrian army soldiers. They were looking for a man who had been spotted with a handgun. Faez and three others were detained and accused of being terrorists. Standing at gunpoint, his hands in the air, he recalls

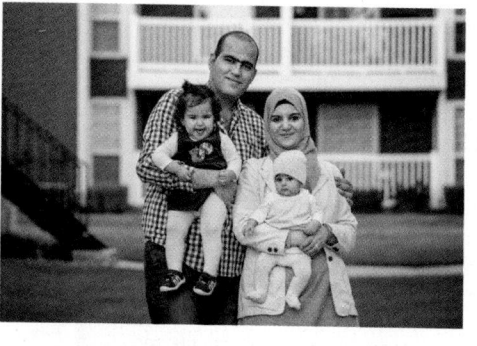

Faez al Sharaa with his family outside of their home in Richardson, Texas, in 2015. Michael Kirby Smith

feeling furious with himself for risking the solo walk to work. "We felt death upon us, and we accepted it," he says now. "I can't describe it in words." He got lucky. At that moment, an old woman barreled into the street, begging the gun-toting soldiers to spare these men. They were her son, her nephew, her neighbors, the old lady pleaded. Faez had never seen the woman before. But the soldiers relented. The stranger saved his life.[54]

Deciding to flee the war-torn nation, Faez, his wife, and his daughter became refugees, paying smugglers to help spirit them into neighboring Jordan.

By 2015 Faez was living with his wife and children in Richardson, Texas, just outside of Dallas. His youngest daughter, Sara, was born in Dallas and is thus an American citizen. Faez and his family were resettled with the help of the United Nations Refugee Agency. They had been subject to an extensive process of investigation, which included "more than a two year process of background checks by several government agencies, including the FBI, Department of Homeland Security and the National Counterterrorism Center."[55]

Faez got a job at Walmart, found an apartment for his family, and bought a used car. According to the *Time* article, "Faez came to believe that the U.S. offered the chance for personal growth and prosperity for his children. He worked hard to improve his English, and has laid out a series of long-term goals, including a higher education degree. 'I would like to make sure to provide for my wife and children,' he says, 'so they can live a happy life.'"[56]

In Paris on the night of November 13, 2015, "gunmen and suicide bombers hit a concert hall, a major stadium, restaurants and bars, almost simultaneously—and left 130 people dead and hundreds wounded."[57] Outside the Stade de France, France's national stadium and one of the places targeted by the terrorists, authorities found a Syrian passport. The passport, most experts agreed, was fake.[58]

In terms of public perception, however, this didn't matter. In France, the rest of Europe, and in the United States, there was a backlash against the policy of welcoming refugees from Syria out of fear that terrorists might use the opportunity to enter Western nations. Following the Paris attacks, Republican governors in thirty-one American states declared that they would block the resettlement of Syrian refugees in their states. While final authority over the nation's immigration policy rests with the federal government and not the states, the states' efforts could at the very least present roadblocks to its implementation.[59]

Texas has been more welcoming than any other state in the nation to refugees from across the globe, including those from Syria. It has taken in more Syrian refugees than any state except California. Many Christian, Jewish, and Islamic members of Texas's faith-based agencies have advocated for welcoming Syrian refugees with open arms and helped them find housing and jobs.

However, in the aftermath of the Paris attacks and in the sharply divided partisan environment of American national politics, Texan hospitality came under question. Bee Moorhead, executive director of a faith-based group in Texas working with refugee agencies, said in a *Los Angeles Times* article, "Texans, it is in our DNA to exhibit Southern hospitality. But when politicians ratchet up the rhetoric, the people who maybe are already disposed to bigotry feel like they've gotten the license they need." The same article reported that "Texas Agriculture Commissioner Sid Miller has posted photos on Facebook of refugees and snakes, saying, 'Can you tell me which of these rattlers won't bite you?'"[60]

In December 2015, the attorney general of Texas, under the leadership of Republican governor Greg Abbott, sued the U.S. government—along with a nonprofit organization—to block the resettlement of six Syrian refugees in the state, citing security concerns.[61] These six refugees were members of the family of Faez al Sharaa: his half-brother, Tamman; Tamman's wife and two children; and Faez's parents. Faez's efforts to bring members of his extended family to his new home in north Texas had been caught up in the contentious politics of American foreign policy. "The clock is ticking," said the leader of a North Texas nonprofit resettlement and advocacy organization. "What is the state going to do? Are they going to meet Faez's brother at the airport and send him away?"[62] Though the attorney general dropped the restraining order shortly afterwards, the fate of many Syrian refugees who want to come to the U.S. remains in legal limbo.

Reflecting upon his path to the United States, Faez expressed a very practical but profound belief in the American dream: "The best thing [about Texas] is the opportunity for employment. . . . Here, anyone who has a goal to pursue or a dream, it is possible for them to reach that goal and reach that dream here."[63]

CONCLUSION
America in Progress

We began this book with a tale about Thomas Jefferson writing a draft of the Declaration of Independence—a complicated story. We ended with the story of Faez al Sharaa working at a Walmart in Texas to support his family after fleeing the violence of Syria—also a complicated story. In between we have engaged with many other narratives, not one of them simple. That is why they are in this book. Powerful stories are not simple; they are not supposed to be. That is why they get told and retold.

What are the problems with the nation's public policies? Which of these issues deserve attention? Which level of government—federal, state, or local—is best suited to provide solutions in the public sector? What are Americans' constitutional guarantees, and how might public policies support or undermine these guarantees? These are all important questions with which you will have to consider—and make your own thoughts heard.

The stories in this book have all been introduced to drive home and make real this fact: At the end of the day, American government is, and has always been, about people—their hopes, struggles, successes, and failures. The conclusions to these stories were never predetermined, and they were always contested. Even though it may not seem like it, contributing to the quilt of American government is never beyond the reach of those who participate in it. Many of those who offered a patch, or even just a thread, to this quilt probably never expected that they would do so. But they did. In 1892 American poet Walt Whitman asked what good one person could possibly do in such a big, scary, and often impersonal world. He asked what meaning one life, one story, could possibly have. His answer was this: "That the powerful play goes on, and you may contribute a verse."[64]

And so, we end with the most important question of all: What are the pieces that you will contribute to this quilt? When you add your own voice to the stories of American government, you might be surprised by what gets told in the chapters not yet written.

CHAPTER REVIEW

This chapter's main ideas are reflected in the Learning Objectives. By reviewing them here you should be able to **remember** the key points and **know** these terms that are central to the topic.

13.1 Understand the steps in the policymaking process and the different forms of domestic social policy in America today.

REMEMBER...

- There are many components to American public policy. Social welfare policy consists of governmental efforts to improve or protect the health, safety, education, and opportunities for citizens and residents.

- Economic policy consists of the efforts to regulate and support the economy in order to protect citizens' financial well-being and to support businesses in the global financial system.

- Foreign policy refers to the ways in which the United States engages with their counterparts in other nations in order to advance its interests.

- The stages of public policymaking include problem definition, agenda setting, policy formulation and adoption, budgeting, implementation, evaluation, and termination.

- Social insurance programs are financed by payroll taxes paid by individuals and do not have income-based requirements to receive these benefits. Need-based assistance programs differ in that their benefits are allocated only to individuals demonstrating specific needs.

KNOW...

- *domestic policy*: policy designed to improve the social welfare of citizens (p. 415)

- *economic policy:* the efforts of government to regulate and support the economy in order to protect and expand citizens' financial well-being and economic prospects and to support businesses in the global financial system (p. 415)

- *entitlement programs*: programs wherein one receives a set of benefits regardless of income provided one meets certain categorical requirements, such as age or a minimum number of years of payroll contributions (p. 420)

- *foreign policy*: the ways in which political actors in a nation engage others at home and abroad in order to advance their nation's interests, protect and secure national security, and support national commercial interests (p. 415)

- *implemented*: enacting public policies on the ground (p. 419)

- *need-based assistance*: social welfare programs whose benefits are allocated to individuals demonstrating specific needs (p. 421)

- *policy entrepreneurs*: individuals in government, academic institutions, think tanks, interest groups, and other venues who try to shape the political agenda and get their solutions implemented (p. 419)

- *public policy*: the intentional use of governmental power to secure the health, welfare, opportunities, and national security of citizens (p. 414)

- *social insurance program*: a program such as Social Security that is financed by payroll taxes paid by individuals and that does not have income-based requirements to receive their benefits (p. 420)

- *social welfare policies*: governmental efforts designed to improve or protect the health, safety, education, and opportunities for citizens and residents (p. 417)

- *unfunded mandate*: when the federal government institutes a policy that members of state governments do not feel has been properly funded (p. 419)

13.2 Understand the U.S. approach to fiscal policy and the tools that are used to measure and implement those policies.

REMEMBER...

- The federal government uses fiscal policy to shape national economic outcomes through taxation and spending policies and decisions.

- Different theories about the role government should play in the economy exist, including laissez-faire, command-and-control, and mixed economic systems.

- Economists use different indicators to measure the health of the economy.

- Different schools of thought explain what causes business cycles: monetary, Keynesian, and supply-side theorists. These differ in what they view as the primary driver and the best solution to maintain stability.

- The federal government raises money through taxes. If the government takes in more money than it spends, it runs a surplus. If not, it holds a deficit.

KNOW...

- *budget deficit*: when the federal government takes in less money than it spends (p. 426)

- *budget surplus*: when the federal government takes in more money than it spends (p. 426)

- *business cycle*: the fluctuation of economic activity around a long-term trend with periods of expansion and contraction (p. 425)

- *command-and-control economy*: a type of economic policy in which government dictates much of a nation's economic activity, including the amount of production and prices for goods (p. 424)

- *Federal Reserve System*: the central bank of the United States (p. 427)

- *fiscal policy*: a set of activities through which government tries to lower unemployment, support economic activity, and stabilize the economy by using policies of taxation and spending (p. 423)

- *gross domestic product (GDP)*: a measure of the total value of goods and services produced by American economic activity (p. 424)

- *inflation*: the rise in the prices of goods and services purchased by individuals (p. 424)

- *interest rates*: the rates paid to borrow money (p. 427)

- *laissez-faire economy*: a type of economic policy in which governments intrude as little as possible in the economic transactions between citizens and businesses (p. 424)

- *mixed economy*: a type of economic policy in which many economic decisions are left to individuals and businesses; federal government also plays a role in shaping these decisions (p. 424)

- *monetary policy*: a set of economic policy tools designed to regulate the amount of money in the economy (in circulation and in the deposits) (p. 427)

- *unemployment rate*: the percentage of the total labor force that is unemployed (p. 424)

13.3 Summarize the events that have shaped changes in America's approach to the world and the actors involved in formulating policy.

REMEMBER...

- Since the nation's founding, U.S. foreign policy has swung between periods of relative isolationism and increased foreign engagement and intervention.

- The president and Congress are primarily responsible for the formulation and implementation of American foreign policy. Power is divided between the two branches. The president is able to act with greater speed and more information than Congress.

- Conflict *within* the structures and agencies of the executive and legislative branches may be as consequential to foreign policy outcomes as conflicts *between* the two branches.

KNOW...

- *Arab Spring*: a series of protests taking place across North Africa and the Middle East beginning in early 2010 that led to democratic reforms in some nations and civil war and chaos in others (p. 435)

- *Cold War*: the period of time between 1945 and 1991 characterized by conflict between the United States and its allies and the Soviet Union and its allies but that did not result in full global war (p. 432)

- *containment*: a Cold War foreign policy strategy designed to restrict expansion of Soviet ideological and military influence, using military force if necessary (p. 432)

- *free trade*: a trade policy characterized by few restrictions on the flow of goods and services across national borders (p. 442)

- *internationalism*: an approach to international affairs that emphasizes close contact and cooperation between nations (p. 430)

- *isolationism*: a foreign policy orientation in which a nation attempts to stay out of foreign entanglements (p. 430)

- *preemptive war*: a type of war in which a state uses its military might to challenge adversaries before they launch attacks or harbor those who might do so (p. 433)

- *protectionism*: restricting access by foreign producers to American markets in order to benefit specific domestic agricultural, industrial, and service providers (p. 442)

- *soft power*: the advancement of a nation's interests by exporting its values and culture abroad (p. 442)

- *terrorism*: the use of violence as a means to achieve political ends (p. 433)

APPENDIX 1
DECLARATION OF INDEPENDENCE

On June 11, 1776, the responsibility to "prepare a declaration" of independence was assigned by the Continental Congress, meeting in Philadelphia, to five members: John Adams, Benjamin Franklin, Thomas Jefferson, Robert Livingston, and Roger Sherman. Impressed by his talents as a writer, the committee asked Jefferson to compose a draft. After modifying Jefferson's draft the committee turned it over to Congress on June 28. On July 2 Congress voted to declare independence; on the evening of July 4, it approved the Declaration of Independence.

In Congress, July 4, 1776,
The Unanimous Declaration of the Thirteen United States of America,

When in the Course of human events, it becomes necessary for one people to dissolve the political bands which have connected them with another, and to assume among the Powers of the earth, the separate and equal station to which the Laws of Nature and of Nature's God entitle them, a decent respect to the opinions of mankind requires that they should declare the causes which impel them to the separation.

We hold these truths to be self-evident, that all men are created equal, that they are endowed by their Creator with certain unalienable Rights, that among these are Life, Liberty and the pursuit of Happiness. That to secure these rights, Governments are instituted among Men, deriving their just powers from the consent of the governed. That whenever any form of Government becomes destructive of these ends, it is the Right of the People to alter or to abolish it, and to institute new Government, laying its foundation on such principles and organizing its powers in such form, as to them shall seem most likely to effect their Safety and Happiness. Prudence, indeed, will dictate that Government long established should not be changed for light and transient causes; and accordingly all experience hath shown, that mankind are more disposed to suffer, while evils are sufferable, than to right themselves by abolishing the forms to which they are accustomed. But when a long train of abuses and usurpations, pursuing invariably the same Object evinces a design to reduce them under absolute Despotism, it is their right, it is their duty, to throw off such Government, and to provide new Guards for their future security. Such has been the patient sufferance of these Colonies; and such is now the necessity which constrains them to alter their former Systems of Government. The history of the present King of Great Britain is a history of repeated injuries and usurpations, all having in direct object the establishment of an absolute Tyranny over these States. To prove this, let Facts be submitted to a candid world.

He has refused his Assent to Laws, the most wholesome and necessary for the public good.

He has forbidden his Governors to pass Laws of immediate and pressing importance, unless suspended in their operation till his Assent should be obtained; and when so suspended, he has utterly neglected to attend to them.

He has refused to pass other Laws for the accommodation of large districts of people, unless those people would relinquish the right of Representation in the Legislature, a right inestimable to them and formidable to tyrants only.

He has called together legislative bodies at places unusual, uncomfortable, and distant from the depository of their Public Records, for the sole purpose of fatiguing them into compliance with his measures.

He has dissolved Representative Houses repeatedly, for opposing with manly firmness his invasions on the rights of the people.

He has refused for a long time, after such dissolutions, to cause others to be elected; whereby the Legislative Powers, incapable of Annihilation, have returned to the People at large for their exercise; the State remaining in the mean time exposed to all the dangers of invasion from without, and convulsions within.

He has endeavored to prevent the population of these States; for that purpose obstructing the Laws of Naturalization of Foreigners; refusing to pass others to encourage their migration hither, and raising the conditions of new Appropriations of Lands.

He has obstructed the Administration of Justice, by refusing his Assent to Laws for establishing Judiciary Powers.

He has made Judges dependent on his Will alone, for the tenure of their offices, and the amount and payment of their salaries.

He has erected a multitude of New Offices, and sent hither swarms of Officers to harass our People, and eat out their substance.

He has kept among us, in times of peace, Standing Armies without the Consent of our legislature.

He has affected to render the Military independent of and superior to the Civil Power.

He has combined with others to subject us to a jurisdiction foreign to our constitution, and unacknowledged by our laws; giving his Assent to their acts of pretended legislation:

For quartering large bodies of armed troops among us:

For protecting them, by a mock Trial, from Punishment for any Murders which they should commit on the Inhabitants of these States:

For cutting off our Trade with all parts of the world:

For imposing taxes on us without our Consent:

For depriving us in many cases, of the benefits of Trial by Jury:

For transporting us beyond Seas to be tried for pretended offences:

For abolishing the free System of English Laws in a neighbouring Province, establishing therein an Arbitrary government, and enlarging its Boundaries so as to render it at once an example and fit instrument for introducing the same absolute rule into these Colonies:

For taking away our Charters, abolishing our most valuable Laws, and altering fundamentally the Forms of our Governments:

For suspending our own Legislature, and declaring themselves invested with Power to legislate for us in all cases whatsoever.

He has abdicated Government here, by declaring us out of his Protection and waging War against us.

He has plundered our seas, ravaged our Coasts, burnt our towns, and destroyed the lives of our people.

He is at this time transporting large armies of foreign mercenaries to compleat the works of death, desolation and tyranny, already begun with circumstances of Cruelty & perfidy scarcely parallel in the most barbarous ages, and totally unworthy the Head of a civilized nation.

He has constrained our fellow Citizens taken Captive on the high Seas to bear Arms against their Country, to become the executioners of their friends and Brethren, or to fall themselves by their Hands.

He has excited domestic insurrections amongst us, and has endeavoured to bring on the inhabitants of our frontiers, the merciless Indian Savages, whose known rule of warfare, is an undistinguished destruction of all ages, sexes and conditions.

In every stage of these Oppressions We have Petitioned for Redress in the most humble terms: Our repeated Petitions have been answered only by repeated injury. A Prince, whose character is thus marked by every act which may define a Tyrant, is unfit to be the ruler of a free People.

Nor have We been wanting in attention to our British brethren. We have warned them from time to time of attempts by their legislature to extend an unwarrantable jurisdiction over us. We have reminded them of the circumstances of our emigration and settlement here. We have appealed to their native justice and magnanimity, and we have conjured them by the ties of our common kindred to disavow these usurpations, which would inevitably interrupt our connections and correspondence. They too have been deaf to the voice of justice and of consanguinity. We must, therefore, acquiesce in the necessity, which denounces our Separation, and hold them, as we hold the rest of mankind, Enemies in War, in Peace Friends.

We, therefore, the Representatives of the United States of America, in General Congress, Assembled, appealing to the Supreme Judge of the world for the rectitude of our intentions, do, in the Name, and by Authority of the good People of these Colonies, solemnly publish and declare, That these United Colonies are, and of Right ought to be Free and Independent States; that they are Absolved from all Allegiance to the British Crown, and that all political connection between them and the State of Great Britain, is and ought to be totally dissolved; and that as Free and Independent States, they have full Power to levy War, conclude Peace, contract Alliances, establish Commerce, and to do all other Acts and Things which Independent States may of right do. And for the support of this Declaration, with a firm reliance on the Protection of Divine Providence, we mutually pledge to each other our Lives, our Fortunes and our sacred Honor.

John Hancock.

New Hampshire:
Josiah Bartlett,
William Whipple,
Matthew Thornton.

Massachusetts-Bay:
Samuel Adams,
John Adams,
Robert Treat Paine,
Elbridge Gerry.

Rhode Island:
Stephen Hopkins,
William Ellery.

Connecticut:
Roger Sherman,
Samuel Huntington,
William Williams,
Oliver Wolcott.

New York:
William Floyd,
Philip Livingston,
Francis Lewis,
Lewis Morris.

Pennsylvania:
Robert Morris,
Benjamin Harris,
Benjamin Franklin,
John Morton,
George Clymer,
James Smith,
George Taylor,
James Wilson,
George Ross.

Delaware:
Caesar Rodney,

George Read,
Thomas McKean.

Georgia:
Button Gwinnett,
Lyman Hall,
George Walton.

Maryland:
Samuel Chase,
William Paca,
Thomas Stone,
Charles Carroll of Carrollton.

Virginia:
George Wythe,
Richard Henry Lee,
Thomas Jefferson,
Benjamin Harrison,
Thomas Nelson Jr.,
Francis Lightfoot Lee,
Carter Braxton.

North Carolina:
William Hooper,
Joseph Hewes,
John Penn.

South Carolina:
Edward Rutledge,
Thomas Heyward Jr.,
Thomas Lynch Jr.,
Arthur Middleton.

New Jersey:
Richard Stockton,
John Witherspoon,
Francis Hopkinson,
John Hart,
Abraham Clark.

APPENDIX 2
ARTICLES OF CONFEDERATION

To all to whom these Presents shall come, we the undersigned Delegates of the States affixed to our Names send greeting.

Articles of Confederation and perpetual Union between the states of New Hampshire, Massachusetts-bay Rhode Island and Providence Plantations, Connecticut, New York, New Jersey, Pennsylvania, Delaware, Maryland, Virginia, North Carolina, South Carolina and Georgia.

Article I

The Stile of this Confederacy shall be **"The United States of America"**.

Article II

Each state retains its sovereignty, freedom, and independence, and every power, jurisdiction, and right, which is not by this Confederation expressly delegated to the United States, in Congress assembled.

Article III

The said States hereby severally enter into a firm league of friendship with each other, for their common defense, the security of their liberties, and their mutual and general welfare, binding themselves to assist each other, against all force offered to, or attacks made upon them, or any of them, on account of religion, sovereignty, trade, or any other pretense whatever.

Article IV

The better to secure and perpetuate mutual friendship and intercourse among the people of the different States in this Union, the free inhabitants of each of these States, paupers, vagabonds, and fugitives from justice excepted, shall be entitled to all privileges and immunities of free citizens in the several States; and the people of each State shall free ingress and regress to and from any other State, and shall enjoy therein all the privileges of trade and commerce, subject to the same duties, impositions, and restrictions as the inhabitants thereof respectively, provided that such restrictions shall not extend so far as to prevent the removal of property imported into any State, to any other State, of which the owner is an inhabitant; provided also that no imposition, duties or restriction shall be laid by any State, on the property of the United States, or either of them.

If any person guilty of, or charged with, treason, felony, or other high misdemeanor in any State, shall flee from justice, and be found in any of the United States, he shall, upon demand of the Governor or executive power of the State from which he fled, be delivered up and removed to the State having jurisdiction of his offense.

Full faith and credit shall be given in each of these States to the records, acts, and judicial proceedings of the courts and magistrates of every other State.

Article V

For the most convenient management of the general interests of the United States, delegates shall be annually appointed in such manner as the legislatures of each State shall direct, to meet in Congress on the first Monday in November, in every year, with a power reserved to each State to recall its delegates, or any of them, at any time within the year, and to send others in their stead for the remainder of the year.

No State shall be represented in Congress by less than two, nor more than seven members; and no person shall be capable of being a delegate for more than three years in any term of six years; nor shall any person, being a delegate, be capable of holding any office under the United States, for which he, or another for his benefit, receives any salary, fees or emolument of any kind.

Each State shall maintain its own delegates in a meeting of the States, and while they act as members of the committee of the States.

In determining questions in the United States in Congress assembled, each State shall have one vote.

Freedom of speech and debate in Congress shall not be impeached or questioned in any court or place out of Congress, and the members of Congress shall be protected in their persons from arrests or imprisonments, during the time of their going to and from, and attendence on Congress, except for treason, felony, or breach of the peace.

Article VI

No State, without the consent of the United States in Congress assembled, shall send any embassy to, or receive any embassy from, or enter into any conference, agreement, alliance or treaty with any King, Prince or State; nor shall any person holding any office of profit or trust under the United States, or any of them, accept any present, emolument, office or title of any kind whatever from any King, Prince or foreign State; nor shall the United States in Congress assembled, or any of them, grant any title of nobility.

No two or more States shall enter into any treaty, confederation or alliance whatever between them, without the consent of the United States in Congress assembled, specifying accurately the purposes for which the same is to be entered into, and how long it shall continue.

No State shall lay any imposts or duties, which may interfere with any stipulations in treaties, entered into by the United States in Congress assembled, with any King, Prince or State, in pursuance of any treaties already proposed by Congress, to the courts of France and Spain.

No vessel of war shall be kept up in time of peace by any State, except such number only, as shall be deemed necessary by the United States in Congress assembled, for the defense of such State, or its trade; nor shall any body of forces be kept up by any State in time of peace, except such number only, as in the judgement of the United States in Congress assembled, shall be deemed requisite to garrison the forts necessary for the defense of such State; but every State shall always keep up a well-regulated and disciplined militia, sufficiently armed and accoutered, and shall provide and constantly have ready for use, in public stores, a due number of filed pieces and tents, and a proper quantity of arms, ammunition and camp equipage.

No State shall engage in any war without the consent of the United States in Congress assembled, unless such State be actually invaded by enemies, or shall have received certain advice of a resolution being formed by some nation of Indians to invade such State, and the danger is so imminent as not to admit of a delay till the United States in Congress assembled can be consulted; nor shall any State grant commissions to any ships or vessels of war, nor letters of marque or reprisal, except it be after a declaration of war by the United States in Congress assembled, and then only against the Kingdom or State and the subjects thereof, against which war has been so declared, and under such regulations as shall be established by the United States in Congress assembled, unless such State be infested by pirates, in which case vessels of war may be fitted out for that occasion, and kept so long as the danger shall continue, or until the United States in Congress assembled shall determine otherwise.

Article VII

When land forces are raised by any State for the common defense, all officers of or under the rank of colonel, shall be appointed by the legislature of each State respectively, by whom such forces shall be raised, or in such manner as such State shall direct, and all vacancies shall be filled up by the State which first made the appointment.

Article VIII

All charges of war, and all other expenses that shall be incurred for the common defense or general welfare, and allowed by the United States in Congress assembled, shall be defrayed out of a common treasury, which shall be supplied by the several States in proportion to the value of all land within each State, granted or surveyed for any person, as such land and the buildings and improvements thereon shall be estimated according to such mode as the United States in Congress assembled, shall from time to time direct and appoint.

The taxes for paying that proportion shall be laid and levied by the authority and direction of the legislatures of the several States within the time agreed upon by the United States in Congress assembled.

Article IX

The United States in Congress assembled, shall have the sole and exclusive right and power of determining on peace and war, except in the cases mentioned in the sixth article—of sending and receiving ambassadors—entering into treaties and alliances, provided that no treaty of commerce shall be made whereby the legislative power of the respective States shall be restrained from imposing such imposts and duties on foreigners, as their own people are subjected to, or from prohibiting the exportation or importation of any species of goods or commodities whatsoever—of establishing rules for deciding in all cases, what captures on land or water shall be legal, and in what manner prizes taken by land or naval forces in the service of the United States shall be divided or appropriated—of granting letters of marque and reprisal in times of peace—appointing courts for the trial of piracies and felonies commited on the high seas and establishing courts for receiving and determining finally appeals in all cases of captures, provided that no member of Congress shall be appointed a judge of any of the said courts.

The United States in Congress assembled shall also be the last resort on appeal in all disputes and differences now subsisting or that hereafter may arise between two or more States concerning boundary, jurisdiction or any other causes whatever; which authority shall always be exercised in the manner following. Whenever the legislative or executive authority or lawful agent of any State in controversy with another shall present a petition to Congress stating the matter in question and praying for a hearing, notice thereof shall be given by order of Congress to the legislative or executive authority of the other State in controversy, and a day assigned for the appearance of the parties by their lawful agents, who shall then be directed to appoint by joint consent, commissioners or judges to constitute a court for hearing and determining the matter in question: but if they cannot agree, Congress shall name three persons out of each of the United States, and from the list of such persons each party shall alternately strike out one, the petitioners beginning, until the number shall be reduced to thirteen; and from that number not less than seven, nor more than nine names as Congress shall direct, shall in the presence of Congress be drawn out by lot, and the persons whose names shall be so drawn or any five of them, shall be commissioners or judges, to hear and finally determine the controversy, so always as a major part of the judges who shall hear the cause shall agree in the determination: and if either party shall neglect to attend at the day appointed, without showing reasons, which Congress shall judge sufficient, or being present shall refuse to strike, the Congress shall proceed to nominate three persons out of each State, and the secretary of Congress shall strike in behalf of such party absent or refusing; and the judgement and sentence of the court to be appointed, in the manner before prescribed, shall be final and conclusive; and if any of the parties shall refuse to submit to the authority of such court, or to appear or defend their claim or cause, the court shall nevertheless proceed to pronounce sentence, or judgement, which shall in like manner be final and decisive, the judgement or sentence and other proceedings being in either case transmitted to Congress, and lodged among the acts of Congress for the security of the parties concerned: provided that every commissioner, before he sits in judgement, shall take an oath to be administered by one of the judges of the supreme or superior court of the State, where the cause shall be tried, 'well and truly to hear and determine the matter in question, according to the best of his judgement, without favor, affection or hope of reward': provided also, that no State shall be deprived of territory for the benefit of the United States.

All controversies concerning the private right of soil claimed under different grants of two or more States, whose jurisdictions as they may respect such lands, and the States which passed such grants are adjusted, the said grants or either of them being at the same time claimed to have originated antecedent to such settlement of jurisdiction, shall on the petition of either party to the Congress of the United States, be finally determined as near as may be in the same manner as is before presecribed for deciding disputes respecting territorial jurisdiction between different States.

The United States in Congress assembled shall also have the sole and exclusive right and power of regulating the alloy and value of coin struck by their own authority, or by that of the respective States—fixing the standards of weights and measures throughout the United States—regulating the trade and managing all affairs with the Indians, not members of any of the States, provided that the legislative right of any State within its own limits be not infringed or violated—establishing or regulating post offices from one State to another, throughout all the United States, and exacting such postage on the papers passing through the same as may be requisite to defray the expenses of the said office—appointing all officers of the land forces, in the service of the United States, excepting regimental officers—appointing all the officers of the naval forces, and commissioning all officers whatever in the service of the United States—making rules for the government and regulation of the said land and naval forces, and directing their operations.

The United States in Congress assembled shall have authority to appoint a committee, to sit in the recess of Congress, to be denominated 'A Committee of the States', and to consist of one delegate from each State; and to appoint such other committees and civil officers as may be necessary for managing the general affairs of the United States under their direction—to appoint one of their members to preside, provided that no person be allowed to serve in the office of president more than one year in any term of three years; to ascertain the necessary sums of money to be raised for the service of the United States, and to appropriate and apply the same for defraying the public expenses—to borrow money, or emit bills on the credit of the United States, transmitting every half-year to the respective States an account of the sums of money so borrowed or emitted—to build and equip a navy—to agree upon the number of land forces, and to make requisitions from each State for its quota, in proportion to the number of white inhabitants in such State; which requisition shall be binding, and thereupon the legislature of each State shall appoint the regimental officers, raise the men and cloath, arm and equip them in a solid-like manner, at the expense of the United States; and the officers and men so cloathed, armed and equipped shall march to the place appointed, and within the time agreed on by the United States in Congress assembled. But if the United States in Congress assembled shall, on consideration of circumstances judge proper that any State should not raise men, or should raise a smaller number of men than the quota thereof, such extra number shall be raised, officered, cloathed, armed and equipped in the same manner as the quota of each State, unless the legislature of such State shall judge that such extra number cannot be safely spread out in the same, in which case they shall raise, officer, cloath, arm and equip as many of such extra number as they judge can be safely spared. And the officers and men so cloathed, armed, and equipped, shall march to the place appointed, and within the time agreed on by the United States in Congress assembled.

The United States in Congress assembled shall never engage in a war, nor grant letters of marque or reprisal in time of peace, nor enter into any treaties or alliances, nor coin money, nor regulate the value thereof, nor ascertain the sums and expenses necessary for the defense and welfare of the United States, or any of them, nor emit bills, nor borrow money on the credit of the United States, nor appropriate money, nor agree upon the number of vessels of war, to be built or purchased, or the number of land or sea forces to be raised, nor appoint a commander in chief of the army or navy, unless nine States assent to the same: nor shall a question on any other point, except for adjourning from day to day be determined, unless by the votes of the majority of the United States in Congress assembled.

The Congress of the United States shall have power to adjourn to any time within the year, and to any place within the United States, so that no period of adjournment be for a longer duration than the space of six months, and shall publish the journal of their proceedings monthly, except such parts thereof relating to treaties, alliances or military operations, as in their judgement require secrecy; and the yeas and nays of the delegates of each State on any question shall be entered on the journal, when it is desired by any delegates of a State, or any of them, at his or their request shall be furnished with a transcript of the said journal, except such parts as are above excepted, to lay before the legislatures of the several States.

Article X

The Committee of the States, or any nine of them, shall be authorized to execute, in the recess of Congress, such of the powers of Congress as the United States in Congress assembled, by the consent of the nine States, shall from time to time think expedient to vest them with; provided that no power be delegated to the said Committee, for the exercise of which, by the Articles of Confederation, the voice of nine States in the Congress of the United States assembled be requisite.

Article XI

Canada acceding to this confederation, and adjoining in the measures of the United States, shall be admitted into, and entitled to all the advantages of this Union; but no other colony shall be admitted into the same, unless such admission be agreed to by nine States.

Article XII

All bills of credit emitted, monies borrowed, and debts contracted by, or under the authority of Congress, before the assembling of the United States, in pursuance of the present confederation, shall be deemed and considered as a charge against the United States, for payment and satisfaction whereof the said United States, and the public faith are hereby solemnly pledged.

Article XIII

Every State shall abide by the determination of the United States in Congress assembled, on all questions which by this confederation are submitted to them. And the Articles of this Confederation shall be inviolably observed by every State, and the Union shall be perpetual; nor shall any alteration at any time hereafter be made in any of them; unless such alteration be agreed to in a Congress of the United States, and be afterwards confirmed by the legislatures of every State.

And Whereas it hath pleased the Great Governor of the World to incline the hearts of the legislatures we respectively represent in Congress, to approve of, and to authorize us to ratify the said Articles of Confederation and perpetual Union. Know Ye that we the undersigned delegates, by virtue of the power and authority to us given for that purpose, do by these presents, in the name and in behalf of our respective constituents, fully and entirely ratify and confirm each and every of the said Articles of Confederation and perpetual Union, and all and singular the matters and things therein contained: And we do further solemnly plight and engage the faith of our respective constituents, that they shall abide by the determinations of the United States in Congress assembled, on all questions, which by the said Confederation are submitted to them. And that the Articles thereof shall be inviolably observed by the States we respectively represent, and that the Union shall be perpetual.

In Witness whereof we have hereunto set our hands in Congress. Done at Philadelphia in the State of Pennsylvania the ninth day of July in the Year of our Lord One Thousand Seven Hundred and Seventy-Eight, and in the Third Year of the independence of America.

Agreed to by Congress 15 November 1777
In force after ratification by Maryland, 1 March 1781

APPENDIX 3
CONSTITUTION OF THE UNITED STATES

The United States Constitution was written at a convention that Congress called on February 21, 1787, for the purpose of recommending amendments to the Articles of Confederation. Every state but Rhode Island sent delegates to Philadelphia, where the convention met that summer. The delegates decided to write an entirely new constitution, completing their labors on September 17. Nine states (the number the Constitution itself stipulated as sufficient) ratified by June 21, 1788.

The Framers of the Constitution included only six paragraphs on the Supreme Court. Article III, Section 1, created the Supreme Court and the federal system of courts. It provided that "[t]he judicial power of the United States, shall be vested in one supreme Court," and whatever inferior courts Congress "from time to time" saw fit to establish. Article III, Section 2, delineated the types of cases and controversies that should be considered by a federal—rather than a state—court. But beyond this, the Constitution left many of the particulars of the Supreme Court and the federal court system for Congress to decide in later years in judiciary acts.

We the People of the United States, in Order to form a more perfect Union, establish Justice, insure domestic Tranquillity, provide for the common defence, promote the general Welfare, and secure the Blessings of Liberty to ourselves and our Posterity, do ordain and establish this Constitution for the United States of America.

Article I

Section 1. All legislative Powers herein granted shall be vested in a Congress of the United States, which shall consist of a Senate and House of Representatives.

Section 2. The House of Representatives shall be composed of Members chosen every second Year by the People of the several States, and the Electors in each State shall have the Qualifications requisite for Electors of the most numerous Branch of the State Legislature.

No Person shall be a Representative who shall not have attained to the age of twenty five Years, and been seven Years a Citizen of the United States, and who shall not, when elected, be an Inhabitant of that State in which he shall be chosen.

[Representatives and direct Taxes shall be apportioned among the several States which may be included within this Union, according to their respective Numbers, which shall be determined by adding to the whole Number of free Persons, including those bound to Service for a Term of Years, and excluding Indians not taxed, three fifths of all other Persons.][1] The actual Enumeration shall be made within three Years after the first Meeting of the Congress of the United States, and within every subsequent Term of ten Years, in such Manner as they shall by Law direct. The Number of Representatives shall not exceed one for every thirty Thousand, but each State shall have at Least one Representative; and until such enumeration shall be made, the State of New Hampshire shall be entitled to chuse three, Massachusetts eight, Rhode-Island and Providence Plantations one, Connecticut five, New-York six, New Jersey four, Pennsylvania eight, Delaware one, Maryland six, Virginia ten, North Carolina five, South Carolina five, and Georgia three.

When vacancies happen in the Representation from any State, the Executive Authority thereof shall issue Writs of Election to fill such Vacancies.

The House of Representatives shall chuse their Speaker and other Officers; and shall have the sole Power of Impeachment.

Section 3. The Senate of the United States shall be composed of two Senators from each State, [chosen by the Legislature thereof,][2] for six Years; and each Senator shall have one Vote.

Immediately after they shall be assembled in Consequence of the first Election, they shall be divided as equally as may be into three Classes. The Seats of the Senators of the first Class shall be vacated at the Expiration of the second Year, of the second Class at the Expiration of the fourth Year, and of the third Class at the Expiration of the sixth Year, so that one third may be chosen every second Year; [and if Vacancies happen by Resignation, or otherwise, during the Recess of the Legislature of any State, the Executive thereof may make temporary Appointments until the next Meeting of the Legislature, which shall then fill such Vacancies.][3]

No Person shall be a Senator who shall not have attained to the Age of thirty Years, and been nine Years a Citizen of the United States, and who shall not, when elected, be an Inhabitant of that State for which he shall be chosen.

The Vice President of the United States shall be President of the Senate, but shall have no Vote, unless they be equally divided.

The Senate shall chuse their other Officers, and also a President pro tempore, in the Absence of the Vice President, or when he shall exercise the Office of President of the United States.

The Senate shall have the sole Power to try all Impeachments. When sitting for that Purpose, they shall be on Oath or Affirmation. When the President of the United States is tried, the Chief Justice shall preside: And no Person shall be convicted without the Concurrence of two thirds of the Members present.

Judgment in Cases of Impeachment shall not extend further than to removal from Office, and disqualification to hold and enjoy any Office of honor, Trust or Profit under the United States: but the Party convicted shall nevertheless be liable and subject to Indictment, Trial, Judgment and Punishment, according to Law.

Section 4. The Times, Places and Manner of holding Elections for Senators and Representatives, shall be prescribed in each State by the Legislature thereof;

but the Congress may at any time by Law make or alter such Regulations, except as to the Places of chusing Senators.

The Congress shall assemble at least once in every Year, and such Meeting shall [be on the first Monday in December],[4] unless they shall by Law appoint a different Day.

Section 5. Each House shall be the Judge of the Elections, Returns and Qualifications of its own Members, and a Majority of each shall constitute a Quorum to do Business; but a smaller Number may adjourn from day to day, and may be authorized to compel the Attendance of absent Members, in such Manner, and under such Penalties as each House may provide.

Each House may determine the Rules of its Proceedings, punish its Members for disorderly Behaviour, and, with the Concurrence of two thirds, expel a Member.

Each House shall keep a Journal of its Proceedings, and from time to time publish the same, excepting such Parts as may in their Judgment require Secrecy; and the Yeas and Nays of the Members of either House on any question shall, at the Desire of one fifth of those Present, be entered on the Journal.

Neither House, during the Session of Congress, shall, without the Consent of the other, adjourn for more than three days, nor to any other Place than that in which the two Houses shall be sitting.

Section 6. The Senators and Representatives shall receive a Compensation for their Services, to be ascertained by Law, and paid out of the Treasury of the United States. They shall in all Cases, except Treason, Felony and Breach of the Peace, be privileged from Arrest during their Attendance at the Session of their respective Houses, and in going to and returning from the same; and for any Speech or Debate in either House, they shall not be questioned in any other Place.

No Senator or Representative shall, during the Time for which he was elected, be appointed to any civil Office under the Authority of the United States, which shall have been created, or the Emoluments whereof shall have been encreased during such time; and no Person holding any Office under the United States, shall be a Member of either House during his Continuance in Office.

Section 7. All Bills for raising Revenue shall originate in the House of Representatives; but the Senate may propose or concur with Amendments as on other Bills.

Every Bill which shall have passed the House of Representatives and the Senate, shall, before it become a Law, be presented to the President of the United States; If he approve he shall sign it, but if not he shall return it, with his Objections to that House in which it shall have originated, who shall enter the Objections at large on their Journal, and proceed to reconsider it. If after such Reconsideration two thirds of that House shall agree to pass the Bill, it shall be sent, together with the Objections, to the other House, by which it shall likewise be reconsidered, and if approved by two thirds of that House, it shall become a Law. But in all such Cases the Votes of both Houses shall be determined by yeas and Nays, and the Names of the Persons voting for and against the Bill shall be entered on the Journal of each House respectively. If any Bill shall not be returned by the President within ten Days (Sundays excepted) after it shall have been presented to him, the Same shall be a Law, in like Manner as if he had signed it, unless the Congress by their Adjournment prevent its Return, in which Case it shall not be a Law.

Every Order, Resolution, or Vote to which the Concurrence of the Senate and House of Representatives may be necessary (except on a question of Adjournment) shall be presented to the President of the United States; and before the Same shall take Effect, shall be approved by him, or being disapproved by him, shall be repassed by two thirds of the Senate and House of Representatives, according to the Rules and Limitations prescribed in the Case of a Bill.

Section 8. The Congress shall have Power To lay and collect Taxes, Duties, Imposts and Excises, to pay the Debts and provide for the common Defence and general Welfare of the United States; but all Duties, Imposts and Excises shall be uniform throughout the United States;

To borrow Money on the credit of the United States;

To regulate Commerce with foreign Nations, and among the several States, and with the Indian Tribes;

To establish an uniform Rule of Naturalization, and uniform Laws on the subject of Bankruptcies throughout the United States;

To coin Money, regulate the Value thereof, and of foreign Coin, and fix the Standard of Weights and Measures;

To provide for the Punishment of counterfeiting the Securities and current Coin of the United States;

To establish Post Offices and post Roads;

To promote the Progress of Science and useful Arts, by securing for limited Times to Authors and Inventors the exclusive Right to their respective Writings and Discoveries;

To constitute Tribunals inferior to the supreme Court;

To define and punish Piracies and Felonies committed on the high Seas, and Offences against the Law of Nations;

To declare War, grant Letters of Marque and Reprisal, and make Rules concerning Captures on Land and Water;

To raise and support Armies, but no Appropriation of Money to that Use shall be for a longer Term than two Years;

To provide and maintain a Navy;

To make Rules for the Government and Regulation of the land and naval Forces;

To provide for calling forth the Militia to execute the Laws of the Union, suppress Insurrections and repel Invasions;

To provide for organizing, arming, and disciplining, the Militia, and for governing such Part of them as may be employed in the Service of the United States, reserving to the States respectively, the Appointment of the Officers, and the Authority of training the Militia according to the discipline prescribed by Congress;

To exercise exclusive Legislation in all Cases whatsoever, over such District (not exceeding ten Miles square) as may, by Cession of particular States, and the Acceptance of Congress, become the Seat of the Government of the United States, and to exercise like Authority over all Places purchased by the Consent of the Legislature of the State in which the Same shall be, for the Erection of Forts, Magazines, Arsenals, dock-Yards, and other needful Buildings;—And

To make all Laws which shall be necessary and proper for carrying into Execution the foregoing Powers, and all other Powers vested by this Constitution in the Government of the United States, or in any Department or Officer thereof.

Section 9. The Migration or Importation of such Persons as any of the States now existing shall think proper to admit, shall not be prohibited by the Congress prior to the Year one thousand eight hundred and eight, but a Tax or duty may be imposed on such Importation, not exceeding ten dollars for each Person.

The Privilege of the Writ of Habeas Corpus shall not be suspended, unless when in Cases of Rebellion or Invasion the public Safety may require it.

No Bill of Attainder or ex post facto Law shall be passed.

No Capitation, or other direct, Tax shall be laid, unless in Proportion to the Census or Enumeration herein before directed to be taken.[5]

No Tax or Duty shall be laid on Articles exported from any State.

No Preference shall be given by any Regulation of Commerce or Revenue to the Ports of one State over those of another; nor shall Vessels bound to, or from, one State, be obliged to enter, clear, or pay Duties in another.

No Money shall be drawn from the Treasury, but in Consequence of Appropriations made by Law; and a regular Statement and Account of the Receipts and Expenditures of all public Money shall be published from time to time.

No Title of Nobility shall be granted by the United States: And no Person holding any Office of Profit or Trust under them, shall, without the Consent of the Congress, accept of any present, Emolument, Office, or Title, of any kind whatever, from any King, Prince, or foreign State.

Section 10. No State shall enter into any Treaty, Alliance, or Confederation; grant Letters of Marque and Reprisal; coin Money; emit Bills of Credit; make any Thing but gold and silver Coin a Tender in Payment of Debts; pass any Bill of Attainder, ex post facto Law, or Law impairing the Obligation of Contracts, or grant any Title of Nobility.

No State shall, without the Consent of the Congress, lay any Imposts or Duties on Imports or Exports, except what may be absolutely necessary for executing its inspection Laws: and the net Produce of all Duties and Imposts, laid by any State on Imports or Exports, shall be for the Use of the Treasury of the United States; and all such Laws shall be subject to the Revision and Controul of the Congress.

No State shall, without the Consent of Congress, lay any Duty of Tonnage, keep Troops, or Ships of War in time of Peace, enter into any Agreement or Compact with another State, or with a foreign Power, or engage in War, unless actually invaded, or in such imminent Danger as will not admit of delay.

Article II

Section 1. The executive Power shall be vested in a President of the United States of America. He shall hold his Office during the Term of four Years, and, together with the Vice President, chosen for the same Term, be elected, as follows:

Each State shall appoint, in such Manner as the Legislature thereof may direct, a Number of Electors, equal to the whole Number of Senators and Representatives to which the State may be entitled in the Congress: but no Senator or Representative, or Person holding an Office of Trust or Profit under the United States, shall be appointed an Elector.

[The Electors shall meet in their respective States, and vote by Ballot for two Persons, of whom one at least shall not be an Inhabitant of the same State with themselves. And they shall make a List of all the Persons voted for, and of the Number of Votes for each; which List they shall sign and certify, and transmit sealed to the Seat of the Government of the United States, directed to the President of the Senate. The President of the Senate shall, in the Presence of the Senate and House of Representatives, open all the Certificates, and the Votes shall then be counted. The Person having the greatest Number of Votes shall be the President, if such Number be a Majority of the whole Number of Electors appointed; and if there be more than one who have such Majority, and have an equal Number of Votes, then the House of Representatives shall immediately chuse by Ballot one of them for President; and if no Person have a Majority, then from the five highest on the list the said House shall in like Manner chuse the President. But in chusing the President, the Votes shall be taken by States, the Representation from each State having one Vote; A quorum for this Purpose shall consist of a Member or Members from two thirds of the States, and a Majority of all the States shall be necessary to a Choice. In every Case, after the Choice of the President, the Person having the greatest Number of Votes of the Electors shall be the Vice President. But if there should remain two or more who have equal Votes, the Senate shall chuse from them by Ballot the Vice President.][6]

The Congress may determine the Time of chusing the Electors, and the Day on which they shall give their Votes; which Day shall be the same throughout the United States.

No Person except a natural born Citizen, or a Citizen of the United States, at the time of the Adoption of this Constitution, shall be eligible to the Office of President; neither shall any Person be eligible to that Office who shall not have attained to the Age of thirty five Years, and been fourteen Years a Resident within the United States.

In Case of the Removal of the President from Office, or of his Death, Resignation, or Inability to discharge the Powers and Duties of the said Office,[7] the Same shall devolve on the Vice President, and the Congress may by Law provide for the Case of Removal, Death, Resignation or Inability, both of the President and Vice President, declaring what Officer shall then act as President, and such Officer shall act accordingly, until the Disability be removed, or a President shall be elected.

The President shall, at stated Times, receive for his Services, a Compensation, which shall neither be encreased nor diminished during the Period for which he shall have been elected, and he shall not receive within that Period any other Emolument from the United States, or any of them.

Before he enter on the Execution of his Office, he shall take the following Oath or Affirmation:—"I do solemnly swear (or affirm) that I will faithfully execute the Office of President of the United States, and will to the best of my Ability, preserve, protect and defend the Constitution of the United States."

Section 2. The President shall be Commander in Chief of the Army and Navy of the United States, and of the Militia of the several States, when called into the actual Service of the United States; he may require the Opinion, in writing, of the principal Officer in each of the executive Departments, upon any Subject relating to the Duties of their respective Offices, and he shall have

Power to grant Reprieves and Pardons for Offences against the United States, except in Cases of Impeachment.

He shall have Power, by and with the Advice and Consent of the Senate, to make Treaties, provided two thirds of the Senators present concur; and he shall nominate, and by and with the Advice and Consent of the Senate, shall appoint Ambassadors, other public Ministers and Consuls, Judges of the supreme Court, and all other Officers of the United States, whose Appointments are not herein otherwise provided for, and which shall be established by Law: but the Congress may by Law vest the Appointment of such inferior Officers, as they think proper, in the President alone, in the Courts of Law, or in the Heads of Departments.

The President shall have Power to fill up all Vacancies that may happen during the Recess of the Senate, by granting Commissions which shall expire at the End of their next Session.

Section 3. He shall from time to time give to the Congress Information of the State of the Union, and recommend to their Consideration such Measures as he shall judge necessary and expedient; he may, on extraordinary Occasions, convene both Houses, or either of them, and in Case of Disagreement between them, with Respect to the Time of Adjournment, he may adjourn them to such Time as he shall think proper; he shall receive Ambassadors and other public Ministers; he shall take Care that the Laws be faithfully executed, and shall Commission all the Officers of the United States.

Section 4. The President, Vice President and all civil Officers of the United States, shall be removed from Office on Impeachment for, and Conviction of, Treason, Bribery, or other high Crimes and Misdemeanors.

Article III

Section 1. The judicial Power of the United States, shall be vested in one supreme Court, and in such inferior Courts as the Congress may from time to time ordain and establish. The Judges, both of the supreme and inferior Courts, shall hold their Offices during good Behaviour, and shall, at stated Times, receive for their Services, a Compensation, which shall not be diminished during their Continuance in Office.

Section 2. The judicial Power shall extend to all Cases, in Law and Equity, arising under this Constitution, the Laws of the United States, and Treaties made, or which shall be made, under their Authority; —to all Cases affecting Ambassadors, other public Ministers and Consuls; —to all Cases of admiralty and maritime Jurisdiction; —to Controversies to which the United States shall be a Party; —to Controversies between two or more States; —between a State and Citizens of another State;[8] —between Citizens of different States; —between Citizens of the same State claiming Lands under Grants of different States, and between a State, or the Citizens thereof, and foreign States, Citizens or Subjects.[8]

In all Cases affecting Ambassadors, other public Ministers and Consuls, and those in which a State shall be Party, the supreme Court shall have original Jurisdiction. In all the other Cases before mentioned, the supreme Court shall have appellate Jurisdiction, both as to Law and Fact, with such Exceptions, and under such Regulations as the Congress shall make.

The Trial of all Crimes, except in Cases of Impeachment, shall be by Jury; and such Trial shall be held in the State where the said Crimes shall have been committed; but when not committed within any State, the Trial shall be at such Place or Places as the Congress may by Law have directed.

Section 3. Treason against the United States, shall consist only in levying War against them, or in adhering to their Enemies, giving them Aid and Comfort. No Person shall be convicted of Treason unless on the Testimony of two Witnesses to the same overt Act, or on Confession in open Court.

The Congress shall have Power to declare the Punishment of Treason, but no Attainder of Treason shall work Corruption of Blood, or Forfeiture except during the Life of the Person attainted.

Article IV

Section 1. Full Faith and Credit shall be given in each State to the public Acts, Records, and judicial Proceedings of every other State. And the Congress may by general Laws prescribe the Manner in which such Acts, Records and Proceedings shall be proved, and the Effect thereof.

Section 2. The Citizens of each State shall be entitled to all Privileges and Immunities of Citizens in the several States.

A Person charged in any State with Treason, Felony, or other Crime, who shall flee from Justice, and be found in another State, shall on Demand of the executive Authority of the State from which he fled, be delivered up, to be removed to the State having Jurisdiction of the Crime.

[No Person held to Service or Labour in one State, under the Laws thereof, escaping into another, shall, in Consequence of any Law or Regulation therein, be discharged from such Service or Labour, but shall be delivered up on Claim of the Party to whom such Service or Labour may be due.]⁹

Section 3. New States may be admitted by the Congress into this Union; but no new State shall be formed or erected within the Jurisdiction of any other State; nor any State be formed by the Junction of two or more States, or Parts of States, without the Consent of the Legislatures of the States concerned as well as of the Congress.

The Congress shall have Power to dispose of and make all needful Rules and Regulations respecting the Territory or other Property belonging to the United States; and nothing in this Constitution shall be so construed as to Prejudice any Claims of the United States, or of any particular State.

Section 4. The United States shall guarantee to every State in this Union a Republican Form of Government, and shall protect each of them against Invasion; and on Application of the Legislature, or of the Executive (when the Legislature cannot be convened) against domestic Violence.

Article V

The Congress, whenever two thirds of both Houses shall deem it necessary, shall propose Amendments to this Constitution, or, on the Application of the Legislatures of two thirds of the several States, shall call a Convention for proposing Amendments, which, in either Case, shall be valid to all Intents and Purposes, as Part of this Constitution, when ratified by the Legislatures of three fourths of the several States, or by Conventions in three fourths thereof, as the one or the other Mode of Ratification may be proposed by the Congress; Provided [that no Amendment which may be made prior to the Year One thousand eight hundred and eight shall in any Manner affect the first and fourth Clauses in the Ninth Section of the first Article; and][10] that no State, without its Consent, shall be deprived of its equal Suffrage in the Senate.

Article VI

All Debts contracted and Engagements entered into, before the Adoption of this Constitution, shall be as valid against the United States under this Constitution, as under the Confederation.

This Constitution, and the Laws of the United States which shall be made in Pursuance thereof; and all Treaties made, or which shall be made, under the Authority of the United States, shall be the supreme Law of the Land; and the Judges in every State shall be bound thereby, any Thing in the Constitution or Laws of any State to the Contrary notwithstanding.

The Senators and Representatives before mentioned, and the Members of the several State Legislatures, and all executive and judicial Officers, both of the United States and of the several States, shall be bound by Oath or Affirmation, to support this Constitution; but no religious Test shall ever be required as a Qualification to any Office or public Trust under the United States.

Article VII

The Ratification of the Conventions of nine States, shall be sufficient for the Establishment of this Constitution between the States so ratifying the Same.

Done in Convention by the Unanimous Consent of the States present the Seventeenth Day of September in the Year of our Lord one thousand seven hundred and Eighty seven and of the Independence of the United States of America the Twelfth. IN WITNESS whereof We have hereunto subscribed our Names,

George Washington, President and deputy from Virginia, and thirty-eight other delegates.

[The language of the original Constitution, not including the Amendments, was adopted by a convention of the states on September 17, 1787, and was subsequently ratified by the states on the following dates: Delaware, December 7, 1787; Pennsylvania, December 12, 1787; New Jersey, December 18, 1787; Georgia, January 2, 1788; Connecticut, January 9, 1788; Massachusetts, February 6, 1788; Maryland, April 28, 1788; South Carolina, May 23, 1788; New Hampshire, June 21, 1788.

Ratification was completed on June 21, 1788.

The Constitution subsequently was ratified by Virginia, June 25, 1788; New York, July 26, 1788; North Carolina, November 21, 1789; Rhode Island, May 29, 1790; and Vermont, January 10, 1791.]

AMENDMENTS

Amendment I

(First ten amendments ratified December 15, 1791.)

Congress shall make no law respecting an establishment of religion, or prohibiting the free exercise thereof; or abridging the freedom of speech, or of the press; or the right of the people peaceably to assemble, and to petition the Government for a redress of grievances.

Amendment II

A well regulated Militia, being necessary to the security of a free State, the right of the people to keep and bear Arms, shall not be infringed.

Amendment III

No Soldier shall, in time of peace be quartered in any house, without the consent of the Owner, nor in time of war, but in a manner to be prescribed by law.

Amendment IV

The right of the people to be secure in their persons, houses, papers, and effects, against unreasonable searches and seizures, shall not be violated, and no Warrants shall issue, but upon probable cause, supported by Oath or affirmation, and particularly describing the place to be searched, and the persons or things to be seized.

Amendment V

No person shall be held to answer for a capital, or otherwise infamous crime, unless on a presentment or indictment of a Grand Jury, except in cases arising in the land or naval forces, or in the Militia, when in actual service in time of War or public danger; nor shall any person be subject for the same offence to be twice put in jeopardy of life or limb; nor shall be compelled in any criminal case to be a witness against himself, nor be deprived of life, liberty, or property, without due process of law; nor shall private property be taken for public use, without just compensation.

Amendment VI

In all criminal prosecutions, the accused shall enjoy the right to a speedy and public trial, by an impartial jury of the State and district wherein the crime shall have been committed, which district shall have been previously ascertained by law, and to be informed of the nature and cause of the accusation; to be confronted with the witnesses against him; to have compulsory process for obtaining witnesses in his favor, and to have the Assistance of Counsel for his defence.

Amendment VII

In Suits at common law, where the value in controversy shall exceed twenty dollars, the right of trial by jury shall be preserved, and no fact tried by a jury, shall be otherwise re-examined in any Court of the United States, than according to the rules of the common law.

Amendment VIII

Excessive bail shall not be required, nor excessive fines imposed, nor cruel and unusual punishments inflicted.

Amendment IX

The enumeration in the Constitution, of certain rights, shall not be construed to deny or disparage others retained by the people.

Amendment X

The powers not delegated to the United States by the Constitution, nor prohibited by it to the States, are reserved to the States respectively, or to the people.

Amendment XI (Ratified February 7, 1795)

The Judicial power of the United States shall not be construed to extend to any suit in law or equity, commenced or prosecuted against one of the United States by Citizens of another State, or by Citizens or Subjects of any Foreign State.

Amendment XII (Ratified June 15, 1804)

The Electors shall meet in their respective states and vote by ballot for President and Vice-President, one of whom, at least, shall not be an inhabitant of the same state with themselves; they shall name in their ballots the person voted for as President, and in distinct ballots the person voted for as Vice-President, and they shall make distinct lists of all persons voted for as President, and of all persons voted for as Vice-President, and of the number of votes for each, which lists they shall sign and certify, and transmit sealed to the seat of the government of the United States, directed to the President of the Senate; — The President of the Senate shall, in the presence of the Senate and House of Representatives, open all the certificates and the votes shall then be counted; — The person having the greatest number of votes for President, shall be the President, if such number be a majority of the whole number of Electors appointed; and if no person have such majority, then from the persons having the highest numbers not exceeding three on the list of those voted for as President, the House of Representatives shall choose immediately, by ballot, the President. But in choosing the President, the votes shall be taken by states, the representation from each state having one vote; a quorum for this purpose shall consist of a member or members from two-thirds of the states, and a majority of all the states shall be necessary to a choice. [And if the House of Representatives shall not choose a President whenever the right of choice shall devolve upon them, before the fourth day of March next following, then the Vice-President shall act as President, as in the case of the death or other constitutional disability of the President. —][11] The person having the greatest number of votes as Vice-President, shall be the Vice-President, if such number be a majority of the whole number of Electors appointed, and if no person have a majority, then from the two highest numbers on the list, the Senate shall choose the Vice-President; a quorum for the purpose shall consist of two-thirds of the whole number of Senators, and a majority of the whole number shall be necessary to a choice. But no person constitutionally ineligible to the office of President shall be eligible to that of Vice-President of the United States.

Amendment XIII (Ratified December 6, 1865)

Section 1. Neither slavery nor involuntary servitude, except as a punishment for crime whereof the party shall have been duly convicted, shall exist within the United States, or any place subject to their jurisdiction.

Section 2. Congress shall have power to enforce this article by appropriate legislation.

Amendment XIV (Ratified July 9, 1868)

Section 1. All persons born or naturalized in the United States, and subject to the jurisdiction thereof, are citizens of the United States and of the State wherein they reside. No State shall make or enforce any law which shall abridge the privileges or immunities of citizens of the United States; nor shall any State deprive any person of life, liberty, or property, without due process of law; nor deny to any person within its jurisdiction the equal protection of the laws.

Section 2. Representatives shall be apportioned among the several States according to their respective numbers, counting the whole number of persons in each State, excluding Indians not taxed. But when the right to vote at any election for the choice of electors for President and Vice President of the United States, Representatives in Congress, the Executive and Judicial officers of a State, or the members of the Legislature thereof, is denied to any of the male inhabitants of such State, being twenty-one years of age,[12] and citizens of the United States, or in any way abridged, except for participation in rebellion, or other crime, the basis of representation therein shall be reduced in the proportion which the number of such male citizens shall bear to the whole number of male citizens twenty-one years of age in such State.

Section 3. No person shall be a Senator or Representative in Congress, or elector of President and Vice President, or hold any Office, civil or military, under the United States, or under any State, who, having previously taken an oath, as a member of Congress, or as an officer of the United States, or as a member of any State legislature, or as an executive or judicial officer of any State, to support the Constitution of the United States, shall have engaged in insurrection or rebellion against the same, or given aid or comfort to the enemies thereof. But Congress may by a vote of two-thirds of each House, remove such disability.

Section 4. The validity of the public debt of the United States, authorized by law, including debts incurred for payment of pensions and bounties for services in suppressing insurrection or rebellion, shall not be questioned. But neither the United States nor any State shall assume or pay any debt or obligation incurred in aid of insurrection or rebellion against the United States, or any claim for the loss or emancipation of any slave; but all such debts, obligations and claims shall be held illegal and void.

Section 5. The Congress shall have power to enforce, by appropriate legislation, the provisions of this article.

Amendment XV (Ratified February 3, 1870)

Section 1. The right of citizens of the United States to vote shall not be denied or abridged by the United States or by any State on account of race, color, or previous condition of servitude.

Section 2. The Congress shall have power to enforce this article by appropriate legislation.

Amendment XVI (Ratified February 3, 1913)

The Congress shall have power to lay and collect taxes on incomes, from whatever source derived, without apportionment among the several States, and without regard to any census or enumeration.

Amendment XVII (Ratified April 8, 1913)

The Senate of the United States shall be composed of two Senators from each State, elected by the people thereof, for six years; and each Senator shall have one vote. The electors in each State shall have the qualifications requisite for electors of the most numerous branch of the State legislatures.

When vacancies happen in the representation of any State in the Senate, the executive authority of such State shall issue writs of election to fill such vacancies: *Provided,* That the legislature of any State may empower the executive thereof to make temporary appointments until the people fill the vacancies by election as the legislature may direct.

This amendment shall not be so construed as to affect the election or term of any Senator chosen before it becomes valid as part of the Constitution.

Amendment XVIII (Ratified January 16, 1919)

Section 1. After one year from the ratification of this article the manufacture, sale, or transportation of intoxicating liquors within, the importation thereof into, or the exportation thereof from the United States and all territory subject to the jurisdiction thereof for beverage purposes is hereby prohibited.

Section 2. The Congress and the several States shall have concurrent power to enforce this article by appropriate legislation.

Section 3. This article shall be inoperative unless it shall have been ratified as an amendment to the Constitution by the legislatures of the several States, as provided in the Constitution, within seven years from the date of the submission hereof to the States by the Congress.[13]

Amendment XIX (Ratified August 18, 1920)

The right of citizens of the United States to vote shall not be denied or abridged by the United States or by any State on account of sex.

Congress shall have power to enforce this article by appropriate legislation.

Amendment XX (Ratified January 23, 1933)

Section 1. The terms of the President and Vice President shall end at noon on the 20th day of January, and the terms of Senators and Representatives at noon on the 3d day of January, of the years in which such terms would have ended if this article had not been ratified; and the terms of their successors shall then begin.

Section 2. The Congress shall assemble at least once in every year, and such meeting shall begin at noon on the 3d day of January, unless they shall by law appoint a different day.

Section 3.[14] If, at the time fixed for the beginning of the term of the President, the President elect shall have died, the Vice President elect shall become President. If a President shall not have been chosen before the time fixed for the beginning of his term, or if the President elect shall have failed to qualify, then the Vice President elect shall act as President until a President shall have qualified; and the Congress may by law provide for the case wherein neither a President elect nor a Vice President elect shall have qualified, declaring who shall then act as President, or the manner in which one who is to act shall be selected, and such person shall act accordingly until a President or Vice President shall have qualified.

Section 4. The Congress may by law provide for the case of the death of any of the persons from whom the House of Representatives may choose a President whenever the right of choice shall have devolved upon them, and for the case of the death of any of the persons from whom the Senate may choose a Vice President whenever the right of choice shall have devolved upon them.

Section 5. Sections 1 and 2 shall take effect on the 15th day of October following the ratification of this article.

Section 6. This article shall be inoperative unless it shall have been ratified as an amendment to the Constitution by the legislatures of three-fourths of the several States within seven years from the date of its submission.

Amendment XXI (Ratified December 5, 1933)

Section 1. The eighteenth article of amendment to the Constitution of the United States is hereby repealed.

Section 2. The transportation or importation into any State, Territory, or possession of the United States for delivery or use therein of intoxicating liquors, in violation of the laws thereof, is hereby prohibited.

Section 3. This article shall be inoperative unless it shall have been ratified as an amendment to the Constitution by conventions in the several States, as provided in the Constitution, within seven years from the date of the submission hereof to the States by the Congress.

Amendment XXII (Ratified February 27, 1951)

Section 1. No person shall be elected to the office of the President more than twice, and no person who has held the office of President, or acted as President, for more than two years of a term to which some other person was elected President shall be elected to the office of the President more than once. But this Article shall not apply to any person holding the office of President when this Article was proposed by the Congress, and shall not prevent any person who may be holding the office of President, or acting as President, during the term within which this Article becomes operative from holding the office of President or acting as President during the remainder of such term.

Section 2. This article shall be inoperative unless it shall have been ratified as an amendment to the Constitution by the legislatures of three-fourths of the several States within seven years from the date of its submission to the States by the Congress.

Amendment XXIII (Ratified March 29, 1961)

Section 1. The District constituting the seat of Government of the United States shall appoint in such manner as the Congress may direct:

A number of electors of President and Vice President equal to the whole number of Senators and Representatives in Congress to which the District would be entitled if it were a State, but in no event more than the least populous State; they shall be in addition to those appointed by the States, but they shall be considered, for the purposes of the election of President and Vice President, to be electors appointed by a State; and they shall meet in the District and perform such duties as provided by the twelfth article of amendment.

Section 2. The Congress shall have power to enforce this article by appropriate legislation.

Amendment XXIV (Ratified January 23, 1964)

Section 1. The right of citizens of the United States to vote in any primary or other election for President or Vice President, for electors for President or Vice President, or for Senator or Representative in Congress, shall not be denied or abridged by the United States or any State by reason of failure to pay any poll tax or other tax.

Section 2. The Congress shall have power to enforce this article by appropriate legislation.

Amendment XXV (Ratified February 10, 1967)

Section 1. In case of the removal of the President from office or of his death or resignation, the Vice President shall become President.

Section 2. Whenever there is a vacancy in the office of the Vice President, the President shall nominate a Vice President who shall take office upon confirmation by a majority vote of both Houses of Congress.

Section 3. Whenever the President transmits to the President pro tempore of the Senate and the Speaker of the House of Representatives his written declaration that he is unable to discharge the powers and duties of his office, and until he transmits to them a written declaration to the contrary, such powers and duties shall be discharged by the Vice President as Acting President.

Section 4. Whenever the Vice President and a majority of either the principal officers of the executive departments or of such other body as Congress may by law provide, transmit to the President pro tempore of the Senate and the Speaker of the House of Representatives their written declaration that the President is unable to discharge the powers and duties of his office, the Vice President shall immediately assume the powers and duties of the office as Acting President.

Thereafter, when the President transmits to the President pro tempore of the Senate and the Speaker of the House of Representatives his written declaration that no inability exists, he shall resume the powers and duties of his office unless the Vice President and a majority of either the principal officers of the executive departments or of such other body as Congress may by law provide, transmit within four days to the President pro tempore of the Senate and the Speaker of the House of Representatives their written declaration that the President is unable to discharge the powers and duties of his office. Thereupon Congress shall decide the issue, assembling within forty-eight hours for that purpose if not in session. If the Congress, within twenty-one days after receipt of the latter written declaration, or, if Congress is not in session, within twenty-one days after Congress is required to assemble, determines by two-thirds vote of both Houses that the President is unable to discharge the powers and duties of his office, the Vice President shall continue to discharge the same as Acting President; otherwise, the President shall resume the powers and duties of his office.

Amendment XXVI (Ratified July 1, 1971)

Section 1. The right of citizens of the United States, who are eighteen years of age or older, to vote shall not be denied or abridged by the United States or by any State on account of age.

Section 2. The Congress shall have power to enforce this article by appropriate legislation.

Amendment XXVII (Ratified May 7, 1992)

No law varying the compensation for the services of the Senators and Representatives shall take effect, until an election of Representatives shall have intervened.

Source: U.S. Congress, House, Committee on the Judiciary, *The Constitution of the United States of America, as Amended,* 100th Cong., 1st sess., 1987, H Doc 100–94.

Notes

1. The part in brackets was changed by section 2 of the Fourteenth Amendment.
2. The part in brackets was changed by the first paragraph of the Seventeenth Amendment.
3. The part in brackets was changed by the second paragraph of the Seventeenth Amendment.
4. The part in brackets was changed by section 2 of the Twentieth Amendment.
5. The Sixteenth Amendment gave Congress the power to tax incomes.
6. The material in brackets was superseded by the Twelfth Amendment.
7. This provision was affected by the Twenty-fifth Amendment.
8. These clauses were affected by the Eleventh Amendment.
9. This paragraph was superseded by the Thirteenth Amendment.
10. Obsolete.
11. The part in brackets was superseded by section 3 of the Twentieth Amendment.
12. See the Nineteenth and Twenty-sixth Amendments.
13. This amendment was repealed by section 1 of the Twenty-first Amendment.
14. See the Twenty-fifth Amendment.

APPENDIX 4
FEDERALIST NO. 10

The Same Subject Continued: The Union as a Safeguard Against Domestic Faction and Insurrection.

From the New York Packet
Friday, November 23, 1787.

Author: James Madison

To the People of the State of New York:

AMONG the numerous advantages promised by a wellconstructed Union, none deserves to be more accurately developed than its tendency to break and control the violence of faction. The friend of popular governments never finds himself so much alarmed for their character and fate, as when he contemplates their propensity to this dangerous vice. He will not fail, therefore, to set a due value on any plan which, without violating the principles to which he is attached, provides a proper cure for it. The instability, injustice, and confusion introduced into the public councils, have, in truth, been the mortal diseases under which popular governments have everywhere perished; as they continue to be the favorite and fruitful topics from which the adversaries to liberty derive their most specious declamations. The valuable improvements made by the American constitutions on the popular models, both ancient and modern, cannot certainly be too much admired; but it would be an unwarrantable partiality, to contend that they have as effectually obviated the danger on this side, as was wished and expected. Complaints are everywhere heard from our most considerate and virtuous citizens, equally the friends of public and private faith, and of public and personal liberty, that our governments are too unstable, that the public good is disregarded in the conflicts of rival parties, and that measures are too often decided, not according to the rules of justice and the rights of the minor party, but by the superior force of an interested and overbearing majority. However anxiously we may wish that these complaints had no foundation, the evidence, of known facts will not permit us to deny that they are in some degree true. It will be found, indeed, on a candid review of our situation, that some of the distresses under which we labor have been erroneously charged on the operation of our governments; but it will be found, at the same time, that other causes will not alone account for many of our heaviest misfortunes; and, particularly, for that prevailing and increasing distrust of public engagements, and alarm for private rights, which are echoed from one end of the continent to the other. These must be chiefly, if not wholly, effects of the unsteadiness and injustice with which a factious spirit has tainted our public administrations.

By a faction, I understand a number of citizens, whether amounting to a majority or a minority of the whole, who are united and actuated by some common impulse of passion, or of interest, adversed to the rights of other citizens, or to the permanent and aggregate interests of the community.

There are two methods of curing the mischiefs of faction: the one, by removing its causes; the other, by controlling its effects.

There are again two methods of removing the causes of faction: the one, by destroying the liberty which is essential to its existence; the other, by giving to every citizen the same opinions, the same passions, and the same interests.

It could never be more truly said than of the first remedy, that it was worse than the disease. Liberty is to faction what air is to fire, an aliment without which it instantly expires. But it could not be less folly to abolish liberty, which is essential to political life, because it nourishes faction, than it would be to wish the annihilation of air, which is essential to animal life, because it imparts to fire its destructive agency.

The second expedient is as impracticable as the first would be unwise. As long as the reason of man continues fallible, and he is at liberty to exercise it, different opinions will be formed. As long as the connection subsists between his reason and his self-love, his opinions and his passions will have a reciprocal influence on each other; and the former will be objects to which the latter will attach themselves. The diversity in the faculties of men, from which the rights of property originate, is not less an insuperable obstacle to a uniformity of interests. The protection of these faculties is the first object of government. From the protection of different and unequal faculties of acquiring property, the possession of different degrees and kinds of property immediately results; and from the influence of these on the sentiments and views of the respective proprietors, ensues a division of the society into different interests and parties.

The latent causes of faction are thus sown in the nature of man; and we see them everywhere brought into different degrees of activity, according to the different circumstances of civil society. A zeal for different opinions concerning religion, concerning government, and many other points, as well of speculation as of practice; an attachment to different leaders ambitiously contending for pre-eminence and power; or to persons of other descriptions whose fortunes have been interesting to the human passions, have, in turn, divided mankind into parties, inflamed them with mutual animosity, and rendered them much more disposed to vex and oppress each other than to co-operate for their common good. So strong is this propensity of mankind to fall into mutual animosities, that where no substantial occasion presents itself, the most frivolous and fanciful distinctions have been sufficient to kindle their unfriendly passions and excite their most violent conflicts. But the most common and durable source of factions has been the various and unequal distribution of property. Those who hold and those who are without property have ever formed distinct interests in society. Those who are creditors, and those who are debtors, fall under a like discrimination. A landed interest, a manufacturing interest, a mercantile interest, a moneyed interest, with many lesser interests, grow up of necessity in civilized nations, and divide them into different classes, actuated by different sentiments and views. The regulation of these various and interfering interests forms the principal task of modern legislation, and involves the spirit of party and faction in the necessary and ordinary operations of the government.

No man is allowed to be a judge in his own cause, because his interest would certainly bias his judgment, and, not improbably, corrupt his integrity. With equal, nay with greater reason, a body of men are unfit to be both judges and parties at the same time; yet what are many of the most important acts of legislation, but so many judicial determinations, not indeed concerning the rights of single persons, but concerning the rights of large bodies of citizens? And what are the different classes of legislators but advocates and parties to the causes which they determine? Is a law proposed concerning private debts? It is a question to which the creditors are parties on one side and the debtors on the other. Justice ought to hold the balance between them. Yet the parties are, and must be, themselves the judges; and the most numerous party, or, in other words, the most powerful faction must be expected to prevail. Shall domestic manufactures be encouraged, and in what degree, by restrictions on foreign manufactures? are questions which would be differently decided by the landed and the manufacturing classes, and probably by neither with a sole regard to justice and the public good. The apportionment of taxes on the various descriptions of property is an act which seems to require the most exact impartiality; yet there is, perhaps, no legislative act in which greater opportunity and temptation are given to a predominant party to trample on the rules of justice. Every shilling with which they overburden the inferior number, is a shilling saved to their own pockets.

It is in vain to say that enlightened statesmen will be able to adjust these clashing interests, and render them all subservient to the public good. Enlightened statesmen will not always be at the helm. Nor, in many cases, can such an adjustment be made at all without taking into view indirect and remote considerations, which will rarely prevail over the immediate interest which one party may find in disregarding the rights of another or the good of the whole.

The inference to which we are brought is, that the CAUSES of faction cannot be removed, and that relief is only to be sought in the means of controlling its EFFECTS.

If a faction consists of less than a majority, relief is supplied by the republican principle, which enables the majority to defeat its sinister views by regular vote. It may clog the administration, it may convulse the society; but it will be unable to execute and mask its violence under the forms of the Constitution. When a majority is included in a faction, the form of popular government, on the other hand, enables it to sacrifice to its ruling passion or interest both the public good and the rights of other citizens. To secure the public good and private rights against the danger of such a faction, and at the same time to preserve the spirit and the form of popular government, is then the great object to which our inquiries are directed. Let me add that it is the great desideratum by which this form of government can be rescued from the opprobrium under which it has so long labored, and be recommended to the esteem and adoption of mankind.

By what means is this object attainable? Evidently by one of two only. Either the existence of the same passion or interest in a majority at the same time must be prevented, or the majority, having such coexistent passion or interest, must be rendered, by their number and local situation, unable to concert and carry into effect schemes of oppression. If the impulse and the opportunity be suffered to coincide, we well know that neither moral nor religious motives can be relied on as an adequate control. They are not found to be such on the injustice and violence of individuals, and lose their efficacy in proportion to the number combined together, that is, in proportion as their efficacy becomes needful.

From this view of the subject it may be concluded that a pure democracy, by which I mean a society consisting of a small number of citizens, who assemble and administer the government in person, can admit of no cure for the mischiefs of faction. A common passion or interest will, in almost every case, be felt by a majority of the whole; a communication and concert result from the form of government itself; and there is nothing to check the inducements to sacrifice the weaker party or an obnoxious individual. Hence it is that such democracies have ever been spectacles of turbulence and contention; have ever been found incompatible with personal security or the rights of property; and have in general been as short in their lives as they have been violent in their deaths. Theoretic politicians, who have patronized this species of government, have erroneously supposed that by reducing mankind to a perfect equality in their political rights, they would, at the same time, be perfectly equalized and assimilated in their possessions, their opinions, and their passions.

A republic, by which I mean a government in which the scheme of representation takes place, opens a different prospect, and promises the cure for which we are seeking. Let us examine the points in which it varies from pure democracy, and we shall comprehend both the nature of the cure and the efficacy which it must derive from the Union.

The two great points of difference between a democracy and a republic are: first, the delegation of the government, in the latter, to a small number of citizens elected by the rest; secondly, the greater number of citizens, and greater sphere of country, over which the latter may be extended.

The effect of the first difference is, on the one hand, to refine and enlarge the public views, by passing them through the medium of a chosen body of citizens, whose wisdom may best discern the true interest of their country, and whose patriotism and love of justice will be least likely to sacrifice it to temporary or partial considerations. Under such a regulation, it may well happen that the public voice, pronounced by the representatives of the people, will be more consonant to the public good than if pronounced by the people themselves, convened for the purpose. On the other hand, the effect may be inverted. Men of factious tempers, of local prejudices, or of sinister designs, may, by intrigue, by corruption, or by other means, first obtain the suffrages, and then betray the interests, of the people. The question resulting is, whether small or extensive republics are more favorable to the election of proper guardians of the public weal; and it is clearly decided in favor of the latter by two obvious considerations:

In the first place, it is to be remarked that, however small the republic may be, the representatives must be raised to a certain number, in order to guard against the cabals of a few; and that, however large it may be, they must be limited to a certain number, in order to guard against the confusion of a multitude. Hence, the number of representatives in the two cases not being in proportion to that of the two constituents, and being proportionally greater in the small republic, it follows that, if the proportion of fit characters be not less in the large than in the small republic, the former will present a greater option, and consequently a greater probability of a fit choice.

In the next place, as each representative will be chosen by a greater number of citizens in the large than in the small republic, it will be more difficult for unworthy candidates to practice with success the vicious arts by which elections are too often carried; and the suffrages of the people being more free, will be more likely to centre in men who possess the most attractive merit and the most diffusive and established characters.

It must be confessed that in this, as in most other cases, there is a mean, on both sides of which inconveniences will be found to lie. By enlarging too much the number of electors, you render the representatives too little acquainted with all their local circumstances and lesser interests; as by reducing it too much, you render him unduly attached to these, and too little fit to comprehend and pursue great and national objects. The federal Constitution forms a happy combination in this respect; the great and aggregate interests being referred to the national, the local and particular to the State legislatures.

The other point of difference is, the greater number of citizens and extent of territory which may be brought within the compass of republican than of democratic government; and it is this circumstance principally which renders factious combinations less to be dreaded in the former than in the latter. The smaller the society, the fewer probably will be the distinct parties and interests composing it; the fewer the distinct parties and interests, the more frequently will a majority be found of the same party; and the smaller the number of individuals composing a majority, and the smaller the compass within which they are placed, the more easily will they concert and execute their plans of oppression. Extend the sphere, and you take in a greater variety of parties and interests; you make it less probable that a majority of the whole will have a common motive to invade the rights of other citizens; or if such a common motive exists, it will be more difficult for all who feel it to discover their own strength, and to act in unison with each other. Besides other impediments, it may be remarked that, where there is a consciousness of unjust or dishonorable purposes, communication is always checked by distrust in proportion to the number whose concurrence is necessary.

Hence, it clearly appears, that the same advantage which a republic has over a democracy, in controlling the effects of faction, is enjoyed by a large over a small republic,—is enjoyed by the Union over the States composing it. Does the advantage consist in the substitution of representatives whose enlightened views and virtuous sentiments render them superior to local prejudices and schemes of injustice? It will not be denied that the representation of the Union will be most likely to possess these requisite endowments. Does it consist in the greater security afforded by a greater variety of parties, against the event of any one party being able to outnumber and oppress the rest? In an equal degree does the increased variety of parties comprised within the Union, increase this security. Does it, in fine, consist in the greater obstacles opposed to the concert and accomplishment of the secret wishes of an unjust and interested majority? Here, again, the extent of the Union gives it the most palpable advantage.

The influence of factious leaders may kindle a flame within their particular States, but will be unable to spread a general conflagration through the other States. A religious sect may degenerate into a political faction in a part of the Confederacy; but the variety of sects dispersed over the entire face of it must secure the national councils against any danger from that source. A rage for paper money, for an abolition of debts, for an equal division of property, or for any other improper or wicked project, will be less apt to pervade the whole body of the Union than a particular member of it; in the same proportion as such a malady is more likely to taint a particular county or district, than an entire State.

In the extent and proper structure of the Union, therefore, we behold a republican remedy for the diseases most incident to republican government. And according to the degree of pleasure and pride we feel in being republicans, ought to be our zeal in cherishing the spirit and supporting the character of Federalists.

PUBLIUS.

APPENDIX 5
FEDERALIST NO. 51

The Structure of the Government Must Furnish the Proper Checks and Balances Between the Different Departments

From the New York Packet.
Friday, February 8, 1788.

Author: James Madison

To the People of the State of New York:

TO WHAT expedient, then, shall we finally resort, for maintaining in practice the necessary partition of power among the several departments, as laid down in the Constitution? The only answer that can be given is, that as all these exterior provisions are found to be inadequate, the defect must be supplied, by so contriving the interior structure of the government as that its several constituent parts may, by their mutual relations, be the means of keeping each other in their proper places. Without presuming to undertake a full development of this important idea, I will hazard a few general observations, which may perhaps place it in a clearer light, and enable us to form a more correct judgment of the principles and structure of the government planned by the convention.

In order to lay a due foundation for that separate and distinct exercise of the different powers of government, which to a certain extent is admitted on all hands to be essential to the preservation of liberty, it is evident that each department should have a will of its own; and consequently should be so constituted that the members of each should have as little agency as possible in the appointment of the members of the others. Were this principle rigorously adhered to, it would require that all the appointments for the supreme executive, legislative, and judiciary magistracies should be drawn from the same fountain of authority, the people, through channels having no communication whatever with one another. Perhaps such a plan of constructing the several departments would be less difficult in practice than it may in contemplation appear. Some difficulties, however, and some additional expense would attend the execution of it. Some deviations, therefore, from the principle must be admitted. In the constitution of the judiciary department in particular, it might be inexpedient to insist rigorously on the principle: first, because peculiar qualifications being essential in the members, the primary consideration ought to be to select that mode of choice which best secures these qualifications; secondly, because the permanent tenure by which the appointments are held in that department, must soon destroy all sense of dependence on the authority conferring them.

It is equally evident, that the members of each department should be as little dependent as possible on those of the others, for the emoluments annexed to their offices. Were the executive magistrate, or the judges, not independent of the legislature in this particular, their independence in every other would be merely nominal. But the great security against a gradual concentration of the several powers in the same department, consists in giving to those who administer each department the necessary constitutional means and personal motives to resist encroachments of the others. The provision for defense must in this, as in all other cases, be made commensurate to the danger of attack. Ambition must be made to counteract ambition. The interest of the man must be connected with the constitutional rights of the place. It may be a reflection on human nature, that such devices should be necessary to control the abuses of government. But what is government itself, but the greatest of all reflections on human nature? If men were angels, no government would be necessary. If angels were to govern men, neither external nor internal controls on government would be necessary. In framing a government which is to be administered by men over men, the great difficulty lies in this: you must first enable the government to control the governed; and in the next place oblige it to control itself.

A dependence on the people is, no doubt, the primary control on the government; but experience has taught mankind the necessity of auxiliary precautions. This policy of supplying, by opposite and rival interests, the defect of better motives, might be traced through the whole system of human affairs, private as well as public. We see it particularly displayed in all the subordinate distributions of power, where the constant aim is to divide and arrange the several offices in such a manner as that each may be a check on the other that the private interest of every individual may be a sentinel over the public rights. These inventions of prudence cannot be less requisite in the distribution of the supreme powers of the State. But it is not possible to give to each department an equal power of self-defense. In republican government, the legislative authority necessarily predominates. The remedy for this inconveniency is to divide the legislature into different branches; and to render them, by different modes of election and different principles of action, as little connected with each other as the nature of their common functions and their common dependence on the society will admit. It may even be necessary to guard against dangerous encroachments by still further precautions. As the weight of the legislative authority requires that it should be thus divided, the weakness of the executive may require, on the other hand, that it should be fortified.

An absolute negative on the legislature appears, at first view, to be the natural defense with which the executive magistrate should be armed. But perhaps it would be neither altogether safe nor alone sufficient. On ordinary occasions it might not be exerted with the requisite firmness, and on extraordinary occasions it might be perfidiously abused. May not this defect of an absolute negative be supplied by some qualified connection between this weaker department and the weaker branch of the stronger department, by which the latter may be led to support the constitutional rights of the former, without being too much detached from the rights of its own department? If the principles on which these observations are founded be just, as I persuade myself they are, and they be applied as a criterion to the several State constitutions, and to the federal Constitution it will be found that if the latter does not perfectly correspond with them, the former are infinitely less able to bear such a test.

There are, moreover, two considerations particularly applicable to the federal system of America, which place that system in a very interesting point of view. First. In a single republic, all the power surrendered by the people is submitted to the administration of a single government; and the usurpations are guarded against by a division of the government into distinct and separate departments. In the compound republic of America, the power surrendered by the people is first divided between two distinct governments, and then the portion allotted to each subdivided among distinct and separate departments. Hence a double security arises to the rights of the people. The different governments will control each other, at the same time that each will be controlled by itself. Second. It is of great importance in a republic not only to guard the society against the oppression of its rulers, but to guard one part of the society against the injustice of the other part. Different interests necessarily exist in different classes of citizens. If a majority be united by a common interest, the rights of the minority will be insecure.

There are but two methods of providing against this evil: the one by creating a will in the community independent of the majority that is, of the society itself; the other, by comprehending in the society so many separate descriptions of citizens as will render an unjust combination of a majority of the whole very improbable, if not impracticable. The first method prevails in all governments possessing an hereditary or self-appointed authority. This, at best, is but a precarious security; because a power independent of the society may as well espouse the unjust views of the major, as the rightful interests of the minor party, and may possibly be turned against both parties. The second method will be exemplified in the federal republic of the United States. Whilst all authority in it will be derived from and dependent on the society, the society itself will be broken into so many parts, interests, and classes of citizens, that the rights of individuals, or of the minority, will be in little danger from interested combinations of the majority.

In a free government the security for civil rights must be the same as that for religious rights. It consists in the one case in the multiplicity of interests, and in the other in the multiplicity of sects. The degree of security in both cases will depend on the number of interests and sects; and this may be presumed to depend on the extent of country and number of people comprehended under the same government. This view of the subject must particularly recommend a proper federal system to all the sincere and considerate friends of republican government, since it shows that in exact proportion as the territory of the Union may be formed into more circumscribed Confederacies, or States oppressive combinations of a majority will be facilitated: the best security, under the republican forms, for the rights of every class of citizens, will be diminished: and consequently the stability and independence of some member of the government, the only other security, must be proportionately increased. Justice is the end of government. It is the end of civil society. It ever has been and ever will be pursued until it be obtained, or until liberty be lost in the pursuit. In a society under the forms of which the stronger faction can readily unite and oppress the weaker, anarchy may as truly be said to reign as in a state of nature, where the weaker individual is not secured against the violence of the stronger; and as, in the latter state, even the stronger individuals are prompted, by the uncertainty of their condition, to submit to a government which may protect the weak as well as themselves; so, in the former state, will the more powerful factions or parties be gradually induced, by a like motive, to wish for a government which will protect all parties, the weaker as well as the more powerful.

It can be little doubted that if the State of Rhode Island was separated from the Confederacy and left to itself, the insecurity of rights under the popular form of government within such narrow limits would be displayed by such reiterated oppressions of factious majorities that some power altogether independent of the people would soon be called for by the voice of the very factions whose misrule had proved the necessity of it. In the extended republic of the United States, and among the great variety of interests, parties, and sects which it embraces, a coalition of a majority of the whole society could seldom take place on any other principles than those of justice and the general good; whilst there being thus less danger to a minor from the will of a major party, there must be less pretext, also, to provide for the security of the former, by introducing into the government a will not dependent on the latter, or, in other words, a will independent of the society itself. It is no less certain than it is important, notwithstanding the contrary opinions which have been entertained, that the larger the society, provided it lie within a practical sphere, the more duly capable it will be of self-government. And happily for the REPUBLICAN CAUSE, the practicable sphere may be carried to a very great extent, by a judicious modification and mixture of the FEDERAL PRINCIPLE.

PUBLIUS.

APPENDIX 6
POLITICAL PARTY AFFILIATIONS IN CONGRESS AND THE PRESIDENCY, 1789-2017

Year	Congress	House Majority party	House Principal minority party	Senate Majority party	Senate Principal minority party	President
1789–1791	1st	AD-38	Op-26	AD-17	Op-9	F (Washington)
1791–1793	2nd	F-37	DR-33	F-16	DR-13	F (Washington)
1793–1795	3rd	DR-57	F-48	F-17	DR-13	F (Washington)
1795–1797	4th	F-54	DR-52	F-19	DR-13	F (Washington)
1797–1799	5th	F-58	DR-48	F-20	DR-12	F (John Adams)
1799–1801	6th	F-64	DR-42	F-19	DR-13	F (John Adams)
1801–1803	7th	DR-69	F-36	DR-18	F-13	DR (Jefferson)
1803–1805	8th	DR-102	F-39	DR-25	F-9	DR (Jefferson)
1805–1807	9th	DR-116	F-25	DR-27	F-7	DR (Jefferson)
1807–1809	10th	DR-118	F-24	DR-28	F-6	DR (Jefferson)
1809–1811	11th	DR-94	F-48	DR-28	F-6	DR (Madison)
1811–1813	12th	DR-108	F-36	DR-30	F-6	DR (Madison)
1813–1815	13th	DR-112	F-68	DR-27	F-9	DR (Madison)
1815–1817	14th	DR-117	F-65	DR-25	F-11	DR (Madison)
1817–1819	15th	DR-141	F-42	DR-34	F-10	DR (Monroe)
1819–1821	16th	DR-156	F-27	DR-35	F-7	DR (Monroe)
1821–1823	17th	DR-158	F-25	DR-44	F-4	DR (Monroe)
1823–1825	18th	DR-187	F-26	DR-44	F-4	DR (Monroe)
1825–1827	19th	AD-105	J-97	AD-26	J-20	DR (John Q. Adams)

Year	Congress	House Majority party	House Principal minority party	Senate Majority party	Senate Principal minority party	President
1827–1829	20th	J-119	AD-94	J-28	AD-20	DR (John Q. Adams)
1829–1831	21st	D-139	NR-74	D-26	NR-22	DR (Jackson)
1831–1833	22nd	D-141	NR-58	D-25	NR-21	D (Jackson)
1833–1835	23rd	D-147	AM-53	D-20	NR-20	D (Jackson)
1835–1837	24th	D-145	W-98	D-27	W-25	D (Jackson)
1837–1839	25th	D-108	W-107	D-30	W-18	D (Van Buren)
1839–1841	26th	D-124	W-118	D-28	W-22	D (Van Buren)
1841–1843	27th	W-133	D-102	W-28	D-22	W (W. Harrison)
						W (Tyler)
1843–1845	28th	D-142	W-79	W-28	D-25	W (Tyler)
1845–1847	29th	D-143	W-77	D-31	W-25	D (Polk)
1847–1849	30th	W-115	D-108	D-36	W-21	D (Polk)
1849–1851	31st	D-112	W-109	D-35	W-25	W (Taylor)
						W (Fillmore)
1851–1853	32nd	D-140	W-88	D-35	W-24	W (Fillmore)
1853–1855	33rd	D-159	W-71	D-38	W-22	D (Pierce)
1855–1857	34th	R-108	D-83	D-42	R-15	D (Pierce)
1857–1859	35th	D-131	R-92	D-35	R-20	D (Buchanan)
1859–1861	36th	R-113	D-101	D-38	R-26	D (Buchanan)
1861–1863	37th	R-106	D-42	R-31	D-11	R (Lincoln)
1863–1865	38th	R-103	D-80	R-39	D-12	R (Lincoln)
1865–1867[1]	39th	U-145	D-46	U-42	D-10	U (Lincoln)
						U (A. Johnson)
1867–1869	40th	R-143	D-49	R-42	D-11	R (A. Johnson)
1869–1871	41st	R-170	D-73	R-61	D-11	R (Grant)
1871–1873	42nd	R-139	D-104	R-57	D-17	R (Grant)
1873–1875	43rd	R-203	D-88	R-54	D-19	R (Grant)
1875–1877	44th	D-181	R-107	R-46	D-29	R (Grant)
1877–1879	45th	D-156	R-137	R-39	D-36	R (Hayes)
1879–1881	46th	D-150	R-128	D-43	R-33	R (Hayes)
1881–1883	47th	R-152	D-130	R-37	D-37	R (Garfield)
						R (Arthur)

(Continued)

(Continued)

Year	Congress	House Majority party	House Principal minority party	Senate Majority party	Senate Principal minority party	President
1883–1885	48th	D-200	R-119	R-40	D-36	R (Arthur)
1885–1887	49th	D-182	R-140	R-41	D-34	D (Cleveland)
1887–1889	50th	D-170	R-151	R-39	D-37	D (Cleveland)
1889–1891	51st	R-173	D-159	R-37	D-37	R (B. Harrison)
1891–1893	52nd	D-231	R-88	R-47	D-39	R (B. Harrison)
1893–1895	53rd	D-220	R-126	D-44	R-38	D (Cleveland)
1895–1897	54th	R-246	D-104	R-43	D-39	D (Cleveland)
1897–1899	55th	R-206	D-134	R-46	D-34	R (McKinley)
1899–1901	56th	R-185	D-163	R-53	D-26	R (McKinley)
1901–1903	57th	R-198	D-153	R-56	D-29	R (McKinley)
						R (T. Roosevelt)
1903–1905	58th	R-207	D-178	R-58	D-32	R (T. Roosevelt)
1905–1907	59th	R-250	D-136	R-58	D-32	R (T. Roosevelt)
1907–1909	60th	R-222	D-164	R-61	D-29	R (T. Roosevelt)
1909–1911	61st	R-219	D-172	R-59	D-32	R (Taft)
1911–1913	62nd	D-228	R-162	R-49	D-42	R (Taft)
1913–1915	63rd	D-290	R-127	D-51	R-44	D (Wilson)
1915–1917	64th	D-231	R-193	D-56	R-39	D (Wilson)
1917–1919	65th	D-216	R-210	D-53	R-42	D (Wilson)
1919–1921	66th	R-237	D-191	R-48	D-47	D (Wilson)
1921–1923	67th	R-300	D-132	R-59	D-37	R (Harding)
1923–1925	68th	R-225	D-207	R-51	D-43	R (Coolidge)
1925–1927	69th	R-247	D-183	R-54	D-40	R (Coolidge)
1927–1929	70th	R-237	D-195	R-48	D-47	R (Coolidge)
1929–1931	71st	R-267	D-163	R-56	D-39	R (Hoover)
1931–1933	72nd	D-216	R-218	R-48	D-47	R (Hoover)
1933–1935	73rd	D-313	R-117	D-59	R-36	D (F. Roosevelt)
1935–1937	74th	D-322	R-103	D-69	R-25	D (F. Roosevelt)
1937–1939	75th	D-333	R-89	D-75	R-17	D (F. Roosevelt)
1939–1941	76th	D-262	R-169	D-69	R-23	D (F. Roosevelt)
1941–1943	77th	D-267	R-162	D-66	R-28	D (F. Roosevelt)
1943–1945	78th	D-222	R-209	D-57	R-38	D (F. Roosevelt)
1945–1947	79th	D-243	R-190	D-56	R-38	D (F. Roosevelt)
						D (Truman)

Year	Congress	House Majority party	House Principal minority party	Senate Majority party	Senate Principal minority party	President
1947–1949	80th	R-246	D-188	R-51	D-45	D (Truman)
1949–1951	81st	D-263	R-171	D-54	R-42	D (Truman)
1951–1953	82nd	D-234	R-199	D-48	R-47	D (Truman)
1953–1955	83rd	R-221	D-213	R-48	D-46	R (Eisenhower)
1955–1957	84th	D-234	R-201	D-48	R-47	R (Eisenhower)
1957–1959	85th	D-233	R-200	D-49	R-47	R (Eisenhower)
1959–1961	86th	D-283	R-153	D-64	R-34	R (Eisenhower)
1961–1963	87th	D-262	R-175	D-64	R-36	D (Kennedy)
1963–1965	88th	D-258	R-176	D-67	R-33	D (Kennedy)
						D (L. Johnson)
1965–1967	89th	D-295	R-140	D-68	R-32	D (L. Johnson)
1967–1969	90th	D-248	R-187	D-64	R-36	D (L. Johnson)
1969–1971	91st	D-243	R-192	D-58	R-42	R (Nixon)
1971–1973	92nd	D-255	R-180	D-54	R-44	R (Nixon)
1973–1975	93rd	D-242	R-192	D-56	R-42	R (Nixon)
						R (Ford)
1975–1977	94th	D-291	R-144	D-60	R-37	R (Ford)
1977–1979	95th	D-292	R-143	D-61	R-38	D (Carter)
1979–1981	96th	D-277	R-158	D-58	R-41	D (Carter)
1981–1983	97th	D-242	R-192	R-53	D-46	R (Reagan)
1983–1985	98th	D-269	R-166	R-54	D-46	R (Reagan)
1985–1987	99th	D-253	R-182	R-53	D-47	R (Reagan)
1987–1989	100th	D-258	R-177	D-55	R-45	R (Reagan)
1989–1991	101st	D-260	R-175	D-55	R-45	R (G. H. W. Bush)
1991–1993	102nd	D-267	R-167	D-56	R-44	R (G. H. W. Bush)
1993–1995	103rd	D-258	R-176	D-57	R-43	D (Clinton)
1995–1997	104th	R-230	D-204	R-52	D-48	D (Clinton)
1997–1999	105th	R-226	D-207	R-55	D-45	D (Clinton)
1999–2001	106th	R-223	D-211	R-55	D-45	D (Clinton)
2001–2003	107th	R-221	D-212	D-50	R-50	R (G. W. Bush)
2003–2005	108th	R-229	D-204	R-51	D-48	R (G. W. Bush)
2005–2007	109th	R-232	D-202	R-55	D-44	R (G. W. Bush)

(Continued)

(Continued)

Year	Congress	House		Senate		President
		Majority party	Principal minority party	Majority party	Principal minority party	
2007–2009	110th	D-233	R-202	D-49	R-49	R (G. W. Bush)
2009–2011	111th	D-254	R-175	D-57	R-40	D (Obama)
*2011–2013	112th	D-193	R-242	D-53	R-47	D (Obama)
2013–2015	113th	R-232	D-200	D-53	R-45	D (Obama)
2015–2017	114th	R-246	D-188	R-54	D-44	D (Obama)
2017–	115th	R-241	D-194	R-52	D-46	R (Trump)

Sources: For data through the 33rd Congress, see U.S. Bureau of the Census, *Historical Statistics of the United States, Colonial Times to 1970* (Washington, D.C.: Government Printing Office, 1975), 1083–1084; for data after the 33rd Congress, see U.S. Congress, Joint Committee on Printing, *Official Congressional Directory* (Washington, D.C.: Government Printing Office, 2008), 553–554; for 2008 election data see *CQ Politics Election 2008*, www.cqpolitics .com/wmspage.cfn?parm1=2. See also http://innovation.cq.com/election_night08?tab2=f; for 2010 election data, see http://www.rollcall.com/politics/. For 2012 election data, see the Office of the Clerk of the U.S. House of Representatives, http://clerk.house.gov/member_info/cong.aspx.

Notes: Figures are for the beginning of the first session of each Congress. Key to abbreviations: AD—Administration; AM—Anti-Masonic;

D—Democratic; DR—Democratic-Republican; F—Federalist; J—Jacksonian; NR—National Republican; Op—Opposition; R—Republican;

U—Unionist; W—Whig.

1. The Republican Party ran under the Union Party banner in 1864.

APPENDIX 7
SUMMARY OF PRESIDENTIAL ELECTIONS, 1789-2016

Year	No. of states	Candidates		Electoral vote		Popular vote	
1789[a]	10	Fed.		Fed.		—[b]	
		George Washington		69			
1792[a]	15	Fed.		Fed.		—[b]	
		George Washington		132			
1796[a]	16	Dem.-Rep.	Fed.	Dem.-Rep.	Fed.	—[b]	
		Thomas Jefferson	John Adams	68	71		
1800[a]	16	Dem.-Rep.	Fed.	Dem.-Rep	Fed.	—[b]	
		Thomas Jefferson	John Adams	73	65		
		Aaron Burr	Charles Cotesworth Pinckney				
1804	17	Dem.-Rep.	Fed.	Dem.-Rep	Fed.	—[b]	
		Thomas Jefferson	Charles Cotesworth Pinckney	162	14		
		George Clinton	Rufus King				
1808	17	Dem.-Rep.	Fed.	Dem.-Rep	Fed.	—[b]	
		James Madison	Charles Cotesworth Pinckney	122	47		
		George Clinton	Rufus King				

(Continued)

(Continued)

Year	No. of states	Candidates		Electoral vote		Popular vote	
1812	18	Dem.-Rep.	Fed.	Dem.-Rep	Fed.	—[b]	
		James Madison	George Clinton	128	89		
		Elbridge Gerry	Jared Ingersoll				
1816	19	Dem.-Rep.	Fed.	Dem.-Rep	Fed.	—[b]	
		James Monroe	Rufus King	183	34		
		Daniel D. Tompkins	John Howard				
1820	24	Dem.-Rep	—[c]	Dem.-Rep	—[c]	—[b]	
		James Monroe		231			
		Daniel D. Tompkins					
1824[d]	24	Dem.-Rep	Dem.-Rep	Dem.-Rep	Dem.-Rep.	Dem.-Rep	Dem.-Rep
		Andrew Jackson	John Q. Adams	99	84	151,271	113,122
		John C. Calhoun	Nathan Sanford			41.3%	30.9%
1828	24	Dem.-Rep.	Nat.-Rep.	Dem.-Rep.	Nat.-Rep.	Dem.-Rep.	Nat.-Rep.
		Andrew Jackson	John Q. Adams	178	83	642,553	500,897
		John C. Calhoun	Richard Rush			56.0%	43.6%
1832[e]	24	Dem.	Nat.-Rep.	Dem.	Nat.-Rep.	Dem.	Nat.-Rep.
		Andrew Jackson	Henry Clay	219	49	701,780	484,205
		Martin Van Buren	John Sergeant			54.2%	37.4%
1836[f]	26	Dem.	Whig	Dem.	Whig	Dem.	Whig
		Martin Van Buren	William H. Harrison	170	73	764,176	550,816
		Richard M. Johnson	Francis Granger			50.8%	36.6%
1840	26	Dem.	Whig	Dem.	Whig	Dem.	Whig
		Martin Van Buren	William H. Harrison	60	234	1,128,854	1,275,390
		Richard M. Johnson	John Tyler			46.8%	52.9%

Year	No. of states	Candidates		Electoral vote		Popular vote	
		Dem.	Whig	Dem.	Whig	Dem.	Whig
1844	26	James Polk	Henry Clay	170	105	1,339,494	1,300,004
		George M. Dallas	Theodore Frelinghuysen			49.5%	48.1%
1848	30	Lewis Cass	Zachary Taylor	127	163	1,233,460	1,361,393
		William O. Butler	Millard Fillmore			42.5%	47.3%
1852	31	Franklin Pierce	Winfield Scott	254	42	1,607,510	1,386,942
		William R. King	William A. Graham			50.8%	43.9%

Year	No. of states	Candidates		Electoral vote		Popular vote	
		Dem.	Rep.	Dem.	Rep.	Dem.	Rep.
1856[g]	31	James Buchanan	John C. Fremont	174	114	1,836,072	1,342,345
		John C. Breckinridge	William L. Dayton			45.3%	33.1%
1860[h]	33	Stephen A. Douglas	Abraham Lincoln	12	180	1,380,202	1,865,908
		Herschel V. Johnson	Hannibal Hamlin			29.5%	39.8%
1864[i]	36	George B. McClellan	Abraham Lincoln	21	212	1,812,807	2,218,388
		George H. Pendleton	Andrew Johnson			45.0%	55.0%
1868[j]	37	Horatio Seymour	Ulysses S. Grant	80	214	2,708,744	3,013,650
		Francis P. Blair Jr.	Schuyler Colfax			47.3%	52.7%
1872[k]	37	Horace Greeley	Ulysses S. Grant		286	2,834,761	3,598,235
		Benjamin Gratz Brown	Henry Wilson			43.8%	55.6%
1876	38	Samuel J. Tilden	Rutherford B. Hayes	184	185	4,288,546	4,034,311
		Thomas A. Hendricks	William A. Wheeler			51.0%	47.9%
1880	38	Winfield S. Hancock	James A. Garfield	155	214	4,444,260	4,446,158
		William H. English	Chester A. Arthur			48.2%	48.3%
1884	38	Grover Cleveland	James G. Blaine	219	182	4,874,621	4,848,936
		Thomas A. Hendricks	John A. Logan			48.5%	48.2%

(Continued)

(Continued)

Year	No. of states	Candidates Dem.	Candidates Rep.	Electoral vote Dem.	Electoral vote Rep.	Popular vote Dem.	Popular vote Rep.
1888	38	Grover Cleveland	Benjamin Harrison	168	233	5,534,488	5,443,892
		Allen G. Thurman	Levi P. Morton			48.6%	47.8%
1892[l]	44	Grover Cleveland	Benjamin Harrison	277	145	5,551,883	5,179,244
		Adlai E. Stevenson	Whitelaw Reid			46.1%	43.0%
1896	45	William J. Bryan	William McKinley	176	271	6,511,495	7,108,480
		Arthur Sewall	Garret A. Hobart			46.7%	51.0%
1900	45	William J. Bryan	William McKinley	155	292	6,358,345	7,218,039
		Adlai E. Stevenson	Theodore Roosevelt			45.5%	51.7%
1904	45	Alton B. Parker	Theodore Roosevelt	140	336	5,028,898	7,626,593
		Henry G. Davis	Charles W. Fairbanks			37.6%	56.4%
		John W. Kern	James S. Sherman			43.0%	51.6%
1912[m]	48	Woodrow Wilson	William H. Taft	435	8	6,293,152	3,486,333
		Thomas R. Marshall	James S. Sherman			41.8%	23.2%
1916	48	Woodrow Wilson	Charles E. Hughes	277	254	9,126,300	8,546,789
		Thomas R. Marshall	Charles W. Fairbanks			49.2%	46.1%
1920	48	James M. Cox	Warren G. Harding	127	404	9,140,884	16,133,314
		Franklin D. Roosevelt	Calvin Coolidge			34.2%	60.3%
1924[n]	48	John W. Davis	Calvin Coolidge	136	382	8,386,169	15,717,553
		Charles W. Bryant	Charles G. Dawes			28.8%	54.1%
1928	48	Alfred E. Smith	Herbert C. Hoover	87	444	15,000,185	21,411,991
		Joseph T. Robinson	Charles Curtis			40.8%	58.2%
1932	48	Franklin D. Roosevelt	Herbert C. Hoover	472	59	22,825,016	15,758,397
		John N. Garner	Charles Curtis			57.4%	39.6%

Year	No. of states	Candidates Dem.	Candidates Rep.	Electoral vote Dem.	Electoral vote Rep.	Popular vote Dem.	Popular vote Rep.
1936	48	Franklin D. Roosevelt	Alfred M. Landon	523	8	27,747,636	16,679,543
		John N. Garner	Frank Knox			60.8%	36.5%
1940	48	Franklin D. Roosevelt	Wendell L. Willkie	449	82	27,263,448	22,336,260
		Henry A. Wallace	Charles L. McNary			54.7%	44.8%
1944	48	Franklin D. Roosevelt	Thomas E. Dewey	432	99	25,611,936	22,013,372
		Harry S. Truman	John W. Bricker			53.4%	45.9%
1948°	48	Harry S. Truman	Thomas E. Dewey	303	189	24,105,587	21,970,017
		Alben W. Barkley	Earl Warren			49.5%	45.1%
1952	48	Adlai E. Stevenson II	Dwight D. Eisenhower	89	442	27,314,649	33,936,137
		John J. Sparkman	Richard M. Nixon			44.4%	55.1%
1956ᵖ	48	Adlai E. Stevenson II	Dwight D. Eisenhower	73	457	26,030,172	35,585,245
		Estes Kefauver	Richard M. Nixon			42.0%	57.4%
1960�q	50	John F. Kennedy	Richard M. Nixon	303	219	34,221,344	34,106,671
		Lyndon B. Johnson	Henry Cabot Lodge			49.7%	49.5%
1964	50*	Lyndon B. Johnson	Barry Goldwater	486	52	43,126,584	27,177,838
		Hubert H. Humphrey	William E. Miller			61.1%	38.5%
1968ʳ	50*	Hubert H. Humphrey	Richard M. Nixon	191	301	31,274,503	31,785,148
		Edmund S. Muskie	Spiro T. Agnew			42.7%	43.4%
1972ˢ	50*	George McGovern	Richard M. Nixon	17	520	29,171,791	47,170,179
		Sargent Shriver	Spiro T. Agnew			37.5%	60.7%
1976ᵗ	50*	Jimmy Carter	Gerald R. Ford	297	240	40,830,763	39,147,793
		Walter F. Mondale	Robert Dole			50.1%	48.0%
1980	50*	Jimmy Carter	Ronald Reagan	49	489	35,483,883	43,904,153
		Walter F. Mondale	George H. W. Bush			41.0%	50.7%

(Continued)

(Continued)

Year	No. of states	Candidates Dem.	Candidates Rep.	Electoral vote Dem.	Electoral vote Rep.	Popular vote Dem.	Popular vote Rep.
1984	50*	Walter F. Mondale	Ronald Reagan	13	525	37,577,185	54,455,075
		Geraldine Ferraro	George H. W. Bush			40.6%	58.8%
1988[u]	50*	Michael S. Dukakis	George H. W. Bush	111	426	41,809,074	48,886,097
		Lloyd Bentsen	Dan Quayle			45.6%	53.4%
1992	50*	William J. Clinton	George H. W. Bush	370	168	44,909,326	39,103,882
		Albert Gore	Dan Quayle			43.0%	37.4%
1996	50*	William J. Clinton	Robert J. Dole	379	159	47,402,357	39,198,755
		Albert Gore	Jack F. Kemp			49.2%	40.7%
2000	50*	Albert Gore	George W. Bush	266	271	50,992,335	50,455,156
		Joseph I. Lieberman	Richard B. Cheney			48.4%	47.9%
2004	50*	John Kerry	George W. Bush	252	286	59,026,013	62,025,554
		John Edwards	Richard B. Cheney			47.3%	50.7%
2008	50*	Barack Obama	John McCain	365	173	69,498,459	59,948,283
		Joe Biden	Sarah Palin			52.9%	45.6%
2012	50*	Barack Obama	Mitt Romney	332	206	62,611,250	59,134,475
		Joe Biden	Paul Ryan			51.5%	48.5%
2016**	50*	Hillary Clinton	Donald Trump	232	306	64,827,442	62,494,402
		Tim Kaine	Mike Pence			(48.2%)	(46.4%)

Sources: Harold W. Stanley and Richard G. Niemi, *Vital Statistics on American Politics, 2007–2008* (Washington, D.C.: CQ Press, 2008), 26–30; *CQ Press Guide to U.S. Elections*, 5th ed. (Washington, D.C.: CQ Press, 2006), 715–719; for the 2008 election: for presidential race electoral vote data, see *CQ Politics Election 2008*, http://innovation.cq.com/election_night08?tab2=f. For presidential race popular vote data, see the *New York Times*'s Presidential Big Board, http://elections.nytimes.com/2008/results/president/votes.html. 2012 election data calculated from Politico, 2012 Presidential Election, http://www.politico.com/2012-election/map/#/President/2012/.

Note: Dem.-Rep.–Democratic-Republican; Fed.–Federalist; Nat.-Rep.–National-Republican; Dem.–Democratic; Rep.–Republican.

a. Elections from 1789 through 1800 were held under rules that did not allow separate voting for president and vice president.

b. Popular vote returns are not shown before 1824 because consistent, reliable data are not available.

c. 1820: One electoral vote was cast for John Adams and Richard Stockton, who were not candidates.

d. 1824: All four candidates represented Democratic-Republican factions. William H. Crawford received 41 electoral votes and Henry Clay received 37 votes. Because no candidate received a majority, the election was decided (in Adams's favor) by the House of Representatives.

e. 1832: Two electoral votes were not cast.

f. 1836: Other Whig candidates receiving electoral votes were Hugh L. White, who received 26 votes, and Daniel Webster, who received 14 votes.

g. 1856: Millard Fillmore, Whig-American, received 8 electoral votes.

h. 1860: John C. Breckinridge, southern Democrat, received 72 electoral votes. John Bell, Constitutional Union, received 39 electoral votes.

i. 1864: Eighty-one electoral votes were not cast.

j. 1868: Twenty-three electoral votes were not cast.

k. 1872: Horace Greeley, Democrat, died after the election. In the Electoral College, Democratic electoral votes went to Thomas Hendricks, 42 votes; Benjamin Gratz Brown, 18 votes; Charles J. Jenkins, 2 votes; and David Davis, 1 vote. Seventeen electoral votes were not cast.

l. 1892: James B. Weaver, People's Party, received 22 electoral votes.

m. 1912: Theodore Roosevelt, Progressive Party, received 88 electoral votes.

n. 1924: Robert M. La Follette, Progressive Party, received 13 electoral votes.

o. 1948: J. Strom Thurmond, States' Rights Party, received 39 electoral votes.

p. 1956: Walter B. Jones, Democrat, received 1 electoral vote.

q. 1960: Harry Flood Byrd, Democrat, received 15 electoral votes.

r. 1968: George C. Wallace, American Independent Party, received 46 electoral votes.

s. 1972: John Hospers, Libertarian Party, received 1 electoral vote.

t. 1976: Ronald Reagan, Republican, received 1 electoral vote.

u. 1988: Lloyd Bentsen, the Democratic vice-presidential nominee, received 1 electoral vote for president.

* Fifty states plus the District of Columbia.

**Election data current as of November 29, 2016.

GLOSSARY

abolitionist movement
a political struggle to end slavery and free all slaves.

absentee ballots
votes completed and submitted by a voter prior to the day of an election.

achievement gap
the persistent differences in school performance of students of majority ethnicity and higher incomes versus those of minority ethnicity and lower incomes.

adversarial system
a legal structure in which two opposing sides present their case in the most persuasive way possible.

affirmative action
a policy designed to address the consequences of previous discrimination by providing advantages to individuals based upon their identities.

agency capture
when agencies tasked with regulating businesses, industries, or other interest groups are populated by individuals with close ties to the very firms that they are supposed to regulate.

agenda setting
the media's ability to highlight certain issues and bring them to the attention of the public.

aggregating
a process through which Internet and other news providers relay the news as reported by journalists and other sources.

The Alien and Sedition Acts
four separate laws passed under the administration of President John Adams that, among other things, restricted the freedom of speech and the press.

Albany Plan
a proposal for a union of British colonies in North America in which colonial legislatures would choose delegates to form an assembly under the leadership of a chief executive appointed by Great Britain.

amendment
a constitutional provision for a process by which changes may be made to the Constitution.

the American dream
The idea that individuals should be able to achieve prosperity through hard work, sacrifice, and their own talents.

American exceptionalism
the belief in the special character of the United States as a uniquely free nation based on its history and its commitment to democratic ideals and personal liberty.

American political culture
a shared set of beliefs, customs, traditions, and values that define the relationship of Americans to their government and to other American citizens.

Antifederalists
the name taken by those opposed to the proposed Constitution; the Antifederalists favored stronger state governments.

appellate jurisdiction
the authority of a court to hear and review decisions made by lower courts in that system.

apportionment
the process of determining the number of representatives for each state using census data; states are divided into congressional districts that have at least one representative each.

appropriation
the process through which congressional committees allocate funds to executive branch agencies, bureaus, and departments.

Arab Spring
a series of protests taking place across North Africa and the Middle East beginning in early 2010 that led to democratic reforms in some nations and civil war and chaos in others.

Articles of Confederation and Perpetual Union
a constituting document calling for the creation of a union of thirteen sovereign states in which the states, not the union, were supreme.

Astroturf lobbying
when a group presents the façade of grassroots support that does not exist on its own or would not exist without the "purchase" of support by the lobbying firm itself.

bail
an amount of money posted as a security to allow the charged individual to be freed while awaiting trial.

ballot roll-off
when voters do not cast votes for a set of races with which they are not familiar and for which they may not have traditional cues.

bill of rights
a list of fundamental rights and freedoms that individuals possess. The first ten amendments to the United States Constitution are referred to as the Bill of Rights.

bipolarity
a distribution of power in the international system where two states exert most of the power and influence.

block grant
a type of grant-in-aid that gives state officials more authority in the disbursement of the federal funds.

brief
legal document presented by plaintiffs, defendants, and, at times, other interested parties outlining their arguments in a case.

broadcast media
outlets for news and other content that rely on mass communications technology to bring stories directly into people's homes; these media sources are subject to stricter content regulations than cable television outlets and alternative sources of information.

Brown v. Board of Education
a landmark 1954 Supreme Court ruling that overturned *Plessy v. Ferguson* and declared legal segregation in public education to be in conflict with the equal protection clause of the Fourteenth Amendment.

budget deficit
when the federal government takes in less money than it spends.

budget resolution
a step in the budgeting process in which Congress provides broad outlines for federal spending.

budget surplus
when the federal government takes in more money than it spends.

bureaucrat
an official employed within a government bureaucracy.

bureaucratic adjudication
when the federal bureaucracy settles disputes between parties that arise over the implementation of federal laws and presidential executive orders or determine which individuals or groups are covered under a regulation or program.

bureaucratic discretion
the power to decide how a law is implemented and, at times, what Congress actually meant when it passed a given law.

bureaucratic drift
when bureaucracies stray from their established goals and devote their energies and efforts to peripheral tasks.

business cycle
the fluctuation of economic activity around a long-term trend, with periods of expansion and contraction.

capitalist system
a way of structuring economic activity in which private firms are allowed to make most or all of the decisions involving the production and distribution of goods and services.

categorical grants
grants-in-aid provided to states with specific provisions on their use.

caucus
a process through which a state's eligible voters gather to discuss candidates and issues and select delegates to represent their preferences in later stages of the nomination process.

Central Intelligence Agency (CIA)
the federal agency charged with collecting intelligence around the world to protect national security.

certiorari
the process through which most cases reach the Supreme Court; after four justices concur that the Court should hear the case, a writ of certiorari is issued to the lower court to request the relevant case records.

challenger
a candidate for office who does not currently hold office.

charter schools
public schools that are funded only by taxpayer money and subject to many of the same regulations as traditional public schools but that are accountable primarily to their founding document (their charter) and that have greater curricular and professional autonomy.

citizen journalists
nonprofessionals who cover or document news and events or offer their own analyses of them.

civic education
the transmission of information about the political world and civic norms to learners.

civic engagement
working to improve society through political and nonpolitical action.

civil disobedience
the intentional refusal to obey a law in order to call attention to its injustice.

civil law
a category of law covering cases involving private rights and relationships between individuals and groups.

civil liberties
fundamental rights and freedoms of citizens the protection of which involves restricting the power of a government.

civil rights
fundamental guarantees ensuring equal treatment and protecting against discrimination under the laws of a nation.

clear and present danger test
a Supreme Court tool to evaluate whether or not forms of political expression constitute such a threat to national security as to warrant restriction.

clientele agencies
organizations that act to serve and promote the interests of their clients.

closed primary
a primary election in which only registered voters from a particular political party may vote.

cloture
a procedure through which senators can end debate on a bill and proceed to action, provided three-fifths of senators agree to it.

coattail effect
a phenomenon that occurs when a presidential candidate's increasing popularity results in increased support for congressional candidates of the same party.

Cold War
the period of time between 1945 and 1991 characterized by conflict between the United States and its allies and the Soviet Union and its allies but that did not result in full global war.

collective action
political action that occurs when individuals contribute their energy, time, or money to a larger group goal.

collective good
also called a public good; some benefit or desirable outcome that individuals can enjoy or profit from even if they do not help achieve or secure it.

command-and-control economy
a type of economic policy in which government dictates much of a nation's economic activity, including the amount of production and prices for goods.

commerce clause
a part of the Constitution that grants Congress the authority to regulate business and commercial activity.

commercial bias
the shaping of the content and focus of news based upon the desire to capture news consumers.

committee chairs
leaders of the subunits of congressional committees who have authority over the committee's agenda.

Committee on Rules (House)
a powerful committee that determines when a bill will be subject to debate and vote on the House floor, how long the debate will last, and whether amendments will be allowed on the floor.

communist system
a way of structuring economic activity in which a government exerts complete control over the production and distribution of goods and services.

concurrent powers
powers granted to both states and the federal government in the Constitution.

confederal systems
structures of governance in which the subnational governments retain the majority of the granted authority.

Congressional Budget Office (CBO)
the federal agency tasked with producing independent analyses of budgetary and economic issues to support the congressional budget process.

consideration
a combination of cognition and affect that contributes to any one answer to any one question or evaluation.

constituencies
bodies of voters in a given area who elect a representative or senator.

constitution
a document that defines and creates a people politically, sets out the fundamental principles of governance, and creates the rules and institutions through which a people choose to self-govern.

Constitutional Convention
a meeting held in Philadelphia in 1787 at which state delegates met to fix the Articles of Confederation.

constitutional interpretation
the process of applying the Constitution in assessing whether or not a law, part of a law, or an action by a governmental official is or is not in conflict with that of the Constitution.

constitutional republic
a form of government in which people vote for elected representatives to make laws and policies and in which limits on the ability of that government to restrict individual rights are placed in a constituting document that is recognized as the highest law of the land.

consumer price index (CPI)
an economic measure that is used to assess price changes associated with the cost of living.

containment
a Cold War foreign policy strategy designed to restrict expansion of Soviet ideological and military influence, using military force if necessary.

cooperative federalism
a vision of American federalism in which the states and the national government work together to shape public policy.

criminal law
a category of law covering actions determined to harm the community itself.

critical election
a major national election that signals a change either in the balance of power between two major parties or the emergence of a new party system.

Daughters of Liberty
a group of colonial-era women who participated in the boycotting of British goods.

de facto segregation
a separation of individuals based on identity that arises not by law but because of other factors, such as residential housing patterns.

defendant
a person or group against whom a case is brought in court.

deflation
when a cascading series of defaults arises because there is not enough money to pay off outstanding debt.

de jure segregation
the separation of individuals based on their characteristics, such as race, intentionally and by law.

delegates
people who act as voters' representatives at a convention to select their party's presidential nominee.

democracy
a system of government where power is held and political decisions made by the people in that society.

demographics
the grouping of individuals based on shared characteristics, such as ancestry, race, ethnicity, and gender.

Department of Defense
the executive branch department responsible for formulating and enacting American defense policy and managing the United States Armed Forces.

Department of Homeland Security
the executive branch department responsible for overseeing and implementing policies enacted to respond to national disasters, secure transit points to and within the United States, and protect the nation's borders.

Department of State
the cabinet department primarily responsible for diplomatic relationships with other nations.

deregulation
the reduction or elimination of government power in a particular industry, usually in order to create more competition within the industry.

descriptive representation
the degree to which a body of representatives in a legislature does or does not reflect the diversity of that nation's identities and lived experiences.

desegregation
the act of eliminating laws or practices that separate individuals based upon racial identity.

devolution
the transfer of power over public policy back to the states in order to shrink the size of the federal government and allow states to have more authority to determine how taxpayer dollars should be spent.

digital divide
divisions in society that are driven by access to and knowledge about technologies; these gaps often fall along the lines of partisanship, class, race, and ethnicity.

direct democracy
a political system in which citizens vote directly on public policies.

direction
the focus of an individual's opinion.

director of national intelligence
the head of all of the intelligence agencies in the United States.

discretionary spending
spending for programs and policies at the discretion of Congress and the president.

divided government
a situation that occurs when control of the presidency and one or both chambers of Congress is split between the two major parties.

domestic policy
policy designed to improve the social welfare of citizens.

double jeopardy
the prosecution of an individual more than once for the same crime.

dual federalism
a view of American federalism in which the states and the nation operate independently in their own areas of public policy.

due process clause
the clause in the Fourteenth Amendment that restricts state governments from denying their citizens the right to due process of law.

earmark
an addition to a piece of legislation that directs specific funds to projects within districts or states.

economic equality
when wealth is relatively evenly distributed across society.

economic interest groups
groups that organize to advocate on behalf of the economic interests of their members.

economic policy
the efforts of government to regulate and support the economy in order to protect and expand citizens' financial well-being and economic prospects and to support businesses in the global financial system.

economic recession
a period of decline in economic activity, typically defined by two consecutive quarters of negative GDP growth.

economy
the systems and organizations through which a society produces and distributes goods and services.

Electoral College
a process for electing the president that involves the voting population choosing a slate of electors who are pledged to vote for a nominee in the presidential election.

elites
a small number of individuals (who tend to have well-informed and well-reasoned opinions).

elitist theory
a theory of governmental influence that focuses on the advantages that certain interests have in the political process based on the unequal distribution of economic and political power.

entitlement programs
programs wherein one receives a set of benefits regardless of income provided one meets certain categorical requirements, such as age or a minimum number of years of payroll contributions.

enumerated powers
powers explicitly granted to the government via the Constitution.

equal protection clause
a clause of the Fourteenth Amendment that serves as the constitutional basis for the assault on educational segregation in the courts and for the assertion of civil rights for Americans of many different identities in many different areas of public and private life.

Equal Rights Amendment
a proposed but not ratified amendment to the Constitution that sought to guarantee equality of rights based upon sex.

Equal time rule
a regulation that requires American radio and television broadcast networks to provide equal time for political candidates to present their views on issues.

essentialism
the risks posed by linking individuals' lived experiences to policy preferences, whether by identifying those individuals by those policies or excluding them from advocating different policy objectives.

European Union (EU)
an association of European countries formed in the 1990s for the purpose of achieving political and economic integration.

exclusionary rule
a rule governing the inadmissibility of evidence obtained without a proper warrant.

executive agreement
an agreement between a president and another nation that does not have the same durability in the American system as a treaty but that may carry important foreign policy consequences.

executive branch
the branch of government charged with putting the nation's laws into effect.

Executive Office of the President
a collection of offices within the White House organization designed primarily to provide information to the president.

executive orders
directions made by presidents to the executive branch departments that often contain nothing more than instructions to be carried out by agencies, bureaus, and departments but that may at times be considered to be acts of presidential lawmaking.

executive political appointees
employees at high levels in the federal bureaucracy who serve at the pleasure of the president and are subject to presidential removal.

exit poll
a survey conducted outside of a polling place in which individuals are asked who or what they just voted for and why.

executive privilege
a right claimed by presidents to keep confidential certain conversations, records, and transcripts from outside scrutiny, especially that of Congress.

exploratory committee
a group that helps determine whether a potential candidate should run for office and that helps lay the groundwork for the campaign.

extended republic
a republic so large and diverse, with so many factions vying for power, that no one faction is able to assert its will over all of the others.

faction
a group of self-interested people who use the government to get what they want, trampling the rights of others in the process.

fairness doctrine
a federal rule that expanded regulations for American political news coverage beyond just the provision of time for candidates to the content of the coverage itself.

faithless elector
a party elector who changes his or her mind in between the general election and the Electoral College vote.

federal bureaucracy
the organizations and suborganizations within the executive branch that are tasked with putting the laws of the nation into effect.

Federal Bureau of Investigation (FBI)
the federal agency charged with carrying out investigations for the attorney general and with safeguarding national security, primarily within the United States.

federal civil service
the permanent professional branches of government concerned with administrative functions, excluding the armed forces and political appointments.

federal courts of appeals
the middle level of the federal judiciary; these courts review and hear appeals from the federal district courts.

federal district courts
the lowest level of the federal judiciary; these courts usually possess original jurisdiction in cases that originate at the federal level.

federalism
a structure of governance that places the people's authority in two or more levels of government.

Federalist Papers
a series of eighty-five essays written by Alexander Hamilton, James Madison, and John Jay and published between 1787 and 1788 that lay out the theory behind the Constitution.

Federalists
the name taken by supporters of the proposed Constitution; the Federalists called for a strong national government.

federal judiciary
the branch of the federal government that interprets and applies the laws of the nation.

Federal Reserve System
the central bank of the United States.

federal systems
structures of governance that divide a people's sovereignty between two or more levels of government.

felon disenfranchisement
the denial of voting rights to Americans who have been convicted of felonies.

Fifteenth Amendment
an amendment to the Constitution passed in 1870 affirming the voting rights of all freedmen.

filibuster
a tactic through which an individual senator may postpone action on a piece of legislation.

fire alarm oversight
a term that describes congressional oversight procedures primarily in response to problems or complaints.

fiscal policy
a set of activities through which government tries to lower unemployment, support economic activity, and stabilize the economy by using policies of taxation and spending.

focus group
a small group of individuals assembled for a directed conversation during which one hopes to uncover patterns of thinking about issues and individuals.

foreign policy
the ways in which political actors in a nation engage others at home and abroad in order to advance their nation's interests, protect and secure national security, and support national commercial interests.

Fourteenth Amendment
an amendment to the Constitution passed in 1868 affirming the citizenship of all persons born or naturalized in the United States and, for the first time in the history of the Constitution, placing explicit restrictions on the laws of states that sought to abridge the privileges and immunities of citizens of the United States.

framing
influencing people's interpretations of news, events, or issues through the presentation of the context.

freedom of expression
a fundamental right affirmed in the First Amendment to speak, publish, and act in the political space.

free riders
individuals who enjoy collective goods without help to secure them.

free trade
a trade policy characterized by few restrictions on the flow of goods and services across national borders.

front-loading
when a state pushes its primary or caucus to a date as early in the season as possible to become more instrumental in the nomination process.

full faith and credit clause
a portion of the Constitution that generally requires states to honor licenses and judicial outcomes of other states.

gender gap
a term that refers to the fact American women are more likely to identify with and vote for Democratic Party candidates than men, who are more likely to vote for Republican Party candidates.

gerrymandering
the intentional use of redistricting to benefit a specific interest or group of voters.

get out the vote (GOTV)
efforts to mobilize voters or potential voters.

going public
a strategy through which presidents reach out directly to the American people with the hope that the people will, in turn, put pressure upon their representatives and senators to press for a president's policy goals.

government
a system of rules and institutions that defines and shapes the contours of public action.

government corporations
organizations that act as businesses within the federal government, charging fees for their services but still subject to governmental control and possible financial subsidization.

government interest groups
organizations that act to secure the interests of local, state, or foreign governments in the political process.

grand jury
a group of citizens who, based on the evidence presented to them, conclude whether or not a person is to be indicted and subsequently tried in a court of law.

grants-in-aid
federal money provided to states to implement public policy objectives.

Great Compromise
an agreement for a plan of government that drew upon both the Virginia and New Jersey Plans; it settled issues of state representation by calling for a bicameral legislature with a House of Representatives apportioned proportionately and a Senate apportioned equally.

The Great Depression
a period defined by the most significant economic crisis in American history.

gridlock
a situation in which Congress's ability to legislate is slowed or stopped by its inability to overcome divisions, especially those based on partisanship.

gross domestic product (GDP)
a measure of the total value of goods and services produced by American economic activity.

hate speech
speech that has no other purpose but to express hatred, particularly toward members of a group identified by racial or ethnic identity, gender, or sexual orientation.

horse race phenomenon
coverage of political campaigns that focuses more on the drama of the campaign than on policy issues.

hyperinflation
extremely rapid or out of control inflation brought on by excessive printing of money and a loss of faith in a currency.

impeachment
the process for removing federal officials

implementation
the enactment of public policies on the ground.

implied powers
powers not textually granted to a government but considered valid in order to carry out the enumerated powers.

inalienable rights
rights that exist before and above any government or its power.

incentives
inducements that leaders of a bureaucracy can offer to their employees to spur successful performance.

income-based repayment
a type of loan repayment plan in which individual student debtors could have their loan payments reduced and eventually forgiven based on their incomes and ability to pay off these significant debts.

incumbency advantage
institutional advantages held by those already in office who are trying to fend off challengers in an election.

incumbent
a political official who is currently in office.

independent executive agency
agencies otherwise similar to cabinet departments but existing outside of the cabinet structure and usually having a narrower focus of mission.

independent regulatory agencies
organizations that exist outside of the major cabinet departments and whose job is to monitor and regulate specific sectors of the economy.

inflation
the rise in the prices of goods and services purchased by individuals.

infotainment
a merging of information and entertainment in a way designed to attract viewers and gain market share.

inside lobbying
when lobbyists contact members of Congress or their staff directly to advocate for their group's position.

intelligence community
the collective name for all of the intelligence agencies in the United States and their members.

intensity
the strength of involvement and preference of an individual's opinion.

interagency rivalry
when two or more agencies are charged with a similar mandate, an outcome that becomes more likely in times of budget cuts and competition for scarce or dwindling appropriations.

interest groups
voluntary associations of people who come together with an agreed-upon set of political and policy objectives and who attempt to pull the levers of political power in service of these defined goals.

interest rates
the rates paid to borrow money.

intergovernmental lobbying
efforts by state and local governments to act in Washington on behalf of their own interests.

internationalism
an approach to international affairs that emphasizes close contact and cooperation between nations.

Intolerable Acts
a term used in the American colonies to refer to a series of laws enacted by Great Britain in response to the Boston Tea Party.

investigative journalism
an approach to newsgathering in which reporters dig into stories, often looking for instances of corruption or failures to uphold the interests of citizens.

iron triangle
the coordinated (and mutually beneficial) activities of interest groups, Congress, and the bureaucracy to achieve shared policy goals, sometimes against the general interests of society or specific groups within it.

isolationism
a foreign policy orientation in which a nation attempts to stay out of foreign entanglements.

issue network
the webs of influence between interest groups, policymakers, and policy advocates.

Joint Chiefs of Staff
an advisory body reporting to the president on military operations.

judicial activism
a philosophy of constitutional interpretation that asserts justices should wield the power of judicial review when needed.

judicial branch
the institution responsible for hearing and deciding cases via a system of federal courts.

judicial restraint
a philosophy of constitutional interpretation that asserts justices should be cautious in overturning laws.

judicial review
the authority of the highest court in a political system to determine if a law is or is not in conflict with a government's highest law, which in the United States is the Constitution.

laissez-faire economics
a type of economic policy in which governments intrude as little as possible in the economic transactions between citizens and businesses.

legal segregation
the separation by law of individuals based upon their racial identities.

legislative branch
in a divided government, the institution responsible for making laws.

legislative deliberation
the considered argument and discussion of the issues by congressional representatives.

Lemon test
A three-pronged test developed by the Supreme Court to determine whether a law or action by the federal or a state government violates the establishment clause.

libel
expression in written form or similarly published media that defames a person's character.

liberty
social, political, and economic freedoms.

linked fate
a theory of group identification that describes ways in which individuals tie their own life chances to those of a group.

lobbying
interacting with government officials in order to advance a group's goals in the area of public policy.

logroll
an exchange of political favors, such as when legislators trade votes to support one another's proposed legislation.

majority
when a candidate receives more than 50 percent of the vote.

majority-minority district
a district in which voters of a minority ethnicity constitute an electoral majority within that electoral district.

majority party leader
the head of the party with the most seats in Congress, chosen by the party's members.

malapportionment
the uneven distribution of the population between legislative districts.

Marbury v. Madison (1803)
a Supreme Court decision that established judicial review over federal laws.

markup
a process during which a bill is revised prior to a final vote in Congress.

Marshall Plan
a Cold War policy wherein loans and aid were made available to the nations of Western Europe; it also established organizations of economic cooperation.

masses
the majority of individuals (who tend to be less well informed).

mass media
sources of information that appeal to a wide audience, including newspapers, radio, television, and Internet outlets.

material rewards
a type of tangible benefit made available to members and contributors of a group.

media effects
the power of the news media in shaping individuals' political knowledge, preferences, and political behavior.

merit system
a system of hiring and promotion based on competitive testing results, education, and other qualifications rather than politics and personal connections.

minimalist paradigm
a theory of public opinion that emphasizes how most people fall short of what we expect them to know, think about, and pay attention to in the complicated world of politics and policy.

minority party leader
the head of the party with the second-highest number of seats in Congress, chosen by the party's members.

Miranda rights
the right not to speak and to have an attorney present during questioning; these rights must be given by police to individuals suspected of criminal activity.

mixed economy
a type of economic policy in which many economic decisions are left to individuals and businesses, but the federal government also plays a role in shaping these decisions.

monetary policy
a set of economic policy tools designed to regulate the amount of money in the economy (in circulation and in the deposits).

Monroe Doctrine
a policy that asserted American interests in and primacy over actions in the Western hemisphere.

Motor Voter Law
a law allowing Americans to register to vote when applying for or renewing their driver's licenses and making it easier for Americans with disabilities to register to vote.

national convention
a meeting where delegates officially select their party's nominee for the presidency.

national debt
the sum of all previously incurred annual federal deficits.

National Security Council
an advisory body that provides the president with intelligence, analysis, and advice on critical matters of national security.

natural rights
rights that people have inherently that are not granted by any government.

necessary and proper clause
a part of the Constitution that grants the federal government the authority to pass laws required to carry out its enumerated powers. Also called the elastic clause.

need-based assistance
social welfare programs whose benefits are allocated to individuals demonstrating specific needs.

negative campaign advertisements
campaign ads that attack an opponent or opponents and try to raise doubts in voters' minds about them.

negative freedoms
fundamental liberties the protection of which is ensured by restricting governmental action and authority.

net neutrality
a Federal Communications Commission (FCC) rule that requires Internet service providers to treat all data and content providers equally and not discriminate based upon content or bandwidth demands.

neutrality test
a Supreme Court test for examining questions of free expression that allows restrictions upon religious expression, provided that laws doing so not single out one faith, or faith over nonfaith.

The New Deal
a set of policies passed during the administration of President Franklin Roosevelt in order to combat the Great Depression.

New Jersey Plan
a plan of government that preserved many of the provisions in the Articles of Confederation, including the unicameral legislature with equal votes for each states, but that strengthened the confederal government.

news media
the variety of sources providing information and covering events, including newspapers, television, radio, the Internet, and social media.

niche journalism
media that caters to fragmented and specialized audiences.

Nineteenth Amendment
a 1920 amendment to the Constitution that prevented states from denying the right to vote based on sex.

nomination
the formal process through which parties choose their candidates for political office.

nonattitudes
a term referring to the lack of stable and coherent opinions on political issues and candidates.

North American Free Trade Agreement (NAFTA)
a regional trade agreement made between the United States, Canada, and Mexico designed to increase trade between the nations.

North Atlantic Treaty Alliance (NATO)
an alliance created during the Cold War that requires America and all other members to come to the military aid of each other in case of attack.

obscenity and pornography
text, images, or video that depicts sexual activity in ways offensive to the broader community and that lacks any artistic merit.

Office of Management and Budget (OMB)
the executive branch office whose purpose is to assist the president in setting national spending priorities.

open primary
a primary election in which all eligible voters may vote, regardless of their partisan affiliation.

open seat election
an election in which no incumbent is seeking reelection.

oral arguments
presentations made by plaintiffs and attorneys before the Supreme Court.

original jurisdiction
the authority of a court to act as the first court to hear a case, which includes the finding of facts in the case.

outside (or grassroots) lobbying
a type of lobbying that focuses on reaching constituents and mobilizing them to pressure their representatives rather than pressuring the representatives directly.

oversight
efforts by Congress to ensure that executive branch agencies, bureaus, and cabinet departments, as well as their officials, are acting legally and in accordance with congressional goals.

partisan bias
the slanting of political news coverage in support of a particular political party or ideology.

partisan polarization
when an individual's stance on a given issue, policy, or person is more likely to be strictly defined by their identification with a particular political party (e.g., Democrat or Republican) or ideology (e.g., liberal or conservative).

partisan press
media outlets or organizations that promote a particular political ideology or support a political party.

party identification
the degree to which an individual identifies with and supports a particular political party.

party ideology
a set of stances shaped by an underlying philosophy about key issues and the proper role of government in society and then communicated to voters.

party platform
a set of positions and policy objectives that members of a political party agree to.

party systems
periods of stability of the composition of political parties and the issues around which they coalesce, brought on by shorter periods of intense change.

path dependence
the way in which a set of political outcomes shapes future possibilities for political action.

Pendleton Act
(or Civil Service Reform Act of 1883) created the first United States Civil Service Commission to draw up and enforce rules on hiring, promotion, and tenure of office within the civil service.

penny press
nineteenth-century American newspapers that sold for only one cent each, thus increasing the size of the audience that could afford to purchase them.

plaintiff
a person or group who brings a case in court.

plea bargaining
a legal process in which the plaintiff and defendant agree to an outcome prior to the handing out of a verdict.

Plessy v. Ferguson
a Supreme Court case in 1896 that upheld legal racial segregation.

pluralism
a theory of governmental influence that views the distribution of political power among many competing groups as serving to keep any one of them in check.

plurality
when a candidate receives more votes than any other candidate.

polarization
a sharp ideological distance between political parties.

police patrol oversight
a term that describes congressional oversight as a process of constant monitoring rather than responding to specific crises.

police powers
a category of reserved powers that includes the protection of people's health, safety, and welfare.

policy agenda
the set of issues to which government officials, voters, and the public attend.

policy diffusion
the process through which states emulate and adopt policies enacted by other states.

policy entrepreneurs
individuals in government, academic institutions, think tanks, interest groups, and other venues who try to shape the political agenda and get their solutions implemented.

policy feedback
the idea that policies, once enacted, open up and close off future policy options, especially because of the effects of policy on politics and political actors.

political action committees
organizations that raise money to support chosen candidates and defeat others.

political efficacy
a person's belief that she or he can make effective political change.

political equality
when members of a society possess the same rights under the laws of the nation.

political ideology
a set of beliefs about the desired goals and outcomes of a process of governance.

political institutions
the rules, laws, and structures that channel and shape political action.

political mobilization
efforts by members of American political parties to turn out the vote and encourage their members to get others to do so.

political participation
the different ways in which individuals take action to shape the laws and policies of a government.

political party
an organized group of candidates, officeholders, voters, and activists that work together to elect candidates to political office.

political patronage
filling administrative positions as a reward for support, rather than solely on merit.

political propaganda
attempts to shape governmental actions and laws by changing people's beliefs and opinions.

political science
the systematic study of the ways in which ideas, individuals, and institutions shape political outcomes.

political socialization
the variety of experiences and factors that shape our political values, attitudes, and behaviors.

politics
the process of influencing the actions of officials and the policies of a nation, state, locality, or community.

positive freedoms
fundamental rights and freedoms that require action by individuals to express and by governments to secure.

power elite
a group composed of the top echelons of people in the business world, government, and military.

precedent
a judicial decision that guides future courts in handling similar cases.

preemptive war
a type of war in which a state uses its military might to challenge adversaries before they launch attacks or harbor those who might do so.

presidential pardon
the presidential authority to forgive an individual and set aside punishment for a crime.

presidential primaries
elections in which a state's voters choose delegates who support a particular candidate for nomination.

priming
shaping individuals' interpretations of news or events by highlighting certain details or contexts.

principal-agent problem
the challenge that arises when one actor, the principal, tasks another, the agent, to carry out the principal's wishes in the presence of uncertainty and unequal information.

prior restraint
the suppression of material prior to publication on the grounds that it might endanger national security.

privacy
a right not enumerated in the Constitution but affirmed by Supreme Court decisions that covers individuals' decisions in their private lives, including decisions regarding reproductive rights and sexuality.

private bureaucracies
privately owned corporations and companies that carry out specific tasks according to a prescribed set of rules and procedures.

private contractors
nongovernmental workers hired by the federal bureaucracy to provide goods and services in support of federal activity.

privatization
shifting control over the provision of certain governmental functions from the federal bureaucracy to the private sector.

probable cause
reasonable belief that a crime has been committed or that there is evidence indicating so.

procedural justice
a judicial standard requiring that fairness be applied to all participants equally.

proportional representation system
a structure of electoral representation in which parties are represented in government according to their candidates' overall share of the vote.

protectionism
restricting access by foreign producers to American markets in order to benefit specific domestic agricultural, industrial, and service providers.

protest
a public demonstration designed to call attention to the need for action or change.

proxy wars
wars in which major powers support different sides but do not directly go to war with each other.

public interest groups
groups that act on behalf of the collective interests of a broad group of individuals, many of who may not be members or contributors to the organization.

public opinion
the sum of individual attitudes about government, policies, and issues.

public opinion surveys
systematic attempts to make inferences about the opinions of large numbers of individuals by carefully sampling and asking questions of a small, randomly assigned sample of the larger population.

public policy
the intentional use of governmental power to secure the health, welfare, opportunities, and national security of citizens.

purposive benefits
rewards in the form of satisfaction from working with others to achieve a common goal or purpose.

push poll
a negative campaign tactic disguised as a survey in which a candidates' opponent or opponents are portrayed in an unfavorable way.

question order
a concern in measuring public opinion having to do with how the sequencing of questions affects responses.

question wording
a concern in measuring public opinion having to do with how the way a question is phrased affects responses.

race of interviewer effects
the shaping of survey responses due to the racial identities of respondents and interviewers.

random digit dialing
when potential survey respondents are selected by computer-generated random numbers.

random selection
how participants are selected from the population for inclusion in the study.

Reagan Doctrine
a foreign policy agenda under President Ronald Reagan offering American assistance, including military training and weaponry, to anticommunist groups.

realignment
a major shift in allegiance to the political parties that is often driven by changes in the issues that unite or divide voters.

recess appointment
occurs when Congress is not in session and the president appoints a person to fill a position that would normally require the advice and consent of the Senate. Unless the person is formally confirmed when the Senate reconvenes, the position ends at the conclusion of that session of Congress.

recruitment
the process through which political parties identify potential candidates.

redistricting
states' redrawing of the electoral district boundaries following each census.

registration requirements
the set of rules that govern who can vote and how, when, and where they vote.

representation
the act of "standing for" one's constituents in government.

representative democracy
a political system in which voters select representatives who then vote on matters of public policy.

republics
governments ruled by representatives of the people.

reserved powers
powers reserved to the states if not textually granted to the federal government.

respondents
individuals who answer a survey.

responsible party model
a proposal for party reform that emphasized cohesive party positions that presents voters with a clear set of choices and allows members' voices to be effectively incorporated into party positions on issues.

retrospective voting
reflecting back on an incumbent's past performance in an election.

revolving door phenomenon
the movement of individuals between government and lobbying positions.

roll-call vote
a recorded vote on a bill.

Roosevelt Corollary
a policy that asserted that the United States was the guarantor of political, military, and economic stability in Latin America and the Caribbean.

rulemaking
the process through which the federal bureaucracy fills in critical details of a law.

runoff election
an election that is held between the two candidates with the highest total votes if no one candidate scores a majority.

salience
the centrality of an individual's opinion in the sense of the opinion's ability to shape the individual's views on other issues or candidates.

sample
the subgroup of individuals from the larger population one wants to measure the opinions of.

sampling error
error in a statistical analysis arising from the unrepresentativeness of the sample taken.

school choice
a type of reform that allows parents and guardians to choose their students' schools and produces competition between the schools themselves to attract students.

scientific poll
when pollsters try to gain an understanding of a large group of individuals by obtaining the opinions of a carefully chosen small sample of the group, although they are aware of the limitations of the effort.

Second Continental Congress
an assembly of delegates from the thirteen British colonies in America that drafted and approved the Declaration of Independence, conducted the Revolutionary War, and created the governmental structure that followed the war.

secretary of defense
the head of the Department of Defense.

secretary of state
the head of the Department of State.

selective benefits
goods that are made available only to those who join or contribute to a group.

selective incorporation
the piecemeal process through which the Supreme Court has affirmed that almost all of the protections within the Bill of Rights also apply to state governments.

self-selected listener opinion polls (or SLOP polls)
a survey in which respondents choose to respond to a survey prompt on their own.

senatorial courtesy
a traditional norm in which presidents consult with senators from the states when considering potential nominees to the lower levels of the federal judiciary.

Senior Executive Service (SES)
federal employees with higher-level supervisory and administrative responsibilities who are paid and treated more like vice presidents of businesses than political figures.

separate but equal
the doctrine that racial segregation was constitutional so long as the facilities for blacks and whites were roughly equal.

separation of powers
a design of government that distributes powers across institutions in order to avoid making one branch too powerful on its own.

Seven Years' War
a war principally between France and Great Britain and other European nations that was fought across the globe.

Shays's Rebellion
a grassroots popular uprising against the government of Massachusetts.

signing statements
text written by presidents while signing a bill into law that usually consists of political statements or reasons for signing the bill but that might also include a president's interpretation of the law itself.

single-member plurality system
a structure of electoral representation in which a candidate and the party that he or she represents must win the most votes in a state or district in order to be represented in government.

slander
expression in spoken form that defames a person's character.

social benefits
rewards in the form of new connections or access to networks that members of a group receive through their participation.

social contract
an agreement in which people give to their governments the ability to rule over them to ensure an orderly and functioning society.

social equality
when no individual's social status is inherently higher than another's.

social insurance programs
programs such as Social Security that are financed by payroll taxes paid by individuals and that do not have income-based requirements to receive their benefits.

socialist system
a way of structuring economic activity in which private firms are allowed to operate and make decisions over production and distribution but with significant governmental involvement to ensure economic equality.

social media
forms of electronic communication that enable users to create and share content or to participate in social networking.

social movements
voluntary associations of individuals who come together to change things or keep things from changing, but they often do so by calling attention to a set of injustices or wrongs in order to get policymakers to act and to educate the public about the issue.

social welfare policies
governmental efforts designed to improve or protect the health, safety, education, and opportunities for citizens and residents.

socioeconomic status (SES)
a measure that captures an individual's wealth, income, occupation, and educational attainment.

soft news
stories that focus on celebrity and personality rather than political or economic issues.

soft power
the advancement of a nation's interests by exporting its values and culture abroad.

solicitor general
a presidential appointee who represents the federal government in the Supreme Court.

Sons of Liberty
a group initially formed of merchants and workingmen in response to the Stamp Act that resisted Great Britain and its tax policies.

Speaker of the House
the leader of the House of Representatives, chosen by an election of its members.

split-ticket voting
when a voter chooses a candidate from one party for one office and a candidate from a different party for another position on the ballot.

spoils system
the practice of cleaning house of one's opponents and installing supporters in their place following a successful election.

stability
the degree of change over time, in different contexts, or in response to differently worded survey questions of a particular opinion.

Stamp Act of 1765
a highly unpopular law designed to raise revenue by requiring the purchase of stamps for newspapers, legal papers, and other documents.

standard operating procedures
the sets of rules governing the behavior of bureaucrats.

standards-based reforms
reforms that set specific state or nationwide student achievement goals, rewards for success, and, most notably, consequences for failure.

standing
the legal ability to bring a case in court.

state and local bureaucracies
public organizations below the federal level designed to carry out specific tasks according to a prescribed set of rules and procedures.

State of the Union Address
the annual, constitutionally required transmittal of information from the president to Congress updating that branch on the state of national affairs.

state sovereignty resolutions
state legislative measures that affirm the sovereignty of states under the Tenth Amendment.

states' rights
the idea that American states have the authority to self-govern, even when in conflict with national laws.

statute
a written law established by a legislative body.

stereotype
a preconceived, often oversimplified idea about something that people apply as a filter to the world.

straw poll
an unofficial tally of opinion or support at a meeting or event.

substantive representation
the degree to which elected representatives or senators represent the interests and policy preferences of their constituents.

suffrage
the right to vote in political elections.

Sugar Act
a law passed by Great Britain in 1764 that taxed sugar and molasses and angered New England merchants.

superdelegates
members of the Democratic Party—usually elected officials or party activists—who are not pledged to any certain candidate based on the outcomes of their state's primary or caucus.

super PACs
political action committees permitted to spend unlimited amounts of money in a campaign, though these actions must not be coordinated with that campaign.

superpower
an extremely powerful state that is capable of influencing international events and the actions of other less powerful states.

supremacy clause
a part of the Constitution that establishes the Constitution and the laws of the nation passed under its authority as the highest laws of the nation.

Supreme Court
the highest level of the federal judiciary, which was established in the Constitution and serves as the highest court in the nation.

swing states
states where no one political party tends to dominate national elections.

symbolic speech
protected expression in the form of images, signs, and other symbols.

terrorism
the use of violence as a means to achieve political ends.

third party
(or minor party) a political party operating over a limited period of time in competition with two other major parties.

Thirteenth Amendment
an amendment to the Constitution passed in 1865 prohibiting slavery within the United States.

Three-fifths Compromise
an agreement reached by delegates at the Constitutional Convention that ensured that a slave would count as three-fifths of a person for a state's representation.

top-two primary system
an electoral system in which candidates, regardless of party, compete in the primary elections, with the top two vote-getters, regardless of party, advancing to the general election.

Trans-Pacific Partnership (TPP)
a regional trade agreement struck between twelve nations in the Pacific Rim, including Mexico, Australia, and East Asian and South American nations.

turf wars
when bureaucrats compete to take duties and responsibilities away from one another's departments or keep their opponents from doing so.

tyranny
the suppression of the rights of a people by those holding power.

tyranny of the majority
when a large number of citizens use the power of their majority to trample on the rights of a smaller group.

tyranny of the minority
when a small number of citizens tramples on the rights of the larger population.

unemployment rate
the percentage of the total labor force that is unemployed.

unfunded mandate
when the federal government institutes a policy that members of state governments do not feel has been properly funded.

unipolarity
a distribution of power in the international system where one state exerts most of the power and influence.

unitary systems
structures of governance that place the people's sovereignty in a national government, with subnational governments deriving their authority from it.

United Nations
an international organization formed in 1945 to promote international dialogue and cooperation.

unorthodox lawmaking
a term that refers to ways in which legislative activity, especially on major bills, is often more fluid than described in a traditional textbook description.

veto
the power of a president to reject a bill passed by Congress, sending it back to the originating branch with objections noted.

Virginia Plan
a plan of government calling for a strong national government with three branches of government and a bicameral legislature, with legislators elected using proportional representation.

voter turnout
the number of eligible voters who actually participate in an election versus the total number of eligible voters.

voucher program
an educational policy that distributes public funds to parents and guardians, allowing them to send their students to private and alternative schools.

War Powers Resolution
A law passed over President Nixon's veto that restricts the power of the president in committing the nation's armed forces into combat or situations of likely combat.

warrant
a writ issued by a judge authorizing some activity.

weighting
a procedure in which the observed results of a survey are adjusted according to what is known about specific proportions in the larger population.

whip
an individual in the House or Senate, chosen by his or her party members, whose job is to ensure party unity and discipline.

wire service
an organization that gathers and reports on news and then sells the stories to other outlets.

writ of habeas corpus
a statement demanding that authorities in charge of a person's detention establish the reasons for that detention.

yellow journalism
an approach to reporting employed in the nineteenth century that relied on sensational headlines and emotional language to persuade readers and sell newspapers.

NOTES

CHAPTER 1

1. Tony Mauro, "Bible Club vs. School Lands in High Court," *USA Today*, January 8, 1990.
2. Ibid.
3. 98 Stat. 1302, 20 U.S.C. §§ 4071-4074. Cornell University Law School, Legal Information Institute, https://www.law.cornell.edu/uscode/text/20/4071.
4. Nat Hentoff, "A Bible Study Club in a Public School?" *Washington Post*, March 14, 1989.
5. *Board of Education of Westside Community Schools v. Mergens* by and through Mergens, 496 U.S. 226 (1990).
6. Robert K. Skolrood, "Don't Bar Bible Clubs from Schools," *USA Today*, January 10, 1990.
7. *Board of Education of Westside Community Schools v. Mergens*.
8. Ruth Marcus, "Schools Brace for Fallout from Bible-Club Ruling: Some Officials Fear Disruptive Groups Will Enter through Door Opened by Court to Religion," *Washington Post*, June 11, 1990.
9. *Boyd County High School Gay Straight Alliance v. Board of Education of Boyd County, KY*, 258 F. Supp. 2d 667 (E.D. Ky. 2003).
10. Ibid. The ACLU had sent the letter in September before the meeting in which the decision to deny was taken.
11. Ibid.
12. Ibid.
13. Ibid.
14. American Civil Liberties Union, "ACLU Wins Settlement for Kentucky School's Gay-Straight Alliance," February 3, 2014, https://www.aclu.org/news/aclu-wins-settlement-kentucky-schools-gay-straight-alliance.
15. National Legal Foundation, "Welcome," www.nlf.net.
16. Philip Bump, "48 Percent of Millennials Think the American Dream Is Dead. Here's Why," *Washington Post*, December 10, 2015, https://www.washingtonpost.com/news/the-fix/wp/2015/12/10/48-percent-of-millennials-think-the-american-dream-is-dead-heres-why. The authors obtained their data from Harvard Institute of Politics, "Harvard IOP Fall 2015 Poll: Trump, Carson Lead Republican Primary; Sanders Edging Clinton among Democrats, Harvard IOP Poll Finds," December 10, 2015, http://iop.harvard.edu/survey/details/harvard-iop-fall-2015-poll.
17. Samuel Huntington, *American Politics: The Promise of Disharmony* (Cambridge, MA: Harvard University Press, 1983); John Kingdon, *America the Unusual* (New York: St. Martin's Press, 1999).
18. John Winthrop, "A Model of Christian Charity," 1630, The Winthrop Society, http://winthropsociety.com/doc_charity.php.
19. Paraphrasing Eric Foner, *Give Me Liberty! An American History* (New York: W. W. Norton, 2006), 36.
20. George Brown Tindall and David E. Shi, *America: A Narrative History*, brief 2nd ed. (New York: W. W. Norton, 1989), 16.
21. Foner, *Give Me Liberty!*, 43.
22. Charles M. Andrews, *The Colonial Background of the American Revolution* (New Haven, CT: Yale University Press, 1924), 42-44.
23. Global war began in 1756, while conflict in the colonies started two years earlier. Other major European powers became involved in various theaters in the war.
24. The colonies that sent representatives were Connecticut, Maryland, Massachusetts, New Hampshire, New York, Pennsylvania, and Rhode Island.
25. Eleven of the thirteen colonies were included in Franklin's proposed plan; Georgia and Delaware were not. Virginia and Massachusetts would each have had seven of the forty-eight total seats, being the largest and wealthiest colonies.
26. Richard Hofstadter, William Miller, and Daniel Aaron, *The American Republic*, Vol. 1 (Upper Saddle River, NJ: Prentice Hall, 1970), 144.
27. Merrill Jensen, *The Founding of a Nation* (Indianapolis: Hackett, 2004), 4-5.
28. Literacy rates varied significantly by gender and race.
29. Philip Davidson, *Propaganda and the American Revolution, 1763-1783* (Chapel Hill: University of North Carolina Press, 1941), xiii.
30. Andrews, *The Colonial Background of the American Revolution*, 64-65.
31. Thomas Paine, *Common Sense* (New York: Buccaneer Books, 1976), 63, 69.
32. Eric Foner, *Tom Paine and Revolutionary America* (New York: Oxford University Press, 1976), 74.
33. Jensen, *The Founding of a Nation*, 99.
34. New York, New Hampshire, Virginia, North Carolina, and Georgia did not send delegates. Support in several of these colonies was strong, but royal governors prevented them from sending delegates.
35. "Newspaper Account of the Boston Massacre," in *English Historical Documents: Volume IX, American Colonial Documents to 1776*, ed. Merrill Jensen (New York: Oxford University Press, 1955), 749.
36. Andrews, *The Colonial Background of the American Revolution*, 157.

37. Jensen, *The Founding of a Nation*, 33. Citing "John Adams to Hezekiah Niles," in *The Works of John Adams*, Vol. X, ed. C. F. Adams (Boston, 1850–56), 283.

38. Foner, *Give Me Liberty!*, 53.

39. Jackson Turner Main, *The Social Structure of Revolutionary America* (Princeton, NJ: Princeton University Press, 1965), 221–227.

40. Ibid., 221.

41. Ibid., 123.

42. Sylvia R. Frey, *Water from the Rock: Black Resistance in a Revolutionary Age* (Princeton, NJ: Princeton University Press, 1991), 17.

43. Sylvia R. Frey, "Liberty, Equality, and Slavery: The Paradox of the American Revolution," in *The American Revolution: Its Character and Limits*, ed. Jack P. Greene (New York: New York University Press, 1987), 230. Quoting Thomas Hutchinson, *Strictures upon the Declaration of the Congress at Philadelphia* (London, 1776), 9–10.

44. Ibid., 73.

45. Thomas J. Davis, "Emancipation Rhetoric, Natural Rights, and Revolutionary New England: A Note on Four Black Petitions in Massachusetts, 1773–1777," *The New England Quarterly* 62, no. 2 (June 1989): 248–263.

46. Ibid., 255–256. Citing Herbert Aptheker, ed., *Documentary History of the Negro People in the United States*, Vol. 1 (New York: International Publishers), 7–8.

47. Ruth Bogin, "'Liberty Further Extended': A 1776 Antislavery Manuscript by Lemuel Haynes," *The William and Mary Quarterly* 40, no. 1 (January 1983): 94.

48. Elaine F. Crane, "Dependence in the Era of Independence: The Role of Women in a Republican Society," in *The American Revolution: Its Character and Limits*, ed. Jack P. Greene (New York: New York University Press, 1987).

49. Joan R. Gunderson, *To Be Useful to the World: Women in Revolutionary America*, Rev. ed. (Chapel Hill: University of North Carolina Press, 2006), 23.

50. Mary Beth Norton, *Liberty's Daughters: The Revolutionary Experience of American Women, 1750–1800* (Boston: Little, Brown, 1980), 22.

51. Sara M. Evans, *Born for Liberty: A History of Women in America* (New York: The Free Press, 1989), 48.

52. Carol Berkin, *Revolutionary Mothers: Women in the Struggle for America's Independence* (New York: Alfred A. Knopf, 2005), 21.

53. Ibid., 44.

54. Ibid., 46.

55. Russell Shorto, *The Island at the Center of the World: The Epic Story of Dutch Manhattan and the Forgotten Colony That Shaped America* (New York: Doubleday, 2004), 50.

56. See, for example, Gail D. MacLeitch, *Imperial Entanglements: Iroquois Change and Persistence on the Frontiers of Empire* (Philadelphia: University of Pennsylvania Press, 2011); Karim M. Tiro, *The People of Standing Stone: The Oneida Nation from the Revolution through the Era of Removal* (Amherst: University of Massachusetts Press, 2011).

57. Hofstadter et al., *The American Republic*, 167.

58. The Articles of Confederation and Perpetual Union (see Chapter 2).

59. "The Virginia Resolutions for Independence," in Jensen, *English Historical Documents*, 867–868.

CHAPTER 2

1. Madison's two papers were titled "Notes of Ancient and Modern Confederacies," written in the spring of 1786, and "Vices of the Political System of the United States," written in the spring of 1787.

2. Robert Livingston Schuyler, *The Constitution of the United States: An Historical Survey of Its Formation* (New York, 1923), 90.

3. William Waller Hening, "Virginia Laws for Blacks—17C & 18C," in *Laws of Virginia, 1619–1792* (1823), I–III. For more on Madison's ambivalence toward slavery, see William Lee Miller, *The Business of May Next: James Madison and the Founding* (Charlottesville: University Press of Virginia, 1992), 177–184.

4. Charles M. Andrews, *The Colonial Background of the American Revolution* (New Haven, CT: Yale University Press, 1924), 26.

5. Merrill Jensen, *The Articles of Confederation: An Interpretation of the Social-Constitutional History of the American Revolution, 1774–1781* (Madison: University of Wisconsin Press, 1948), 150.

6. Robert W. Hoffert, *A Politics of Tensions: The Articles of Confederation and American Political Ideals* (Niwot: University Press of Colorado, 1992), 86.

7. Article 2.

8. Andrews, *The Colonial Background of the American Revolution*, 44.

9. This idea of term limits is one that we continue to debate today. For a discussion of challenges of coordination under the Articles of Confederation, see Keith L. Dougherty, *Collective Action under the Articles of Confederation* (New York: Cambridge University Press, 2001).

10. Jensen, *The Articles of Confederation*, 240.

11. "We do Each one of us, acknowledge our Selves to be Inlisted . . . in colo Hazeltons Regiment of Regulators . . . for Suppressing of tyrannical government in the Massachusetts State." "Report of the Commissioners, April 27, 1787," in David P. Szatmary, *Shays' Rebellion: The Making of an Agrarian Insurrection* (Amherst: University of Massachusetts Press, 1980), 63.

12. James MacGregor Burns, *The Vineyard of Liberty* (New York: Alfred A. Knopf, 1982), 14.

13. Szatmary, *Shays' Rebellion*.

14. Louise B. Dunbar, "A Study of 'Monarchical' Tendencies in the United States from 1776 to 1801," in *The Papers of James Madison: Volume 9, 9 April 1786–24 May 1787*, ed. Robert A. Rutland and William M. E. Rachal (Chicago: University of Chicago Press, 1975), 162.

15. "Letter from George Washington to James Madison, November 5, 1786," in Rutland and Rachal, *The Papers of James Madison*, 162.

16. George Washington had been reluctant to be a delegate in part because the Society of the Cincinnati, an organization of former Revolutionary War officers of which he had been a president, was to meet in Philadelphia at the same time. The society was viewed with mistrust due to its potential to form a new aristocracy. See Catherine Drinker Bowen, *Miracle at Philadelphia: The Story of the Constitutional Convention, May to September 1787* (Boston: Little, Brown, 1966).

17. Ira Stoll, *Samuel Adams: A Life* (New York: Free Press, 2008), 229–230.

18. Patrick Henry, "Virginia Ratifying Convention, June 4 and 5, 1788," in *The Essential Antifederalist*, 2nd ed., ed. W. B. Allen and Gordon Lloyd (New York: Rowman & Littlefield, 2002), 130.

19. See, for example, Gordon S. Wood, "The Origins of the Constitution," in *This Constitution: A Bicentennial Chronicle* (The American Political Science Association, 1987).

20. Max Farrand, ed., *The Records of the Federal Convention of 1787, Volume I* (New Haven, CT: Yale University Press, 1911), xi.

21. "Notes of James Madison, May 29, 1787," in Farrand, *Records of the Federal Convention*, 15.

22. Bowen, *Miracle at Philadelphia*, 22.

23. Though Madison would state that the entire Virginia delegation was responsible for it. See Bowen, *Miracle at Philadelphia*.

24. Ibid., 18.

25. "Notes of James Madison, June 9, 1787," in Farrand, *Records of the Federal Convention*, 179.

26. Bowen, *Miracle at Philadelphia*, 116.

27. Ibid., 285.

28. Ibid., 492.

29. "Notes of Robert Yates, July 2, 1787," in Farrand, *Records of the Federal Convention*, 519.

30. "Notes of James Madison, May 29, 1787," in Farrand, *Records of the Federal Convention*, 531.

31. It is also known as Connecticut Compromise, after Roger Sherman, a Connecticut delegate, member of the committee, and author of the proposal. One state delegation was split.

32. For an analysis of Madison's strategic shift, see Miller, *The Business of May Next*, 78–80.

33. Bowen, *Miracle at Philadelphia*, 115.

34. Richard E. Neustadt, *Presidential Power and the Modern Presidents: The Politics of Leadership from Roosevelt to Reagan* (New York: The Free Press, 1990), 29.

35. Also called the Committee of Eleven.

36. Bruce Ackerman, *We the People: Foundations* (Cambridge, MA: Harvard University Press, 1991).

37. Native Americans not paying taxes would not count at all.

38. James Madison, *Federalist No. 54*, in *The Federalist Papers*, ed. George W. Carey and James McClellan (Indianapolis: Liberty Fund, 2001), 283.

39. James Madison, "James Madison to Robert I. Evans, June 15, 1819," Library of Congress, June 15, 1819, https://www.loc.gov/item/mjm018592.

40. Madison, *Federalist No. 51*, 269.

41. James Madison, *Federalist No. 10*, in Carey and McClellan, *The Federalist Papers*, 44.

42. Ibid., 43.

43. Ibid., 46.

44. Alexander Hamilton, *Federalist No. 9*, in Carey and McClellan, *The Federalist Papers*, 41.

45. Alexander Hamilton, *Federalist No. 16*, in Carey and McClellan, *The Federalist Papers*, 76–77.

46. W. B. Allen and Gordon Lloyd, *The Essential Antifederalist*, 2nd ed. (New York: Rowan & Littlefield, 2002), xxiii.

47. Ibid., xxiii.

48. "Centinel Letter I, October 5, 1787," in Allen and Lloyd, *The Essential Antifederalist*, 102–103. See also Herbert J. Storing, *What the Antifederalists Were For* (Chicago: University of Chicago Press, 1981), 57.

49. "Brutus Essay V, December 13, 1787," in Allen and Lloyd, *The Essential Antifederalist*, 119.

50. See Storing, *What the Antifederalists Were For*.

51. See Kate Davies, *Catharine Macaulay and Mercy Otis Warren: The Revolutionary Atlantic and the Politics of Gender* (New York: Oxford University Press, 2005).

52. Mercy Otis Warren, *Observations on the New Constitution, and on the Federal and State Conventions, by a Columbian Patriot* (Washington, DC: Library of Congress, 1788).

53. William H. Riker, *The Strategy of Rhetoric: Campaigning for the American Constitution* (New Haven, CT: Yale University Press, 1996).

54. Ibid., 211.

55. Douglass C. North and Barry R. Weingast, "Constitutions and Commitment: The Evolution of Institutions Governing Public Choice in Seventeenth-Century England," *The Journal of Economic History* 49, no. 4 (December 1989): 803–832.

56. Donald S. Lutz, "From Covenant to Constitution in American Political Thought," in *Covenant, Polity, and Constitutionalism*, ed. Daniel Elezar and John Kincaid (Lanham, MD: University Press of America, 1983).

57. Edward S. Corwin, "The Constitution as an Instrument and as a Symbol," *The American Political Science Review* 30, no. 6 (December 1936): 1071–1085. See also Edward S. Corwin, *The "Higher Law" Background of American Constitutional Law* (Ithaca, NY: Great Seal Books, 1928).

CHAPTER 3

1. Joel Roberts, "Dying Woman Loses Medical Marijuana Case," CBSNews.com, March 14, 2007, www.cbsnews.com/news/dying-woman-loses-medical-marijuana-case.

2. Dan Reed, "Medicinal Pot Users Renew Legal Challenge," *San Jose Mercury News*, October 10, 2002; available from Lexis-Nexis Academic.

3. Brian Anderson, "Women File Suit for Continued Access to Marijuana," *Contra Costa Times*, October 10, 2002; available from Lexis-Nexis Academic.

4. "Declaration of Diane Monson in Support of Motion for Preliminary Injunction," *Raich v. Ashcroft*, 248 F. supp 2d 918 (ND Cal. 2003).

5. Comprehensive Drug Abuse and Control Act of 1970, 84 Stat. 1236.

6. Ibid.

7. "Declaration of Diane Monson."

8. Anderson, "Women File Suit for Continued Access to Marijuana."

9. Richard Willing, "Medical-Pot Fight Goes to Justices," *USA Today*, November 26, 2004; available from Lexis-Nexis Academic.

10. U.S. Constitution, art. 6.

11. U.S. Constitution, art. 1, sec. 8.

12. Ibid.

13. Ibid.

14. U.S. Constitution, art. 1, sec. 2, 4; art. 2, sec. 1.

15. U.S. Constitution, art. 5.

16. U.S. Constitution, art. 1, sec. 10.

17. Richard E. Neustadt, *Presidential Power and the Modern Presidents: The Politics of Leadership from Roosevelt to Reagan* (New York: The Free Press, 1990), 29.

18. Daniel J. Elazar, *American Federalism: A View from the States* (New York: Thomas Y. Crowell Company, 1972), 190.

19. Richard Willing, "Justices Doubtful about Medical Marijuana," *USA Today*, November 30, 2004; available from Lexis-Nexis Academic.

20. *Gonzales v. Raich.*

21. *Wickard v. Filburn*, 317 U.S. 111 (1942).

22. Paul E. Peterson, *The Price of Federalism* (Washington, DC: Brookings Institution, 1995), 12.

23. Reagan Ali and M. David, "Obama Effectively Tells Supreme Court to Legalize Marijuana," *Counter Current News*, January 17, 2016, http://countercurrentnews.com/2016/01/obama-tells-supreme-court-to-legalize.

24. Ariane de Vogue, "Obama Admin Weighs in on Legalized Marijuana at the Supreme Court," CNN.com, December 16, 2015, www.cnn.com/2015/12/16/politics/supreme-court-marijuana-colorado-obama.

25. Editorial, "Trump and Sessions Are Ignoring Voters' Overwhelming Support for Medical Marijuana, Will Congress Listen? *Los Angeles Times*, September 9, 2017, www.latimes.com/opinion/editorials/la-ed-medical-marijuana-20170909-story.html.

26. *McCulloch v. Maryland*, 17 U.S. (4 Wheat.) 316 (1819).

27. *Gibbons v. Ogden*, 22 U.S. (9 Wheat.) 11 (1824).

28. Ibid.

29. *Barron v. Mayor and City Council of Baltimore*, 32 U.S. 243 (1833).

30. This interpretation would change during the process of incorporation, which began in the twentieth century (see Chapter 4).

31. James Bryce, *The American Commonwealth*, Vol. I (New York: Macmillan and Co., 1888), 432.

32. *Tarble's Case*, 80 Wall. 397 (1871).

33. The Northwest Ordinance of 1787, for example, stated, "Religion, morality, and knowledge, being necessary to good government and the happiness of mankind, schools and the means of education shall forever be encouraged." Henry Steele Commager, ed., *Documents of American History*, 8th ed. (New York: Appleton-Century-Crofts, 1968), 131.

34. *Slaughterhouse Cases*, 83 U.S. (16 Wall.) 36 (1873).

35. Ronald M. Labbé and Jonathan Lurie, *The Slaughterhouse Cases: Regulation, Reconstruction, and the Fourteenth Amendment* (Lawrence: University Press of Kansas, 2003), 211.

36. *Plessy v. Ferguson*, 163 U.S. 537 (1896).

37. Mark V. Tushnet, *The NAACP's Legal Strategy against Segregated Education, 1925–1950* (Chapel Hill: University of North Carolina Press, 1987), 21.

38. Elazar, *American Federalism*, 33.

39. Ibid., 47–48.

40. See *United States v. E.C. Knight Company*, 156 U.S. 1 (1895); *Hammer v. Dagenhart*, 247 U.S. 251 (1918).

41. National Drought Mitigation Center, "Drought in the Dust Bowl Years," http://drought.unl.edu/DroughtBasics/DustBowl/DroughtintheDustBowlYears.aspx.

42. Jean Edward Smith, *FDR* (New York: Random House, 2007), 15.

43. Arthur M. Schlesinger Jr., *The Age of Roosevelt, Vol II: The Coming of the New Deal* (Boston: Houghton Mifflin Company, 1958), 4.

44. See the Banking Act of 1933, the Securities Act of 1933, and the Securities Exchange Act of 1934.

45. Amity Shlaes, *The Forgotten Man: A New History of the Great Depression* (New York: HarperCollins, 2007), 150

46. Ibid., 151.

47. Schlesinger, *The Age of Roosevelt*, 121.

48. Alan Brinkley, *Franklin Delano Roosevelt* (New York: Oxford University Press, 2010), 52.

49. Steven Horwitz, "The Story of the Schechter Brothers," George Mason University History News Network, http://historynewsnetwork.org/blog/57574.

50. The brothers were charged with violating the Code of Fair Competition for the Live Poultry Industry of the Metropolitan Area in and about the City of New York.

51. Shlaes, *The Forgotten Man,* 220.

52. Ibid., 227.

53. See also *Panama Refining Co. v. Ryan*, 293 U.S. 388 (1935).

54. *Schechter Poultry Corp. v. United States* 295 U.S. 495 (1935).

55. Ibid.

56. Ibid.

57. Jeff Shesol, *Supreme Power: Franklin Roosevelt vs. the Supreme Court* (New York: W.W. Norton, 2010), 2–3.

58. Pub. L. 74-271, 49 Stat 620-648 (1935). The programs were collectively called Old-Age, Survivors, and Disability Insurance (OASDI), commonly referred to as Social Security. Aid to Dependent Children was later renamed Aid to Families with Dependent Children (AFDC), which was abolished in 1996 and replaced with Temporary Assistance to Needy Families (TANF).

59. Shesol, *Supreme Power*, 3–4.

60. Joseph F. Zimmerman, *Contemporary American Federalism: The Growth of National Power* (New York: Praeger, 1992), 118.

61. Ibid., 118–119.

62. Lawrence D. Brown, James W. Fossett, and Kenneth T. Palmer, *The Changing Politics of Federal Grants* (Washington, DC: Brookings Institution, 1984), 7.

63. Ibid., 8.

64. "Acceptance Speeches: Reagan: 'Time to Recapture Our Destiny,'" in *CQ Almanac 1980*, 36th ed. (Washington, DC: Congressional Quarterly, 1981), available at http://library.cqpress.com/cqalmanac/cqal80-860-25879-1173673.

65. John D. Nugent, *Safeguarding Federalism: How States Protect Their Interests in National Policymaking* (Norman: University of Oklahoma Press, 2009), 6.

66. James Madison, *Federalist* No. 46, in *The Federalist Papers*, ed. George W. Carey and James McClellan (Indianapolis: Liberty Fund, 2001), 246.

67. Nugent, *Safeguarding Federalism*, 56.

68. Peterson, *Price of Federalism*, 45.

69. Nugent, *Safeguarding Federalism*, 66. Quoting Bryan Schweitzer, "Montana Governor on 'REAL ID' Act," by Melissa Block (host), National Public Radio's *All Things Considered*, March 7, 2008.

70. *United States v. Lopez*, 514 US 549 (1995).

71. *Printz v. United States*, 521 US 898 (1997).

72. "Angel McClary Raich," angeljustice.org, http://angeljustice.org/angel/Angel_Raichs_Bio.html.

73. Alaska, California, Colorado, Maine, Massachusetts, Nevada, Oregon, and Washington.

74. Office of National Drug Control Policy, "Marijuana Resource Center: State Laws Related to Marijuana," https://obamawhitehouse.archives.gov/ondcp/state-laws-related-to-marijuana

75. "Number of Legal Medical Marijuana Patients (as of March 1, 2016)," ProCon.org, March 3, 2016, http://medicalmarijuana.procon.org/view.resource.php?resourceID=005889.
76. James M. Cole, "Memorandum for All United States Attorneys," U.S. Department of Justice, August 29, 2013, https://www.justice.gov/iso/opa/resources/3052013829132756857467.pdf.

CHAPTER 4

1. U.S. Constitution, art. 4, sec. 1.
2. *United States v. Windsor.*
3. Justin Jones, "The Godmother of Gay Marriage: Edie Windsor's Passionate Life," The Daily Beast, March 18, 2015, www.thedailybeast.com/articles/2015/03/18/the-godmother-of-gay-marriage-edie-windsor-s-passionate-life.html.
4. Chris Geidner, "Two Years after His Husband's Death, Jim Obergefell Is Still Fighting for the Right to Be Married," BuzzFeed.com, March 22, 2015, www.buzzfeed.com/chrisgeidner/his-huband-died-in-2013-but-jim-obergefell-is-still-fighting#.ldrnVM0Ag.
5. Ibid.
6. Richard Wolf, "Grieving Widower Takes Lead in Major Gay Marriage Case," *USA Today*, April 10, 2015, www.usatoday.com/story/news/nation/2015/04/10/supreme-court-gay-marriage-obergefell/25512405.
7. *Griswold v. Connecticut*, 381 U.S. 479 (1965).
8. *Lawrence v. Texas*, 539 U.S. 558 (2003). In its ruling, the Court overturned *Bowers v. Hardwick*, 478 U.S. 186 (1986).
9. *Roe v. Wade*, 410 U.S. 113 (1973).
10. Ibid.
11. Catherine Drinker Bowen, *Miracle at Philadelphia: The Story of the Constitutional Convention, May to September 1787* (1966; Boston: Little, Brown, 1985), 244.
12. U.S. Constitution, art. 3, sec. 3.
13. Irving Brant, *The Bill of Rights: Its Origin and Meaning* (New York: The Bobbs-Merrill Company, Inc., 1965), 39.
14. Alexander Hamilton, *Federalist* No. 84, in *The Federalist*, ed. George W. Carey and James McClellan (Indianapolis: Liberty Fund, 2001), 447.
15. *Annals of Congress*, House of Representatives, 1st Cong., 1st sess. (June 8, 1789), 440–441. Available at http://memory.loc.gov/ammem/amlaw/lwac.html.
16. Two of the proposed twelve did not receive enough votes to secure ratification. The first involved apportionment of seats in the House of Representatives, the second restricted Congress's ability to raise its own pay. This latter amendment was ratified, but not until 1992 (Twenty-Seventh Amendment). Amendments are typically proposed including a date of expiry, but this was not the case for the two unratified, originally proposed amendments.
17. *Gitlow v. New York.* In *Chicago, Burlington & Quincy Railroad Company v. Chicago*, 166 U.S. 226 (1897), the Supreme Court had already applied the Fifth Amendment's due process clause to state actions in its reasoning, though ruling against the plaintiffs.
18. *Gitlow v. New York.*
19. *McDonald v. Chicago*, 561 U.S. 742 (2010).
20. *Everson v. Board of Education,* 330 U.S. 1 (1947). *Board of Education v. Allen*, 392 U.S. 236 (1968).
21. *Abington School District v. Schempp.* Quoting Madison, "A Memorial and Remonstrance," in *The Constitution & Religion: Leading Supreme Court Cases on Church and State,* ed. Robert S. Alley (Amherst, MA: Prometheus Books, 1999), 30. *Engle v. Vitale*, 370 U.S. 421 (1962).
22. *Cantwell v. Connecticut*, 310 U.S. 296 (1940).
23. "The Sedition Act (1798)," in *Documents of American History*, 8th ed., ed. Henry Steele Commager (New York: Appleton-Century-Crofts, 1968), 177–178.
24. Paul E. Peterson, *The Price of Federalism* (Washington, DC: Brookings Institution, 1995), 8.
25. *Abrams v. United States*, 250 U.S. 616 (1919).
26. *Brandenburg v. Ohio*, 395 U.S. 444 (1969).
27. Ibid.
28. *New York Times v. United States*, 403 U.S. 713 (1971).
29. *United States v. O'Brien*, 391 U.S. 367 (1968).
30. *Morse v. Frederick*, 551 U.S. 393 (2007).
31. *Texas v. Johnson*, 491 U.S. 397 (1989). See also *Spence v. Washington*, 418 U.S. 405 (1974).
32. The definitions of legal terms in this section are informed by Bryan A. Garner, ed., *Black's Law Dictionary*, 8th ed. (St. Paul, MN: Thompson/West, 2004).
33. *Chaplinksy v. State of New Hampshire*, 315 U.S. 586 (1942).
34. *Roth v. United States*, 354 U.S. 476 (1957).
35. *Miller v. California*, 413 U.S. 15 (1973).
36. *Reno v. American Civil Liberties Union et al.*, 521 U.S. 844 (1997).
37. *De Jonge v. Oregon*, 299 U.S. 353 (1937). See also *Edwards v. South Carolina*, 372 U.S. 229 (1963).
38. Noting, however, that the process of incorporating these rights has involved the Fourteenth Amendment as well.
39. National Firearms Act (1934).
40. *United States v. Miller*, 307 U.S. 174 (1939).
41. *District of Columbia v. Heller*, 554 U.S. 570 (2008).
42. *McDonald v. Chicago.* A similar law in Oak Park, a suburb of Chicago, was also overturned.
43. U.S. Constitution, art. 1, sec. 9.
44. John Rawls, *A Theory of Justice* (Cambridge, MA: Belknap Press of Harvard University Press, 1999).
45. *Katz v. United States*, 389 U.S. 347 (1967).
46. See *Warden v. Hayden*, 387 U.S. 294 (1967).
47. *Mapp v. Ohio*, 367 U.S. 643 (1961).
48. *United States v. Sokolow*, 490 U.S. 1 (1989).
49. *Horton v. California*, 496 U.S. 128 (1990).
50. *Miranda v. Arizona*, 384 U.S. 436 (1966). Miranda was retried without the illegally obtained evidence but was convicted based on other evidence, including identification by the victim and the testimony of his girlfriend.
51. *Klopfer v. North Carolina*, 386 U.S. 213 (1967).
52. *Powell v. Alabama*, 287 U.S. 45 (1932).
53. *Johnson v. Zerbst*, 304 U.S. 458 (1938).
54. *Gideon v. Wainwright*, 372 U.S. 335 (1963).
55. *Wiggins v. Smith*, 539 U.S. 510 (2003).
56. The Court's decision in *Furman v. Georgia*, 408 U.S. 238 (1972) invalidated the use of the death penalty according to the state laws at the time, finding them arbitrary and discriminatory. Rewritten death penalty statutes were held constitutional in *Gregg v. Georgia*, 428 U.S. 153 (1976).
57. *Atkins v. Virginia*, 536 U.S. 304 (2002).
58. *Roper v. Simmons*, 543 U.S. 551 (2005).
59. *Dred Scott v. Sandford*, 60 U.S. 393 (1857).
60. *Plessy v. Ferguson*, 163 U.S. 737 (1896).

61. *Brown v. Board of Education*, 98 F. Supp. 797.
62. Quoted in Richard Kluger, *Simple Justice: The History of* Brown v. Board of Education *and Black America's Struggle for Equality* (New York: Vintage Books, 1977), 574.
63. *Brown v. Board of Education of Topeka*, 347 U.S. 483 (1954).
64. It was said that Justice Frankfurter told Justice Reed, who was most likely to dissent, that "a dissent is written for the future, but that there was no future for segregation." Jack Greenberg, *Crusaders in the Courts: How a Dedicated Band of Lawyers Fought for the Civil Rights Revolution* (New York: Basic Books, 1994), 198.
65. Juan Williams, *Eyes on the Prize: America's Civil Rights Years, 1954–1965* (New York: Viking Penguin, 1987), 35.
66. Ibid., 34.
67. *Gayle v. Browder*, 352 U.S. 903 (1956).
68. Clayborne Carson, ed., *The Autobiography of Martin Luther King, Jr.* (New York: Warner Books, 1998), 184.
69. Ibid., 187.
70. "White Clergymen Urge Local Negroes to Withdraw from Demonstrations," *Birmingham News*, April 13, 1963, Birmingham Public Library Digital Collections, http://bplonline.cdmhost.com/cdm/singleitem/collection/p4017coll2/id/746/rec/8.
71. Parts of the letter were also written on paper later smuggled in or provided to King by his attorneys.
72. *Regents of the University of California v. Bakke*, 438 U.S. 265 (1978).
73. *Gratz v. Bollinger*, 539 U.S. 244 (2003).
74. *Gunner v. Bollinger*, 539 U.S. 306 (2003).
75. See Eleanor Flexner, *Century of Struggle: The Woman's Rights Movement in the United States* (Cambridge, MA: Belknap Press, 1959); and Edwin W. Small and Miriam R. Small, "Prudence Crandall: Champion of Negro Education," *The New England Quarterly* 17, no. 4 (December 1944): 506–529.
76. Flexner, *Century of Struggle*, 39.
77. Kathryn Kish Sklar, *Women's Rights Emerges within the Antislavery Movement: A Brief History with Documents* (Binghamton, NY: State University of New York, 2000), 1.
78. Sally G. McMillen, *Seneca Falls and the Origins of the Women's Rights Movement* (New York: Oxford University Press, 2008), 167.
79. Betty Friedan, *The Feminine Mystique* (New York: Dell Publishing Co., 1963), 351.
80. National Organization for Women, "National Organization for Women (N.O.W.) Statement of Purpose, 1966," https://now.org/about/history/statement-of-purpose/
81. The distinction originally appeared in a footnote to Justice Harlan Fiske Stone's opinion in *United States v. Carolene Products Co.* 304 U.S. 144 (1938).
82. Molefi Kete Asante, "Racing to Leave the Race: Black Postmodernists Off-Track," *The Black Scholar* 23 (Summer/Fall 1993): 50–51.

CHAPTER 5

1. "Police-Community Reform and the Two Fergusons," Editorial, *St. Louis Post-Dispatch,* December 3, 2014, www.stltoday.com/news/opinion/columns/the-platform/editorial-police-community-reform-and-the-two-fergusons/article_c486f098-588a-5951-af85-036d74bd6999.html.
2. Leah Thorsen, "Shooting of Teen by Ferguson Police Officer Spurs Angry Backlash," *St. Louis Post-Dispatch*, August 10, 2014; available from Lexis-Nexis Academic.
3. "Ferguson Timeline," *St. Louis Post-Dispatch,* August 2, 2015; available from Lexis-Nexis Academic.
4. Tim Barker, "Ferguson-Area Businesses Cope with Aftermath of Weekend Riot," *St. Louis Post-Dispatch*, August 12, 2014; available from Lexis-Nexis Academic.
5. Joe Holleman and Kevin Johnson, "Ferguson Notes Ferguson Police Shooting," *St. Louis Post-Dispatch*, November 22, 2014. (Lexis-Nexis Academic Universe).
6. Amanda Paulson, "In Ferguson's Wake, Outcries Arise about Police Shootings in Other Cities," *The Christian Science Monitor*, August 19, 2014; available from Lexis-Nexis Academic.
7. "When Does a Moment Become a Movement?," *Washington Post*, August 24, 2014; available from Lexis-Nexis Academic.
8. Christine Byers, "Darren Wilson Resigns from Ferguson Police Department: 'It Is My Hope That My Resignation Will Allow the Community to Heal,'" *St. Louis Post-Dispatch*, November 30, 2014; available from Lexis-Nexis Academic.
9. Frances Robles and Michael S. Schmidt, "Shooting Accounts Differ as Holder Schedules Visit," *New York Times*, August 20, 2014; available from Lexis-Nexis Academic.
10. See Paul M. Sniderman, Richard A. Brody, and Philip E. Tetlock, *Reasoning and Choice: Explorations in Political Psychology* (New York: Cambridge University Press, 1991).
11. Angus Campbell et al., *The American Voter* (Chicago: University of Chicago Press, 1960), 151.
12. Philip E. Converse, "The Nature of Belief Systems in Mass Publics," in *Ideology and Discontent,* ed. David E Apter (London: The Free Press of Glencoe, 1964), 212.
13. Michael Delli Carpini and Scott Keeter, *What Americans Know about Politics and Why It Matters* (New Haven, CT: Yale University Press, 1996).
14. John Zaller, *The Nature and Origins of Mass Opinion* (New York: Cambridge University Press, 1992).
15. While Zaller also maintains the traditional distinction between elite and mass opinion, his work emphasizes the ability of masses to draw on political elites in the process of constructing opinions.
16. Samuel L. Popkin, *The Reasoning Voter: Communication and Persuasion in Political Campaigns* (Chicago: University of Chicago Press, 1991), 212.
17. Arthur Lupia and Mathew D. McCubbins, *The Democratic Dilemma: Can Citizens Learn What They Need to Know?* (New York: Cambridge University Press, 1998).
18. Wendy M. Rahn, "The Role of Partisan Stereotypes in Information Processing about Political Candidates," *American Journal of Political Science* 37, no. 2 (1993): 472–496.
19. See James Surowiecki, *The Wisdom of Crowds* (New York: Doubleday, 2004).
20. Benjamin I. Page and Robert Y. Shapiro, *The Rational Public: Fifty Years of Trends in Americans' Policy Preferences* (Chicago: University of Chicago Press, 1992), 14.

21. Robert D. Behn, "What Right Do Public Managers Have to Lead?" *Public Administration Review* 58, no. 3 (1998): 209–224.

22. James M. Druckman, "The Implications of Framing Effects for Citizen Competence," *Political Behavior* 23, no. 3 (Sep. 2001): 225–256.

23. Pew Research Center, "Questionnaire Design," www.pewresearch.org/methodology/u-s-survey-research/questionnaire-design.

24. Darren W. Davis and Brian D. Silver, "Stereotype Threat and Race of Interviewer Effects in a Survey on Political Knowledge," *American Journal of Political Science* 47, no. 1 (2003): 33–45.

25. Julie Bosman, "Bruised and Weary, Ferguson Struggles to Heal," *New York Times*, October 7, 2014; available from Lexis-Nexis Academic.

26. "Police-Community Reforms and the Two Fergusons."

27. Bosman, "Bruised and Weary"; Fred I. Greenstein, "The Benevolent Leader: Children's Images of Political Authority," *The American Political Science Review* 54, no. 4 (1960): 934–943; David Easton and Robert D. Hess, "The Child's Political World," *Midwest Journal of Political Science* 6, no. 3 (1962): 229–246. For a deeper view of the effectiveness of parent-child transmission of political attitudes and values, see M. Kent Jennings and Richard G. Niemi, "The Transmission of Political Values from Parent to Child," *The American Political Science Review* 62, no. 1 (1968): 169–184.

28. Christopher H. Achen, "Parental Socialization and Rational Party Identification," *Political Behavior* 24, no. 2 (2002): 151–170.

29. See Kenneth P. Langton and M. Kent Jennings, "Political Socialization and the High School Civics Curriculum in the United States," *The American Political Science Review* 62, no. 3 (1968): 852–867.

30. David E. Campbell, *Why We Vote: How Schools and Communities Shape Our Civic Life* (Princeton, NJ: Princeton University Press, 2006).

31. Lee H. Ehman, "The American School in the Political Socialization Process," *Review of Educational Research* 50, no. 1 (1980): 99–119.

32. Lisa Brown, "Hundreds of Protesters March to Ferguson Police Department," *St. Louis Post-Dispatch*, August 21, 2014; available from Lexis-Nexis Academic.

33. David Hunn, "No Charges for Wilson, Arson, Rioting Erupt in Ferguson Decision: Federal Inquiries Continue," *St. Louis Post-Dispatch*, November 25, 2014; available from Lexis-Nexis Academic.

34. Pew Research Center, "Stark Racial Divisions in Reactions to Ferguson Police Shooting," August 18, 2014, www.people-press.org/files/2014/08/8-18-14-Ferguson-Release.pdf.

35. See for example, Morris P. Fiorina, *Culture War? The Myth of a Polarized America* (New York: Longman/Pearson, 2011).

36. Michael Dawson, *Black Visions: The Roots of Contemporary African American Political Ideologies* (Chicago: University of Chicago Press, 2001).

37. Dennis Chong and Dukhong Kim, "The Experiences and Effects of Economic Status among Racial and Ethnic Minorities," *American Political Science Review* 100, no. 3 (2006): 335–351.

38. Evelyn M. Simien, "Race, Gender, and Linked Fate," *Journal of Black Studies* 35, no. 5 (2005): 529.

39. Pew Research Center, "Stark Racial Divisions."

40. Bosman, "Bruised and Weary, Ferguson Struggles to Heal."

41. Julie Hirschfeld Davis, "Calling for Calm in Ferguson, Obama Cites Need for Improved Race Relations," *New York Times*, August 19, 2014.

42. "When Does a Moment Become a Movement?"

43. Lauren Carroll, "Rand Paul Says Federal Program Incentivizes Police Militarization," *Tampa Bay Times*, August 21, 2014; available from Lexis-Nexis Academic.

44. Patrick Jonsson, "How Current Events Might Play into America's Shift in Favor of Gun Rights," *Christian Science Monitor*, December 11, 2014; available from Lexis-Nexis Academic.

45. Ibid.

46. Pew Research Center, "Sharp Racial Divisions in Reactions to Brown, Garner Decisions: Many Blacks Expect Police-Minority Relations to Worsen," December 8, 2014, www.people-press.org/2014/12/08/sharp-racial-divisions-in-reactions-to-brown-garner-decisions.

47. "1 Person Shot, Crowd Scatters as Gunshots Ring out Late Sunday in Ferguson," *St. Louis Post-Dispatch*, August 10, 2015; available from Lexis-Nexis Academic.

48. Mitch Smith, "A Year on, Ferguson Killing Is Recalled," *New York Times*, August 8, 2015, www.nytimes.com/2015/08/09/us/a-year-on-ferguson-killing-is-recalled.html?_r=0.

49. Zeeshan Aleem, "The First Democratic Debate Proved That Black Lives Matter Is Making a Difference," Policy.Mic, October 14, 2015, http://mic.com/articles/126730/the-first-democratic-debate-proved-that-black-lives-matter-is-making-a-difference.

50. Ibid.

51. Ibid.

52. Ibid.

53. Lilly Fowler, "Members of the Congressional Black Caucus Arrive in Ferguson to Pledge Their Support," *St. Louis Post-Dispatch*, January 19, 2015; available from Lexis-Nexis Academic.

54. Ibid.

55. Jeremy Kohler, "Prominent Ferguson Protesters Publish Anti-Police Violence Policy Platform," *St. Louis Post-Dispatch*, August 22, 2015; available from Lexis-Nexis Academic.

56. Ibid.

57. Pew Research Center, "Across Racial Lines, More Say Nation Needs to Make Changes to Achieve Racial Equality," August 5, 2015, www.people-press.org/2015/08/05/across-racial-lines-more-say-nation-needs-to-make-changes-to-achieve-racial-equality; Scott Clement, "A Year after Ferguson, 6 in 10 Americans Say Changes Are Needed to Give Blacks and Whites Equal Rights," *Washington Post*, August 5, 2015, https://www.washingtonpost.com/news/the-fix/wp/2015/08/05/what-changed-since-ferguson-americans-are-far-more-worried-about-black-rights.

58. John W. Kingdon, *Agendas, Alternatives, and Public Policies*, 2nd ed. (New York: Longman, 2003), 1.

59. Mark Trumbull, "How Differently Do Blacks and Whites View Ferguson? Here Are the Numbers," *The Christian Science Monitor*, November 21, 2104; available from Lexis-Nexis Academic.

60. Bosman, "Bruised and Weary, Ferguson Struggles to Heal."

CHAPTER 6

1. Eric Johnson, @Heyheygj, "Full Transcript: Hillary Clinton at Code 2017, *Recode*, May 31, 2017, https://www.recode.net/2017/5/31/15722218/hillary-clinton-code-conference-transcript-donald-trump-2016-russia-walt-mossberg-kara-swisher.

2. Ibid.

3. Ibid.

4. Office of the Director of National Intelligence, "Assessing Russian Activities and Intentions in Recent US Elections," January 6, 2017, ICA 2017-01D, ii.

5. President Donald J. Trump, @realDonald Trump, January 4, 2017, https://twitter.com/realdonaldtrump/status/816620855958601730?lang=en.

6. David French, "A Beginner's Guide to the Trump/Russia Controversy," *The National Review*, March 31, 2017, www.nationalreview.com/article/446339/donald-trump-russia-2016-election-controversy-explained.

7. Patrick Novotny, *The Press in American Politics, 1787–2012* (Denver, CO: Praeger, 2014), 1.

8. Ibid., 2.

9. Max Farrand, ed., *The Records of the Federal Convention of 1787, Volume II* (New Haven, CT: Yale University Press, 1911), 334.

10. Michael Schudson, *Discovering the News: A Social History of American Newspapers* (New York: Basic Books, Inc., 1978), 15–16.

11. Ibid., 18.

12. John D. Stevens, *Sensationalism and the New York Press* (New York: Columbia University Press, 1991).

13. Associated Press, "AP's History," www.ap.org/company/history/ap-history.

14. David Protess, *The Journalism of Outrage: Investigative Reporting and Agenda Building in America* (New York: Guilford Press, 1991).

15. Novotny, *The Press in American Politics*, 96.

16. Jeffrey M. Berry and Sarah Sobieraj, *The Outrage Industry: Political Opinion Media and the New Incivility* (New York: Oxford University Press, 2014), 7.

17. Jules Witcover, "Brian Williams' Fib: Embellished Stories May Be the Norm in Politics, But They're a Career-Killer in Journalism," *Baltimore Sun*, February 10, 2015.

18. James Carson, "What Is Fake News? Its Origins and How it Grew in 2016," *The Telegraph*, March 16, 2017, www.telegraph.co.uk/technology/0/fake-news-origins-grew-2016.

19. Project Veritas, "American Pravda: CNN Producer Says Russia Narrative 'Bullsh*t," https://www.youtube.com/watch?v=jdP8TiKY8dE.

20. Ibid.

21. Project Veritas, "Van Jones: Russia Is 'Nothing burger'—American Pravda: CNN Part 2," https://www.youtube.com/watch?v=I2G360HrSAs.

22. Michael M. Grynbaum, "3 CNN Journalists Resign After Retracted Story on Trump Ally," *New York Times*, June 26, 2017, https://www.nytimes.com/2017/06/26/business/3-cnn-journalists-resign-after-retracted-story-on-trump-ally.html.

23. Jake Tapper, "Trump: 'I Think it Was Russia' Behind Election Hacks," CNN.com, January 11, 2017, www.cnn.com/videos/politics/2017/01/11/jake-tapper-defends-donald-trump-intelligence-report-fake-news-sot.cnn.

24. Gloria Goodale, "Brian Williams Suspended: How Big a Blow Was Dealt to Network News?," *The Christian Science Monitor*, February 10, 2015; available from Lexis-Nexis Academic.

25. Michael Parkin, "Taking Late Night Comedy Seriously: How Candidate Appearances on Late Night Television Can Engage Voters," *Political Research Quarterly* 63, no. 1 (2010): 3–15.

26. Matthew A. Baum and Angela S. Jamison, "The Oprah Effect: How Soft News Helps Inattentive Citizens Vote Consistently." *The Journal of Politics* 68, no. 4 (2006): 946–959.

27. Matthew A. Baum, "Sex, Lies, and War: How Soft News Brings Foreign Policy to the Inattentive Public," *The American Political Science Review* 96, no. 1 (2002): 91–109.

28. Jody Baumgartner and Jonathan S. Morris, "The Daily Show Effect: Candidate Evaluations, Efficacy, and American Youth." *American Politics Research* 34, no. 3 (2006): 341–367.

29. Thomas E. Patterson, "Doing Well and Doing Good," Faculty Research Working Paper Series, RWP01-001 (Cambridge, MA: John F. Kennedy School of Government, Harvard University, 2000).

30. See, for example, Bernard Goldberg, *Bias: A CBS Insider Exposes How the Media Distort the News* (New York: Perennial, 2002).

31. See, for example, William Schneider and I. A. Lewis, "Views on the News," *Public Opinion* 8, no. 4 (1985): 6–13.

32. D. Domke et al., "The Politics of Conservative Elites and the 'Liberal Media' Argument," *Journal of Communication* 49, no. 4 (1999): 35–58.

33. Larry J. Sabato, *Feeding Frenzy: How Attack Journalism Has Transformed American Politics* (New York: Free Press, 1991).

34. Amber Athey, "Study: Broadcast Networks Obsessed with Russia," *The Daily Caller*, June 27, 2017. http://dailycaller.com/2017/06/27/study-broadcast-networks-obsessed-with-russia.

35. Garrett Hardin, "The Tragedy of the Commons," *Science* 162, no. 3859 (1968): 1243–1248.

36. *Annual Report of the Federal Radio Commission to the Congress of the United States for the Fiscal Year Ended June 30, 1927* (Washington, DC: Government Printing Office, 1927), 1.

37. Ibid.

38. Federal Communications Commission, "Telecommunications Act of 1996," https://transition.fcc.gov/telecom.html.

39. Doris A. Graber, *Mass Media and American Politics*, 8th ed. (Washington, DC: CQ Press, 2010), 52.

40. "Applicability of the Fairness Doctrine in the Handling of Controversial Issues of Public Importance," 29 Fed. Reg. 10426 (1964). Quoted in Kathleen Ann Ruane, "Fairness Doctrine: History and Constitutional Issues," (Washington, DC: Congressional Research Service, 2011), 2.

41. Graber, *Mass Media and American Politics*, 53.

42. This section also draws heavily on Cathleen O'Connell (Director) and Michelle Ferrrari and A. Brad Schwartz (telescript and story), "American Experience: War of the Worlds," *WBGH*, aired October 29, 2013.

43. John Gosling, *Waging the War of the Worlds: A History of the 1938 Radio Broadcast and Resulting*

Panic (Jefferson, NC: McFarland & Company, 2009), 34.

44. Howard Koch, Original Script for Radio, "The War of the Worlds," reprinted in A. Brad Schwartz, *Broadcast Hysteria: Orson Welles's War of the Worlds and the Art of Fake News* (New York: Hill and Wang, 2015), 202.

45. Ibid., 202–203.

46. A. Brad Schwartz, *Broadcast Hysteria: Orson Welles's War of the Worlds and the Art of Fake News* (New York: Hill and Wang, 2015), 77.

47. Koch, Original Script, 218.

48. Schwartz, *Broadcast Hysteria*, 103.

49. Bernard R. Berelson, Paul F. Lazarsfeld, and William N. McPhee, *Voting: A Study of Opinion Formation in a Presidential Campaign* (Chicago: University of Chicago Press, 1954).

50. James N. Druckman and Kjersten R. Nelson, "Framing and Deliberation: How Citizens' Conversations Limit Elite Influence," *American Journal of Political Science* 47, no. 4 (2003): 730. See also Thomas E. Nelson, Rosalee A. Clawson, and Zoe M. Oxley, "Media Framing of a Civil Liberties Conflict and Its Effect on Tolerance," *American Political Science Review* 91, no. 3 (1997): 567–583.

51. Harold Lasswell, "The Structure and Function of Communication in Society," in *Mass Communications*, ed. Wilbur Schram (Urbana: University of Illinois Press, 1969), 103, as discussed in Graber, *Mass Media and American Politics*, 5.

52. Graber, *Mass Media and American Politics*, 5.

53. Pew Research Center, "What Americans Know: 1989–2007," April 15, 2007, www.people-press .org/files/legacy-pdf/319.pdf.

54. Markus Prior, *Post-Broadcast Democracy: How Media Choice Increases Inequality in Political Involvement and Polarizes Elections* (New York: Cambridge University Press, 2007).

55. Prior, *Post-Broadcast Democracy*, 142.

56. Andrea Caumont, "Who's Not Online? 5 Factors Tied to the Digital Divide," Pew Research Center, November 8, 2013, www.pewresearch.org/fact-tank/2013/11/08/whos-not-online-5-factors-tied-to-the-digital-divide.

CHAPTER 7

1. Jonathan Rauch, "The Secret to Saner Elections? Stronger State Parties," *Los Angeles Times*, March 22, 2016, www.latimes.com/opinion/op-ed/la-oe-0322-rauch-state-parties-20160322-story.html.

2. "Transcript of the Democratic Presidential Debate in Milwaukee," *New York Times*, February 11, 2016, www.nytimes.com/2016/02/12/us/politics/transcript-of-the-democratic-presidential-debate-in-milwaukee.html?_r=0.

3. Chuck McCutcheon, "Young Voters," *CQ Researcher*, October 2, 2015, http://library. cqpress.com/cqresearcher/document.php? id=cqresrre2015100203.

4. Joshua Gillin, "Bush Says Trump Was a Democrat Longer than a Republican 'in the Last Decade,'" PolitiFact, August 24, 2015, www.politifact.com/florida/statements/2015/aug/24/jeb-bush/bush-says-trump-was-democrat-longer-republican-las.

5. Ibid.

6. "'This Week' Transcript: Gov. John Kasich," ABC News, December 27, 2015, http://abcnews. go.com/Politics/week-transcript-gov-john-kasich/ story?id=35959367.

7. Nicholas Confessore and Karen Yourish, "Measuring Donald Trump's Mammoth Advantage in Free Media," *New York Times*, March 15, 2016, www.nytimes .com/2016/03/16/upshot/measuring-donald-trumps-mammoth-advantage-in-free-media.html.

8. Michael Cooper Jr., "A Message from Trump's America," *U.S. News & World Report*, March 9, 2016, www.usnews.com/news/the-report/articles/2016-03-09/a-message-from-trumps-america.

9. V. O. Key Jr., *Politics, Parties, and Pressure Groups*, 5th ed. (New York: Cromwell, 1964).

10. Rauch, "The Secret to Saner Elections?"

11. Drew DeSilver, "So Far, Turnout in This Year's Primaries Rivals 2008 Record," Pew Research Center, March 8, 2016, www.pewresearch.org/fact-tank/2016/03/08/so-far-turnout-in-this-years-primaries-rivals-2008-record.

12. Marty Cohen et al., *The Party Decides: Presidential Nominations before and after Reform* (Chicago: University of Chicago Press, 2008), 3.

13. John H. Aldrich, *Why Parties? The Origin and Transformation of Political Parties in America* (Chicago: University of Chicago Press, 1995), 26.

14. Jeffrey M. Jones, "Democratic, Republican Identification near Historical Lows," Gallup, January 11, 2016, www.gallup.com/poll/188096/ democratic-republican-identification-near-historical-lows.aspx?g_ source=Politics&g_medium=lead& g_campaign=tiles.

15. Tom Price, "Polarization in America," *CQ Researcher*, February 28, 2014, http://library. cqpress.com/cqresearcher/document.php? id=cqresrre2014022800.

16. D. Stephen Voss, "Will Superdelegates Pick the Democratic Nominee? Here's Everything You Need to Know," *Washington Post*, February 26, 2016, https://www.washingtonpost.com/news/monkey-cage/wp/2016/02/26/will-superdelegates-pick-the-democratic-nominee-heres-everything-you-need-to-know.

17. John H. Aldrich, *Why Parties?*, 261. See also V. O. Key Jr., "A Theory of Critical Elections," *The Journal of Politics* 17, no. 1 (February 1955): 3–18.

18. Amy Kittelstrom, "Ignorance, Racism and Rage," *Salon*, April 9, 2016, https://www.salon .com/2016/04/09/ignorance_racism_and_rage_ the_gops_transformation_to_the_party_of_stupid_ started_long_before_donald_trump/

19. "Political Parties and Elections," in *CQ Press Guide to Congress*, 7th ed. (Washington, DC: CQ Press, 2013), 997–1000.

20. Ibid., 1002.

21. Nixon Presidential Library and Museum Collection, "Silent Majority," https://www.nixonlibrary.gov/ forresearchers/find/subjects/silent-majority.php.

22. Napp Nazworth, "Barna: Romney Got Lowest Level of Evangelical Support since Dole," *Christian Post*, December 5, 2012, www.christianpost.com/news/barna-romney-got-lowest-level-of-evangelical-support-since-dole-86145.

23. Robert Reich, "Robert Reich Sees the Future: Why America's Two-Party System May Collapse," Alternet.org, March 22, 2016, https://www.alternet .org/election-2016/robert-reich-sees-futurewhy-americas-two-party-system-may-collapse

24. The debates about the dominance of the two-part system continue.

25. Kristina Nwazota, "Third Parties in the U.S. Political Process," PBS NewsHour, July 26, 2004, www.pbs.org/newshour/updates/politics-july-dec04-third_parties.

26. "2000 Presidential Election Results," U.S.ElectionAtlas.org, http://uselectionatlas.org/RESULTS/national.php?year=2000.

27. Christopher J. Devine and Kyle C. Kopko, "5 Things You Need to Know about How Third-Party Candidates Did in 2016," Washington Post, November 15, 2016, https://www.washingtonpost.com/news/monkey-cage/wp/2016/11/15/5-things-you-need-to-know-about-how-third-party-candidates-did-in-2016.

28. U.S. Constitution, art. 1, sec. 4.

29. Morris P. Fiorina, Retrospective Voting in American National Elections (New Haven, CT: Yale University Press, 1981).

30. Mark Hugo Lopez, Ana Gonzalez-Barrera, and Jens Manuel Krogstad, "Chapter 4: Top Issues in This Year's Election for Hispanic Voters," Pew Research Center, October 29, 2014, www.pewhispanic.org/2014/10/29/chapter-4-top-issues-in-this-years-election-for-hispanic-voters.

31. Center for Responsive Politics, "2016 Presidential Race," OpenSecrets.org, https://www.opensecrets.org/pres16.

32. Jonathan Berr, "Election 2016's Price Tag: $6.8 Billion," CBSNews.com, November 8, 2016. www.cbsnews.com/news/election-2016s-price-tag-6-8-billion.

33. John G. Geer, In Defense of Negativity: Attack Ads in Presidential Campaigns (Chicago: University of Chicago Press, 2006), 13.

34. Buckley v. Valeo, 424 U.S. 1 (1976).

35. Citizens United v. Federal Election Commission, 558 U.S.__ (2010).

36. The size of the House was fixed at 435 members by the Reapportionment Act of 1929. The number rose to 437 for a time after the admission of Alaska and Hawaii as states, but it has stayed at 435 since the apportionment following the 1960 census. Washington, D.C., has three nonvoting delegates in the House.

37. Ibid., 13.

38. Wesberry v. Sanders, 376 U.S. 1 (1964); Reynolds v. Sims, 377 U.S. 533 (1964).

39. Davis v. Bandemer, 478 U.S. 109 (1986).

40. Vieth v. Jubelirer, 541 U.S. 267 (2004).

41. League of United Latin American Citizens v. Perry, 548 U.S. 399 (2006). The Court ruled that the proposed Texas Twenty-Fifth District violated the rights of Hispanic Americans protected under provisions of the Voting Rights Act of 1965.

42. Robert Barnes, "Supreme Court to Hear Potentially Landmark Case on Partisan Gerrymandering," Washington Post, June 19, 2017, https://www.washingtonpost.com/politics/courts_law/supreme-court-to-hear-potentially-landmark-case-on-partisan-gerrymandering/2017/06/19/d525237e-5435-11e7-b38e-35fd8e0c288f_story.html?utm_term=.57020b353b78.

43. Thornburg v. Gingles, 478 U.S. 30 (1986); the Voting Rights Act of 1965.

44. Shaw v. Reno, 509 U.S. 630 (1993).

45. California's voting age population was twenty-eight million in 2010 and Wyoming's was 428,000, according to the 2010 census. U.S. Census Bureau, Statistical Abstract of the United States: 2012, www.census.gov/compendia/statab.

46. Frances E. Lee, "Representation and Public Policy: The Consequences of Senate Apportionment for the Geographic Distribution of Federal Funds," The Journal of Politics 60, no. 1 (February 1998): 34–62.

47. Gary C. Jacobson, The Politics of Congressional Elections, 8th ed. (New York: Pearson, 2012), 27.

48. Ibid., 27–28.

49. David R. Mayhew, Congress: The Electoral Connection (New Haven, CT: Yale University Press), 5. See also David R. Mayhew, "Congressional Elections: The Case of the Vanishing Marginals," Polity 6, no. 3 (Spring 1974): 295–317.

50. Mayhew, Congress, 49–77.

51. Alan I. Abramowitz, Brad Alexander, and Matthew Gunning, "Incumbency, Redistricting, and the Decline of Competition in U.S. House Elections," The Journal of Politics 68, no. 1 (February 2006): 82.

52. Sidney Verba and Norman H. Nie, Participation in America: Political Democracy and Social Equality (New York: Harper & Row, 1972), 46–48.

53. Russell J. Dalton, "The Myth of the Disengaged American," Comparative Study of Electoral Systems (CSES), 2005, www.cses.org/resources/results/POP_Oct2005_1.htm.

54. Anthony Downs, An Economic Theory of Democracy (New York: HarperCollins: 1957), 233.

55. Raymond E. Wolfinger and Steven J. Rosenstone, Who Votes? (New Haven, CT: Yale University Press, 1980).

56. See Eric Plutzer, "Becoming a Habitual Voter: Inertia, Resources, and Growth in Young Adulthood," American Political Science Review 96, no. 1 (March 2002): 41–56.

57. Symm v. United States, 439 U.S. 1105 (1979).

58. Laura Fitzpatrick, "College Students Still Face Voting Stumbling Blocks," Time, October 14, 2008, http://content.time.com/time/nation/article/0,8599,1849906,00.html.

59. Center for American Women and Politics, Eagleton Institute of Politics, Rutgers, the State University of New Jersey, "Fact Sheet: Gender Differences in Voter Turnout," October 2015, www.cawp.rutgers.edu/sites/default/files/resources/genderdiff.pdf.

60. Angus Campbell et al., The American Voter (Chicago: University of Chicago Press, 1960).

61. Steven J. Rosenstone and John Mark Hansen, Mobilization, Participation, and Democracy in America (New York: Macmillan Publishing Company, 1993).

62. USA.gov, "Voter Registration Deadlines for the General Election by State," https://www.usa.gov/voter-registration-deadlines.

63. National Conference of State Legislatures, "Online Voter Registration," May 9, 2016, www.ncsl.org/research/elections-and-campaigns/electronic-or-online-voter-registration.aspx.

64. Attack of the Crab Monsters (roughly 39:24 into the film), YouTube, https://www.youtube.com/watch?v=-RA12RHnYIA.

CHAPTER 8

1. Chairman Ben. S. Bernanke, "The Economic Outlook," testimony before the Joint Economic Committee, United States Congress, March 28, 2007, www.federalreserve.gov/newsevents/testimony/bernanke20070328a.htm.

2. U.S. Department of the Treasury, "The Financial Crisis Response in Charts," April 2012, www.treasury.gov/resource-center/data-chart-center/Documents/20120413_FinancialCrisis Response.pdf.

3. Henry M. Paulson Jr., *On the Edge: Inside the Race to Stop the Collapse of the Global Financial System* (New York: Business Plus, 2010), 63.

4. Helen Kennedy, "Economy Is Headin' for Cliff! OK Bailout Soon or Else, Says Treasury Chief," *New York Daily News*, September 22, 2008; available from Lexis-Nexis Academic.

5. Ibid.

6. Kevin G. Hall, "Is It Safe to Trust a Wall Street Veteran with a Wall Street Bailout?," *McClatchy Newspapers*, September 21, 2008; available from Lexis-Nexis Academic.

7. Jeffrey H. Birnbaum, "Vital Part of Housing Bill Is Brainchild of Banks," *Washington Post*, June 25, 2008, www.washingtonpost.com/wp-dyn/content/article/2008/06/24/AR2008062401389.html.

8. Jenny Anderson, Vikas Bajaj, and Leslie Wayne, "Big Financiers Start to Lobby for Wider Aid," *New York Times*, September 21, 2008, www.nytimes.com/2008/09/22/business/22lobby.html?_r=0.

9. Jerry Zremski, "Bailout Plan Hit by Backlash; Congress Expresses Outrage; Reflects Taxpayers' Mood amid Call for Quick Action," *Buffalo News* (New York), September 24, 2008; available from Lexis-Nexis Academic.

10. Tony Pugh, "Groups Say Bailout Doesn't Do Enough for Struggling Homeowners," Knight Ridder Washington Bureau, September 23, 2008; available from Lexis-Nexis Academic.

11. Juan Gonzalez, "Bailout Dish Has Heaping Side of Pork," *New York Daily News*, October 3, 2008; available from Lexis-Nexis Academic.

12. Alexis de Tocqueville, *Democracy in America*, trans. George Lawrence, ed. J. P. Mayer (New York: Harper Perennial Modern Classics, 1966), 9.

13. For a historical treatment of these ideas, see Arthur M. Schlesinger, "Biography of a Nation of Joiners," *The American Historical Review* 50, no. 1 (October 1944): 1–25.

14. James Madison, *Federalist No. 54*, in *The Federalist Papers*, ed. George W. Carey and James McClellan (Indianapolis: Liberty Fund, 2001), 44.

15. Robert A. Dahl, *Who Governs? Democracy and Power in an American City* (New Haven, CT: Yale University Press, 1961), 3.

16. C. Wright Mills, *The Power Elite* (New York: Oxford University Press, 1956), 4–5.

17. E. E. Schattschneider, *The Semisovereign People: A Realist's View of Democracy in America* (Hinsdale, IL: The Dryden Press, 1960), 32.

18. David B. Truman, *The Governmental Process: Political Interests and Public Opinion* (New York: Alfred A. Knopf, 1962), 5. Truman used the term *pressure groups* to describe the phenomenon.

19. Mancur Olson, *The Logic of Collective Action: Public Goods and the Theory of Groups* (Cambridge, MA: Harvard University Press, 1965), 2. Italics are the author's.

20. Paul Samuelson, "The Pure Theory of Public Expenditure," *The Review of Economics and Statistics* 36, no. 4 (November 1954): 387–389. Technically, the characteristic is called *nonexcludability*. Public goods also exhibit the characteristic of *nonrivalry*, referring to the fact that the consumption of the good by one individual does not reduce its availability to others.

21. Olson, *The Logic of Collective Action*, 14–15.

22. David C. King and Jack L. Walker, "The Provision of Benefits by Interest Groups in the United States," *The Journal of Politics* 54, no. 2 (May 1992): 394–426.

23. Deniz Igan, Prachi Mishra, and Thierry Tressel, "A Fistful of Dollars: Lobbying and the Financial Crisis," National Bureau of Economic Research Working Paper 17076, May 2001, www.nber.org/papers/w17076.

24. Erika Lovely, "Wall St. Ramps Up Lobbying on Hill," Politico, June 3, 2010, www.politico.com/news/stories/0610/38091.html.

25. Ibid.

26. Sandy Mackenzie, "The Impact of the Financial Crisis on Older Americans," *Insight on the Issues, AARP Public Policy Institute* 19 (December 2008): 11.

27. Anthony J. Nownes, *Total Lobbying: What Lobbyists Want (and How They Try to Get it)* (New York: Cambridge University Press, 2006), 6.

28. Center for Responsive Politics, "Lobbying Database," OpenSecrets.org, 2014, https://www.opensecrets.org/lobby. Their figures were calculated from data obtained from the Senate Office of Public Records.

29. Kay Lehman Schlozman and John T. Tierney, *Organized Interests and American Democracy* (New York: Harper & Row, 1986), 148–157.

30. Joseph White, "Making Connections to the Appropriations Process," in *The Interest Group Connection: Electioneering, Lobbying, and Policymaking in Washington*, 2nd ed., ed. Paul S. Herrnson, Ronald G. Shaiko, and Clyde Wilcox (Washington, DC: CQ Press, 2005), 164–188.

31. Administrative Procedure Act of 1946.

32. Scott R. Furlong, "Exploring Interest Group Participation in Executive Policymaking," in Herrnson et al., *The Interest Group Connection*, 282–297.

33. Marver Bernstein, *Regulating Business by Independent Commission* (Princeton, NJ: Princeton University Press, 1955).

34. Karen O'Connor, "Lobbying the Justices or Lobbying for Justice? The Role of Organized Interests in the Judicial Process," in Herrnson et al., *The Interest Group Connection*, 331.

35. Gregory A. Caldeira and John R. Wright, "Organized Interests and Agenda Setting in the U.S. Supreme Court," *The American Political Science Review* 82, no. 4 (December 1988): 1109–1127.

36. Lee Epstein and C. K. Rowland. "Debunking the Myth of Interest Group Invincibility in the Courts." *The American Political Science Review* 85, no. 1 (March 1991): 205–217.

37. *Citizens United v. Federal Election Commission*, 558 U.S. ___ (2010).

38. Norman J. Ornstein and Shirley Elder, *Interest Groups, Lobbying, and Policymaking* (Washington, DC: CQ Press, 1978), 88.

39. Ken Kollman, *Outside Lobbying: Public Opinion and Interest Group Strategies* (Princeton, NJ: Princeton University Press, 1998), 80.

40. Kenneth M. Goldstein, *Interest Groups, Lobbying, and Participation in America* (New York: Cambridge University Press, 1999), 125.

41. Grant McConnell, *Private Power & American Democracy* (New York: Alfred A. Knopf, 1966), 5.

42. Kay Lehman Schlozman, "What Accent the Heavenly Chorus? Political Equality and the American Pressure System," *The Journal of Politics* 46, no. 4 (November 1984): 1006–1032.

43. Dara Z. Strolovitch, *Affirmative Advocacy: Race, Class, and Gender in Interest Group Politics* (Chicago: University of Chicago Press, 2007).

44. Maud Dillingham, "Top 5 Targets of Occupy Wall Street," *The Christian Science Monitor*, October 24, 2011; available from Lexis-Nexis Academic.

45. Ibid.

46. John Wellington Ennis, "Three Years Later, What Has Come of Occupy Wall Street?," *Huffington Post*, September 17, 2014, www.huffingtonpost.com/john-wellington-ennis/three-years-later-what-ha_b_5833682.html.

47. James C. McKinley Jr., "At the Protests, the Message Lacks a Melody," *New York Times*, October 19, 2011; available from Lexis-Nexis Academic.

48. Harold Brubaker, "'Occupy Wall Street' Protest Movement Seeks a Philadelphia Foothold," *The Philadelphia Inquirer*, October 2, 2011; available from Lexis-Nexis Academic.

49. Brad Knickerbocker, "Occupy Wall Street Protest 'about People Claiming Some Autonomy,'" *The Christian Science Monitor*, October 2, 2011; available from Lexis-Nexis Academic.

50. Jonathan Easley, "GOP: Dems Mum on Anti-Semitism from Occupy Wall Street Protestors," The Hill.com, October 20, 2011; available from Lexis-Nexis Academic.

51. Alice Speri, "Struggling to Make 'the 99%' More Representative of Reality," *New York Times*, October 29, 2011; available from Lexis-Nexis Academic.

52. Ibid.

53. Letter to the Editor, *New York Times*, November 17, 2011; available from Lexis-Nexis Academic.

54. Gloria Goodale, "Occupy Wall Street: Time to Become More Overtly Political?," *The Christian Science Monitor*, November 16, 2011; available from Lexis-Nexis Academic.

55. See, for example, Dennis Chong, *Collective Action and the Civil Rights Movement* (Chicago: University of Chicago Press, 1991).

56. This section draws upon Ken Kollman, *The American Political System* (New York: W. W. Norton, 2012), 378–379.

57. Christian Davenport, "How Social Movements Die—the Blog Entry (Book on the Way)," Mobilizing Ideas, The Center for the Study of Social Movements at the University of Notre Dame, December 2, 2013, https://mobilizingideas.wordpress.com/2013/12/02/how-social-movements-die-the-blog-entry-book-on-the-way.

58. Edwin Amenta, "Failure Is Not an Option," Mobilizing Ideas, The Center for the Study of Social Movements at the University of Notre Dame, December 2, 2013, https://mobilizingideas.wordpress.com/2013/12/02/failure-is-not-an-option.

59. Erik W. Johnson, "Social Movement Size, Organizational Diversity and the Making of Federal Law," *Social Forces* 86, no. 3 (2008): 967–993.

60. John W. Kingdon, *Agendas, Alternatives, and Public Policies*, updated 2nd ed. (Boston: Longman 2011).

61. David S. Meyer and Steven A. Boutcher, "Signals and Spillover: *Brown v. Board of Education* and Other Social Movements," *Perspectives on Politics* 5, no. 1 (2007): 81–93.

CHAPTER 9

1. Hanna Fenichel Pitkin, *The Concept of Representation* (Berkeley: University of California Press, 1972).

2. Angela Fritz, "We Hereby Name This Winter Storm 'Snowzilla,'" *Washington Post*, January 22, 2016, https://www.washingtonpost.com/news/capital-weather-gang/wp/2016/01/21/poll-name-this-winter-storm.

3. Bridget Bowman, "Senate Women Rule as Work Begins after Blizzard," *Roll Call*, January 26, 2016, www.rollcall.com/wgdb/senate-women-rule-as-work-begins-after-blizzard. The original article substituted "our" for "are."

4. Ballotpedia, "114th United States Congress," https://ballotpedia.org/114th_United_States_Congress.

5. There had been a total of four women serving in the Senate at some point during the 102nd Congress. Jocelyn Burdick, D-ND, had served as an interim appointee before retiring in December 1992, and Dianne Feinstein's, D-CA, success in the election on November 3, 1992, enabled her to serve out the remainder of the term of interim appointee John F. Seymour, R-CA. The numbers for the House of Representatives do not include nonvoting delegates.

6. Chris Chrystal, "Democratic Women Battle for 2 California Senate Seats," UPI, May 31, 1992, www.upi.com/Archives/1992/05/31/Democratic-women-battle-for-2-California-Senate-seats/6261707284800.

7. Debra L. Dodson, et al., *Voices, Views, Votes: The Impact of Women in the 103rd Congress* (New Brunswick, NJ: Center for American Women and Politics, Eagleton Institute of Politics, Rutgers, 1995), 2.

8. Although they are only required by the Constitution to live in the states that they represent, members of the House are, by custom, expected to maintain a residence in their electoral district.

9. James Madison, *Federalist* No. 52, in *The Federalist Papers*, ed. George W. Carey and James McClellan (Indianapolis: Liberty Fund, 2001), 273.

10. Also referred to as The Congressional Budget Control and Impoundment Act of 1974, P.L. 93-344.

11. Mathew McCubbins and Thomas Schwartz, "Congressional Oversight Overlooked: Police Patrols versus Fire Alarms," *American Journal of Political Science* 28 (1984): 165–179.

12. If the president is being tried for impeachment, the chief justice of the Supreme Court presides (U.S. Constitution, art. 1, sec. 3).

13. Clara Bingham, "Queens of the Hill: Will the Newly Empowered Women Lawmakers Clean up Congress?" *Washington Monthly*, January–February 2007.

14. Michael X. Delli Carpini and Ester R. Fuchs, "The Year of the Woman? Candidates, Voters, and the 1992 Election," *Political Science Quarterly* 108, no. 1 (1993): 34–35.

15. Barbara Mikulski et al., *Nine and Counting: The Women of the Senate* (New York: Perennial, 2001), 48–49.

16. "The Year of the Woman. Then and Now: Women in U.S. Politics in 1992 and 2008," International Museum of Women, Global Fund for Women, http://exhibitions.globalfundforwomen.org/exhibitions/women-power-and-politics/elections/year-woman.

17. Linda L. Fowler and Robert D. McClure, *Political Ambition: Who Decides to Run for Congress* (New Haven, CT: Yale University Press, 1989), xii. See also Jennifer L. Lawless, *Becoming a Candidate: Political Ambition and the Decision to Run for Office* (New York: Cambridge University Press, 2012).

18. Clyde Wilcox, "Why Was 1992 the 'Year of the Woman?' Explaining Women's Gains in 1992," in *The Year of the Woman: Myths and Realities*, ed. Elizabeth Adell Cook et al. (Boulder, CO: Westview Press, 1994), 5.

19. Mikulski et al., *Nine and Counting*, 44.

20. Candice J. Nelson, "Women's PACs in the Year of the Woman," in Cook et al., *The Year of the Woman*, 183.

21. Debra L. Dodson, "Whatever Happened to the 'Year of the Woman?'" *The Public Perspective* (August/September, 1996), 5.

22. Jean R. Schoedel and Bruce Snyder, "Patty Murray: The Mom in Tennis Shoes Goes to the Senate," in Cook et al., *The Year of the Woman*, 60–61.

23. "Leadership PACs," OpenSecrets.org, www.opensecrets.org/industries/indus.php?ind=Q03.

24. Richard F. Fenno Jr., *Congressmen in Committees* (Boston: Little, Brown, 1973).

25. Barbara Sinclair. *Unorthodox Lawmaking: New Legislative Processes in the U.S. Congress*, 2nd ed. (Washington, DC: CQ Press, 2000), 33.

26. Ibid., 3.

27. Ibid., 14.

28. Ibid., 15.

29. Ibid., 52.

30. The term *filibuster* has also been generally used to describe several other delaying tactics in the Senate.

31. Sinclair, *Unorthodox Lawmaking*, 43.

32. Carl Hulse, "Trump Gets a Win He Wasn't Counting On: He Saved the Filibuster," *New York Times*, May 3, 2017, https://www.nytimes.com/2017/05/03/us/politics/trump-filibuster.html?rref=collection%2Ftimestopic%2FFFilibusters%20and%20Debate%20Curbs&action=click&contentCollection=timestopics&region=stream&module=stream_unit&version=latest&contentPlacement=2&pgtype=collection&_r=0.

33. Ibid.

34. Sinclair, *Unorthodox Lawmaking*, 58.

35. See Charles M. Cameron, *Veto Bargaining: Presidents and the Politics of Negative Power* (New York: Cambridge University Press, 2000).

36. Pitkin, *The Concept of Representation*, 114.

37. Richard F. Fenno Jr., *Home Style: House Members in Their Districts* (New York: HarperCollins, 1978).

38. John W. Kingdon, *Congressmen's Voting Decisions*, 3rd ed. (Ann Arbor: University of Michigan Press, 1989).

39. Fenno, *Home Style*.

40. Jane Mansbridge calls the former *promissory representation* and the latter *anticipatory representation*. Jane Mansbridge, "Rethinking Representation," *American Political Science Review* 97, no. 4 (November 2003): 515–528.

41. R. Douglas Arnold, *The Logic of Congressional Action* (New Haven, CT: Yale University Press, 1990).

42. Ibid.

43. Tracy Sulkin, *Issue Politics in Congress* (New York: Cambridge University Press, 2005).

44. Richard L. Hall, *Participation in Congress* (New Haven, CT: Yale University Press, 1996).

45. "1994 Committee Supplement: Senate Judiciary," *CQ Weekly*, March 5, 1994, http://library.cqpress.com/cqweekly/wr103403788.

46. Dodson et al., *Voices, Views, Votes*, 13.

47. See Morris P. Fiorina, Samuel J. Abrams, and Jeremy C. Pope, *Culture War? The Myth of a Polarized America*, 3rd ed. (New York: Longman, 2011); and Alan I. Abramowitz, *The Disappearing Center: Engaged Citizens, Polarization, and American Democracy* (New Haven, CT: Yale University Press, 2010).

48. Jane Mansbridge, "Should Blacks Represent Blacks and Women Represent Women? A Contingent 'Yes,'" *The Journal of Politics* 61, no. 3 (August 1999): 628.

49. Ibid., 632.

50. Carol M. Swain, *Black Faces, Black Interests: The Representation of African Americans in Congress* (Cambridge, MA: Harvard University Press, 1995), 5.

51. Mansbridge, "Should Blacks Represent Blacks?," 637.

52. Pitkin, *The Concept of Representation*, 114.

53. Mansbridge, "Should Blacks Represent Blacks?," 634.

54. John W. Kingdon, *Agendas, Alternatives, and Public Policies*, 2nd ed. (New York: Longman, 2003).

55. Mansbridge, "Rethinking Representation," 522.

56. Mikulski et al., *Nine and Counting*, 197.

57. Kevin Robillard and Elana Schor, "Van Hollen to Serve as DSCC Chair," Politico.com, November 18, 2016, www.politico.com/story/2016/11/chris-van-hollen-dscc-chair-231621.

CHAPTER 10

1. Dina Temple-Rastan, "Kill and Tell: Inside the President's Terrorist Hunt," *Washington Post*, June 17, 2012, B01; available from Lexis-Nexis Academic.

2. Mark Mazzetti, Charlie Savage, and Scott Shane, "A U.S. Citizen in America's Cross Hairs," *New York Times*, March 10, 2013, A1; available from Lexis-Nexis Academic.

3. "Details of Al-Awlaki's Death," *Yemen Times*, October 3, 2011; available from Lexis-Nexis Academic.

4. Ibid.

5. Scott Shane, "Judging a Long, Deadly Reach," *New York Times*, October 1, 2011, A1; available from Lexis-Nexis Academic.

6. Charlie Savage, "Top U.S. Security Official Says 'Rigorous Standards' Used for Drone Strikes," *New York Times*, May 1, 2012, A8; available from Lexis-Nexis Academic.

7. Scott Shane and Souad Mekhennet, "From Condemning Terror to Preaching Jihad," *New York Times*, May 9, 2010, A1; available from Lexis-Nexis Academic.

8. Scott Shane and Mark Mazzetti, "A Newly Religious Immigrant Is Linked to a Militant Yemeni-American Cleric," *New York Times*, May 7, 2010, A13; available from Lexis-Nexis Academic.

9. Anthony Shadid and David D. Kirkpatrick, "As the West Celebrates a Cleric's Death, the Mideast Shrugs," *New York Times*, October 2, 2011, A14; available from Lexis-Nexis Academic.

10. Shane and Mekhennet, "From Condemning Terror to Preaching Jihad."

11. Ibid.

12. Charlie Savage, "Secret U.S. Memo Made Legal Case to Kill a Citizen," *New York Times*, October 9, 2011, A1; available from Lexis-Nexis Academic.

13. Scott Shane, "A Legal Debate as C.I.A. Stalks a U.S. Jihadist," *New York Times*, May 10, 2010, A1; available from Lexis-Nexis Academic.

14. Ulysses S. Grant unsuccessfully sought a third term in 1880.

15. In some states, widows with property were allowed to participate in public and political life.

16. Max Farrand, *The Framing of the Constitution of the United States* (New Haven, CT: Yale University Press, 1913), 163.

17. Many of these titles are in Clinton Rossiter, *The American Presidency*, 2nd ed. (Baltimore: Johns Hopkins University Press, 1987).

18. U.S. Constitution, art. 2, sec. 1.

19. U.S. Constitution, art. 2, sec. 1; art. 2, sec. 3.

20. U.S. Constitution, art. 2, sec. 2.

21. U.S. Constitution, art. 2, sec. 2, 3.

22. U.S. Constitution, art. 2, sec. 3.

23. Charles M. Cameron, *Veto Bargaining: Presidents and the Politics of Negative Power* (New York: Cambridge University Press, 2000).

24. U.S. Constitution, art. 2, sec. 2.

25. Edward S. Corwin, *Presidential Power and the Constitution: Essays* (Ithaca, NY: Cornell University Press, 1976), 163.

26. U.S. Constitution, art. 2, sec. 2.

27. U.S. Constitution, art. 1, 3.

28. U.S. Constitution, art. 2, sec. 2.

29. U.S. Constitution, art. 2, sec. 4.

30. The chief justice presides only when presidents are impeached. Otherwise, the presiding office of the Senate would chair the proceedings.

31. Michael D. Shear and Michael R. Gordon, "63 Hours: From Chemical Attacks to Trump's Strikes in Syria," *New York Times*, April 7, 2017, https://www.nytimes.com/2017/04/07/us/politics/syria-strike-trump-timeline.html?_r=0.

32. Benjamin I. Page and Mark P. Petracca, *The American Presidency* (New York: McGraw-Hill Book Company, 1983), 40.

33. "Starting from Baltimore: The Northern Troops Mobbed and Fired Upon," *New York Times*, April 19, 1861; available from ProQuest Historical Newspapers.

34. "Testimony of William Lynch, September 9, 1861," Quoted in Jonathan W. White, *Abraham Lincoln and Treason in the Civil War: The Trials of John Merryman* (Baton Rouge: Louisiana State University Press, 2011), 13. The reported comments were most likely not referring to the racial identity of the soldier but used as a derogatory remark.

35. "The Battle of Baltimore: Detailed Account of the Affair," *New York Times*, April 19, 1861; available from ProQuest Historical Newspapers.

36. Brian McGinty, *The Body of John Merryman: Abraham Lincoln and the Suspension of Habeas Corpus* (Cambridge, MA: Harvard University Press, 2011), 67.

37. Edward S. Corwin, *Presidential Power and the Constitution: Essays* (Ithaca, NY: Cornell University Press, 1976), 130.

38. Ibid.

39. Fort McHenry.

40. *Ex parte Merryman*, 17 Fed. Cases 146 (1861).

41. McGinty, *The Body of John Merryman*.

42. George William Brown, *Baltimore and the Nineteenth of April 1861: A Study of the War* (Baltimore: Johns Hopkins University Press, 1887), 88.

43. *Ex parte Merryman*. The legal term *ex parte* refers to a decision that affects one party only or a suit that is brought by or on behalf of one individual. Justice Taney, in standard practice at the time, also served as a circuit court judge, with Baltimore included in his circuit. Scholars continue to debate whether Justice Taney was properly acting as chief justice of the Supreme Court (which the *Merryman* opinion so identifies him as) or in his role as circuit judge when he issued the opinion.

44. Brown, *Baltimore and the Nineteenth of April 1861*, 89.

45. U.S. Constitution, art. 1, sec. 9.

46. *Ex parte Merryman*.

47. Page and Petracca, *The American Presidency*, 51.

48. Habeas Corpus Suspension Act of March 3, 1863, 12 Stat 755 (1863).

49. Corwin, *Presidential Power and the Constitution*, 112, 158.

50. U.S. Constitution, art. 1, sec. 9.

51. Page and Petracca, *The American Presidency*, 42.

52. Norman C. Thomas and Joseph A. Pika, *The Politics of the Presidency*, rev. 4th ed. (Washington, DC: CQ Press, 1997), 25.

53. Page and Petracca, *The American Presidency*, 47.

54. Ibid., 54.

55. Paul F. Boller Jr., *Presidential Anecdotes*, rev. ed. (New York: Oxford University Press, 1996), 208. Quoting from William F. McCombs, *Making Woodrow Wilson President* (New York: 1921).

56. America formally entered the war in 1917.

57. Thomas and Pika, *The Politics of the Presidency*, 28.

58. The German invasion of Poland in September 1, 1939, is commonly used to mark the beginning of World War II. Formal American involvement in the war, apart from aid to Great Britain, lasted from 1941 to 1945. Japan's invasion and occupation of much of Northeast Asia in 1937 might be said to mark the beginning of the war in Asia. (Rossiter, *The American Presidency*, 11).

59. Corwin, *Presidential Power and the Constitution*, 165.

60. He had assumed office from the vice presidency on November 22, 1963, when President Kennedy was assassinated.

61. Pub. L. No. 93-148, 87 Stat. 555 (November 7, 1973). Codified in 50 U.S.C. 33, Sections 1541-48 (1973). It is also called the War Powers Act, which was the title of the version of the joint resolution passed in the Senate.

62. Louis Fisher and David Gray Adler, "The War Powers Resolution: Time to Say Goodbye," *Political Science Quarterly* 113, no. 1 (1998): 1.

63. War Powers Resolution, Section 2(a).

64. War Powers Resolution, Section 2(c).

65. War Powers Resolution, Section 4(a). The president must notify both the Speaker of the House and the president of the Senate pro tempore.

66. War Powers Resolution, Section 5(b).

67. See Fisher and Adler, "The War Powers Resolution."

68. Congress authorized military operations in Afghanistan in Authorization for Use of Military Force, Pub. L. 107-40 (2001) and in Iraq in Authorization for Use of Military Force against Iraq Resolution of 2002, Pub. L. 107-243 (2002).

69. Authorization for Use of Military Force, Section 2(a).

70. James David Barber, *The Presidential Character: Predicting Performance in the White House*, 4th ed. (Englewood Cliffs, NJ: Prentice Hall, 1992).

71. Max Farrand, *The Framing of the Constitution of the United States* (New Haven, CT: Yale University Press, 1913), 169.

72. U.S. Constitution, art. 1, sec. 3.

73. The *Report of the President's Committee on Administrative Management* (1937), also known as the Brownlow Committee Report. The Reorganization Act of 1939 provided the legislative authorization for President Roosevelt's reorganization of the executive branch.

74. For a challenge to the argument that divided government necessarily leads to legislative gridlock, see David R. Mayhew, *Divided We Govern: Party Control, Lawmaking, and Investigations, 1946–1990* (New Haven, CT: Yale University Press, 1991).

75. Rossiter, *The American Presidency*, 54, 56.

76. Page and Petracca, *The American Presidency*, 118. Quoting J. D. Richardson, ed., *Messages and Papers of the Presidents* (New York, 1879), 3.

77. Samuel Kernell, *Going Public: New Strategies of Presidential Leadership* (Washington, D.C.: CQ Press, 2007), 1–2.

78. James A. Stimson, "Public Support for American Presidents: A Cyclical Model," *The Public Opinion Quarterly* 40, no. 1 (1976): 1–21.

79. See, for example, Mark J. Rozell, "The Law: Executive Privilege: Definition and Standards of Application," *Presidential Studies Quarterly* 29, no. 4 (1999): 918–930.

80. *United States v. Nixon*, 418 U.S. 683 (1974).

81. Kenneth R. Mayer, *With the Stroke of a Pen: Executive Orders and Presidential Power* (Princeton, NJ: Princeton University Press, 2001).

82. Executive Order 9066, 7 *Federal Register* 1407 (February 19, 1942).

83. *Korematsu v. United States*, 323 U.S. 214 (1944).

84. Ibid.

85. *Youngstown Sheet & Tube Co. v. Sawyer*, 343 U.S. 579 (1952). The president's order was Executive Order No. 10340, 16 Federal Register 3503 (April 8, 1952).

86. William G. Howell, *Power without Persuasion: The Politics of Direct Presidential Action* (Princeton, NJ: Princeton University Press, 2003), 14.

87. See Barber, *Presidential Character*.

88. Richard E. Neustadt, *Presidential Power and the Modern Presidents: The Politics of Leadership from Roosevelt to Reagan* (New York: The Free Press, 1990), 163.

89. Ibid., 30.

90. Mark Mazzetti, "American Drone Strike in Yemen Was Aimed at Awlaki," *New York Times*, May 7, 2011, A11; available from Lexis-Nexis Academic.

91. Thomas E. Cronin and Michael A. Genovese, *The Paradoxes of the American Presidency*, 2nd ed. (New York: Oxford University Press, 2004).

CHAPTER 11

1. Tamara Lush, "For Forecasting Chief, No Joy in Being Right," *St. Petersburg Times*, August 30, 2005, 3A; available from Lexis-Nexis Academic.

2. Ibid.

3. Deana Poole and Pat Beall, "New Orleans Emptying: Katrina on Path to Bring Disaster," *Palm Beach Post*, August 28, 2005, 1A; available from Lexis-Nexis Academic.

4. Donald F. Kettl, *The Next Government of the United States: Why Our Institutions Fail Us and How to Fix Them* (New York: W. W. Norton, 2009), 18.

5. Poole and Beall, "New Orleans Emptying."

6. John Ashton, "Thousands Flee as Hurricane Nears U.S. Coast," *Birmingham Post*, August 29, 2005, 9; available from Lexis-Nexis Academic.

7. Tina Hesman, "Most People Killed by Katrina Were Elderly, Researcher Finds," *St. Louis Post-Dispatch*, February 17, 2006, A5; available from Lexis-Nexis Academic.

8. Bryan Dean and Ryan McNeill, "Facing the Future: Hurricane Survivors Express Thanks to State," *The Oklahoman*, September 5, 2005. 1A; available from Lexis-Nexis Academic.

9. Max Weber, "The Permanent Character of the Bureaucratic Machine," in *From Max Weber: Essays in Sociology*, ed. H. H. Gerth and C. Wright Mills (New York: Oxford University Press, 1959), 229.

10. Max Weber, *Economy and Society: An Outline of Interpretive Sociology*, trans. and ed. Guenther Roth and Claus Wittich (Berkeley: University of California Press, 1978), 987. The work was first published in Germany, posthumously, in 1922.

11. Ibid., 957–958.

12. Ibid., 975.

13. Chester I. Barnard, *The Functions of the Executive* (1938; Cambridge, MA: Harvard University Press, 1968), 72.

14. Barnard, *The Functions of the Executive*, 82.

15. James Q. Wilson, *Bureaucracy: What Government Agencies Do and Why They Do It* (New York: Basic Books, 1989), 173.

16. Wilson calls this category of bureaucracies "coping organizations." Wilson, *Bureaucracy*, 175.

17. Public education is largely governed by the states, not the federal government; however, the illustration applies to the actions of federal bureaucrats as well.

18. See Scott F. Abernathy, *No Child Left Behind and the Public Schools* (Ann Arbor: University of Michigan Press, 2007), 25–45.

19. James Q. Wilson, "The Rise of the Bureaucratic State," *The Public Interest* 41 (Fall 1975): 77.

20. U.S. Constitution, art. 2, sec. 2.

21. Roughly 1,350 of 6,500 presidentially nominated officials require Senate confirmation.

22. U.S. Constitution, art. 2, sec. 2 and 4.

23. Leonard D. White, *The Federalists: A Study in Administrative History* (New York: The Macmillan Company, 1948), 20.

24. *Myers v. United States*, 272 U.S. 52 (1926).

25. White, *The Federalists*, 258. Quoting George Washington to Edward Rutledge, 21 March 1789.

26. White, *The Federalists*, 259.

27. Ibid., 222.

28. David H. Rosenbloom, *Federal Service and the Constitution: The Development of the Public Employment Relationship* (Ithaca, NY: Cornell University Press, 1971), 35. See also Brian J. Cook, *Bureaucracy and Self-Government: Reconsidering the Role of Public Administration in American Politics* (Baltimore: The Johns Hopkins University Press, 1996), 45.

29. The Department of Agriculture was given full cabinet status in 1889.

30. Stephen Skowronek, Building a New American State: The Expansion of National Administrative Capacities, 1877–1920 (New York: Cambridge University Press, 1982).

31. Theda Skocpol, *Protecting Soldiers and Mothers: The Political Origins of Social Policy in the United*

States (Cambridge, MA: Belknap Press of Harvard University Press, 1992). Professor Skocpol also examined the gendered aspects of American social welfare policy and how the degree to which recipients were seen as "deserving" shaped the policies themselves.

32. In *The Jungle* (1906), Upton Sinclair described unhealthy and dangerous working conditions in the meatpacking industry, which helped secure the passage of the Pure Food and Drug Act as well as the Federal Meat Inspection Act of 1907.

33. The National Security Act of 1947 also reorganized the cabinet structure of the departments and agencies involved in defense.

34. Public Law 88-352 (78 Stat. 241).

35. Thomas A. Garrett and Russell M. Rhine, "On the Size and Growth of Government," *Federal Reserve Bank of St. Louis Review* 88, no. 1 (January/February 2006): 13–30.

36. Richard W. Stevenson, "After Katrina's Lesson, Bush Is Heading to Texas," *New York Times*, September 23, 2005, p. A1

37. The U.S. armed forces, which are part of the executive branch, have a different organizational structure, though the secretary of defense and deputy and assistant secretaries are political appointees.

38. For a foundational study of the challenges of implementation, see Jeffrey L. Pressman and Aaron Wildavsky, *Implementation*, 3rd ed. (Berkeley: University of California Press, 1984).

39. Michael Lipsky, *Street-Level Bureaucracy: Dilemmas of the Individual in Public Services* (New York: Russell Sage Foundation, 1980).

40. Cornelius M. Kerwin, *Rulemaking: How Government Agencies Write Laws and Make Policy* (Washington, DC: CQ Press, 1994), 4.

41. Kenneth J. Meier, "Representative Bureaucracy: A Theoretical and Empirical Exposition," in *Research in Public Administration*, ed. James Perry (Greenwich, CT: JAI Press, 1993).

42. Sally Coleman Selden, *The Promise of Representative Bureaucracy: Diversity and Responsiveness in a Government Agency* (Armonk, NY: ME Sharpe, 1997).

43. Charles T. Goodsell, *The Case For Bureaucracy: A Public Administration Polemic*, 2nd ed. (Chatham, NJ: Chatham House Publishers, Inc., 1985), 63.

44. William A. Niskanen, "The Peculiar Economics of Bureaucracy," *The American Economic Review* 58, no. 2 (May 1968): 293–305.

45. John Brehm and Scott Gates, *Working, Shirking, and Sabotage: Bureaucratic Responses to a Democratic Public* (Ann Arbor: University of Michigan Press, 1997).

46. For a classic study of the challenges posed by outside pressures on bureaucrats and how bureaucratic agencies deal with them, see Herbert Kaufman, *The Forest Ranger: A Study in Administrative Behavior* (Washington, DC: Resources for the Future, 1960).

47. Joel D. Aberbach, *Keeping a Watchful Eye: The Politics of Congressional Oversight* (Washington, DC: Brookings Institution, 1990), 4.

48. The legislative and judicial branches also contain bureaucratic organizations, though these are few in number and small in size compared to the departments, agencies, and bureaus in the executive branch.

49. U.S. Government Accountability Office, "Preliminary Observations on Hurricane Response," February 1, 2006. GAO-06-365R, www.gao.gov/assets/100/94002.pdf.

50. Mathew D. McCubbins and Thomas Schwartz, "Congressional Oversight Overlooked: Police Patrols versus Fire Alarms," *American Journal of Political Science* 28, no. 1 (February 1984): 165–179.

51. Herbert Kaufman, "Fear of Bureaucracy: A Raging Pandemic," *Public Administration Review* 41, no. 1 (1981), 6.

52. William Douglas and Steven Thomas, "On Katrina Anniversary, Bush Returns to Gulf Coast," Knight Ridder Washington Bureau, August 28, 2006; available from Lexis-Nexis Academic.

53. John J. Dilulio Jr., Gerald Garvey, and Donald F. Kettl, *Improving Government Performance: An Owner's Manual* (Washington, DC: Brookings Institution, 1993), 64.

54. David Osborne and Ted Gaebler, *Reinventing Government: How the Entrepreneurial Spirit Is Transforming the Public Sector* (New York: Plume/Penguin Books, 1993), xix.

55. Wilson, *Bureaucracy*, 134–136. Professor Wilson did not necessarily condemn efforts at privatization, instead pointing out differences in mandates and structure. In the provision of services in which outputs and outcomes are difficult to measure—such as education—he pointed out that parents, and not supervisors, might be more effective at measuring the quality of the product (364).

56. Select Bipartisan Committee to Investigate the Preparation for and Response to Hurricane Katrina, *A Failure of Initiative: Final Report of the Select Bipartisan Committee to Investigate the Preparation for and Response to Hurricane Katrina* (Washington, DC: Government Printing Office, 2006), 17.

57. Brad Delong, "Katrina Reveals the Presidential Flaws," *Financial Times*, September 7, 2005, 13; available from Lexis-Nexis Academic.

58. Sarah Ladislaw, "Hurricane Sandy: Evaluating the Response One Year Later," *Center for Strategic and International Studies*, November 4, 2013, https://www.csis.org/analysis/hurricane-sandy-evaluating-response-one-year-later.

CHAPTER 12

1. The title refers to Alexander Hamilton's characterization in *Federalist* No. 78 of the federal judiciary as "least dangerous to the political rights of the Constitution." Alexander Hamilton, *Federalist* No. 78, in *The Federalist Papers*, ed. George W. Carey and James McClellan (Indianapolis: Liberty Fund, 2001), 402. Alexander M. Bickel also chose the phrase from the title of his critique of judicial power, *The Least Dangerous Branch: The Supreme Court at the Bar of Politics* (Indianapolis: Bobbs-Merrill Educational Publishing, 1962).

2. Robert Barnes and Michael A. Fletcher, "Riskiest Choice on Obama's List Embodies His Criteria; President and Judge Cite Her Life Experience," *Washington Post*, May 27, 2009; available from Lexis-Nexis Academic.

3. Charlie Savage, "Conservatives Map Strategies on Court Fight," *New York Times*, May 17, 2009; available from Lexis-Nexis Academic.

4. Ibid.

5. Sonia Sotomayor, "A Latina Judge's Voice," *Berkeley La Raza Law Journal* 13, no. 1 (Spring 2002): 87–93.

6. David S. Broder, "After Bork—and Obama; Confirmation Fights Still Echo," *Washington Post*, June 4, 2009; available from Lexis-Nexis Academic.

7. "GOP Senator Sums Up Sotomayor Issue," *Washington Post*, June 7, 2009; available from Lexis-Nexis Academic.

8. Peter Baker and Neil A. Lewis, "Judge Focuses on Rule of Law at the Hearings," *New York Times*, July 14, 2009; available from Lexis-Nexis Academic.

9. N. C. Aizenman, "For Latinos, Confirmation Is an Emotional Moment," *Washington Post*, August 7, 2009; available from Lexis-Nexis Academic.

10. Forrest McDonald, *Novus Ordo Seclorum: The Intellectual Origins of the Constitution* (Lawrence: University Press of Kansas, 1985), 253.

11. The delegates did debate the need to raise judges' salaries to keep up with changes in the cost of living, but they ultimately left the issue of pay raises out of the document.

12. U.S. Constitution, art. 3, sec. 1.

13. U.S. Constitution, art. 2, sec. 2.

14. McDonald, *Novus Ordo Seclorum*, 254–255.

15. U.S. Constitution, art. 3, sec. 1.

16. U.S. Constitution, art. 2, sec. 1.

17. U.S. Constitution, art. 6.

18. The term *jurisdiction* is also applied in other contexts, such as the authority of a specific law enforcement agency to investigate a case. However, we will focus only on the jurisdiction of courts in this chapter.

19. Hamilton, *Federalist* No. 78, in Carey and McClellan, *The Federalist Papers*, 402.

20. Ibid.

21. "The Judiciary Act of 1789," in *Documents of American History*, 6th ed., ed. Henry Steele Commager (New York: Appleton-Century-Crofts, Inc., 1958), 153.

22. Ibid., 155.

23. John Adams and Alexander Hamilton were not always in complete agreement. Adams and other Federalists sometimes expressed misgivings about Hamilton's ardent nationalism.

24. Jefferson's party is often referred to as the Democratic-Republican Party, though it was more commonly called the Republican Party at the time. "Jeffersonian Republicans" is also a commonly used label today.

25. "Thomas Jefferson, First Inaugural Address, 4 March 1801," in *Basic Writings of Thomas Jefferson*, ed. Philip S. Foner (New York: Wiley Book Company, 1944), 333.

26. U.S. Constitution, art. 3, sec. 1.

27. Kathryn Turner, "Federalist Policy and the Judiciary Act of 1801," *The William and Mary Quarterly* 22, no. 1 (January 1965): 32. Turner noted that as many of the provisions in the Judiciary Act of 1801 had been introduced prior to the election, there were other reasons for these provisions, particularly a desire to strengthen the power of the national government. The electoral results, however, "gave a driving urgency to the fight for its passage" (32).

28. David Loth, *Chief Justice: John Marshall and the Growth of the Republic* (New York: W. W. Norton, 1949), 176.

29. Oliver Ellsworth, the former chief justice, had retired shortly before.

30. The four plaintiffs were William Marbury, Dennis Ramsay, Robert Townsend Hope, and William Harper.

31. *Marbury v. Madison*, 5 U.S. 137 (1803).

32. For fans of the television and film series *Star Trek*, Marshall's dilemma might be seen as one of America's first political Kobayashi Maru scenarios. In *Star Trek* lore, Captain James T. Kirk only defeated the no-win training scenario by cheating, something that several historians and scholars have accused Marshall of doing in his interpretation and reading of the Constitution and Judiciary Act of 1789.

33. *Marbury v. Madison*.

34. Ibid.

35. Ibid.

36. Section 13 of the Judiciary Act of 1789.

37. *Marbury v. Madison*.

38. "Thomas Jefferson to Abigail Adams, Monticello, VA, 11 September 1804," in Foner, *Basic Writings of Thomas Jefferson*, 670.

39. *Dred Scott v. Sandford*, 60 U.S. 393 (1857).

40. For cases heard on appeal, the petitioner is the party that lost in the lower court and the respondent is the other party in the case.

41. Another category of law, called procedural law, refers to proceedings and rules through which laws are enforced, such as how law enforcement officials interact with those accused of crimes.

42. Many of the definitions of legal terms in this chapter are informed by Bryan A. Garner, ed., *Black's Law Dictionary*, 8th ed. (St. Paul, MN: Thompson/West, 2004).

43. The relevant federal law is the Controlled Substances Act (1970). Under that act, marijuana, along with heroin, ecstasy, and other substances, is classified as one having a high potential for abuse and no accepted medical use.

44. As of September 2016, thirty states had the death penalty. (Death Penalty Information Center, "States with and without the Death Penalty," www.deathpenaltyinfo.org/states-and-without-death-penalty.) The U.S. government also has the authority to impose the death penalty for conviction under certain federal laws. In addition, the military retains the death penalty for conviction of certain offenses under the Uniform Code of Military Justice, though it has not been carried out since 1961.

45. Two states, Texas and Oklahoma, have separate state supreme courts for criminal and civil cases.

46. U.S. Constitution, art. 3, sec. 2.

47. A small set of cases may bypass the appellate courts in this process, such as those involving voting rights and aspects of the 1964 Civil Rights Act.

48. The Supreme Court automatically hears a small set of cases on appeal—those involving voting rights and congressional redistricting. Unless overturned by the Supreme Court, appellate court decisions are binding but only within the jurisdiction of that specific court of appeals. Such jurisdictions (excepting the D.C. and federal circuits) are geographically determined.

49. The opposition files a "brief in opposition to a petition for a writ of certiorari." Briefs in opposition

are only mandatory in capital cases. U.S. Supreme Court, *Rules of the Supreme Court of the United States*, Rule 15, www.supremecourt.gov/ctrules/2013RulesoftheCourt.pdf.

50. Ibid., Rule 10.

51. Only attorneys admitted to the Bar of the Court may file amicus curiae briefs (*Rules of the U.S. Supreme Court*, Rule 37).

52. Gregory A. Caldiera and John R. Wright, "Amici Curiae before the Supreme Court: Who Participates, When, and How Much?," *The Journal of Politics* 52, no. 3 (August 1990): 782–806.

53. See, for example, Timothy R. Johnson, Paul J. Wahlbeck, and James F. Spriggs Jr., "The Influence of Oral Arguments on the U.S. Supreme Court," *American Political Science Review* 100, no. 1 (February 2006): 99–113.

54. Another option for the Court is to send it back to the lower court under the status of review being improvidently granted. In such a case, the Court has decided that after review it now chooses not to give a full hearing to the case. If so, the lower ruling stands, but the Court has not officially weighed in on that ruling.

55. Bickel, *The Least Dangerous Branch*, 17.

56. For historical perspectives on the countermajoritarian difficulty, see Sylvia Snowiss, *Judicial Review and the Law of the Constitution* (New Haven, CT: Yale University Press, 1990). Also see Barry Friedman, "The History of the Countermajoritarian Difficulty, Part One: The Road to Judicial Supremacy," *New York University Law Review* 73, no. 2 (May 1998): 333–433.

57. Bickel, *The Least Dangerous Branch*, 29–33.

58. James B. Thayer, "The Origin and Scope of the American Doctrine of Constitutional Law," *Harvard Law Review* 7, no. 3 (October 25, 1893): 144.

59. Jack Knight and Lee Epstein, "The Norm of Stare Decisis," *American Journal of Political Science* 40, no. 4 (November 1996): 1018–1035. For an analysis that challenges the use of stare decisis, especially when crafting dissenting opinions, see Jeffrey A. Segal and Harold J. Spaeth, "The Influence of Stare Decisis on the Votes of United States Supreme Court Justices," *American Journal of Political Science* 40, no. 4 (November 1996): 971–1003.

60. Glendon A. Schubert, *The Judicial Mind: The Attitudes and Ideologies of Supreme Court Justices, 1946–1963* (Evanston, IL: Northwestern University Press, 1965).

61. Jeffrey A. Segal and Albert D. Cover, "Ideological Values and the Votes of U.S. Supreme Court Justices," *American Political Science Review* 83, no. 2 (June 1989): 557–565.

62. Walter F. Murphy, *Elements of Judicial Strategy* (Chicago: University of Chicago Press, 1964), 3–4.

63. Ibid., 35–36.

64. Charles M. Cameron, et al., "Strategic Auditing in a Political Hierarchy: An Informational Model of the Supreme Court's *Certiorari* Decisions," *American Political Science Review* 94, no. 1 (March 2000): 101–116.

65. James F. Spriggs II, Forrest Maltzman, and Paul J. Wahlbeck, "Bargaining on the U.S. Supreme Court: Justices' Responses to Majority Opinion Drafts," *The Journal of Politics* 61, no. 2 (May 1999): 485–506.

66. The cases listed under the year 1929 were decided in 1930 following Hughes's confirmation as chief justice in February 1930.

67. Kevin T. McGuire and James A. Stimson, "The Least Dangerous Branch Revisited: New Evidence on Supreme Court Responsiveness to Public Preferences," *The Journal of Politics* 66, no. 4 (November 2004): 1018–1035.

68. Leonard D. White, *The Federalists: A Study in Administrative History* (New York: The Macmillan Company, 1948), 259–260.

CHAPTER 13

1. Opinion, "American Dreamers," *New York Times*, DATE?, https://www.nytimes.com/interactive/projects/storywall/american-dreamers.

2. Department of Homeland Security, "Consideration of Deferred Action for Childhood Arrivals (DACA)," https://www.uscis.gov/humanitarian/consideration-deferred-action-childhood-arrivals-daca.

3. Opinion, "American Dreamers."

4. Bradley Jones, "Americans' Views of Immigration Marked by Widening Partisan, Generational Divides," Pew Research Center, April 15, 2016, www.pewresearch.org/fact-tank/2016/04/15/americans-views-of-immigrants-marked-by-widening-partisan-generational-divides.

5. Audrey Singer, Nicole Prchal Svajlenka, and Jill H. Wilson, "Local Insights from DACA for Implementing Future Programs for Unauthorized Immigrants," Brookings Metropolitan Policy Program, April, 2015, p. 2, https://www.brookings.edu/wp-content/uploads/2016/06/BMPP_Srvy_DACAImmigration_June3b.pdf.

6. James Barragán, "Immigration hard-liners try to force Trump's hand on DACA," *Dallas Morning News*, https://www.dallasnews.com/news/immigration/2017/07/03/immigration-hardliners-try-force-trumps-hand-daca.

7. Tal Kopan, "States try to force Trump's hand on DACA," *CNN*, July 1, 2017, www.cnn.com/2017/06/30/politics/trump-daca-bind/index.html.

8. Michael D. Shear and Julie Hirschfeld Davis, "Trump Moves to End DACA and Calls on Congress to Act," *New York Times*, September 5, 2017, https://www.nytimes.com/2017/09/05/us/politics/trump-daca-dreamers-immigration.html?mcubz=0.

9. Stephanie Ewert, "U.S. Population Trends: 2000 to 2060," U.S. Census Bureau, October 15, 2015, www.ncsl.org/Portals/1/Documents/nalfo/USDemographics.pdf.

10. My thanks go to Professor John J. Dilulio Jr. for his thoughts on this topic learned mostly through an independent study on the bureaucracy at Princeton to which he was so generous to agree.

11. John W. Kingdon, *Agendas, Alternatives, and Public Policies*, 2nd ed. (New York: Longman, 2003), 1.

12. Theda Skocpol, *Protecting Soldiers and Mothers: The Political Origins of Social Policy in the United States* (Cambridge, MA: Belknap Press of Harvard University Press, 1992).

13. Suzanne Mettler, "Bringing the State Back in to Civic Engagement: Policy Feedback Effects of the G.I. Bill for World War II Veterans," *The American Political Science Review* 96, no. 2 (June 2002).

14. Jeffrey L. Pressman and Aaron Wildavsky, *Implementation*, 3rd ed. (Berkeley: University of California Press, 1984).

15. Pub. L. 74-271, 49 Stat 620-648 (1935). The programs were collectively called Old-Age, Survivors, and Disability Insurance (OASDI) and commonly referred to as Social Security. Aid to Dependent Children was later renamed Aid to Families with Dependent Children (AFDC), which was abolished in 1996 and replaced with Temporary Assistance to Needy Families (TANF).

16. Office of the Assistant Secretary for Planning and Evaluation, "2015 Poverty Guidelines," January 22, 2015, http://aspe.hhs.gov/2015-poverty-guidelines.

17. The Republican Party gained fifty-four seats in the House of Representatives and eight seats in the Senate.

18. John Maynard Keynes, *The General Theory of Employment, Interest, and Money* (New York: Harcourt, Brace, & Company, 1936).

19. The purchase price, about three cents per acre, included a payment of $11.25 million and forgiveness of $3.75 million in debt. Jesse Greenspan, "8 Things You May Not Know about the Louisiana Purchase," History in the Headlines, www.history.com/news/8-things-you-may-not-know-about-the-louisiana-purchase.

20. "The First Barbary War," The Jefferson Monticello, https://www.monticello.org/site/research-and-collections/first-barbary-war.

21. It should be noted that combatants from occupied nations—Poland, for example—also made major contributions to the allied war effort.

22. Steven W. Hook, *U.S. Foreign Policy: The Paradox of World Power*, 4th ed. (Washington, DC: CQ Press, 2013), 47.

23. American allies France and Great Britain were also clearly victors, but their industries and economies had been devastated by the European fighting.

24. Winston S. Churchill, "Sinews of Peace," Speech delivered at Westminster College, Fulton, Missouri, March 5, 1946.

25. North Atlantic Treaty Organization, The North Atlantic Treaty, Article I, www.nato.int/cps/en/natolive/official_texts_17120.htm.

26. "Full Text of Colin Powell's Speech," *Guardian*, February 5, 2003, https://www.theguardian.com/world/2003/feb/05/iraq.usa.

27. See, for example, "Former Aide: Powell WMD Speech 'Lowest Point in My Life,'" CNN.com, August 23, 2005, www.cnn.com/2005/WORLD/meast/08/19/powell.un.

28. Mark Thompson, "How Disbanding the Iraqi Army Fueled ISIS," *Time*, May 28, 2015, http://time.com/3900753/isis-iraq-syria-army-united-states-military.

29. Amanda Bennett, "Daesh? ISIS? Islamic State? Why What We Call the Paris Attackers Matters," *Washington Post*, November 25, 2015, https://www.washingtonpost.com/news/in-theory/wp/2015/11/25/daesh-isis-islamic-state-why-what-we-call-the-paris-attackers-matters.

30. Yasmine Ryan, "How Tunisia's Revolution Began," Al Jazeera, January 26, 2011, www.aljazeera.com/indepth/features/2011/01/201112612181595485483.html.

31. Mohamed Eishinnawi, "Arab Spring Became Brutal Winter, Analysts Say," VOA News, January 19, 2016, www.voanews.com/content/arab-spring-brutal-winter-analysts-say/3153382.html.

32. The Sykes-Picot Agreement of 1916.

33. Max Fisher, "9 Questions about S*yria You Were Too Embarrassed to Ask*," Washington Post, August 29, 2013, https://www.washingtonpost.com/news/worldviews/wp/2013/08/29/9-questions-about-syria-you-were-too-embarrassed-to-ask.

34. Martin Chulov, *"Isis: The Inside Story,"* Guardian, December 11, 2014, www.theguardian.com/world/2014/dec/11/-sp-isis-the-inside-story.

35. "'They Cut Off Heads': Syrians Speak to RT about ISIS Atrocities," RT.com, December 1, 2015, https://www.rt.com/news/324120-isis-sex-slavery-trafficking.

36. "Public Backs Diplomatic Approach in Syria, but Distrusts Syria and Russia," Pew Research Center, September 16, 2013, www.people-press.org/2013/09/16/public-backs-diplomatic-approach-in-syria-but-distrusts-syria-and-russia.

37. James O. Goldsborough, "California's Foreign Policy," *Foreign Affairs* 72, no. 2 (Spring 1993): 88.

38. Edward S. Corwin, ed., *The Constitution of the United States of America: Analysis and Interpretation* (Washington, DC: Government Printing Office, 1952), 470.

39. The Intelligence Reform and Terrorism Prevention Act of 2004.

40. Richard E. Neustadt, *Presidential Power and the Modern Presidents: The Politics of Leadership from Roosevelt to Reagan* (New York: The Free Press, 1990), 29.

41. It is also called the War Powers Act, which was the title of the version of the joint resolution passed in the Senate.

42. Louis Fisher and David Gray Adler, "The War Powers Resolution: Time to Say Goodbye," *Political Science Quarterly* 113, no. 1 (1998): 1.

43. War Powers Resolution, Section 2(c).

44. War Powers Resolution, Section 4(a). The president must notify both the Speaker of the House and the president of the Senate pro tempore.

45. War Powers Resolution, Section 5(b).

46. The most recent formal declaration was against Hungary, Romania, and Bulgaria on June 5, 1942; however, the most consequential declaration in that conflict was a declaration of war against Japan on December 8, 1941, and Germany and Italy on December 11, 1941.

47. See Fisher and Adler, "The War Powers Resolution."

48. Catherine E. Shoichet and Tom Watkins, "Strike against Syria? Obama Backs It, but Wants Congress to Vote," CNN.com, August 31, 2013, www.cnn.com/2013/08/31/world/meast/syria-civil-war.

49. "Q&A: Syria Chemical Weapons Disarmament Deal," BBC News, January 30, 2014, www.bbc.com/news/world-middle-east-23876085.

50. Joseph Nye, *Soft Power: The Means to Success in World Politics* (New York: Public Affairs Books, 2004).

51. Avi Asher-Schapiro "The Young Men Who Started Syria's Revolution Speak about Daraa, Where It All Began," Vice News, March 15, 2016, https://news.vice.com/article/the-young-men-who-started-syrias-revolution-speak-about-daraa-where-it-all-began.

52. Hugh Macleod, "How Schoolboys Began the Syrian Revolution," CBS News, April 26, 2011, www.cbsnews.com/news/how-schoolboys-began-the-syrian-revolution.

53. Joe Sterling, "Daraa: The Spark That Lit the Syrian Flame," CNN.com, March 1, 2012, www .cnn.com/2012/03/01/world/meast/syria-crisis-beginnings.

54. Alex Altman, "A Syrian Refugee Story: Inside One Family's Two-Year Odyssey from Daraa to Dallas," *Time*, http://time.com/a-syrian-refugee-story.

55. Ben Russell, "Syrian Family Finds Opportunity in North Texas," 5NBCDFW.com, www.nbcdfw.com/news/local/Syrian-Family-Finds-Opportunity-in-North-Texas-353149931.html.

56. Altman, "A Syrian Refugee Story."

57. "Paris Attacks: What Happened on the Night," BBC News, December 9, 2015, www.bbc.com/news/world-europe-34818994.

58. Ishaan Tharoor, "Were Syrian Refugees Involved in the Paris Attacks? What We Know and Don't Know," *Washington Post*, November 17, 2015, https://www.washingtonpost.com/news/worldviews/wp/2015/11/17/were-syrian-refugees-involved-in-the-paris-attacks-what-we-know-and-dont-know.

59. Haley Sweetland Edwards, "Why Texas' Attempt to Block a Syrian Refugee Family Probably Won't Work," *Time*, December 3, 2015, http://time .com/4134620/texas-lawsuit-to-block-syrian-refugees.

60. Molly Hennessey Fiske, "Meet Two Syrian Families in Texas Who Had the Welcome Mat Pulled out from under Them," *Los Angeles Times*, December 3, 2015, www.latimes.com/nation/la-na-syrian-texas-20151204-story.html.

61. Jon Kamp, "Texas Sues to Stop Resettlement of Six Syrian Refugees," *Wall Street Journal*, December 3, 2015, www.wsj.com/articles/texas-sues-to-stop-resettlement-of-six-syrian-refugees-1449101946. The lawsuit also sought to block resettlement of members of another family.

62. Fiske, "Meet Two Syrian Families in Texas."

63. Russell, "Syrian Family Finds Opportunity in North Texas."

64. Walt Whitman, "O Me! O Life!," *Leaves of Grass* (Champaign, IL: Project Gutenberg, 1892).

INDEX